Portugal

Julia Wilkinson
John King

LONELY PLANET PUBLICATIONS
Melbourne • Oakland • London • Paris

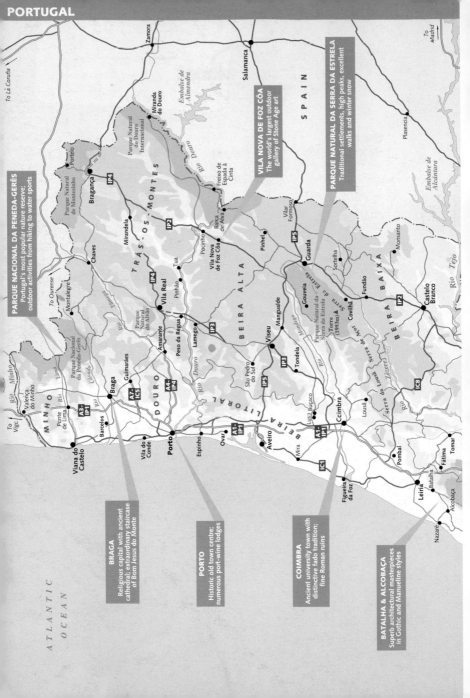

PARQUE NACIONAL DA PENEDA-GERÊS
Portugal's most popular nature reserve;
outdoor activities from hiking to water sports

VILA NOVA DE FOZ CÔA
The world's largest outdoor
gallery of Stone Age art

PARQUE NATURAL DA SERRA DA ESTRELA
Traditional settlements, high peaks, excellent
walks and winter snow

BRAGA
Religious capital with ancient
cathedral; extraordinary staircase
of Bom Jesus do Monte

PORTO
Historic old town centre;
numerous port-wine lodges

COIMBRA
Ancient university town with
distinctive fado tradition; fine Roman ruins

BATALHA & ALCOBAÇA
Superb architectural masterpieces
in Gothic and Manueline styles

ATLANTIC OCEAN

SPAIN

TRÁS-OS-MONTES

BEIRA ALTA

BEIRA BAIXA

BEIRA LITORAL

DOURO

MINHO

To La Coruña
To Vigo
To Ourense
To Madrid

Zamora
Salamanca
Plasencia

Miranda do Douro
Bragança
Portelo
Chaves
Montalegre
Mirandela
Vila Real
Pinhão
Tua
Amarante
Peso da Régua
Lamego
Freixo de Espada à Cinta
Pocinho
Vila Nova de Foz Côa
Barca de Alva
Pinhel
Vilar Formoso
Guarda
Sortelha
Monsanto
Gouveia
Covilhã
Fundão
Manteigas
Viseu
Mangualde
Tondela
São Pedro do Sul
Castelo Branco
Luso
Buçaco
Coimbra
Lousã
Aveiro
Mira
Figueira da Foz
Pombal
Leiria
Batalha
Fátima
Tomar
Alcobaça
Nazaré
Espinho
Ovar
Vila do Conde
Porto
Braga
Guimarães
Barcelos
Ponte de Lima
Valença do Minho
Viana do Castelo

Parque Natural do Douro Internacional
Parque Natural de Montesinho
Parque Nacional da Peneda-Gerês
Parque Natural do Alvão
Parque Natural da Serra da Estrela
Torre (1993m)

Rio Minho
Rio Lima
Rio Cávado
Rio Douro
Rio Tâmega
Rio Côa
Rio Tejo
Rio Mondego
Rio Zêzere
Serra da Lousã
Serra de Açor
Serra da Estrela

Embalse de Almendra
Embalse de Alcántara

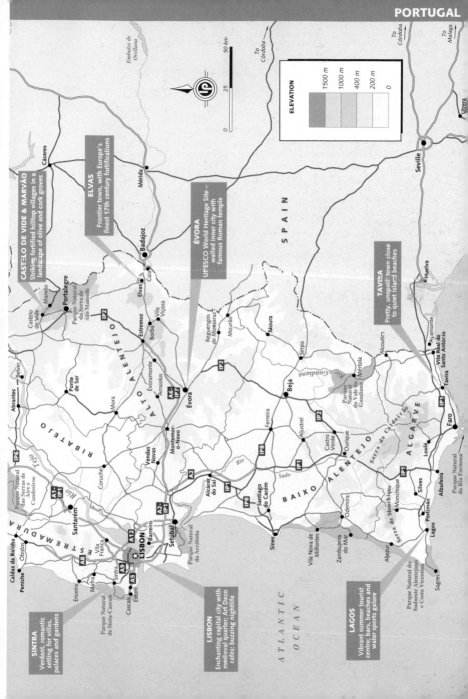

PORTUGAL

ELEVATION

1500 m
1000 m
400 m
200 m
0

25   50 km

CASTELO DE VIDE & MARVÃO
Striking, fortified hilltop villages in a landscape of olive and cork groves

ELVAS
Frontier town, with Europe's finest 17th century fortifications

ÉVORA
UNESCO World Heritage Site – walled inner city with famous Roman temple

TAVIRA
Pretty, unspoilt town close to quiet island beaches

SINTRA
Verdant, romantic setting for villas, palaces and gardens

LISBON
Enchanting capital city with medieval quarter, Art Deco cafés; buzzing nightlife

LAGOS
Vibrant summer tourist centre; bars, beaches and water sports galore

To Córdoba
To Málaga

Embalse de Orellana

Cáceres
Mérida
Badajoz

SPAIN

Seville
Huelva
Utrera

To Córdoba

ATLANTIC OCEAN

Caldas da Rainha
Peniche
Óbidos
Ericeira
Mafra
Vila Franca
Santarém
Abrantes
Belver
Castelo de Vide
Marvão
Portalegre
Caia
Elvas
Badajoz

ESTREMADURA
RIBATEJO
ALTO ALENTEJO

Parque Natural das Serras de Aire e Candeeiros
Parque Natural da Serra de São Mamede

Ponte de Sor
Mora
Arraiolos
Évoramonte
Estremoz
Borba
Vila Viçosa
Reguengos de Monsaraz
Mourão
Moura
Serpa
Mértola
Alcoutim

Rio Tejo
Rio Guadiana
Rio Sado

Coruche
Montemor-o-Novo
Vendas Novas
Évora
Ferreira
Beja
Aljustrel
Castro Verde
Ourique

Sintra
Cascais
Estoril
Parque Natural de Sintra-Cascais
LISBON
Barreiro
Setúbal
Parque Natural da Arrábida
Alcácer do Sal
Santiago do Cacém
Sines
Vila Nova de Milfontes
Zambujeira do Mar
Odemira

BAIXO ALENTEJO
Parque Natural do Vale do Guadiana

ALGARVE
Serra do Caldeirão
Serra de Monchique

Aljezur
Sagres
Lagos
Portimão
Silves
Monchique
Albufeira
Loulé
Faro
Tavira
Vila Real de Santo António
Ayamonte

Parque Natural do Sudoeste Alentejano e Costa Vicentina
Parque Natural da Ria Formosa

IP6
IP2
IP2
IP8
IP1
IP2
IP1
IP1
A6
IP7
A2
IP1
A2
IP1
IP8
A1
IP1
A8
A5
A9
A12
IP7

Portugal
2nd edition – April 1999
First published – May 1997

Published by
Lonely Planet Publications Pty Ltd A.C.N. 005 607 983
192 Burwood Rd, Hawthorn, Victoria 3122, Australia

Lonely Planet Offices
Australia PO Box 617, Hawthorn, Victoria 3122
USA 150 Linden St, Oakland, CA 94607
UK 10a Spring Place, London NW5 3BH
France 1 rue du Dahomey, 75011 Paris

Photographs
All of the images in this guide are available for licensing from
Lonely Planet Images.
email: lpi@lonelyplanet.com.au

Front cover photograph
Decorated pots from the Alto Alentejo, a region famous for its pottery
(Carlos Costa)

ISBN 0 86442 623 2

Contents – Text

1

2 Contents – Text

AROUND LISBON 191

THE ALGARVE 218

THE ALENTEJO 278

ESTREMADURA & RIBATEJO 323

THE BEIRAS 359

THE DOURO 405

THE MINHO 448

TRÁS-OS-MONTES 491

LANGUAGE 515

GLOSSARY 522

ACKNOWLEDGMENTS 525

INDEX 536

MAP LEGEND back page

METRIC CONVERSION inside back cover

Contents – Maps

INTRODUCTION

FACTS ABOUT PORTUGAL

GETTING AROUND

LISBON

AROUND LISBON

THE ALGARVE

THE ALENTEJO

ESTREMADURA & RIBATEJO

THE BEIRAS

THE DOURO

THE MINHO

TRÁS-OS-MONTES

MAP LEGEND – SEE BACK PAGE

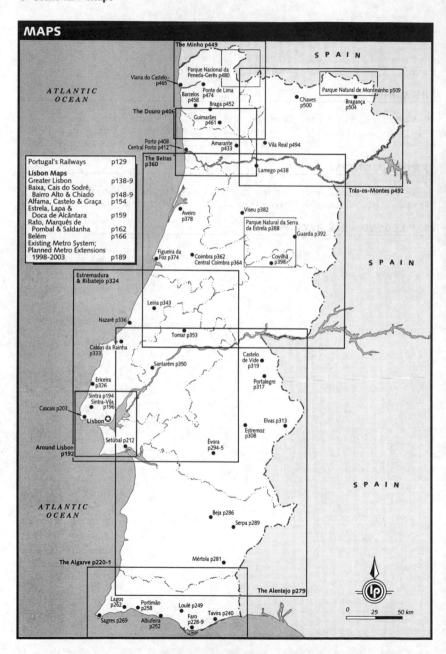

MAPS

SPAIN

ATLANTIC OCEAN

The Minho p449

Parque Nacional da Peneda-Gerês p480

Viana do Castelo p465

Parque Natural de Montesinho p509

Barcelos p458
Ponte de Lima p474
Braga p452

Chaves p500
Bragança p504

The Douro p406

Guimarães p461

The Belras p360

Porto p408
Central Porto p412

Amarante p433
Vila Real p494

Lamego p438

Trás-os-Montes p492

Aveiro p378

Viseu p382

Parque Natural da Serra da Estrela p388
Guarda p392

SPAIN

Figueira da Foz p374
Coimbra p362
Central Coimbra p364
Covilhã p398

Estremadura & Ribatejo p324

Leiria p343

Nazaré p336

Tomar p353

Caldas da Rainha p333

Santarém p350

Castelo de Vide p319

Portalegre p317

Ericeira p326

Sintra p194
Sintra-Vila p196

Cascais p203
Lisbon

Elvas p313

Estremoz p308

Around Lisbon p192

Setúbal p212

Évora p294-5

SPAIN

ATLANTIC OCEAN

Beja p286

Serpa p289

The Algarve p220-1

Mértola p281

The Alentejo p279

Lagos p262
Portimão p258
Loulé p249
Tavira p240

Sagres p269
Albufeira p252
Faro p228-9

0   25   50 km

The Authors

Julia Wilkinson & John King

Julia left home with her first backpack at the age of four. She only got to the end of the road, but has been a travel junkie ever since. After university in England she headed for Australia but got side-tracked in Hong Kong, where she worked in publishing and radio until going freelance as a writer and photographer. Since then she has travelled throughout Asia, writing for international publications. She has contributed to guidebooks on Hong Kong, Tibet and Laos and is the author of guidebooks on Thailand and Portugal and of Lonely Planet's *Lisbon*. Julia has also helped update the Portugal chapters of Lonely Planet's *Western Europe* and *Mediterranean Europe* guides. To get away from the road, she takes to the skies, flying hot-air balloons.

John grew up in the USA, and in earlier 'incarnations' has been a university physics teacher and an environmental consultant. In a rash moment in 1984 he headed off for a look at China and ended up living there for half a year. During that time he and Julia crossed paths in Lhasa, the Tibetan capital. After surviving a three month journey across China and Pakistan they decided anything was possible and, in 1988, John took up travel writing, starting with the first edition of Lonely Planet's *Karakoram Highway*. He is also co-author of Lonely Planet's *Central Asia*; *Russia, Ukraine & Belarus*; *Pakistan*; *Czech & Slovak Republics*; and *Prague*.

After two decades in Hong Kong, Julia and John are now based in south-west England with their son, Kit (who looks set to don *his* first backpack), and daughter, Lia.

From the Authors

We are indebted to art lecturer and architecture specialist Carol Rankin for her major contribution to our special architecture section; Algarve-based author and ornithologist Clive Viney for his eagle's-eye review of Flora & Fauna; Marco Oliveira for his wide-ranging and thorough review of Porto nightlife; and Lisbon resident Peter Gilbert for a very helpful review of our Lisbon nightlife entries.

Once again we are very grateful to Pilar Pereira of ICEP in London for logistical support and patient responses to many queries. Many thanks also to Malcolm Ginsberg of AB Airlines and to Geraldine Aherne at TAP Air Portugal.

In Portugal, certain municipal tourist offices stood out from the others. Thanks in particular to Miguel Gonzaga and Vitor Carriço of Lisbon's Visitors & Convention Bureau, and to the formidable troika of Marco Oliveira, Maria José Braga and Joana Firmino at the Porto office. Others who went beyond the call of duty were Ana Seixas Palma (Beja), Anabela Pereira (Bragança), Marie Theresa Gomes (Coimbra), Abílio Viegas (Faro), Amélia Paulo Vieira (Sintra), Maria do Rosário Graça (Vila Real) and staff at Aveiro, Ericeira, Estremoz, Évora and Tavira.

Dra Helena Taborda of the Metropôlitano de Lisboa, Dr João Carlos Farinha of the Instituto da Conservação da Natureza (ICN) and Sra Ana Cardoso Santos of the Instituto Nacional de Estatística helped us chase down elusive facts. From Gonçalo Diniz of ILGA-Portugal came a drumroll of good information on Portugal's gay scene. Luís Ramos at the Gouveia office of the Parque Natural da Serra da Estrela brought us up-to-date on the park. Anabela Esteves told us much that was new about the Associação de Desenvolvimento das Regiões (ADERE) and a bit more about Ponte da Barca. A tip of the hat also to 'JP' at Residencial Montalto in Covilhã.

A special obrigada from Julia to Maurice Clyde of Os Caminheiros do Algarve/Walkers (OCDAW), not only for information on The Algarve Way, but for mending her puncture in the back of beyond; and to John Hole for a memorably fast balloon flight over Castelo Branco's endless forests.

Many people in the UK provided essential and first-rate support, including Peter Mills of Rail Europe; Sue Copper of Eurolines; Pieter Beelen of Eurail; Paul Gowen, Touring Information & Research Manager at the RAC; and Sue Hall of the Cyclists' Touring Club. We are also indebted to staff at several STA Travel offices, especially Leah Ullness in New Zealand and Julie Thomas in London, and to Fiona Lang at Flight Centres International in Melbourne.

Cheers to Sacha Pearson at Lonely Planet's Oakland office for answers to numerous USA queries and Dan Levin at the Melbourne office for computer help.

This Book

Julia Wilkinson and John King researched and wrote the first edition of *Portugal*. For this second edition, Julia worked on the southern and central Portugal chapters and John covered the mountains and the north.

From the Publisher

This second edition of *Portugal* was edited in Lonely Planet's London office by Christine Stroyan, with help from Paul Bloomfield, Katrina Browning and Dorinda Talbot. Angie Watts coordinated the mapping – updating the maps and drawing several new ones – assisted by Michelle Lewis, Sara Yorke, Tony Battle, Tom Fawcett, Andrew Smith, Anthony Phelan and Lisa Borg. Angie designed the book with Michelle's assistance and put together the colour pages with Tony. Dorinda Talbot and Corinne Simçock proofread the book and Dorinda helped with indexing, along with Tim Ryder and David Rathborne. Nicky Castle drew the illustrations, Lonely Planet Images supplied the photographs, Dale Buckton designed the cover and Tony Battle provided the cute cockerel chapter end. Piotr Czajkowski drew the colour map and Anthony drew the climate charts. Special thanks are due to Simon Calder, who thoroughly revised the Getting There & Away chapter, and to Katrina, who struggled through Sydney flu to get this book to the printers.

Thanks, too, to the many people in the Melbourne office who answered questions and provided information – Leonie Mugavin checked out the Health section and answered numerous travel queries, Martin Hughes read through the sections on bullfighting and Paul Clifton checked the Gay & Lesbian Travellers section. Verity Campbell and Carolyn Papworth advised on Women Travellers and Quentin Frayne sorted out the language chapter. In the Oakland office, Sacha Pearson helped with US travel information.

THANKS

Many thanks to the travellers who used the last edition and wrote to us with helpful hints, advice and interesting anecdotes. Your names appear in the back of this book.

Foreword

ABOUT LONELY PLANET GUIDEBOOKS

The story begins with a classic travel adventure: Tony and Maureen Wheeler's 1972 journey across Europe and Asia to Australia. Useful information about the overland trail did not exist at that time, so Tony and Maureen published the first Lonely Planet guidebook to meet a growing need.

From a kitchen table, then from a tiny office in Melbourne (Australia), Lonely Planet has become the largest independent travel publisher in the world, an international company with offices in Melbourne, Oakland (USA), London (UK) and Paris (France).

Today Lonely Planet guidebooks cover the globe. There is an ever-growing list of books and there's information in a variety of forms and media. Some things haven't changed. The main aim is still to help make it possible for adventurous travellers to get out there – to explore and better understand the world.

At Lonely Planet we believe travellers can make a positive contribution to the countries they visit – if they respect their host communities and spend their money wisely. Since 1986 a percentage of the income from each book has been donated to aid projects and human rights campaigns.

Updates Lonely Planet thoroughly updates each guidebook as often as possible. This usually means there are around two years between editions, although for more unusual or more stable destinations the gap can be longer. Check the imprint page (following the colour map at the beginning of the book) for publication dates.

Between editions up-to-date information is available in two free newsletters – the paper *Planet Talk* and email *Comet* (to subscribe, contact any Lonely Planet office) – and on our Web site at www.lonelyplanet.com. The *Upgrades* section of the Web site covers a number of important and volatile destinations and is regularly updated by Lonely Planet authors. *Scoop* covers news and current affairs relevant to travellers. And, lastly, the *Thorn Tree* bulletin board and *Postcards* section of the site carry unverified, but fascinating, reports from travellers.

Correspondence The process of creating new editions begins with the letters, postcards and emails received from travellers. This correspondence often includes suggestions, criticisms and comments about the current editions. Interesting excerpts are immediately passed on via newsletters and the Web site, and everything goes to our authors to be verified when they're researching on the road. We're keen to get more feedback from organisations or individuals who represent communities visited by travellers.

Lonely Planet gathers information for everyone who's curious about the planet – and especially for those who explore it first-hand. Through guidebooks, phrasebooks, activity guides, maps, literature, newsletters, image library, TV series and Web site we act as an information exchange for a worldwide community of travellers.

Research Authors aim to gather sufficient practical information to enable travellers to make informed choices and to make the mechanics of a journey run smoothly. They also research historical and cultural background to help enrich the travel experience and allow travellers to understand and respond appropriately to cultural and environmental issues.

Authors don't stay in every hotel because that would mean spending a couple of months in each medium-sized city and, no, they don't eat at every restaurant because that would mean stretching belts beyond capacity. They do visit hotels and restaurants to check standards and prices, but feedback based on readers' direct experiences can be very helpful.

Many of our authors work undercover, others aren't so secretive. None of them accept freebies in exchange for positive write-ups. And none of our guidebooks contain any advertising.

Production Authors submit their raw manuscripts and maps to offices in Australia, USA, UK or France. Editors and cartographers – all experienced travellers themselves – then begin the process of assembling the pieces. When the book finally hits the shops some things are already out of date, we start getting feedback from readers, and the process begins again ...

WARNING & REQUEST

Things change – prices go up, schedules change, good places go bad and bad places go bankrupt – nothing stays the same. So, if you find things better or worse, recently opened or long since closed, please tell us and help make the next edition even more accurate and useful. We genuinely value all the feedback we receive. Julie Young coordinates a well-travelled team that reads and acknowledges every letter, postcard and email and ensures that every morsel of information finds its way to the appropriate authors, editors and cartographers for verification.

Everyone who writes to us will find their name in the next edition of the appropriate guidebook. They will also receive the latest issue of *Planet Talk*, our quarterly printed newsletter, or *Comet*, our monthly email newsletter. Subscriptions to both newsletters are free. The very best contributions will be rewarded with a free guidebook.

Excerpts from your correspondence may appear in new editions of Lonely Planet guidebooks, the Lonely Planet Web site, *Planet Talk* or *Comet*, so please let us know if you *don't* want your letter published or your name acknowledged.

Send all correspondence to the Lonely Planet office closest to you:

Australia: PO Box 617, Hawthorn, Victoria 3122
UK: 10A Spring Place, London NW5 3BH
USA: 150 Linden St, Oakland CA 94607
France: 1 rue du Dahomey, Paris 75011

Or email us at: talk2us@lonelyplanet.com.au

For news, views and updates see our Web site: www.lonelyplanet.com

HOW TO USE A LONELY PLANET GUIDEBOOK

The best way to use a Lonely Planet guidebook is any way you choose. At Lonely Planet we believe the most memorable travel experiences are often those that are unexpected, and the finest discoveries are those you make yourself. Guidebooks are not intended to be used as if they provide a detailed set of infallible instructions!

Contents All Lonely Planet guidebooks follow the same format. The Facts about the Country chapter or section gives background information ranging from history to weather. Facts for the Visitor gives practical information on issues like visas and health. Getting There & Away gives a brief starting point for researching travel to and from the destination. Getting Around gives an overview of the transport options when you arrive.

The peculiar demands of each destination determine how subsequent chapters are broken up, but some things remain constant. We always start with background, then proceed to sights, places to stay, places to eat, entertainment, getting there and away, and getting around information – in that order.

Heading Hierarchy Lonely Planet headings are used in a strict hierarchical structure that can be visualised as a set of Russian dolls. Each heading (and its following text) is encompassed by any preceding heading that is higher on the hierarchical ladder.

Entry Points We do not assume guidebooks will be read from beginning to end, but that people will dip into them. The traditional entry points are the list of contents and the index. In addition, however, there is a complete list of maps and an index map illustrating map coverage.

There's also a colour map that shows highlights. These highlights are dealt with in greater detail in the Facts for the Visitor chapter, along with planning questions and suggested itineraries. Each chapter covering a geographical region begins with a locator map and another list of highlights. Once you find something of interest in a list of highlights, turn to the index.

Maps Maps play a crucial role in Lonely Planet guidebooks and include a huge amount of information. A legend is printed on the back page. We seek to have complete consistency between maps and text, and to have every important place in the text captured on a map. Map key numbers usually start in the top left corner.

Although inclusion in a guidebook usually implies a recommendation we cannot list every good place. Exclusion does not necessarily imply criticism. In fact there are a number of reasons why we might exclude a place – sometimes it is simply inappropriate to encourage an influx of travellers.

Introduction

Portugal has long been overlooked on the traveller's European itinerary. This is a land apart, at the westernmost corner of Europe, its development hindered for hundreds of years by poverty and political turmoil. Ruled by Romans and Moors for centuries, and perennially in the threatening shadow of Spain, it emerged as a nation state in the 12th century and established its independence and frontiers during the following century (making it one of Europe's oldest countries). Two hundred years later its mariners ventured into the unknown, ultimately discovering a sea route to India and turning Portugal into one of the richest and most powerful kingdoms in the western hemisphere. The gold and glory were short-

lived, however; Portugal slipped into chaos and obscurity on the forgotten hem of Europe.

Wracked by political upheaval, including 48 years of dictatorship and a revolution in 1974, Portugal has only recently begun to emerge from the shadows. In 1986 it joined the European Union (EU) and looked forward to a future within Europe. Thanks largely to massive EU funding, changes since then have been fast and furious: new highways to Spain, new urban development, new enterprises and new confidence. But the long isolation, especially the xenophobic period of dictatorship under Salazar, has left much of the country extraordinarily, often appealingly, old-fashioned. This

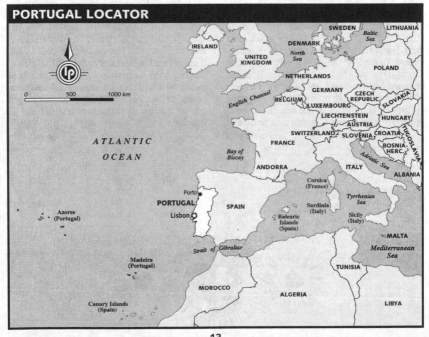

includes the capital, Lisbon, which, despite ferocious redevelopment pre and post-Expo '98, remains one of Europe's most attractive and relaxing cities.

Although stretches of the country's 800km of Atlantic coast are terribly polluted and the southern Algarve coastline has long catered to mass tourism (and paid the price with its ugly coastal development), there's plenty left that's wild, unspoilt and stunningly beautiful. That's true of the interior too. For such a small country there's a remarkable natural diversity, ranging from the south's undulating plains and Mediterranean landscapes to the north's dramatic mountain ranges and lush valleys.

While the south, particularly the Alentejo, is chequered with vast farming estates (originally founded by the Romans) and yawning vistas of cork oaks and wheat, the north reflects an even older agricultural system of tiny smallholdings producing maize, vegetables and vines. Socially, too, there are obvious north-south divisions: southern Portuguese tend to be outgoing and 'Mediterranean', whereas northerners are more conservative and religious, taking their festivals and folklore very seriously indeed. In parts of the rural north, where EU funds have yet to trickle down, life has changed little in hundreds of years. Poverty is so ingrained that many families depend on money sent by menfolk who have emigrated to France and Germany in search of

work, following a tradition dating from the 17th and 18th centuries. Their home villages of granite and shale houses, bullock carts and donkeys seem hardly touched by Portugal's new winds of progress, though even here roads are now being upgraded and farm machinery introduced.

As a traveller in this little-explored corner of Europe you've got some enviable choices to make: stick to the Algarve with its lively resorts, golf courses and water sports; loiter in Lisbon with its upbeat attitude and lively nightlife, including music ranging from *fado* – Portugal's own soul-searing blues – to immigrant African sounds; trek into remote mountains where the Portuguese themselves rarely go; follow a cultural trail through the art and architecture of a number of UNESCO World Heritage Sites, including Évora, Porto, Batalha and Alcobaça; or meander up the beautiful Lima, Douro and Minho river valleys in the north.

Of course there are hiccups – reliable information is hard to come by and many officials are incurably inefficient. On the other hand, transport and accommodation are excellent and reasonably priced. Food, if not refined, is certainly plentiful, and Portuguese wine is perhaps the country's best and most addictive bargain. Add to this a generous supply of sunshine and you've got one of the most attractive destinations in Europe.

Carving Up Portugal

Traditionally, Portugal was composed of seven loosely defined provinces (*províncias*) – the Minho (named after the Rio Minho), the Douro (named after the Rio Douro), Trás-os-Montes (beyond the mountains), the Beira (border), the Estremadura (furthest from the Rio Douro), the Alentejo (beyond the Rio Tejo) and the Algarve (after the Moorish *al-gharb*, meaning west country).

In the 1830s the boundaries of these provinces were firmed up and they were subdivided into administrative districts (*distritos*), each named after its main town. In the 1930s three provinces were broken into smaller pieces: the Beira into Beira Litoral (coastal), Beira Alta (upper) and Beira Baixa (lower), the Estremadura into Estremadura and Ribatejo, and the Alentejo into Alto Alentejo and Baixo Alentejo.

The chapters of this book correspond to the traditional provinces defined by the 1830s borders, with the exception of separate chapters for Lisbon and its environs, and the inclusion in the Douro chapter of the entire Douro valley all the way to the Spanish border (even though some towns in the valley are properly part of Beira Alta or Trás-os-Montes).

To complicate matters, ICEP, the Portuguese tourism authority, has invented its own geographically based *regiões de turismo* (tourism regions). Its brochures and maps, and the locations of regional tourist offices, are all based on these regions, whose borders don't correspond exactly with any of the political ones.

PROVINCES & DISTRICTS

REGIÕES DE TURISMO

Facts about Portugal

HISTORY
Pre-Roman & Roman

The Iberian Peninsula has been inhabited for at least 500,000 years. The earliest evidence of human habitation in Portugal includes recently discovered Palaeolithic inscriptions near Vila Nova de Foz Côa in the Douro. The first distinct cultures can be traced to the Neolithic-era *castro* culture of fortified hilltop settlements and to settlements in the lower Tejo valley dating from 5500 BC.

In the first millennium BC, Celtic people started to trickle into the Iberian Peninsula, settling in northern and western areas of Portugal around 700 BC. The resulting hybrid Celtic-castro culture was responsible for dozens of *citânias* or fortified villages (especially in the Minho), complete with defence walls and moats. Many, including the formidable citânia of Briteiros near Braga, continued to be used right up to Roman times.

Further south, Phoenician traders, followed by Greeks and Carthaginians, set up coastal stations and mined metals inland. The Carthaginians held sway until their defeat by the Romans in the Second Punic War (218-202 BC).

When the Romans swept into southern Portugal in 210 BC, they expected an easy victory. But they hadn't reckoned on the Lusitani, a Celtic warrior tribe which was based between the Tejo (Tagus) and Douro rivers and which resisted ferociously for half a century. Only when their brilliant leader, Viriathus, was tricked and assassinated in 139 BC did resistance collapse.

By 19 BC the Romans had managed to subdue all traces of Lusitanian independence. Under Decimus Junius Brutus and Julius Caesar a capital was established at Olisipo (Lisbon) in 60 BC and other major colonies were founded at Scallabis (Santarém), Bracara Augusta (Braga), Pax Julia (Beja) and Ebora (Évora).

Around 25 BC, Augustus divided this part of the Roman Empire – called Hispania Ulterior and consisting of southern Spain and the whole of Portugal – into several provinces, including Lusitania (south of the Douro) and Baetica (Andalusia). In the 3rd century AD, the Minho became part of a new province called Gallaecia (Galicia). Around this time, Christianity was established, with important bishoprics at Évora and Braga.

By the 5th century, when the Roman Empire had all but collapsed, Portugal's inhabitants had been under Roman rule for 600 years. What did they get from it? Most usefully, roads and bridges (still in evidence throughout Portugal), but the Romans also left them wheat, barley, olives and vines; a system of large farming estates (called *latifúndios* and still in existence in the Alentejo); a legal system; and, above all, a Latin-derived language. No other invader left Portugal such an important legacy.

Moors & Christians

The gap left by the Romans was quickly filled by barbarian invaders from beyond the Pyrenees: Vandals, Alans, Visigoths and Suevi. The Germanic Suevi had the greatest impact, settling between the Minho and Douro rivers in the years after 400 AD, and ruling from Braga and Portucale (Porto). For a time·they had a tenuous control over most of the peninsula, but from 469 onwards, Arian Christian Visigoths got the upper hand, encouraged by the Romans.

Internal disputes paved the way for the Visigoths' downfall and Portugal's next great wave of invaders: in 711, Muslim forces from North Africa were invited to help a Visigoth faction. The Moors were only too ready to move north. Commanded by Tariq ibn Ziyad, they rapidly occupied Portugal's southern coastal region. Egyptians settled in the Beja and Faro area, while Syrians mostly settled between Faro and

Seville, an area they called al-Gharb al-Andalus (the word Algarve comes from this). The north – known as the county of Portucale – remained unstable, unsettled and predominantly Christian.

Under the Moors (who established a capital at Silves, then called Shelb), southerners enjoyed a peaceful and productive period. The new rulers were tolerant of Jews and Christians. Christian smallholding farmers, called Mozarabs, were allowed to keep working their land and were encouraged to try out new methods of irrigation and new crops, especially citrus and rice. It was in this period, too, that Arabic words began to filter into the Portuguese language, and Arabic influences into the local cuisine – in particular an obsession with cakes and desserts of unsurpassable sweetness.

Meanwhile, in the north of the peninsula, Christian powers were gaining strength. The symbolic kick-start to the Reconquista (which did not really begin in earnest for another three centuries) was a Christian victory over a small force of Moors in 718 at Covadonga in the Asturias, northern Spain. From here the tiny kingdom of Asturias-León expanded, gradually absorbing Castile, Aragon, Galicia and the province of Portucale (including Porto, which was taken in 868).

By the 11th century, when the Moors controlled most of southern Portugal as well as southern and eastern Spain, Portucale had become an important regional power, for a time autonomous under the dynastic rule of Mumadona Dias and her family. By 1064 Coimbra fell within the Christian sphere, governed by a Mozarab. In 1085 Alfonso VI, king of the Christian kingdoms of León and Castile, took the bull by the horns and thrashed the Moors in their Spanish heartland of Toledo. A colourful character, Alfonso is said to have secured Seville by winning a game of chess with its cultured emir. But the following year, he faced a tougher enemy, the ruthless Almoravids from Morocco, who answered the emir's call for help, defeated Alfonso and drove out the Mozarabs. Worse was

follow with the arrival of even more fanatical Almohads.

When Alfonso in turn called for foreign help, European crusaders were quick to rally to his side against the 'infidels'. Among them were Henri of Burgundy and his cousin Raymond, who won not only battlefield glory but the hands of Alfonso's daughters. Henri married Teresa (and became Count of Portucale), and Raymond married Urraca (and became Lord of Galicia and Coimbra).

On Alfonso's death in 1109, things got messy: Urraca's son, Alfonso Raimúndez (later Alfonso VII), took control of León, while Teresa (regent for her son, Afonso Henriques, after the death of her husband in 1112) favoured a union with Galicia, thanks to her dalliance with a Galician. But she reckoned without the nationalist ideas of her son.

In 1128, Afonso Henriques took up arms against her, defeating her forces near his capital, Guimarães. At first he had to bow to the superior power of his cousin, Alfonso VII of León. But on the basis of a dramatic victory against the Moors in 1139 at Ourique (in present-day Alentejo), Afonso Henriques began calling himself King (Dom) of Portugal in 1143, a title confirmed in 1179 by the pope (on condition extra tribute was paid, of course). By then he had also retaken Santarém and Lisbon from the Moors (crusaders en route to the Holy Land had helped with the siege of Lisbon in 1147).

By the time Afonso Henriques died in 1185, the Portuguese frontier was secure to the Rio Tejo. Yet despite assistance frequently given by the crusaders (another lot helped capture Silves in 1189), it was almost another century before the Alentejo and the Algarve were wrested from the Moors.

In 1297, after several disputes with neighbouring Castile, the boundaries of the Portuguese kingdom (much the same then as they are today) were given official recognition in the Treaty of Alcañices. The kingdom of Portugal had arrived.

The Burgundian Era

During the Reconquista, the 400,000 inhabitants of the country – most of whom lived in the north – were faced with more than war and turmoil: in the wake of Christian victories they faced the arrival of new rulers and new Christian settlers (especially in Trás-os-Montes and the Beiras, and later in the Algarve). Powerful military orders like the Knights Templar (see the boxed text under Tomar in the Estramadura & Ribatejo chapter) and the Hospitallers took control of much of the land south of the Rio Tejo, while the Cisterian monks developed the Alcobaça area.

The Church and its wealthy clergy were the greediest landowners – so much so that the Crown had to hold frequent royal commissions to recover illegally taken land. Next in the landowning pecking order came a hundred or so nobles from the aristocratic warrior class, followed by a thousand or so minor nobles. During the rule of Afonso Henriques' son, Sancho I, many municipalities (*concelhos*) were enfranchised and given special privileges embodied in charters. Enfranchisement extended to some Muslims, too, although enslavement of Moors persisted in some places right up to the 13th century and segregated living areas for Moors – *mourarias* – were widespread.

Although in theory free, most common people were actually still subjects of the landowning classes, working on their lord's land, their rights controlled by the terms of the charters. In the south, especially, many were also recruited as foot soldiers for ongoing raids into Muslim territory. The first hint of democratic rule came with the establishment of the *cortes* (parliament): an assembly of nobles and clergy who first met in 1211 at Coimbra, which was then the capital. Municipal representation – allowing commoners (mostly wealthy merchants) to attend the cortes – followed in 1254 under Afonso III. Six years later, the capital was moved to Lisbon.

But although Afonso III deserves recognition for many important administrative changes, and for standing up to the power of the Church, it was his son Dinis (1279-1325) who started to really shake Portugal into shape. A far-sighted, cultured man, he brought the judicial system under royal control, suppressed the dangerously powerful Knights Templar by refounding them as the Order of Christ, initiated progressive afforestation programmes and encouraged internal trade. He also cultivated music, the arts and education, founding a university in Lisbon in 1290, which later transferred to Coimbra.

His foresight was spot-on when it came to defending Portugal's borders: Dom Dinis built or rebuilt some 50 fortresses along the eastern frontier with Castile, and signed a pact of friendship with England in 1308, the basis of a future, long-lasting alliance.

It was none too soon. Within 60 years of Dinis' death, Portugal was at war with Castile over rival claims to the Portuguese throne. Fernando I, the last of the Burgundian kings, had done much to provoke the clash by playing a dangerous game of alliances with both Castile and the English (as represented by John of Gaunt, Duke of Lancaster). He had, for instance, promised his only legitimate child, Beatriz, to John of Gaunt's nephew when the English arrived in 1381 to help with an invasion of Castile. In the event, Fernando made peace with the Castilians halfway through the campaign and offered Beatriz to Juan I of Castile instead, thereby throwing Portugal's future into Castilian hands.

On Fernando's death in 1383, his wife, Leonor Teles, ruled as regent but she, too, was entangled with the Spanish, having long had a Galician lover. While nobles and bishops supported her, the merchant classes turned to a truly Portuguese candidate: João, Grand Master of the Order of Avis, and a son (albeit illegitimate) of Fernando's father, Pedro I. João assassinated Leonor's lover, Leonor fled to the King of Castile, and the Castilians duly invaded. But João had the support of the common people, who rose in revolt not only against the invaders but also against Castilian nobles who had settled in Portugal.

The showdown came in 1385 when João faced an imposing force of Castilians at Aljubarrota. Even with Nuno Álvares Pereira (the 'Holy Constable') as his military right-hand man, and a force of English archers as support, the odds were stacked against him. João vowed to build a monastery to the Virgin if he won – and he did.

This victory sealed Portugal's independence – and also delivered the superb architectural legacy of Batalha Abbey. It also sealed Portugal's alliance with England: the 1386 Treaty of Windsor formalising the alliance was followed by the marriage of João to John of Gaunt's daughter, Philippa of Lancaster. Peace with Castile was finally concluded in 1411. Portugal was ready to look further afield for adventure.

The Age of Discoveries

Morocco was the obvious first outlet for João's military energies, and in 1415 Ceuta fell to his forces. Although his successor, Duarte, failed in the first bid to capture Tangier in 1437, these advances marked the start of something very big indeed. It was João's third son, Prince Henry 'the Navigator', who focused the spirit of the age – a combination of crusading zeal, love of martial glory and desire for gold and riches – into extraordinary explorations across the seas which transformed the small kingdom into a great imperial power (see the boxed text 'Henry the Navigator' on the next page).

By the 1460s the Cape Verde islands had been discovered and the Gulf of Guinea had been reached. And in 1487 Bartolomeu Dias rounded the Cape of Good Hope.

The way was now open to India: in 1497, during the reign of Manuel I (who titled himself 'Lord of the Conquest, Navigation, and Commerce of India, Ethiopia, Arabia and Persia'), Vasco da Gama reached Calicut in southern India. With gold (and slaves) from Africa and spices from the East, Portugal soon became enormously wealthy.

Spain, however, had also jumped on the exploration bandwagon and was soon disputing some of Portugal's claims to foreign land. Christopher Columbus' 1492 'discovery' of America for Spain led to a fresh outburst of jealous conflict. It was resolved by the pope with the extraordinary Treaty of Tordesillas of 1494, by which the world was divided between the two great powers along a line 370 leagues west of the Cape Verde islands. Spain won the lands to the west of the line, Portugal those to the east – including Brazil, the existence of which they may have known about already (it was officially claimed for Portugal in 1500).

In the following years, as its explorers reached Timor, China and eventually Japan, Portugal consolidated its power and world trading status with garrison ports and strategic trading and missionary posts: Goa in 1510, Malacca in 1511, Hormoz in 1515 and Macau in 1557. Back home, the monarchy, taking its 'royal fifth' of trading profits, became the richest in Europe, and the lavish Manueline style of architecture (named after Dom Manuel I) marked the exuberance of the age (most visibly in the Mosteiro dos Jerónimos and Torre de Belém near Lisbon).

It couldn't last, of course. By the 1570s, the huge cost of expeditions and maintenance of the overseas empire began to take a

The Portuguese in Australia

It is believed by many historians that Portuguese explorers reached the Australian coast in the 16th century, 2½ centuries before the arrival of the recognised discoverer, Captain James Cook. At least one Australian historian, Kenneth McIntyre, is convinced that by 1536 the Portuguese had secretly mapped three-quarters of the island's coastline. In September 1996 a 500-year-old Portuguese coin was found by a treasure hunter on the Mornington Peninsula, on the Victorian coast, adding further weight to this theory.

Prince Henry the Navigator

Henrique, Infante de Portugal (Prince of Portugal), was born in present-day Porto in 1394. By the time he died 66 years later he had almost single-handedly set Portugal on course for its so-called Age of Discoveries, turning it from Spain's little brother into a wealthy maritime power, and in the process transforming seaborne exploration from a groping, semirandom process to a near science.

At the age of 18, Henry and his older brothers, Duarte and Pedro, keen to prove themselves in battle, convinced their father to invade Ceuta in Morocco. The city fell with ease in 1415 and Henry was appointed its governor. Though he spent little time there this stirred his interest in North Africa and, with several ships now at his disposal, he began to sponsor exploratory voyages. Two of his pro-tégés discovered (or rediscovered, as Genoese sailors had stumbled across them in the 14th century) the islands of Porto Santo and Madeira.

Henry's likeness on the Padrão dos Descobrimentos in Belém

In 1419 Henry became governor of the Algarve, moved to the south coast and began collecting the best sailors, map makers, shipbuilders, instrument makers and astronomers he could find in order to get Portuguese explorers as far out into the world as possible. The next year, at the age of 26, he became Grand Master of the Order of Christ, which superseded the crusading Knights Templar, and his efforts went into high gear thanks to money available through the order. His strategy was as much religious as com-mercial, aimed at sapping the power of the Islamic world by siphoning off its trade and, ultimately, by finding a way around it by sea, all the while converting newly discovered peoples. All his ships bore the trademark red cross of the Order of Christ on their sails. Henry took no vows, though he lived simply and chastely, and remained single all his life.

Madeira and the Azores were the first lands to be discovered in 1419 and 1427 (colonisa-tion followed in 1445). In 1434 Gil Eanes sailed beyond the much-feared Cape Bojador on the West African coast, breaking a maritime superstition that this was the end of the world. The newly designed, highly manoeuvrable Portuguese caravel made this possible.

In 1437 Henry and his younger brother, Prince Fernando, embarked on a disastrous attempt to take Tangier. Despite his guilt about his part in the expedition (during which his brother was taken hostage, to die six years later still in captivity), Henry continued his work. In 1441, as unease was mounting over his lavish spending on exploration, ships began re-turning with West African gold and slaves. Within a few years the slave trade was galloping, and Henry's interest gradually began to turn from exploration to commerce. He founded his own trading company in Lagos, having been granted by Afonso V the sole right to trade on the coast of Guinea. The last great discovery to which Henry was witness was of several of the Cape Verde islands by the Venetian Alvise Cá da Mosto and the Portuguese Diogo Gomes. The furthest his sailors got in his lifetime was present-day Sierra Leone, or possibly Côte d'Ivoire. His last military adventure, at the age of 64, was the capture, with Afonso, of Alcácer Ceguer in Morocco. Two years later, on 13 November 1460, he died at Sagres – heavily in debt in spite of revenues from the slave and gold trade.

EXPLORATION BY THE PORTUGUESE

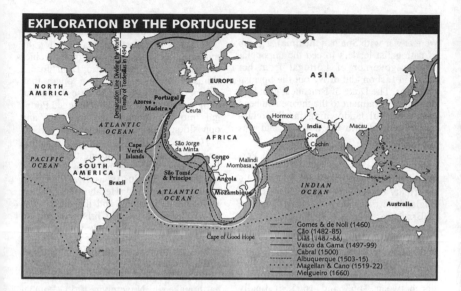

NORTH AMERICA
EUROPE
ASIA
Demarcation Line Dividing the World (Treaty of Tordesillas in 1494)
Portugal
Azores
Madeira
Ceuta
ATLANTIC OCEAN
Hormoz
India
Macau
Goa
AFRICA
Cochin
São Jorge da Minta
Cape Verde Islands
Congo
Malindi
Mombasa
PACIFIC OCEAN
SOUTH AMERICA
Brazil
São Tomé & Príncipe
Angola
Mozambique
ATLANTIC OCEAN
INDIAN OCEAN
Australia
Cape of Good Hope

Gomes & de Noli (1460)
Cão (1482-85)
Diás (1487-88)
Vasco da Gama (1497-99)
Cabral (1500)
Albuquerque (1503-15)
Magellan & Cano (1519-22)
Melgueiro (1660)

toll. The new riches went little further than the monarchy and nobility, while domestic agriculture declined and prices in Europe fell. The expulsion of many commercially minded refugee Spanish Jews in 1496 and the subsequent persecution of converted Jews – New Christians, or *marranos* – during the Inquisition (see under Religion later in this chapter) only worsened the financial situation.

The final straw came in 1557 when the young idealist prince Sebastião took the throne, determined to bring Christianity to Morocco. He rallied a huge force of 18,000 and set off in 1578, only to be disastrously defeated at the Battle of Alcácer-Quibir. Dom Sebastião and 8000 others were killed, including most of the Portuguese nobility. Over the next few years, his aged successor, Cardinal Henrique, had to drain the royal coffers to ransom those captured.

On Henrique's death in 1580, Sebastião's uncle, Felipe II of Spain, claimed the throne, defeated Portuguese forces at the battle of Alcântara and the following year was crowned Felipe I of Portugal. This marked the end of the Avis dynasty and centuries of independence, the end of Portugal's golden age and its glorious moment on the world stage.

Spain's Rule & Portugal's Revival

The start of Spanish rule looked promising: Felipe I promised to preserve Portugal's autonomy and to pay frequent visits to the long-ignored cortes. But common people strongly resented Spanish rule and held onto the dream that Sebastião was still alive: pretenders to the Sebastião role continued to pop up until 1600. And though Felipe was honourable, his successors were considerably less so, using Portugal to raise money and men for Spain's wars overseas and appointing Spaniards to Portuguese offices of government.

Meanwhile, Portugal's overseas empire was slipping out of its grasp. In 1622 the English seized Hormoz, and by the 1650s the Dutch had taken Malacca, Ceylon and part of Brazil.

Portuguese resentment finally exploded in 1640 when an attempt was made to recruit Portuguese forces to crush a revolt in Catalonia. Encouraged by the French (who were at war with Spain at the time), a group of nationalist leaders forced the unpopular woman governor of Portugal from her office in Lisbon and drove out the Spanish garrisons. The Duke of Bragança, grandson of a former claimant to the throne and head of a powerful landowning family, reluctantly stepped into the hot seat and was crowned João IV.

With a hostile Spain on the doorstep, Portugal searched for allies and in 1654 it signed a treaty with England, followed by the Treaty of 1661 by which Charles II of England married João's daughter, Catherine of Bragança, promising arms and men for the war with Spain in return for Portugal ceding Tangier and Bombay. Preoccupied with wars elsewhere, Spain made only half-hearted attempts to recapture Portugal and, after losing a series of battles on the frontier between 1663 and 1665, it finally recognised Portuguese independence with the 1668 Treaty of Lisbon.

The moves towards democracy which had begun over 400 years earlier with municipal representation at the cortes now stalled under João's successors. The Crown hardly bothered to call the cortes, thanks to its renewed financial independence following the discovery of gold and precious stones in Brazil at the end of the 17th century. Economically, too, the country was in trouble: after a burst of economic sense, when Pedro II's Superintendent of Finance managed to boost exports and restrict the import of luxury goods, came another era of profligate expenditure, epitomised by the gigantic Baroque monastery palace in Mafra, which required a workforce of 50,000 between 1717 and 1735.

The most notable event on the economic front was the 1703 Methuen Treaty, which stimulated Anglo-Portuguese trade with preferential terms for the import of English textiles and the export of Portuguese wines to England. But even this wasn't the boon it first appeared, as it increased Portugal's dependency on Britain, hurt the local textile industry and distracted from efforts to increase the production of wheat.

Into this chaos stepped a man for the moment: the Marquês de Pombal, chief minister of the hedonistic Dom José I (himself more interested in opera than affairs of state). Popularly described as an enlightened despot, Pombal dragged Portugal into the modern era, crushing any opposition with brutal efficiency.

He reformed trade and industry by setting up state monopolies, curbing the power of British merchants and boosting agriculture and domestic industry as Brazilian gold production declined. He abolished slavery in mainland Portugal and the distinctions between old and 'new' Christians. Pombal also founded royal schools and reformed the universities, eliminating the influence of the Jesuits and establishing faculties of science.

When Lisbon suffered a devastating earthquake in November 1755, Pombal acted swiftly and pragmatically to deal with the crisis and to rebuild the city. He was by then at the height of his power. In the following years he got rid of his main enemies – the most powerful Jesuits and several noble families – by accusing them of a mysterious attempt on the king's life in 1758.

He may well have continued his autocratic rule had it not been for the accession of the extremely devout Dona Maria I in 1777. The anticlerical Pombal was promptly dismissed, put on trial and charged with various offences, though he was not imprisoned. Although his religious legislation was repealed, his economic, agricultural and educational policies were largely maintained, helping the country back towards prosperity. But turmoil once again was on the horizon, as Napoleon swept through Europe.

The Dawn of a Republic

In 1793 Portugal found itself back at war when it joined England in sending naval forces against revolutionary France. After a few years of uneasy peace, Napoleon threw

Portugal an ultimatum: close your ports to British shipping or we'll invade.

There was no way Portugal could turn its back on Britain, upon whom it depended for half its trade (especially in cloth and wine) and for protection of its sea routes. In 1807 Portugal's royal family fled to Brazil (where they stayed for 14 years), and General Junot led Napoleon's forces right into Lisbon, sweeping Portugal into the so-called Peninsular War (France's invasion of Spain and Portugal which lasted until 1814).

Invoking the British alliance, Portugal soon had the help of Sir Arthur Wellesley (later Duke of Wellington) and Viscount William Beresford, leading a force of seasoned British troops. After a series of setbacks, the joint Portuguese-British army finally drove the French back across the Spanish border in 1811.

Free but seriously weakened, Portugal was administered by Beresford while João VI and his court remained in Brazil. In 1810 Portugal had lost a profitable intermediary role when it gave Britain the right to trade directly with Brazil. The next humiliation was João's proclamation of Brazil as a kingdom united with Portugal in 1815. With soaring debts and dismal trade, Portugal was at one of the lowest points in its history, reduced to a de facto colony of Brazil and a protectorate of Britain.

Meanwhile, resentment simmered in the army, not only over the unpopular Beresford but over lack of pay and promotion. Influenced by liberal ideas circulating in Spain, a group of rebel officers took advantage of Beresford's absence from the country in 1820 to convene a cortes and draw up a new, liberal constitution (finalised in 1822). Based on the ideals of the Enlightenment, it abolished clerical privileges and the rights of the nobility, and instituted a single-chamber parliament, to be chosen every two years by an electorate that excluded clergy.

Faced with this *fait accompli*, João returned and accepted its terms – though his wife and his son Miguel were bitterly

opposed to it, a sentiment that won widespread support in rural areas. João's elder son, Pedro, also had other ideas: left behind to govern Brazil, he immediately snubbed the constitutionalists by declaring Brazil independent in 1822 and himself its emperor. When João died in 1826, leaving no obvious successor, the stage was set for civil war.

Offered the crown, Pedro first drew up a new, less liberal charter and then abdicated in favour of his seven-year-old daughter Maria, provided she marry her uncle Miguel and he vowed to accept the new constitution. In 1827, Miguel took the oath and was appointed regent, only to abolish Pedro's constitution – still considered unpalatably progressive to many Portuguese – proclaim himself king and revert to the old monarchist system. Liberals rallied under Pedro and, encouraged by French, British and Spanish liberals, forced Miguel to surrender at Évoramonte in May 1834.

Revolutionary zeal quickly led to changes, notably the abolition of the religious orders in 1834. Pedro died the same year but his daughter Maria, now Queen of Portugal at the age of 15 (Pedro's son became Emperor of Brazil), kept his flame alive with her fanatical support of his 1826 charter. Radical supporters of the liberal 1822 constitution were even more active and vociferous. By 1846, with urban discontent exacerbated by economic recession, the prospect of civil war loomed once again. The Duke of Saldanha (a 'Chartist' supporting the 1826 charter) sought the intervention of the British and Spanish, and peace was restored in 1847 with the Convention of Gramido.

Between 1851 and 1856, Saldanha governed the country, steering it through more stable waters. A compromise was reached between the progressive and conservative liberals by using the charter of 1826 but restricting suffrage to 36,000 voters (this was increased to 500,000 by 1910), and by rotating power between the so-called 'Historicals' (radicals) and the 'Regenerators' (moderates such as Saldanha).

Another notable Regenerator was Fontes Pereira de Melo, who created a Ministry of Public Works and set about modernising the country's infrastructure with new roads, bridges, railways, ports and the establishment of an electric telegraph network.

Although these improvements helped the economy, Portugal remained in dire straits at the turn of the century. The country's industrial growth lagged behind that of its European neighbours, budgets were rarely balanced, and foreign (notably British) involvement left a quarter of Portugal's trade and industry out of its control. With the development of tobacco manufacture and sardine canning industries, rural areas were depopulated in favour of the cities, and emigration (especially to Brazil) became increasingly popular among villagers of the poor northern Minho area, their remittances a vital prop to the country's balance of payments.

Much was changing, but for many the changes weren't happening fast enough. Industrial workers were poorly paid and protected, their organisations lacking political clout. Urban discontent was growing, as was support for socialism and trade unions. The humiliation suffered when Britain forced Portugal to withdraw its claim to land between Angola and Mozambique in 1890 was another blow to the monarchist government.

A radical, nationalist republican movement started to sweep the urban lower middle classes in Lisbon, Porto and the south. When Dom Carlos allowed his premier, João Franco, to rule dictatorially, resentment exploded in an attempted republican coup in 1908. It failed, but the following month the king and crown prince were assassinated while driving through the streets of Lisbon.

Carlos' younger son, Manuel II, and his ministers feebly tried to appease the republicans, but it was too late. On 5 October 1910, after an uprising by military officers, a republic was declared. Manuel 'the Unfortunate' sailed into exile in Britain where he died in 1932.

The Rise & Fall of Salazar

Hopes were high among republicans after their landslide victory in the 1911 elections, but it was soon clear that the sentiment expressed in the 1910 national anthem ('Oh sea heroes, oh noble people ... raise again the splendour of Portugal ...!') wasn't going to be satisfied any time soon. Under the increasingly dominant leadership of Afonso Augusto da Costa's leftist Democrat Party, power was maintained by a combination of patronage and a divisive form of anticlericalism that was bitterly opposed in rural areas. Particularly controversial was the disestablishment of the Roman Catholic Church and the internationally criticised persecution of Catholics.

Meanwhile the economy was in tatters, the more so because of the strain of military operations in WWI, when Portugal made its economically disastrous decision to join the Allies. In the recessionary postwar years, political chaos deepened: republican factions squabbled, workers and their unions were repressed despite frequently exercising their new right to strike, and the military became increasingly powerful. The new republic soon had a reputation as Europe's most unstable regime. Between 1910 and 1926 there were 45 changes of government, often brought about through military intervention. Yet another coup in May 1926 heralded the familiar round of new names and faces. One, however, rose above all the others – António de Oliveira Salazar.

A renowned professor of economics at Coimbra University, Salazar was appointed finance minister by the new president, General Óscar Carmona, and given sweeping powers to bring order to Portugal's economy. This he did with such success that by 1932 he was prime minister, a post he was to hold for 36 years. In 1933 he announced a new constitution and a 'New State' – a corporatist republic that was nationalistic, Catholic, authoritarian and repressive.

All political parties were banned except for the National Union, a loyalist movement that provided the National Assembly

António de Oliveira Salazar headed an authoritarian regime which lasted for 44 years.

(which replaced the cortes when the New State was declared) with all its elected members. Strikes were banned and workers were organised into national syndicates or associations controlled by employers. Censorship, propaganda and brute force kept society in order. The feared Polícia Internacional e de Defesa do Estado (PIDE) was the most sinister development, a secret force that used imprisonment and torture to suppress opposition. Not surprisingly, various attempted coups during Salazar's rule came to nothing.

The only good news during this period was that the economy markedly improved. The country's debt was reduced, as was its dependence on British investment, and although agriculture stagnated due to lack of mechanisation, industry and infrastructure development responded well. Throughout the 1950s and 1960s Portugal experienced an annual industrial growth rate of between 7 and 9%.

Internationally, Salazar played two hands, unofficially supporting Franco's Nationalists during the Spanish Civil War, and allowing the British to use airfield facilities in the Azores during WWII despite official neutrality (and despite continuing to sell wolfram to the Germans until 1944). In 1997 it was discovered that he had also authorised the transfer of Nazi-looted gold from Switzerland to Portugal – around 44 tonnes according to Allied records, some allegedly transferred to a Bank of Portugal account in New York and only a tenth of it repaid after the war.

But it was something else on the international scene that finally brought down Salazar's regime: decolonisation. Refusing to relinquish the colonies, Salazar was faced with increasingly costly military expeditions that were internationally deplored and domestically unpopular, even among the military. In 1961, Goa was occupied by India and local nationalists rose up in Angola. Similar guerrilla movements were soon established in Portuguese Guinea and Mozambique.

In the event, Salazar himself didn't have to face the consequences. In 1968 he had a stroke, dying two years later. His successor, Marcelo Caetano, made some attempt at reform, which only stirred up more unrest. Military officers who sympathised with African freedom fighters grew reluctant to serve in colonial wars. Several hundred of them formed the Movimento das Forças Armadas (MFA) and, led by General Costa Gomes and General António de Spínola, carried out a nearly bloodless coup on 25 April 1974, later nicknamed the Revolution of the Carnations (the victorious soldiers apparently stuck carnations in the barrels of their rifles). But although the coup was generally popular (a record 92% of voters turned out in April 1975 to vote for the new Constituent Assembly), the year following it was to be marked by unprecedented chaos and confusion.

From Revolution to Democracy

The first major change took place where the revolution had begun – in the African colonies. Independence was granted almost immediately to the newly named Guinea-Bissau, and this was followed the next year by the decolonisation of the Cape Verde islands, São Tomé e Príncipe, Mozambique and Angola. Civil war broke out in Angola, and when East Timor was relinquished, it was immediately invaded by Indonesia, whose subsequent massacre of the Timorese and continuing occupation is still widely resented.

For Portugal, too, the effects of decolonisation were turbulent. Suddenly it had to cope with nearly a million refugees from the African colonies – a social upheaval that it managed remarkably well.

Politically and economically, however, the country was in a mess. There were widespread strikes and a tangle of political ideas and parties, although the two most powerful groups were the communists (who dominated the trade unions) and a radical wing of the MFA. Private banking, insurance firms, transport and the media were nationalised and peasant farmers seized some of the huge latifúndio estates in the Alentejo to establish their own communal farms (few of which succeeded and most of which were later returned to their owners).

As political parties polarised and MFA factions splintered, divisions in the country became increasingly obvious, with traditional conservatives in the north led by Mário Soares and his Partido Socialista (PS; Socialist Party) and revolutionaries in the south. In August 1975 a more moderate government was formed, bitterly opposed by the Partido Comunista Português (PCP; Communist Party) and the extreme left. Finally, on 25 November 1975, a radical leftist coup was crushed by moderate forces from the army under General Ramalho Eanes. The revolution had ended.

The Rocky Road to Stability

A new constitution of April 1976 committed Portugal to a blend of socialism and democracy, with a powerful president, an assembly elected by universal suffrage, and a Council of the Revolution to control the armed forces. After parliamentary elections, Mário Soares formed a minority government and General Eanes won the presidential election.

Only a year later, Soares' government faltered and there followed a series of attempts at government by coalitions and nonparty candidates, including Portugal's first female prime minister, Maria de Lurdes Pintassilgo. In the 1980 parliamentary elections a new political force emerged to govern the country – the conservative Aliança Democrática (AD; Democratic Alliance), a combination of right-leaning parties led by the social democrat, Francisco de Sá Carneiro.

After Carneiro's death in a plane crash that same year, Francisco Pinto Balsemão took over as prime minister and persuaded socialists in the assembly to agree to constitutional changes to establish full civilian rule. These included abolition of the Council of the Revolution and a reduction of presidential powers. Marxist phraseology disappeared from the constitution. Other about-turns favoured by both the public and the government were reprivatisation of the economy and the abolition of communal farming methods. The first steps were also taken to join the European Community (EC), renamed the European Union (EU) in 1992.

It was partly to satisfy the requirements for EC admission and to keep the IMF (International Monetary Fund) happy that a new coalition government of socialists and social democrats under Mário Soares was forced to implement a strict economic policy and a programme of modernisation. Not surprisingly, the belt-tightening wasn't popular. The most vocal critics were Soares' right-wing partners in the Partido Social Democrata (PSD; Social Democrat Party), led by the dynamic Aníbal Cavaco Silva. Communist trade unions in the industrial and transport sectors organised strikes.

Adding to the unrest was an increase in urban terrorism, carried out mainly by the radical left-wing Forças Populares de 25 Abril (FP-25). In June 1984 more than 40 terrorist suspects were arrested, including the former revolutionary leader Lieutenant Colonel Otelo Saraiva de Carvalho. Controversial legislation established a new security intelligence agency.

By June 1985 the coalition government had collapsed over disagreements about labour and agricultural reform. In October elections the PSD emerged a narrow winner, forming a minority government led by Cavaco Silva. Not that this was the end of Soares' political career: in the presidential elections of February 1986, the veteran socialist leader became president, the country's first civilian head of state for 60 years. Another political record was achieved in 1987, when parliamentary elections returned Cavaco Silva and the PSD with the first clear majority since 1974. With a repeat performance four years later, it looked as if Portugal had finally reached calm waters.

In January 1986 Portugal was admitted to the EU, after nine years of negotiations. Flush with EU funds, it now raced ahead of many of its equally poor neighbours, recording an unprecedented 4.5 to 5% annual economic growth rate. The new prosperity gave Cavaco Silva the power to push ahead with his programme of radical economic reform and free enterprise. Privatisation continued and fundamental changes were made to agriculture, education and the media.

But there was considerable resistance among industrial workers to attempts at reforming labour laws (to the employees' disadvantage). The 1980s saw major strikes: in March 1988 an estimated 1.5 million workers participated in a 24 hour general strike, and in January 1989 10,000 protested in Lisbon. The controversial legislation was finally passed in February 1989 but unrest continued, with demands by various sectors of the workforce that wage increases should match inflation.

Despite its troubles, the PSD kept most of its seats in 1989 elections to the European Parliament. But in municipal elections the PSD, stricken by corruption scandals, suffered a serious reverse, and the PS, backed by the communists and the greens, took control of Lisbon and other major cities. The canny Cavaco Silva fought back with a surprise reshuffle of his cabinet

in January 1990, removing the scandal-tainted ministers. But further scandal erupted in February when the socialist governor appointed by Soares to rule Macau (the Chinese territory administered by Portugal until 1999) was involved in a bribery accusation.

Nevertheless, the hugely popular Soares won an outright victory in the presidential elections in 1991. Even more surprisingly, the PSD renewed its absolute majority in the legislative elections that followed. The electorate may have been disgusted by scandals and worried about unemployment, inflation and the severe shortcomings in the health and education services, but they were still attracted by the PSD's promise of continued growth and stability.

Portugal Today

It was soon obvious that these promises were going to be hard to keep. In 1992, the year Portugal held the presidency of the European Community, EC trade barriers fell and Portugal was faced with the threat of competition, which would particularly affect its small and middle-sized companies. Fortunes diminished as recession set in, and disillusion with the PSD grew as Europe's single market revealed the backwardness of Portugal's agricultural sector. Uncontrolled profiteering, corruption and industrial pollution were also undermining the PSD's reputation and detracting from the improvements that had been made to the infrastructure, transport, health and welfare services.

Politically, too, trouble was brewing. Tensions between the socialist Soares and his centre-right prime minister became increasingly evident, with President Soares frequently exercising his right of veto to stall or modify controversial legislation.

Throughout 1993 and 1994 there were strikes (mainly in support of wage increases), charges of corruption (among other cases, the minister of finance was investigated over missing EU funds) and student demonstrations due to increased fees. The government was still further shaken when

Amnesty International expressed concern over allegations of torture by Portuguese police and prison officers.

In the local elections in 1993 and elections to the European Parliament, voters gave the PS more seats than the PSD. By the end of 1994, although the government managed to survive a vote of no confidence, criticism was increasingly public, with the president warning darkly of a 'dictatorship of the majority'.

Cavaco Silva saw the writing on the wall. In an astute move, which many saw as a way to save his reputation for coming presidential elections, he resigned as PSD leader in January 1995. He continued as prime minister until elections in October, when the PS, under the dynamic leadership of 46-year-old António Guterres, gained the largest number of seats (although without an overall majority) and 10% more votes than the PSD.

As expected, Cavaco Silva ran for the presidency in January 1996 on the expiry of Soares' second and last term of office. But his defeat by the socialist mayor of Lisbon, Jorge Sampaio, confirmed popular weariness of him. These two elections marked the end of the PSD's decade in power, and the first time since 1974 that the president and prime minister both came from the same party (socialist).

António Guterres led his party's election campaign on a platform of social reform but in most ways he offers little change in his programme of government. Indeed, one of his first announcements was that two years of economic stringency lay ahead before the government could meet its pledges on social reform. But the uneasy coalitions and economic instability of the 1970s and early 1980s are over. The business community is reassured by Guterres' commitment to budgetary rigour and his success in qualifying for European and Monetary Union in 1999.

The atmosphere is one of cautious optimism that Guterres can fulfil at least some of his promises, such as regional devolution in mainland Portugal and the establishment of a minimum guaranteed income. But if improvements in health care, education and policing take too long the market-oriented socialists could well be in trouble.

GEOGRAPHY

Together with Ireland, Portugal lies at the westernmost edge of Europe. Covering an area of 92,389 sq km and measuring only 560km north to south and 220km east to west, it's one of Europe's smallest countries (about the size of Austria). But it's also one of the most geographically diverse. Bordered on the west and south by the Atlantic Ocean and on the east and north by Spain (a country five times bigger), it offers everything from dramatic mountain ranges and lush, green valleys in the north to flat, dry plains and undulating landscapes in the south. You can take your pick of beaches from over 830km of coastline and your choice of mountain hiking from a series of *serras* (mountain ranges) that reach their highest point with Torre (1993m) in the Serra da Estrela range.

Dividing the country roughly in half is the Rio Tejo, which flows north-east to south-west, draining into the Atlantic at Lisbon, one of Portugal's few natural harbours. To the north of the Tejo are most of the country's mountains: 90% of the land here rises above 400m, although only a fraction is higher than 700m. This region, together with Spanish Galicia, comprises the mountainous border of the Meseta (a major plateau region of the Iberian Peninsula), which is also the source of three of Portugal's most important rivers, the Douro, the Tejo and the Guadiana.

While the fertile and heavily populated north-western Minho region is characterised by rolling plateaus and rivers flowing through deep gorges, the adjacent provinces of Beira Alta (upper Beira), Douro and Trás-os-Montes (behind the mountains) are marked by high plateaus of granite, schist and slate. This region rises to 800m and is known as the *terra fria* (cold country). In the southern and eastern stretches of the Alto Douro (in southern

Trás-os-Montes) is the region known as *terra quente* (hot country), a landscape of sheltered valleys with dark schists that trap the heat, thereby creating the perfect microclimate (described by locals as 'nine months of winter and three months of hell') for growing Portugal's port wine grapes.

Further south, the high Beira plains are *serra* country, featuring several major mountain ranges, notably the Serra da Estrela, a continuation of Spain's central sierras. The chain extends south-west to the Serra de Açor and Serra da Lousã, some of the loveliest and least visited ranges in the land.

The border between Beira Baixa (lower) and Alto (upper) Alentejo along the Rio Tejo is marked by the sudden drop of the plateau from an altitude of 480m to 215m. South-west of here is the low-lying and often marshy coastline of Beira Litoral and Estremadura, stretching southwards along the Atlantic seaboard and characterised by lagoons and salt marshes at the river mouths. Inland, between the Rio Tejo and the Rio Guadiana, the Alto Alentejo features a series of plateaus, a continuation of the Spanish tablelands. Further south, in northern Baixo Alentejo, are ridges of quartz and marble, and a vast undulating landscape of wheat, cork and olive trees, which rarely rises above 150m.

This southern half of the country is predominantly flat: some 63% of the country below 400m is found here. Only the eastern Serra do Caldeirão and western Serra de Monchique break the monotony, acting as a division between the provinces of the Alentejo and the Algarve. They also act as a buffer against the northern climate for the Algarve, which basks in the protected Mediterranean climate that encourages its semitropical landscapes.

The islands of Madeira and the Azores (originally colonised in the 15th century) are also part of metropolitan Portugal, although too far away to be considered in a peninsular visit: Madeira (a popular destination in its own right) lies 900km to the south-west (off the west coast of Africa), while the nine-island archipelago of the Azores is spread in the Atlantic Ocean about 1440km west of Lisbon.

The last remaining overseas territory still under Portuguese administration is Macau, which returns to Chinese rule at the end of 1999.

CLIMATE

Portugal falls within both Atlantic and Mediterranean climatic zones. The Atlantic influences the country the most, especially in the north-west, where the weather is noticeably milder and damper than in the rest of the country. As much as 2000mm of rain a year can fall here (2500mm on higher ground), compared to 300mm in the interior of the Algarve and the national average of 1100mm. The Atlantic also moderates the dry Mediterranean climate of the southern coast, where summer temperatures average a comfortable maximum of 28°C. Average summer maximums in Lisbon and Porto are slightly less (27°C and 25°C), and rain is rare everywhere in July and August. Even winters are mild in coastal regions, averaging 13°C in Lisbon, 12°C in Porto and 16°C in Faro.

Inland, there's greater variation, thanks to continental winds from the interior. Summers can be painfully hot in the upper Douro valley and the Alentejo (expect temperatures as high as 40°C), with drought often lasting for a month or more. In the south, drought can last even longer. Spanish influences (high pressure conditions from the Meseta plateau region), as well as Siberian anticyclones, are also responsible for the relatively severe winters in the Serra da Estrela and the north-east; temperatures often drop to freezing in Bragança in January. In the Serra da Estrela you can usually ski from January to March, or join the traffic jams in search of the last remnants of snow on Torre as late as May. The national winter average temperature, however, is a mild 11°C.

Sun seekers get a warm welcome in Portugal: there's an average 12 hours of sunshine a day during a typical Algarve

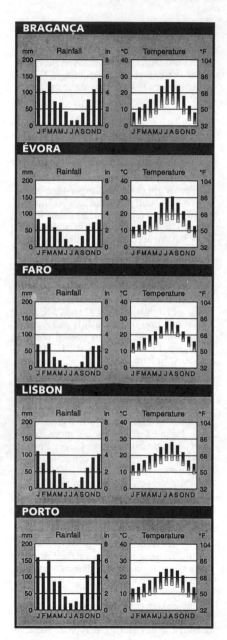

summer (six hours in the winter). In the north this drops to about four hours daily in winter but a balmy 10 in summer.

ECOLOGY & ENVIRONMENT

Portugal has been slow to wake up to its environmental problems, notably soil erosion, pollution, rubbish disposal and the effects of mass tourism on fragile coastal areas. Of growing concern, too, are the spread of eucalyptus plantations (see the boxed text on the next page), and the first stages of desertification in some areas.

For visitors, mass tourism is the most obvious problem, especially in the overdeveloped southern Algarve, with its ugly hotel, villa and apartment block complexes. Building restrictions were widely ignored after the 1974 revolution and although they are now back in place, the damage has already been done around Albufeira, Lagos and Portimão.

Elsewhere, too, the sudden influx of summer visitors – as many as 40,000 on a village population of 2000 is not uncommon – causes enormous pressure as services and infrastructure are stretched to the limit.

But it's industrial development that is to blame for some of Portugal's most polluted seasides: you'd be wise to stay well clear of the seas around heavily populated or industrial centres like Porto and Sines.

Water – or rather the lack of it – is at the heart of another controversial issue. Four years of drought in the mid-1990s – the worst dry cycle this century – raised concern about Spain's mammoth National Hydrographic Plan, a scheme that includes diverting water from the rainy north to the south of the country. Unfortunately for Portugal, three of its most important rivers – the Douro, the Tejo and the Guadiana – rise in Spain. And like Spain, Portugal desperately needs this water for agriculture (which accounts for 76% of water use in Portugal), hydroelectric production and for the environment generally. If Spain's plan goes ahead, Portugal's water supplies – especially from the Douro – could be seriously affected. Of more immediate concern is the

The Eucalyptus Onslaught

One of Portugal's biggest consumers of water is the eucalyptus. Quick to grow (it's tall enough for felling in 10 years), it's one of the most profitable trees on the market, much in demand by paper pulp companies. By the 1990s, paper pulp was earning Portugal as much as US$2 billion a year. Eucalyptus plantations have continued to spread over the hillsides throughout the country, much to the concern of many local farmers who are seeing their traditional smallholdings of olive and cork disappear. Environmental groups are even more vociferous, arguing that the eucalyptus drains the soil both of water and nutrients, and that the huge plantations are destroying the region's wildlife habitat.

According to Marion Kaplan in her book *The Portuguese*, government officials have tried to reassure the protesters by saying that eucalyptus forests will be kept to a maximum of 20% of the forest area (in 1989 it was already at 14%). But as Carlos Pimenta, Portuguese member of the European Parliament, has said: '... short-term private profit almost always has won over the defence of our common values and heritage of those living or yet to be born. Public awareness and information are important in the fight to save our habitat'.

Guadiana, vital for irrigating the arid Alentejo plains. Work is well advanced on a giant dam at Alqueva, near Beja, but Spain has increased its consumption of water from the Guadiana and plans to even take more. Spain's response to alarm is that Portugal is worrying too much as the plan has yet to get the official go-ahead. Plentiful rain in 1995 and 1996 temporarily stalled worries but if the cycle of drought continues, the tug-of-war over the rivers will escalate.

Environmental Organisations

Portugal's most active environmental group is Quercus: the Associação Nacional de Conservação da Natureza (National Association for the Conservation of Nature; ☎ 01-778 84 74, fax 778 77 49, email quercus@mail.telepac.pt), based at Bairro do Calhau, Parque Florestal de Monsanto, 1500 Lisbon. Founded in 1986, it has some 10,000 members and 19 branch offices, including Aveiro, Beja, Braga, Bragança, Coimbra, Covilhã, Faro, Guarda, Porto, Portalegre, Viana do Castelo and Vila Real, as well as four Centros de Educação Ambiental, or environmental education centres (Lisbon, Leiria, Monsanto and Porto).

In addition to carrying out studies of Portugal's flora, fauna and ecosystems, members bring issues to the attention of the public and government through regular campaigns. Many branch offices also arrange field trips to natural parks or reserves. If you read Portuguese, you'll find its monthly magazine, *Teixo*, packed with environmental horror stories.

Another group that arranges weekend trips to environmentally special areas is GEOTA: Grupo de Estudos de Ordenomento do Território e Ambiente (Environment Study Group; ☎ 01-395 61 20, fax 395 53 16), Travessa do Moinho de Vento 17, 1200 Lisbon. Trips cost from 5000$00 to 10,000$00 per person.

Less obviously active groups include Liga para a Proteção da Natureza (League for the Protection of Nature; ☎ 01-778 00 97), Estrela do Calhariz de Benfica 187, Lisbon, and Associação Portuguesa de Ecologia e Amigos da Terra (Portuguese Association of Ecology and Friends of the Earth; ☎ 01-395 18 66), Calçada Marquês de Abrantes 10, 3/f, Lisbon.

FLORA & FAUNA
Flora

Like its climate, Portugal's flora is a blend of Mediterranean and Atlantic ingredients. Before the land was reshaped by humans, oaks dominated the vegetation – deciduous species in the north and evergreens in the south. Today, little of the natural forest remains and prairies of scrubland prevail over much of the country.

In the sunny southern provinces of the Algarve and the Alentejo, Mediterranean flowers set the countryside ablaze in spring and early summer. Especially striking are white and purple rockroses (*gum cistus*). The pretty but troublesome Bermuda buttercup – an invasive and herbicide-resistant plant of South African origin – turns the fields of the Algarve brilliant yellow from November to May. Orchid lovers will find a wide variety thriving in the Algarve, especially in the limestone soil around Faro.

Moving north into the rainier, more mountainous regions, species typical of temperate Europe take over: gorse, heather and broom cover the hillsides, while sweet chestnut and Scots pine occur in the woods. Oaks are common, as well as elm and poplar.

As many as a third of Portugal's species are of foreign origin. Early settlers in the south cultivated the first vines and planted citrus trees, while the Moors introduced almonds, carobs, figs, palms and the large white irises commonly seen lining the roadsides (they once graced graveyards). Portuguese explorers and colonists brought back many foreign plants, including the gaudy purple or yellow Hottentot fig (a native of South Africa), which generates huge mats of succulents; and the prickly pear cactus, believed to have been introduced from the Americas by Christopher

Cork

Travel through the vast Alentejo plains and you'll see thousands of them: tall, round-topped evergreen trees with glossy, holly-like leaves, and wrinkled bark that's often stripped, leaving a strangely naked, ochre trunk. One of Portugal's most profitable indigenous products – *quercus suber* or cork oak – grows abundantly throughout the country, supplying some 700 factories with about 170,000 tons of cork a year, a third of which is manufactured by one family firm, Corticeira Amorim. Lucky Amorim: Portugal's prodigious cork output accounts for 60% of world output, twice that of Spain – not bad for a product that's as slow and traditional to make as a vintage port wine. Cultivators have to wait 20 years before they can cut the first bark (probably 30 years before the bark is of commercial quality), and then cut (always by hand) as skilfully as a barber to guarantee future harvests for the next 100 years or so of the tree's life.

So valuable is this tree that there's a law against stripping its bark until the tree's circumference has reached a certain size. And from then on it can only be stripped every ninth year. Such repeated strippings are possible because the tree continually grows new tissue, though care has to be taken not to damage the deeper layers.

Cork has long been prized for its lightness (it's only one-fifth as heavy as water) and its insulating and watertight qualities. More versatile than any synthetic product, it's used for everything from footwear to floor-covers, gaskets to girders, baseball bats to fishing-rod handles. And most obviously, of course, it's used as a bottle stopper. Spirits such as whisky and gin gave up cork in the 1960s, cheap wine resorted to plastic, and synthetic cork stoppers from Norway barged in on the market, but for superior wines there's no alternative. The world's wine producers obviously agree – 25 billion corks are used a year. Cork's all-natural assets (no smell, no taste, no toxicity) make it the unbeatable bottle stopper for posh wines such as champagne, which is particularly fussy about its corks. Portugal comes up with the goods: about 30 million corks a day, and 500 million a year just for champagne.

European bee-eater.

The Mediterranean chameleon: a shy creature that's hard to spot.

The greater flamingo winters in the Reserva Natural do Sapal de Castro Marim.

The purple gallinule, alias purple swamp-hen or sultan chicken.

Black-winged stilt.

Portuguese handicrafts range from pots and baskets to textiles and wooden toys and, of course, the ubiquitous Barcelos cockerel, a national icon, reputed to have saved the life of an innocent man.

Columbus. And in Sintra you'll see exotic thuja firs, enormous sequoias and araucarias which were planted as fashionable novelties in the 18th and 19th centuries.

More recently, vast plantations of Australian eucalyptus and commercial pines have transformed huge areas into dreary swaths of thirsty monoculture.

Two other vitally important commercial trees that have crafted Portugal's landscape and lifestyle are the olive and cork oak. Since Roman times both have been grown and harvested in harmony with the environment, providing not only income but protection for many kinds of flora and fauna. Although the olive prefers the sunny climate of the south, it's also taken root in parts of the north. The cork oak, too, pre dominates in the south, especially in the dry plains of the Alentejo.

Fauna

Portugal's fauna is typical of southern Europe, although a few North African species have also found their way here. Unfortunately, most mammals are nocturnal and hard to spot. The most likely mammals to be encountered are hedgehogs, rabbits, hares and bats. In more remote areas you might come across the occasional fox, deer, otter or even a party of foraging wild boar. Portugal's rarest mammals are the Iberian wolf and Iberian lynx (see Endangered Species later in this section).

Two well-established North African species are the genet, a spotted, catlike mammal with weasel characteristics, and the Egyptian mongoose. While genets spend the day hiding, mongooses are diurnal; they're quite often seen crossing quieter roads in the Algarve. Portugal's most extraordinary North African settler, however, is the Mediterranean chameleon, introduced about 70 years ago and found in coastal areas of the eastern Algarve (see the boxed text 'Now You See Me, Now You Don't …' in the Algarve chapter).

Among other reptile species, it's worth noting that the venomous Lataste's viper and Montpellier snake do occur (despite

The Portuguese Water-Dog

What do you get when you cross a dog and a duck? Answer: the Portuguese (or Algarve) water-dog. This curious breed (no descendant of the duck) looks very like a poodle at first glance, with its clipped black or brown hair. However, it has the unique characteristic of webbed feet (strictly speaking, a membrane between the toes). This makes it a great little swimmer, able to dive down to depths of 6m.

Traditionally these pedigree dogs have been a fisherman's best friend: they can dive for fish that have escaped from nets, paddle from boat to shore with ropes in their mouths and retrieve broken nets drifting in the sea. Now practically extinct (dog fanciers in the USA have snapped up many in recent years), they're getting a new lease of life at the Quinta de Marim headquarters of the Parque Natural da Ria Formosa, where there's a special programme for breeding the species and restoring its unique place in the webbed-feet, wagging-tail world.

reports that Portugal has no venomous snakes). Fortunately, neither of these two snakes is deadly.

Portugal's birdlife is a rich mix of temperate and Mediterranean species plus migrants, including Audouin's gull, the black tern and the pied flycatcher. Outside protected areas, birds are often hard to spot – hunting and habitat loss have both taken their toll – but in reserves such as the Reserva Natural do Sapal de Castro Marim and the Parque Natural da Ria Formosa (see the boxed texts in the Algarve chapter) you stand a pretty good chance of seeing several different wetland species, including flamingos, egrets, herons, spoonbills, and many species of shore birds, gulls and terns.

Keep an eye out, too, for some of Portugal's more unusual birds – lesser kestrels at Mértola, purple gallinules (see the boxed text 'Golf & Gallinules' in the Algarve chapter) in the Parque Natural da Ria Formosa, bustards and sandgrouse on the plains of the Alentejo, and Iberian specialities such as the great spotted cuckoo, red-winged nightjar, rufous bushchat, spectacled warbler and azure-winged magpie. Several of these species, along with birds such as the hoopoe, bee-eater and Sardinian warbler, can easily be seen in the protected farmland and scrubland of the Parque Natural da Ria Formosa.

For details of specialised bird-watching tours in Portugal run by overseas operators, see Organised Tours in the Getting There & Away chapter.

Endangered Species Portugal's protected areas (see the next section) harbour several endangered birds, including the Spanish imperial eagle and the tawny owl in the Parque Nacional da Peneda-Gerês, and the purple gallinule in the Parque Natural da Ria Formosa. Ria Formosa is also home to the strictly protected Mediterranean chameleon. Outside the parks, you're most likely to see an endangered or strictly protected species in the southern Alentejo – in Mértola, which hosts the country's largest nesting colony of lesser kestrels between March and September, or in the Castro

Verde region, a favourite haunt of the great bustard, Europe's heaviest bird (adult males can weigh up to 18kg).

Among endangered mammal species in Portugal, one of the rarest is the Iberian wolf. Its last major hide-out is in the eastern Parque Natural de Montesinho (Trás-os-Montes) and adjacent protected areas of Spain. There are also declining numbers of dolphins in the Sado Estuary, south of Setúbal, and a few Iberian lynx hiding out in the lynx reserve of the Reserva Natural da Serra da Malcata in Beira Alta. However, your chances of seeing a wolf or a lynx in the wild are practically nil.

National Parks

Strictly speaking, Parque Nacional da Peneda-Gerês is the only national park in Portugal. The other parks are called *parques naturais* (natural parks). You're unlikely to notice the difference: Peneda-Gerês meets certain international requirements (including reasonably undisturbed ecosystems of scientific/educational value and the setting aside of research-only areas), while a *parque natural* features both natural or seminatural and landscaped areas where human activities have integrated with nature.

Wolves

It's thought that there are fewer than 200 Iberian wolves left in Portugal (out of an estimated 1500 in the entire Iberian Peninsula). Most of these are believed to live in the Parque Natural de Montesinho in north-eastern Trás-os-Montes. Although it is fully protected by law, the wolf is still illegally shot, trapped or poisoned. As elsewhere in the world, it is widely feared and hated for supposedly attacking cattle and domestic animals (though in fact many of these attacks are by wild dogs).

Now in danger of extinction in Portugal (an estimated 20 wolves are illegally killed every year), the wolf has at least some friends working on its behalf: Grupo Lobo, an independent, nonprofit association established in 1985, wins support for the wolf and the preservation of its habitat by publishing booklets and pamphlets and operating a travelling exhibition. It also helps run the Centro de Recuperação do Lobo Ibérico (recuperation centre) in Malveira, about 40km north of Lisbon (see the boxed text under Mafra in the Around Lisbon chapter). You can support the cause by joining Grupo Lobo for 3000$00 a year or by 'adopting' a wolf at the centre. For more information, write to CRLI, Apartado 61, 2665 Malveira.

Portugal's Parks & Nature Reserves

Following are contact details for Portugal's national/natural parks and reserves:

1 *Parque Nacional da Peneda-Gerês*
   (☎ 053-600 34 80, fax 61 31 69)
   Quinta das Parretas, Rodovia, 4700 Braga
2 *Parque Natural de Montesinho*
   (☎ 073-38 14 44, fax 38 11 79)
   Bairro Salvador Nunes Teixeira, Lote 5, 5300 Bragança
3 *Parque Natural do Douro Internacional*
   (☎ 0936-47 01 88)
   Temporary Contact: Apartado 34, 6440 Figueira de Castelo Rodrigo
4 *Parque Natural do Alvão*
   (☎ 059-32 41 38, fax 7 38 69)
   Praceta do Tronco, Cruz das Almas, Lote 17, 5000 Vila Real
5 *Reserva Natural das Dunas de São Jacinto*
   (☎ 034-83 10 63, fax 039-490 10 29)
   Mata Nacional do Choupal, 3000 Coimbra
6 *Parque Natural da Serra da Estrela*
   (☎ 075-98 23 82, fax 98 23 84)
   Rua I de Maio 2, Valezado, 6260 Manteigas
7 *Reserva Natural da Serra da Malcata*
   (☎ 077-9 44 67, fax 9 45 80)
   Rua dos Bombeiros Voluntários, 6090 Penamacor
8 *Reserva Natural do Paúl de Arzila*
   (☎ 039-98 10 06, fax 490 10 29)
   Mata Nacional do Choupal, 3000 Coimbra
9 *Reserva Natural da Berlenga*
   (☎ 062-78 79 10, fax 78 79 30)
   Porto da Areia Norte, Estrada Marginal, 2520 Peniche
10 *Parque Natural das Serras de Aire e Candeeiros*
   (☎ 043-9 01 68, fax 9 26 05)
   Jardim Municipal, 2040 Rio Maior
11 *Reserva Natural do Paúl do Boquilobo*
   (☎/fax 049-82 05 50)
   Quinta do Paul, Brogueira, Apartado 27, 2350 Torres Novas
12 *Parque Natural da Serra de São Mamede*
   (☎ 045-2 36 31, fax 2 75 01)
   Rua General Conde Jorge de Avilez 22, 7300 Portalegre
13 *Reserva Natural do Estuário do Tejo*
   (☎ 01-234 17 42, fax 234 16 54)
   Avenida Combatentes da Grande Guerra 1, 2890 Alcochete
14 *Parque Natural de Sintra-Cascais*
   (☎ 01-923 51 16, fax 923 51 41)
   Rua General Alves Roçadas 10, 2710 Sintra
15 *Parque Natural da Arrábida*
   (☎ 065-52 40 32, fax 3 72 56)
   Praça da República, 2900 Setúbal

16 *Reserva Natural do Estuário do Sado*
   (☎ 065-52 40 32, fax 3 72 56)
   Praça da República, 2900 Setúbal
17 *Parque Natural do Sudoeste Alentejano e Costa Vicentina*
   (☎ 083-2 27 35, fax 2 28 30)
   Rua Serpa Pinto 32, 7630 Odemira
18 *Parque Natural do Vale do Guadiana*
   (☎ 086-61 10 84, fax 61 10 85)
   Rua Dr António José de Almeida, 7750 Mértola
19 *Reserva Natural do Sapal de Castro Marim e Vila Real de Santo António*
   (☎ 081-53 11 41, fax 53 12 57)
   Castelo de Vila, 8950 Castro Marim
20 *Parque Natural da Ria Formosa*
   (☎ 089-70 41 34, fax 70 41 65)
   Quinta de Marim, Quelfes, 8700 Olhão

An additional trans-border 'international' park is under development, but few details were available at the time of research:

Tejo Internacional
(☎/fax 077-20 20 87)
Rua Vaz Preto 116, 6060 Idanha-a-Nova
(Beira Baixa, around Castelo Branco)

There are also eight *reservas naturais* (nature reserves), three *áreas de paisagens protegidas* (areas of protected landscape), 10 *sítios classificados* (classified sites) and five *monumentos naturais* (natural monuments). Altogether, these protected areas cover 651,554 hectares – 7.3% of Portugal's land area. A new park, the Tejo Internacional (in the Castelo Branco area), is under development.

The Instituto da Conservação da Natureza, or ICN (☎ 01-352 33 17, fax 314 31 03, Web site www.icn.pt/), Rua Ferreira Lapa 29A, 1150 Lisbon, is the government agency responsible for overall park management, publicity and policy. It has some general information, but individual park offices are usually better equipped and staffed and have maps, brochures and information on local trails and accommodation. Standards of maintenance and facilities vary greatly, however, and hopeful hikers may be disappointed: 'trails' often turn out to be roads or nothing at all; the park 'map' a glossy leaflet for motorists; and 'park accommodation' a couple of huts geared (and priced) for school groups.

But the parks do feature vast areas of unspoilt mountains, forests and coastal lagoons. The reluctance of most Portuguese to go walking anywhere, let alone venture into remote areas, means you can find some incredibly quiet, isolated spots. We describe the best of the parks in the respective regional chapters.

GOVERNMENT & POLITICS

Portugal has been a sovereign republic since 1910, when it overthrew its monarchy. But western-style, multiparty democracy only came after the 1974 Revolution of the Carnations, which removed the authoritarian Salazar-era government. According to the 1976 constitution (revised in 1982 to remove Marxist elements and reduce the power of the president, and again in 1989), Portugal's chief of state is the president of the republic, directly elected by universal suffrage for a maximum of two consecutive five-year terms. Presidents still have wide powers, including the power to dissolve parliament and veto laws. They also appoint the prime minister (following the results of parliamentary elections) and, on the prime minister's proposal, can appoint or dismiss other members of government, principally the cabinet.

The prime minister is responsible both to the president and to the Assembléia da República, the national legislature. This single-chamber body has 230 members (including four representing Portuguese abroad), who are elected for four years by popular vote under a system of proportional representation. Portugal also has 25 representatives in the European Parliament: the last EP elections in 1994 saw the PS (Partido Socialista) winning 10 seats and the PSD (Partido Social Democrata) winning nine, with the rest divided among other parties.

Portuguese citizens can cast their first vote when they're 18 years old. From then on men can also be called up for compulsory military service – anything from four to 18 months – although they have a right to conscientious objection.

Local tiers of government in the country's 18 districts consist of 305 municipal *concelhos*, or councils, and 4209 *freguesias*, or parishes within those councils, each governed by an assembly elected by popular vote under a system of proportional representation. The PS currently controls most municipal councils.

Since 1976 the archipelagoes of Madeira and the Azores have been recognised as autonomous regions and have their own governments, legislatures and administrations. Macau, Portugal's last overseas dependent territory, is governed by special statute and reverts to Chinese rule at the end of 1999.

Portugal's two main political parties are the ruling left-of-centre PS and the opposition right-of-centre PSD. Other major opposition parties include the conservative Centro Democrática Social (CDS; Social Democratic Centre), now more commonly referred to as the Partido Popular (PP;

Popular Party); and the Coligação Democrático Unitária (CDU; United Democratic Coalition), which links the hardline communists of the Partido Comunista Português with other left-wing parties such as the greens (Partido Ecologista Os Verdes, or PEV).

The October 1995 elections saw the return of the PS after 10 years of single-party rule by the PSD under Aníbal Cavaco Silva. The new prime minister, António Guterres, managed this political coup by swinging his party behind free-market, pro-European policies, promising social improvements while reassuring financial markets of a continued commitment to budgetary rigour and the discipline of European monetary union. The electorate, tired of the complacent, scandal-tainted PSD, gave the PS its biggest victory since it began fighting elections in 1974: 112 of the 230 seats in the national legislature, compared with 72 in the election of 1991. The PSD trailed behind with 88 seats, while the PP and communist-led CDU each won 15.

Since achieving the widely unexpected goal of qualifying for European monetary union in 1998, and maintaining a healthy economic climate, Guterres is riding high. However, his confidence rating suffered a serious blow in November 1998 when an overwhelming 63% of voters rejected a referendum on his plans for regional devolution – one of the main planks of Guterres' 1995 election campaign. The regionalisation was intended to spread prosperity more evenly between the country's relatively rich Atlantic coast and the poorer rural hinterlands, but voters were persuaded against the plan by the two main opposition parties – the PSD and the PP – which decided after the referendum to unite as a new party, the Democratic Alternative, to fight the October 1999 parliamentary elections.

Even if he wins the elections, Guterres may well be robbed of a parliamentary majority by this new opposition alliance. He also has to worry about growing disillusionment with the EU among voters, as competition stiffens in the wake of the European single market and the GATT (General Agreement on Tariffs and Trade) agreements. Portugal's economy is also in danger of overheating, which will lead to a nasty scenario of greater unemployment if wages rise faster than productivity. And Guterres still has to meet electoral promises of higher spending on education, health and welfare, a tricky challenge since he has also promised not to raise taxes.

He has a major ally in the president, Jorge Sampaio, a socialist and two-term Lisbon mayor. His victory marked the first time since 1974 that the prime minister and president have come from the same party – a great advantage for Guterres as he walks the tightrope of office.

ECONOMY

Not so long ago, Portugal was among the poorest nations in Europe, its economy a shambles, its inflation and unemployment rates appalling, its trade deficit a nightmare, and its workforce thoroughly demoralised. Now its growth rate (around 3.5%) is the second highest in Europe after Finland, its unemployment (7%) one of the lowest, and its inflation tamed to an impressive 2.4%.

The dramatic turnaround started in 1985 when the austere economist, Aníbal Cavaco Silva, and his centre-right PSD came to power. The following year Portugal joined the EC (now EU). Over the next decade the government introduced a wide range of structural reforms, extensively deregulating and liberalising the economy and launching an ambitious privatisation programme (see the boxed text 'Peak of Privatisation' on the next page). The EC began pumping funds in (an astounding US$12.8 million a day for the rest of this century) and, helped by dollar exchange rates and falling oil prices, Portugal's economy started to revive. Soon it was showing the highest growth rate in Europe and increases in real wages of more than 2%. This honeymoon coincided with political stability and sound monetary policy, resulting in increasing prosperity for many Portuguese.

But in 1992 recession reared its head. That was also the year of the single European market, when trade and employment barriers were removed, the year Portugal ratified the Maastricht Treaty on European Union. Financial pressure rose as the country faced the Maastricht Treaty's stringent demands for European and Monetary Union (EMU) in 1999. The first signs of a recovery came in 1994 when foreign markets expanded and exports started to surge.

To everyone's astonishment, when the March 1998 EMU deadline arrived, Portugal fulfilled the criteria in style, with a budget deficit down to 2.5% (better than Germany's), a declining debt of 62% of GDP and dramatically falling interest rates.

The economic picture for the next few years looks even more encouraging: fuelled by massive infrastructure investment (most notably the US$3 billion Expo '98 site and new Vasco da Gama bridge in Lisbon), the country is enjoying unprecedented growth. Unemployment is expected to fall to 6.6% and real wages to increase by 1.2%.

But these healthy figures mask some dismal realities. Years of rapid growth have widened the gulf between rich and poor, with many farmers in the provinces struggling harder than ever and a small but growing number of urban poor. Education levels and facilities in these areas are appalling and unemployment is well above the national average. Despite its glossy public face, Portugal is still the second poorest country in the EU after Greece, with typical wages only two-thirds the EU average. Taxation and social security systems urgently need reforming, as do the justice and health systems. With the ending of the EU's massive funding programme by the year 2000 and few major infrastructure projects ahead (except for a new Lisbon airport), the socialist government is being urged to tackle these problems now, while economic expansion lasts.

One of the government's biggest economic burdens is an inefficient agriculture sector. Some 11% of the workforce is still engaged in agriculture, forestry and fishing, but the contribution of this sector to the GDP has been dropping steadily since 1990. Agriculture's only notable success stories are in tomato paste and cork – Portugal is the world's largest exporter of both commodities.

By contrast, the services sector (real estate, banking, financial services, wholesale and tourism) is booming: it now employs 57% of the population (compared with 35% a decade ago), with tourism alone accounting for 15% of Portgual's GDP. In 1995, 9.7 million tourists (and 22.9 million day-visitors, largely from Spain) contributed US$4403 million in foreign exchange earnings.

The manufacturing sector still has important traditional industries, such as metal products and machinery, textiles and clothing, footwear, cork, wood and paper pulp. But the headline-grabbing action is in

Peak of Privatisation

As the millennium draws to a close, so too will one of Europe's most extensive programmes of privatisation. Portugal's gung-ho sale of some of its most important companies (including electricity and telecommunications utilities) was launched by the old centre-right government in 1989 and has been pursued even more enthusiastically by the current socialist government. It will reach its peak in 1999 with the sell-off of a further 17 companies including the national airline, TAP Air Portugal.

The revenue raised (an estimated US$4.4 billion from this latest sale alone) has helped reduce the public debt and lower Portugal's fiscal deficit. It's also made Portugal a nation of shareholders: more than 750,000 people applied for shares in the initial public offering of the national power utility in 1997, and 250,000 in a secondary offering of Portugal Telecom.

industrial parks with massive manufacturing projects funded by foreign investment. While projects like these are welcomed for the employment they generate, growing investment by Spain in the recently privatised services sector is viewed with alarm by many Portuguese, who see their country's business slipping into the hands of their least liked European neighbour.

However, Portugal's economic future undoubtedly lies with Spain and its other European partners. In 1995, EU countries (notably France, Germany, Spain and the UK) accounted for some 77% of Portugal's foreign trade and 78% of foreign direct investment.

POPULATION & PEOPLE

Portugal has an estimated population of 10 million. Around 17% is under 15 years of age and 15% over 65. As with the rest of southern Europe, the over-65 age group in Portugal is growing rapidly (it's more than doubled over the past 30 years). This, plus wider eligibility for state pensions, is putting a serious strain on the social security system.

The vast majority of the population lives in rural areas, although the urban population has increased dramatically since the 1960s. At that time, urban population was 22% of the total; now it's 36% (still low compared to other European countries: Britain's urban population, for instance, is 89%). One of the major reasons for the urban increase was the arrival of nearly a million refugees in 1974 and 1975, following the independence of Portugal's African colonies – Angola, Cape Verde, Guinea-Bissau, Mozambique and São Tomé e Príncipe. These immigrants (both legal and illegal) make up Portugal's major ethnic groups (the 39,500 Cape Verdeans are the biggest single group). There is also a small resident Gypsy population.

The 1960s and 1970s were times of population change for other reasons, too. Ever since gold and diamonds were discovered in Brazil in the 17th century, the Portuguese have sought their fortunes (or simply a better chance of survival) overseas, notably during the 18th and 19th centuries (in Brazil) and in the 1950s and 1960s elsewhere in Europe (especially France and Germany). According to Marion Kaplan in her book *The Portuguese*, some 1.3 million Portuguese emigrated between 1886 and 1926, and a similar number between 1926 and 1966. That second wave of émigrés included young men avoiding conscription to the Portuguese forces sent abroad during the wars of independence in the African colonies.

Although now, for the first time in ages, there are more immigrants than emigrants, Portugal's emigration rate is still one of the highest in Europe (some 1.7 million emigrated over the past three decades) and its overseas population is one of the largest. It is estimated that about three million Portugúese live or work abroad, causing a serious depletion of social security contributions. Brazil, South Africa, America and Canada have the largest settlements, and

Saudade

It's been described as a great nostalgia for the glorious past, a fathomless yearning, and a longing for home, but unless you're Portuguese you'll probably never really grasp the uniquely Portuguese passion of *saudade*. Its musical form is the aching sorrow expressed in *fado* songs – a melancholic submission to the twists and turns of fate. In Portuguese and Brazilian poetry it's a mystical reverence for nature, a brooding sense of loneliness that became especially popular among 19th and early 20th century poets who fostered a cult of *saudosismo*. In tangible form it's the return of thousands of émigrés to their home villages every August, drawn not just by family ties but by something much deeper – a longing for all that home and Portugal represents: the heroism of the past, the sorrows of the present, and wistful hopes for the future.

France and Germany the largest number of temporary workers. In August or at Christmas, when the émigrés return for holidays, you can see how their home villages revive and how wealthy these young men appear compared with those left behind.

The northern Minho province, where most of the émigrés originate, is one of the poorest and most densely peopled regions. The population there is growing at several times the country-wide rate, and population density is over 165 people per sq km, compared with fewer than 20 per sq km in the Alentejo.

Unlike most other European countries, the vast majority of Portuguese people are very similar in appearance, sharing typical Mediterranean features such as brown eyes and dark hair. But the country's many invaders and settlers – from Celts and Carthaginians in the north and coastal areas to Romans and North African Muslims mainly in the south – have left recognisable traits, too. You'll also notice a distinctive north-south social division – the northerners tend to seem more religious and conservative than their easy-going compatriots in the south.

The thousands of African and mixed-race immigrants who flooded into Portugal in 1974-75 have integrated well into Portuguese society (among the more famous is the well-loved footballer, Eusébio, who came from Mozambique). African music is all the rage in Lisbon, with an increasing number of African nightclubs opening. Although Portugal has one of the lowest percentages of avowed racists in the EU (only 3% of the population, compared with Belgium's 22% and Britain's 8%), incidents of racism do occur. There have been sporadic violent attacks on blacks, mostly by skinheads. And as the current era of wealth exacerbates social divisions, immigrants may well face tougher times.

In our text, the population figures given are for the town. Where this figure is not available, the figure given is for the *concelho*, or municipality, of the town, indicated by (municipality).

EDUCATION

The state of Portugal's education system is embarrassingly awful. Portugal has the biggest proportion of employees with a 'low level' of education in the EU – 75% (the equivalent figure for Germany is 18%). According to a 1995 report by the Organisation for Economic Cooperation and Development (OECD), over 47% of Portuguese people between the ages of 15 and 64 have little or no ability to read or do sums.

The Salazar regime is to blame: for four decades it invested as little as possible in education, and there were only four years of compulsory schooling.

Today, there's free (voluntary) preschool education for three to six-year-olds, and nine years of compulsory education (from age six to 15), provided free of charge in state schools. Private schools supplement the state schools. Secondary education, which is not compulsory, lasts for three years. Higher education is provided at the country's 18 universities and at 98 other higher education establishments, such as regional technical colleges.

According to figures, 99% of the school-age population enrol in basic and secondary education, but the reality is that many children leave school early to find work. The OECD found that less than half of those between the ages of five and 29 are actually in full-time education. And only 8% of the relevant age group continue in education long enough to get a degree (half as many as in France, for instance).

The system itself exacerbates the problems. There's a serious lack of teachers and schools (city kids have to go to schools in shifts), opportunities for vocational education are limited and the education system is excessively centralised. According to the OECD, this has meant large numbers of people leaving school with low skills. Many are still waiting for the new socialist government to do its own sums correctly and find the money (probably from the EU) to fulfil promises of reforms and improvements to the system.

PORTUGAL'S
ARCHITECTURE

Pre-Roman

An isolated clearing in a tranquil Alentejan olive grove near Évora is the setting for one of the earliest and most memorable prehistoric architectural sites in Portugal: the Cromeleque dos Almendres (Almendres Cromlech). This vast oval of some 95 monoliths is the finest cromlech (a circle or oval of huge boulders used for funerary purposes) in the Iberian Peninsula.

All over Portugal – and particularly in the Alentejo – you'll come across other similar funerary and religious structures, built during the Neolithic and Megalithic eras some five to six thousand years ago. Particularly impressive are the dolmens, or funerary chambers. Rectangular, polygonal or round in shape, they are reached by a corridor of stone slabs and covered with earth to create an artificial mound. The most striking example is the Anta Grande do Zambujeiro, or Great Dolmen of Zambujeiro, also near Évora. It's the largest dolmen in Europe, with six stones, each 6m high, forming a huge chamber. Single monoliths, or menhirs, often carved with phallic or religious symbols, also dot the countryside like a lingering army of stone sentinels. See the boxed text 'Dolmens, Menhirs & Other Mysteries' in the Alentejo chapter for more on these Stonehenge-like wonders of Portugal.

With the arrival of the Celts (800-200 BC) came the first established hilltop settlements called *castros*. You can find some of the best examples in the northern Minho province, notably the Citânia de Briteiros near Braga. At this evocative hilltop site the ruins are particularly well-preserved (several buildings have even been remodelled) and you can literally step into Portugal's past. The stone dwelling huts were built in circular or elliptical shapes and the entire complex was surrounded by a defensive outer wall of dry stone. This style is typical of northern *citânias* (towns). In the south the huts tended to be rectangular, and they would all have been roofed and separated from each other by alleyways. Funerary buildings from this period often incorporated a furnace for incinerating the dead.

Previous Page: Manueline motifs were still being used in the 19th and 20th century, as seen in this sea monster decorating the Palácio Nacional da Pena in Sintra.

Left: Stone Age dolmens (temple tombs) are found on the high plateaus of the Minho and Trás-os-Montes, and on the plains of the Alentejo.

One of the most arresting artefacts recovered from Briteiros – a slab of carved stone thought to have been the front of a funerary monument – can be seen, together with other sculptural remains, in Guimarães, at the excellent Museu Martins Sarmento (named after the archaeologist who excavated the site in 1875).

Roman & Early Christian (3rd century BC to 8th century AD)

The Romans, who invaded the Iberian Peninsula in 218 BC, left a wealth of architectural evidence – roads, bridges, and towns complete with forums (market places), villas, public baths and aqueducts. Much of it remains unexcavated, and although nearly all of Portugal's major cities are built on Roman foundations, these have mostly been covered over or destroyed. However, at Portugal's most extensive Roman site, Conimbriga (near Coimbra), you'll find an entire Roman town under excavation. Revealed so far are some stunning mosaics, as well as other typically Roman architectural features – columns used for structural or decorative purposes, elaborately carved entablatures and classical ornamentation.

A much smaller excavation of a villa at Milreu (near Faro in the Algarve) has some tantalising fragments of fish mosaics in a former bathing chamber. The most spectacular Roman ruin of all is the famous Temple of Diana in Évora, with its elaborately carved Corinthian columns. This is the best preserved temple of its kind in the entire Iberian Peninsula, and the only Roman bit of Évora that remains (it survived so well because it was walled-up in the Middle Ages, and was even used as a slaughterhouse for a while).

The various Teutonic tribes who invaded after the fall of Rome in the early 5th century left little architectural mark apart from a few churches built by the Visigoths (a pugnacious bunch of Arian Christians who booted out the earlier Vandals and Alani). Although these churches have been heavily restored over the centuries they still reveal their basic Roman basilical outline: a rectangular building divided by columns into a nave and two aisles. For some of the best examples check out the Igreja de São Gião (near Nazaré), the Capela de São Pedro de Balsemão (near Lamego) and the Igreja de Santa Amaro (in Beja). The most unusual is the Igreja de São Frutuoso, near Braga, which is Byzantine (Graeco-Asiatic) in character, with a centralised plan in the shape of a Greek cross.

The Visigoths also rebuilt the Roman town of Idanha-a-Velha; parts of the cathedral in this once-grand and now eerily quiet backwater village near Castelo Branco date from this time. Many other Visigothic churches were destroyed by the Moors after they kicked out the Visigoths in 711 AD.

Moorish (8th to 12th centuries)

Unlike Spain, Portugal has no complete buildings left from the Moorish period. But you can find the odd arch or wall, bits of fortresses and, most atmospheric of all, remains of Moorish quarters – the overlooked little town of Moura, in the Alentejo, has a notable Moorish quarter. Not far from Moura, in Mértola, you'll also find a distinctive former mosque converted into a church.

The Moors did, however, introduce important elements which have persisted in Portuguese architecture to this day, particularly in the south of the country. It's thanks to the Moors, for instance, that Portugal houses sport so many horseshoe arches and patios, along with wrought-iron work and whitewash, plentiful ornamentation and the use of water as a decorative element both inside and outside. To discover some of the strongest Moorish vibes, wander round the old back streets of Algarve towns such as Silves (a former Moorish capital), Tavira and Olhão.

Romanesque (11th to late 13th centuries)

During the successful Christian Reconquista of the country from the Moors (completed by 1297), virtually all the Moors' mosques were destroyed and replaced by churches or cathedrals, often on the same site. They followed the simple, robust Romanesque style of architecture – rounded arches, thick walls and heavy vaulting – which was originally introduced to Portugal by Burgundian monks. Often, too, as with Coimbra's dour example, these cathedrals were more like fortified castles than religious strongholds because of the continuing military threat from the Moors and, later, the Castilians.

More delicate Romanesque touches can be found in several small, lovely churches (notably the Igreja de São Salvador at Bravães, near Ponte da Barca in the Minho), where portals often display fine geometric animal or plant motifs in their archivolts (spot the monkeys and oxen on the one at Bravães). Although castles and other fortifications were also built at this time, there's only one remaining complete example of a secular building – Bragança's Domus Municipalis, a quaint and endearing little five-sided building which is the country's oldest town hall.

Gothic (12th to 15th centuries)

The Gothic style of architecture graces some of the most aesthetically pleasing religious architecture in the country. The earliest and most spectacular example is the dramatically austere church and cloister of the Mosteiro de Santa Maria de Alcobaça. Begun in 1178, the abbey is considered one of the finest examples of Cistercian architecture in Europe, with a soaring lightness and simplicity strongly influenced by the style of the French Cistercian abbey at Clairvaux. Distinctive Gothic touches include pointed (not rounded) arches and rib vaults, while the beautifully proportioned interior follows Cistercian rules by being completely devoid of sculpture. Perhaps the most memorable corner of Alcobaça is the simple, square Cloisters of Silence. If it reminds you of the cathedral cloisters of Coimbra, Lisbon and Évora, it's because the Cloisters of Silence served as their model (and the model for many other strikingly simple cloisters throughout the land).

Simplicity went right out the window, however, with the construction of the Mosteiro de Santa Maria da Vitória (Mosteiro da Batalha) at the end of the 14th century. Portuguese, Irish and French architects all worked on this breathtaking monument over the following two centuries (even then, the final chapels were left unfinished). Looking at all the ornamentation, you'd think they were each trying to outdo one another. The combination of their different skills and the changing architectural fashions of their times – from Flamboyant (late) Gothic to Gothic Renaissance to Manueline (see the following section) – makes this the most impressive and stimulating Gothic building in Portugal. Free from the constraints of Cistercian rules, it reveals far more decorative elements than the monastery at Alcobaça (especially in its Gothic Royal Cloisters and Chapter House), while the eye-catching flying buttresses are typical of the style called English Perpendicular Gothic.

Meanwhile, secular architecture was also enjoying something of a Gothic boom, thanks to the need for constant fortifications against the Moors and to the castle-building fervour of the 13th century ruler,

Pillory Power

Portugal's *pelourinhos*, or pillories, are a distinctive feature of nearly every town and village, especially in the northern Minho and Trás-os-Montes provinces. Believed to have originated in Roman times, these stone columns became prominent in Portugal around the 12th century and were in use for some 500 years. Originally, they were devoid of decoration and served as a form of punishment: criminals were chained from hooks at the top (earlier versions had cages) or locked into attached handcuffs. But increasingly, pillories became a symbol of municipal power – which is why you'll see most of them beside town halls, cathedrals or monasteries, the most common seats of jurisdiction at the time. During the 16th century Manueline era, pillories became elaborate works of art and were often topped by Dom Manuel's motifs of an armillary sphere and cross of the Order of Christ, while the stone column itself was carved into rope-like coils.

Some of the more unusual pillories in Portugal include the 16th century one in Elvas, covered with stone dots; a hexagonal pillory in Barcelos, topped by a graceful granite lantern; and the curiously pagan pillory of Soajo, carved with a crude smiling face.

Dom Dinis. Dozens of impressive castles (such as Almourol, Estremoz, Óbidos and Bragança) date from this time, many featuring massive double perimeter walls and an inner square tower. Even townsfolk got in on the Gothic act, adding classically simple Gothic stone doorways and windows to their plain granite houses (look for them especially in Castelo de Vide and Marvão, in northern Alentejo).

Manueline (late 15th to mid-16th centuries)

Manueline is the term given to a specifically Portuguese variety of late Gothic architecture. A highly decorative style, it roughly coincided with the reign of Dom Manuel I (1495-1521), although it continued long after and still crops up today (check out the mind-boggling neo-Manueline Palace Hotel do Buçaco in Luso, built in the early years of the 20th century).

It was during Dom Manuel's reign that Vasco da Gama and his peers were exploring the seas as far as India and discovering new lands and new wealth for Portugal. The confidence of this Age of Discoveries was expressed in sculptural creations of extraordinary inventiveness, drawing heavily on nautical themes: ropes, coral and anchors in twisted stone topped by ubiquitous armillary spheres (a navigational device which became the personal symbol of Dom Manuel) and the Cross of the Order of Christ (the symbol of the religious-military order, formerly the Knights Templar, which largely financed and inspired Portugal's explorations).

The style first emerged in Setúbal's Igreja de Jesus, designed in the 1490s by Diogo de Boitaca, a Frenchman who had settled in Portugal. He gave the church large twisted columns reminiscent of thick cables, and smaller columns and rib vaulting which look like twisted ropes. The fashion quickly caught on in cathedrals and churches elsewhere; in these buildings architectural styles soar up like ocean waves amid a plethora of spiral decoration (aptly described by the eccentric 18th century English novelist William Beckford as 'scollops and twistifications').

Outstanding Manueline masterpieces worth going out of your way to see are the Mosteiro dos Jerónimos at Belém (masterminded largely by Diogo de Boitaca and João de Castilho), and Diogo de Arruda's fantastically sculpted window in the Chapter House of Tomar's Convento de Cristo, which boasts an abundance of maritime detail and illustrates the style's preoccupation with exotic plants and decoration. Other famous Manueline creations include the Torre de Belém, a Manueline and Moorish concoction also created by Diogo de Boitaca and his brother Francisco (both of whom, significantly, had worked in North Africa), and the

Left: Armillary sphere topped by the Cross of the Order of Christ, a typical Manueline device.

Mosteiro da Batalha's Unfinished Chapels, which are incredible examples of the style at its most flamboyant.

Among the few secular Manueline examples that remain are parts of the Palácio Nacional de Sintra (added during Dom Manuel's reign). As the style progressed, it assimilated flatter Plateresque designs (named after the ornate Spanish work of silversmiths, or *plateros*) and Italian Renaissance ornamentation.

Renaissance (16th century)

The Portuguese were slow to take up this style, which was a return to Roman classical designs and proportions. One of its protagonists, the Italian Andrea Sansovino, is thought to have spent some time in Portugal but he made little impression. The Quinta da Bacalhoa, a private house built at Vila Nogueira de Azeitão (near Setúbal) in the late 15th century, is believed to be his only notable contribution. It was left to the French decorative sculptor Nicolas Chanterène to be the pioneer of Renaissance ideas. From around 1517 onwards, his influence was noticeable both in sculpture and in decorative elements of architecture.

Entire Renaissance buildings are rare in Portugal, but among the best are the Great Cloisters in Tomar's Convento de Cristo, which were designed by the Spanish Diogo de Torralva in the late 16th century, the small Igreja de Nossa Senhora da Conceição nearby, and the Convento de Bom Jesus at Valverde, just outside Évora.

Mannerist (mid/late 16th to late 17th centuries)

Sober, serious and severe: the Mannerist style reflects the spirit of its time, coinciding as it did with the years of Spanish rule (1580-1640) and the predominant influence of the Inquisition and the Jesuits. It persisted throughout much of the 17th century. Take a look at Lisbon's Igreja de São Vicente de Fora, built between 1582 and 1627 by Felipe Terzi, and you can see a typical example (which served as a model for many other churches) of balanced Mannerist classicism.

Baroque (late 17th to mid/late 18th centuries)

When independence from Spain was firmly re-established and the influence of the Inquisition was on the wane, Portugal burst out in Baroque fever – an architectural style that was exuberant, theatrical and meant to appeal to the senses. Nothing could possibly match the imaginative Manueline flourish, but in terms of flamboyance the Baroque style (named, incidentally, after the Portuguese word for a rough pearl, *barroco*) clearly surpassed it. At its height in the 18th century (almost a century after it had been popular in Italy), it was characterised by curvaceous forms, huge monuments and spatially complex schemes.

Financed by the 17th century gold and diamond discoveries in Brazil, and encouraged by the extravagant Dom João V, local and foreign (particularly Italian) artists created mind-bogglingly opulent Baroque masterpieces. A hallmark of the architecture at this time was the awesome use of *talha dourada* (gilded woodwork), lavished on church interiors throughout the land, particularly Aveiro's Convento de Jesus, Lisbon's Igreja de São Roque and Porto's Igreja de São Francisco.

The Baroque of central and southern Portugal tended to be more restrained than that of the north. Examples include the chancel of Évora's cathedral, and the Palácio Nacional de Mafra. Designed by the German architect João Frederico Ludovice to rival the similar palace-monastery of San Lorenzo de El Escorial (near Madrid), the Mafra version is relatively sober in style, but so immense it took 15,000 labourers working every day for 13 years to complete.

Meanwhile, the Tuscan painter and architect Nicolau Nasoni (who settled in Porto around 1725) introduced a more lively, ornamental Baroque style to the north of the country. It was Nasoni who was responsible for Porto's Torre dos Clérigos and Igreja da Misericórdia, as well as the whimsical Solar de Mateus near Vila Real (made internationally famous as the image on Mateus Rosé wine-bottle labels). In the middle of the 18th century, a notable school of architecture evolved in Braga (largely thanks to the patronage of several wealthy archbishops). Local artists such as André Soares built churches and palaces in a very decorative style, heavily influenced by Augsburg engravings from southern Germany: Soares' Casa do Raio, in Braga, and much of the monumental staircase of the nearby Bom Jesus do Monte are typical examples of this period's ornamentation.

Only when the gold ran out did the Baroque fad fade. At the end of the 18th century, local architects had a quick flirtation with Rococo architecture (best exemplified by Mateus Vicente's Palácio de Queluz which was started in 1747) before embracing neoclassicism.

Neoclassical (mid-18th to 19th centuries)

After Lisbon suffered its devastating earthquake in 1755, the Marquês de Pombal invited architect Eugenio dos Santos to rebuild the main Baixa area in a plain style using classical elements that could easily be constructed and repeated. This revolutionary new 'Pombaline' style featured a grid pattern marked by unadorned houses and wide avenues. It had a knock-on effect and led to a reaction against the excesses of the Baroque period in other parts of the country. In Porto, for instance, the Hospital de Santo António and Feitoria Inglesa (Factory House) – both designed by Englishmen – show a noticeable return to sober Palladian and classical designs. Lisbon's early 19th century Palácio Nacional da Ajuda (the last great royal palace to be built) was also designed on neoclassical lines and served as the inspiration for the elegantly restrained Palácio de Brejoeira (near Monção, in the Minho).

VITOR VIEIRA

Top: The prehistoric Cromleque dos Alendres is thought to have been the site of both social and religious functions.

Middle Left: Flamboyant Gothic architecture dominates the Claustro Real of the Mosteiro de Santa Maria da Vitória at Batalha.

Middle Right: The polychrome marble interior of the Baroque basilica at the Palácio Nacional de Mafra.

Bottom Left: The tall columns and vaulted Manueline roof of the Mosteiro dos Jerónimos in Belém survived the earthquake which devasted much of Lisbon in 1755.

Bottom Right: A variety of religious and secular characters adorn the ornate south portal of the Mosteiro dos Jerónimos in Belém.

JULIA WILKINSON

JULIA WILKINSON

BETHUNE CARMICHAEL

JOHN KING

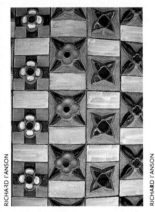

Wherever you turn in Portugal you'll see azulejos covering public and private buildings, inside and out. The art of azulejos is still going strong and colourful modern murals sit alongside earlier styles.

Azulejos

There's no question which decorative art is Portugal's finest: painted tiles, known as *azulejos* (probably after the Arabic *al zulaycha*, which means polished stone), cover everything from church interiors to train stations, house façades to fountains, all over Portugal. While the Portuguese can't claim to have invented the technique – they learnt about it from the Moors, who picked it up from the Persians – they have certainly used azulejos more imaginatively and consistently than any other nation.

Some of the earliest 16th century tiles to be found in Portugal (for instance, at Sintra's Pálacio Nacional) are of Moorish origin and are geometric in style. But after the Portuguese captured Ceuta (then in Morocco) in 1415, they began to investigate the art more thoroughly for themselves. The invention of the majolica technique by the Italians in the 16th century, enabling colours to be painted directly onto the wet clay over a layer of white enamel, gave the Portuguese the impetus they needed, and the azulejo craze began.

The first truly Portuguese tiles started to appear in the 1580s, gracing churches such as Lisbon's Igreja de São Roque and Santarém's Igreja de Marvila. Initially, these azulejos were multicoloured and mostly geometric, reflecting carpet or tapestry patterns, but in the late 17th century a fashion began for huge azulejo panels in churches and cloisters, and on houses and public buildings, illustrating everything from cherubs to picnics, saints to bucolic landscapes. Every nobleman had to have his azulejo hunting panel or poetic allegory (as in Lisbon's Quinta dos Marquês da Fronteira), every church its life of Christ or the saints (as in Lisbon's Igreja São Vicente de Fora). Indeed, such was the growing azulejo craze that the quality of production and colouring eventually suffered and the blue-and-white tiles produced by the Dutch Delft company were able to take over the market.

With the 18th century arrived the great Portuguese azulejo masters António de Oliveira Bernardes and his son Policarpo, who revived the use of both blue-and-white and polychrome Portuguese tiles, producing brilliant panels that perfectly complemented their surroundings. Rococo themes and flavours (such as the seasons and continents in polychromatic colours) also appeared, decorating fountains, stairways (Lamego's Igreja de Nossa Senhora dos Remédios) and sacristies (Lisbon's Convento da Madre de Deus). Only towards the end of the century did a more simple style and colour scheme emerge, reflecting the neoclassical movement in architecture. By then, the industrial manufacture of azulejos had started to cause another decline in quality, as did the rapid need for huge quantities of azulejos after the 1755 Lisbon earthquake.

New, imaginative uses of azulejos still appeared in the 19th century – among them, the large azulejo figures in restaurants such as Lisbon's popular Cervejaria da Trindade. The Art Nouveau and Art Deco movements took the art of azulejo even further into the public domain, with some fantastic façades and interiors for shops and restaurants, kiosks and residential buildings created by Rafael Bordalo Pinheiro, Jorge Colaço and others. Azulejos still have their place in contemporary Portuguese life: Maria Keil and Júlio de Resende are two of the leading artists, responsible for creating some stunning wall mosaics and murals.

For the complete history of this uniquely Portuguese art, visit the Museu Nacional do Azulejo in Lisbon.

19th Century & Modern

In the early 19th century virtually all new building of major monuments came to a halt. This was partly due to the aftereffects of the Peninsular War (1807-14), and partly because a liberal decree in 1834 dissolved the religious orders, allowing their many buildings to be appropriated by the state and thus obviating the need for new commissions. Some former monasteries are still used by the government today – notably Lisbon's Benedictine Mosteiro de São Bento, which is now the seat of parliament (the Palácio da Assembleia da República).

When new buildings did emerge they tended to draw on all the architectural styles of the past, from Moorish (as in Lisbon's Rossio station) to neoclassical (Porto's stock exchange, the Palácio da Bolsa). A distinctly French influence can also be seen in many of the grand apartment blocks and office buildings built in several major cities at this time. Towards the end of the 19th century the increased use of iron and steel reflected Portugal's emergence as a growing industrial nation. Train stations (Lisbon's Alcântara, Campanha and Rossio stations) and other grand buildings (notably Porto's Palácio de Cristal, which was modelled on London's Crystal Palace and no longer stands) were covered in iron and glass. Gustave Eiffel arrived on the scene to build iron bridges across the rivers Minho, Lima and Douro, and his followers were responsible for several other Eiffel-look-a-like bridges, as well as the eye-catching Elevador de Santa Justa in Lisbon.

One of the most delightful movements during this period was the Art Nouveau fad, which resulted in a number of beautifully decorated cafés and shops (particularly in Lisbon, Porto and Braga), many of them still drawing admiring customers today (check out Lisbon's Versailles café or Braga's Café Astória).

Art Nouveau was a short-lived burst of carefree, decorative fancy: the later years of repressive rule under the Salazar dictatorship produced notably severe and communistic state-commissioned pieces of architecture (look and groan at Coimbra University's dull faculty buildings, for instance, which replaced elegant 18th century neoclassical ones). And with a growing middle class and increasing industrialisation, many ugly buildings and blocks of flats sprang up on city outskirts. There are, of course, exceptions, such as Lisbon's Palácio da Justiça in the Campolide district, and the modern, purpose-built Museu Calouste Gulbenkian and its adjacent galleries and concert halls, which date from the 1960s.

Since the 1974 Revolution, although the urban sprawl has continued, many contemporary architects are also producing impressive schemes. Portugal's leading architect, Álvaro de Siza Vieira (winner of the prestigious Pritzger Prize), is restoring with notable sensitivity (and slowness!) the historic Chiado shopping district of central Lisbon, following a major fire in 1988. He also produced the impressive Pavilhão de Portugal (Portuguese National Pavilion) for Expo '98. The award-winning and startling postmodern Amoreiras shopping complex, by Tomás Taveira, is another notable contribution to Lisbon's contemporary skyline (see Shopping in the Lisbon chapter).

Fortunately, due to a combination of national and local laws and rulings made since 1974, it is no longer permissible to knock down old buildings of historical or architectural interest: instead, they must be restored or incorporated into new schemes. A fine example of this recent trend is the headquarters of the Association of Portuguese Architects, in Lisbon, which combines its original neoclassical façade with a striking contemporary interior.

Vernacular (Domestic) Architecture

A relatively unsung aspect of architecture is so-called 'vernacular architecture', the shapes and forms in a region's common buildings that arise naturally over the centuries in response to climate, land use and other constraints. In Portugal, the north is a land of granite, a hard material perfect for constructing thick-walled houses with slate roofs that keep out the cold winter winds and rain. The houses are built on two floors: the lower one used for animals and storage, and the upper one (reached by an outside staircase) for living space. In the coastal Beiras, the local limestone is used for two-storey houses (often with a 1st floor, south-facing veranda) that are faced with painted stucco or, occasionally, *azulejo* tiles (see the boxed text earlier in this section). Typically, their floors are connected by internal staircases and their roofs covered with red clay tiles.

On the coast near Aveiro, several villages are famous for their candy-striped, painted houses built of wood from nearby pine forests. Further south, in the Ribatejo and Alentejo provinces, the brick houses are long, single-storey structures, stuccoed and whitewashed, and with a single colour (usually blue) used to outline the architectural features. In order to keep out the searing summer heat the houses have few doors and windows, while their fireplaces and chimneys are huge to provide much-needed winter warmth and spaces to smoke the meat and sausages typical of the region. It's in the Alentejo, too, that you'll find the most extravagant housing material: around Estremoz, the plentiful supply of local marble ensures its generous use in everything from palaces and town houses to kerbs and walls.

By contrast, the Algarve's houses, built of clay or stone, appear quite modest. When the roofs of red tiles are replaced by flat terraces (used for drying produce or catching rainwater) they can also take on a North African or Moorish appearance. Another Moorish influence – very characteristic of the Algarve – is the shape and design of the decorative pierced chimneys. Typical, too, of Mediterranean houses are the Algarve's shaded porches and arcaded verandas at ground level. A fine book on the vernacular architecture of Portugal and Spain is Norman F Carver Jr's *Iberian Villages*, published in 1988.

ARTS
Music

Fundamental to Portugal's history of musical expression is its folk music, which you can hear throughout the country at almost every festival. It traces its roots to the medieval troubadour, and is traditionally accompanied by a band of guitars, violins, clarinets, harmonicas and various wooden percussion instruments. In fact, the instruments are often more attractive than the singing, which could generously be described as a high-pitched repetitive wail.

You can't argue with its roots, though: songs invariably deal with harvesting, sowing and other aspects of life on the land. If the foot-tapping rhythms get to you, it's easy to find cassette tapes at local markets and weekly fairs: groups from the Alentejo and Minho are said to be the best.

Far more enigmatic is Portugal's most famous style of music, *fado*. These melancholic chants – performed as a set of three songs, each one lasting three minutes – are also said to have their roots in troubadour songs (although African slave songs have had an influence too). They're traditionally sung by one performer accompanied by a 12 string Portuguese *quitarra* (a pear-shaped guitar), and often a Spanish guitar as well. Fado emerged in the 18th century in Lisbon's working-class districts of Alfama and Mouraria and gradually moved upmarket. A more academic version developed later in the university town of Coimbra.

The greatest modern *fadista* is Amália Rodrigues. Pick up a copy of her greatest hits (or the double CD set *O Melhor*) to hear what fado should sound like. Unfortunately she no longer sings live – her 55 year singing career ended in 1995 after a lung operation – but her septuagenarian sister, Celeste, still pulls in the crowds. Another performer to watch out for is the dynamic young singer Mísia, who has experimented with instrumentation and commissioned poets to write lyrics. Venues for live fado in

Fado Uproar

There are two styles of *fado* music: one comes from Lisbon and the other from the university town of Coimbra. The Lisbon style is still considered by aficionados to be the most genuine, but there's something about Coimbra's roving bands of romantic, fado-singing students during their May celebration week that pulls at the heartstrings far more effectively than the Lisbon performers in their nightclubs.

Indeed, in many ways, the Coimbra singers surpass their Lisbon colleagues in tradition. When singer Manuela Bravo announced in 1996 that she was going to record a CD of Coimbra fados, there was an outcry by the fado department of Coimbra University. Why? Because Coimbra fado – which praises the beauty of women – is traditionally sung by men only. Her opponents, described by Bravo's supporters as 'Salazaristic, old-fashioned and musty', warned that the gutsy *fadista* would 'debauch' tradition.

To their horror, she won the support of one of Portugal's best fado guitarists, António Pinho Brojo. Even the Mayor of Coimbra got involved (on her side), and the album, *Intenções*, went ahead. Alas, the entire issue disappeared from sight almost as soon as it had appeared, allegedly bought up by a local pharmaceutical company, and Bravo's CD is nearly impossible to find now.

Lisbon, Coimbra, Porto and other towns are recommended under the Entertainment sections for each town.

Both fado and traditional folk songs – and, increasingly, 'foreign' strains from Europe and Africa – have shaped Portugal's modern folk music scene (now known as *música popular*). It began to attract attention in the 1960s, when contemporary musicians like José Afonso joined with modern poets to start a new musical movement dealing with social and political issues. Often censored during the Salazar years, its lyrics became overtly political after 1974, with singers using their performances to support various revolutionary factions. Today's *música popular* has successfully returned to its roots, thanks to singer-songwriters and instrumentalists like Carlos Paredes. Notable groups include Brigada Victor Jara, Trovante and the widely known Madredeus (whose blend of traditional and contemporary music has been described as a 'window into the Portuguese soul').

Another increasingly popular genre in Lisbon is contemporary African jazz and rock. Dozens of African nightclubs now resonate to the rhythms of the former African colonies. Among big names are Cesária Évora from Cape Verde, Guem from Angola and Kaba Mane from Guinea-Bissau.

Literature

Portuguese literature has been moulded by foreign influences since the 13th century, particularly by Spain's literary styles and standards (from the 15th to 17th centuries nearly every major Portuguese writer wrote in both Portuguese and Spanish).

Nonetheless, Portuguese literature retains a distinct temperament and individuality. Two major styles dominate: lyric poetry and realistic fiction. The most outstanding literary figure is Luís Vaz de Camões (1524-80). This 16th century poet enjoyed little fame or fortune in his lifetime. Only after his death was his genius recognised, thanks largely to an epic poem, *Os Lusiadas*

(The Lusiads). Ostensibly, it relates the historic sea voyage by Vasco da Gama to India in 1497, but it is also a superbly lyrical song of praise to the greatness of the Portuguese spirit, written when Portugal was still one of the most powerful countries in the western world. When it was first published in 1572 it received few plaudits. Over 400 years later, it is considered the national epic, its poet a national hero.

In the 19th century a tide of Romanticism swept the Portuguese literary scene. The chief figure in this movement was poet, playwright and Romantic novelist Almeida Garrett (1799-1854), who devoted much of his life to stimulating political awareness through his writings. Among his most notable works is the novel, *Viagens na Minha Terra* (Travels in My Homeland), an allegory of contemporary political events. Despite being Portugal's most talented playwright since the 16th century court dramatist, Gil Vicente, he was exiled for his political liberalism.

Garrett's contemporary, Alexandre Herculano (also exiled), was meanwhile continuing the long Portuguese tradition of historical literature (which flourished most strongly during the 16th century Age of Discoveries) by creating an enormous body of work – most notably his magnum opus, *História de Portugal*.

Towards the end of the 19th century several other writers emerged, among them José Maria Eça de Queirós, who introduced realism to Portuguese literature with his powerful 1876 novel, *O Crime do Padre Amaro* (The Sin of Father Amaro). His other works include the entertaining narratives, *Os Maias* (The Maias) and *A Illustre Casa de Ramires* (The Illustrious House of Ramires). Some of his best short stories are included in a well-translated collection published by Carcanet, *The Anarchist Banker and Other Portuguese Stories*.

Fernando Pessoa (1888-1935), author of the 1934 *Mensagem* (Message), is posthumously regarded as the most extraordinary poet of his generation; his four different poet-personalities (which he referred to as heteronyms) created four distinct strains of poetry and prose. *A Centenary Pessoa*, published in English, provides a fascinating insight into his work.

The Salazar dictatorship that spanned much of the early modern era suppressed creativity and freedom of expression. Several writers suffered during this period, including the poet and storyteller Miguel Torga, whose background in tough Trás-os-Montes gave a radical individualism to his writings (so much so that one of his novels was banned); and Maria Velho da Costa, one of the three authors of *Novas Cartas Portuguesas* (The Three Marias: New Portuguese Letters), whose modern feminist interpretation of the 17th century *Letters of a Portuguese Nun* so shocked the Salazar regime that its authors were put on trial.

The post-Salazar literary scene is dominated by figures like António Lobo Antunes and José Saramago, winner of the 1998 Nobel Prize for Literature. Saramago's international reputation is based on works like *Memorial do Convento* (Memorial of the Convent), which combines astute realism with poetic fancy. José Cardoso Pires, who died in 1998, was another popular writer; his finest novel, *Balada da Praia dos Cães* (Ballad of Dog's Beach), is a gripping thriller based on a real political assassination in the Salazar era. In Portugal's former colonies (particularly Brazil), writers such as Jorge Amado are also making a mark on modern Portuguese-language literature.

Painting

The earliest examples of visual art in Portugal are several treasure-troves consisting of 20,000-year-old Palaeolithic paintings and carvings; the most impressive are those along the Rio Côa near Vila Nova de Foz Côa in Beira Alta (see the boxed text 'Rock Art in the Vale do Côa' in the Douro chapter).

The cave dwellers' modern successors have been heavily influenced by French, Italian and Flemish styles. The first major exception was the 15th century primitive painter Nuno Gonçalves, whose polyptych of the *Adoration of St Vincent* (now in Lisbon's Museu Nacional de Arte Antiga) is a unique tapestry-style revelation of contemporary Portuguese society.

The Manueline school of the 16th century also produced some uniquely Portuguese paintings, remarkable for their delicacy, realism and luminous colours. The big names of this school are Vasco Fernandes (known as Grão Vasco) and Gaspar Vaz, who both worked from Viseu (their best works can be seen in Viseu's excellent Museu de Grão Vasco). In Lisbon, other outstanding Manueline artists were Jorge Afonso (court painter to Dom Manuel I), Cristóvão de Figueiredo and Gregório Lopes.

The Renaissance era produced more notable sculpture than painting (see the following section), but the 17th century saw a woman artist, Josefa de Óbidos, make waves with her rich still lifes (see the boxed text under Óbidos in the Estremadura & Ribatejo chapter). In the late 18th century, Domingos António de Sequeira produced wonderful portraits. The 19th century saw an artistic echo of the naturalist and Romantic movements, expressed particularly strongly in the works of Silva Porto and Marquês de Oliveira, while Sousa Pinto excelled as a pastel artist in the early 20th century.

José Saramago is the first Portuguese writer to win the Nobel Prize for Literature.

Naturalism continued to be the dominant trend through the 20th century, although Amadeo de Souza Cardoso struck out on his own impressive path of Cubism and Expressionism, and Maria Helena Vieria da Silva became noted as the country's finest abstract painter (although she lived and worked in Paris for most of her life). Other eminent artists in the contemporary art world include Almada Negreiros (often called the father of Portugal's modern art movement) and Guilherme Santa-Rita. Their works and many others can best be seen in Lisbon's Centro de Arte Moderna and Porto's Museu Nacional Soares dos Reis.

Sculpture

Sculptors have excelled in many periods of Portugal's history. Among the first memorable creations are the carved tombs of the 12th to 14th centuries, such as the beautifully ornate limestone tombs of Inês de Castro and Dom Pedro in the Mosteiro de Alcobaça, where the detailed friezes are still impressive despite vandalism by French soldiers in 1811.

During the Manueline era, sculptors including Diogo de Boitaca went wild with uniquely Portuguese seafaring fantasies and exuberant decoration (see the special section 'Portugal's Architecture' earlier in this chapter). At the same time, foreign influences were seeping in: first, a Flemish style (thanks to resident Flemish masters Olivier de Gand and Jean d'Ypres), followed in the 16th century by the Flamboyant Gothic and Plateresque styles from Spanish Galicia and Biscay. The Biscayan artists João and Diogo de Castilho created the most outstanding work during this time, often combining their native styles with Manueline (for example, the cloisters of the Mosteiro dos Jerónimos in Lisbon).

During the Renaissance period, it was the turn of the French: several French artists who had settled in Coimbra, including Nicolas Chanterène and Jean de Rouen, excelled in sculpting doorways, pulpits, altarpieces and low reliefs. The ornate pulpit in Coimbra's Igreja de Santa Cruz is regarded as Chanterène's masterpiece. Foreign schools continued to influence Portuguese sculptors in the 18th century Baroque era, when Dom João V took advantage of all the foreign artists helping with the construction of the Convento do Mafra to found a school of sculpture. Its first principal was the Italian, Alexander Giusti, but its most famous Portuguese teacher was Joaquim Machado de Castro (the museum named after him in Coimbra contains some of the finest sculptures and paintings in Portugal). Castro's work inevitably shows strong influences from the classical and Romantic traditions of France and Italy, especially in the terracotta figures of his Baroque manger scenes.

A century later, the work of António Soares dos Reis reflects similar influences, although Soares also tried to create something uniquely Portuguese (and impossibly intangible) by attempting to portray in sculpture the melancholic feeling of saudade (see the boxed text 'Saudade' earlier in this chapter). At the turn of the 20th century, two names were prominent: Francisco Franco, and the prolific sculptor António Teixeira Lopes (a pupil of Soares dos Reis), whose most famous works are his series of children's heads. These, along with work by Soares, are on display in the Museu Nacional Soares dos Reis, in Porto.

Cinema & the Performing Arts

Portugal's film industry is practically nonexistent, with just half a dozen or so films produced each year. The only internationally famous director is Manoel de Oliveira, described by the British *Guardian* newspaper as 'the most eccentric and the most inspired of cinema's world masters'. Now nearly 90 years old, the ex-racing driver has made 18 films (all except three after he turned 60), including the recent *The Convent*, with Catherine Deneuve and John Malkovich. Oliveira's rather theatrical films are often controversial, demanding to be interpreted on different levels. His latest offering, *Journey to the Beginning of the World*, features the late Italian actor Marcello Mastroianni.

Classic theatre, too, is still finding its feet after the repressive Salazar years, though many small theatres in Lisbon and the provinces are now flourishing, thanks largely to the support of the generous Gulbenkian Foundation. This is one of the few private arts sponsors in Portugal: state funding of cinema, orchestras, opera, ballet and theatre is still very common.

Far more exciting are the independent 'fringe' performing arts, such as the puppet theatres of Porto and Évora (Porto even has an international puppet festival in March), and a circus school in Lisbon. Further information is given under Entertainment in the Porto and Évora sections, and in the boxed text 'Chapitô' in the Lisbon chapter.

Handicrafts & Indigenous Arts

You only have to visit the big weekly markets in Portugal to see the astounding range of handicrafts that are available – from ceramics, embroidery and lacework to baskets, painted furniture and carved ox yokes. The Algarve, Alentejo and Minho regions produce some of the finest work, although nearly every area has its speciality. In addition to the *artesanato* (artisan) shops where these handicrafts are for sale, you can also often find items not available elsewhere at turismos and rural museums (for example, in the Barcelos and Beja turismos and São Bras de Alportel's museum). Porto's Centro Regional de Artes Tradicionais (CRAT; Regional Centre for Traditional Arts & Crafts) is another good source (see Shopping under Porto in the Douro chapter). For detailed information about the crafts and artisans of the Algarve and Alentejo region, check out John & Madge Measures' book, *Southern Portugal: Its People, Traditions & Wildlife*.

The ceramics are, perhaps, the most impressive (and the most frustratingly inconvenient to cart around, though the major artesanato shops can offer a packing and shipping service). The most famous pottery centres are São Pedro do Corval and Estremoz (both in the Alentejo), where the pottery is often encrusted with marble chips; Barcelos in the Minho (brightly coloured pots and cockerels); Coimbra in the Beiras (predominantly green and geometric wares); and Caldas da Rainha in Estremadura (cabbage leaf designs). Despite Caldas da Rainha's tendency to frivolity in ceramics (such as suggestive phallic ornaments), the town holds the important Feira Nacional da Cerâmica (National Ceramics Fair) every year. The Algarve, too, is packed with great pottery, especially huge, Roman-style amphora jugs.

Baskets made from rush, willow, cane or rye straw are widely available, while other rural necessities still being fashioned for practical use (although increasingly for tourist souvenirs as well) are the fabulous painted wooden furniture of the Alentejo (made in miniature sizes, too), along with the carved wooden ox yokes of the Minho region. Traditional wooden toys, model boats and ox carts are other carved wooden specialities (check out Estremoz and Nazaré), while tiny straw figures dressed in traditional rural costume are some of Portugal's cutest souvenirs.

Hand-embroidered linen, especially tablecloths and place mats, is a flourishing handicraft throughout Portugal. Weaving (especially woollen blankets) is also a long-established tradition, particularly in the Algarve and southern Alentejo, where the craft has recently been revived and boosted by women's cooperatives and initiatives such as LEADER (established by the EU to assist rural development projects) and IN LOCO (aimed at revitalising the Serra do Caldeirão region of the Algarve). There are several weaving strongholds in the Algarve, including Mértola, Odemira and Alté (which is also famous for its crochet work), where women take great pride in their work.

Lace and filigree jewellery are less widespread. Although filigree jewellery has been famous in Portugal since the 18th century, its crafting is now limited mainly to the Porto area and Minho province, where the women's traditional costumes (seen at folk dances and festivals) include lavish adornments of intricate filigree jewellery.

Lace is traditionally found along the coast ('where there are nets, there is lace,' goes the popular saying), although there are several inland places that are famous for lace, including Loulé and Silves in the Algarve. Two of the few places where children are actually taught the art of bobbin lace (from the age of six) are Silves and Vila do Conde in the Minho, renowned for its lace for centuries. The latter also hosts an annual crafts fair every July, which is well worth visiting if you want to track down some of the best northern handicrafts.

SOCIETY & CONDUCT
Traditional Culture
Thanks to a strong Catholic influence and decades of repression under Salazar, Portugal remains a traditional and conservative country. *Romarias* (religious festivals in honour of a patron saint) are taken seriously everywhere, especially in the Minho where they can last for days. Solemn processions are a hallmark of these events, with a candle or banner carried to a sanctuary where devotees kiss the feet of the saint's statue. Sometimes there's a long pilgrimage to a hilltop chapel attended by participants from all over the region. And nearly always there's a finale of lay festivities, featuring a fairground atmosphere of family picnics, dances and fireworks.

The many festivals where folk dancing is the central attraction are much livelier. They take place all over Portugal, mainly in spring and summer, but again the north presents the most flamboyant versions. Here each village sends an ensemble, all in brilliantly embroidered costumes, the women draped in gold chains and necklaces, the children clad in identical versions of their parents' outfits.

The only modern activity to rival the popularity of the folk dance is football: customers in bars and restaurants are glued to the TV on big match days (see Spectator Sports in the Facts for the Visitor chapter), and almost every village and town fields a team. Some traditional group entertainments requiring a certain amount of dedication (such as the *pauliteiros*, or stick dancers, of Miranda do Douro in Trás-os-Montes) are finding it hard to compete with this relatively new obsession.

One cultural activity impervious to changing times is the lingering fondness among men for cafés and squares. As in most Mediterranean countries, men of all ages seem to spend hours in their local café gossiping over coffee or wine, or gathering in the cobbled squares to watch the world go by. City women often have their own afternoon tête-à-têtes in a *salão de chá* (tea room) or *pastelaria* (cake shop), but they aren't nearly as dedicated to this national pastime as their menfolk.

Dos & Don'ts
Generally, the Portuguese share characteristics of friendliness and an unhurried approach to life: in other words, expect smiles and warmth (especially if you speak some Portuguese) but don't expect punctuality or brisk efficiency. This lassitude may sometimes drive you mad, but displays of anger will get you nowhere.

Travellers may also experience an irritating face-saving technique when Portuguese offer information: if you're asking directions (or even for information in a turismo) you'll rarely hear the words *Não sei* (I don't know). You'll invariably get a reply, even if it's not correct. Be sure to seek a second opinion if the answer is important.

Portuguese pride comes into play with language, too: they may be neighbours with Spain but, after centuries of rivalry and hostility, the last thing they want to hear is Spanish. Try English, French, even German – or, best of all, Portuguese, however clumsy it may sound to you. Politeness is so highly valued that simply addressing someone in Portuguese (*senhor* for men, *senhora* for women, *senhora dona* followed by the Christian name for an elderly or respected woman) will earn you lots of points. A handshake is the norm when you're introduced to someone, although you may well get a light peck on each cheek from a young person.

In traditionally minded rural areas (especially up north), outlandish dress may cause offence. And while beachwear (and even nudity on some beaches) is acceptable in coastal tourist resorts, shorts and skimpy tops on a visit to a church will draw frowns. If you're visiting the authorities (such as the police or an immigration office), you'll get more help if you're well dressed.

Treatment of Animals

Hunting It's not as bad as in France, but the urge to shoot any wild bird or animal within range is deep-rooted among Portuguese men. There are over 250,000 licensed hunters in the land, and many more unlicensed ones taking their private pot shots. Migratory birds are a favourite target, as well as rabbit, quail, partridge, duck and wild boar. Indeed, almost anything from wolves to songbirds can fall prey to this passion.

Since 1988, hunting has become more organised with newly defined hunting zones. It's also become a popular and profitable business with special *zona de caça* hunting reserves geared specifically for visitors or private associations. These are often created from the large estates of the Alentejo region and have facilities for both game and clay-pigeon shooting. Red deer, pheasant and red-legged partridge are the most popular species reared for hunters in these zones, but even the protected wild boar can be culled under licence when its numbers are considered excessive.

There are laws, of course. During open season, hunting is restricted to Thursday, Sunday and public holidays. Landowners can forbid hunting on their land (red and white metal markers by the roadside indicate what areas are out of bounds), and the trapping of small birds is illegal. But policing the laws is almost impossible. Even organised hunting reserves aren't as simple

a solution as they appear: at the very least they hinder rural development and also affect long-established grazing rights. And birds of prey – although themselves protected – suddenly find they're unwelcome intruders as they swoop up the profits from the land that was once freely theirs.

Bullfighting This is an even more controversial subject than hunting. Although bullfighting is not as popular in Portugal as it is in Spain, it's still considered by many Portuguese people to be a spectacular form of 'entertainment' and a noble tradition dating back 2000 years. At least 300 *touradas*, or bullfights, are held every March-to-October season (traditionally from Easter Sunday to All Saints' Day), many in tourist areas such as the Algarve (especially Albufeira). To calm foreigners, posters often declare, 'The bull isn't killed!'. But the bulls do suffer and they are killed (after the show). You just don't get to see the final blow.

Supporters point out that the Portuguese *tourada* is far less brutal and bloody than the Spanish version. There's a good deal more skilled horsemanship, artistry, valour and bravado. The most obvious differences are that the bull is initially fought by a man on horseback, then by a team of young men who tackle the bull by hand; and the fight is not to the death (at least, not in public: the gory death of a nobleman, Count dos Arcos, in 1799, put a stop to that). Another difference is that the bull's horns are covered in leather or capped with metal balls.

But this hardly disguises the fact that bullfighting is cruel. If you must see for yourself, first read the Spectator Sports section in the Facts for the Visitor chapter.

The anti-bullfighting lobby in Portugal is vocal but small. Most Portuguese people are either impartial or surprised at the fuss. If you feel strongly about it you can write to the turismo or the *câmara municipal* (town hall) of Albufeira and/or other places that promote bullfighting for the entertainment of tourists.

The following international organisations can be contacted for information and suggestions for action:

People for the Ethical Treatment of Animals (PETA)
UK: (☎ 0171-388 4922, fax 388 4925; from 22 April 2000 ☎ 020-7388 4922, fax 7388 4925) PO Box 3169, London NW1 2JF
USA: (☎ 757-622 PETA, fax 622 1078) 501 Front St, Norfolk VA 23510

World Society for the Protection of Animals (WSPA)
Canada: (☎ 416-369 0044, fax 369 0147, email 102232.3627@compuserve.com) 44 Victoria St, Suite 1310, Toronto, Ontario M5C 1Y2
UK: (☎ 0171-793 0540, fax 793 0208; from 22 April 2000 ☎ 020-7793 0540, fax 7793 0208, email wspanq@gn.apc.org) 2 Langley Lane, London SW8 1TJ
USA: (☎ 617-522 7000, fax 522 7077, email wspa@world.std.com) PO Box 190, Boston MA 02130

Liga Portuguese dos Direitos dos Animais (Portuguese League for Animal Rights)
(☎ 01-458 18 18, fax 457 84 13) Rua José Costa Mamede 9, 2775 Carcavelos.

RELIGION

As freedom of religion is part of the constitution there is no state religion in Portugal, but Roman Catholicism is the dominant faith, adhered to by roughly 95% of the population. Other Christian denominations include Anglicans, Evangelists, Baptists, Congregationalists, Methodists, Jehovah's Witnesses and Mormons. There are also some 15,000 Muslims and about 2000 Jews.

Christianity has been a major force in shaping Portugal's history. It first reached Portugal in the 1st century AD, thriving despite pagan invaders. By the 3rd century, bishoprics had been established in Braga, Évora, Faro and Lisbon. After the Moors

The Jews of Portugal

Communities of Jews first became prominent in Portugal in medieval times. They wielded power and influence as bankers, financiers, court doctors, tax collectors, astronomers and map makers. Although the Afonsine Ordinance of 1446 decreed that they must live in segregated Jewish quarters, called *judiaria*, they faced relatively little harassment. Indeed, when Spain's zealous Catholic rulers Ferdinand and Isabella expelled Jews from their country in 1492, Portugal's João II offered temporary refuge to an estimated 60,000 of them. Many settled in Guarda, Belmonte, Bragança, Tomar and Viana do Castelo.

But five years later, Portugal's new king, Manuel I, was forced to show his anti-Semitic credentials as a condition of marrying the Spanish rulers' daughter, Isabella. He offered the Jews a choice: 'conversion' to Christianity (with no inquiry made into their beliefs for 20 years) or emigration. Not surprisingly, many scorned the offer and left (Holland was a popular destination).

Those who remained – now known as New Christians, or *marranos* – faced the horrors of the Inquisition, launched by João III in 1540. Thousands were tortured, imprisoned or burnt at the stake. In 1989, President Soares offered a public apology to the Jews for this horrific period of persecution.

Today, some 2000 Jews live in Portugal, with the largest community in Belmonte, in Beira Alta. Traces of judiarias can still be found in many towns. Castelo de Vide has the country's oldest synagogue (dating from the 13th century) – a tiny and discreet little house, tucked into a cobbled lane. Tomar's former synagogue, used by the Jewish community for only a few years before Manuel's conversion order, now serves as a major Luso-Hebraic museum, displaying gifts from Jewish visitors from all over the world.

invaded in 711, Christians (and Jews) were initially allowed freedom of worship, but with the arrival of the fanatical Almoravids in the early 11th century, the Christian Reconquista picked up speed. Crusaders en route to the Holy Land from England, France, Germany and Holland frequently helped the kings of Portugal defeat the Moors – notably at Lisbon in 1147 and Silves in 1189.

Other Christian forces that influenced Portugal's development at this time were the Cistercians (a Benedictine order which was responsible for enriching agriculture and architecture around Alcobaça) and powerful Christian military orders such as the Knights Templar (later reorganised into the Order of Christ). It was the wealth and vast resources of the Order of Christ that largely financed Portugal's overseas explorations in the 15th century.

But Christianity has also been responsible for some of the darkest moments in Portugal's history, notably the Inquisition, started in the 1530s by João III and his staunch Catholic Spanish wife. Thousands of victims, including many Jews, were tortured, imprisoned or burnt at the stake at public sentencing ceremonies known as autos-da-fé. The terror was only really suppressed in 1820.

Today's Catholic Church is still powerful and highly respected. Sunday masses are widely attended (though more in the north than the south), as are the many religious festivals honouring local patron saints. One of Europe's most important centres of pilgrimage is at Fátima (see the Estremadura & Ribatejo chapter), where up to 100,000 pilgrims congregate every 12 to 13 May and 12 to 13 October, many walking for miles to get there, or creeping towards the sanctuary on bended knees.

Northern Portugal has always been the most religious part of the country, though certain festivals (such as the celebrations in June for St Anthony, St John and St Peter: Os Santos Populares) are celebrated with fervour throughout the land. In the north,

too, you're most likely to see more bizarre expressions of faith. On a hill above Ponte de Lima is a tiny chapel dedicated to St Ovido, patron saint of ears. The walls are covered with votive offerings of wax ears, given by devotees in hope of, or in thanks for, a cured ear affliction. Similar chapels (adorned with wax limbs of all kinds) can be found even inside churches, revealing a pragmatic sort of tolerance by the Catholic Church.

The continuing influence of the Church was most recently evident in June 1998, when Portugal held its first-ever referendum to vote on one of society's most controversial moral issues: should women be allowed to terminate pregnancies in the first 10 weeks at approved medical facilities (as already allowed in most other European countries)? Parliament had already voted in support and the referendum was held to ratify that decision. The Roman Catholic Church supported opposition campaigns and encouraged their clergy to speak out against the bill, and in the lowest turnout ever recorded (only 32% of eligible citizens voted), the proposal was narrowly defeated. With the embarrassing defeat of the referendum vote, the government has now agreed to abandon the legislation.

LANGUAGE

The national language of Portugal is, naturally, Portuguese. For more about the Portuguese language, some useful phrases and a food glossary, see the Language chapter later in this book.

In Lisbon, Porto, most of the Algarve and other main tourist destinations you'll find English spoken fairly widely (and always in turismos), but as soon as you move into the countryside, English-speakers become rare (especially among older folk; the young can usually speak a few words). In areas such as the Minho, where emigrant workers have spent time in France or Germany, you'll find many people speak some French or German.

Facts for the Visitor

PLANNING

When to Go

Portugal's climate is temperate, and you'll find agreeable weather just about everywhere from April through September or October, and almost year-round in the Algarve. Spring (late March and April) and early autumn (late September and October) bring spectacular foliage. July and August are mostly dry except in the far north; the Algarve, the Alentejo and the upper Douro valley can get ferociously hot then.

Higher areas such as the Serra da Estrela and the ranges of Peneda-Gerês, and much of the Minho and Trás-os-Montes, are a bit showery in summer and uncomfortably cold and wet in winter. Overall, the wettest season is from November through March, and the wettest regions are the Minho and the Serra da Estrela. Snowfall is substantial only in the Serra da Estrela, where skiers will find basic facilities. The ski season lasts from January to March, and February is best.

For more about the weather, see Climate in the Facts about Portugal chapter.

If you're going for beaches, remember that Portugal faces the blustery Atlantic, not the Mediterranean. The further north you go, the colder the water and the bigger the waves. Only in sheltered, shallow areas of the eastern Algarve, in summer, could you call the water warm.

Certain local festivals and celebrations are worth going out of your way for, particularly Carnaval (the three days leading up to Ash Wednesday) and Easter; dates for these vary from year to year – for details, see Public Holidays & Special Events later in this chapter.

The peak tourist season is roughly from mid-June through August or September; *pensões* (guesthouses) and hotels tend to charge peak-season prices during Carnaval and Easter week as well. For these times, you'll probably have to prebook middle or top-end accommodation anywhere from a few days to a few weeks ahead. Outside the peak season, crowds thin out, rooms are plentiful, and room and admission prices may drop by as much as 50% (prices in this book are for peak season). The Algarve is the exception: peak season here runs for much of the year, from late February through November.

What Kind of Trip?

Take a tour if you have very little time or want guaranteed comfort every night, though there's enough cheap long-distance transport, budget accommodation and helpful tourist offices in most places to make unstructured travel entirely feasible.

Despite its small size, Portugal is so different from one end to the other that you cannot get an accurate feel for it in any one place. Nevertheless, you could easily fill a fortnight just with Lisbon, or Porto and the Douro valley, or beaches in the Algarve, or walking/cycling around the Minho or Trás-os-Montes.

There's plenty of nightlife in the cities, so solo travellers needn't be lonely. Portugal is very child-friendly too, making it a happy place for family travel. Don't count on finding work if you want to stay in the country for a long spell.

Maps

Road & Tourist Maps Lonely Planet publishes its own full-colour, illustrated, indexed, 1:400,000 *Portugal travel atlas*. Another good road map is Michelin's *Portugal*, No 440, at 1:400,000. Even more up-to-date (but without Michelin's Lisbon enlargement and its very useful index) is the 1:350,000 *Mapa das Estradas*, published and sold by the Automóvel Club de Portugal (see under Car & Motorcycle in the Getting Around chapter for addresses).

Foto-Vista publishes a few good, clear tourist maps showing major roads and

Highlights

Following is a list to help you find the best of everything in Portugal, from a quiet beach to a rowdy festival.

Architecture
Mosteiro dos Jerónimos at Belém (Lisbon); Mosteiro de Santa Maria da Vitória at Batalha and Mosteiro de Alcobaça (Estremadura); Convento de Cristo, Tomar (Ribatejo); the monumental baroque stairways of Nossa Senhora dos Remédios, Lamego (Douro) and Bom Jesus do Monte, Braga (Minho)

Art Deco Cafés
Café A Brasileira, Lisbon; Café Aliança, Faro (Algarve); Café Santa Cruz, Coimbra (Beiras); Café Majestic, Porto; the Vianna and the Astória, Braga (Minho)

Azulejos
Igreja do Carmo, Porto; the train stations in São Bento (Minho), Porto and Aveiro (Beira Litoral); Museu Nacional do Azulejo, Lisbon; Igreja de São João Evangelista, Évora (Alentejo); Igreja São Lourenço, Almancil (Algarve)

Beaches
Barril on the Ilha de Tavira (Algarve); Praia de Odeceixe (north-western Algarve); São Martinho do Porto, south of Nazaré (Estremadura); São Jacinto, north of Aveiro (Beiras)

Children's Parks
Jardim da Estrela, Lisbon; Gouveia (Beiras); riverside adventure playground at Viana do Castelo (Minho)

Festivals
Easter week, Braga (Minho); Festa de São João, 16 to 24 June, Porto and Festa de Santo António, 12 to 13 June, Lisbon; Festa dos Tabuleiros (Feast of Trays), first Sunday in July every four years, Tomar (Ribatejo); Romaria da Nossa Senhora da Agonia, third weekend in August, Viana do Castelo (Minho); Feiras Novas, mid-September, Ponte de Lima (Minho)

Fortresses, Castles & Walled Towns
Valença do Minho (Minho); Bragança (Trás-os-Montes); Monsanto and Sortelha (Beiras); Óbidos (Estremadura); Marvão, Elvas, Monsaraz and Mértola (Alentejo)

---

attractions, including *Lisbon* (1:13,400) and the *Algarve* (1:176,000). Some tourist offices dispense an adequate 1:600,000 *Carta Turística* of the entire country, published by Guia Turístico do Norte (though its motorways are not up-to-date). Tourist offices also sell glossier regional maps with useful town maps on the reverse. The most handsome tourist map we found anywhere was Edições Livro Branco's bilingual fold-

out of the Rio Douro valley, *Rio Douro: Porto-Barca d'Alva*, available for about 1000$00 from major bookshops.

The Instituto Geográfico do Exército (see the next section) also publishes a 1:10,000 *Lisbon* map.

Topographic Maps Cyclists and trekkers will probably want topographic maps. IGeoE, the Instituto Geográfico do Exérci-

Highlights

Hill & Mountain Treks
Parque Nacional da Peneda-Gerês (Minho); Parque Natural da Serra da Estrela (Beiras); Parque Natural de Montesinho (Trás-os-Montes); Sintra (Around Lisbon)

Markets
Barcelos (Minho); Caldas da Rainha (Estremadura); Ponte de Lima (Minho); Feira da Ladra, Lisbon

Miscellaneous
Espigueiros (granaries) at Lindoso and Soajo (Minho); the Iron-Age *berrões* (stone pigs) of Trás-os-Montes; ossuaries (bone chapels) in the Igreja de São Francisco, Évora (Alentejo), and Igreja do Carmo, Faro (Algarve); Europe's most south-westerly corner at Cabo de São Vicente (Algarve)

Museums
Fundação Calouste Gulbenkian, Lisbon; Museu Soares dos Reis, Porto; Museu do Abade de Baçal, Bragança (Trás-os-Montes); Museu Martins Sarmento, Guimarães (Minho); Museu Machado de Castro, Coimbra (Beiras)

Other Beautiful Towns of Historical Interest
Évora (Alentejo); Guimarães (Minho); Coimbra (Beiras)

Pre-Roman Remains
Citânia de Briteiros, near Guimarães (Minho); menhirs and dolmens (standing stones) in the Évora region (Alentejo)

Roman Ruins
Conimbriga, near Coimbra (Beiras); Roman temple at Évora (Alentejo)

Surfing & Windsurfing
Praia do Guincho and Praia das Maçãs, west of Sintra (Around Lisbon); Praia da Ribeira de Ilhas, Ericeira (Estremadura); Figueira da Foz (Beira Litoral)

Trams
The No 28 through Lisbon's Bairro Alto, Alfama and Castelo districts

to (Army Geographic Institute), publishes 1:25,000 topographic maps of the entire country, as well as series at 1:50,000, 1:100,000 and 1:250,000. These maps date from 1991 and include reservoirs and most motorways, though they tend to be poor on currently used trails.

The civilian IPCC, or Instituto Português de Cartográfia e Cadastro (Portuguese Institute of Cartography & Registry), publishes 1:50,000 topographic maps called *Carta Corográfica*, but these lack the detail and precision of the military ones. IPCC also has older 1:100,000 topographic maps.

Both the IGeoE and the IPCC have outlets in Lisbon (see Maps under Orientation in the Lisbon chapter), and all IGeoE sheets are available at the Porto Editora bookshop in Porto (see the next section). Sheets start at about 1000$00 each.

Other Map Sources A variety of road maps and army and civilian topographic maps is available from mail-order map shops outside Portugal. Probably the widest range of Portugal maps of every sort is at GeoCenter ILH (☎ 0711-788 93 40, fax 788 93 54), Schockenriedstrasse 44, D-70565 Stuttgart, Germany. Other reliable mail-order firms are:

Michael Chessler Books (toll-free ☎ 800 654 8502, ☎ 303-670 0093) PO Box 2436, Evergreen, CO 80439, USA

Omni Resources (☎ 910-227 8300, fax 227 3748, Web site www.omnimap.com/) 1004 S Mebane St, PO Box 2096, Burlington, NC 27216-2096, USA

Stanfords (☎ 0171-836 1321; from 22 April 2000 ☎ 020-7836 1321) 12-14 Long Acre, Covent Garden, London WC2E 9LP, UK

The Travel Bookshop (☎ 02-9241 3554, fax 9241 3159) 6 Bridge St, Sydney 2000, NSW, Australia

MapQuest (Web site www.mapquest.com/) is an online map service that includes an 'interactive atlas'. You can't buy maps from them, but you can customise and print out their online maps.

A Portuguese bookshop that stocks all IGeoE maps is Livraria Porto Editora (☎ 02-200 76 81), Praça Dona Filipa de Lencastre 42, Porto. There's also a branch in Lisbon (Map Greater Lisbon). A few local outfits stock topographic maps covering nearby national and natural parks; see the sections on the various parks and reserves for convenient sources.

Turismos (tourist offices) in larger towns have street maps of varying utility. National and natural park information offices, in designated towns in or near the parks, usually have a simple, often schematic, park map that is of little use for trekking or cycling.

What to Bring

Of course, bring as little as you can; get it to a bare minimum and then cut it in half! This is Europe, not Central Asia, and you can find most comforts and essentials in small-town *supermercados* and big-city *hipermercados*. Pharmacies stock a wide range of medicines as well as tampons and *preservativos* (condoms). You needn't even worry about clothes too much: weekly markets in most sizeable towns usually have a few Gypsy dealers selling cheap clothing, and shoes are a bargain everywhere.

Seasoned travellers will already have a secure money belt. Other helpful items are a day pack, penknife, universal sink plug, sunscreen lotion, lip salve, sunhat, sunglasses, torch, adapter plug, compass, a few clothes pegs, a length of cord as a washing line, and a small sewing kit. For a suggested medical kit see the Health section later in this chapter.

The Portuguese are conservative about dress, and except for beaches and coastal Algarve towns, it's rare to see shorts and short sleeves – except on tourists. Take more modest clothes to cover up with in churches and very rural areas where skimpy clothes might offend. You might need a sweater in the Algarve as late as March, and certainly in the Serra da Estrela even in early May, but you'll hardly use it elsewhere (of course you'll need many more layers in the mountains in winter). If you plan to spend much time outside July and August in the showery north, a collapsible umbrella is more comfortable than a raincoat. All of these items are available in local shops too.

For suggested documents to take along, see the Visas & Documents section of this chapter.

SUGGESTED ITINERARIES

The following suggested itineraries cover most of Portugal's worthy destinations, leaving you to work out local excursions. They assume that one day each week is spent in transit.

One Week

Lisbon Area
   Lisbon, Belém and Sintra (four days); Óbidos and Nazaré (two days)
Porto & the Douro
   Porto and Vila Nova de Gaia (three days); Amarante and Lamego (three days)

The Algarve
  Sagres and Cabo de São Vicente (two days); Lagos (two days); Tavira and Ilha de Tavira (two days)

Two Weeks
Lisbon to the Algarve
  Lisbon, Belém and Sintra (four days); the Costa Vicentina (down the west coast of the Alentejo and Algarve through Odemira to Cabo de São Vicente), Sagres and Cabo São Vicente (three days); Lagos (two days); Tavira and the Ilha de Tavira (three days); depart Faro
Lisbon to the Spanish Border
  Lisbon, Belém and Sintra (five days); Évora and Monsaraz (three days); Estremoz and Elvas (two days); Castelo de Vide and Marvão (two days)
Lisbon to Porto
  Lisbon, Belém and Sintra (four days); Óbidos and Nazaré (two days); Coimbra and Luso (two days); Lamego (one day); from Peso da Régua to Porto by train or by cruise boat down the Rio Douro; Porto and Vila Nova de Gaia (three days)
Porto, the Douro & the Minho
  Porto and Vila Nova de Gaia (three days); Viana do Castelo and Ponte de Lima (three days); Braga and Guimarães (three days); Parque Nacional da Peneda-Gerês (three days); return to Porto by train or by cruise boat down the Douro from Peso da Régua

One Month
Central Portugal
  Lisbon, Belém and Sintra (six days); Évora, Estremoz and Elvas (four days); Marvão and Castelo de Vide (two days); Parque Natural da Serra da Estrela (three days); Coimbra and Luso (three days); Lamego, Amarante and Mondim de Basto (four days); from Peso da Régua to Porto by train or by cruise boat down the Douro; Porto and Vila Nova de Gaia (four days); depart Porto
Lisbon & Southern Portugal
  Lisbon, Belém and Sintra (six days); Óbidos, Nazaré, Batalha and Tomar (three days); Évora, Monsaraz and Elvas (four days); Beja, Serpa and Mértola (three days); Tavira, Ilha de Tavira and Parque Natural da Ria Formosa (four days); Lagos (three days); Sagres and Cabo de São Vicente (three days); depart Faro or Lisbon
Lisbon & Northern Portugal
  Lisbon, Belém and Sintra (five days); Coimbra (two days); Parque Natural da Serra da Estrela (three days); Lamego, Amarante and Mondim de Basto (four days); take a train from Peso da Régua or cruise down the Rio Douro; Porto and Vila Nova de Gaia (four days); Braga (two days); Parque Nacional da Peneda-Gerês (three days); Bragança and Parque Natural de Montesinho (three days); return to Porto

RESPONSIBLE TOURISM

Mass tourism has had a huge impact on the Algarve coast (see Ecology & Environment in the Facts about Portugal chapter). Not that this deters visitors: of the nearly 10 million tourists who come to Portugal each year, at least half go to the Algarve, for its fine climate, beaches and facilities. Supposedly 'eco-friendly' activities like jeep safaris, on the increase in this area, inevitably damage once-remote habitats.

Organised walks are a fine way to see the country, and you can get first-hand knowledge of local environmental issues on the regular walks organised by Quercus, the country's leading environmental organisation (see Ecology & Environment in the Facts about Portugal chapter).

In many popular destinations (such as Évora, Óbidos or Monsaraz), the summer influx of tourists puts a real strain on local infrastructure, ancient buildings and the environment. One way to minimise your own impact – and probably enjoy yourself more – is to avoid visiting in the high season.

Spending your pounds or dollars in less-visited areas is another way to even out tourism's financial impact, while simultaneously broadening your enjoyment and understanding of the country. Many remote park areas (such as the Parque Natural de Montesinho in Trás-os-Montes) are working hard to attract visitors and are worth the extra effort to visit. See the Accommodation section in this chapter for alternative ideas on where to stay in rural areas.

TOURIST OFFICES
Local Tourist Offices

The state's umbrella tourism organisation is Investimentos, Comércio e Turismo de Portugal (ICEP; ☎ 01-793 01 03, fax 794 08 26), Avenida 5 de Outubro 101, Lisbon.

Locally managed *postos de turismo* (tourist offices, usually signposted *turismo*) are everywhere; they can provide brochures and varying degrees of help with sights and accommodation. Often they are run by the *câmara municipal* (town hall). ICEP has its own turismos, with good regional information, in the main town of each of its *regiões de turismo* (see the boxed text 'Carving up Portugal' after the Introduction).

Some bigger cities, such as Lisbon, Porto and Coimbra, have both municipal and ICEP national turismos, the latter concentrating on country-wide information. ICEP also has information desks at Lisbon, Porto and Faro airports.

Tourist Offices Abroad

ICEP-affiliated trade and tourism offices abroad include the following:

Brazil
(☎ 011-288 8744, fax 288 2877)
Alameda Santos 905, 12th floor, 01419-001 São Paulo
(☎ 021-233 8736, fax 233 7424)
Avenida President Vargas 62, 20071-000 Rio de Janeiro
Canada
(☎ 416-921 7376, fax 921 1353)
60 Bloor St West, Suite 1005, Toronto, Ontario M4W 3B8
(☎ 514-282 1264, fax 499 1450)
500 Sherbrooke St West, Suite 940, Montreal, Quebec H3A 3C6
France
(☎ 01 47 42 55 57, fax 01 42 66 06 89)
7 Rue Scribe, 75009 Paris
Germany
(☎ 030-8 82 10 66, fax 8 83 18 51)
Kurfürstendamm 203, 10719 Berlin
(☎ 069-23 40 94, fax 23 14 33)
Schäfergasse 17, 60313 Frankfurt/Main
Ireland
(☎ 01-670 9133, fax 670 9141)
54 Dawson St, Dublin 2
The Netherlands
(☎ 070-328 12 39, fax 328 00 25)
Paul Gabriëlstraat 70, 2596 VG, Den Haag
Spain
(☎ 91-522 4408, fax 522 2382)
Gran Via 27, 1st floor, 28013 Madrid
(☎ 93-301 4416, fax 318 5068)
Calle Bruc, 50, 4th floor, 08010 Barcelona

UK
(☎ 0171-494 1441, fax 494 1868; from 22 April 2000 ☎ 020-7494 1441, fax 7494 1868)
22-25a Sackville St, London W1X 1DE
USA
(☎ 212-719 3985 or toll-free ☎ 800 PORTUGAL, fax 764 6137)
590 Fifth Ave, 4th floor, New York, NY 10036-4785
(☎ 202-331 8222, fax 331 8236)
1900 L St NW, Suite 310, Washington, DC 20036

VISAS & DOCUMENTS
Passport

Check your passport's date of expiry – you may have trouble getting a visa if it expires during or soon after your proposed visit. Also, make sure there are some blank pages left in it.

Police in Portugal are empowered to check your ID papers at any time, so always carry your passport with you.

Visas

No visa is required (for any length of stay) for nationals of EU countries. Those from Australia, Canada, New Zealand and the USA can stay up to 90 days in any half-year without a visa. Others, including nationals of Hong Kong, South Africa and Singapore, need a visa and may need to produce evidence of financial independence, such as a fixed sum of money plus an additional amount per day of their stay, unless they are the spouse or child of EU citizens.

The general requirements for entry to Portugal also apply to other signatories of the 1990 Schengen Convention on the abolition of mutual border controls, namely Austria, the Benelux countries (Belgium, the Netherlands and Luxembourg), France, Germany, Italy, Portugal and Spain. Denmark, Finland, Greece and Spain are expected to have put the agreement into effect by 1999. Once you've entered one of these countries you shouldn't need a passport to move between them. Similarly, a visa valid for any of them ought to be valid for them all, but check with the relevant consulates.

Visa Extensions To extend a visa or 90 day period after arriving in Portugal, contact the foreigners' registration office, called Serviço de Estrangeiros e Fronteiras (☎ 01-346 61 41, 352 31 12), at Avenida António Augusto de Aguiar 20 in Lisbon. It's open from 9 am to 3 pm on weekdays only. Major tourist towns also have branch Serviço de Estrangeiros e Fronteiras offices. As entry regulations are already liberal, you'll need convincing proof of employment or financial independence, or a pretty good story, if you're asking to stay longer.

Photocopies

It's wise to carry photocopies of the data pages of your passport and visa, to ease paperwork headaches should they be lost or stolen. Other copies you might want to carry are of your credit card and travellers cheque numbers (plus the telephone numbers for cancelling or replacing them), airline tickets, travel insurance policy, birth certificate and any documents related to possible employment. Keep the copies in a separate place from the originals.

Travel Insurance

A travel insurance policy to cover theft, loss and medical problems is a good idea. You should cover yourself for the worst case, such as an accident or illness requiring hospitalisation and a flight home. If you can't afford to do that, you certainly can't afford to deal with a medical emergency abroad.

A wide variety of policies is available; your travel agent will have recommendations. The international policies handled by youth/student travel agencies are good value. Check the small print: some policies specifically exclude 'dangerous activities' such as scuba diving or even trekking. If these are on your agenda, get another policy or ask about an amendment (for an extra premium) that includes them.

You may prefer a policy that pays doctors or hospitals directly rather than one that requires you to pay and claim later, though in Portugal you'll usually find immediate cash payment is expected. If you have to claim later, make sure you keep all documentation. Some policies ask you to call back (reverse charge) to a centre in your home country, where an immediate assessment of your problem is made.

EU citizens are eligible for free emergency medical treatment if they have an E111 certificate. See Predeparture Planning under Health later in this chapter for more details.

Driving Licence & Permits

Nationals of EU countries need only their home driving licences, although holders of the UK's old green licences are advised to get an International Driving Permit (IDP). Portugal also accepts licences issued in Brazil, Switzerland and the USA. Others should consider getting an IDP through an automobile licensing department or automobile club in their home country.

For information on paperwork and insurance see the Car & Motorcycle section in the Getting There & Away chapter.

Student, Youth & Senior Cards

Numerous discounts are available to full-time students and to those who are under 26 years of age or 60 and over. These include reductions on domestic and international transport, museum admission, accommodation and, in some cases, restaurant meals. See Money later in this chapter for more information.

Hostel Card

Portugal's network of *pousadas da juventude* and *centros de alojamento* (see Hostels under Accommodation later in this chapter) is part of the Hostelling International (HI) network, and an HI card from your hostelling association at home entitles you to the standard cheap rates.

Camping Card International

Formerly known as a Camping Carnet, the Camping Card International (CCI) can be presented instead of your passport when you register at camping grounds affiliated to the Federation Internationale de Camping et de Caravanning (FICC). It guarantees third-party insurance for any damage you may cause, and is sometimes good for discounts. Certain camping grounds run by local camping clubs may be used by foreigners only if they have a CCI.

The CCI is available to members of most national automobile clubs, except in the USA; the RAC in the UK charges members UK£4 for one. It's also issued by camping clubs affiliated to FICC, such as the Camping & Caravanning Club (☎ 01203-694995) in the UK, and the Federação Portuguesa de Campismo e Caravanismo, or FPCC (☎ 01-812 68 90, fax 812 69 18), Avenida Coronel Eduardo Galhardo 24-C, 1170 Lisbon.

Bicycle Information

If you're cycling around Portugal on your own machine, seasoned bicycle tourists suggest carrying a written description and a photograph of it (to help police in case it's stolen), and proof of ownership.

EMBASSIES & CONSULATES
Portuguese Embassies & Consulates

Portuguese embassies and consulates abroad include the following:

Australia
  Embassy:
  (☎ 02-6290 1733, fax 6290 1957)
  23 Culgoa Circuit, O'Malley, ACT 2606
  Consulate:
  (☎ 02-9326 1844, fax 9327 1607)
  132 Ocean St, Edgecliff, Sydney, NSW 2027
Brazil
  Embassy:
  (☎ 061-321 34 34, fax 225 52 96)
  Avenida das Nações, Lote 2-CEP, 70402
  Brasilia
  Consulate:
  (☎ 021-233 73 23, fax 233 74 24)
  Avenida Presidente Vargas 62, CEP 20091
  Estado Rio Janeiro
Canada
  Embassy:
  (☎ 613-729 0883, fax 729 4236)
  645 Island Park Drive, Ottawa, Ontario
  K1Y OB8

  Consulate:
  (☎ 514-499 0359, fax 499 0366)
  2020 Rue de l'Université, 17th floor,
  Montreal, Quebec H3A 2A5
  Consulate:
  (☎ 416-360 8260, fax 360 0350)
  121 Richmond St West, 7th floor, Toronto,
  Ontario M5H 2K1
France
  Embassy:
  (☎ 01 47 27 35 29, fax 01 47 55 00 40)
  3 Rue de Noisiel, 75116 Paris
  Consulate:
  (☎ 01 44 06 88 90, fax 01 45 85 09 58)
  187 Rue de Chevaleret, 75013 Paris
  Consulate:
  (☎ 04 91 76 12 82, fax 04 91 71 42 45)
  29 Rue Wulfran Puget 13008, Marseilles
  Consulate:
  (☎ 05 56 52 19 50, fax 05 56 52 46 09)
  11 Rue Henri Rodel, 33000
  Bordeaux
Germany
  Embassy:
  (☎ 0228-36 30 11, fax 35 28 64)
  Ubierstrasse 78, 53173 Bonn
  Consulate:
  (☎ 040-34 00 47, fax 34 57 30)
  Gansemarkt 23-1, 20354 Hamburg 36
  Consulate:
  (☎ 0711-226 50 13, fax 226 25 14)
  Königstrasse 20/1, 70173
  Stuttgart
Ireland
  Embassy:
  (☎ 01-289 4416, fax 289 2849)
  Knock Sinna House, Knock Sinna, Fox Rock,
  Dublin 18
The Netherlands
  Embassy:
  (☎ 070-363 02 17, fax 361 55 89)
  Bazarstraat 21, 2518 AG, The Hague
  Consulate:
  (☎ 010-411 15 40, fax 414 98 89)
  Willemskade 18, 3016 Rotterdam
New Zealand
  Embassy:
  (☎ 09-309 1454, fax 308 9061)
  85 Forte St, Remuera, Auckland 5
Spain
  Embassy:
  (☎ 91-261 78 08, fax 411 01 72)
  Calle del Pinar 1, 28046 Madrid
  Consulate:
  (☎ 91-445 46 00, fax 445 46 08)
  Paseo del General Martinez Campos 11-1,
  Madrid

Consulate:
(☎ 93-318 81 50, fax 318 59 12)
Ronda de São Pedro 7-1, Barcelona
UK
Embassy:
(☎/fax 0171-235 5331; from 22 April 2000
☎/fax 020-7235 5331)
11 Belgrave Square, London SW1X 8PP
Consulate:
(☎ 0171-581 8722, fax 581 3085; from 22
April 2000 ☎ 020-7581 8722, fax 7581 3085)
62 Brompton Rd, London SW3 1BJ
USA
Embassy:
(☎ 202-328 8610, fax 462 3726)
2125 Kalorama Rd NW, Washington,
DC 20008
Consulate:
(☎ 212-246 4580, fax 459 0190)
630 Fifth Ave, Suite 310 378,
New York, NY 10111
Consulate:
(☎ 451-921 1443, fax 346 1440)
3298 Washington St, San Francisco,
CA 94115

Embassies & Consulates in Portugal

Your embassy or consulate in Portugal is
the best first stop in any emergency, but
there are some things it cannot do for you.
It can't get local laws or regulations waived
because you're a foreigner, investigate a
crime, provide legal advice or representation in court cases, get you out of jail,
provide you with a ticket home, or lend you
money. A consul can, however, issue emergency passports, contact relatives and
friends, advise on how to transfer funds,
provide lists of reliable local doctors,
lawyers and interpreters, and visit you if
you've been arrested or jailed. Foreign embassies and consulates in Portugal include:

Brazil
Embassy:
(☎ 01-726 77 77, fax 726 76 23)
Estrada das Laranjeiras 144, Lisbon
Consulate:
(☎ 01-322 01 00, fax 347 39 26)
Praça Luís de Camões 22, Lisbon
Consulate:
(☎ 02-610 62 78)
Rua Fernão Vaz Dourado 62, Porto

Canada
Embassy:
(☎ 01-347 48 92, fax 342 56 28)
Edifício MCB, Avenida da Liberdade 144,
Lisbon
Consulate:
(☎ 089-80 37 57)
Rua Frei Lourenço de Santa Maria 1,
Faro
France
Embassy:
(☎ 01-60 81 21, fax 397 83 27)
Rua Santos-o-Velho 5, Lisbon
Consulate:
(☎ 395 60 56, fax 395 39 81)
Calçada Marquês de Abrantes 123,
Lisbon
Consulate:
(☎ 02-609 48 05, fax 606 42 05)
Rua Eugénio de Castro 352, Porto
Germany
Embassy:
(☎ 01-352 39 61, 885 38 46)
Campo dos Mártires da Pátria 38, Lisbon
Consulate:
(☎ 089-80 31 48)
Avenida da República 166, Faro
Ireland
Embassy:
(☎ 01-396 15 69, fax 397 73 63)
Rua da Imprensa à Estrela 1, Lisbon
The Netherlands
Embassy:
(☎ 01-396 11 63, fax 396 64 36)
Rua do Sacramento à Lapa 6, Lisbon
Consulate:
(☎ 089-2 09 03)
Largo Dr Francisco Sá Carneiro 52, Faro
Spain
Embassy & Consulate:
(embassy ☎ 01-347 23 81, fax 342 53 76,
consulate ☎ 347 27 92)
Rua do Salitre 3, Lisbon
Consulate:
(☎ 02-510 16 85, fax 510 19 14)
Rua de Dom João IV 341, Porto
Consulate:
(☎ 051-2 21 22)
Avenida Espanha, Valença do Minho
Consulate:
(☎ 081-54 48 88)
Avenida Ministro Duarte Pacheco,
Vila Real de Santo António
UK
Embassy:
(☎ 01-392 40 00, fax 397 67 68)
Rua de São Domingos à Lapa 37, Lisbon

Consulate:
(☎ 392 41 60, fax 392 41 88)
Rua da Estrela 4, Lisbon
Consulate:
(☎ 082-41 78 00, fax 41 78 06)
Largo Francisco A Maurício 7, Portimão
Consulate:
(☎ 02-618 47 89, fax 610 04 38)
Avenida da Boavista 3072, Porto
USA
Embassy & Consulate:
(embassy ☎ 01-726 66 00, fax 726 91 09,
consulate ☎ 727 33 00, fax 726 91 09)
Avenida das Forças Armadas, Lisbon

There are no embassies for Australia or New Zealand in Portugal, but both countries have honorary consuls in Lisbon. Australian citizens can call ☎ 01-353 07 50 on weekdays between 1 and 2 pm; the nearest Australian embassy is in Paris. New Zealand citizens should call ☎ 01-357 41 34 during business hours; the nearest New Zealand embassy is in Rome.

CUSTOMS

There's no limit on the amount of foreign currency you can bring into Portugal. Customs regulations say visitors (at least those who need a visa) must bring in a minimum of 10,000$00 plus 2000$00 per day of their stay, but this isn't stringently enforced. If you leave with more than 100,000$00 in escudos or 500,000$00 in foreign currency you may have to prove that you brought in at least this much.

The duty-free allowance for travellers over 17 years of age coming from non-EU countries is: 200 cigarettes (or 100 cigarillos or 50 cigars or 250g of tobacco); 1L of alcohol which is over 22% alcohol by volume, or 2L of wine or beer.

Within the EU, duty-free shopping is scheduled to be abolished on 30 June 1999. Travellers will still be able to bring in alcohol and tobacco which they have paid duty on in another EU country, provided they are for personal use only. The amounts that officially constitute personal use are: 800 cigarettes (400 cigarillos, 200 cigars or 1kg of tobacco) and either 10L of spirits, 20L of fortified wine, 60L of sparkling wine or a mind-boggling 90L of still wine, or 110L of beer!

You can also bring in enough coffee and tea for personal use. You cannot bring fresh meat into the country.

MONEY
Currency

The unit of Portuguese currency is the *escudo*, further divided into 100 *centavos*. Prices are usually denoted with a $ sign between escudos and centavos; for example, 25 escudos 50 centavos is written 25$50.

Portuguese notes currently in circulation are 500$00, 1000$00, 2000$00, 5000$00 and 10,000$00. Coin denominations are 1$00, 2$50, 5$00, 10$00, 20$00, 50$00, 100$00 and 200$00, though coins smaller than 5$00 are rarely used. Nowadays market prices tend to be rounded to the nearest 10$00. The Portuguese frequently refer to 1000$00 as *um conto*.

Many goods and services are now priced in both escudos and euros (the new single European currency). The exchange rate of most European currencies, including the escudo, is fixed against the euro for non-cash transactions such as cheques, credit cards and electronic transfers. By 1 January 2002, euro notes and coins will be circulated and bank accounts will operate in euros. The escudo will be replaced entirely by the euro from 1 July 2002.

Exchange Rates

Rates at the time of printing were:

country	unit		escudos
Australia	A$1	=	106$00
Canada	C$1	=	113$00
euro	€1	=	200$48
France	1FF	=	30$75
Germany	DM1	=	102$00
Ireland	I£1	=	257$50
Japan	¥100	=	152$50
New Zealand	NZ$1	=	91$00
Spain	100 ptas	=	122$00
UK	UK£1	=	284$00
USA	US$1	=	173$00

Exchanging Money

Portuguese banks and private exchange bureaux accept most foreign currencies, but they're free to set their own fees and rates. Thus a bureau's low commission may be offset by an unfavourable exchange rate. If you need to watch every penny, you'll have to shop around, calculator in hand.

Travellers cheques are easily exchanged, but although rates are about 1% better than for cash, they are very poor value in Portugal because additional fees are so high. Banks, especially, charge exorbitant commission fees: around 2500$00 (in addition to government taxes of about 140$00) for each transaction of any size. You can do much better at private exchange bureaux, though even they usually charge around 1000$00 for each transaction. The exception is American Express travellers cheques, which can be exchanged with no commission fee at Top Tours, Portugal's American Express representative. Top Tours has branches in Lisbon, Porto, Braga, Aveiro, Cascais and Setúbal).

Fees for exchanging Eurocheques are low – typically 500$00 to 800$00 per transaction – though for the cheques and the accompanying card you also pay an annual subscription fee of about US$15.

A more sensible alternative is a Visa, Access/MasterCard, American Express or similar card. Nearly every town has 24-hour Multibanco automated teller machines (ATMs), where you can use your card to get a cash advance in escudos. All you need is your PIN number from home. There is a handling charge of about 1.5% per transaction, and exchange rates are reasonable. Cards are also accepted by many shops, hotels and a small but increasing number of guesthouses and restaurants.

Portuguese ATMs occasionally spit out cards with a message like 'communication failure', or tell you your PIN number is wrong. A second try or another ATM will often work, but bear in mind that three 'wrong PIN number' messages may invalidate your card. After two such warnings you'd be advised to seek help from a bank.

A small stash of cash (pounds sterling or US dollars) is useful for such emergencies.

Foreign cash can also be changed (for higher commission) in the automatic 24 hour cash exchange machines found in most tourist destinations (but rarely elsewhere).

Security

Keeping your money secure is largely a matter of common sense: see Crime under Dangers & Annoyances later in this chapter.

In addition to looking after your cash, be careful, too, when you pay for something with a credit card: complete the 'total' box on the sales slip yourself, add a currency symbol before it with no space in between and be sure only one sales slip is imprinted.

Costs

Although costs are beginning to rise as Portugal falls into fiscal step with the EU, this is still one of the cheapest places to travel in Europe.

On a rock-bottom budget – staying in hostels or camping grounds, and mostly self-catering – you could squeeze by on about 4000$00 (US$22) a day per person in the high season (excluding long-distance travel). With budget accommodation and the occasional inexpensive restaurant meal, daily costs would hover around 5000$00 (US$27). Travelling with a companion and timing your trip to take advantage of off-season discounts, you could eat and sleep in relative style for about 14,000$00 (US$75) for two. Outside major tourist areas, prices dip appreciably.

Discounts Numerous discounts are available to full-time students and teachers, and to travellers aged under 26 or 60 and over.

The international student identity card (ISIC) and teacher's card (ITIC) are aimed at travel-related costs such as reductions on airline fares and cheap or free admission to museums. Valid for a year, they're available from youth-oriented travel agencies such as Campus Travel, STA Travel, Council Travel and Travel CUTS, and from the Portuguese youth-travel agencies Tagus

Travel and Jumbo Expresso. Check the Web site www.istc.org/ for more information.

However, other youth-card schemes (especially Euro26 and Go25) are more widely recognised in Portugal. These provide more general discounts, for example in shops and cinemas, as well as some accommodation and travel. Also valid for a year, they're available from most youth-travel agencies for about UK£6. For more information on Euro26 see their Web site www.euro26 .org/. More general information on ISIC, ITIC and Go25, and application forms, is at www.ciee.org/idcards/index.htm.

Portugal's own under-26 youth card, the Cartão Jovem, is available to documented foreign residents as well as Portuguese. It costs 1100$00 from youth-travel agents and Instituto Português da Juventude offices (see the boxed text 'Youth Centres' under Accommodation later in this chapter). It can get you limited reductions on train travel, as well as discounts in many shops and some hotels.

Many similar discounts are also available in Portugal to travellers aged 60 and over with a seniors' card. In addition, the Rail Europe Senior (RES) Card gives you about

How Much in Portugal?

Following are some typical unit costs in Portugal. Prices for accommodation vary according to the season.

Bed in a youth hostel dormitory*	1500$00 to 2900$00	(US$8 to US$16)
Small tent at a camp site (two people)	650$00 to 1700$00	(US$3.50 to US$9)
Double room in a lower-end *pensão**	3500$00 to 5000$00	(US$19 to US$27)
Double in a mid-range hotel*	6000$00 to 12,000$00	(US$32 to US$65)
Double in a Pousada de Portugal*	15,600$00 to 29,600$00	(US$84 to US$160)
Three course meal in a medium-grade restaurant (minus drinks)*	1700$00 to 3000$00	(US$9 to US$16)
Big Mac	440$00	(US$2.40)
Ordinary espresso coffee (*bica*)	70$00	(US$0.38)
Portuguese beer (300mL)		
draught	200$00	(US$1.10)
bottle from supermarket	120$00	(US$0.65)
Portuguese wine (1L)	500$00 to 1200$00	(US$2.70 to US$6.50)
Pack of Portuguese cigarettes	about 330$00	(US$1.78)
Three minute local call from a Credifone (card) telephone	25$00	(US$0.14)
Museum admission	250$00 to 600$00	(US$1.35 to US$3.20)
Train, 2nd class IC, per 100km	about 640$00	(US$3.50)
Coach, long-distance, per 100km	about 600$00	(US$3.25)
Petrol, 1L of 95 octane unleaded	165$00	(US$0.89)

* = high season

30% off the fare on international journeys. To be eligible for this card you must have a local senior citizens' railcard, the availability of which depends on the country you're in. In Britain, Senior Railcards (UK£18) and RES Cards (UK£5) are sold at staffed train stations (or contact one of the British Rail offshoots, such as Connex ☎ 0870 603 0405).

For information on discounts for children see Travel with Children, later in this chapter.

Tipping & Bargaining

If you're satisfied with the service, a reasonable restaurant tip is about 10% of the bill. For a snack at a *cervejaria* (bar serving snacks), *pastelaria* (cake shop) or café, a bit of loose change is enough. Taxi drivers appreciate 10% of the fare, and petrol station attendants 50$00 or so.

Good-humoured bargaining is acceptable in markets but you'll find the Portuguese tough opponents! Off season, you can sometimes even bargain down the price of accommodation.

Taxes & Refunds

A 17% sales tax, called IVA (Imposto Sobre Valor Acrescentado), is levied on hotel and other accommodation, restaurant meals, car rental and some other bills. If you are a tourist who resides outside the EU, you can claim an IVA refund on goods from shops that are members of the Europe Tax-Free Shopping Portugal scheme (displayed on a sign in the window and/or on the till). The minimum purchase required for a refund is currently 11,700$00 in any one shop. The shop assistant fills in a cheque for the amount of the refund (minus an administration fee). Items *not* covered by this refund scheme include grocery-store food, books, prescription lenses, hotel costs and car rental.

When you leave Portugal you present the goods, the cheque and your passport at the Tax-Free Shopping refund counter at customs for cash, a postal order or credit-card refund. This service is available only at Lisbon and Porto airports. If you leave overland, talk to customs at your final EU border point. Further information (including a list of participating shops) is in the free *Shopping in Portugal* brochure, available at Lisbon airport's international departures concourse. Or call Europe Tax-Free Shopping Portugal, ☎ 01-840 88 13 in Lisbon.

POST & COMMUNICATIONS
Sending Mail

Correio normal (posted in red letter boxes) refers to ordinary post, including air mail, while *correio azul* (literally blue post, posted in the blue letter boxes) refers to priority or express post. For ordinary postcards and letters up to 20g postage costs 140$00 to destinations outside Europe, 100$00 to non-EU European destinations and 85$00 to EU destinations (except within Portugal, which costs 50$00). International correio azul costs a minimum of 350$00 for a 20g letter.

Stamps are sold not only at post offices, but also at numerous kiosks and shops with a red *Correios – selos* (Stamps) sign, as well as from coin-operated vending machines. 'By airmail' is *por avião* in Portuguese; 'by surface mail' is *via superfície*. For delivery to the USA or Australia, allow eight to 10 days; delivery times for Europe are four to six days.

A 4 to 5kg parcel sent surface mail to the UK would cost 5300$00 (about US$28). Economy air (or surface airlift, SAL) costs about a third less than ordinary air mail, but usually arrives a week or so later. Printed matter is cheapest (and simplest) to send in batches of under 2kg.

Don't post anything important or valuable if you can't afford to lose it. Always use registered mail for sending important documents.

Receiving Mail

Most towns have a *posta restante* service at the central post office. Letters should be addressed with name (family name first, capitalised and underlined), c/o posta

Addresses

Addresses in Portugal are written with the street name first, followed by the building number. An alphabetical tag on the number, for example 2-A, indicates an adjacent entrance or building. Floor numbers may be included, with a degree symbol, so 15-3° means entrance No 15, 3rd floor. The further abbreviations D, dir or Dta (for *direita*, right), or E, esq or Esqa (for *esquerda*, left), tell you which door to go to. Floor numbering is by European convention: the 1st floor is one flight up from the ground floor. R/C (*rés do chão*) means ground floor.

restante, central post office, town name. Lisbon's central post office is on Praça Comércio; Porto's is on Praça General Humberto Delgado.

To collect mail, you must show your passport. A charge of 60$00 is levied for each item of mail collected. Unclaimed letters are normally returned after a month.

Telephone

All calls within, and out of, Portugal are charged according to the number of *impulsos* (literally beeps), or units, used; their duration varies according to the destination, time of day and how and where you make the call. Calls are cheapest from 9 pm to 9 am, and all day Saturday and Sunday.

Aside from home telephones, the cheapest and most convenient way to call anywhere is from a card-operated Credifone, using a *cartão telefónico* (phonecard). These are widely available from newsagents, tobacconists and telephone offices for 625$00 (50 beeps), 1250$00 (100), 1500$00 (120) or 1875$00 (150). A youth or student card should get you a discount of 10% on them.

At the time of research the charge per beep with a Credifone was 12$50. Coin-operated telephones cost 20% more, and a metered telephone in a hotel or café three to

five times as much. Charges from a home telephone are about 20% less than from a Credifone. In addition to the per-beep charge, it costs an extra beep's worth just to make a domestic connection (hence you must insert a minimum of 30$00 for a local call on a coin-phone), and three to make an international connection.

There are plenty of public telephones around. For a slightly higher charge you can also make calls from booths in Portugal Telecom offices and post offices, where you pay over the counter after your call is finished.

Local Calls For local calls a single beep lasts over six minutes in economy periods, or three minutes otherwise. For a regional call (under 50km away) it's 33 seconds, and for a national call 12 seconds.

Portugal's directory enquiries number is ☎ 118, and operators will search by address as well as by name. Any ☎ 0800 number (called *linha verde*, or green line) is tollfree. Those with a ☎ 0808 code (*linha azul*, or blue line) are charged at local rates from anywhere in the country.

Long-Distance & International Calls
Following are some sample international charges at the time of research, using a card during economy periods:

country	per minute	3 minutes
Australia	213$39	565$17
EU	131$77	320$00
USA	156$93	395$78

For international enquiries or assistance, or to make a reverse-charge (*pago no destino*) call, with the help of multilingual operators, dial ☎ 099 (for Europe, Algeria, Morocco and Tunisia) or ☎ 098 (for other overseas destinations). From Portugal, the international access code is ☎ 00.

Country-Direct Service To make a collect or credit-card call you can dial direct (for an extra charge) to operators in at least 38 countries. Among these are:

Australia	☎ 05017 61 10
Brazil	☎ 05017 55 10
Canada	☎ 05017 12 26
France	☎ 0505 00 33
Germany	☎ 0505 00 49
Ireland	☎ 0505 03 53
The Netherlands	☎ 0505 00 31
New Zealand	☎ 05017 64 00
Spain	☎ 0505 00 34
UK	☎ 0505 00 44
USA (AT&T)	☎ 05017 12 88
(MCI)	☎ 05017 12 34
(Sprint)	☎ 05017 18 77
(TRT)	☎ 05017 18 781

Calls to Portugal To call Portugal from abroad, dial the international access code of the country you're in, plus ☎ 351 (the country code for Portugal), plus the area code (minus its initial zero), then the number. Important Portugal telephone codes include ☎ 01 for Lisbon and ☎ 02 for Porto; others are listed with each town in this book.

Many old five-digit telephone numbers in Portugal are now being changed; if any listed in the text no longer work, call the local turismo for help.

Telephone Rental Telecel rents mobile phones from their shops in Lisbon, Porto and Faro airports. The minimum three day charge is about 4800$00 plus 150$00 per minute for national calls or 262$00 per minute for European calls – considerably higher than ordinary rates.

Fax

Post offices operate a domestic and international fax service called Corfax, costing 850$00 for the first page to Europe and 1000$00 to North America or Australia. However, only half the post office form is available for your message. And to collect a fax at the post office you pay 250$00 per page. A guesthouse with a fax is almost certain to be cheaper. See also Telephone & Fax under Information in the Lisbon chapter for a computer shop with cheap fax service.

National Emergency Numbers

The nationwide emergency telephone number is ☎ 112, for fire and other emergencies as well as for the police. Unfortunately, you're unlikely to reach an English speaker (at least until June 1999, when all should be answered in English and French as well as Portuguese).

For medical emergencies it's probably better to contact the local hospital (phone numbers are provided in the text). The emergency number for snake bites and poisoning is ☎ 01-795 01 43.

For more routine police matters (and direct access to the fire brigade) there are also telephone numbers for each town or district, as noted.

Email & Internet Access

Apart from Lisbon, Porto and a few other towns, few places in Portugal yet boast cybercafés. But an excellent alternative is the branches of the Instituto Português da Juventude, or IPJ, a state-funded network of youth centres (see the boxed text 'Youth Centres' under Accommodation later in this chapter). These usually have a library with free Internet access (via standard Web browsers) on a limited number of computers, at least during certain hours on weekdays. If you have a Web-based email account such as Hotmail (www.hotmail .com) or Yahoo! Mail (www.yahoo.com), you're all set. There's rarely any technical expertise at hand. For some handy Portuguese terms see the boxed text on the next page. These facilities are intended for use by Portuguese young people, not visitors, so please don't overuse or misuse them.

Some municipal libraries, and a few larger Portugal Telecom offices, also have free Internet access. Cybercafés charge anywhere from 200$00 to 800$00 per hour of online time. Where we've found cybercafés, we've listed them under each town's Information or Post & Communications section.

It's also possible to access your own email account, but you'll need to have three pieces of information: your incoming (POP or IMAP) mail server name, your account name and your password. Your ISP or network supervisor will be able to give you these and tell you how it's done; get familiar with the process for doing this before you leave home.

If you've got your own laptop/palmtop and modem, and an account with a server with POPs (local access points) in Portugal, you might be able to log on from your hotel room for the cost of a local or long-distance call. Major Internet service providers, such as CompuServe (www.compuserve.com), AOL (www.aol.com) and IBM Net (www.ibm.net), have dial-in nodes in Portugal. Along with your computer you may need a power-plug adapter and possibly a frequency adapter, easiest to buy before you leave home. Also note that PCMCIA card-modems may or may not work once you leave your home country – and you won't know for sure until you try; the safest option is to buy a reputable global modem before you leave home, or a card-modem in Portugal if you'll be staying there for a while.

Unfortunately, many hotel-room telephones are hard-wired into the wall, in which case you'll need a kit with tiny screwdriver, clips, plugs and, preferably, a line tester. These are available from Web-based dealers such as Magellan's (www.magellans.com) and Konexx (www.konexx.com). With luck you'll find a telephone jack. Most hotel jacks in Portugal are USA standard (RJ-11). A few aren't, and for these you'll need an adapter, available from a local electronics shop or a Web-based 'shop'.

It's not always easy to distinguish between tone and pulse systems: if you can't connect with your dialler software set to one, try the other. Get on and off quickly; calls are expensive in Portugal and even more so from hotels.

Be sure the hotel doesn't have a digital telephone exchange, which can blow your

Portuguese Internet Jargon

If you surf the Web at a Portuguese cybercafé you may have to do it in Portuguese. Following is a bit of useful Portuguese cyber-speak:

File	Ficheiro
New	Novo
Open	Abrir
Close	Fechar
Save	Guardar
Save As ...	Guardar como ...
Print	Imprimir
Exit	Sair
Edit	Editar
Cut	Cortar
Copy	Copiar
Paste	Colar
Help	Ajuda
Bookmark	Marcador
Search	Procurar

modem. You can always plug safely into an analog data line such as the hotel's fax line.

A problem with ordinary lines in Portugal is the faint 'beeps' that mark *impulsos* or units of calling time. These can interfere with modem connections. The solution is an in-line filter, available from many computer shops, or the Web-based shops mentioned earlier. Data lines like those at Telecom offices, IJPs and cybercafés don't have this problem.

For more information on travelling with a portable computer, see www.teleadpt.com or www.warrior.com.

An alternative for those planning a long stay is an Internet package from one of Portugal's providers, whose multiple POPs mean cheaper calls. Portugal Telecom's Telepac is the most accessible unless you speak Portuguese. Their Netpac, sold at Telecom offices, includes dialler software, Netscape Navigator and 30 hours of online time usable within two months. At the time of writing this cost 6950$00 (Windows 95) or 9500$00 (Windows 3.1 or Macintosh), and you can top up the account at any Multibanco ATM, at 2500/3000/4000$00 for a further 15/20/30 hours.

INTERNET RESOURCES
The World Wide Web is a rich resource for travellers. You can research your trip, hunt down bargain air fares, book hotels, check on weather conditions or chat with locals and other travellers about the best places to visit (or avoid!).

One of the best places to start your Web explorations is the Lonely Planet Web site (www.lonelyplanet.com). Here you'll find succinct summaries on travelling to most places on earth, postcards from other travellers and the Thorn Tree bulletin board, where you can ask questions before you go or dispense advice when you get back. You can also find travel news and updates to many of our most popular guidebooks, and the subWWWay section links you to the most useful travel resources elsewhere on the Web. Lonely Planet's Portugal page is at www.lonelyplanet.com/dest/eur/por.htm.

Other good travel-related, English-language Web sites include the following three, with links to sights, practicalities, maps, airfares, entertainment, books, personal narratives, news, weather, features and more:

A Collection of Home Pages about Portugal
    www.well.com/user/ideamen/portugal.html
Portugal Info
    www.portugal-info.net/
Portugal for Travellers
    nervo.com/pt/

More general links are at:

AEIOU
    www.aeiou.pt/
    (mainly in Portuguese)
Excite City.Net
    www.city.net/countries/portugal/
    (includes links to the home pages of about
    20 Portuguese towns)
SAPO (Servidor de Apontades Portugueses)
    www.sapo.pt/
    (mainly in Portuguese)

Yahoo! Portugal
    www.yahoo.com/regional_information
    /countries/portugal/

A good site about Lisbon (though it's not updated very often) is www.eunet.pt/Lisboa/i/lisboa.html, with listing of museums, bars and clubs, and recommendations on restaurants and places to see. Portugal's state-run tourism organisation, ICEP (see Tourist Offices earlier in this chapter), has its own, pretty good site at www.portugal-insite.pt.

For information on access to email, see the Post & Communications section earlier in this chapter.

BOOKS
Few shops outside Lisbon, Porto and major towns in the Algarve have a decent supply of English-language books about the country, so it's worth visiting your local bookshop, or Web-based 'shops' such as Condé Nast Traveller (www.cntraveller.co.uk/) and Amazon (www.amazon.com/), before you go. Check the Spain listings on these sites too – Portugal often gets lumped in with it.

Most books are published in different editions by different publishers in different countries. Your local bookshop or library is best placed to advise you on the availability of the following recommendations and order them for you.

Lonely Planet
If you're planning making your journey wider than just Portugal, consider taking one of Lonely Planet's comprehensive multicountry guides: *Europe on a shoestring*, *Western Europe* or *Mediterranean Europe*. For a short break to Lisbon there's the Lonely Planet *Lisbon* city guide. And how's your Portuguese? Lonely Planet can help in that department too, with its *Western Europe phrasebook*.

Other Guidebooks
A good book for serious footwork is Bethan Davies & Ben Cole's *Walking in Portugal*, with routes around Lisbon, Porto, Coimbra,

Parque Nacional da Peneda-Gerês, and the Serra da Estrela, Montesinho and Serra de São Mamede natural parks. Less single-minded pedestrians will like Brian & Eileen Anderson's small-format *Landscapes of Portugal* series, featuring both car tours and walks, in separate books on the Algarve; Sintra, Cascais and Estoril; and Costa Verde, Minho and Peneda-Gerês.

Among many regional guidebooks, one of the best is expatriate residents John & Madge Measures' *Southern Portugal: Its People, Traditions & Wildlife*, with loving detail on the archaeology, landscapes, agriculture, flora, fauna and local products of scores of little-visited places in the Algarve and southern Alentejo. Another nice perspective is that of *Exploring Rural Portugal*, by Joe Staines and Lia Duarte.

If you'll be riding the rails around the Iberian Peninsula, Norman Renouf's *Spain & Portugal by Rail* is full of network maps and charts (see the introduction to the Train section in the Getting There & Away chapter for details of how to order this book).

If you've got the dosh to stay in Portugal's converted manor houses, palaces and castles, Sam & Jane Ballard's *Pousadas of Portugal* will tell you about every room, and how to cross the country without staying anywhere else.

Travel

Rose Macaulay's entertaining and by now well-known collections, *They Went to Portugal* and *They Went to Portugal Too*, follow the experiences of a wide variety of English visitors from medieval times through the 19th century. These are recommended 'companion' books, easy to enjoy in small doses.

Travels in My Homeland by Almeida Garrett, one of Portugal's best known Romantic writers and public figures, is a philosophical tour of 19th century Portugal, an early home-grown travelogue.

History & Politics

Small and useful enough to tote around is David Birmingham's *A Concise History of Portugal*, modestly illustrated, academic but very readable, and covering events up to its 1993 publication. Similarly user-friendly is *Portugal: A Companion History* by José Hermano Saraiva, which has a handy historical gazetteer. Too big to take along, but one of the best English-language general histories, is AH de Oliveira Marques' *History of Portugal*.

Good specific references on the discoveries are *Prince Henry the Navigator* by John Ure, and CR Boxer's *The Portuguese Seaborne Empire, 1415-1825*. For insights into the Salazar years, look at António de Figueiredo's *Portugal: Fifty Years of Dictatorship*. A good reference on the events of 1974 is *Revolution & Counter-Revolution in Portugal* by Martin Kayman.

Portugal is just one player in Daniel J Boorstin's classic *The Discoverers*, an original and panoramic look at nothing less than the way humans keep discovering their world. The author is one of the most respected and readable of modern historians. Chapters on Portugal include the discovery of a sea route to India, Portugal's rivalry with Spain, and the slave trade.

Food & Drink

Edite Vieira's *The Taste of Portugal* is more than a cookbook: its selected recipes from all of Portugal's regions are spiced with cultural background information and lively anecdotes. There is also a section on wines, and an appendix on the sort of vegetarian dishes you wish you could find in Portuguese restaurants. Another good cookbook is Maite Manjon's *The Home Book of Portuguese Cookery*.

Richard Mayson's brisk, readable *Portugal's Wines & Wine-Makers: Port, Madeira & Regional Wines* is a good introduction to the country's favourite product, and includes a history of Portuguese wine making. Another good resource is Jan Read's *The Wines of Portugal*. Sarah Bradford's *The Englishman's Wine*, revised in 1978 as *The Story of Port*, is the definitive history of the port-wine trade and of the British colony in Porto.

Art & Architecture

An appealing book on the region's vernacular architecture, with fine black and white photographs, is Norman F Carver Jr's *Iberian Villages* (1988). Though it's Spain-oriented, the Portuguese towns of Lindoso, Mértola, Monsanto, Albufeira, Calcadinha, Guarda, Loulé and Monsaraz get detailed attention. The author is an architect with a passion for the subject. Unfortunately, the book is out of print.

Among many coffee-table books on Portugal's idiosyncratic architecture are two handsome Portuguese ones by Júlio Gil: *The Finest Castles in Portugal* (photos by Augusto Cabrita) and *The Finest Churches in Portugal* (photos by Nuno Calvet). Another is *Country Manors of Portugal*, with text by Marcus Binney and fine photos by Nicolas Sapieha and Francesco Venturi.

Living & Working in Portugal

How to Live & Work in Portugal, by Sue Tyson-Ward, is a useful little tome for those planning to stay a long time or even settle down in Portugal. It has sections on accommodation (and even buying a house), domestic life, work, money, driving, education, health services and, of course, travel.

If you get seduced by the idea of relocating to Portugal, you may be sobered and amused by *A Cottage in Portugal* by Richard Hewitt, which recounts an American couple's tribulations in renovating a cottage in Sintra.

General

One of the very best all-round books about the Portuguese is Marion Kaplan's perceptive *The Portuguese: The Land & Its People*, first published in 1991 and revised in 1998. Ranging knowledgeably all over the landscape, from literature to the Church, from agriculture to *emigrantes*, its sympathetic feminine perspective seems most appropriate for a country whose men so often seem to be abroad.

An excellent and accessible work on anthropology and folklore is *Portugal: A Book of Folk-Ways* by Rodney Gallop.

Poetry and novels by Portuguese writers, many of which are translated into English, are mentioned under Arts in the Facts about Portugal chapter.

FILMS

Wim Wenders' film *A Lisbon Story* had its world premiere in Lisbon in 1994, the year the capital was named European City of Culture. Originally conceived as a documentary, it acquired a story line as it went along: a movie sound man wanders the streets trying to salvage a film that its director has abandoned, recording the sounds of the city. In the process he falls in love, has a close call with some gangsters and is followed by a pack of school children. In the film Wenders pays tribute to many cinema greats, including Federico Fellini, Charlie Chaplin and the Portuguese director Manoel do Oliveira (see Cinema & the Performing Arts under Arts in the Facts about Portugal chapter).

NEWSPAPERS & MAGAZINES
Portuguese-Language Press

Major Portuguese-language daily newspapers include *Diário de Notícias*, *Público*, *Jornal de Notícias* and the gossip tabloid *Correio da Manhã*, which licks all the others for circulation. Popular weeklies include the *O Independente* newspaper and *Expresso* magazine. *Público* (www.publico.pt/), *Diário de Notícias* (www.dn.pt/) and *Jornal de Notícias* (www.jnoticias.pt/) also have online editions.

Newsstands groan under sports publications – the best on football is *A Bola*. For entertainment listings, check the local dailies. A monthly or seasonal calendar of regional events is also available from turismos in tourist centres such as Lisbon, Porto and the Algarve. The Lisbon and Porto editions of *Público* have classified sections with big what's-on listings.

Foreign-Language Press

Several English-language newspapers are published in Portugal by and for its expatriate population, especially in the Algarve.

These provide entertainment listings and information on regional attractions and events, as well as advertising long-term accommodation, cheap flights, language and other courses, and even work. Best known are *APN* (*Anglo-Portuguese News*), published every Thursday, and the *News*, published fortnightly in regional editions. Another is the weekly *Algarve Resident* magazine. The *News* has an online edition (www.nexus-pt.com/news/index.hts).

In major towns and tourist destinations it's easy to find a range of foreign papers, including the *European*, the *International Herald Tribune*, *Le Monde*, *Le Figaro* and the *Guardian*. They cost the equivalent of US$1.50 to US$3 and are usually a day or two old. At better-stocked newsagents you can also find foreign magazines such as *Paris-Match*, *Le Point*, *L'Express*, *Der Spiegel*, *Bünte* and the *Economist*.

RADIO & TV
Radio
Domestic radio is represented by the state-owned Rádiodifusão Portuguesa (RDP) stations Antena 1 on MW and FM, and Antena 2 and Antena 3 on FM; the private Rádio Comercial and Rádio Renascença; and a clutch of local stations. All broadcasts are in Portuguese. Evening programming includes some helpings of music, with jazz on Antena 1 and rock on Rádio Comercial.

Frequencies vary with locale. Look for Antena 1 at MW 666kHz or FM 95.7MHz in Lisbon; MW 720kHz or FM 96.7MHz in Porto; or MW 720kHz, FM 88.9 or 97.6MHz in the Algarve. For Rádio Comercial try MW 1035kHz or FM 97.4MHz in Lisbon; MW 1170kHz or FM 97.7MHz in Porto; or MW 558kHz or FM 88.1 or 96.1MHz in the Algarve.

English-language broadcasts of the BBC World Service, Voice of America (VOA) and Radio Australia can be picked up on various short-wave frequencies in Portugal. For current frequency and schedule information, contact the BBC at fax 0171-257 8258 (from 22 April 2000 fax 020-7257 8258) or see its Web site at cgi.bbc.co.uk /worldservice/. Contact VOA at fax 202-619 0916, email voa-europe@voa.gov, or its Web site, www.voa.gov/. You can contact Radio Australia at fax 03-9626 1899, email ratx@radioaus.abc.net.au, or Web site www.abc.net.au/ra/.

TV
Portuguese TV consists of the state-run Rádio Televisão Portuguesa (RTP) channels Canal 1 (on VHF) and TV2 (on UHF), plus two private channels, Sociedade Independente de Communicação (SIC) and TV Independente (TVI). The country also has at least 14 cable-TV companies. Portuguese and Brazilian soap operas (*telenovelas*) and lightweight entertainment shows appear to take up the bulk of TV airtime. There are also lots of subtitled foreign movies.

At least a dozen international channels, mostly showing sports, music and movies, also come in via satellite, including CNN and BBC Prime. Some mid-range and many top-end hotels provide satellite TV in their rooms.

VIDEO SYSTEMS
If you want to record or buy video tapes to play back home, you won't get a picture if the image registration systems are different. Portugal uses the PAL video system, which is incompatible with both the French SECAM system and the North American and Japanese NTSC system. Australia and most of Europe use PAL.

PHOTOGRAPHY & VIDEO
Film & Equipment
Most brands of slide film, such as Ektachrome and Fujichrome, as well as print film and 8mm video cassettes, are widely available. Sample prices are about 1600$00 (US$8.65) for a 36 exposure slide film, 930$00 (US$5) for a 36 exposure print film and 890$00 (US$4.80) for a 90 minute video cassette. However, it's best to take camera equipment and more expensive brands of film, like Kodachrome, with you.

You can buy most video accessories in major towns but take along the necessary battery charger, plugs and transformer (plus a few cartridges).

Print film processing is as fast and cheap as anywhere in Europe. Slide and video processing are rare. Imported point-and-shoot cameras are also available in franchise shops and elsewhere, though at significantly marked-up prices.

Technical Tips

Except for the occasional indoor shot with something like 400 ASA/ISO film, you'll rarely need anything faster than about 100 ASA/ISO. Contrast between light and shadow is harshest at high noon; try to get out in the early morning or just before sunset for the gentlest light.

Video cameras now have amazingly sensitive microphones. Filming by the side of a busy road might seem OK when you do it, but may produce only a deafening roar as a sound track when you replay it at home. Another useful tip is to try and film in long takes and not move the camera around too much.

Restrictions

There are no customs limits on equipment for personal use. There are no significant restrictions on what you can shoot in Portugal, though military sites aren't a very good idea. Some museums and galleries forbid flash photography.

Photographing People

Older Portuguese often become serious and frustratingly uncandid when you take their photos, but few will object to it, and many will be delighted. Everybody seems to like having their children photographed! Nevertheless, the courtesy of asking beforehand is always appreciated. 'May I take a photograph' is *Posse tirar uma fotografia, por favor* in Portuguese. Use the same guidelines for video: always ask permission first.

Airport Security

If you carry unprocessed film in your checked baggage, even in a lead-lined 'filmsafe' pouch, you're inviting trouble.

Several international airports now use 'smart' CTX 5000 scanners for checked baggage. These scan first with a mild beam, then zero in ferociously on anything suspicious. A lead pouch would not only be ineffective but would invite further scans, and film inside is virtually certain to be ruined. Even tests by the manufacturer have confirmed this.

On the other hand, scanners for carry-on bags at most major airports are relatively harmless, at least for slow and medium-speed films. There are no plans yet to use the CTX 5000 for carry-on luggage. The moral of the tale is obvious: always carry unprocessed film in your carry-on bags, and if possible get officials to hand-inspect it. They may refuse, though having the film in clear plastic bags (and preferably clear canisters) can help to persuade them.

TIME

Portugal, like Britain, is on GMT/UTC in winter and GMT/UTC plus one hour during summer. This puts it an hour earlier than Spain year-round. Clocks are set forward by an hour on the last Sunday in March and back an hour on the last Sunday in October.

ELECTRICITY

Electricity is 220V, 50Hz. Plugs normally have two round pins, though some have a third, projecting, earth pin. North American appliances will need a transformer if they don't have built-in voltage adjustment.

WEIGHTS & MEASURES

Portugal uses the metric system; see the inside back cover for a conversion guide. Decimals are indicated with commas, and thousands with points.

LAUNDRY

You'll find *lavandarias* providing laundry services at reasonable cost all over the place, though most concentrate on dry-cleaning (*limpar/limpeza a seco*). Those that also do a wash-and-dry service (*lavar e secar*) usually need at least a day or two to do the work. Some may do ironing (*passar a ferro*) as well. Genuine self-service places are still rare. Figure from 1500$00 to 2000$00 for a 5kg load. Your guesthouse proprietor may also be willing to do small loads of laundry.

TOILETS

Public toilets (*sanitários* or *casas de banho*) are few and far between, though Parisian-style, automatically operated street toilets are becoming more common in major cities. Most people, however, go to the nearest café for a drink or pastry and take advantage of the facilities there. Look for the 'WC' sign, or 'H' (for *homens*, men), and 'S' (for *senhoras*, women).

HEALTH

Portugal, like the rest of Europe, presents no serious health risks to the sensible traveller. Your main risks are likely to be insect bites, sunburn, an upset stomach or foot blisters. Some people routinely experience a day or two of 'travellers' diarrhoea' upon arriving in any new country.

Predeparture Planning

Health Insurance Citizens of EU countries are covered for emergency medical treatment throughout the EU on presentation of an E111 certificate, though charges are likely for medications, dental work and secondary examinations, including x-rays and laboratory tests. Ask about the E111 at your local health services department or travel agency at least a few weeks before you go. In the UK you can get the form at the post office.

Most travel insurance policies also include medical cover. For important suggestions about travel insurance, see Visas & Documents earlier in this chapter.

Health Preparations If you wear glasses take a spare pair and your prescription. You can usually get new spectacles made up quickly, cheaply and competently.

If you need a particular medication, take an adequate supply with you, as it may not always be available (though most pharmacies in Portugal are remarkably well equipped). It's wise to carry a legible prescription to show that you legally use the medication – it's surprising how often drugs that are sold over-the-counter in one place are illegal without a prescription elsewhere. Should you need to get more, you're better off knowing the medication's generic name rather than its brand name (which can vary).

Dental care is available in Portugal, but it's not a bad idea to have a routine dental checkup before you leave home.

Immunisations No vaccinations are required for entry into Portugal unless you're coming from an infected area and are destined for the Azores or Madeira, in which case you may be asked for proof of vaccination against yellow fever. There are a few routine vaccinations that are recommended whether you're travelling or not: polio (usually administered during childhood), diphtheria and tetanus (usually administered together in childhood, with a booster every 10 years) and sometimes measles. See your physician or nearest health service about these.

All vaccinations should be recorded on an International Health Certificate, which is available from your physician or government health department. Don't leave jabs until the last minute, as they may have to be spread over some weeks. Some are contraindicated if you're pregnant.

Contraception In Portugal the most widely available form of contraception is condoms (*preservativos*). These are available in all pharmacies (though you may have to ask for them in smaller towns), and sometimes in supermarkets as well. If you're taking the contraceptive pill, it's safest to bring a supply from home.

Basic Rules

Many health problems can be avoided simply by taking good care of yourself, for example washing your hands often, keeping out of the sun when it's very hot, and covering up or using repellent when insects are around. Care in what you eat and drink is also important, though the worst you can expect in Portugal is a temporary stomach upset.

Food Salads and fruit are safe anywhere in Portugal. Ice cream is usually OK, but beware of ice cream that has melted and been refrozen. Take care with shellfish (for example, cooked mussels that haven't opened properly can be dangerous), and avoid undercooked meat, particularly minced meat. Be careful with food that has been cooked and then left to go cold.

Water Tap water is almost always safe to drink in Portugal's towns and cities though you should be wary in small villages: bottled water is sold almost everywhere as an alternative (though non-degradable plastic bottles bring with them a significant environmental impact). Be careful about those rustic-looking roadside springs in rural areas unless you're sure they really are springs and not just surface streams through populated areas or pastureland.

If you're planning any long hikes where you'll depend on natural water, you should know how to purify it. The simplest way is to boil it vigorously; five minutes should be enough at altitudes typical of Portugal. Iodine treatment, available in tablet form (such as Potable Aqua or Globaline), is very effective and is safe for short-term use unless you're pregnant or have thyroid problems. A flavoured powder will disguise the taste of treated water – a good idea if you're travelling with children. Chlorine tablets (such as Puritabs or Steritabs) kill many, but not all pathogens – some parasites, like giardia and amoebic cysts, are not affected by them. The only commercial water filters that stop all pathogens are combined charcoal and iodine-resin filters.

Nutrition If you're travelling hard and fast and therefore missing meals or not eating a balanced diet, it's a good idea to take multivitamin and mineral supplements. Fruits

Medical Kit Check List

Following is a list of items you should consider including in your medical kit – consult your phamacist for brands available in your country.

- ☐ **Aspirin** or **paracetamol** (acetaminophen in the US) – for pain or fever.
- ☐ **Antihistamine** – for allergies, such as hay fever; to ease the itch from insect bites or stings; and to prevent motion sickness.
- ☐ **Antibiotics** – consider including these if you're travelling well off the beaten track; see your doctor, as they must be prescribed, and carry the prescription with you.
- ☐ **Loperamide** or **diphenoxylate** 'blockers' for diarrhoea; **prochlorperazine** or **metaclopramide** for nausea and vomiting.
- ☐ **Rehydration mixture** – to prevent dehydration, eg due to severe diarrhoea; particularly important when travelling with children.
- ☐ **Insect repellent, sunscreen, lip balm** and **eye drops.**
- ☐ **Calamine lotion, sting relief spray** or **aloe vera** – to ease irritation from sunburn and insect bites or stings.
- ☐ **Antifungal cream** or **powder** – for fungal skin infections and thrush.
- ☐ **Antiseptic** (such as povidone-iodine) – for cuts and grazes.
- ☐ **Bandages, Band-Aids (plasters)** and other wound dressings.
- ☐ **Water purification tablets** or **iodine.**
- ☐ **Scissors, tweezers** and a **thermometer** (note that mercury thermometers are prohibited by airlines).
- ☐ **Syringes** and **needles** – in case you need injections in a country with medical hygine problems. Ask your doctor for a note explaining why you have them.
- ☐ **Cold** and **flu tablets, throat lozenges** and **nasal decongestant.**
- ☐ **Multivitamins** – consider for long trips, when dietary vitamin intake may be inadequate.

and vegetables are also good sources of vitamin. In hot weather make sure you drink enough – don't rely on thirst to remind you to drink. Carry a water bottle on long trips. Excessive sweating can lead to loss of salt and therefore muscle cramping; to avoid it, just add a bit more salt to your food than usual.

Medical Treatment

Every Portuguese town of any size has its own *centro de saúde* (state-administered medical centre), typically open from 8 am to 8 pm. Big cities have full-scale hospitals and clinics, with 24-hour emergency services; contact addresses are included under Information in each city. There are also numerous – and pricier – English-speaking private physicians, and in Lisbon even the Hospital Britânico (British Hospital). Your embassy or the local turismo can refer you to the nearest hospital or English-speaking private doctor.

For minor health problems you can pop into a pharmacy (*farmácia*) for advice; these are abundant in larger towns, and usually very well-supplied. They often have English-speaking staff too. Typical daily opening hours are from 9 am to 1 pm and 3 to 7 pm. There's always one pharmacy open after hours; the address of the late-night one is usually posted in the window of the others. Or you can call the general enquiries number ☎ 118 to find out which farmácia in your area is open.

Environmental Hazards

Bites & Stings Bee and wasp stings are usually painful rather than dangerous. Calamine lotion will provide relief and ice packs will reduce the pain and swelling. Mosquitoes are only a minor nuisance in Portugal, and mosquito-borne diseases are virtually unknown in Europe.

Snakes are probably more afraid of humans than the other way round. To minimise your chances of being bitten, wear boots, socks and long trousers when walking through undergrowth where snakes may be present, and tramp heavily to give

them time to flee from you. Don't put your hands into holes and crevices. Campers should be careful when collecting firewood.

Contrary to some people's fears, snake bites do not cause instantaneous death, and antivenenes are usually available. Keep the victim calm and still, wrap the bitten limb tightly, as you would for a sprained ankle, and attach a splint to immobilise it. Then seek medical help, if possible with the dead snake for identification (but don't attempt to catch the snake if there is even a remote possibility of being bitten again). Tourniquets and sucking out the poison are now comprehensively discredited. An emergency number where you can get advice regarding snake bites and poisoning is ☎ 01-795 01 43.

Fungal Infections Fungal infections, which occur with greater frequency in hot weather, are most likely to appear on the scalp, between the toes or fingers (athlete's foot), in the groin and on the body (ringworm). You get ringworm (which is a fungal infection, not a worm) from infected animals or other people.

To prevent fungal infections wear loose, comfortable clothes, avoid artificial fibres, wash frequently and dry yourself carefully. If you get an infection, wash the infected area daily with a disinfectant or medicated soap, and rinse and dry well. Apply an anti-fungal cream or powder, like tolnaftate (Tinaderm). Try to expose the infected area to air or sunlight as much as possible, change all towels and underwear often and wash them in hot water.

Heat Exhaustion Dehydration or salt deficiency can cause heat exhaustion. This is characterised by fatigue, lethargy, headaches, giddiness and muscle cramps; in this case salt tablets may help, but adding extra salt to your food is much better. Vomiting or diarrhoea can also deplete your liquid and salt levels. Take time to acclimatise to high temperatures (don't do anything too physically demanding) and make sure you get sufficient liquids.

Heatstroke This serious, and sometimes fatal, condition can occur if the body's heat-regulating mechanism breaks down and the body temperature rises to dangerous levels. Long, continuous periods of exposure to high temperatures can leave you vulnerable to heatstroke.

Symptoms include feeling unwell, not sweating very much or at all, and high body temperature (39 to 41°C, or 102 to 106°F). Where sweating has ceased, the skin becomes flushed and red. Severe, throbbing headaches and lack of coordination will also occur, and the sufferer may be confused or aggressive. Eventually the victim will become delirious or convulse. Hospitalisation is essential, but meanwhile get victims out of the sun, remove their clothing, cover them with a wet sheet or towel and fan them continually. Give them fluids if they are conscious.

Prickly Heat Prickly heat is an itchy rash caused by excessive perspiration trapped under the skin. It usually strikes people who haven't adjusted to a hot climate. Keeping cool and bathing often, and using a mild talcum or special prickly heat powder should help.

Sun Damage In Portugal, especially on water or sand, you can get sunburnt surprisingly quickly, even through cloud. Wear a hat, use a sunscreen or sunblock, and protect your eyes with good quality sunglasses. Calamine lotion soothes mild sunburn.

Remember that too much sunlight, whether it's direct or reflected (glare) can damage the surface structures and lens of the eye. Good-quality sunglasses – treated to filter out ultraviolet radiation – are vital if you plan to spend much time on or near the beach.

Infectious Diseases

Diarrhoea You may have a mild bout of travellers' diarrhoea on arrival in a new place, but a few dashes to the loo with no other symptoms is not serious. Moderate diarrhoea, with half a dozen loose movements in a day, is more of a nuisance. Dehydration is the main danger, particularly for children, and fluid replacement is the main treatment. Soda water, soft drinks allowed to go flat and diluted 50% with water, or weak black tea with a little sugar, are all good. Stick to a bland diet for a few days. With any diarrhoea more severe than this, get yourself straight to a doctor.

Lomotil or Imodium can stop you up but they don't cure the problem. Use them only when absolutely necessary; for example, if you *must* travel. They are not recommended for children under 12 years old. Do not use them if the person has a high fever or is severely dehydrated.

HIV & AIDS HIV, the Human Immuno-deficiency Virus, develops into AIDS, Acquired Immune Deficiency Syndrome, which is a fatal disease. HIV is a major problem in many countries. Any exposure to blood, blood products or body fluids may put the individual at risk. The disease is often transmitted through sexual contact or dirty needles – vaccinations, acupuncture, tattooing and body piercing can be potentially as dangerous as intravenous drug use. The Portuguese Institute of Blood screens blood that's used for transfusions.

Sexually Transmitted Diseases Gonorrhoea, herpes and syphilis are among these diseases; sores, blisters or rashes around the genitals, discharges or pain when urinating are common symptoms. With some STDs, such as wart virus or chlamydia, symptoms may be less marked or not observed at all especially in women. Syphilis symptoms eventually disappear completely but the disease continues and can cause severe problems in later years. While abstinence from sexual contact is the only 100% effective prevention, using condoms is also effective. Gonorrhoea and syphilis are treated with antibiotics. The different sexually transmitted diseases each require specific antibiotics. There is no cure for herpes or AIDS.

Women's Health
Antibiotic use, synthetic underwear, sweating and contraceptive pills can lead to fungal vaginal infections when travelling in hot climates. Fungal infections are characterised by a rash, itch and discharge. The infection can be treated with a vinegar or lemon-juice douche with yoghurt, or ask a pharmacist for nystatin, miconazole or clotrimazole pessaries or a vaginal cream. Good personal hygiene and wearing loose-fitting clothes and cotton underwear may help prevent these infections.

Some women experience an irregular menstrual cycle on the road because of the upset in routine. Your physician can give you advice about this.

Pregnancy Most miscarriages occur during the first three months of pregnancy, so this is the riskiest time to travel. The last three months should also be spent within reach of good medical care. A baby born as early as 24 weeks has a chance of survival, but only in a good modern hospital. Additional care should be taken to prevent illness and particular attention should be paid to diet and nutrition. Avoid alcohol, nicotine and all unnecessary medication.

WOMEN TRAVELLERS
Despite the official reversal of many traditional attitudes towards women after the 1974 revolution, Portugal remains, at least on the face of it, a man's world. Although 55% of Portuguese university students (and two-thirds of successful graduates) are female, and although women make up over half the total labour force, there are still few women in positions of public trust.

An official organisation called the Comissão para a Igualdade e para os Direitos das Mulheres (Commission for the Equality & Rights of Women) was founded in 1976 to alter public perceptions of women's social status and is a leading advocate of women's rights.

According to women's groups in Portugal (and to a 1994 report by the US State Department, *Portugal Human Rights Practices*), domestic violence against women is a persistent problem. There are no centres for battered women or rape victims, nor are there reliable statistics on either. Sexual harassment in the workplace is fairly common.

Attitudes Towards Women
In traditional, rural areas of Portugal, an unaccompanied foreign woman is considered an oddity. Older villagers may ask women visitors where their husbands are, and fuss over them as if they were in need of protection. Never mind that these same rural areas often seem populated entirely by unaccompanied Portuguese women whose husbands are either working in the fields, gossiping in the bars, employed abroad (often for years at a time), or long dead. In some ultra-conservative pockets of the north, unmarried couples seeking accommodation will frequently save themselves hassles by saying they are married.

However, women travelling on their own in Portugal report few serious problems. Portuguese machismo, when it manifests at all, is irritating rather than dangerous. A bigger risk may be stoked-up male tourists in seaside resorts, particularly in the Algarve.

Safety Precautions
Women should be cautious about where they go after dark, especially in certain areas of Porto and Lisbon (see those cities for details). Hitching is not recommended for solo women anywhere in Portugal.

Organisations
The Comissão para a Igualdade e para os Direitos das Mulheres (other sources refer to the Comissão da Condição Feminina, or Commission on the Status of Women) is at Avenida da República 32, 1093 Lisbon.

GAY & LESBIAN TRAVELLERS
Attitudes towards gay lifestyles range from a dramatically increased level of acceptance in Lisbon, Porto and the Algarve to bafflement in remoter parts of the country.

Lesbians appear to be more or less ignored. In this overwhelmingly Catholic country there is still little understanding of homosexuality, negligible tolerance of it within families, and no public structures to support homosexuals. Although homophobic violence (gay-bashing) is relatively unknown, there is a steady stream of reported discrimination in schools, workplaces and so on.

Lisbon is the only city in Portugal with a substantial range of places for gay/lesbian socialising – restaurants, bars, discos, saunas, beaches and cruising areas (but parks after dark are not a good idea). See the Lisbon chapter (and the boxed text on this page) for more details. Porto and the Algarve have some places to socialise, but there are few elsewhere.

For listings of gay bars, clubs and news, check out ILGA-Portugal's Web site, www.ilga-portugal.org/. A largelyPortuguese-language site is *Portugal GAY* (www.portugalgay.pt); this includes the *Roteiro Portugal Gay Guide*, which lists heaps of gay venues in Lisbon and regional areas, with maps.

Legal Situation

Homosexuality is not illegal in Portugal. In January 1997, the government approved the new penal code recognising the same age of consent (16) between homosexual and heterosexual partners. A Partnership Bill sponsored by the Partido Socialista is also in the pipeline: if passed, it would be a huge step forward for recognition of gay and lesbian couples, allowing those who have lived together for at least two years the same civil rights (excluding adoption) as married couples. Foreigners will also be allowed to stay in the country without the usual bureaucracy if they can prove they have been in a relationship with a Portuguese national for at least two years.

Organisations

Founded in 1995, ILGA-Portugal, a member of the International Lesbian & Gay Association (ILGA), is the nation's official

---

Gay Pride

Gays look back on 1997 as a watershed year for gay awareness in Portugal: this was the year Lisbon city authorities backed the first Gay Pride Festival and a Gay & Lesbian Film Festival, and the city's first Gay & Lesbian Community Centre was opened (see Gay & Lesbian Travellers under Information in the Lisbon chapter). The festivals now take place annually, Gay Pride on the Saturday closest to 28 June and the film festival in September.

---

gay voice. It can be contacted at the Centro Comunitário Gay e Léobico de Lisboa (Lisbon Gay & Lesbian Community Centre; ☎ 01-887 39 18, fax 887 39 22, email ilga-portugal@ilga.org), Rua de São Lazaro 88, Lisbon.

The Movimento Quilt Português, based at the Gay & Lesbian Community Center, is Portugal's contribution to the quilt-making movement in memory of those lost to AIDS. The Gay Opus Associação was recently founded in Lisbon (☎ 01-317 07 72, Apartado 13054, 1096 Lisbon) and Coimbra (☎ 0931 48 88 20, Apartado 1116) to provide social help to isolated gay men.

A bimonthly gay newspaper, *Diferente*, was launched in 1996 and publishes from Apartado 21221, 1131 Lisbon (☎ 01-362 63 16). *Lilas* (Apartado 6104, 2700 Amadora) is a lesbian-oriented periodical, based in a suburb of Lisbon.

DISABLED TRAVELLERS

Portuguese law requires public offices and agencies to provide access and facilities for disabled people. But it does not cover private businesses, and relatively few places in Portugal have special facilities for disabled travellers yet. Lisbon airport is wheelchair-accessible, and all three international airports (Lisbon, Porto and Faro) and most major train stations (particularly international terminals) have toilets with wheelchair access.

Carris, Lisbon's public transport agency, offers a 7 am to midnight minibus dial-a-ride service (☎ 01-758 56 76) for disabled people, at a cost roughly comparable to taxis. They usually need two days notice. A similar system in Porto is operated jointly by STCP (the public transport agency), the local Red Cross (Cruz Vermelha de Portugal, or CVP) and the regional social security agency (Centro Regional de Segurança Social, or CRSS), daily from 7 am to 9 pm; call CRSS on ☎ 02-600 63 53 or CVP on ☎ 02-606 68 72 (fax 606 71 18).

Carris (☎ 01-363 93 43, fax 364 93 99) in Lisbon and the Algarve coach line Frota Azul (☎ 01-795 14 47, fax 937 70 85) sometimes have specially adapted coaches for hire.

The UK's Orange Badge scheme entitles people with severe walking difficulties to certain on-street parking concessions, and there are reciprocal arrangements with other EU countries. While some have specific concessions, Portugal's are rather vague: 'Parking spaces are reserved for badge holders' vehicles ... indicated by signs with the international wheelchair symbol. Badge holders are not allowed to park ... where parking is prohibited by a general regulation or a specific sign'. We saw very few disabled parking spaces around Portugal, and then only in major towns. Orange badges are issued in the UK by local council social services departments, and the UK Department of Transport publishes an explanatory booklet.

The Royal Association for Disability & Rehabilitation (RADAR), publishes a useful guidebook, updated every two years or so, called *European Holidays & Travel Abroad: A Guide for Disabled People*. Its section on Portugal includes transport information and selected accommodation in the Algarve and elsewhere. RADAR (☎ 0171-250 3222, fax 250 0212; from 22 April 2000 ☎ 020-7250 3222, fax 7250 0212) is at 12 City Forum, 250 City Rd, London EC1V 8AF, UK.

ICEP offices abroad (see Tourist Offices earlier in this chapter) can also furnish some information on barrier-free accommodation around the country. It's mainly the top-end hotels that have the capital to spend modifying their doors, toilets and other facilities. For local barrier-free hotels, camping grounds and other facilities, ask at the nearest turismo. Wheelchair-accessible youth hostels are listed in the Accommodation section later in this chapter.

Organisations

The Secretariado Nacional de Rehabilitação (National Rehabilitation Secretariat; ☎ 01-793 65 17, fax 796 51 82), Avenida Conde de Valbom 63, Lisbon, publishes a guide in Portuguese, *Guia de Turismo para Pessoas com Deficiências* (Tourist Guide for Disabled People). It's updated every few years and has sections on barrier-free accommodation (including camping), transport, general information (including shops, restaurants and sights), and help numbers throughout Portugal. It's only available from their (barrier-free) offices, open weekdays from 10 am to noon and 2 to 7 pm.

A private agency that keeps a close eye on new developments and arranges holidays for disabled travellers is Turintegra (☎/fax 01-859 53 32, contact Ms Luisa Diogo), Praça Dr Fernando Amado, Lotc 566-E, 1900 Lisbon. It's also known as APTTO (Associação Portuguesa de Turismo Para Todos, or Portuguese Association for Tourism for All).

The Portuguese Handicapped Persons' Association (☎ 01-388 98 83, fax 387 10 95) is at Largo do Rato, 1250 Lisbon. Other organisations that might provide additional information are ACAPO, the Association of the Blind & Partially Sighted of Portugal (☎ 01-342 20 01, fax 342 85 18), Rua de São José 86-1, 1500 Lisbon; and APS, the Portuguese Association for the Deaf (☎/fax 01-355 72 44).

SENIOR TRAVELLERS

As elsewhere in Europe, travellers aged 60 and over are entitled to various discounts; see the Money section earlier in this chapter for details. They can also get discounted admission to many tourist sights, as noted throughout the book. For a recommended UK tour operator specialising in holidays for seniors, see the Air and Organised Tours sections in the Getting There & Away chapter.

TRAVEL WITH CHILDREN

Portugal is a splendidly child-friendly place. As Marion Kaplan observes in *The Portuguese: The Land & Its People*, 'To the Portuguese, small children, no matter how noisy and ill-behaved, are angels to be adored and worshipped, overdressed and underdisciplined'. Even teenage boys seem to have a soft spot for toddlers. Whenever our two-year-old shrieked with glee or boredom in a restaurant, the only sour faces were those of other (child-free) tourists.

The following sections have some tips for making a trip with kids easier. For more detailed and wide-ranging suggestions (not all of them necessary in Portugal), pick up the current edition of Lonely Planet's *Travel with Children*.

Discounts & Children's Rates

No restaurant we ate in ever objected to providing child-sized portions at child-sized prices. Children under the age of eight are entitled to a 50% discount in hotels and guesthouses if they share their parents' room. Budget places may charge nothing extra at all. Preschool children usually get into museums and other sights free. Children between four and 12 years old get 50% off tickets on Portuguese Railways, and those under four years travel for free.

Supplies

Basic supplies are no problem, unless you want to settle down in a remote hamlet in Trás-os-Montes. Most *minimercados* (groceries or small supermarkets) have at least one or two brands of disposable nappies. Pharmacies are a handy source of baby supplies of all kinds, from bottles and nappies to food supplements. The big chain supermercados stock toys and children's clothes as well.

Health

Portugal presents no significant health risks for kids other than hot beaches and cold mountains. Restaurant food is quite safe except at obviously cheap and grotty places in bigger cities. For more general health information refer to the Health section earlier in this chapter.

Accommodation

The best bets are simple *pensões* (guesthouses), which are accustomed to families with young children and are casual enough to actually enjoy them. Camping grounds are excellent places to meet other children from all over the world, and youth hostels (nearly all of which have private rooms as well as dormitories) are good for meeting older kids. Most hotels and pensões can provide a cot or extra bed.

Food

Most minimercados, and many pharmacies, have various Portuguese and imported brands of tinned baby food, and markets abound in fresh fruit and vegetables.

All but the stuffiest restaurants tolerate kids well. But a constant problem with eating out is the late hour at which restaurants open for the evening meal – 7 pm at the earliest. Most bars and snack bars can produce plain cheese sandwiches or toasted sandwiches throughout the day. Some restaurants may let you in before regular hours and cook up something simple for a child. Lucky you if your child likes homemade soup, as there is often a pot ready to be served as soon as you walk in the door.

Entertainment

From a child's perspective, the best part of Portugal is probably the Algarve, with its warm, calm beaches, water sports (such as water-skiing, sailing, diving, windsurfing) and beachside cafés; a marine park (Zoomarine) with dolphin and seal shows, near Albufeira; a night-time theme park (Planeta Aventura) near Quarteira; and no fewer than three huge water parks along the main N125 highway. Bicycle rental outfits are more plentiful in the Algarve than anywhere else in the country. Some larger Algarve resorts have children's clubs for three to 11-year-olds, which can be booked through some UK tour operators.

Beaches from one end of the country to the other are an obvious source of fun and an outlet for energy, but beware of the Atlantic Ocean's undertow, serious pollution around Sines and Porto, and Portugal's strong midday sun.

Lisbon and Porto may look like pretty stuffy places to a child. But Lisbon's trams and *elevadores* (funiculars) are great fun, its new Oceanarium a treat for all ages, and several of its museums, especially the Museu da Marioneta (Puppet Museum) and Museu de Marinha (Naval Museum) in Belém, pleasantly kid-friendly places. The tram ride to Belém is half the fun. Sintra's horse-and-cart rides and Toy Museum are also just a 40 minute train ride away. In Porto, though the trams have all but disappeared, the Tram Museum is an enthralling alternative and boat rides upriver make an enjoyable jaunt.

Portugal dos Pequenitos is a theme park in Coimbra built especially for young children. Although now rather run-down, its kid-sized miniatures of architectural monuments from all over the old empire are still appealing. And the full-sized castles of Óbidos, Marvão, Castelo de Vide, Valença, Elvas and elsewhere are great for letting old and young imaginations run wild (but keep hold of your toddler on those sheer-drop battlements).

Many towns have now upgraded their playgrounds, although you'll probably still encounter some rusty, decrepit versions. Good *parques infantil* approved by our toddler were in Lisbon's Jardim da Estrela, at Gouveia (Serra da Estrela) and on the riverfront at Viana do Castelo. Larger towns may also have puppet theatres; Évora has a good one. Every sizeable festival comes complete with parades, fireworks, music, dancing and food. In rural areas, especially up north, friendly farmers may offer tractor or donkey rides.

For older children, see local references in this book to horse-riding centres, especially in the Algarve, the Alentejo and the Minho (Parque Nacional da Peneda-Gerês). Also check out the Activities section in this chapter which lists everything from organised summer camps to bicycling, canyoning and trekking tours – enough to keep the most energetic kid entertained.

Childcare

Babysitters Of course you're going there to travel with the kids, but you may long for the occasional few hours on your own. Ask at the turismo if they can recommend a babysitter. Local papers in the Algarve and Lisbon often advertise babysitting services too. Figure on at least 500$00 per hour for anyone with experience.

Many resorts, self-catering apartment complexes and larger hotels have their own childcare facilities staffed by trained nursery nurses. Several UK-based tour operators, such as Sunworld (☎ 0990 550 440, fax 0113-2393275), have special kids' clubs in Algarve resorts.

Infantários Most sizeable towns have one or more private *infantários* that provide daycare for children from three months to six years of age. They aren't meant for tourists (children are typically enrolled by the month or longer), but you might find one with a place for a few weeks in the summer when some families go away. They aren't cheap – typically 14,000$00 to 18,000$00 per month – partly because they serve hot lunches. Turismos can help you find these.

Ludoteca Ludoteca is the name of a string of privately funded kindergartens staffed by professional nursery nurses and equipped with games, toys, art supplies and so on. There are around 100 of them throughout the country, some only for special-needs children. They're meant for the local community, of course (the staff usually speak little English), although some are open to visiting kids. We found accessible ones in

Lisbon (in the grounds of the Museu Calouste Gulbenkian), in the Algarve at Albufeira, and in Évora. Hours vary, but generally they're open during weekdays from 10 to noon and 2 to 5 or 6 pm.

DANGERS & ANNOYANCES
Crime

Portugal has a low crime rate by European standards, but it's on the rise. Crime against foreigners usually involves pickpocketing or bag-snatching, break-ins and theft from cars (especially rental cars), and pilfering from camping grounds. However, there have been reports recently of armed robberies and assaults by gangs of youths on tourists, especially at some beach resorts (including Estoril/Cascais and Lagos) and in parts of Lisbon and Porto (refer to Dangers & Annoyances under the Information section of those cities).

Take the usual precautions: don't carry your wallet, cash or credit cards in your back pocket or an open bag, use a money belt for large sums, don't leave valuables in your car, tent, hotel room or unattended backpack, and use common sense about going out at night. For peace of mind, take out travel insurance. And if you are robbed, do not under any circumstances put up a fight. For emergency numbers see the boxed text under Post & Communications earlier in this chapter.

Your embassy or consulate is the best first stop in any emergency. For a list of consular offices and the services they can provide in Portugal, see Embassies & Consulates earlier in this chapter.

Police If you've been robbed or burgled, you should visit the local police, not just to report the crime but also to get a police report which you'll need if you hope to make an insurance claim. We identify the appropriate office under each major town. Except in larger cities, you won't find much English spoken, and the police report may be in Portuguese too.

In major towns you'll probably deal with the blue-uniformed local constabulary, the Polícia de Segurança Pública (PSP). In rural areas and smaller towns it's more likely to be the nearest post of the leather-booted Guarda Nacional Republicana (GNR). Many older officers of both were part of the state security apparatus under Salazar and can come across as rather stern. Younger officers are usually easier to talk to.

Portuguese Drivers

Driving in Portugal can be terrifying. Normally peace-loving Portuguese men and women can seem to become irascible, deranged speed-freaks behind the wheel. Tailgating on the motorway at 120km/h and passing on blind curves are the norm. Solid lane markings seem to have little meaning. Not surprisingly, Portugal has Europe's highest annual per capita death rate from road accidents.

Motorcycles

Many young Portuguese men love motorcycles, in particular unmuffled dirt-bikes. Even in the remotest villages, these vile machines snarl up and down quiet streets at every hour of the day and night, sundering dreams and setting teeth on edge.

Ocean Currents & Pollution

Atlantic Ocean currents in some coastal areas are notoriously dangerous. Beaches are often marked by coloured flags: red means the beach is closed to all bathing, yellow means swimming is prohibited but wading is fine, green means anything goes. Be very careful about swimming on beaches that are not signposted or otherwise identified as safe. Steer clear, too, of dangerously polluted beaches near heavily industrialised cities such as Porto and Sines.

Smoking

Three-quarters of the Portuguese population seems to smoke and restaurants outside big cities rarely have no smoking areas. There is little you can do but move upwind, outdoors, or on somewhere else. Portugal does not have a high-profile antismoking lobby.

Hunting Season

Much of the Portuguese countryside (especially inland Algarve and the Alentejo) is open for hunting on certain days of the week, mainly from August through to mid-February, and usually on Thursday, Sunday and public holidays. If you're planning any long country walks, check with the local turismo about places and days to avoid.

LEGAL MATTERS

Foreigners here, as elsewhere, are subject to the laws of the host country. Penalties for dealing in, possessing and using illegal drugs are stiff in Portugal, and may include heavy fines or even jail terms.

BUSINESS HOURS

Don't plan on getting much business or shopping done anywhere between the hours of 1 and 3 pm, when the Portuguese give lunch serious and lingering attention.

Most shops are open from 9 or 9.30 am to 1 pm (though many close at noon) and from 3 to 7 pm. The majority are closed on Saturday afternoon (except in December) and Sunday. Shopping centres are usually open every day of the week, from 10 am to 10 or 11 pm or later.

Normal office hours are from 9 am to 1 pm and from 3 to 5 pm, Monday to Friday. Most banks are open for public business on weekdays only from 8.30 am to 2.30 or 3 pm. Typical post office hours are from 9 am to 12.30 pm and 2.30 to 6 pm on weekdays only.

Museums are usually open Tuesday to Saturday from 10 am to 12.30 pm and 2 to 5 pm. If the Monday is a holiday, they are often closed on the following day as well.

PUBLIC HOLIDAYS & SPECIAL EVENTS

The following dates are public holidays in Portugal, when banks, offices, department stores and some shops close, workers get the day off and public transport services are reduced. Most museums and other tourist attractions also close. And on Christmas Day, New Year's Day, Easter and 1 May even turismos close.

1 January
    New Year's Day
February/March (variable)
    Carnaval Tuesday (Shrove Tuesday, about six
    weeks before Easter)
March/April (variable)
    Good Friday
25 April
    Liberty Day (celebrating the 1974 revolution)
1 May
    Labour Day
May/June (variable)
    Corpus Christi
10 June
    Portugal Day, or Camões & the
    Communities Day
15 August
    Feast of the Assumption
5 October
    Republic Day (commemorating the declaration of the Portuguese Republic in 1910)
1 November
    All Saints' Day
1 December
    Independence Day (commemorating the restoration of independence from Spain in 1640)
8 December
    Feast of the Immaculate Conception
25 December
    Christmas Day

Fairs & Festivals

Portugal abounds with *romarias* (religious pilgrimages), *festas* (festivals) and *feiras* (fairs), which bring whole towns or regions to a standstill. At the core of many are religious processions. The further north you go, the more traditional and less touristy these celebrations get. Some are well worth going out of your way to see (though accommodation is often booked up).

Local turismos can tell you what's coming up, and some regional tourist offices (such as the one in the Minho) publish annual timetables of all their events. Bigger turismos may have the countrywide booklet *Fairs, Festivals & Folk Pilgrimages* or the more general and descriptive *Religious Festivals*.

The following are some of the big ones:

February/March
Carnaval
Taking place over the last few days before the start of Lent (about six weeks before Easter), Carnaval was traditionally an occasion for people to let off steam and thumb their noses at public decorum. Things often got out of hand, with mayhem and even murder between feuding families, but since police powers were boosted in the 1970s, it seems to consist mainly of parades and a lot of weirdly made-up kids out begging for sweets. The biggest celebrations are said to be in Loulé (Algarve), Nazaré (Estremadura) and Ovar (Beiras).

March/April
Senhor Ecce Homo
Braga's Easter or Holy Week Festival is the grandest of its kind in the country, featuring a series of vast and colourful processions. The most famous is Senhor Ecce Homo on Maundy Thursday, which is led by barefoot, torch-bearing penitents.

May
Fátima
Two annual pilgrimages to Fátima (Estremadura) celebrate the first and last apparitions of the Virgin Mary to three shepherd children here in 1917. These are strictly religious events, with hundreds of thousands of pilgrims from around the world visiting one of the Catholic world's major holy sites. The pilgrimages take place over 12 to 13 May and 12 to 13 October.

Festa das Cruzes
The Festival of the Crosses in Barcelos (early May) is noted for its processions, folk performances and regional handicrafts exhibits.

June
Feira Nacional da Agricultura
This grand farming and livestock fair, which also includes bullfighting, folk singing and dancing, is held in Santarém (Ribatejo) in the first week of June.

Festa de Santo António
The Festival of St Anthony is an all-night street fair on the 12 to 13 June in the Alfama and Mouraria districts of Lisbon. The 13th is also a municipal holiday there (see Festas dos Santos Populares under Special Events in the Lisbon chapter). Other communities also celebrate St Anthony's day at this time.

Festa de São João
Many communities celebrate St John's Festival (23 to 24 June), but Porto parties for nearly a week beforehand, and the night of the 23rd sees everybody out on the streets cheerfully bashing each other with leeks or plastic hammers. The 24th is a municipal holiday in Porto.

July
Festa dos Tabuleiros
The (Feast of Trays), in Tomar (Ribatejo), is held only once every three or four years during the week preceding the first Sunday in July. It features a procession of girls and boys bearing trays laden with huge loaves of bread (see the boxed text under Tomar in the Estremadura & Ribatejo chapter). The last one was held in 1995.

August
Romaria e Festa da Nossa Senhora da Agonia
The Pilgrimage and Festival of Our Lady of Suffering in Viana do Castelo (Minho) is famed for its parades, fireworks, folk art and handicrafts fair. It takes place on the weekend of the third Sunday in August.

September
Feiras Novas of Ponte de Lima
Featuring a vast market set up on the banks of the Rio Lima, plus folk music, processions and funfairs, the New Fairs of Ponte de Lima in the Minho date back to the 12th century. They are held over three days in mid-September.

October
See Fátima in May.

November
Feira de São Martinho
This national horse fair, held from 3 to 11 November in Golegã (Ribatejo), features horse parades, riding competitions and bullfights, and a final feast of roast chestnuts and young wine.

ACTIVITIES
Organised outdoor activities are a booming industry in Portugal. One of the most useful information resources is the Departamento de Informação aos Jovens at the Instituto Português da Juventude in Lisbon (see the boxed text 'Youth Centres' under Accommodation later in this chapter for contact details). This helpful IPJ headquarters has stacks of files listing almost every adventure club or operator in the country.

IPJ also coordinates (and organises) summer camps and holidays for young people (see under Multiactivity Programmes later in this section).

For more listings of adventure activity operators check out the slim books published by Temas e Debates on *Trekking*, *Canyoning*, *Bungee Jumping*; *Surfing*, *Windsurfing & Funboard* and *Jeep Safaris*, available in major Portuguese bookshops.

For overseas operators organising activity holidays to Portugal, see Organised Tours in the Getting There & Away chapter.

Walking

Despite some magnificent rambling country, walking ranks low among Portuguese passions. There are no national walking clubs and no official cross-country trails, though parks, including Parque Nacional da Peneda-Gerês and Parque Natural da Serra da Estrela, are increasingly starting to mark walking trails, and some areas, such as the Algarve, have clubs of keen amateur walkers who are trying to organise trans-Algarve trails (see the boxed text 'Via Algarviana' under Activities in the Algarve chapter).

Armed with good maps (see Planning earlier in this chapter for map sources) you can turn this to your advantage and have remoter parts of Portugal, especially its national/natural parks, almost to yourself.

Camping is usually restricted to established camping grounds, but most trails pass close enough to villages or towns for you to find accommodation there.

Most of the good walking is in the north. Most challenging is the Serra da Estrela, which includes mainland Portugal's tallest peak, 1993m Torre. Less taxing but at least as beautiful are Parque Nacional da Peneda-Gerês in the Minho; the lovely but little-visited Parque Natural de Montesinho in Trás-os-Montes; and the tiny Parque Natural do Alvão and Serra do Marão range, both near Vila Real. For more on Portugal's parks, see National Parks under Flora & Fauna in the Facts about Portugal chapter.

A Lisbon agency that organises weekend guided walks to remote corners of Portugal is Rotas do Vento (☎ 01-364 98 52, fax 364 98 43, email rotasdovento@mail.telepac.pt, Map Estrela & Doca). A Porto agency with considerable experience in the north is Montes d'Aventura (see Information under Porto in the Douro chapter, and Activities under Parque Nacional da Peneda-Gerês in the Minho chapter). Other agencies with more local expertise are listed in the sections on Setúbal, Monchique, Tavira, and the Serra da Estrela, Peneda-Gerês, Montesinho and Alvão parks.

Quercus (see Ecology & Environment in the Facts about Portugal chapter) organises trips to areas of environmental interest. Some branch offices are more active than others: check with the Lisbon head office (☎ 01-778 84 74, fax 778 77 49, email quercus@mail.telepac.pt). The Liga para a Proteção da Natureza (League for the Protection of Nature) runs short walks in areas of natural interest (see Walking under Activities in the Algarve chapter).

Some books on walking in Portugal are recommended in the Books section earlier in this chapter. For advice about snakes see Bites & Stings under Health earlier in this chapter.

Cycling

Mountain biking is one of the fastest-growing sports in Portugal and there are increasing numbers of outlets where you can rent mountain bikes (*bicyclete tudo terrano*, or BTT), especially in the Algarve and around Parque Nacional da Peneda-Gerês. Prices range from 1500$00 to 3500$00 a day. Guided biking trips are particularly popular in Lagos and Tavira (Algarve) and Setúbal (Around Lisbon).

Near Lisbon, Cabra Montêz (☎ 01-419 5315, mobile ☎ 0931 994 38 40, email cabramontez@hotmail.com) runs good half-day biking tours to Sesimbra, Setúbal and Sintra. Minho-based PlanAlto runs day-long and multiday BTT trips all round the Minho and Trás-os-Montes. See Activities under Parque Nacional da Peneda-Gerês in the Minho chapter for more details. Some câmaras municipais (town halls) also organise biking outings at a very reasonable cost (see under Sintra and Mafra).

For an introduction to cycling, not as an activity but as a way of getting around Portugal, see the Bicycle section in the Getting Around chapter.

Water Sports

Portugal has over 800km of coastline offering some fine surfing and windsurfing, as well as water-skiing, sailing and scuba diving. The northern beaches tend to have bigger waves, and colder water. Prime surfing and windsurfing locations are Praia do Guincho and Praia das Maçãs on the Estoril coast, and Ericeira in the Estremadura. Only the Algarve and the Estoril coast have appreciable support facilities such as equipment rental. Nautilus-Sub (☎ 01-255 1969, fax 255 3900, email nautilus .sub@mail.telepac.pt) is a Lisbon-based outfit which organises scuba-diving courses and activities.

Inland water sports include a limited amount of white-water boating, and plenty of motorised and nonmotorised reservoir boating, particularly in Parque Nacional da Peneda-Gerês and on the Barragem do Castelo de Bode, near Tomar.

Horse Riding

There are many centres for pony and horse riding, especially in the coastal Algarve and Alentejo; some do organised trips. See individual chapters for further details. Typical high-season rates are about 3500$00 an hour.

Golf

Southern Portugal is full of championship-standard golf courses, with a few up north too. The Algarve west of Faro has no fewer than 19 courses, and the Estoril coast has 11. There are three in the Estremadura, two just south of Porto, two in the Minho, near Barcelos and Ponte de Lima, and one at Chaves (Trás-os-Montes). ICEP produces a glossy booklet with detailed descriptions of every one of them. The *Golf in Portugal* Web site (www.ecs.net/golf/portugal/) has information on clubs in, and golf tours to, Portugal.

Tennis

Most top-end hotels in the Algarve have tennis courts. There are clubs with professional instructors at Vilamoura, Vale do Lobo and Carvoeiro (all in the Algarve); Lisbon; and the Tróia Peninsula (south-east of Lisbon).

Jeep Safaris

Numerous outfits in the Algarve, Setúbal Peninsula and Serra de Sintra offer one-day jeep safaris into the foothills. Shop around: some are little more than noisy off-road scrabbles. Perhaps the most responsible of the lot is Horizonte in Salema, which arranges trips into the Parque Natural do Sudoeste Alentejano e Costa Vicentina, including a look at the disappearing rural scene as well as wild landscapes and remote west-coast beaches.

Another reliable safari agency in the Algarve is Riosul. See Jeep Safaris under Activities in the Algarve chapter for contact details for both companies. Planeta Terra is a good agency in Setúbal (see the Around Lisbon chapter).

Canyoning & Hydrospeed

Canyoning is a relatively new adventure sport, tackling all the challenges offered by a canyon: trekking, swimming, abseiling and rock climbing. Hydrospeed is a version of white-water boating, with individual boards and helmets instead of a boat. Several agencies offer tourist programmes in these high-adrenalin activities, including Trilhos and Templar; see the later section on Multiactivity Programmes.

Marathon

Not surprisingly – given Portugal's prominence in track and field (see Spectator Sports later in this chapter) – Lisbon hosts its own international race, the Maratona de Lisboa, or Discoveries Marathon. This takes place annually in late November, and there is also a half-marathon in early March. For more information and contact details see Athletic Events under Special Events in the Lisbon chapter.

Skiing

The only place where you can be sure of snow is around Torre in the Parque Natural da Serra Estrela. Facilities (lifts, equipment rental and so on) are pretty basic. Penhas de Saúde is the major accommodation base. The season is January through March, with reliably good snow only in February.

Multiactivity Programmes

The Instituto Português da Juventude (IPJ) organises adventure summer camps (including biking, canoeing and rock climbing) and voluntary work camps for young people, in locations throughout Portugal. They are open to foreigners, but not much English is spoken. The one to two-week camps (for a maximum of 20 people, in age groups of 12 to 15 or 18 to 30) cost about 1000$00 per person; advance reservations are essential.

Other youth holiday organisers include Associação Crista de Mocidade (☎ 01-388 56 79, fax 387 30 70) and Planeta Terra (☎ 065-53 21 40, email planeta.terra@mail .telepac.pt).

Cabra Montêz (see under Cycling) specialises in mountain-biking trips but also organises horse-riding, walking, paintball and karting activities (often in combination) in the Sintra and Setúbal Peninsula areas. TurAventur in Évora (Alentejo) does group walking, biking and jeep trips across the Alentejo plains. Similar programmes open to individuals are run by Templar in Tomar (Estremadura & Ribatejo).

Trote-Gerês (see Parque Nacional da Peneda-Gerês in the Minho chapter) can arrange trekking, horse-riding, canoeing, cycling and combination trips in Peneda-Gerês. A Porto agency that can do the same at Peneda-Gerês and elsewhere is Montes d'Aventura (see Walking & Trekking earlier in this section).

Trilhos in Porto (Douro) is a leading operator for canyoning and hydrospeed (the latter only during November to May), and can also arrange rock-climbing and walking trips in Peneda-Gerês and elsewhere in the north.

Hot-Air Ballooning

If you've got 25,000$00 to spare you can enjoy some of Europe's most unspoilt aerial vistas from the comfort of a wicker basket. Several operators offer commercial rides, including Hemisférios, based in Alcácer do Sol (see under Setúbal in the Around Lisbon chapter), and Duobalão (☎ 049-2 10 15, fax 2 25 46), based in Abrantes (Ribatejo).

COURSES
Language

For a two hour crash course in Portuguese basics for 3500$00, contact Interlingua in Portimão (☎/fax 082-41 60 30), Lagos (☎/fax 082-76 10 70) or Lagoa (☎ 082-34 14 91). The Cambridge School offers intensive four-week group courses for foreigners from about 79,200$00, plus shorter courses and pricey private lessons; it has branches in Lisbon (☎ 01-352 74 74, fax 353 47 29, Map Saldanha), Porto (☎ 02-56 03 80, fax 510 26 52) and Coimbra (☎ 039-83 49 69, fax 83 39 16). The Lisbon-based Instituto de Línguas e Informática (☎ 01-315 41 16, fax 315 41 19, email instituto@ipfel.pt) runs intensive two-week group courses for 50,000$00 (discounts for students). It also has branches in Porto and Leiria.

CIAL-Centro de Línguas (☎ 01-794 04 48, fax 796 07 83, email cialis@mail .telepac.pt) offers individual lessons at 5200$00 an hour or group lessons from 44,000$00 for a week. Social activities (like visits to museums) are included in the group price. CIAL has centres in Faro (☎ 089-80 76 11, fax 80 31 54) and Porto (☎ 02-332 02 69, fax 208 39 07).

Other Courses

Among other things you can learn while in Portugal are:

Arts and crafts: courses in ceramic pottery, azulejos and traditional Arraiolos carpet-making at the Associação dos Artesãos da Região de Lisboa (☎ 01-796 24 97), Rua de Entrecampos 66, Lisbon; 10-day pottery holidays at Casa de Yavanna (☎/fax 051-83 92 11), Lugar da Insua, Fontoura, 4930 Valença (Minho); eight hour course in ceramics and azulejo-making at CIAL-Centro de Línguas (see Language)

Dance, singing, juggling, circus techniques, TV acting: evening courses from the Collectividade Cultural e Recreativa de Santa Catarina (☎ 01-887 82 25), Costa de Castelo 1, Lisbon

Portuguese gastronomy: eight hour course at CIAL-Centro de Línguas (see Language)

Riding Portugal's famous Lusitano horses: Escola de Equitacao de Alcainça (☎ 061-966 21 22), Rua de São Miguel, Alcainça (near Mafra)

Skydiving: weekend courses from the Associação do Paraquedistas do Minho (☎ 053-62 65 30), Aeroclube de Palmeira, Palmeira

Zen meditation: Centro de Alimentação e Saúde Natural (☎ 01-315 08 98), Rua Mouzinho da Silveira 25, Lisbon

For information on US universities with exchange programmes in Portugal, check out this Web site: www.studyabroad.com/.

WORK

EU nationals can compete for any job in Portugal without a work permit. Non-EU citizens who want to work in Portugal are expected to get a Portuguese work permit before they arrive, with the help of their prospective employer.

Several organisations can help you search for a job in Portugal before you go, and even arrange your work permit. One of the best known is the Work Abroad Program of CIEE, the Council on International Educational Exchange (☎ 212-822 2600, fax 822 2699, email info@ciee.org, www.ciee.org/), 205 East 42nd St, New York, NY 10017-5706.

A Web-based index of library resources on jobs abroad is at www.lib.calpoly.edu /research/quick_facts/overseas.html.

As a traveller, you're more likely to decide after arriving that you need some cash to help extend your travels, though the prospects of on-the-spot work in Portugal are limited unless you have a skill that's scarce. The search will be easier if you've brought along a curriculum vitae, references and certified copies of relevant diplomas or certificates. The odds also improve if you speak passable Portuguese. Except for work where you're paid in kind or in petty cash, you'll probably have to sign a work contract.

The most realistic option is English teaching, but only if you're prepared to stay in one place for at least a few months. A TEFL certificate is a big help, though you may find work without one. See the *páginas amarelas* (Yellow Pages) under Escolas de Línguas for the names of schools in your chosen area. You can also check out classified ads in Portugal's English-language press or if your Portuguese is good enough, in dailies such as *Diário de Notícias* or *Público* (see Newspapers & Magazines earlier in this chapter).

The English-language newspapers may be interested in writers or reporters. Otherwise, there are rare jobs in Algarve bars and in summer you can sometimes pick up day-to-day cash passing out leaflets for bars and clubs in the streets of Lagos or other Algarve towns.

If you plan to stay more than three months, you'll also need a residence permit, from the local Serviço de Estrangeiros e Fronteiras office (see Visas & Documents earlier in this chapter). We have listed some offices in this book or you can ask the local turismo.

A somewhat dated but comprehensive reference for the serious long-term job seeker is Sue Tyson-Ward's paperback, *How to Live & Work in Portugal.*

ACCOMMODATION

Most local turismos have lists of accommodation to suit a wide range of budgets, and can help you find and even book a place to stay. Some turismos scrupulously avoid making recommendations, while others are happy to offer their opinions. The government grades most accommodation with a bewildering and not very useful system of stars.

Prices for most places are seasonal. Typically, high season is mid-June or July through August or September; middle season is April to the middle or end of June, plus September or October; and low season is the rest of the year. The Algarve's busy season runs for most of the year, from late March through November; accommodation here is generally more expensive and more booked up than the rest of the country. Prices jump everywhere during Carnaval and Easter week (dates for these are variable; see Public Holidays & Special Events earlier in this chapter).

You'll have to prebook most mid-range and top-end accommodation for the high season, anywhere from a few days to a few weeks ahead (at many places you'll get a cheaper rate in upmarket hotels if you book through a travel agent).

Prices in Portugal are always for the room – not per person. Single rooms are usually about two-thirds the price of a double (save money and find a friend to travel with!). Many places have a variety of prices (for example, for rooms with/without private bath or window); it's always worth asking. Many, too, will give discounts for longer stays; but again, you must ask.

For a room with a double bed, ask for *um quarto de casal*; for twin beds (usually a bit more expensive), ask for *um duplo*; and for a single room, ask for *um quarto individual*.

In this book we use the following price categories for an establishment's most basic double with toilet and shower or bath: budget (up to 6000$00); mid-range (from 6000$00 to 12,000$00); top end (over 12,000$00).

Camping

Camping is widespread and popular in Portugal, and easily the cheapest option. Depending on facilities, high season prices per night are about 300$00 to 700$00 per adult (or child over 10 years old), plus 200$00 to 500$00 for a small tent and the same again for a car. Lower prices often apply in less touristy regions and in the low season.

The best equipped, biggest (but priciest) camping grounds in the country are run by Orbitur; bookings can be made through Orbitur's central booking office in Lisbon (☎ 01-811 70 00, fax 815 80 45, email info@orbitur.pt, Web site www.orbitur.pt). We note Orbitur sites throughout the book.

The annual *Roteiro Campista* (800$00), sold in larger Portuguese bookshops, is an excellent multilingual guide with details of nearly every camping ground in the country, plus regulations for camping outside these sites.

For information about the Camping Card International, see under Visas & Documents earlier in this chapter.

Hostels

Portugal has a network of 23 *pousadas da juventude* (youth hostels) and nine *centros de alojamento* (accommodation centres), all part of the Hostelling International (HI) network. Centros de alojamento are usually beside the local branch of the Instituto Português da Juventude – until 1997 they belonged to the IJP network (see the boxed text 'Youth Centres' on the next page).

Rates vary – they are higher in more popular hostels, such as those in Lisbon and Porto. A dorm bed in high season costs 1500$00 to 2900$00 (1200$00 to 1900$00 in low season) at pousadas da juventude and 1700$00 (1400$00) at centros de alojamento. Bedlinen is included. Many pousadas da juventude also offer private doubles for 2700$00 to 3600$00 (3200$00 to 6000$00 with bathroom). One at Vilarinho das Furnas has bungalows for four/five people (9000/11,000$00 in high season).

Many pousadas da juventude have kitchens where you can do your own cooking; a continental breakfast is always included in the price, and lunch or dinner costs 900$00. Centros de alojamento have facilities for cooking or serving food.

Six pousadas da juventude (Almada, Catalazete, Lagos, Lisbon, Ovar and Porto) are open 24 hours. The others, and all centros de alojamento, are typically open from 8 am to noon and 6 pm to midnight, though you can usually stash your bags at any hour and come back at opening time to book in.

Ten pousadas da juventude (Almada, Catalazete, Coimbra, Foz do Cávado, Lagos, Leiria, Lisboa, Penhas da Saúde, Porto, Sines) are suitable for wheelchair-users.

Demand is high in summer, so advance reservations are essential. You can book ahead from any hostel to any other in Portugal free of charge, or alternatively pay 160$00 per set of bookings (not per hostel) at Portugal's central HI reservations office, Movijovem (☎ 01-313 88 20, fax 352 14 66, email movijovem@mail.telepac.pt), Avenida Duque d'Ávila 137, Lisbon; you can also book hostels abroad from here.

If you don't already have a card from your national hostel association, you can become a member of HI by paying an extra 400$00 (and having a guest card stamped) at each of the first six hostels you stay in.

There are pousadas da juventude at:

Alentejo
    Sines, Évora
Algarve
    Alcoutim, Lagos, Portimão, Vila Real de
    Santo António
Beiras
    Coimbra, Mira, Ovar, Penhas da Saúde
    (Covilhã), São Pedro do Sul
Douro
    Porto (Vila Nova de Foz Côa pousada was
    under construction at time of research)
Estremadura
    Areia Branca (Lourinha), Leiria, São
    Martinho
Lisbon area
    Almada, Catalazete (Oeiras), Lisbon, Sintra
Minho
    Braga, Fóz do Cávado (Esposende), Vila
    Nova de Cerveira, Vilarinho das Furnas

Centros de alojamento are in: Aveiro, Castelo Branco, Faro, Guarda, Portalegre, Santarém, Setúbal, Vila Real and Viseu.

Private Rooms

Another cheap option, especially in coastal towns, is a *quarto particular* (or simply *quarto*, meaning room), usually just a room

---

Youth Centres

The Instituto Português da Juventude (IPJ; Portuguese Youth Institute) is a state-funded network of youth centres which provide a wide range of facilities to people aged under 30 years old. Its headquarters (☎ 01-352 26 94, email ipj.infor@mail.telepac.pt), Avenida da Liberdade 194, Lisbon, has a Departamento de Informação aos Jovens (Youth Information Department) with stacks of information on courses and adventure activities, as well as notice boards advertising accommodation and things to sell and buy. Check out IJP's Web site at www.sejuventude.pt/.

There are IPJ branches all over the country: Aveiro, Beja, Braga, Bragança, Castelo Branco, Coimbra, Évora, Faro, Guarda, Leiria, Portalegre, Porto, Santarém, Setúbal, Viana do Castelo, Vila Real and Viseu. Most have libraries (with free Internet access), cafés and study rooms, and are great places to meet students and local young people.

---

in a private house. These are easiest to find in summer. Home owners may approach you in the street or at the bus or train station; otherwise watch for 'quartos' signs. Some turismos have lists of private rooms, though most avoid the subject. The rooms are usually clean, cheap (about 3500$00 a double, or around 5000$00 in popular high-season resorts) and free from the restrictions of hostels, and the owners can be interesting characters. A more commercial variant is a *dormida*, or rooming house, where doubles are about 4000$00 in the high season. Prices don't usually vary between seasons, but you may have some success bargaining them down in the low season.

In the smallest rural villages, if you find the public accommodation is full or non-existent, you might find a *casa de povos* (literally, house of the people; like a community hall) where you can crash with the permission of the mayor or other local bigwig. Facilities are likely to be limited to a floor to sleep on and a toilet.

Guesthouses

The most common types of guesthouses, the Portuguese equivalent of bed and breakfasts (B&Bs), are the *residencial* (plural *residenciais*) are the *pensão* (plural *pensões*). Both are graded from one to three stars, and the top-rated establishments are often cheaper and better run than some hotels clinging to one star. Lower-standard places are often ignored by turismos, though they may be the only budget options in town.

High-season rates for a double with private bathroom in the cheapest pensão are about 5000$00; you can expect to pay slightly more for a residencial, where breakfast is often included in the price. There are often cheaper rooms with shared bathrooms. You may also see places confusingly advertised as Pensão Residencial: these are usually pensões with pretensions to being residenciais.

Pensões and residenciais are probably Portugal's most popular form of tourist accommodation, and they tend to fill up in summer. Try to book at least a week ahead in the high season, even two or three weeks ahead in tourist areas or for good-value places. During the low season, rates drop by at least a third.

Some places that don't qualify for, or can't be bothered with, government approval as residenciais may go by the name *residência*. While these aren't graded and guaranteed by the state, some are as good as the approved versions at the lower end of the scale.

A step down are boarding houses, called *hospedarias* or *casas de hóspedes*, where prices are lower and showers and toilets are usually shared.

Hotels

Hotels (*hotel*, plural *hotéis*) are graded from one to five stars. For a double in the high season you'll pay about 12,000$00 to 15,000$00 at the lower end and between 20,000$00 and 40,000$00 at the top end. In the same category, but more like upmarket inns, are the *albergarias* and the pricier *estalagens* (both unstarred). In the low season, prices drop spectacularly, with a doubles in spiffy four star hotels going for as little as 10,000$00. Breakfast is usually included.

In some towns you may find *aparthotels* – whole blocks of self-contained apartments for rent to tourists, managed as hotels.

Room Service (☎ 0171-636 6888, fax 636 6002; from 22 April 2000 ☎ 020-7636 6888, fax 7636 6002, email rooms@ netcomuk.co.uk, Web site www.room-service.co.uk) is a UK-based hotel booking service that can make reservations (often with big discounts) for mid-range and top-end hotels and resorts in Lisbon, the Estoril Coast, Porto and elsewhere in Portugal.

Turismo de Habitação

Under a private (but governemt monitored) scheme called Turismo de Habitação, and smaller schemes known as Turismo Rural and Agroturismo (often collectively referred to as Turihab), you can stay in anything from a farmhouse to a mansion as the guest of the owner. Some also have self-contained cottages, though owners prefer stays of at least three or four days in these.

A hefty book, *Turismo no Espaço Rural*, describing most of them in Portuguese,

English, French and German, is available for about 2500$00 from ICEP tourist offices abroad and in Lisbon and Porto, or from the largest of the Turihab owners' associations, Solares de Portugal (☎ 058-74 16 72, fax 74 14 44, email turihab@mail .telepac.pt), Praça da República 4990, Ponte de Lima. Solares also has a smaller, free catalogue of its own. But unless you plan on Turihabbing every night of your trip and want to book each one, you may not need these books, as nearly all turismos have lists of local Turihab properties.

Prices vary according to quality and season. For a double in high season you'll pay a minimum of 16,500$00 in a Turihab manor house, but just 9500$00 in a farmhouse. In low season, and/or if you book directly with the owner, prices can drop significantly and you can literally stay in a palace for the price of an average B&B elsewhere in Europe.

Pousadas de Portugal

These are deluxe, government-run former castles, monasteries or palaces (plus some new establishments), over 60 in all, usually in areas of natural beauty or historical significance. Doubles in a pousada cost from 15,600$00 to 29,600$00 in the high season, and 10,600$00 to 24,400$00 in the low season. For more information contact ICEP offices abroad or Pousadas de Portugal (☎ 01-848 12 21, fax 840 58 46), Avenida Santa Joana Princesa 10, 1749 Lisbon, or check out their Web site at www.pousadas.pt.

FOOD

Without a shadow of doubt the Portuguese is the most refined, the most voluptuous and succulent cuisine in the world ... We did acquire – thanks to the spices from the Orient, the tangy bits from Brazil and the art of using sugar from sweet-toothed countries, Turkey, India and the Moors of northern Africa – culinary skills, foods, delicacies, recipes, which turned us into a foremost gastronomic people. There is no other country that can boast such an array of national dishes ...

Fialho de Almeida
Os Gatos (1893)

Olive oil, wine and friendship, the older the better.

Portuguese proverb

Don't get your hopes up: most travellers' experiences of Portuguese cuisine don't come close to Almeida's lyrical description. There's no doubt that eating and drinking get serious attention here. But traditional Portuguese cuisine is far from fancy: it's basically the honest fare of farmers and fisherfolk. And that means hearty portions (at cheap prices), lots of fish and meat, rice and potatoes, and a few scraps of lettuce as the standard 'vegetable'.

The only meal that may fail to fill your stomach is *pequeno almoço* (breakfast), which is traditionally just coffee and a bread roll (often taken in a café). *Almoço* (lunch) is a far bigger affair, often lasting at least two hours (usually 1 to 3 pm). Like the *jantar* (evening dinner), it features three courses, including a hot main dish, invariably served with potatoes (and sometimes rice as well). There's a growing trend (especially in the cities) for shorter lunch hours, and smaller, cheaper meals. But even with the full-length affair, you'll find it easy to gorge yourself on a three course meal for under 1800$00 (about US$10), since many main dishes cost less than 1300$00 each. Bargain-hunters will find a wider choice of good-value meals at lunch time (when *pratos do dia* or daily specials, at around 800$00, are the norm) rather than dinner.

Although restaurants open for dinner at about 7 pm (with last orders at around 10.30 pm in cities), most locals don't eat until at least 8 or 9 pm. Restaurants are usually closed for service between 4 and 7 pm, even if they say they're open all day. But you'll always be able to find something to eat somewhere. In addition to the *restaurantes*, hordes of places serve snacks: cafés, café-bars and snack-bars sell sandwiches and cakes as well as coffee, tea and alcoholic drinks throughout the day; many serve simple meals at lunch time, often at the bar counter as well as at tables. Several packed-out lunch eateries in Lisbon are

Caldo Verde

This is the most typical of Portugal's soups and is made with kale (a type of cabbage). The stalk and tough parts of the kale are removed and the rest is shredded finely so that it resembles grass. In Portugal the soup is served with a slice of maize bread and a side dish of small black olives.

Serves 4

500g floury potatoes, peeled and cut into quarters
1L water
salt
3 tbs olive oil
1 onion, finely chopped
250g kale or cabbage leaves, very finely shredded
1 small clove of garlic (optional)
freshly ground black pepper
4 thin slices of *chouriço* (optional)

Cook the potatoes in salted water until they are soft enough for mashing. Remove, mash and return to the water, along with the oil, onion and shredded cabbage, and boil for three to four minutes (the cabbage should not be overcooked or mushy). Season and serve hot. Place a slice of chouriço (a Portuguese spicy pork sausage) in each soup bowl if desired.

almost entirely stand-up. (Nonsmokers may prefer to avoid these rush hours as Portuguese restaurants rarely have nonsmoking sections.)

Another popular place, especially at lunch times, is a *casa de pasto*, a casual eatery with cheap, simple meals. Slightly more upmarket, and popular with locals for both lunch and dinner, is a *tasca*, a simple tavern, often with rustic décor. A *cervejaria*, literally beer house, serves food as well as drinks, while a *marisqueira* specialises in seafood (and is therefore often

expensive). The *churrasqueira* (or *churrascaria*), literally a barbecue or grill, is actually a popular family-style restaurant serving grilled foods, especially chicken.

If you can't face the huge servings (rice and chips with at least two pieces of meat or fish is considered quite normal for an ordinary portion), you can ask for a *meia dose* (half-portion). This is standard practice in many restaurants, though the cost usually works out to be about two-thirds of a *dose*, not half.

Many restaurants advertise an *ementa turística* (tourist menu), a set meal with a choice of dishes and a glass of beer or half-bottle of wine. Sometimes these can be genuine bargains (popular with locals, too); often, however, portions are miserable. Beware, too, of those tempting little titbits of olives and cheese spread or plain bread and butter, which are put on the table at the start of your meal; if you start nibbling them, you'll be charged for them (they're usually listed as a *couvert* or cover charge on the bill, or as *pão e manteiga*, bread and butter). If you don't want them, play it safe and send them back at the outset.

To order the bill, ask for *a conta, se faz favor*. Cafés don't usually charge for service (a tip of small change is acceptable). In other establishments it's almost always included in the bill; if not, it's customary to leave about 10%. A 17% IVA tax may also be added in upmarket restaurants.

Snacks

Snacks include *sandes* (sandwiches), typically with queijo (cheese) or *fiambre* (ham); *prego no pão* (a slab of meat sandwiched in a roll, often with a fried egg as well); *pastéis de bacalhau* (cod fishcakes); and *tosta mista* (toasted cheese and ham sandwich). Prices start at about 250$00. Soups are also cheap (about 200$00) and delicious; see the following section. Keep an eye out for cafés advertising *combinados*: these tasty little bargains, costing about 700$00, are miniature portions of a regular meat or fish dish, invariably served with chips (and sometimes salad).

Main Meals

Before delving into the menu (*a ementa* or *a lista*) it's always worth asking if there's a *prato do dia* (dish of the day) or *especialidade da casa/região* (speciality of the house or region). Greedy tourist-geared eateries may simply suggest the expensive *arroz de marisco* – a rich seafood and rice stew, usually for a minimum of two – but elsewhere you could well end up with some unusual dish that's far more exciting than the standard menu items.

Among *entradas* or starters, best value are the excellent home-made soups. Especially popular is *caldo verde*, a jade-green potato and cabbage soup (see the boxed recipe on the previous page). In areas such as the Serra de Estrela, where local cheeses are famous, you may well find these on the entrada menu, as well as the occasional *queijo fresco* (fresh goat's cheese).

For main meals, *peixe* (fish) and seafood offer exceptional value, especially at seaside resorts, though you'll find fish on menus througout Portugal, even in the remotest corner of the land. There's an amazing variety available, from favourites such as *linguada* and *lulas grelhado* (grilled sole and squid) and *pescada* (hake) to *bife de atúm* (tuna steak), often served in the Algarve smothered in onions, and *espadarte* (swordfish) – sometimes confused in menu translations with *peixe espada* (scabbard fish).

The cheapest fish are the ubiquitous *sardinhas assadas* (charcoal-grilled sardines), a delicious feast when eaten with salad and chilled white wine or port. And you won't get far in Portugal before discovering its favourite fish dish: *bacalhau*, or salted cod, which has been a Portuguese culinary obsession for 400 years (see the boxed text).

For more exotic fish specialities, there's the popular but expensive arroz de marisco (seafood paella); *caldeirada* (fish stew) or *açorda de marisco* (bread-based fish stew); *cataplana*, a combination of shellfish and ham cooked in a sealed wok-style pan and typical of the Algarve region; and all the

---

Bacalhau – the Faithful Friend

The Portuguese have been obsessed with bacalhau – salted cod – since the early 16th century. It was at this time that Portuguese fishing boats started to fish for cod around Newfoundland (claimed by the Corte Real brothers in 1500). The sailors salted and sun-dried their catch to make it last the long journey home, thereby discovering the perfect convenience food both for their compatriot seafaring explorers (who were sailing as far as India at the time) and for their fish-loving but fridgeless folk back home. Indeed, so popular did bacalhau become throughout Portugal that it soon became known as *fiel amigo*, the faithful friend.

Most of today's bacalhau is made from cod imported from Norway and is fairly expensive, but as bacalhau more than doubles in volume after soaking, keeps well and is extremely nourishing, it's still widely popular. If you join the fan club, you're in for a treat – there's said to be a different bacalhau recipe for every day of the year.

It takes a few centuries to get addicted: try the *bacalhau à Gomes de Sá*, a tastier version than most of the 364 other recipes. This one features flaked cod baked with potatoes, onions, hard-boiled eggs and black olives.

---

varieties of shellfish, from *amêijoas* (clams) and *camarões* (shrimps) to *lagostins* (crayfish) and *chocos* (cuttlefish).

The Portuguese are great meat-eaters but choosing a good *carne* (meat) or *aves* (poultry) dish is often hit-and-miss: strike it lucky and you'll find delicious specialities such as *leitão assado* (roast suckling pig), best around Coimbra; *borrego* (lamb), famous in the Alentejo; and *presunto* (smoked ham), delicious in Chaves and Lamego. One of Portugal's rare culinary coups is the widely available *carne de porco à alentejana*, an inspired combination of pork and clams.

Even the cheapest menus invariably feature *vitela* (veal) and *bife* (beef steak), while *coelho* (rabbit) and *cabrito* (kid) are unexpected delights. Most popular of all poultry dishes is *frango* (chicken), which is widely available grilled on outdoor spits (*frango assado*), and perfect for a takeaway meal.

Strike it unlucky, however, and you'll end up with *tripas* (tripe), most famous in Porto; the stomach-sticking *migas alentejanas*, a bread and fatty pork stodge; the unbelievably meaty *cozido à Portuguesa* stew; or worst of all, a bloody bread-based slop called *papas de sarrabulho*.

Desserts & Pastries

Sobremesas (desserts) are surprisingly disappointing in restaurants, though you're in for a treat if a home-cooked *doce* (sweet pudding) such as a *leite creme* (custard) or *mousse de chocolate* is available. More often than not, however, you'll be offered the same old *pudim* (crème caramel), *arroz doce* (sweet rice) or *gelado* (ice cream), often the expensive Ola or Motta commercial varieties.

A variety of fresh fruit is usually available – grapes, of course, along with citrus fruits, apricots, figs and strawberries in season. There's also cheese – the best and most expensive is *queijo da serra*, a Brie-like cheese from the Serra da Estrela region made from pure ewe's milk.

If you're hankering for some really effective tooth-decaying desserts, head for the nearest pastelaria or *casa de chá* (tea house) where you can find the sweetest concoctions imaginable, made from egg yolks and sugar. Nuns of the 18th century created many of the recipes, bestowing tongue-in-cheek names on the results, such as *papos de anjo* (angel's breasts) or *barriga de freira* (nun's belly). Regional specialities in this department include the egg-based *doces de ovos* from Aveiro, and the cheesecakes (*queijadas*) and almond pastries (*travesseiros*) from Sintra.

Vegetarian Food

Vegetarians can have a miserable time in carnivorous Portugal, where meat and offal are consumed with relish. Servings of vegetables just don't figure in traditional cuisine here. And although many restaurants (especially in tourist resort areas) now include a token few vegetarian dishes on their menus, exclusively vegetarian restaurants are few and far between.

The most easily available but utterly boring choices of unadulterated vegetarian fare are *omeleta* (omelettes) and *batatas fritas* (chips), *salada mista* (mixed salad), and *sandes do queijo* (cheese sandwiches). But there are some delicious vegetable soups on nearly every menu – from *sopa de legumes*, the good old vegetable purée stand-by, to the more uniquely Portuguese *sopa à alentejana*, a bread, garlic and poached egg soup (better than it sounds). Even here, however, something that should be reliably vegetarian (the popular green cabbage caldo verde soup, for instance) can often be tainted with slices of *chouriço* (spicy smoked sausage) or bits of fatty pork, and there's no knowing whether the stock is made with meat.

Among more filling dishes, Portuguese specialities that avoid meat are some of the simple peasant *migas* (bread soup) dishes, notably *migas do Ribatejo* and *migas à moda da Beira Litoral*. They look disgusting (their main ingredient is soaked maize bread, with lots of olive oil and garlic to taste), but fit the bill when you're ravenous. Keep an eye out, too, for *arroz de tomate* (tomato rice) or *favas com azeite* (broad beans with olive oil).

Alternatively, head for the markets and do your own vegetarian shopping: in addition to excellent fruit and vegetable stalls (along with fish and meat), you'll nearly always find freshly baked bread and local cheeses – the soft handmade ewe's milk or goat's milk cheeses are well worth trying, and perfect for a picnic. Markets are best on Saturday, worst on Monday and closed on Sunday. They are open from early morning to about 6 pm.

DRINKS
Nonalcoholic Drinks

Surprisingly, *sumo de fruta* (fresh fruit juice) is quite hard to find, although the local Tri Naranjus bottled varieties are a reasonable substitute. But Portuguese *água mineral* (mineral water) is excellent and widely available, either *com gás* (carbonated) or *sem gás* (still).

Coffee drinkers are in for a high time: it's freshly brewed, even in the humblest rural café. And there are dozens of different varieties (see the boxed text below). But countless cups of coffee during the day can add up. *Uma bica* usually costs about 70$00, but it depends where you drink it: a typical Lisbon pastelaria might charge 90$00 if you drink your coffee standing up by the *balcão* (counter), 120$00 at the *mesa* (table) or as much as 200$00 outside at the *esplanada* (street tables).

Chá (tea) is usually served rather weak, in the style of Catherine of Bragança, who is best remembered not for being the wife of Charles II but for starting England on its long love affair with tea (and toast). You can ask for tea *com leite* (with milk) or *com limão* (lemon), but if you ask for *um chá de limão*, you'll get a glass of hot water with a lemon rind (which can actually be quite refreshing).

Also available in cafés and teahouses is *um chocolate quente*, hot chocolate, or simply *um copo de leite*, a glass of milk.

Alcoholic Drinks

Portuguese people like their tipple: you can pick up anything from a glass of beer or wine to a shot of *aguardente* (firewater) at cafés, restaurants and bars throughout the day (and most of the night). And bartenders aren't stingy with their tots, either: most of them don't even bother with spirit measures. A single brandy here often contains the equivalent of a double in the UK or USA.

Coffee Confusion

You practically need a dictionary to order coffee in Portugal: the following are just some of the variations.

um café/uma bica – a small black espresso; the most popular form. If you want coffee really strong, black and punchy, ask for uma bica, not simply um café since many waiters don't believe foreigners want the real thing.

um café duplo – a double dose of a bica

um carioca – a weaker version of a bica

uma bica cheia – a bica filled to the top of the cup

um abatanado (only really understood in the Lisbon area) – a big black coffee, weaker than a café duplo, stronger than a carioca

um garoto (small size) or *um café com leite* – coffee with milk

um pingado – a bica with just a few drops of milk (make those drops brandy and it's *uma bica com uma pinga*).

um galão – a large glass of hot milk with a dash of coffee, popular at breakfast time (*um galão bem escuro* makes it stronger)

um meia de leite or *um meia de leite de máquina* – equal portions of milk and coffee (in a cup)

If you want (heaven forbid) an instant decaffeinated coffee, it's simply *um descafeinado*.

In most places you pay when you're ready to leave (as in a restaurant) but in some foreign-owned bars there's a pay-as-you-order system (*pronto pagamento*).

Wines Portuguese wine offers great value in all its varieties – red, white, or rosé; mature or young (and semisparkling). You can find decent *vinho da casa* (house wine) everywhere, for as little as 300$00 for a 350mL bottle or jug. And for less than 800m$00 you can buy a bottle to please the most discerning taste buds. In shops and supermarkets wine is available by the bottle, box or 5L container (and you can leave your empty bottles at the ubiquitous bottle banks, or at supermarket checkouts).

Restaurant wine lists differentiate not only between *branco* (white) and *tinto* (red), but also between *maduros* (mature wines) and *vinhos verdes* (semisparkling young wines). As there are over a dozen major regional wines (usually produced by cooperatives), with new ones coming onto the market all the time, you're spoilt for choice.

The most famous of the maduro wines are probably the red Dão table wines, produced in an area just north of the Serra da Estrela. Sweet and velvety, they resemble a Burgundy. Other maduros worth trying are the increasingly popular wines from the Alentejo (the reds from Reguengos are excellent); the reds and whites of Buçaco, near Coimbra; the dry, straw-coloured whites of Bucelas in Estremadura; the table wines of Ribatejo, especially the reds of Torres Vedras and whites from Chamusca; and the expensive but very traditional-style red Colares wines (famous since the 13th century) from near Sintra. The vines here, grown on sand dunes, have never been touched by phylloxera (a fungus that has ravaged many a European wine region over the years).

The vinho verde (literally green wine) of the northern Minho and lower Douro valley area is also very popular: young (hence its name) and slightly sparkling, it has a low alcoholic content and comes in red, white and rosé varieties. The white is undoubtedly the best – try it with shellfish. The best known vinho verde label is Casal Garcia, but well worth the extra escudos are the Alvarinho whites, especially those from Quinta da Brejoeira, the reds from Ponte da Barca, and whites from Ponte de Lima.

Portugal's most internationally famous rosé wine is, of course, the sweet, semi-sparkling Mateus rosé. The Portuguese themselves prefer their bubbles either in vinho verde form or as *espumantes naturais* (sparkling wines). The best of these are from the Bairrada region near Coimbra (try some with the local speciality, roast suckling pig) and the Raposeira wines from Lamego. Sweet dessert wines are rare – the *moscatel* from Setúbal and Favaíos, and the Carcavelos wine from Estremadura offer the fruitiest flavours.

Port *Vinho do Porto* (port), a fortified wine made from grapes grown in the Douro valley, can be red or white; dry, medium or sweet. See the Douro chapter for a special section about port and details of visits to the port-wine lodges in Vila Nova de Gaia. There's also a port-wine institute in Lisbon.

Madeira *Vinho da Madeira* (Madeira) is one of the oldest fortified wines of all: vines were first introduced to this Atlantic Ocean island province of Portugal soon after it was claimed by Portuguese explorers in 1419. The English (who called the sweet version of the wine malmsey) became particularly partial to it (the Duke of Clarence drowned in a butt of the stuff). In addition to the malmsey dessert wine, there's a dry apéritif version called *sercial* and a semisweet *verdelho*.

Spirits Portuguese whisky, brandy and gin are all much cheaper than elsewhere in Europe, although the quality isn't as good. If you fancy something with a more unique taste and punch, try some of the aguardente firewaters: *medronho* (made from arbutus berries; see the boxed text 'Monchique's Moonshine' in the Algarve chapter), *figo*

A Glossary of Wines & Labels

adega	winery or cellar
ano	year
branco	white
bruto	extra dry
colheita	a single-harvest vintage tawny port, aged for at least seven years
doce	sweet
engarrofado por ...	bottled by ...
espumante	sparkling
garrafeira	wines of an outstanding vintage, at least three years old for reds and one year for whites
generoso	fortified wine
LBV	late-bottled vintage; a vintage port aged for four to six years in oak casks before bottling
licoroso	sweet fortified wine
meio seco	medium dry
quinta	a country property or wine estate
região demarcada	officially demarcated wine region
reserva	wine from a year of outstanding quality
ruby port	the cheapest and sweetest port wine
seco	dry
tawny port	a sweet or semisweet port, the best of which has been aged for at least 10 years; less likely than a vintage port to give you a hangover
tinto	red
velho	old
vinho branco/tinto	white/red wine
vinho da casa	house wine
vinho do Porto	port wine
vinho maduro	wine matured for more than a year
vinho regionão	a new classification for superior country wines, similar to the French *vins de pays*
vinho verde	young (literally green) wine, slightly sparkling and available in red, white and rosé varieties
vintage character port	a cheap version of a vintage port, blended and aged for about four years
vintage port	the unblended product of a single harvest of outstanding or rare quality, bottled after two years and then aged in the bottle for up to two decades, sometimes more
white port	usually dry, crisp and fresh; popular as an apéritif

(figs), *ginginha* (cherries) and *licor beirão* (aromatic plants) are all delicious – and safe in small doses. For some rough stuff that tries hard to destroy your throat, ask for a *bagaço* (made from grape husks).

Beer Stronger and cheaper than in the UK and the USA, Portugal's *cerveja* (beer) comes in three main brands of lager: Sagres and Cristal, drunk mainly in the south, and Super Bock, which is more popular in the

Top of the Tipplers

In a 1998 survey of EU drinking habits, Portugal ranked a boozy second in the league table of drinkers, with 11.2L of pure alcohol consumed per person per year. Top was Luxembourg, with 11.8L.

north. There's little difference between them. If you take your empty bottles back to a supermarket checkout you'll get a refund on them.

You can order beer in bars by the bottle or on draught – *um imperial* or *um fino* refers to a 300mL glass of draught and costs about 200$00 (equivalent to about 150$00 for a half-pint). Half a litre is called *uma caneca* and 1L, *um girafe*. Bars in tourist resorts often have popular foreign brews such as bitter or stout, pricey at 400$00 for 400mL.

ENTERTAINMENT

Perhaps the commonest forms of entertainment in all of Portugal are its many municipal and regional festivals and fairs. Many are centred on local saints' days and their associated religious processions, or are part of a romaria, or pilgrimage. Whole towns or regions may down tools for several days and revel in music, dance, fireworks, colourful parades, handicrafts fairs or vast animal markets. For more about these events, see the list under Public Holidays & Special Events earlier in this chapter.

Another venerable – and uniquely Portuguese – tradition, is *fado*, the haunting, melancholy Portuguese equivalent of the blues (see Music under Arts in the Facts about Portugal chapter for more on fado). Tourists get stylised versions in the *casas de fado* (fado houses) of Lisbon's Bairro Alto district, and shell out minimum charges of 2000$00 to 3000$00 for it. Locals will tell you where to find the real thing, in little cafés that may stay open most of the night.

The two cities with the most distinctive fado traditions and styles are Lisbon (fado's home) and Coimbra.

More conventional bars, pubs and clubs abound in Lisbon, Porto and the Algarve, and smaller towns often have a disco or two on the outskirts. Many of them go right through until morning.

A number of Portugal's towns sponsor summer cultural programmes, especially music (classical, rock, jazz or folk) and dance (traditional, classical or modern). Probably the best known international music festival is Sintra's in July and August; nearby Cascais and Estoril also host a jazz festival and classical music festival in July. Others of interest include an international festival of Celtic music in Porto in March; and an international film festival in Figueira da Foz in early September. Ask at local turismos about what's coming up, or for the city's monthly or seasonal what's-on bulletin, or check out the entertainment listings in the newspapers.

European and American films (most of them subtitled, not dubbed) seem to edge out local competition in the country's cinemas. Tickets are fairly cheap, typically 700$00 to 800$00; prices are often further reduced one day a week (usually Monday) in an effort to lure audiences away from their videos.

SPECTATOR SPORTS
Football

Football (soccer) is a national obsession, and life' – male life, at any rate, and quite possibly the national economy – comes to a near standstill when there's a big match on, with TVs in bars and restaurants showing nothing else. The season lasts from September through May, and almost every village and town finds enough players to field a team. The three major national teams are FC Porto in Porto (leading champions in the 1998 season), and Benfica (recently plagued by financial scandal) and Sporting in Lisbon. Tickets are fairly cheap; check the papers or ask at local turismos about upcoming matches and venues.

Bullfighting

Bullfighting is still popular in Portugal, despite opposition from local and international welfare organisations. The season runs from March (late April in some places) to October.

A typical *tourada* (bullfight) starts with a huge bull charging into the ring towards a *cavaleiro*, a mounted horseman dressed in elaborate 18th century-style costume and plumed tricorn hat (so far, there's only one female *cavaleira* in Portugal, Marta Manuela). The 500kg bull has his horns capped in metal balls or leather but, despite the handicap, is still a formidable adversary. The cavaleiro sizes him up as his backup team of *peões de brega* (footmen) distract and provoke the bull with capes. Then, with incredible horsemanship, he gallops within inches of the bull's horns and plants a number of short, barbed *bandarilha* spears into the bull's neck.

The next phase of the fight, the *pega*, features a team of eight young, volunteer *forcados* dressed in breeches, white stockings and short jackets, who face the weakened bull barehanded, in a single line. The leader swaggers towards the bull from across the ring, provoking it to charge. Bearing the brunt of the attack, he throws himself onto the animal's head and grabs the horns while his mates rush in behind him to try to immobilise the beast, often being tossed in all directions in the process. Their success marks the end of the contest and the bull is led out of the pen among a herd of steers. Though the rules for Portuguese bullfighting prohibit a public kill, the hapless animal is usually dispatched in private afterwards.

Another style of performance (often the final contest in a day-long tourada) is similar to the Spanish version, with a *toureiro* (on foot) challenging the bull – its horns uncapped – with cape and bandarilhas. Unlike in Spain, however, there's no *picador* on horseback to weaken the bull with lances. It's man against beast. And unlike in Spain, the kill is symbolic only, with a short bandarilha feigning the thrust of a sword.

A History of Bullfighting

The first recorded mention of bullfighting in Portugal is from the Roman historian Strabo, who wrote in the 1st century that 'the peoples inhabiting the coastal regions of the Peninsula like to challenge isolated bulls, which in Hispania are very wild'.

Developing their hunting into a sport, the Celtiberian people used to hold games in Baetica (later known as Andalusia), where wild animals were killed with axes or lances. Combats with bulls were common, too, in ancient Crete, Thessaly and imperial Rome: several amphitheatres were rebuilt for bullfights in the dying days of the Roman Empire.

Portugal's modern version of the bullfight was originally conceived in the 12th century, when the *tourada* was developed as a method to maintain military fitness and prepare kings and nobles for battle on horseback. By the 16th century, the increasing popularity of the bloody spectacle aroused such indignation in the Vatican that Pope Pius V decreed in 1567 that 'exhibitions of tortured beasts or bulls are contrary to Christian duty and piety'. The penalty for violating this decree (which has never been repealed) is excommunication.

Only the gory death of a Portuguese nobleman, Count dos Arcos, in 1799, resulted in a less blatantly cruel version of the tourada in Portugal: from then on, the bull's horns were padded to make it less dangerous and rules amended so that public slaughter of the bulls was prohibited. Today's *cavaleiro* still wears a black handkerchief around his neck in remembrance of the count.

The most traditional bullfights are take place in the bull-breeding Ribatejo province, especially in Santarém during the agricultural fair in June and in Vila Franca de Xira during the town's July and October festivals (which even feature bull runs through the streets). The touradas held in the Algarve and in Lisbon are more tourist oriented.

The fights usually last at least two hours. Tickets (available from agents in advance or from outside the *praça de touros*, or bullring) range from 2500$00 to 4000$00, depending on where you sit: the cheapest are *sol* seats (in the sun). The *sol e sombra* seats provide some shade as the sun moves around, while the most expensive tickets are for the always shady *sombra* seats.

See Treatment of Animals under Society & Conduct in the Facts about Portugal chapter for details on the unpleasant side of the sport.

Athletics

Portugal shines in track and field athletics, especially long-distance events. In 1984 Carlos Lopes won the Olympic gold medal in the men's marathon (and his time still stands as an Olympic 'best'). Rosa Mota won the marathon in the 1982, 1986 and 1990 European Championships and took gold in the 1988 Olympics women's marathon. Manuela Machado followed her success by winning the same race in the 1994 and 1988 Europeans and 1996 Olympics, while Fernanda Ribeiro nosed out China's wunderkind, Wang Junxia, to win the women's 10,000m race in the 1996 Olympics.

SHOPPING

Shopping can be a real pleasure in Portugal: artisans still take pride in producing some fantastic handicrafts, prices are reasonable and there's a great variety of tempting goodies. Particularly good buys are, of course, port (with plenty of choice at cheap prices, at least for the lesser wines); rural handicrafts and pottery; and unique deluxe items such as Arraiolos carpets. For infor-

mation about tax-free shopping see Taxes & Refunds under Money earlier in this chapter.

Gourmet Products

Port wine, Portugal's best known export, is readily available to visitors. To pick up some at the source, visit one or two of the port-wine lodges in Vila Nova de Gaia, across the river from Porto. Or simply pop into any supermarket, where you'll usually find a reasonable selection at modest prices. Lisbon, Porto and other major cities have specialist wine and port shops, too, if you're after something fancier. Other quality foodstuffs are olive oil, numerous varieties of fresh olives, and a mouth-watering range of honeys from all over the country.

Linen, Cotton & Lace

Hand-embroidered linen and cotton, traditional costumes (in children's sizes, too) and lacework (a speciality of coastal fishing towns) are sold at modest prices all over the country, but especially in seaside resorts such as Nazaré and Viana do Castelo. Castelo Branco (in the Beiras) is renowned for embroidered bed covers. Embroidered tablecloths are a common item at the Gypsy markets that materialise regularly on the outskirts of most Portuguese towns – but bargain hard. The home of Portuguese-style bobbin lace is Vila do Conde, north of Porto, though quality work also comes from the eastern Algarve and the seaside town of Peniche, north of Lisbon.

Azulejos & Ceramics

Azulejo souvenirs are tempting buys, especially in Lisbon (which has several azulejo showrooms and a shop at the Museu dos Azulejos), and in Sintra and the Algarve. Souvenir tiles can be remarkably cheap, though made-to-order items get pricey.

Another uniquely Portuguese purchase is ceramics, and not just the trademark Barcelos cockerel that appears ad nauseam in every gift shop in the country. Among quality pottery, both practical and decorative, are the famous black pots of

Shop Names

Many small shops appear to have no name, only a sign indicating their generic speciality, so it's worth learning a few terms. Some examples are: *artesanato* (handicrafts shop), *livraria* (bookshop), *papelaria* (stationery shop), *sapateria* (shoe shop) and *joalheria* (jewellery shop). A *discoteca* can be either a music shop or a discotheque!

Trás-os-Montes, the unique cabbage-leaf crockery of Caldas da Rainha (Estremadura), the earthenware jugs of Estremoz (Alentejo), and some interesting work from Barcelos itself. São Pedro do Corval, near Monsaraz in the Alentejo, is one of Portugal's largest pottery centres.

Rugs, Jewellery & Leather

Those with more money to spend should consider the famous hand-stitched carpets of Arraiolos (now made under contract in many parts of the country), earlier versions of which graced manor houses and castles for centuries. Traditional woollen blankets are a speciality of the Alentejo.

Another good-value but rather expensive purchase is the gold and silver filigree jewellery of the Porto area. Leather goods, especially shoes and bags, are also good value; Porto is full of leather and shoe shops, though the leatherworkers of Loulé and Almodôvar in the Algarve count themselves among the best.

Other Handicrafts

Within range for those on a budget is rush, palm or wicker basketwork, available throughout the country and best tracked down in the ubiquitous municipal markets.

Trás-os-Montes in general is a good place for woven goods and tapestries, and Trás-os-Montes, Beira Alta and Beira Beixa are good for wrought-iron work. Around Nazaré (Estremadura) look for inexpensive, woollen pullovers.

The Alentejo is known for its simple hand-painted wooden furniture; there's a handicrafts centre for this and other crafts at Reguengos de Monsaraz. Cheap souvenirs of native cork are also plentiful.

An eye-catching item for adults or children alike are the beautifully dressed porcelain dolls found everywhere in gift shops, and often considered collector's items in Portugal.

Markets

Every town in Portugal has a *mercado municipal* (municipal market), usually open daily, selling fruit and vegetables, other foods such as freshly baked bread, fresh meat and fish, cakes and local cheeses, and sometimes local handicrafts (such as wicker baskets or pottery). Most sizeable towns also have regular weekly farmers' markets, and many have big, usually monthly, Gypsy markets (often fairly touristy), featuring itinerant hawkers of everything from souvenirs to cheap clothes to kitchenware. For listings check out the what's-on pages of the English-language papers or the turismo's monthly events pamphlet.

Artesanatos

Finally, even if you won't be travelling widely, bear in mind that certain quality *artesanatos* (handicrafts shops), such as Santos Ofícios in Lisbon and Arte Facto in Porto, showcase quality work from all around the country. For more on the crafts of the Algarve and Alentejo in particular, see the excellent regional guide by John & Madge Measures, *Southern Portugal: Its People, Traditions & Wildlife*.

Getting There & Away

AIR

Fares quoted in this section are approximate return fares during peak air-travel season, based on advertised rates at the time of writing. None of them constitutes a recommendation for any airline.

Fares tend to be 40 to 50% lower outside peak season. In North America and Europe, peak season is roughly from June to mid-September plus Christmas. Shoulder season is April to May and mid-September to October. In Australia and New Zealand, peak season is roughly December to January.

Airports & Airlines

Portugal has international airports at Lisbon, Porto and Faro. Lisbon has by far the most scheduled flights, while Faro gets dozens of charters from all over Europe. International carriers with scheduled services to/from all three airports include TAP Air Portugal (the country's recently privatised flagship carrier), PGA Portugália Airlines (Portugal's main domestic airline, which also has some European connections), British Airways (BA), Lufthansa Airlines, Luxair and Air Liberté.

Other airlines that serve Lisbon and Porto only are Alitalia, Iberia, KLM-Royal Dutch Airlines, Sabena, Swissair and Varig. Airlines that fly to/from Lisbon only are Aeroflot, Air France, Delta Air Lines, Lauda Air, Royal Air Maroc, Scandinavian Airlines (SAS), Tunis Air and TWA.

Buying Tickets

World aviation has never been so competitive, making air travel better value than ever. But you have to research the options carefully to make sure you get the best deal. The Internet is a useful resource for checking air fares: many travel agencies and airlines have a Web page.

Some airlines now sell discounted tickets direct to the customer, and it's worth contacting airlines anyway for information on routes and timetables. Sometimes, there is nothing to be gained by going direct to the airline – discounted tickets are released to selected travel agents and specialist discount agencies, and these are often the cheapest deals going.

The exception to this rule is the new breed of 'no-frills' airlines, which mostly sell direct. At the time of writing only Go and AB Airlines of Britain had established links to Lisbon, but Portugal is sure to be on the wish-lists of some of the other leading players (easyJet of Britain, Ryanair of Ireland and Virgin Express of Belgium).

Unlike the 'full-service' airlines, the no-frills carriers often make one-way tickets available at half the return fare – meaning that it is easy to stitch together an open jaw itinerary where you fly in to one city and out of another. You may also be able to arrange an open jaw ticket through a regular airline, particularly if you are flying in from outside Europe.

Round-the-World (RTW) tickets are another possibility and are comparable in price to an ordinary return long-haul flight. Some airlines also offer student/youth fares – a good travel agent should be able to provide information on such deals. Ask about Apex (advance purchase excursion) tickets too – they are often much cheaper. For US and Canadian citizens there is the EurAir Pass, with which you can fly between designated cities in Europe with participating airlines for US$90 per flight. Check out their Web site (www.eurairpass .com) for more details.

You may find the cheapest flights are advertised by obscure agencies. Most such firms are honest and solvent, but there are some rogue fly-by-night outfits around. Paying by credit card generally offers protection since most card issuers will provide refunds if you don't get what you paid for. However, if you feel suspicious about a firm, it's best to steer clear, or only pay a deposit before you get your ticket, then ring the airline to confirm that you are actually booked on the flight before paying the balance. Established outfits, such as those mentioned in this book, offer more security and are almost as competitive as you can get.

Ticketless travel, where your reservation details are contained within an airline computer, is becoming more common. On simple return trips the absence of a ticket can be a benefit, since it is one less thing to worry about. But if you are planning a complicated itinerary which you may wish to amend en route, there is no substitute for the good old paper version.

Travellers with Special Needs

If you have special requirements – you're in a wheelchair, taking the baby, terrified of flying, vegetarian – let the airline know when you book. Restate your needs when you reconfirm, and again when you check in at the airport. With advance warning most international airports can provide escorts from check-in to the plane, and most have ramps, lifts, wheelchair-accessible toilets and telephones. Aircraft toilets, on the other hand, present problems for wheelchair users, who should discuss this early on with the airline and/or their doctor.

Guide dogs for the blind will often have to travel in a specially pressurised baggage compartment with other animals, away from their owner, though smaller guide dogs may be admitted to the cabin. They are subject to the same stiff quarantine laws as any other animal entering or returning to rabies-free countries, such as Britain or Australia.

Children under two years travel for 10% of the standard fare (or free, on some airlines), as long as they don't occupy a seat. They don't get a baggage allowance. Bassinets or 'skycots' – for children weighing up to about 10kg – can usually be provided by the airline if requested in advance. Children between two and 12 years can usually occupy a seat for half to two-thirds the full fare, and do get a baggage allowance. Pushchairs can often be taken as hand luggage.

Departure Tax

Portugal's international departure tax is 2019$00. This is included in the price of any ticket from a scheduled carrier, but payable at check-in in the case of a charter flight.

The UK

Thanks to Britain's long love affair with Portugal (and the UK's cheap fares tradition) there are some excellent deals. Cheap fares appear in the weekend national papers and, in London, in *Time Out*, the *Evening Standard* and *TNT* (a free magazine which is available from bins outside underground stations).

Scheduled flights from London to Lisbon are operated by AB Airlines (☎ 0800 45 88 111) from Gatwick (summer only), BA (☎ 0345 222111) from Gatwick and Heathrow, Go (☎ 0845 60 54321) from Stansted and TAP (☎ 0171-828 0262; from 22 April 2000 ☎ 020-7828 0262) from Heathrow. Fares in 1998 fell as low as UK£60 return, but many of the cheapest flights come with restrictions, such as a minimum stay of one Saturday night and a maximum of one month. Other, less competitive, routes include Heathrow-Faro or Porto (TAP and BA) and Manchester-Porto-Lisbon (Portugália, ☎ 0990 502 048). Charters operate to Faro from all over the UK for fares that are around UK£120 return in the lowest season and upwards of UK£200 at the peak of the summer season.

The UK's best known bargain-ticket agencies are Trailfinders (☎ 0171-937 5400; from 22 April 2000 ☎ 020-7937 5400), Usit Campus (☎ 0171-730 3402; from 22 April 2000 ☎ 020-7730 3402, Web site www.usitcampus.co.uk), Travel CUTS (☎ 0171-637 3161; from 22 April 2000 ☎ 020-7637 3161) and STA Travel (☎ 0171-361 6161; from 22 April 2000 ☎ 020-7361 6161, Web site www.statravel .co.uk). All of these firms have branches

Air Travel Glossary

Baggage Allowance This will be written on your ticket and usually includes one 20kg item to go in the hold, plus one item of hand luggage.

Bucket Shops These are unbonded travel agencies specialising in discounted airline tickets.

Bumped Just because you have a confirmed seat doesn't mean you're going to get on the plane (see Overbooking).

Cancellation Penalties If you have to cancel or change a discounted ticket, there are often heavy penalties involved; insurance can sometimes be taken out against these penalties. Some airlines impose penalties on regular tickets as well, particularly against 'no-show' passengers.

Check-In Airlines ask you to check in a certain time ahead of the flight departure (usually one to two hours on international flights). If you fail to check in on time and the flight is overbooked, the airline can cancel your booking and give your seat to somebody else.

Confirmation Having a ticket written out with the flight and date you want doesn't mean you have a seat until the agent has checked with the airline that your status is 'OK' or confirmed. Meanwhile you could just be 'on request'.

Courier Fares Businesses often need to send urgent documents or freight securely and quickly. Courier companies hire people to accompany the package through customs and, in return, offer a discount ticket which is sometimes a phenomenal bargain. In effect, what the companies do is ship their freight as your luggage on regular commercial flights. This is a legitimate operation, but there are two shortcomings – the short turnaround time of the ticket (usually not longer than a month) and the limitation on your luggage allowance. You may have to surrender all your allowance and take only carry-on luggage.

Full Fares Airlines traditionally offer 1st class (coded F), business class (coded J) and economy class (coded Y) tickets. These days there are so many promotional and discounted fares available that few passengers pay full economy fare.

ITX An ITX, or 'independent inclusive tour excursion', is often available on tickets to popular holiday destinations. Officially it's a package deal combined with hotel accommodation, but many agents will sell you one of these for the flight only and give you phoney hotel vouchers in the unlikely event that you're challenged at the airport.

Lost Tickets If you lose your airline ticket an airline will usually treat it like a travellers cheque and, after inquiries, issue you with another one. Legally, however, an airline is entitled to treat it like cash and if you lose it then it's gone forever. Take good care of your tickets.

MCO An MCO, or 'miscellaneous charge order', is a voucher that looks like an airline ticket but carries no destination or date. It can be exchanged through any International Association of Travel Agents (IATA) airline for a ticket on a specific flight. It's a useful alternative to an onward ticket in those countries that demand one, and is more flexible than an ordinary ticket if you're unsure of your route.

No-Shows No-shows are passengers who fail to show up for their flight. Full-fare passengers who fail to turn up are sometimes entitled to travel on a later flight. The rest are penalised (see Cancellation Penalties).

On Request This is an unconfirmed booking for a flight.

Air Travel Glossary

Onward Tickets An entry requirement for many countries is that you have a ticket out of the country. If you're unsure of your next move, the easiest solution is to buy the cheapest onward ticket to a neighbouring country or a ticket from a reliable airline which can later be refunded if you do not use it. Alternatively, you can get an MCO (see facing page).

Open Jaw Tickets These are return tickets where you fly out to one place but return from another. If available, this can save you backtracking to your arrival point.

Overbooking Airlines hate to fly empty seats and since every flight has some passengers who fail to show up, airlines often book more passengers than they have seats. Usually excess passengers make up for the no-shows, but occasionally somebody gets bumped. Guess who it is most likely to be? The passengers who check in late.

Point-to-Point Tickets These are discount tickets that can be bought on some routes in return for passengers waiving their rights to a stopover.

Promotional Fares These are officially discounted fares, available from travel agencies or direct from the airline.

Reconfirmation At least 72 hours prior to departure time of an onward or return flight, you must contact the airline and 'reconfirm' that you intend to be on the flight. If you don't do this the airline can delete your name from the passenger list and you could lose your seat.

Restrictions Discounted tickets often have various restrictions on them – such as needing to be paid for in advance and incurring a penalty to be altered. Others are restrictions on the minimum and maximum period you must be away, such as a minimum of 14 days or a maximum of one year.

Round-the-World Tickets RTW tickets give you a limited period (usually a year) in which to circumnavigate the globe. You can go anywhere the carrying airlines go, as long as you don't backtrack. The number of stopovers or total number of separate flights is decided before you set off and they usually cost a bit more than a basic return flight.

Stand-by This is a discounted ticket where you only fly if there is a seat free at the last moment. Stand-by fares are usually available only on domestic routes.

Transferred Tickets Airline tickets cannot be transferred from one person to another. Travellers sometimes try to sell the return half of their ticket, but officials can ask you to prove that you are the person named on the ticket. This is less likely to happen on domestic flights, but on an international flight tickets are compared with passports.

Travel Agencies Travel agencies vary widely and you should choose one that suits your needs. Some simply handle tours, while full-services agencies handle everything from tours and tickets to car rental and hotel bookings. If all you want is a ticket at the lowest possible price, then go to an agency specialising in discounted tickets.

Travel Periods Ticket prices vary with the time of year. There is a low (off-peak) season and a high (peak) season, and often a low-shoulder season and a high-shoulder season as well. Usually the fare depends on your outward flight – if you depart in the high season and return in the low season, you pay the high-season fare.

spread throughout London and the UK, and Campus Travel also has outlets in many Hostelling International (HI) shops.

Among agencies specialising in travel to Portugal are Abreu (☎ 0171-229 9905; from 22 April 2000 ☎ 020-7229 9905) and Destination Portugal (☎ 01993-773269, email info@witney.itsnet.co.uk). ICEP, the Portuguese national tourist office (☎ 0171-494 1441, fax 494 1868; from 22 April 2000 ☎ 020-7494 1441, fax 7494 1868), has an exhaustive list of specialist UK agencies, *Tour Operators' Guide: Portugal*. SAGA Flights Service (☎ 01303-711700, Web site www.saga.co.uk) often has good deals for travellers over age 50.

Continental Europe

France Since France has a huge Portuguese immigrant population, there are frequent flights at reasonable prices to/from Paris. During the summer there are nonstop flights from Paris to Lisbon including six a day by TAP (☎ 01 44 86 89 89) – four from Orly and two from Charles de Gaulle – and four a day by Air France (☎ 01 44 08 24 24, reservations ☎ 01 44 08 22 22, Minitel 3615 AF) from Charles de Gaulle. There are indirect flights (via Toulouse, Bordeaux, Lyon or Madrid) with Air France, TAP, Air Liberté and Iberia. Portugália flies daily from Lyon and Nice to Lisbon.

From Orly, TAP goes three times a day to Porto and frequently to Faro. Portugália flies daily from Lyon and Nice to Porto (via Lisbon) and frequently from Nice to Faro (via Lisbon).

Expect to pay at least 1800FF for a Paris-Lisbon adult fare in high season. TAP and Air France offer youth/student prices.

Paris travel agencies specialising in bargain flights include Go Voyages (☎ 01 49 23 26 86, Minitel 3615 GO) and Council Travel (☎ 01 44 55 55 44). STA Travel's Paris agent is Voyages Wasteels (☎ 01 43 25 58 35).

Germany There are plenty of summer flights to/from Germany. The major scheduled carriers are Lufthansa, TAP, Portugália and Iberia, and the major corridors are Frankfurt-Lisbon and Frankfurt-Porto, with several daily flights on each. There are other daily connections to Lisbon from Berlin, Dresden, Hamburg and Munich, and to Porto from Dresden and Nuremburg. At least three flights a week go direct to Faro from Frankfurt, Düsseldorf, Hamburg, Munich and Stuttgart. Other cities with connections to Portugal are Cologne and Hanover.

At the time of research, STA Travel (☎ 069-97 90 71 13) at Leipziger Str 17a, Frankfurt/Main was offering a summer return fare of DM534 (DM494 youth fare) plus taxes, to Lisbon with Swissair. STA has 26 other branches throughout Germany. A similar agency in Berlin is SRS Studenten Reise Service (☎ 030-283 30 94).

Other European Cities KLM flies direct from Amsterdam to both Lisbon and Porto daily, and TAP flies daily to Lisbon and four times a week to Porto. From Brussels, TAP and Sabena have at least two direct flights a day to Lisbon; Portugália goes daily except Saturday to Faro, Lisbon and Porto. From Madrid, TAP goes to Lisbon four to six times a day; Portugália and Iberia go to both Lisbon and Porto several times a day. Portugália also has flights from Barcelona to Faro, Lisbon and Porto almost daily.

Other European destinations served by Portugália include Turin and Milan, with almost daily connections to Lisbon and Porto. TAP has a daily Zürich to Lisbon connection.

In Amsterdam, try the official student travel agency, NBBS Reizen (☎ 020-620 50 71) for up-to-date information.

The USA & Canada

The *Los Angeles Times*, *New York Times*, *San Francisco Examiner*, *Chicago Tribune*, Toronto *Globe & Mail* and *Vancouver Sun* have big weekly travel sections with lots of ads and information.

The main links are from New York to Lisbon: from JFK airport with TAP (a code-share flight with Delta Air Lines) and TWA, and from Newark with Continental Airlines. There is also a handy twice-weekly link from Boston via the Azores to Lisbon with TAP. The cheapest return fares on these direct services are around US$800 in high season. You can save money by travelling off-peak or using an airline from a third country such as Air France via Paris, BA via London or Iberia via Madrid. These are also good options from other points in the USA.

There are currently no direct flights between Canada and Portugal, so travelling via another European city is usually the easiest option. From Montreal or Toronto, the lowest high-season fare is likely to be around C$1200; from Calgary, Edmonton or Vancouver, it's around C$1500.

Two reliable sources of cheap tickets in the USA are STA Travel (toll-free ☎ 800 777 0112, Web site www.sta-travel.com) and Council Travel (toll-free ☎ 800 226 8624, Web site www.counciltravel.com); both of them have offices throughout the country. Canada's best bargain-ticket agency is Travel CUTS (toll-free ☎ 888 838 2887, Web site www.travelcuts.com) with some 50 offices.

Travellers over 50 years old might like to check out SAGA Holidays (toll-free ☎ 800 343 0273) which sometimes offers bargain holiday fares.

Australia & New Zealand

Check the travel agencies' ads in the Yellow Pages, and the Saturday travel sections of the *Sydney Morning Herald* and the Melbourne *Age*.

There are no direct flights from Australasia to Portugal, but there are dozens of indirect routes via third countries. At the time of research Alitalia was offering return flights from Melbourne/Sydney to Lisbon, via Rome, for around A$2000 (A$1900 youth fare).

Your best first step from Australasia might be a bargain flight to London for around A$1800 from Sydney/Melbourne or NZ$2500 from Auckland (NZ$2300 youth

fare) and then a charter flight from London to Faro. Another possibility is a RTW ticket for around A$2200. The fastest, though not the cheapest, route is the one-stop hop via Bangkok.

STA Travel and Flight Centres International are major dealers in cheap air fares. STA (www.statravel.com.au) has offices all over Australia and New Zealand including Melbourne (☎ 03-9349 2411), Sydney (☎ 02-9212 1255, Fast Fare Hotline ☎ 1300 360 960, fax 9281 4183) and Auckland (☎ 09-309 9723, Fast Fare Hotline ☎ 09-366 6673, fax 303 9572). Flight Centres (☎ 131 600, Web site www.flightcentre.com.au) has offices all over Australia and New Zealand, including at 19 Bourke St, Melbourne (☎ 03-9650 2899, fax 9650 3751) and 205-225 Queen St, Auckland (☎ 09-309 6171).

Africa

The former Portuguese colonies of Angola and Mozambique have good links with Lisbon, and TAP also flies from South Africa. There are also good links from Morocco, but from most other points in Africa it will be necessary to change planes at another European point. Sample high-season return fares include: around US$1500 from Luanda, US$1000 from Maputo, US$700 from Johannesburg and US$270 from Casablanca.

South America

Historically, Lisbon was an important stop on the air route between South America and Europe; indeed, the first-ever flight between Heathrow and South America stopped there. Longer-range aircraft mean its importance has declined somewhat, but TAP Air Portugal has a good network to the leading South American cities – Spanish-speaking countries as well as points in Brazil. Other carriers serving Lisbon include Cubana of Cuba and Varig of Brazil.

Sample high-season return fares include: around US$1000 from Rio de Janeiro and US$1300 from Caracas.

LAND
Border Crossings

All overland connections to Portugal go through Spain, of course. The two main rail crossings are at Vilar Formoso (the Paris to Lisbon line) and Marvão-Beirã (the Madrid to Lisbon line). Two other important crossings are at Valença do Minho (Vigo in Spain to Porto) and Caia (Badajoz in Spain to Lisbon).

There are dozens of highway crossings, with fast, high-capacity roads on both sides. For further details see under Car & Motorcycle later in this section. Land border controls between the two countries have virtually disappeared.

Bus

Eurolines With the increase in availability of low air fares, buses no longer offer the cheapest public transport around Europe. But if you can't find a cheap flight or prefer to stay on the ground, buses are a good deal. The easiest way to book tickets is through Eurolines, a consortium of coach operators with offices all over Europe. A coach trip from the UK to Portugal can be pretty tedious, though Eurolines' coaches are fairly comfortable, with reclining seats, on-board toilets, and sometimes air-con. They stop frequently for meals, though you'll save a bit by packing your own munchies.

Discounts depend on the route, but children from four to 12 years typically get 30 to 40% off, while those aged under 26 and seniors get a 10 to 20% discount on some routes. Fares given here are adult fares. It's a good idea to book at least several days ahead in summer.

Among some 200 Eurolines offices in Europe are the following:

Amsterdam
 Eurolines (☎ 020-560 8787, fax 560 8766)
 Rokin 10, and Amstel Bus Station,
 Julianaplein 5
Frankfurt
 Deutsche Touring/Eurolines
 (☎ 069-790 353, fax 706 059,
 Web site www.deutsche-touring.com)
 Am Romerhof 17

London
 Eurolines (bookings ☎ 0990-143 219,
 information ☎ 0171-730 8235, fax 730 8721;
 from 22 April 2000 ☎ 020-7730 8235,
 fax 7730 8721,
 Web site www.eurolines.co.uk/euro1.htm)
 52 Grosvenor Gardens, London SW1
Madrid
 SAIA (☎ 01-528 11 05, fax 468 38 13,
 Web site www.travelcom.es/juliavia)
 Estación Sur de Autobuses
Paris
 Eurolines (☎ 01 49 72 51 51, fax 01 49 72 51
 61, Minitel 3615 EUROLINES,
 Web site www.eurolines.fr)
 Gare Routière Internationale de Paris,
 28 Ave du Général de Gaulle, Bagnolet

In the USA, the Eurolines agent is British Travel International (toll-free ☎ 800 327 6097). Portugal's main Eurolines affiliates are Internorte, Intercentro and EVA/Intersul which, as the names suggest, are based in northern, central and southern Portugal:

Internorte
 (☎ 02-609 32 20, fax 609 95 70)
 Praça da Galiza 96, Porto
Intercentro
 (☎ 01-357 17 45, fax 357 00 39)
 Rua Actor Taborda 55, Lisbon
EVA/Intersul
 (☎ 089-80 33 23)
 Avenida da República, Faro

Eurolines Pass For real coach junkies, the Eurolines Pass gives you unlimited travel between 30 major European cities for 30 days (high season prices of UK£229/199 for adults/youth and seniors) or 60 days (UK£279/249), although Madrid is currently the closest city to Portugal covered by the pass.

Busabout This UK-based budget alternative to Eurolines is aimed at younger travellers, but has no upper age limit. It runs coaches along three interlocking European circuits: the North Zone runs from Paris through Brussels and Amsterdam to Berlin and Prague. It continues to Munich, where it links up with the South Zone (covering Italy, southern France, parts of

Spain, and Lisbon and Faro) and, in winter, the Snow Zone around the Alps. Pick-up points are usually convenient for hostels and camping grounds.

It costs UK£109 (UK£99 for youth and student card holders) for a combined North and South Zone pass for two weeks, and UK£139/159 for the Snow Zone. The add-on from London to Paris is UK£30 return. You can buy Busabout tickets directly from the company (☎ 0181-784 2816; from 22 April 2000 ☎ 020-8784 2816; Web site www.busabout.com) or from suppliers such as Usit Campus and STA Travel. The Euro-bus company, which used to offer a similar service, went out of business in 1998.

ALSA ALSA is an independent Spanish company which has a weekly connection between London and Porto (see under The UK in this section). In the UK it's called SSS International (☎ 0171-233 5727, fax 233 5737; from 22 April 2000 ☎ 020-7233 5727, fax 7233 5737) and is based at 5 Gillingham St, London SW1V 1HN. ALSA's Porto office is the TIAC travel agency (☎ 02-208 85 78, fax 208 86 05), Rua do Campinho 30.

The UK Intercentro/Eurolines operates a year-round London-Lisbon service (via Coimbra) departing from Victoria coach station three times a week. The company also runs coaches to Faro and Lagos twice a week, with an additional Sunday service in summer. All involve a 7½ hour stopover and change of coach in Paris. The adult one-way/return fare to any of these destinations is UK£75/139. London-Lisbon takes about 38 hours.

The ALSA bus comany runs a London-Porto service (via Vilar Formoso, Guarda, Viseu and other points), departing once a week during certain periods only (early April, late June to mid-September, Christmas and New Year); a one-way/return ticket costs UK£79/141. You can buy ALSA tickets through the Eurolines office, and ALSA has its own check-in desk at London's Victoria coach station.

Spain Internorte/Eurolines runs coaches between Madrid and Porto (via Salamanca) four times a week for about 5175/9825 ptas one way/return. Its Paris-Porto run (five times a week) also goes via various Spanish cities including Zamora and Valladolid. Ledesma (a Eurolines affiliate in Spain) operates a Salamanca to Porto service via Zamora (2140 ptas).

Intercentro/Eurolines operates services between Madrid and Lisbon three times a week (daily from mid-May through September); the eight hour trip costs 5850/9350 ptas one way/return. From April through September Intercentro has a Friday service from Barcelona to Lisbon for 11,550/21,950 ptas. SAIA/Eurolines has a Salamanca Lisbon service once weekly for 4000/7200 ptas.

From April through November, Intersul/Eurolines runs from Malaga (via Seville) to Lisbon four times a week for 8150 ptas.

The Algarve coach line EVA runs express buses twice a day between Seville and Faro (via Vila Real de Santo António); the four hour trip costs about 2460 ptas.

Other European Cities Eurolines France offers a range of Portugal connections, including Paris to Lisbon (24 hours) five times a week for 520/910FF and Paris-Braga five times a week for 570/930FF one way/return.

The privately run line IASA (☎ 01 43 53 90 82, fax 01 43 53 49 57 in Paris; ☎ 01-793 64 51, fax 793 62 76 in Lisbon; ☎ 02-208 43 38, fax 31 01 91 in Porto) runs deluxe coaches five times a week, between Paris and Porto (via Braga) for 670FF, and between Paris and Lisbon (via Coimbra) for 695FF. The coaches also stop at various French cities (including Bordeaux) and Spanish cities (including Valladolid).

From Hamburg and Hanover, German Eurolines affiliates run twice a week to Lisbon for DM262/423 one way/return, twice a week to Porto for DM250/403 and once-weekly to Faro and Lagos for DM289/464. Fares from Düsseldorf are slightly lower.

Train

Trains are a popular way to get around Europe – comfortable, frequent and generally on time – and they're a good place to meet other travellers. The cost, though, can be higher than flying, unless you have one of several available rail passes (see the boxed text 'Rail Passes').

Tickets can only be purchased from departure stations or travel agencies. You're unlikely to have problems buying a long-distance ticket as little as a day or two ahead, even in summer. Paris, Amsterdam, Munich and Vienna are major Western European rail hubs.

If you intend to do a lot of rail travel, consider getting a copy of the *Thomas Cook European Timetable*, updated monthly with a complete listing of train schedules, plus information on reservations and supplements. Single issues cost about UK£10 and are available from Thomas Cook Publishing (☎ 01733-505821). Thomas Cook also publishes *Spain & Portugal by Rail* (see Books in the Facts for the Visitor chapter).

International trains are a favourite target for thieves, so always carry your valuables with you, keep your bags in sight (or at least chained to the luggage rack) and make sure your compartment is securely locked at night.

There are two standard long-distance rail journeys into Portugal. One is on the *TGV Atlantique* from Paris to Irún in Spain (where you must change trains), then continuing on the *Rápido Sud-Expresso* across Spain via Vilar Formoso in Portugal to Pampilhosa (where you can change for Porto) and south to Lisbon. The other runs from Paris to Madrid, where you can pick up the *Talgo Lusitânia* via Marvão-Beirã in Portugal to Encontramento (with connections for Porto) and on to Lisbon. Change at Lisbon for the south of Portugal (see Train under Getting There & Away in the Lisbon chapter for details).

The UK From the UK, the cheapest route to Portugal by train is from London to Paris by train-boat-train (using the ferry, hovercraft or Seacat to cross the Channel) and then changing trains (and stations) in Paris for the onward journey to Lisbon via Irún or Madrid. Connex Southeastern (☎ 0870 603 0405, fax 603 0505) handles this London-Paris route and they can sell you tickets for the onward journey to Lisbon, too. A 2nd class return ticket from London to Lisbon costs around UK£195 (UK£178 youth fare), plus a small charge for seat reservation. Tickets are valid for two months and you can break your journey anywhere en route. Another way to save a bit on the ticket cost is to buy two or three separate tickets (London-Paris, Paris-Irún, Irún-Lisbon) from, for example, Rail Europe (see below).

For speed and convenience, the best route is from London Waterloo to Paris via the Channel Tunnel. This can shorten the journey by about six hours (making a London-Lisbon trip possible in about 25 hours), but is more expensive. A 2nd class London-Lisbon fare with no restrictions costs around UK£230/295 one way/return. There are usually reductions for students and seniors.

Channel Tunnel services are run by the Eurostar passenger train service (☎ 0990 186 186; London-Paris) or the Eurotunnel vehicle service (☎ 0990 353 535; Folkestone-Calais). These operators do not sell tickets to Lisbon. Instead, you should consult Rail Europe (☎ 0990 848 848), which is part of French Railways (SNCF) and arranges rail travel between the UK and many European countries. You can also contact Rail Europe in the USA at ☎ 800 4 EURAIL, fax 432 1FAX; and in Canada at ☎ 800 361 RAIL, fax 905-602 4198; or on their Web site www.raileurope.com/. Rail passes (see the boxed text) can be bought from all these offices. See the following France section for equivalent SNCF contact numbers.

Whichever way you get to Paris, the additional cost for a couchette for the overnight Irún-Lisbon section costs around UK£14 or around UK£20 for a sleeper. For travellers under 26 years, special fares are also available through youth travel

Rail Passes

If you're planning a wider European trip, it makes financial sense to get a rail pass. In addition to the following passes, others are available in certain countries only, such as Billets Internationaux de Jeunesse (BIJ) in France. Even with a pass you must still pay for seat and couchette reservations, and supplements on express trains.

Rail Passes for Europeans

Inter-Rail Pass Inter-Rail passes are available to anyone (not just those aged under 26) resident in Europe for six months before starting their travels. The pass divides Europe into zones: for example, zone A is Ireland and the UK; zone E is France, Belgium, the Netherlands and Luxembourg; zone F is Spain, Portugal and Morocco, and so on. A one-zone pass is good for 22 specified, consecutive days of travel; the 2nd class price is UK£229 (UK£159 for those aged under 26). Multizone passes are good for one month's travel and are better value. A two zone pass costs UK£279/209, three zones UK£309/229, and all zones UK£349/259.

Euro Domino Pass The Euro Domino Pass (Freedom Pass in the UK) can be used for a number of consecutive days within a specified month. For Portugal, it costs UK£105 (UK£85 for those aged under 26) for three days, UK$145/115 (five days) or UK£220/185 (10 days).

Rail Europe Senior Card With this card, travellers aged 60 and over can get discounts of up to 30% on international journeys, including to/from Portugal. It's issued by Rail Europe (☎ 0990 848 848 in the UK) and costs UK£5. To be eligible you must have a local senior citizens' railcard. In the UK this is called a Senior Railcard; it costs UK£18 and can be bought at train stations. Alternatively, contact any British rail company (for example, Connex ☎ 0870 603 0405) for an application form.

Rail Passes for Non-Europeans

Eurailpass Eurailpass is the Inter-Rail counterpart for non-European residents. A Eurailpass is valid for unlimited rail travel (1st class for those aged over 26, 2nd class for those under 26) in 17 European countries, including Portugal (but not the UK). It includes most supplements for quality trains (such as ICE and most TGV, Eurocity and InterCity trains). The standard Eurailpass costs from US$538 for 15 days up to US$1512 for three months.

Among many variants is the Eurail Flexipass (Eurail Youth Flexipass for those under 26 years), good for any 10 days (US$654/458) or 15 days (US$862/603) of travel in a two month period; a one month continuous pass costs US$890/623. Further 1st class variants are the Portugal Flexipass (any four days within a 15 day period for US$99) and the Iberic Flexipass (any three days in Portugal and Spain within a two month period for US$198).

Eurailpasses are meant to be purchased before you get to Europe, although you can buy them at a few European locations (including Rail Europe) for about 10% more, provided your passport shows you've been in Europe for less than six months.

Europass This provides unlimited 1st class train travel in five countries (France, Germany, Italy, Spain and Switzerland) with the option of adding Portugal as an 'associate country', for any five days in a two month period. Including Portugal, it costs US$386 (US$309 per adult if two adults are travelling together) or US$261 for those under 26 years. There's also the option of buying an extra 10 days train travel within the two month period.

specialists such as Usit Campus (see the UK section under Air earlier in this chapter).

France The daily train journey from Paris (Gare d'Austerlitz) takes about 20 hours to Lisbon, a little less to Porto. A 2nd class seat to Lisbon is about 850FF (820FF to Porto). Per person prices for a couchette in a six person sleeper are about 900FF, or 985FF in a triple sleeper.

If you book 30 days in advance you can get a 50% reduction (20% reduction with eight days advance booking) for the Paris-Irún section.

In France, SNCF has a nationwide telephone number (☎ 08 36 35 35 35 in French, ☎ 08 36 35 35 39 in English). Or check them out on Minitel (3615 SNCF) or their Web site (web.sncf.fr).

Spain The main rail route is from Madrid to Lisbon via Marvão-Beirã. The nightly journey on the *Talgo Lusitânia* takes 10½ hours; a 2nd class seat is 6700 ptas one way, while a berth in a *turista* (four person) sleeper is 9000 ptas.

Two other well-used routes originating in Spain are Vigo-Porto, which crosses at Valença do Minho (Minho) in Portugal, and Badajoz-Elvas-Lisbon, crossing at Caia (Alentejo) in Portugal. Expresses run on the Vigo to Porto route three times a day.

The daily Paris to Porto/Lisbon train (see the preceding section on France) goes via San Sebastián, Vitória, Burgos, Valladolid and Salamanca in Spain; a 2nd class reserved seat from Salamanca to Porto is about 3770 ptas, a sleeper 6067 ptas.

Connections are tedious on the five hour Badajoz to Lisbon route (two trains a day, both slow regional services, with a change at Entroncamento), but the scenery through the Serra de Marvão is grand.

In the south you can ride the train west from Seville to Huelva; for Algarve destinations you must then change for Ayamonte and take the bus across the border to pick up a Portuguese train at Vila Real de Santo António. From there you can pick up frequent train connections to Faro and Lagos.

Car & Motorcycle

Roads cross the Portugal-Spain border in at least 30 places. The easiest crossings (on the best and biggest roads) are at Valença do Minho, Feces de Abajo (Chaves), Vilar Formoso, Elvas, Vila Verde de Ficalho (Serpa) and Vila Real de Santo António.

Insurance & Documents If you're driving your own car into Portugal, in addition to your passport and driving licence (see under Visas & Documents in the Facts for the Visitor chapter) you must carry vehicle registration (proof of ownership) and insurance documents. If these are in order, you should be able to keep the car in the country for up to six months.

If people other than the registered owner are to drive the car, they'll need written authorisation from the owner. For guidance on how to prepare such a document and validate it, contact your national automobile licensing department or auto club, or the nearest Portuguese consular office.

Motor vehicle insurance with at least third-party cover is compulsory throughout the EU. Your home policy may or may not be extendable to Portugal, and the coverage of some comprehensive policies is automatically reduced to third-party-only outside your home country, unless the insurer is notified. It's a good idea (though not a legal requirement) to get a Green Card from your home insurer before you leave home; this confirms that you have the correct coverage.

If you're stopped by the police you probably won't be allowed to go back to your hotel to fetch these documents. Carry them with you whenever you're driving. If you hire a car, the rental firm will furnish you with registration and insurance papers, plus a rental contract.

Camper Van Travelling in a camper van can be a surprisingly economical option for budget travellers, as it can take care of eating, sleeping and travelling in one convenient package. London is a good place to buy: look in *TNT* magazine and *Loot* newspaper, or go to the van market on Market Rd, London N7 (open daily, but the best days are Saturday and Sunday). Expect to pay at least UK£2000 (US$3200). The most common camper van is the VW based on the 1600cc or 2000cc Transporter, and spare parts are widely available in Europe.

A drawback with camper vans is that they're expensive to buy in spring and hard to sell in autumn. A car and tent might do just as well.

The UK & France The quickest route to Portugal from the UK is by ferry to northern Spain – from Plymouth to Santander with Brittany Ferries (☎ 0990 360 360) or from Portsmouth to Bilbao with P&O Ferries (☎ 0990 980 980).

Both lines make the crossing twice a week in summer, taking about 36 hours. Peak summer fares are about UK£440 for a standard return for car and driver plus about UK£125 per extra adult and cabin accommodation from UK£40 per person. From Santander it's roughly 1000km to Lisbon, 800km to Porto and 1300km to Faro.

An alternative is catching a ferry across the Channel (or using the Eurotunnel vehicle service underneath it) to France and motoring down the coast via Bordeaux, through Spain (via Burgos and Salamanca) into Portugal. From the channel ports of France it's roughly 1900km to Lisbon, 1800km to Porto and 2200km to Faro.

Eurotunnel (☎ 0990 353 535 in UK or ☎ 03 21 00 50 00 in France) runs a 24 hour service (taking 35 minutes) between Folkestone and Calais. The maximum fare in peak season is around UK£300 return for a car and up to nine passengers, but much lower prices are available for off-peak travel.

Among the ferry companies, P&O Stena Line (☎ 0990 707 070) has the most frequent sailings between Dover and Calais, and also covers the Newhaven-Dieppe route (though the future of this link is in some doubt). SeaFrance (☎ 0990 711 711) offers lower fares, and frequencies, on the Dover-Calais route. Fast hovercrafts are run by Hoverspeed (☎ 01304-240241) from Dover to Calais and Folkestone to Boulogne.

One option to reduce driving time for those using this route, or starting in France, is to use Motorail (car transport by rail) for all or part of the trip through France. From Calais to Biarritz (the closest Motorail gets to Portugal) it costs UK£227 for a car and driver. This summer-only service takes 12 hours. For more information, contact Rail Europe's Motorail division in the UK (☎ 0171-203 7000; from 22 April 2000 ☎ 020-7203 7000).

Bicycle

Bicycles can travel by air. You can take yours to pieces and put it in a bag or box but it's much easier to simply wheel it to the check-in desk, where it should be treated as baggage. Check this with the airline well in advance. You may have to fold it down and dismantle it as much as possible so that it takes up less space. Let much (but not all) of the air out of the tyres to prevent them from bursting in the low-pressure baggage hold.

If you're getting to Portugal by train, you can register your bike and send it separately to your destination, or take it with you on the train, usually for an extra charge.

Before you leave home, fill your repair kit with every imaginable spare. You probably won't be able to buy that crucial gizmo for your machine when it breaks down somewhere in the back of beyond. For information on cycling around Portugal, see the Bicycle section in the Getting Around

Any Distinguishing Marks?

As with cars, it's a good idea to pack some sort of document showing you to be the owner of your bicycle, in the unlikely event that the police stop you. Some cyclists also carry photographs and written descriptions of their bicycles, to assist the police if their bike is stolen.

chapter and Activities in the Facts for the Visitor chapter.

SEA

There are no longer any scheduled passenger ferry connections between any of the Algarve ports (including Faro) and North Africa. The closest ports for these trips are in Spain: Tarifa (ferries daily except Sunday to/from Tangier) and Algeciras (ferries daily to/from Tangier; ferries and jetfoils daily to/from Ceuta). There's also a ferry three times a week from Gibraltar to Tangier.

There are, however, a couple of cargo boats with passenger space which stop at Lisbon: the OPDR Tejo (☎ 04503-73675, fax 74437), operated by Kapitan Helmut Hoffman and based in Germany, sails between Rotterdam and the UK via Portugal; and several boats operated by P&O Containers in London (☎ 0171-836 6363, fax 497 0078; after 22 April 2000 ☎ 020-7836 6363, fax 7497 0078) which sail to Australia and New Zealand via Germany and the Netherlands, returning via Portugal. See the earlier Car & Motorcycle section for details on ferry services from the UK to the continent.

For details about car ferries that crisscross the Rio Guadiana between Vila Real de Santo António (Portugal) and Ayamonte (Spain), see under Vila Real de Santo António in the Algarve chapter.

ORGANISED TOURS

Portugal's status as one of Europe's most popular holiday destinations means that there are plenty of flight and accommodation packages on offer – particularly to the Algarve. Outside the peak summer season, this can be the cheapest way to visit Portugal – any half-decent travel agent should be able to find you a cheap deal through massmarket operators such as Airtours and Thomson of Britain, and LTU and Hapag Lloyd of Germany.

For something more specialised, a good listing of some of the UK's specialist tour operators is the free *AITO Directory of Real*

Holidays, an annual index of member companies of the Association of Independent Tour Operators. It's available from AITO (☎ 0181-744 9280, fax 744 3187; from 22 April 2000 ☎ 020-8744 9280, fax 8744 3187).

The London office of ICEP (☎ 0171-494 1441, fax 494 1868; after 22 April 2000 ☎ 020-7494 1441, fax 7494 1868), the Portuguese state tourism organisation, publishes its own UK directory, the *Portugal Tour Operators Guide*.

For domestic tours and activity programmes, see the Organised Tours section in the Getting Around chapter (coach tours) and Activities in the Facts for the Visitor chapter (adventure holidays).

Walking Tours

The UK has several hiking specialists offering escorted small-group packages: the Alternative Travel Group (☎ 01865-513333, fax 310299) runs well-researched walking tours (guided or self-guided, off-the-shelf or tailor-made) with deluxe bed and board.

Other specialist companies are Ramblers Holidays (☎ 01707-331133, fax 333276); Exodus (☎ 0181-675 5550, fax 673 0779; from 22 April 2000 ☎ 020-8675 5550, fax 8673 0779); and Explore Worldwide (☎ 01252-319448, fax 343170; in Australia, ☎ 02-9956 7766, fax 9956 7707).

Gentle walking tours in the Douro valley, with a wine and gourmet-dining angle, are offered by Winetrails (☎ 01306-712111, fax 713504).

For those who are very fit, and good at reading topographic maps, Sherpa Expeditions (☎ 0181-577 2717, fax 572 9788; from 22 April 2000 ☎ 020-8577 2717, fax 8572 9788; email sherpa.sales@dial.pipex .com) offers go-as-you-please self-guided walks in the Parque Nacional da Peneda-Gerês, with route notes, maps and transfer of baggage between hotels provided.

Progressive Travels in the USA (see the following Cycling Tours section) runs one-week guided walking tours of the Algarve, and of the Costa Verde (Minho).

Cycling Tours

In the UK, Rough Tracks (☎ 07000 560 749, email tours@rough-tracks.co.uk, Web site www.rough-tracks.co.uk) offers one week off-road tours to the Minho region, as well as a combination of biking and other sports in the Parque Nacional da Peneda-Gerês. Bike Tours (☎ 01225-310859, fax 480132, email biketours@aol.com) will have you pedalling through the Minho for a week.

In the US, Easy Rider Tours (☎ 978-463 6955, toll-free ☎ 800 488 8332, fax 978-463 6988, email ezrider@shore.net, Web site www.easyridertours.com) has an impressive selection of small-group Portugal itineraries (each with one American and one Portuguese guide), covering the Alentejo, Minho and Costa Azul (around Setúbal).

Guided tours by Blue Marble Travel (☎ 973-326 9533, fax 326 8939) include a four week Trans-Iberian tour and several two week trips around Spain and Portugal.

Progressive Travels (☎ 206-285 1987, toll-free ☎ 800 245 2229, fax 206-285 1988, email progtravinc@earthlink.net) does week-long self-guided Algarve journies, plus guided tours of the Algarve, coastal Algarve/Alentejo, central Portugal, and a Lisbon to Lagos trip for the truly fit.

Toronto-based Butterfield & Robinson (☎ 416-864 1354, toll-free ☎ 800 678 1147, fax 416-864 0541) offers a combined biking and walking tour in the Alentejo and Sintra with deluxe accommodation. Backroads (☎ 510-527 1555, toll-free ☎ 800 462 2848, fax 510-527 1444, email goactive@backroads.com) has a nine day trip from Spain through northern Portugal to Porto. Their Web site is at www.bacroads.com.

Botanical & Bird-Watching Tours

UK-based Naturetrek (☎ 01962-733051, fax 736426, email sales@naturetrek.co.uk), a specialist in bird-watching and botanical tours, runs an eight day excursion around flora and fauna-rich southern Portugal. One-week 'garden holidays' in Estoril and the Lisbon area are offered by the UK senior traveller specialists, SAGA Holidays (☎ 0800 300 500) and Mundi Color Holidays (☎ 0171-828 6021, fax 834 5752; from 22 April 2000 ☎ 020-7828 6021, fax 7834 5752).

Golf, Tennis & Horse-Riding Holidays

Leading UK speicalist operators 3D Golf (☎ 0800 333 323, fax 01292-286424, email sales@3dgolf.co.uk) and Longshot Golf Holidays (☎ 01730-268621, fax 230397, Web site www.longshotgolf.co.uk) offer golfing packages which include car hire and discounted green fees, in the Algarve and on the Estoril coast. See under Carvoeiro in the Algarve chapter for details of a golfing package offered in that resort. The *Golf in Portugal* Web site at www.ccs.net/golf /portugal is a good source of information on golf tours.

Upmarket accommodation with tennis centres, golf courses or horse-riding facilities (including one-week riding holidays in the Algarve) can be arranged by UK-based EHS Travel (☎ 01993-700600, fax 771910, email info@witney.itsnet.co.uk).

Specialist Accommodation

Perhaps all you want is to relax in style in a restored castle, manor house or rural farmhouse (for more on these places, see under Accommmodation in the facts for the Visitor chapter). Several agencies in the UK can make all the arrangements, including Individual Travellers Spain & Portugal (☎ 01798-869485, fax 869343), Kingsland Holidays (☎ 01752-251688, fax 251 699), Unicorn Holidays (☎ 01582-834400, fax 831133) and Vintage Travel (☎ 01954-261431, fax 260 819, email holidays@vintagetravel.co.uk).

For those who want to put their own holidays together, an upmarket Portugal-specialist agency called Witney Travel, operating under the name Destination Portugal (☎ 01993-773269, fax 771910), publishes a series of brochures on top-end hotel, *pousada* and manor house accommodation, and one on air (scheduled and charter) and car-hire prices.

Other Specialist Tours

Among the UK's other specialist operators, Arblaster & Clarke Wine Tours (☎ 01730-893344, fax 892888) and Winetrails (see under Walking Tours earlier in this section) offer wine tours in the Alentejo and the Douro regions. Martin Randall Travel (☎ 0181-742 3355, fax 742 7766; from 22 April 2000 ☎ 020-8742 3355, fax 8742 7766) arranges one-week art and architecture tours.

SAGA Holidays (see Botanical & Bird-Watching Tours earlier in this section) has a one week painting holiday in the Algarve. For details of pottery holidays in northern Portugal see Courses in the Facts for the Visitor chapter.

A reliable Portugal-specialist tour operator in France is Lusitania (☎ 01 44 69 75 12, fax 01 44 69 75 15). Contact ICEP in Paris for a list of other agencies with Portugal programmes.

WARNING

The information in this chapter is particularly vulnerable to change: prices for international travel are volatile, routes are introduced and cancelled, schedules get changed, special deals come and go, and rules and visa requirements are amended. Airlines and governments seem to take a perverse pleasure in making price structures, regulations and restrictions as complicated as possible. Always check directly with the airline or a travel agent to make sure you understand how a fare (and ticket you may buy) works.

You should try to get opinions, quotes and advice from as many airlines and travel agents as possible before you part with any of your hard-earned cash. The details given in this chapter should be regarded as pointers and are not a substitute for your own careful research.

Getting Around

AIR
Domestic Air Services
Flights within mainland Portugal are expensive. For the short distances involved they're hardly worth considering – unless you have an under-26 card, which gets you a 50% discount with PGA Portugália Airlines, the country's main domestic carrier, plus limited discounts from TAP Air Portugal. See Money in the Facts for the Visitor chapter on where to get these cards.

Portugália and TAP both have multiple daily Lisbon-Porto and Lisbon-Faro flights (taking under one hour) year-round. TAP has an evening Lisbon-Faro flight and a morning Faro-Lisbon service connecting with all its international arrivals and departures at Lisbon, plus additional Faro links from April through October. There's almost no way to fly Porto-Faro directly. Portugália has one direct flight from Porto each week, in summer only, but none in the other direction.

Without an under-26 card, a high-season one-way fare (including taxes) with Portugália is about 15,500$00 for Lisbon-Porto and 14,800$00 for Lisbon-Faro. There are no discounts on return tickets.

Domestic Departure Tax
The tax depends on your destination (around 800$00 for a Faro-Lisbon flight, for example) and is invariably included in the ticket price.

BUS
There's a host of small private bus operators, most of them amalgamated into regional companies which together operate a dense network of services. Among the largest are Rede Expressos (Web site www.rede-expressos.pt/index_uk.htm) and the Algarve line, EVA (Web site www.eva-transportes.pt/).

Bus services are of three general types: *expressos* are comfortable, fast, direct

Take the Slow Bus to ...
If you're planning a quick trip anywhere, avoid buses marked *carreiras* (or CR for short). Never mind that *carreiras* means something like 'in a hurry' in Portuguese – these are the slowest of slow local buses, stopping everywhere.

coaches between major cities, *rápidas* are fast regional buses, and *carreiras* stop at every crossroad. The Algarve line EVA also offers a fast deluxe category called *alta qualidade*.

Expressos are generally the best cheap way to get around Portugal (particularly for long trips where the cost per kilometre is lowest), and even in summer you'll have little problem booking a ticket for the next or even the same day. An express coach from Lisbon to Faro takes just under five hours and costs 2200$00 (2550$00 for the luxury four hour EVA express); Lisbon-Porto takes 3½ hours for 2000$00. By contrast the local services, especially up north, can thin out to almost nothing on weekends, especially in summer when school is out.

With an under-26 card you should get a discount of about 20%, at least on long-distance services. Senior travellers can often get up to 50% off.

TRAIN
If you can match your itinerary and pace to a regional service, travelling with Caminhos de Ferro Portugueses (CP; Web site www.cp.pt), the state railway company, is cheaper than going by bus, thanks in part to state subsidies. Trains are generally slower than long-distance buses, though railway lovers consider the relaxed pace an additional plus.

Timetable Gobbledegook

One thing that will drive bus and train travellers up the wall is timetables (*horários*). Schedules change frequently (between school term and summer holidays, between summer and winter), and may be conditional on religious celebrations and holidays. They often differ for each day of the week (work day, work day after a holiday, market day, Tuesday after a Monday holiday, school days that aren't Saturdays and so on). While non-Portuguese speakers will have little trouble with the schedules themselves, the footnotes – which reveal whether a scheduled bus actually departs on the day you want – can be baffling.

Following are some common footnote phrases and their English meanings. Refer to the Language chapter at the back of this guide for the names of months and the days of the week. Sometimes weekdays, instead of being named, are numbered and followed by the *feiras* tag common to all weekday names; thus *2as. feiras (segundas feiras)* means Mondays.

a partir de ...	beginning on ...
aos (Sábados)	on Saturdays
chegada	arrival
de (segunda) a (sexta)	from (Monday) to (Friday)
diariamente or *diário*	daily
dias úteis	working days
efectua(m)-se or *em vigôr*	in force
excepto or *exc* or *não se efectua(m)*	except
feriados nacionais/oficiais	national holidays
ligação de ou para ...	connection from/to ...
no período de aulas/escolas or *nos dias escolares*	during school term (from early September to late June except around Easter and Christmas)
partida	departure
se a dia lôr feriado (or *se feriado*)	if it is a holiday
se a dia seguinte a feriado	if it follows a holiday
se vespera de feriado	if it precedes a holiday
só	only
todos os dias	every day

Now you can figure out that *de 16 Set a 30 Jun, aos Sábados (ou 6as. feiras se feriado) e 2as. feiras (ou 3as. feiras se dia seguinte a feriado)* means 'from 16 September to 30 June, on Saturday (or Friday if the Friday is a holiday) and Monday (or Tuesday if the Tuesday follows a holiday)'!

Incidentally, timetables are a rare commodity in rural areas; stock up on information at tourist offices or bus and train stations in major towns.

Sample 2nd class fares include 2000$00 for Lisbon-Porto and 1850$00 for Lisbon-Faro by fast *interregional* train (see the following section on types of service).

Serious rail-riders may want to buy the *Guia Horário Oficial* (360$00) which covers CP's complete domestic and international timetables. It's available (if not out of print) from *bilheteiras* (ticket windows) at major stations, at least in Lisbon.

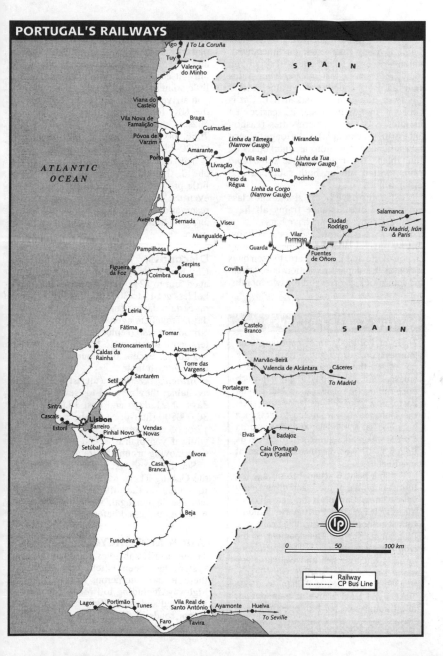

PORTUGAL'S RAILWAYS

Types & Classes of Service

CP operates three main levels of service: *regional* trains (marked R on timetables), which stop everywhere and will drive you crazy; reasonably fast *interregional* trains (marked IR); and express trains, called *rápido* or *intercidade* (marked IC). *Alfa* is a special, marginally faster IC service that operates between northern cities (Lisbon and Porto, for example). CP's long-distance international connections are marked IN on timetables. You may also see *suburbano* trains, which run on both suburban and regional lines.

Most trains have both 1st and 2nd class carriages. Long-distance trains all have restaurant cars and some have bars.

There's a CP Motorail service (car transport by rail) on most major lines, including Lisbon-Porto and Lisbon-Faro. Fifteen days notice at the departure station is required, and return tickets are valid for two months.

Narrow-Gauge Railways

Three of Portugal's most appealing train journeys, on narrow-gauge track climbing up out of the Douro valley, have been emasculated. The Linha da Tâmega, which once ran up from Livração to Mondim de Basto, now goes only as far as Amarante; the Linha da Tua from Tua to Bragança now ends at Mirandela; and the Linha da Corgo, which once stretched from Peso da Régua to Chaves, has been truncated at Vila Real.

But in a belated attempt to salvage the tourist potential of these and other Douro valley lines, Caminhos de Ferro Portugueses, ICEP (the Portuguese national tourist authority) and something called the Programme for the Development of the Douro have jointly restored several historic engines and coaches and will run them along several lines, starting with Régua-Vila Real and Régua-Pinhão in 1999. Tickets will be available at train stations and through selected tour operators.

Reservations

Tickets can only be purchased from the departure station or a travel agent. Discounted and other special tickets can be purchased only at certain main-line stations. There's little point in buying domestic tickets before you arrive in Portugal, but it is possible. In the UK, for example, tickets can be purchased through Wasteels (☎ 0171-834 7066, fax 630 7628; from 22 April 2000 ☎ 020-7834 7066, fax 7630 7628).

You can book tickets up to 20 days ahead, though in most cases you'll have little problem booking one for the next or even the same day, even in summer. Seat reservations are usually mandatory on IC and Alfa trains and are included in the ticket price.

Discounts

Children under four years travel free; those aged four to 12 go at half-price. Youth cardholders get 15 to 30% off R and IR services on certain days (usually Tuesday to Thursday). Travellers aged 65 and over can get a *cartão dourado* (senior card) at ticket counters, entitling them to half-price travel on weekdays, except on suburban commuter trains at rush hour.

Bilhetes turísticos (tourist tickets) are available; they're valid for seven days, 14 days or 21 days and cost 18,000/42,000/30,000$00 (half-price for those aged under 12 or 65 and over), but they're only worthwhile if you plan to spend a great deal of time moving around by train.

See the boxed text in the Train section of the Getting There & Away chapter for information on the different rail passes you can use in Portugal, including some that must be purchased before you arrive.

CAR & MOTORCYCLE

Thanks to EU subsidies, the country's road system has been extensively upgraded; there are now numerous long stretches of highway, including toll roads. Main roads are sealed and generally in good condition. Minor roads in the countryside often have surprisingly little traffic.

The downside of driving here is your road-mates. Courtesy is almost nonexistent. Portuguese drivers, men and women alike, seem guided by two principles: take the fastest route between here and there, and look mortality in the eye en route. Portugal's annual per capita death rate from road accidents is Europe's highest. The coastal roads of the Algarve, and the Lisbon-Cascais A5, are especially dangerous.

City driving tends to be nightmarish, not least in Portugal's many small walled towns, where roads can taper down to donkey-cart size before you know it. Fiendish one-way systems (usually the only way for towns to cope with cars in their narrow lanes) can trap you and force you far out of your way. Parking is often metered within city centres (about 60$00 to 80$00 per hour, but free on Saturday afternoon and Sunday), and in small towns may be restricted to the outskirts.

A common sight in larger towns is the down-and-outers who hang around squares and parking lots, wave you into the space you've just found for yourself, and ask for payment for this 'service'. Of course it's a kind of amateur protection racket and there's no need to give them anything, but many Portuguese drivers do, and 50$00 or 100$00 might keep your car out of trouble.

For information on what to bring in the way of documents, see Car & Motorcycle in the Getting There & Away chapter.

Assistance

Automóvel Club de Portugal (ACP), Portugal's national auto club, provides medical, legal and breakdown assistance for its members. But anyone can get good road information and maps from its head office (☎ 01-356 39 31, fax 357 47 32) at Rua Rosa Araújo 24, Lisbon. Branch offices in Aveiro, Braga, Bragança, Coimbra, Évora, Faro, Porto, Vila Real and elsewhere can also help.

If you belong to a national auto club which is a member of the Fédération Internationale de l'Automobile or the Alliance de Tourisme (as nearly all major national auto clubs are), you can also use ACP's emergency services, and get discounts on maps and other products. Among clubs which qualify are: the AA and RAC, the Australian Automobile Association, the Canadian Automobile Association, the New Zealand Automobile Association and the American Automobile Association.

Highways & Toll-Roads

Portugal's modest network of *estradas* (highways) is gradually spreading across the country. Top of the range are *auto-estradas* or motorways, all of them *portagens* (toll-roads). The longest of these is the 304km Lisbon-Porto road, the shortest the northbound lanes of the 2km Ponte de Abril 25 over the Tejo at Lisbon. Other stretches include Porto-Braga, Porto-Amarante and Lisbon-Cascais. The present total of 740km of toll-roads charges cars and motorcycles 9$00 to 10$00 per kilometre (2790$00 for Lisbon-Porto, for example).

Highway nomenclature can be baffling. Motorway numbers prefixed with an E are Europe-wide designations. Portugal's toll-roads are prefixed with an A. Highways in the country's *rede fundamental* (main network) are prefixed IP (*itinerário principal*), and subsidiary ones IC (*itinerário complementar*). Some highways have several designations, and numbers that change in mid-flow; for example the Lisbon-Porto road is variously called E80, E01, A1 and IP1.

Numbers for the main two-lane *estradas nacionais,* or national roads, have no prefix letter on some road maps (such as the one published by the Automóvel Club de Portugal), while on other maps, including the Michelin No 440 map, they're prefixed by N. We use the N prefix in this book.

ACP emergency help numbers are ☎ 01-942 50 95 (Lisbon) for southern Portugal, and ☎ 02-830 11 27 (Porto) for northern Portugal.

Road Rules

You may not believe it after seeing what Portuguese drivers can do, but there are rules. To begin with, as with the rest of continental Europe, driving is on the right, overtaking is on the left and most signs use international symbols.

Except when marked otherwise, speed limits for cars (without a trailer) and motorcycles are 60km/h in built-up areas, 90km/h outside towns and villages, and 120km/h on motorways. If you've held your driving licence for less than a year, you're restricted to 90 km/h even on motorways and your car must display a '90' disk, available from any ACP office.

Safety belts must by law be worn in both front and back seats and children under 12 years may not travel in the front seat. It is compulsory for motorcyclists and their passengers to wear helmets, and motorcycles must have their headlights on day and night.

The police are authorised to impose on-the-spot fines for speeding and parking (in escudos) and must issue a receipt for them. It may even cost you more to argue, as one reader discovered after parking in a Lisbon official's reserved space: 'The official and a police officer stood next to my car while I ran down to the bank and got the money (the fine was growing with each additional minute that I queried the officer).' Typical parking fines are about 5000$00.

Give Way to the Right

An important rule to remember is that traffic from the right usually has priority. Portugal has lots of non-right-angle, ambiguously marked intersections, so this rule is more important here than it might be elsewhere.

Drinking & Driving

The maximum legal blood-alcohol level for anyone behind the wheel is a mere 0.05%. If you drink and drive and are caught, you can expect to spend the night in a lockup, and the next morning in a courtroom.

Fuel

Fuel is expensive: 165$00 or more for a litre of 95-octane *sem chumbo* (unleaded petrol) and 115$00 for *gasóleo* (diesel). Unleaded petrol is readily available and there are plenty of self-service stations. Major credit cards are accepted at many, but not all, stations.

Rental

To rent a car in Portugal you must be at least 23 years old and have held your licence for over one year. There are dozens of car rental firms in the country, from international outfits such as Avis, Hertz, Budget and Europcar down to modest local ones. The biggest selections are at Lisbon, Porto and Faro airports. Because of the competition, everybody's rates in the Algarve are lower than elsewhere. Recommended car rental firms are listed in the text under various towns.

The best deals are often arranged from abroad, either as part of a package with your flight, or through an international firm. From the UK, for example, for the smallest car expect to pay about UK£140 for seven days in the high season or UK£65 in the low season. Renting in Portugal, figure on at least 45,000$00 (including tax, insurance and unlimited kilometres) from a local agency in the high season, but as much as 60,000$00 from the Portuguese branches of international firms. Rental companies usually insist on payment up front.

For a modest additional fee you can get personal insurance through the rental company, unless you're covered by your home policy (see Insurance & Documents under Car & Motorcycle in the Getting There &

Road Distances (km)

	Aveiro	Beja	Braga	Bragança	Castelo Branco	Coimbra	Évora	Faro	Guarda	Leiria	Lisbon	Portalegre	Porto	Santarém	Setúbal	Viana do Castelo	Vila Real	Viseu
Aveiro	---																	
Beja	383	---																
Braga	129	504	---															
Bragança	287	566	185	---														
Castelo Branco	239	271	366	299	---													
Coimbra	60	329	178	314	191	---												
Évora	305	78	426	488	191	251	---											
Faro	522	166	643	732	437	468	244	---										
Guarda	163	369	260	197	102	161	291	535	---									
Leiria	126	273	244	402	179	72	195	412	233	---								
Lisbon	256	183	372	530	264	202	138	296	402	146	---							
Portalegre	276	178	403	390	93	222	100	344	193	172	219	---						
Porto	71	446	58	216	308	123	368	585	202	189	317	339	---					
Santarém	188	195	309	464	181	134	117	346	295	78	80	147	251	---				
Setúbal	299	143	420	575	316	246	105	256	406	189	47	186	362	123	---			
Viana do Castelo	144	515	50	211	▪▪▪	191	441	658	276	262	387	412	73	324	435	---		
Vila Real	169	528	94	120	261	199	450	683	159	282	412	352	98	349	460	150	---	
Viseu	86	415	185	228	177	86	366	554	75	158	288	268	127	220	331	241	113	---

Away chapter). A minimum of third-party coverage is compulsory throughout the EU.

Rental cars are especially at risk of break-ins in larger towns; do not leave anything of value visible in your car.

Motorcycles or scooters can be rented from Gesrent in Lisbon, Gesrent and AA Castanheira in Cascais, and various outlets throughout the Algarve. See under Cascais in the Around Lisbon chapter, and Getting Around in the Algarve chapter, for typical prices.

BICYCLE

Mountain biking is amazingly popular here: the 1997 and 1998 world cross-country biking championships (Taça do Mundo de Cross Country) were held in Portugal.

Out on the highway, the biggest problem is Portuguese drivers, who are among Europe's rudest and craziest (be sure to dress colourfully so you stand out). Second biggest is Portuguese back roads: a few are still paved with little stone blocks that can shake your teeth loose.

Portugal has few dedicated bicycle lanes (but see Bicycle under Getting Around in the Lisbon chapter for one running along the Rio Tejo).

Where to Go

Possible itineraries are numerous – in the mountainous national/natural parks of the north, along the coast or across the Alentejo plains. Lisbon's Monsanto park area and the hills around Silves (both chosen for the world cross-country championships) are also worth exploring. Most veteran cyclists recommend Parque Nacional da Peneda-Gerês. More demanding is the Serra da Estrela (which serves as the Tour de Portugal's 'mountain run'). Another favourite is the Serra do Marão range between Amarante and Vila Real.

Local clubs organise regular *Passeio BTT* trips: check out their flyers (often found at turismos) for ideas or get in touch and ask to join their excursions.

Guided trips are often available in popular tourist destinations (see Activities in the Facts for the Visitor chapter for locally arranged tours, and the Organised Tours section in the Getting There & Away chapter for tours arranged from abroad).

Transporting Your Bicycle

You can take your bike on any regional (R) or interregional (IR) train as accompanying baggage for 1500$00, regardless of the distance. Arrange this with the *bagagem* (left luggage office) at the departure station, at least several hours in advance. For a small surcharge, regional coach lines might take your bike along, but big ones such as Internorte and Intercentro probably won't. It's up to the driver, so ask first. Agreement may be more likely if you dismantle the bike so it looks as small as possible.

Resources

For listings of national events and bike shops, pick up a copy of the monthly Portuguese *Bike Magazine*.

The Cyclists' Touring Club (CTC) in the UK (☎ 01483-417217, fax 426994, email cycling@ctc.org.uk, Web site www.ctc .org.uk/) publishes a useful, free information booklet on cycling in Portugal for its members. This also has suggested route information for the Coimbra-Porto region and for the Algarve and Alentejo. CTC also offers tips on bikes, spares, insurance and so on, and can put you in touch with others who've cycled in Portugal.

Other useful information is in the Bicycle and Organised Tours sections of the Getting There & Away chapter.

Rental

There are numerous places to rent bikes, especially in the Algarve and other areas geared to tourists. Prices range from about 1500$00 to 3500$00 a day. Rental outfits are noted in the text.

HITCHING

Hitching is never entirely safe anywhere, and we don't recommend it. Travellers who decide to hitch should understand that they are taking a small but potentially serious risk. In any case, it doesn't look like an easy way to get around Portugal, and it may take considerable time and patience. Almost nobody stops on major highways, and on smaller roads drivers tend to be going short distances. You can meet some interesting characters, but you may only advance from one field to the next!

BOAT

Other than river cruises along the Rio Douro from Porto (see the Douro chapter) and along the Rio Tejo from Lisbon, the only main waterborne transport left in Portugal is cross-river ferries. The longest routes are the Transtejo commuter ferries across the Rio Tejo between Lisbon and Cacilhas, Montijo and Seixal, and the Transado ferries that make the 30 minute trip across the mouth of the Rio Sado between Setúbal and Tróia (see the Lisbon and Around Lisbon chapters for details).

LOCAL TRANSPORT
Bus

Except in big cities such as Lisbon there's little reason to take a municipal bus, since most attractions tend to be within walking distance. Most areas have regional bus services, for better or worse (for more on these see the Bus section earlier in this chapter).

Underground

Lisbon's underground system, the Metro, was considerably upgraded and expanded in time for Expo '98 and is still growing. See Getting Around in the Lisbon chapter for more details.

Taxi

Taxis offer good value over short distances, especially for two or more people, and are usually plentiful in larger towns. Ordinary taxis are usually marked A for *aluguer* (for hire) on the door, number plate or elsewhere. These use meters and are available on the street or at taxi ranks. In many towns you can book a taxi by telephone, for a surcharge of a few hundred escudos. See under the Getting Around sections of individual towns for taxi telephone numbers.

The fare on weekdays during daylight hours is 250$00 flag fall (for the first 350m or so) plus roughly 60$00 per kilometre. A fare of 500$00 will usually get you across town. Once a taxi leaves the city limits you pay a higher fare, and possibly the cost of a return trip (whether you take it or not). Rates are also higher at night and on weekends and holidays. It's best to insist on the meter, although it's possible to negotiate a flat fare. If you have a sizeable load of baggage you'll pay a further 300$00.

Except for those who lurk at international airports, drivers are, on the whole, quite honest, even in Lisbon and the Algarve.

In larger cities, including Lisbon, you'll also see meterless taxis marked 'T' (for *turismo*) hired out by private companies for excursions. Rates for these are higher (but standardised). The drivers are honest and polite, and speak foreign languages.

Other Transport

Enthusiasts for stately progress should not miss the trams of Lisbon and Porto, an endangered species. Also worth trying are the *elevadores* (funiculars and elevators) in Lisbon, Bom Jesus do Monte (Braga), Nazaré and elsewhere.

What's in a Street Name

All over Portugal the same street names keep cropping up. Their significance is as follows:

Rua/Avenida

25 de Abril	the date when the 1974 Revolution of the Carnations began
5 de Outubro	the date in 1910 when the monarchy was overthrown and a republic established
1 de Dezembro	the date in 1640 when Portuguese independence was restored after Spanish rule
da Liberdade	referring to the freedom established by the 1974 revolution
dos Restauradores	the restorers of independence after Spanish rule
Afonso de Albuquerque	the viceroy of India who expanded Portugal's empire; he conquered Goa in 1510, Malacca in 1511 and Hormoz in 1515
Miguel Bombarda	a distinguished psychiatrist and leading republican figure, whose murder by a deranged patient in October 1910 precipitated the revolution
Pedro Álvares Cabral	the 'discoverer' of Brazil (in 1500)
Luís de Camões	Portugal's most famous 16th century poet
Manuel Cardoso	a 17th century composer
João de Deus	a 19th century lyric poet
Almeida Garrett	a 19th century poet, playwright and novelist
Alexandre Herculano	a 19th century historian
Alexandre Serpa Pinto	a late-19th century African explorer
Cândido dos Reis	distinguished rear admiral and republican supporter of the 1910 revolution
Gil Vicente	a 16th century court dramatist

ORGANISED TOURS

Gray Line (☎ 01-352 25 94, fax 316 04 04), based at Avenida Praia da Vitória 12-B, Lisbon, organises coach tours of three to seven days to selected regions of Portugal, usually through travel agents or upper-end tourist hotels. The AVIC coach company (☎ 058-82 97 05), Avenida Combatentes 206, Viana do Castelo, does full-day tours of the Douro, Minho and Lima valleys.

The Algarve has several coach operators offering a choice of day trips in the region as well as further afield. See under Getting Around in the Algarve chapter for details.

Adventure holidays and tours – mountain biking, trekking, jeep safaris and so on – are described under Activities in the Facts for the Visitor chapter; see individual towns for details of Portuguese operators. For adventure and specialist interest tours to Portugal from abroad, see Organised Tours in the Getting There & Away chapter.

Lisbon

☎ 01 • pop 572,370

Lisbon is an enticing tangle of past and present – funky and old-fashioned, unpretentious and quirky, booming with new money and new confidence. Its position on seven low hills beside the Rio Tejo (River Tagus) was the main attraction for traders and settlers in centuries past, and it's still a stunning site. Add today's cultural diversity together with a laid-back ambience and an architectural time-warp, and you have one of Europe's most enjoyable cities. And, despite rising prices, it's still good value for money, cheap enough to remain a base as you explore beyond the city limits.

It's also small and manageable enough to explore on foot. Even its muscle-busting hills are tamed by a bevy of *elevadors* (funiculars) and cranky old trams, so leave your car in the lot and let somebody else get you through the nightmarish traffic and one-way streets.

At Lisbon's heart are wide, tree-lined avenues graced by Art Nouveau buildings, mosaic pavements and outdoor cafés. The Alfama district below Castelo de São Jorge is a warren of narrow streets redolent of the city's Moorish and medieval past. Seen from the river – one of the city's many great viewpoints – Lisbon appears as an impressionist picture of low-rise ochre and pastel, punctuated by church towers and domes.

But it has also suffered massive redevelopment in recent years. Although the Alfama and Chiado districts have seen some sensitive restoration projects, many fine old buildings have given way to office blocks. Once-sleepy old Lisbon is on a helter-skelter ride to modernisation, thanks to an expanding economy and the attention it got as host to the millennium's last exposition, Expo '98.

The resulting contrasts are arresting: in the shadow of glittering high-rises are the seedy backstreets of Alfama and Cais do Sodré, where you'd be wise not to wander

HIGHLIGHTS

- Admire the superb Manueline architecture of the Mosteiro dos Jerónimos in Belém
- Wander (in daylight) through the lanes of the Alfama, down to the riverside and up to Castelo São Jorge
- Trundle on tram No 28 from the Baixa, east into the Alfama and west into the Bairro Alto
- Bar-hop through the Bairro Alto, pausing for a taste of port or fado
- See in the dawn at the nightspots of Alcântara or Doca de Santo Amaro
- Savour cultural treasures at the Museu Calouste Gulbenkian, the Museu Nacional de Arte Antiga and the Museu Nacional do Azulejo
- Gawp at the gilded extravagance of the Capela de São João Baptista

at night. And despite frenzied traffic, the city's squares have a caravanserai character, with lingering lottery ticket-sellers, shoeshiners, itinerant hawkers and pavement artists.

You'll find an abundance of history and culture, from Belém's Manueline masterpieces to the world-class Museu Calouste Gulbenkian. You'll hear the angst-filled strains of fado (which originated here in the Alfama) alongside African rhythms from a new generation of clubs responding to a surging demand for the music of the former African colonies. Traditionalists may disapprove, but this is a city on the move.

GREATER LISBON

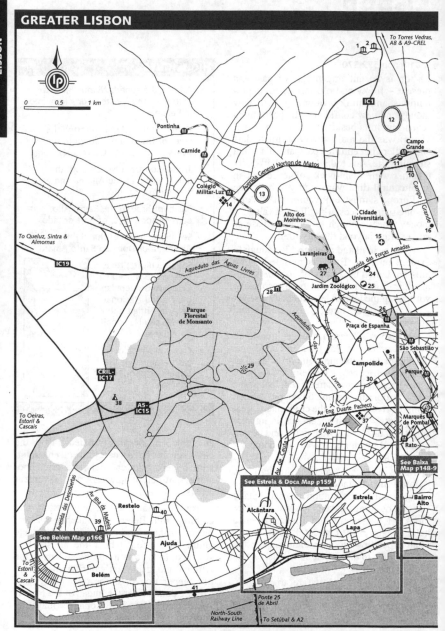

To Torres Vedras,
A8 & A9-CREL

IC1

12

Campo
Grande

11

10

Pontinha

Carnide

Campo Grande

Avenida General Norton de Matos

Colégio
Militar-Luz

14

13

Alto dos
Moinhos

Cidade
Universitária

To Queluz, Sintra &
Almornas

15

16

IC19

Aqueduto das Águas Livres

Laranjeiras

Avenida das Forças Armadas

27

24

28

Jardim Zoológico

25

Parque
Florestal
de Monsanto

26

Praça de Espanha

São Sebastião

31

CRIL-
IC17

Campolide

Parque

29

30

38

A5-
IC15

Av Eng Duarte Pacheco

Marquês
de Pombal

To Oeiras,
Estoril &
Cascais

Mãe
d'Água

37

Rato

See Baixa
Map p148-9

See Estrela & Doca Map p159

Avenida das Descobertas

Restelo

40

Alcântara

Estrela

Bairro
Alto

39

Av. Ilha da Madeira

Ajuda

Lapa

See Belém Map p166

To
Estoril
& Cascais

Belém

41

North-South
Railway Line

Ponte 25
de Abril

To Setúbal & A2

Aqueduto das Águas Livres

Av. de Ceuta

0   0.5   1 km

GREATER LISBON

To Porto & A1

To Ponte de Vasco da Gama

Aeroporto de Lisboa

Av Cidade do Porto

Av Dr Alfredo Bensaúde

● 3

Olivais Norte

Oriente Train & Metro Station

● 5
● 6
● 7

Avenida Marechal Craveiro Lopes

Av Marechal

Cabo Ruivo

Doca dos Olivais

● 8

Olivais

Gomes da Costa

Av do Santo Cindestável

Avenida Infante Dom Henrique

● 9

Avenida Almirante Gago Coutinho

Chelas

Alvalade

Av dos Estados Unidos da América

Roma

17 ●

Entre Campos

23

18

22

19

Bela Vista

Campo Pequeno

20

Areeiro

Estrada de Chelas

Avenida Infante Dom Henrique

Alameda

Olaias

Av Almirante Reis

Saldanha

See Saldanha Map p162

República

Arroios

32

Rua Morais Soares

Xabregas

Picoas

33

Anjos

34

Intendente

Av Almirante Reis

35

Avenida

36

Rio Tejo

Restauradores

Martim Moniz

Graça

Rossio Train Station

Rossio

Castelo

Santa Apolónia Train Station

Baixa-Chiado

Baixa

Alfama

See Alfama Map p154

Cais do Sodré Train & Metro Station

To Cacilhas & Almada

To Montijo & Seixal

To Barreiro

Av Infante Dom Henrique

PLACES TO STAY
32 Pensão Louro
38 Campismo de Câmara
   Municipal de Lisboa

OTHER
1 Museu Nacional do Teatro
2 Museu National do Traje
3 Instituto Geográfico
   do Exército
4 Olivais Swimming Pool
5 Lisbon Exhibition Centre
6 Multifunctional Pavilion
7 Sony Place
8 Oceanarium
9 Feira do Relógio
10 Museu da Cidade
11 Mafrense Bus Station
12 Estádio José de Alvalade
13 Estádio da Luz
14 Centro Comercial Colombo
15 Santa Maria Hospital School
16 Biblioteca Nacional
17 Livraria Porto Editora
18 Teatro Maria Matos
19 Areeiro Swimming Pool
20 Tagus Travel
21 Praça de Touros
22 Jumbo Expresso
23 Apeadeiro de Entrecampos
   Train Station
24 US Embassy & Consulate
25 Brazilian Embassy
26 Bus Station for Cacilhas
   & Setúbal Peninsula
27 Jardim Zoológico
28 Quinta dos Marquêses
   da Fronteira
29 Highest Point in Lisbon
30 Restaurante Numero Um
31 Palácio da Justiça
33 Igreja de Penha de França
34 Museu Nacional do Azulejo
35 Museu da Água
36 Cerâmica Viúva Lamego
37 Complexo das Amoreiras
39 Museu Nacional de Etnológia
40 Museu do Palácio
   Nacional da Ajuda
41 Tejo Bike

When you're ready to get off, you have a variety of options: day trips to the massive monastery at Mafra or the Rococo palace at Queluz, seaside frolics in Cascais, or walks in the wooded hills of Sintra. For information on these places, and more, see the Around Lisbon chapter.

HISTORY

Legend has it that Lisbon was founded by Ulysses but it was probably the Phoenicians who first settled here 3000 years ago, attracted by the fine harbour and strategic hill of São Jorge. They called the city Alis Ubbo (delightful shore). Others soon recognised its delightful qualities too: Greeks displaced Phoenicians, and were themselves booted out by Carthaginians.

In 205 BC the Romans arrived in the city, known by then as Olisipo, and held on to it until 5th century AD. Julius Caesar raised its rank (and changed its name to Felicitas Julia), making it the most important city in Lusitania. After the Romans, and a succession of northern tribes, the Moors arrived in 714 from North Africa. They fortified the city they called Lissabona and fended off the Christians for 400 years.

But in 1147, after a four month siege (see the boxed text in the Castelo section later in this chapter), Christian fighters under Dom Afonso Henriques recaptured the city with the help of Anglo-Norman crusaders. Just over a century later, in 1260, Afonso III declared Lisbon's pre-eminence by moving his capital here from Coimbra.

Since then, Lisbon has had more than its fair share of glory and tragedy. In the 15th and 16th centuries it was the opulent seat of a vast empire after Vasco da Gama discovered a sea route to India. In the 17th century, gold was discovered in Brazil, further boosting the city's importance. Merchants flocked here from all over the world, trading in gold and spices, silks and precious stones. During the reign of Dom Manuel I,

Lisbon's Great Earthquake

It was 9.30 am on All Saints' Day, 1 November 1755, when the earth lurched under Lisbon. Residents were caught inside churches, celebrating High Mass, as three major tremors hit in quick succession. So strong were they that their effects were felt as far away as Scotland and Jamaica. In their wake came an even more devastating fire – kindled by thousands of votive candles – and a tidal wave that submerged the quay and destroyed the lower town.

At least 13,000 of the city's 270,000 inhabitants perished (some estimates put it at three times as many) and much of the city was ruined. Lisbon had known earthquakes before – notably in 1531 and 1597 – but nothing on this scale.

Portugal's European neighbours immediately offered aid and commiseration. England sent food and pickaxes. In France there arose a lively exchange between Voltaire and Rousseau on the doctrine of providence: Voltaire's *Poème sur le désastre de Lisbonne* was followed by an account of the earthquake in his philosophical novel *Candide*, published in 1759.

Dom João I's chief minister, the redoubtable Marquês de Pombal, was the man of the moment, efficiently coping with the aftermath (though it was actually the Marquês de Alorna who uttered the famous words 'we must bury the dead, and feed the living'), and rebuilding the city in a revolutionary new style.

Lisbon recovered, but many of its glorious monuments and works of art had gone. It lost its role as Europe's leading port and finest city. Once revered by Luís de Camões as 'the princess of the world ... before whom even the ocean bows', the city had finally bowed before nature.

the extravagant style of architecture that came to be called Manueline – typified by the Mosteiro dos Jerónimos at Belém – complemented Lisbon's role as the world's most prosperous trading centre. But it was an extravagance that crumbled into rubble in the massive earthquake of 1755.

Lisbon never regained its power and prestige after the earthquake. In November 1807 Napoleon's forces occupied the city (to be driven from Portugal four years later by a joint British-Portuguese force) and Lisbon slid with the rest of the country into political chaos and insurrection.

In 1908, at the height of the turbulent republican movement, Dom Carlos and his eldest son were assassinated as they rode in a carriage through the streets of Lisbon. Over the next 16 years there were 45 changes of government, another high-profile assassination (President Sidónio Pais, at Rossio station in 1918), and a cloak-and-dagger period during WWII when Lisbon (which was officially neutral) developed a reputation as a nest of spies.

Two bloodless coups (in 1926 and 1974) have rocked the city, but it was the massive influx of refugees from the former African colonies from 1974 to 1975 that had the most radical effect on Lisbon, straining its housing resources but also introducing an exciting new element.

The 1980s and 1990s saw Lisbon revitalised. Portugal's entry into the European Community in 1986 coincided with a stable, centre-right government which lasted a record 10 years. Massive EU funding has boosted redevelopment (especially welcome after a major fire in 1988 destroyed the Chiado district) and put Lisbon back in the limelight, first as European City of Culture in 1994 and then as host of Expo '98. Its role today may not be as glorious as in Vasco da Gama's time but it's certainly reclaiming a place on the European stage.

ORIENTATION

Lisbon nestles among seven hills on the northern side of Portugal's finest natural harbour, the wide mouth of the Rio Tejo.

The hills – Estrela, Santa Catarina, São Pedro de Alcântara, São Jorge, Graça, Senhora do Monte and Penha de França – are fine places for bird's-eye views of this very photogenic city. São Jorge is topped by Lisbon's famous *castelo*, and each of the others by a church or a *miradouro* (lookout point).

Other places to get your bearings and shoot off film are the Elevador de Santa Justa and Parque Eduardo VII. The city's highest point (230.5m) is within the military fortress in the huge Parque Florestal de Monsanto, west of the centre.

At the river's edge is the grand Praça do Comércio, the traditional gateway to the city. Behind it march the latticework streets of the Baixa (lower) district, up to the twin squares of Praça da Figueira and Praça Dom Pedro IV – the latter known to virtually everybody as Rossio or Largo Rossio.

Here the city forks along two main arteries. Lisbon's splendid main street, Avenida da Liberdade – more a long park than a boulevard – stretches 1.5km north-west from the Rossio and the adjacent Praça dos Restauradores to Praça Marquês de Pombal and the huge Parque Eduardo VII. The other fork is the main commercial artery of Avenida Almirante Reis (which later becomes Avenida Almirante Gago Coutinho), running north, straight as an arrow, for almost 6km from Praça da Figueira (where it's called Rua da Palma) to the airport.

From the Baixa it's a steep climb west, through a wedge of upmarket shopping streets called the Chiado, over Rua da Misericórdia and into the pastel mini-canyons of the Bairro Alto, Lisbon's traditional centre for dining and nightlife. Eastwards from the Baixa it's another climb to the Castelo de São Jorge and the ancient, maze-like Alfama district around it.

River ferries depart from Praça do Comércio and from Cais do Sodré to the west of it. Lisbon's four long-haul train stations are Cais do Sodré, Santa Apolónia (1.5km east of Praça do Comércio), Rossio and Barreiro (across the Tejo). Oriente (one of Expo '98's associated developments) is

Lisbon's newest and biggest intermodal terminal, combining bus, train and metro stations on the north-eastern outskirts of town.

The city's main long-distance bus terminal, Arco do Cego, is on Avenida João Crisóstomo, near Saldanha metro station. There's another bus terminal at Praça de Espanha for buses to the Setúbal Peninsula. Other bus companies (mainly serving southern destinations) run from Campo das Cebolas, at the end of Rua da Alfândega, a few blocks east of Praça do Comércio, and there are buses to northern destinations from Campo Grande metro station. See Getting There & Away later in this chapter for more details on trains and buses out of Lisbon.

In addition to the metro and a network of city bus lines, ageing trams clank picturesquely around the hills, and smart new ones run 6km west from Praça da Figueira, past the port district of Alcântara, to on the waterfront suburb of Belém.

With the exception of Belém and the Oceanarium, Lisbon's main attractions are within walking distance of one another and public transport (when you need it at all) works well. Streets are generally well marked and buildings clearly numbered. Note, however, that the names of many smaller streets, and some big ones, change every few blocks.

Lisbon is connected south across the Tejo to the Costa da Caparica and Setúbal Peninsula by the immense, 70m-high Ponte 25 de Abril, Europe's longest suspension bridge (which is due to start carrying trains by late 1999). The new Vasco da Gama bridge – at 18km Portugal's longest river crossing – reaches across the Tejo further north, from Sacavem (near the former Expo site) to Montijo, providing a convenient bypass for north-south traffic.

Maps

Staff at the turismos on Praça dos Restauradores and Rua Jardim do Regedor (Map Baixa & B Alto) dispense a free but microscopic city map (some overseas Portuguese tourist offices still have its superior 1:15,000 predecessor). For map junkies and long-term residents, the 230 page *Guia Urbano* city atlas noses into every corner at about 1:5300; it costs 1800$00 and you can get it from the turismo on Restauradores. Also sold at the Restauradores turismo is *Mapas Turísticos* (1200$00), a book of adequate maps of Lisbon, Oeiras, Cascais and Sintra, plus accommodation, restaurant and other listings. The oblique-perspective, detailed *Lisbon City Map – Vista Aérea Geral*, 1100$00 from kiosks and bookshops, is good for spotting landmarks.

The Instituto Português de Cartográfia e Cadastro (Portuguese Institute of Cartography & Registry; ☎ 381 96 00, 386 96 00, fax 381 96 99), Rua Artilharia Um 107, sells topographic maps of Portugal; it's open weekdays from 9 am to 4 pm.

The Instituto Geográfico do Exército (Army Geographic Institute; ☎ 852 00 63,

---

Map Name Abbreviations

For easier reading, references to several map names throughout this chapter have been abbreviated as follows:

Map	Abbreviation	Page(s)
Baixa, Cais do Sodré, Bairro Alto & Chiado	Baixa & B Alto	148-9
Alfama, Castelo & Graça	Alfama	154
Estrela, Lapa & Doca de Alcântara	Estrela & Doca	159
Rato, Marquês de Pombal & Saldanha	Saldanha	162

Post Expo '98

Expo '98, the last world exposition of the millennium, was held in Lisbon from May to September 1998, hosting a record 130 countries and international organisations and over eight million visitors. But this wasn't just a chance for Portugal to capture the limelight and promote the Expo theme – The Oceans: a Heritage for the Future. Expo preparations gave Lisbon the incentive for major infrastructure and urban regeneration projects.

Within the city the metro was upgraded and expanded in all directions and a new major intermodal station, the Estação do Oriente, built at the Expo site. The 18km Vasco da Gama bridge was completed across the Rio Tejo, providing an essential bypass for north-south traffic.

The Expo site itself has seen the greatest changes. Built on 60 hectares of the city's northeastern riverfront, it was once an industrial area of rusting containers, abandoned rubbish, a redundant oil refinery and lakes of oil and gasoline. It's now the focus of Portugal's largest urban regeneration project – Expo Urbe – aiming to transform 70% of Expo's facilities and their surroundings into a vibrant new neighbourhood. Included in the 340 hectare project are residential, office and commercial buildings, housing for 5000 people, a 900 boat recreational harbour and an 80 hectare park (the Tejo & Trancão City Park), once a refuse landfill site.

Expo facilities at the centre of this revived area include the former North International Area (now the new Lisbon Exhibition Centre), the Utopia Pavilion (now a Multifunctional Pavilion for shows and concerts), and the Oceans Pavilion, now Europe's largest Oceanarium.

The Expo Urbe project will continue until 2009. If all goes according to plan, housing and work opportunities will then be available for up to 20,000 people.

852 02 71, fax 853 21 19, email igeoe@ igeoe.pt, Web site www.igeoe.pt) sells military topographic maps at its headquarters on Avenida Dr Alfredo Bensaúde (Map Greater Lisbon) in the far north-eastern Olivais Norte district. It's open weekdays from 9 am to noon and 1.30 to 4.30 pm. See under Planning in the Facts for the Visitor chapter for more on these maps.

Guidebooks

The Real Lisbon is an English-language version of a popular, if rather outdated, guide to Lisbon's food, entertainment and shops; it's sold in city bookshops and at the turismo on Praça dos Restauradores.

ANA, the airport authority, regularly updates its free *Your Guide: Lisboa* with lists of shops, restaurants, top-end hotels and nightlife; pick one up at the ANA counter at airport arrivals or at the airport turismo.

INFORMATION
Tourist Offices

ICEP has a large turismo (☎ 346 63 07, fax 346 87 72) in the Palácio Foz on Praça dos Restauradores (a block north of Rossio train station). It's open daily from 9 am to 8 pm, with general information about Portugal as well as specific information on Lisbon. Service ranges from cheerful to breathtakingly rude. There is also an ICEP turismo (☎ 849 43 23), open daily from 6 am to 2 am, at the airport.

The Turismo de Lisboa Visitors and Convention Bureau (☎ 343 36 72, fax 346 33 14) deals specifically with Lisbon inquiries from its office at Rua Jardim do Regedor 50, across Praça dos Restauradores from the ICEP turismo. It's open daily from 9 am to 6 pm. This is also the place to pick up a Lisboa Card (see the boxed text).

A useful freebie at both turismos is the monthly what's-on *Agenda Cultural*. You

LISBON

Lisboa Card

Holders of this card get free travel on nearly all city transport, including the metro; free admission to most of the city's museums and monuments; and discounts from 15 to 50% on bus and tram tours, river cruises and other admission charges. There are 24, 48 and 72 hour versions costing 1700$00, 2800$00 or 3600$00 respectively (or 660$00, 1000$00 and 1400$00 for children from five to 11 years) – excellent value if you plan on cramming lots of sights into a short stay.

You can buy the Lisboa Card from the city turismo at Rua Jardim do Regedor 50 and other outlets, including the central post office on Praça do Comércio, and in Belém at the Mosteiro dos Jerónimos and the Museu Nacional dos Coches.

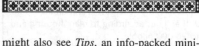

might also see *Tips*, an info-packed mini-guide, and the free *Guia Gay e Lésbico* (Gay & Lesbian Guide to Lisbon) leaflet should be available here.

Another more lively guide to entertainment and useful contacts is the monthly *Lisboa em ...*, 200$00 from various outlets, such as Planet's computer stationery store at Avenida da República 41A.

Money

Nearly every bank has a Multibanco ATM. There are several 24 hour exchange machines where you can exchange foreign banknotes for escudos – there's one opposite Rossio train station at Rua 1 de Dezembro 118-A and another near Praça do Comércio at Rua Augusta 24. Be wary of using these after dark. There are other machines at the airport and Santa Apolónia station.

Your best bet for changing cash or travellers cheques is a private exchange bureau, such as Gabriel de Carvalho at Rossio 41, open daily until 10 pm (closed Sunday morning), or Cota Câmbios at Rua Áurea 283, open daily except Sunday until 7 pm.

The latter even buys foreign coins from 3 to 5 pm on weekdays.

General banking hours are roughly from 8.30 am to 3 pm on weekdays only, though the exchange at Banco Borges e Irmão, Avenida da Liberdade 9-A, is open until 7.30 pm on weekdays and alternate Saturdays. All the money-changing places listed here are shown on Map Baixa & B Alto.

Top Tours (see Travel Agencies later in this section) is Lisbon's American Express (Amex) representative. Here, you can cash Amex travellers cheques commission-free, and Amex cards can be used for cash advances at back-home rates.

Among French banks in Lisbon are Banque National de Paris (☎ 343 08 04), Avenida Liberdade 16; Crédit Lyonnais (☎ 347 58 00), Rua da Conceição 92, in the Baixa; and Société Générale (☎ 383 34 73), Avenida Engenheiro Duarte Pacheco. Barclays Bank has headquarters (☎ 791 11 00) at Avenida da República 50.

Post & Communications

Post The most convenient post office (☎ 347 11 22) around the Rossio is in the pink building opposite the turismo on Praça dos Restauradores. It's open weekdays to 10 pm and weekends to 6 pm.

The not-so-central central post office on Praça do Comércio (Map Baixa & B Alto), open weekdays only to 6.30 pm, is the place for poste restante: mail addressed to Posta Restante, Central Correios, Terreiro do Paço, 1100 Lisboa, will go to counter 13 or 14 here. There is also a 24 hour post office at the airport.

Amex credit card and travellers cheque holders can have mail sent to the Amex representative, Top Tours (see Travel Agencies later in this section).

Telephone & Fax With a Credifone card you can make international direct dial (IDD) calls from most street telephones. At Portugal Telecom booths in post offices, and the Portugal Telecom office at Rossio 68 (open daily until 11 pm), you can pay when you're done.

Faxes can be sent from post offices but Planet, the computer and stationery store (see Email & Internet Access in this section), charges 420$00 a page to Europe (and 120$00 to receive a page) – half the post office price.

At the front of the *páginas amarelas* (Yellow Pages) in the telephone directory there's a list of headings useful to visitors, in English and other languages. There is also a privately operated 'talking yellow pages' in Portuguese on ☎ 795 22 22.

For information on renting mobile phones, see the Post & Communications section in the Facts for the Visitor chapter.

Email & Internet Access Some reliable places to log onto the Internet are:

Ciber Chiado
(☎ 346 67 22, fax 342 82 50, email info@cnc.pt) at Café no Chiado, Largo do Picadeiro 12 (Map Baixa & B Alto); Monday from 11 am to 7 pm, Tuesday to Friday from 11 am to 1 pm, Saturday from 7 pm to 1 am; 300$00 per 15 minutes

Espaço Ágora
(☎ 346 03 90); student-oriented complex near Cais do Sodré (also see Universities in this chapter), with an Internet room; daily from 3 pm to 2 am; 300$00 per 30 minutes

Planet
(☎ 792 81 00, fax 793 41 24); savvy chain of computer, photocopying and stationery stores; main shop, Avenida da República 41A (Map Saldanha), daily from 7 am to 2 am, terminals from 9 am; branch (☎ 321 90 40), Rua da Misericórdia 78 (Map Baixa & B Alto), weekdays from 9 am to 11 pm (assistance until 10 pm) and weekends 11 am to 10 pm; 200$00 per 15 minutes, 50% less from Saturday noon to Sunday 10 pm, 30% more any day after 10 pm

Quiosque Internet
(☎ 352 22 92); a public users' centre on the ground floor of the Edifício Portugal Telecom building by Picoas metro station (Map Saldanha); some technical help available; weekdays only, from 9 am to 5 pm; 180$00 per 30 minutes

Web Café
(☎ 342 11 81, email web1@mail.esoterica.pt); small, friendly cybercafé-bar, Rua do Diário de Notícias 126 (Map Baixa & B Alto); daily 2 pm to 2 am; 175$00 per 15 minutes

Travel Agencies

The city's youth-oriented travel agencies are Tagus Travel and Jumbo Expresso. Tagus (☎ 352 55 09 for air tickets, ☎ 352 59 86 for other services, fax 353 27 15, Web site www.viagenstagus.pt) is at Rua Camilo Castelo Branco 20 (Map Saldanha); there's another branch (☎ 849 15 31) at Praça de Londres (metro Areeiro). Both are open on weekdays and on Saturday morning.

Jumbo Expresso (☎ 793 92 64, fax 793 92 67, email jumbotravel@mail.telepac.pt) is at Avenida da República 97 (Map Greater Lisbon). Tagus and Jumbo also sell ISIC cards. Wasteels (☎ 357 96 55), Avenida António Augusto de Aguiar 88 (Map Saldanha), is another student-geared outfit.

Top Tours (☎ 315 50 05, fax 315 58 73, email toptoursid@mail.telepac.pt), Avenida Duque de Loulé 108 (Map Saldanha), is a useful mainstream travel agency. It's also Lisbon's Amex representative, so holders of Amex cards or travellers cheques can get commission-free currency exchange and cash advances, help with lost cards or cheques, and can have mail and faxes held or forwarded (use the postcode 1050). It's open weekdays only, from 9.30 am to 1 pm and 2.30 to 6.30 pm.

Bookshops

The city's best bookshop is Livraria Bertrand, which has at least half a dozen branches; the original and biggest branch (☎ 342 19 41) is at Rua Garrett 73 in Chiado (Map Baixa & B Alto). There are branches in the Amoreiras shopping centre (Map Greater Lisbon) and the Centro Cultural de Belém (Map Belém). The closest bookshop to the Rossio is Livraria Diário de Notícias at Rossio 11, with a modest range of guides and maps.

The only shop devoted entirely to Lisbon – history, art and architecture, with a few titles in English – is the elegant Livraria Municipal at Avenida da República 21-A (Map Saldanha). Nearby at Avenida Marquês de Tomar 38 is the city's only exclusively French bookshop, Librairie Française. Livraria Buchholz, at Rua Duque de Palmela 4 (Map Saldanha), has a huge collection of literature in Portuguese, English, French and German. For a wide range of exclusively English-language books, visit Livraria Britânica at Rua de São Marçal 83 (Map Baixa & B Alto).

For second-hand books, there are a few dusty shops on Calçada do Carmo behind Rossio train station and stalls in the arcade near the Praça do Comércio end of Rua Augusta (Map Baixa & B Alto).

Libraries

Lisbon's best *bibliotecas* are the General Arts Library of the Fundação Calouste Gulbenkian (☎ 793 51 31, fax 793 51 39) at Avenida de Berna 56 (Map Saldanha; metro Praça de Espanha), and the Biblioteca Nacional (☎ 795 01 30, 797 47 41) at Campo Grande 83 (Map Greater Lisbon). The municipal library (☎ 797 13 26) is in the Palácio das Galveias (metro Campo Pequeno).

Universities

The Universidade de Lisboa, 5km northwest of the Rossio, has its own metro station, Cidade Universitária. The most prestigious university is the private Universidade Católica, near Sete Ríos. There are nearly a dozen other private universities in Lisbon.

A more convenient place to meet students is the Espaço Ágora (☎ 342 47 01, fax 342 47 04) at Avenida da Ribeira das Naus, Cais do Sodré (Map Baixa & B Alto). Run by the Associação Academica de Lisboa, this prefab complex has a computer room, study rooms and a café (open 24 hours, with discounts for students), plus good notice boards. During term time it's open almost round the clock.

Cultural Centres

The reading room of the USA's Abraham Lincoln Center (☎ 357 01 02), Avenida Duque de Loulé 22-B (Map Saldanha), has a huge stock of American books and magazines and is open weekdays from 2 to 5.30 pm.

The good library at the British Council (☎ 347 61 41, fax 347 61 52, email info@ britcounpt.org), Rua de São Marçal 174 (Map Baixa & B Alto), is open Monday to Saturday from 2 to 6 pm. Take bus Nos 15 or 58 from Rua da Misericórdia.

At Avenida Luís Bívar 91 (Map Saldanha) are the Institut Franco-Portugais de Lisbonne (☎ 311 14 00) and the Alliance Française (☎ 315 88 06). There is also a reading room (☎ 352 01 49) at the German embassy, Campo dos Mártires da Pátria 37 (Map Saldanha).

Gay & Lesbian Travellers

The Centro Comunitário Gay e Lésbico de Lisboa (Lisbon Gay & Lesbian Community Centre; ☎ 887 39 18, fax 887 39 22) opened in 1997 at Rua de São Lazaro 88 (Map Baixa & B Alto; bus No 100 from Praça da Figueira). Its café, library, Internet terminal and counselling facilities are open daily from 4 to 9 pm.

Laundry

Lave Neve self-service laundry (☎ 346 61 05), Rua da Alegria 37 (Map Baixa & B Alto), is open Tuesday to Friday from 10 am to 1 pm and 3 to 7 pm, plus Monday and Saturday morning.

Medical Services

Farmácias (pharmacies) are plentiful in Lisbon. A competent one near the centre is Farmácia Estácio at Rossio 62.

The Hospital Britânico (British Hospital; ☎ 395 50 67, 397 63 29 out of office hours), at Rua Saraiva de Carvalho 49, has English-speaking staff and doctors. Other large hospitals include São José (☎ 886 01 31), Rua José António Serrano (Map Baixa & B Alto), and Santa Maria Hospital School (☎ 352 94 40, 797 51 71), Avenida Professor Egas Moniz (Map Greater Lisbon).

Emergency

There's a 24 hour, English-speaking, tourist-oriented police subsection (Subsecção de Turismo) in the courtyard at the PSP section office, Rua Capelo 13 in

Chiado. Call ☎ 346 61 41, ext 279, or the country-wide emergency number ☎ 112.

Dangers & Annoyances

Lisbon has a low crime rate by European standards, but it's on the rise. Most crime against foreigners involves pickpocketing, bag-snatching or car break-ins. Use a money belt and keep cameras and other tourist indicators out of sight. There have also been isolated assaults by gangs of kids as young as 11 or 12 in deserted metro stations or late at night in nightclub neighbourhoods like Bairro Alto. For this reason it's probably unwise to explore the bars and nightclubs in this area alone.

It's certainly risky to wander alone after dark in the back streets of Alfama and Cais do Sodré. A woman reader even encountered flashers in broad daylight in Parque Eduardo VII. Train stations attract dodgy types. Another reader suggests not boarding your train until there are plenty of other people in the carriage.

Other places in the Lisbon area with a small but growing reputation for assaults on tourists and racist crime are the Estoril-Cascais beach resorts and the Setúbal region. Extra police were mobilised during 1998 specifically to patrol the beaches and holiday zones.

What's Free

Many of the museums are free on Sunday morning, as noted in the text. Free cultural events include music and dance performances at the Bar Terraço of the Centro Cultural de Belém, weekdays from 7 to 9 pm. The Centro also has a programme of free weekend performances in July and August.

During the Festa de Santo António (12 to 13 June) and on other summer weekends, free concerts are often held at churches and former churches, for example the Basílica da Estrela, Igreja de São Roque and the Sé.

From mid-July to mid-August the Lisboa Mexe-me music festival (see Special Events later in this chapter) takes place in the streets of various areas.

BAIXA & THE RIVERFRONT

Following the 1755 earthquake, one of the few people who kept his head was the autocratic Marquês de Pombal, Dom José I's chief minister. He put Lisbon on the road to recovery, and took the opportunity to rebuild the city centre as quickly as possible, in a severe and simple, low-cost, easily managed style.

The entire area from the riverside to the Rossio was reborn as a grid of wide, commercial streets (with pavements), each dedicated to a trade. The memory of these districts lives on in the Baixa's north-south street names – Áurea (formerly Ouro, gold), Sapateiros (shoemakers), Correeiros (saddlers), Prata (silver), Douradores (gilders) and Fanqueiros (cutlers).

This lower town remains the de facto heart of Lisbon. Down the middle runs pedestrianised Rua Augusta, the old street of the cloth merchants, now overflowing with cafés, restaurants, shops and banks. A number of the city's bus and tram lines funnel through Praça do Comércio at the Baixa's riverside end, or Rossio and Praça da Figueira at its upper end. All the sights in this section are shown on Map Baixa & B Alto.

From Praça do Comércio to Cais do Sodré

Before the earthquake, Praça do Comércio was called Terreiro do Paço (Palace Square), after the royal Palácio da Ribeira that overlooked it until the morning of 1 November 1755. Most visitors coming by river or sea in bygone days would have arrived here. It was also from here that Dom João VI and his court fled to Brazil in 1807. The huge square still feels like the entrance to the city, thanks to Joaquim Machado de Castro's bronze **equestrian statue** of Dom José I, the 18th century, arcaded **ministries** along three sides and Verissimo da Costa's **Arco da Victória**, the arch opening onto Rua Augusta.

At the north-western corner of the square, by the post office, is the spot where Dom Carlos and his son Luís Filipe were

LISBON

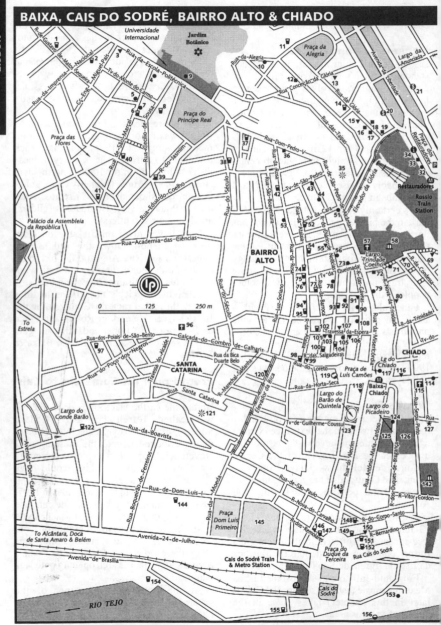

BAIXA, CAIS DO SODRÉ, BAIRRO ALTO & CHIADO

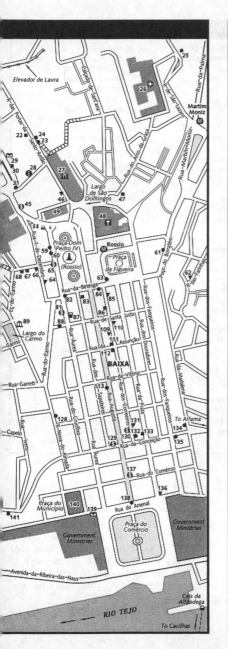

PLACES TO STAY
12 Residencial Nova Avenida
16 Pensão Monumental
17 Hotel Suiço-Atlântico
18 Pensão Pérola de Baixa
19 Pensão Iris
22 Pensão Residencial Florescente
30 Pensão Imperial
33 Orion Eden Lisboa
36 Pensão Londres
43 Pensão Globo
47 Pensão Residencial Gerês
61 Pensão Residencial Alcobia
67 Pensão Estação Central
68 Pensão Henriquez
71 Pensão Duque
72 Pensão Estrela de Ouro
83 Pensão Arco da Bandeira
86 Pensão Moderna
111 Albergaria Insulana
112 Pensão Aljubarrota
133 Pensão Prata
141 Residencial Nova Silva

PLACES TO EAT
3 Confeitaria Císter
13 O Fumeiro
15 Restaurante O Brunhal
46 Gambrinus
55 A Transmontana
62 Algures na Mouraria
64 Café Nicola
66 Celeiro
69 Restaurante O Sol
70 Casa Transmontana
76 Ali-a-Papa
80 Cervejaria da Trindade
85 Restaurante João do Grão
91 Sinal Vermelho
94 Pap'Açorda
99 Tendinha da Atalaia
101 Tasca do Manel
106 O Cantinho do Bem Estar
107 A Primavera
109 Lagosta Vermelha
110 Restaurante Ena Pãi
116 Café A Brasileira
118 La Brasserie de l'Entrecôte
120 Restaurante Alto Minho
131 Restaurante Yin-Yang
136 Martinho da Arcada
143 Pano Mania
146 Restaurante Porto de Abrigo
150 Caneças

continued ...

LISBON

BAIXA & B ALTO

OTHER
1 Memorial
2 Trumps
4 Casa Achilles
5 Livraria Britânica
6 Bar Áqua no Bico
7 British Council
8 Bric-a-Bar
9 Casa das Cortiças
10 Lave Neve
11 Hot Clube de Portugal
14 Ritz Clube
20 Banco Borges e Irmão
21 Banque Nacional de Paris
23 Loja da Música
24 Coliseu dos Recreios
25 Gay & Lesbian Community
     Centre
26 Hospital São José
27 Palácio dos Condes de
     Almada
28 Turismo & Lisboa
     Card Office
29 Post Office
31 ABEP Ticket Agency
32 Virgin Megastore
34 Turismo
35 Miradouro de São Pedro
     de Alcântara
37 Pavilhão Chinês
38 Snob Bar
39 Finalmente
40 Bar 106
41 Tatoo
42 Nova
44 Pais em Lisboa
45 Foreign Exchange Machine
48 Igreja de São Domingos
49 Teatro Nacional de Dona
     Maria II

50 Portugal Telecom Office
51 Solar do Vinho do Porto
52 Primas
53 O Forcado
54 Frágil
56 Web Café
57 Igreja de São Roque;
     Capela de São João
     Baptista
58 Museu de Arte Sacra
59 Farmácia Estácio
60 Valentim de Carvalho
63 Carris Ticket Kiosk
65 Gabriel de Carvalho
73 Café Luso
74 Arroz Doce
75 Portas Largas
77 Os Três Pastorinhos
78 Adega Mesquita
79 Planet
81 Cota Câmbios
82 Livraria Diário de Notícias
84 Manuel Tavares
87 Discoteca Amália
88 Elevador de Santa Justa
89 Convento do Carmo;
     Museu Arqueológico do
     Carmo
90 Lisboa à Noite
92 Adega do Machado
93 Tertúlia
95 A Capela
96 Igreja de Santa Catarina
97 Incógnito
98 Ma Jong
100 Soul Factory Bar
102 7° Céu
103 Adega do Ribatejo
104 Café Suave
105 Nono

108 A Severa
113 Madeira House
114 Livraria Bertrand
115 Basilica da Nossa Senhora
     dos Mártires
117 Vista Alegre
119 Brazilian Consulate
121 Miradouro de Santa Catarina
122 B.Leza
123 Fábrica Sant'Ana
124 Ciber Chiado
125 Teatro Municipal
     de São Luís
126 Teatro Nacional de São
     Carlos
127 Police Subsection
     for Tourists
128 Teresa Alecrim
129 Crédit Lyonnais
130 Banco Comércial Portuguesa
132 Núcleo Arqueológico
134 Santos Ofícios
135 Napoleão
137 Foreign Exchange Machine
138 Arco da Victória
139 Central Post Office
140 Câmara Municipal
142 Museu do Chiado
144 Absoluto
145 Mercado da Ribeira
147 Ó Gilíns Irish Pub
148 Jamaica
149 British Bar
151 California
152 Hennessy's Irish Pub
153 Espaço Ágora;
     Ágora Café
154 Rock City
155 Bar do Rio
156 Car Ferry to Cacilhas

assassinated in 1908. Just west of here is a smaller square, **Praça do Município**, dominated by Lisbon's 1874 *câmera municipal* (town hall) on the eastern side, the former marine arsenal on the southern side and a finely carved, 18th century *pelourinho* (pillory) at the centre.

Continuing west for another 400m along Rua do Arsenal, you arrive at Lisbon's other main riverfront plaza, Praça do Duque da Terceira, better known by its riverfront name, **Cais do Sodré**. Here there are more

government offices, consulates, the Transtejo car ferry and the Cais do Sodré train station (for Cascais and the Estoril coast).

A few short blocks west of the square is the city's kinetic main market, the domed **Mercado da Ribeira** – officially the Mercado Municipal 24 de Julho. Get here early in the morning to see feisty vendors hawking vegetables, fruit, seafood and more.

From here, Avenida 24 de Julho runs for 3km along the river to the Port of Lisbon and the warehouse district of Alcântara and Doca de Santa Amaro. This strip is a major axis for Lisbon's nightlife (see Entertainment later in this chapter). A pleasant way to return to Praça do Comércio is along the breezy riverfront promenade.

For the route east of the Praça do Comércio, see under Alfama, Castelo & Graça.

Central Baixa

Under the streets of the Baixa is the **Núcleo Arqueológico**, a web of tunnels believed to be the remnants of a **Roman spa** and probably dating from the 1st century AD. You can descend into the mouldy depths – via the offices of Banco Comércial Portuguesa at Rua dos Correeiros 9 – on a guided tour which is run by the Museu da Cidade (see the Greater Lisbon section). Tours times are Thursday at 3, 4 and 5 pm, and Saturday hourly from 10 am to noon and 3 to 5 pm.

Alternatively you can rise above the Baixa at a stately pace. From the eastern end of Rua da Conceição the **No 28 tram** clanks up into the Alfama and Graça districts. At the other end of the Baixa, the **Elevador de Santa Justa**, an incongruously huge but charming wrought-iron lift designed by Raul Mésnier du Ponsard (a follower of Gustave Eiffel) and completed in 1902, will hoist you 32m above Rua de Santa Justa to a viewing platform and café at eye level with the Convento do Carmo ruins in the Chiado district.

Rossio & Praça da Figueira

This pair of plazas forms the gritty heart of the Baixa, with transport to everywhere, lots of cafés from which to watch a cross-section of Lisbon's multicultural population and hustlers and hawkers preying cheerfully on visitors.

In the middle of the Rossio is a **statue**, allegedly of Dom Pedro IV, after whom the square is formally named. The story goes that it's actually a statue of Emperor Maximilian of Mexico and was abandoned in Lisbon en route from France to Mexico after news arrived of Maximilian's assassination. On the northern side of the square is

Rolling Motion Square

This was the nickname given to the Rossio by early English visitors because of the undulating mosaic pattern of its pavements (also seen elsewhere in the city). These mosaics were first installed by prison labour gangs during the 19th century and are now mostly in evidence around the fountains.

They may make you seasick, but they're more sensible than they look. Hand-cut white limestone and grey basalt cubes are pounded into a bed of sand, making a hard surface which nevertheless lets the rainwater through. In the course of street works they're simply dug up and reused.

the restored 1846 **Teatro Nacional de Dona Maria II**, its façade topped by a statue of 16th century playwright Gil Vicente.

In less orderly times the Rossio was the scene of animal markets, fairs and bullfights. The theatre was built on the site of a palace in which the unholiest excesses of the Portuguese Inquisition took place during the 16th to 19th centuries. Around the corner, just to the north of Praça da Figueira, is the **Igreja de São Domingos**. In this vast church's pre-earthquake incarnation the Inquisition's judgements, or autos-da-fé, were handed down.

Across Largo de São Domingos from the church is the **Palácio dos Condes de Almada**, also called the Palácio da Independéncia or Palácio da Restauração, where the *restauradores* (nationalist leaders) met for the last time in 1640 before rising against the Spanish occupation.

CHIADO & BAIRRO ALTO

These two districts, lying above the Baixa to the west, make a perfect pair for day and night exploration. The Chiado, a wedge of wide streets roughly between Rua do Crucifixo and Rua da Misericórdia, is the posh place for shopping and for loitering in cafés. The Bairro Alto, a fashionable residential district in the 17th century (and still boasting some fine mansions), is now better known as the raffish heartland of Lisbon nightlife. All the sights in this section are shown on Map Baixa & B Alto.

It's in the Chiado that you'll get the best impression of the destruction wrought by fire and earthquake: the ruins of the **Convento do Carmo**, uphill from Rua Garrett, stand as stunning testimony to the 1755 earthquake. Only the Gothic arches, walls and flying buttresses remain of what was once one of Lisbon's largest churches. It was built in 1423 under the orders of Nuno Álvares Pereira, Dom João I's military commander (who became religious after a life of war and spent his last eight years in this Carmelite retreat).

Now the ruins are an open-air home to the curious **Museu Arqueológico do Carmo** (Carmo Archaeological Museum; ☎ 346 04 73), where you can normally see the carved tomb of Fernando I, Luso-Romano statuary, a 3500-year-old Egyptian mummy and preserved Peruvian skulls. Unfortunately, the metro works have caused the temporary closure of the museum.

By contrast, the gutted buildings that have pockmarked the Chiado since a massive fire in 1988 are being (very) slowly rebuilt and restored by architect Álvaro de Siza Vieira, in the Chiado's old style. One survivor of the fire is the **Teatro Nacional de São Carlos** in Rua Serpa Pinto – Lisbon's opera house and the city's largest, most handsome theatre, built in the 1790s in imitation of Naples' San Carlos Theatre. It stands opposite the smaller Teatro Municipal de São Luís.

Nearby, in the former Convento de São Francisco at Rua Serpa Pinto 4, is the **Museu do Chiado** (Chiado Museum; ☎ 343 21 48), which has a respectable collection of Portuguese art from approximately 1850 to 1950. Among painters represented are Rafael Bordalo Pinheiro, José de Almada Negreiros, Amadeo de Souza Cardoso and Maria Helena Vieira da Silva. The museum is open from 10 am to 6 pm (closed all day Monday and Tuesday morning); admission costs 400$00 (free on Sunday morning).

Two funiculars – the **Elevador da Glória** and **Elevador da Bica** – provide stately entrance to the Bairro Alto and are worth the ride in any case. The Elevador da Glória climbs from near Praça dos Restauradores to gardens and a superb viewpoint atop one of Lisbon's seven hills, **São Pedro de Alcântara**. Across the road is the **Solar do Vinho do Porto** (see the boxed text in the Entertainment section), where you can sample port wine in a salubrious setting.

Strike uphill along Rua Dom Pedro V, past Praça do Principe Real, to the hillside **Jardim Botânico** (botanical garden), a great place for a picnic. It's open from 9 am to 8 pm (from 10 am at weekends, and closing at 6 pm in winter); admission costs 200$00. The main entrance is on Rua da Escola Politécnica.

In the opposite direction from Elevador da Glória, it's a short walk downhill to Largo Trindade Coelho and the late-16th century Jesuit **Igreja de São Roque**, whose dull façade is one of Lisbon's biggest deceptions. Inside are chapels stuffed with gold, marble and Florentine azulejos, and the *pièce de résistance*: the **Capela de São João Baptista**, to the left of the altar. Commissioned in 1742 by Portugal's most extravagant king, Dom João V, this chapel was designed and built in Rome by the Italian architect Luigi Vanvitelli, using the most expensive materials possible, including amethyst, alabaster, agate, lapis lazuli and Carrara marble. After its consecration by Pope Benedict XIV it was dismantled and shipped to Lisbon for what was then a staggering UK£225,000. Check out the intricate marble mosaics which, from a modest distance, look just like paintings.

If you still haven't seen enough churchly extravagance, pop next door to the **Museu de Arte Sacra** (Museum of Ecclesiastical Art; ☎ 346 03 61), also known as the Museu de São Roque, in the church's former convent. Inside is a mind-boggling array of gold-threaded vestments, bejewelled mitres and gem-encrusted chalices. The museum is open daily except Monday, from 10 am to 5 pm. Admission to the church and museum costs 150$00 (free on Sunday).

From the southern end of the Bairro Alto (walking distance from Cais do Sodré) the **Elevador da Bica** creeps up to Rua do Loreto, a few blocks west of Praça de Luís Camões. Riding this gives you a chance to explore unsung **Santa Catarina**, a compact, maze-like district bright with fluttering laundry, and alive with balcony gossip, chattering kids and caged songbirds. The name comes from the 17th century **Igreja de Santa Catarina** in Calçada do Combro de Calhariz, largely rebuilt after the 1755 earthquake but still full of pre-earthquake gilded woodwork and with a gloriously ornate Baroque organ. Downhill, at the end of Rua Marechal Saldanha, on another of Lisbon's seven hills, is the **Miradouro de Santa Catarina**, offering a bird's-eye view of the river and the Ponte 25 de Abril.

ALFAMA, CASTELO & GRAÇA

This area east and north-east of the Baixa is Lisbon's oldest and most historically interesting district. It's also one of the most rewarding areas for walkers and photographers, thanks to a warren of medieval streets in the Alfama district and outstanding views from three of Lisbon's seven hills – São Jorge, Graça and Senhora do Monte.

Alfama

The Alfama was inhabited by the Visigoths as far back as the 5th century, and remnants of a Visigothic town wall remain. But it was the Moors who gave the district its shape and atmosphere, as well as its name: the Arabic *alhama* means springs or bath, probably a reference to hot springs found near Largo das Alcaçarias. In Moorish times this was an upper-class residential area. After earthquakes brought down many of its mansions (and post-Moorish churches) it reverted to a working-class and fisherfolk quarter. It was one of the few districts to ride out the 1755 earthquake.

The Alfama's tangled alleys (*becos* and *travessas*) and vertiginous stairways make a

sharp contrast to the Baixa's prim streets. Plunging from the castle to the river, with lanes often narrow enough to shake hands across, it has a village atmosphere; you can quickly feel like an intruder if you take a wrong turn into someone's back yard. With a somewhat unruly reputation, it's not a good place to wander alone at night, but by day it's a lively enclave of taverns and tiny grocery stores, sizzling sardine smells and squawking budgies.

In the early morning, women sell fresh fish from their doorways and hang laundry from their windows. Not so long ago they would have congregated at public open-air laundries, but in recent years many houses have been modernised under the Reabilitação Urbana d'Alfama project, an urban improvement programme run by the government. This scheme has inevitably led to some gentrification and commercialisation in the main streets. For a real rough-and-tumble atmosphere, visit during the Festas dos Santos Populares in June (see Special Events later in this chapter).

Walking east from the Praça do Comércio in Baixa, you'll come to the **Igreja da Conceição Velha** on the north side of Rua da Alfândega. Its finely carved Manueline façade was rebuilt and reattached to the church after the earthquake.

Further along, where Rua dos Bacalhoeiros merges with Rua da Alfândega, is the startling early-16th century **Casa dos Bicos** (House of Points) – a folly built by Afonso de Albuquerque, a former viceroy of India. Its prickly façade was restored in the early 1980s. On the ground floor, an outfit calling itself Comemorações dos Descobrimentos hawks Age of Discoveries souvenirs and Portuguese-language pamphlets, and there's a display of bits of the old Moorish city wall and brick streets.

From here it's an easy stroll up to the Alfama's most important religious monument, the **Sé**. Alternatively, you can walk or take tram No 28 along from Rua da Conceição in the Baixa. The Romanesque cathedral was built in 1150, soon after the city was recaptured from the Moors by

LISBON

ALFAMA, CASTELO & GRAÇA

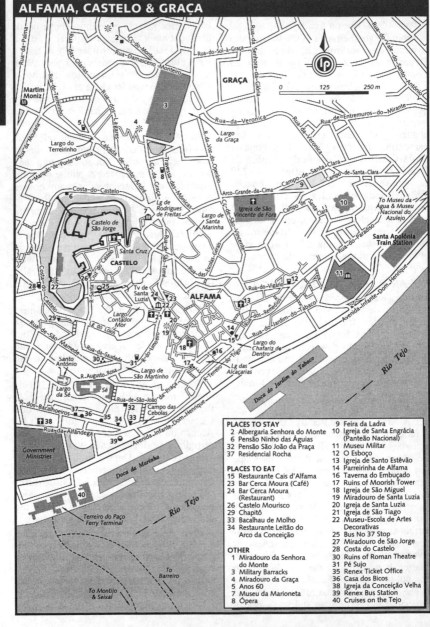

PLACES TO STAY
2 Albergaria Senhora do Monte
6 Pensão Ninho das Águias
32 Pensão São João da Praça
37 Residencial Rocha

PLACES TO EAT
15 Restaurante Cais d'Alfama
23 Bar Cerca Moura (Café)
24 Bar Cerca Moura (Restaurant)
26 Castelo Mourisco
29 Chapitô
33 Bacalhau de Molho
34 Restaurante Leitão do Arco da Conceição

OTHER
1 Miradouro da Senhora do Monte
3 Military Barracks
4 Miradouro da Graça
5 Anos 60
7 Museu da Marioneta
8 Ópera
9 Feira da Ladra
10 Igreja de Santa Engrácia (Panteão Nacional)
11 Museu Militar
12 O Esboço
13 Igreja de Santo Estêvão
14 Parreirinha de Alfama
16 Taverna do Embuçado
17 Ruins of Moorish Tower
18 Igreja de São Miguel
19 Miradouro de Santa Luzia
20 Igreja de Santa Luzia
21 Igreja de São Tiago
22 Museu-Escola de Artes Decorativas
25 Bus No 37 Stop
27 Miradouro de São Jorge
28 Costa do Castelo
30 Ruins of Roman Theatre
31 Pé Sujo
35 Renex Ticket Office
36 Casa dos Bicos
38 Igreja da Conceição Velha
39 Renex Bus Station
40 Cruises on the Tejo

Afonso Henriques. He was wary enough to want the church built like a fortress (its French architects designed a similar fortress cathedral for Coimbra). It's been extensively restored and is now rather dull, but check out the Baroque organs and intricate Baroque crib by Machado de Castro in a chapel off the north aisle. The Gothic cloister is open daily except Monday, from 10 am to 1 pm and 2 to 6 pm; admission costs 100$00 (free on Sunday). Religious paraphernalia on display in the sacristy (same hours, 400$00) includes São Vicente relics in a mother-of-pearl casket (see the boxed text 'St Vincent' in the Algarve chapter).

Across the road is the **Igreja de Santo António**, built in 1812 on the site of St Anthony's birthplace. A small museum here devoted to the city's favourite saint is open Tuesday to Saturday, from 10 am to 1 pm and 2 to 6 pm (admission 165$00).

Behind the cathedral, Rua de São João da Praça runs downhill to Largo de São Rafael and a ruined **Moorish tower**, part of the Moors' original town wall. The old **Jewish quarter** is adjacent, marked by tiny Rua da Judiaria. Along Rua de São Miguel and Rua de São Pedro, as far as Largo do Chafariz de Dentro ('fountain within the walls'), are most of the Alfama's shops, restaurants and cafés.

Uphill from the Sé, along Rua Augusto Rosa, you can double back along Rua da Saudade to see the unmemorable ruins of a **Roman theatre** (supposedly consecrated by Nero in 57 BC), before topping out at two stunning viewpoints: the **Miradouro de Santa Luzia** and, a little further on, **Largo das Portas do Sol** (the 'sun gateway', originally one of the seven gateways into the Moorish city).

Other worthwhile sights here are the **Igreja da Santa Luzia**, with azulejos depicting the capture of the castle from the Moors, and the **Museu-Escola de Artes Decorativas** (☎ 886 21 83), Largo das Portas do Sol 2. This museum-school is owned and run by the private Fundação Ricardo do Espírito Santo Silva, founded in 1953 to showcase banker Espírito Santo Silva's striking collection of 16th to 19th century furniture and other decorative articles. The foundation also provides adjacent workshop space to cabinet-makers, silversmiths, bookbinders and other artisans working with traditional methods. All of this, plus a souvenir shop, restaurant, library and temporary exhibitions, is housed on several floors of an elegant 18th century palace, the Palácio Azurara (which itself sports some fine original azulejos). It's open daily except Tuesday, from 10 am to 5 pm; admission

---

St Anthony

Although St Vincent is Lisbon's official patron saint, *lisboêtas* are fonder of St Anthony, despite the fact that he spent most of his life in France and Italy. Born in Lisbon in 1195 and baptised in the Sé, he first joined the Augustinian Order in the Convent de São Vicente de Fora before switching to the Franciscans (in 1220) in Coimbra. After illness forced him back from an African trip, he divided his time between France and Italy, dying near Padua in 1231.

Revered in Italy as St Anthony of Padua, or simply Il Santo, his humanistic preachings and concern for the poor made him internationally famous. Less than a year after his death he was canonised. Many miracles are attributed to him but he's especially renowned for his help in fixing marriages: many single women still ask for his help in finding husbands and newly wed couples leave gifts of thanks at the Igreja de Santo António.

Elsewhere in the Alfama you'll notice many houses decorated with azulejo panels depicting the miracles he performed. But the best time to feel the city's affection is during the Festa de Santo António from 12 to 13 June (see Special Events later in this chapter).

costs 900$00 (free to art students and children up to 12 years).

Castelo

A short, steep climb from Largo das Portas do Sol via Travessa de Santa Luzia brings you to the **Castelo de São Jorge** (or catch bus No 37 from Praça da Figueira). From its Visigothic beginnings in the 5th century, the castle was later fortified by the Moors in the 9th century, sacked by Christians in the 12th century and used as a royal residence from the 14th to 16th centuries – and as a prison in every century.

What remains has been considerably tarted up for tourists. Within the massive battlements are everything from a posh restaurant and open-air café to strutting peacocks and craft hawkers. Best of all, 10 towers and shady terraces offer great panoramas over the city and river.

The inner area is now the focus of an archaeological survey, ahead of the possible construction of an underground car park. Roman and Islamic remains are anticipated: this was once an elite residential neighbourhood for the Moors, whose mosque stood on the site of the nearby Igreja de Santa Cruz.

Little remains of the former palace, Paço de Alcáçova, built by Dom Dinis on the site of a Moorish palace in the south corner (it was already in ruins by the 17th century), but the nearby medieval quarter of Bairro de São Jorge, around Rua Santa Cruz do Castelo, still retains some of its original flavour.

North of the castle is the former **Mouraria** quarter, where the Moors lived after the Christian reconquest. It's now rather sombre, though Rua da Mouraria has been modernised and pedestrianised.

Graça

North-east of the castle lies the Graça district. Following Rua de São Tomé up from Largo das Portas do Sol, you pass Largo de Rodrigues de Freitas. At No 13 is the intriguing **Museu da Marioneta** (Puppet Museum; ☎ 886 33 04), crammed with everything from finger puppets to life-size creations. Note the traditional 19th century

---

The Siege of Lisbon

The reconquest of Lisbon in 1147 is one of the more unsavoury chapters in Portugal's early history. Afonso Henriques, Count of Porto, had already thrashed the Moors at Ourique in 1139 (and started calling himself King of Portugal) and his sights were now on Lisbon. Short of experienced troops, he persuaded a ruffian band of English, Flemish, French and German adventure-crusaders on their way to Palestine to give him a hand.

'Do not be seduced by the desire to press on with your journey,' begged the Bishop of Porto on the king's behalf, 'for the praiseworthy thing is not to have been to Jerusalem, but to have lived a good life while on the way.'

This (and an offer of all the enemy's loot if the city was taken) persuaded them, and in June 1147 the siege of the Castelo de São Jorge began. The Moors were at first contemptuous – 'How many times within your memory have you come hither with pilgrims and barbarians to drive us hence?' – and managed to hold out for 17 weeks.

But in October the castle's defences gave way and the 'Christian' forces (described more correctly by a contemporary reporter as 'plunderers, drunkards and rapists ... men not seasoned with the honey of piety') showed their true colours by pillaging their way through the city, despite assurances of leniency for the losers from Afonso himself. The only good man among them appears to have been one Gilbert of Hastings, an English priest who later became Bishop of Lisbon.

Portuguese puppets and an Asian collection, including elephant puppets from Myanmar. A tiny theatre has occasional weekend performances for children. The museum is open daily except Monday, from 10 am to 1 pm and 2 to 7 pm; admission costs 500$00.

Uphill from here, Calçada da Graça leads to a splendid viewpoint, the **Miradouro da Graça**, atop one of Lisbon's seven hills. To the right is a former Augustinian convent, which now serves as a barracks, and about 700m beyond the convent (turn left off Largo da Graça into Rua Damasceno Monteiro, then bear right up Calçada do Monte) is the area's third major viewpoint, on another of Lisbon's hills, the **Miradouro da Senhora do Monte**. This is the best point in town for views of the castle, Mouraria and city centre.

Two cultural eye-openers lie within walking distance to the east of Largo de Rodrigues de Freitas (tram No 28 also passes close by). Dominating the scene is the huge dome of the **Igreja de Santa Engrácia**. When work began on this church in 1682, it was to be one of Lisbon's grandest. After almost three centuries of dithering and neglect, it was inaugurated in 1966 as a sombre and rather incongruous Panteão Nacional (National Pantheon), with marble cenotaphs to historic and literary figures (among them Vasco da Gama and Henry the Navigator), and the tombs of former presidents. The best thing about it is the view from the roof. It's open daily except Monday, from 10 am to 5 pm; admission costs 250$00.

Far more impressive is the nearby **Igreja de São Vicente de Fora** (*fora* refers to the church being outside the old city wall). Built in Mannerist style by the master of the Italian Renaissance, Felipe Terzi, between 1582 and 1627, its wide nave and coffered vault are striking in their simplicity. In the cloisters are 18th century azulejos depicting La Fontaine's fables. The former refectory (open daily from 9 am to 12.30 pm and 3 to 5.30 pm; 200$00) is now a mausoleum containing the black marble tombs of almost the entire Bragança dynasty, from João IV

(died 1656) to Manuel II (died 1932, in exile in England).

On Saturday and on Tuesday morning, the **Feira da Ladra** flea market is in full swing in nearby Campo de Santa Clara (see the boxed text 'Markets' under Shopping later in this chapter). The Bragança mausoleum is a spooky place then, with the sounds of the flea market resonating through one wall and Mass through the other.

Santa Apolónia

Just west of Santa Apolónia station, on Largo do Museu de Artilharia, is the **Museu Militar** (Military Museum; ☎ 888 21 31). Its main claim to fame is its artillery collection, said to be the world's biggest. War freaks can also look at other armaments, medals and patriotic paintings. It's open daily except Monday, from 10 am to 5 pm; admission costs 300$00.

North-east of Santa Apolónia are two more museums. The **Museu da Água** (Water Museum; ☎ 813 55 22), devoted to Lisbon's water supply over the centuries, won the Council of Europe's Museum Prize in 1990. Lisbon only got a dependable water supply in the 18th century and what an amazing project it was (see the boxed text 'The Aqueduct of Free Waters' under Greater Lisbon later in this chapter).

The museum, in a former pumping station, is open daily except Sunday and Monday, from 10 am to 12.30 pm and 2 to 5 pm; admission costs 300$00. Take bus Nos 104 or 105 from Santa Apolónia (the 104 comes from Praça Comércio, the 105 from Praça da Figueira). Get off the bus four stops after Santa Apolónia station and walk up Calçada dos Barbadinhos, turn right into Rua do Alviela and walk to the end.

A few stops further on is the **Museu Nacional do Azulejo** (National Azulejos Museum; ☎ 814 77 47), Rua Madre de Deus 4, perhaps the city's most attractive museum. A splendid array of tiles from as early as the 15th century (plus displays on how they're made) is integrated into the elegant buildings of the former convent of Igreja de Nossa Senhora da Madre de Deus. Among highlights are a 36m-long panel depicting pre-earthquake Lisbon and a lovely mural, *Our Lady of Life* by Marçal de Matos (dating from about 1580). There are also some charming 20th century azulejos. For more on azulejos, see the special section 'Portugal's Architecture' in the Facts about Portugal chapter.

The church, with its own beautiful tiles (and walls and ceiling crowded with paintings on the life of St Francis), the Manueline cloister, and the stupendous Baroque chapel and adjacent rooms of carved, gilded wood are highlights in their own right. There's also an excellent restaurant here (see Places to Eat later in this chapter). The complex was founded for the Poor Clare order of nuns in 1509 by Dona Leonor, wife of Dom João II. It's open Tuesday from 2 to 6 pm and Wednesday to Sunday from 10 am to 6 pm; admission costs 350$00.

ESTRELA, LAPA & DOCA DE ALCÂNTARA

Those with the stamina can ascend another of Lisbon's seven hills, Estrela, and explore the surrounding district of the same name to the west of the Bairro Alto. The attractions are limited, though the view from the hill is fine.

The easiest way to get there is on westbound tram No 28 from Rua da Conceição (Baixa), tram No 25 from Cais do Sodré or bus No 13 from Praça do Comércio. The most interesting way on foot is through Santa Catarina (see the earlier Chiado & Bairro Alto section), via Praça de Luís Camões, Calçada do Combro de Calhariz and Calçada da Estrela, up to the Basílica da Estrela.

As you leave Santa Catarina, head north on Avenida Dom Carlos I to Largo de São Bento and the imposing **Palácio da Assembleia da República** (also called the Palácio da Assembleia Nacional), Portugal's parliament, the nucleus of which is the 17th century former convent of São Bento. The

national assembly has convened here since 1833. At the rear is a vast public park and several other buildings, including the official residence of the prime minister.

At the top of Calçada da Estrela are the massive dome and belfries of the **Basílica da Estrela**. Completed in 1790 by order of Dona Maria I (whose tomb is here) in gratitude for bearing a male heir, the church is all elegant neoclassicism outside and chilly, echoing Baroque inside. Its best feature is the view across Lisbon from the dome, the weight of which was ingeniously spread over three concentric structures by architect Mateus Vicente de Oliveira. Also check out the life-size Christmas manger, with figures carved by Joaquim Machado de Castro (better known for the statue of Dom José I in Praça do Comércio). The church is open daily from 7.30 am to 7 pm (closed lunch time).

Across the road is a big, beautiful public park, the **Jardim da Estrela**. Beyond this lies a patch of heresy in this Catholic land, the Protestant **Cemitério dos Ingleses** (English Cemetery), founded in 1717 under the terms of the Treaty of 1654 with England. Among expatriates at rest here are novelist Henry Fielding (author of *Tom Jones*), who died during a visit to Lisbon for his health in 1754. At the far corner is all that remains of Lisbon's old Jewish cemetery.

To the south of Estrela is Lapa, Lisbon's diplomatic quarter. The main attraction (besides the bars and nightclubs of Avenida 24 de Julho and Doca de Santo Amaro; see Entertainment later in this chapter) is the first-class **Museu Nacional de Arte Antiga** (National Museum of Ancient Art; ☎ 396 41 51), in a 17th century palace at Rua das Janelas Verdes 9. Here is the official national collection of works by Portuguese painters, the largest such collection in the country. Also on display are other 14th to 20th century European works, including some by Hieronymus Bosch, Piero della Francesca and Albrecht Dürer, and an extensive collection of applied art.

The most outstanding item is undoubtedly the *Panels of São Vicente* by Nuno

ESTRELA, LAPA & DOCA DE ALCÂNTARA

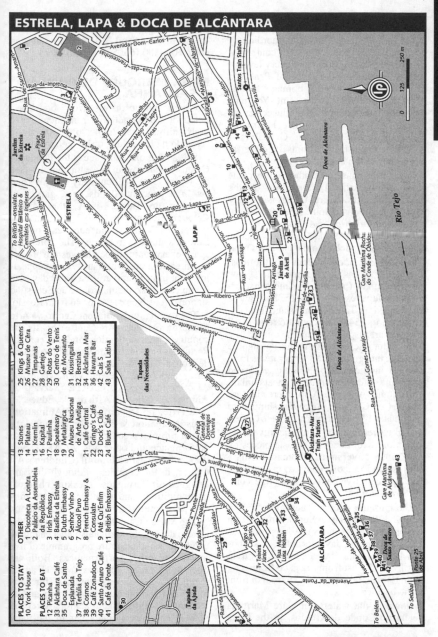

PLACES TO STAY
10 York House

PLACES TO EAT
12 Picanha
33 Alcântara Café
35 Doca de Santo
   Esplanada
37 Tertúlia do Tejo
38 Cosmos
39 Café Zonadoca
40 Santo Amaro Café
41 Café da Ponte

OTHER
1 Discoteca A Lontra
2 Palácio da Assembleia
   da República
3 Irish Embassy
4 Basílica da Estrela
5 Dutch Embassy
6 Senhor Vinho
7 Álcool Puro
8 French Embassy &
   Consulate
9 Até Qu'Enfim
11 British Embassy

13 Stones
14 Plateau
15 Kremlin
16 Kapital
17 Paulinha
18 Speakeasy
19 Metalúrgica
20 Museu Nacional
   de Arte Antiga
21 Café Central
22 Gringo's Café
23 Dock's Club
24 Blues Café

25 Kings & Queens
26 Museu de Cêra
27 Timpanas
28 Gatejo
29 Rotas do Vento
30 Centro de Tenis
   de Monsanto
31 Kussinguila
32 Benzina
34 Alcântara Mar
36 Havana Bar
42 Cais S
43 Salsa Latina

Gonçalves, most brilliant of the Flemish-influenced Portuguese painters prominent in the 15th century. The six extraordinarily detailed panels show a crowd of contemporary Portuguese figures from every level of society (including the Duke of Bragança and his family) paying homage to São Vicente, Portugal's patron saint. You may recognise the frequently reproduced central panels, which include Prince Henry the Navigator in his floppy hat. Gonçalves is thought to have painted himself in the far left corner of the central left panel.

Few of the museum's other works come close, though the *Annunciation* by the Flemish artist-monk Frei Carlos is a lovely work of luminous colour. After the apocalyptic *Temptation of St Anthony* by Bosch, it's a relief to move on to gentler works by Dürer, Holbein, della Robia and Van Dyck.

Japanese *namban* screens are the most interesting items in the museum's new wing. Namban (meaning southern barbarians), the Japanese name for the Portuguese who landed on Tanegaxima island in southern Japan in 1543, has come to refer to all Japanese art inspired by this encounter. The 16th century screens show the Portuguese arrival in intriguing detail. Other items from this era include Afro-Portuguese carved tusks and Indo-Portuguese chests inlaid with mother-of-pearl. Also interesting are samples of Chinese porcelain shipped to Lisbon and 18th century Portuguese copies.

Don't overlook the fantastic silverware collection, with dozens of masterpieces by the French silversmith Thomas Germain and his son François-Thomas, made in the late 18th century for the Portuguese court and royal family.

The museum is open Tuesday from 2 to 6 pm and Wednesday to Sunday from 10 am to 6 pm (closed Monday). Admission costs 500$00 (free Sunday morning). Take bus Nos 40 or 60 from Praça da Figueira or tram Nos 15 or 18 west from Praça do Comércio. From Estrela, take tram No 25 from in front of the basilica.

Down at the waterfront Gare Marítima Rocha do Conde de Óbidos, in the Doca de Alcântara, is a **Museu de Cêra** (Wax Museum), open daily except Monday from 11 am to 2 pm and 3 to 8 pm; admission costs 1000$00 (650$00 for children).

RATO, MARQUÊS DE POMBAL & SALDANHA

Northern and north-western Lisbon has a hotchpotch of attractions, from hothouses to high culture, reachable on foot along Avenida da Liberdade or by metro or bus.

Saldanha's one must-see is the Fundação Calouste Gulbenkian museum complex (see the boxed text). Meticulously designed and set in a peaceful, landscaped garden at Avenida de Berna 45-A, the **Museu Calouste Gulbenkian** (☎ 793 51 31) is surely Portugal's finest museum, and one of Europe's unsung treasures. The collection spans every major epoch of western art and much eastern art, with hardly an unappealing item in it. Spend at least a full day here if you can. Take the metro to São Sebastião station or bus Nos 31, 41 or 46 from Rossio.

The foundation's adjacent **Centro de Arte Moderna** (Modern Art Centre) boasts the country's best collection of 20th century Portuguese art, including works by Amadeo de Souza Cardoso, José de Almada Negreiros and Maria Helena Vieira da Silva. Also based here is ACARTE (Serviço de Animação, Criação Artistica e Educação pela Arte, or Department of Animation, Artistic Creation & Education through Art), which promotes contemporary Portuguese performance and other arts. ACARTE runs the **Centro Artístico Infantil** (Children's Art Centre) in the complex; although they are designed for Portuguese-speaking children, its exhibitions and related activities may also be of interest to young foreign visitors.

The Museu Calouste Gulbenkian and the Centro de Arte Moderna also host changing exhibitions and an entire programme of live music and other performances. Both are open daily except Monday from 11 am to 5 pm. Admission costs 500$00 for each museum (free on Sunday morning and to students, children and seniors over 65 years). There is a snack bar in the main

Hitch a ride on the Elevador de Santa Justa.

Looking across Lisbon to Castelo de São Jorge.

Gothic arches in the ruined Convento do Carmo.

Figures from Portugal's Age of Discoveries appear on the Padrão dos Descobrimentos in Belém.

The Eléctrico das Colinas tram passes through Alfama on its tour of Lisbon's hills.

Museu Calouste Gulbenkian Highlights

Among the classical and oriental art collections, some of the most memorable items are in the **Egyptian Room**: an exquisite 2700-year-old alabaster bowl, small female statuettes (each with a different hairstyle), a modern-looking sculpture of a priest's head and a series of bronze cats. In the adjoining **Greek and Roman** section, note the 2400-year-old Attic vase, Roman glassware in magical colours and an absorbing collection of Hellenic coins with finely carved heads and figures.

In the **Oriental Islamic Art** collection are some fine 16th and 17th century Persian carpets (note the black-hatted Portuguese explorers in their boats on one). Turkish faïence and azulejos from the same era glow with brilliant greens and blues, rust-reds and turquoise feather patterns, while 14th century mosque lamps from Syria have strikingly sensuous shapes. The adjoining Armenian collection includes illuminated manuscripts and books from the 16th to 18th centuries.

The **Chinese and Japanese** collection features a rich display of porcelain, lacquer, jade and celadon. Especially lovely are the 19th century Japanese prints of flowers and birds by Sugakudo.

The huge **European Art** section is arranged in chronological order, from medieval ivories and manuscripts to paintings from the 15th to

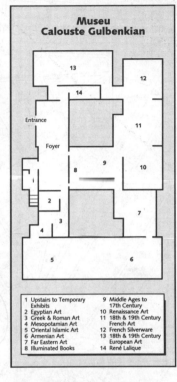

19th centuries. You'll recognise a few names – Rembrandt (see his sad *Figure of an Old Man*), Van Dyck (a rather spookier old man), Rubens (his second wife, Hélène Fourment, painted with more than his usual passion). Perhaps loveliest of all is the 15th century *Portrait of a Girl* by Ghirlandaio. Other pleasures from this era include a white marble *Diana* by Houdon and a trio of 16th century Italian tapestries portraying naughty, chubby cherubs in a cherry orchard.

Eighteenth and 19th century European art is comprehensively represented with Aubusson tapestries, fabulous if often fussy furniture (including items from Versailles), Sèvres porcelain, silverware and intricate clocks. Outstanding paintings in the collection are Gainsborough's *Mrs Lowndes*, two atmospheric La Tour portraits and some typically turbulent Turners. There's a whole room of works by Francesco Guardi and a passionate *Spring Kiss* by Rodin.

Finally, fans of Art Nouveau will appreciate the magical jewellery of French designer **René Lalique**: fantasies in the form of coronets and hair combs, brooches and necklaces.

LISBON

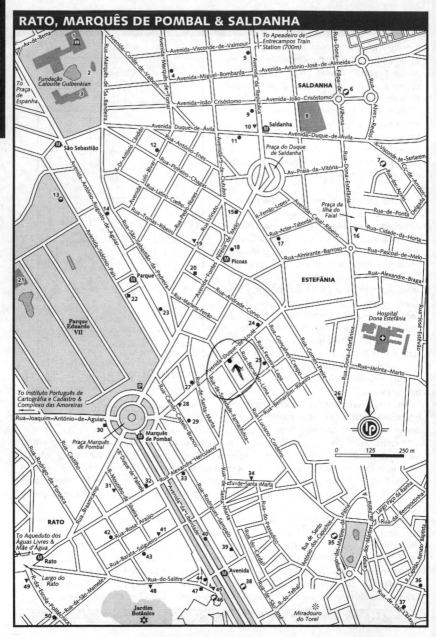

RATO, MARQUÊS DE POMBAL & SALDANHA

RATO, MARQUÊS DE POMBAL & SALDANHA

PLACES TO STAY		45	Cervejaria Ribadouro	23	Serviço de Estrangeiros
15	Residencial Lisbonense	48	Restaurante Os Tibetanos		e Fronteiras (Foreigners'
20	Pousada da Juventude	49	Real Fábrica		Registration Service)
22	Hotel Miraparque			24	Abraham Lincoln Center
26	Pensão Residencial Princesa	**OTHER**		25	Instituto da Conservação
30	Hotel Fénix	1	Museu Calouste Gulbenkian		da Natureza (ICN)
33	Hotel Presidente	2	Centro Artístico Infantil	27	Top Tours
39	Hotel Britânia	3	Centro de Arte Moderna	29	Tagus Travel
47	Pensão Residencial 13	4	Librairie Française	32	Livraria Buchholz
	da Sorte	5	Planet	35	German Embassy
50	Casa de São Mamede	6	Argentine Embassy	36	Olaria do Desterros
		7	Argentine Consulate	37	Os Ferreiros
PLACES TO EAT		8	Arco do Cego Bus Terminal	38	Canadian Embassy
10	Versailles	9	Livraria Municipal	40	Instituto Português
16	Restaurante Espiral	11	Movijovem		da Juventude (IPJ)
19	Li Yuan	12	Institut Franco-Portugais de	42	Automóvel Club de
28	Balcão do Marquês		Lisbonne; Alliance Française		Portugal (ACP)
31	Centro de Alimentação	13	Bus Tour Terminal	43	Instituto da Cinemateca
	e Saúde Natural	14	Wasteels		Portuguesa
34	Restaurante Estrela de	17	Intercentro Bus Linea	44	Cambridge School
	Santa Marta	18	Quiosque Internet	46	Spanish Embassy &
41	Big Apple Restaurante	21	Estufas		Consulate

museum building and a restaurant in the Centro de Arte Moderna.

When you need a breather, the **Parque Eduardo VII** is down the road, at the top of Avenida da Liberdade. Recently extended, the park – named after England's Edward VII, who visited Lisbon in 1903 – provides a fine escape, especially in its so-called **estufas** (greenhouses), the estufa fria (cool) and estufa quente (hot), which have an exotic collection of tropical and subtropical plants. They're open daily from 9 am to 6 pm and admission costs 95$00; access is easiest from Rua Castilho on the west side of the park. There's also a good children's area in the park. Take the metro to Parque or Marquês de Pombal or bus Nos 31, 41 or 46 from Rossio.

GREATER LISBON

Among limited attractions in Lisbon's northern suburbs is its Moorish-style **praça de touros** (bullring), across Avenida da República from Campo Pequeno metro station. See the Spectator Sports section later in this chapter for information on the action there.

Two metro stops north of the Parque Eduardo VII is the somewhat depressing **Jardim Zoológico** (zoo; ☎ 726 93 49). As the Liga Portuguesa dos Direitos do Animal (Portuguese League for Animal Rights) reported in 1998, most of the animals are housed in appalling conditions and the administration's concern seems to be 'profit and the amusement of people', with many animals made to perform senseless tricks. The dolphin show is more professional but heavy on chatter and slapstick. The zoo is open daily from 10 am to 8 pm in summer (6 pm in winter; admission costs 1800$00 (1400$00 for children aged three to 11). It's close to Jardim Zoológico metro station.

More uplifting is the **Quinta dos Marquêses da Fronteira** (☎ 778 20 23), Largo de São Domingos de Benfica 1, a 10 minute walk south-west of the zoo. This 17th century mansion, still inhabited, is known for its fabulous, manicured gardens and its abundant azulejos. It's open from 10.30 am to noon, daily except Sunday. Guided tours of the house cost 1000$00 (including admission to the gardens); admission to the gardens only costs 300$00.

Calouste Gulbenkian

Calouste Sarkis Gulbenkian, born to Armenian parents in Istanbul in 1869, was one of the 20th century's wealthiest men and best known philanthropists, and an astute and generous patron of the arts years before he struck it rich in Iraqi oil. His great artistic coup was the purchase of works from Leningrad's Hermitage between 1928 and 1930, when the young Soviet Union desperately needed hard currency.

In his later years he adopted Portugal as his home and bequeathed to it his entire, stupendous art collection – snubbing Britain (though he had British citizenship) after it foolishly labelled him a 'technical enemy' for working as an economic adviser in Paris at the time of the Vichy government. He lived in Portugal from 1942 until his death in 1955. In 1969 his art collection was moved into its own purpose-built quarters, Lisbon's Museu Calouste Gulbenkian.

Gulbenkian also bestowed on Portugal an extraordinary artistic, educational, scientific and charitable foundation that has become Portugal's main cultural life force. The Fundação Calouste Gulbenkian, with assets now exceeding US$1billion and a budget bigger than some Portuguese ministries, funds architectural restoration and the construction of libraries, museums, schools, hospitals, clinics and centres for disabled people all over the country. In Lisbon, as well as running the Museu Calouste Gulbenkian, it has endowed the adjacent Centro de Arte Moderna, built concert halls and galleries, and gathered together its own Orquestra Gulbenkian, Coro (Choir) Gulbenkian and a contemporary dance ensemble called Ballet Gulbenkian.

The foundation's main offices (☎ 793 51 31, fax 793 51 39, email info@gulbenkian.pt) are at Avenida de Berna 45-A, 1067 Lisbon. Its Portuguese-language Web site (www.gulbenkian .pt) is worth a dip for more information on the museum and other projects supported by the foundation, and a monthly agenda of cultural events.

Further out to the north are three museums in former palaces. The **Museu da Cidade** (City Museum; ☎ 759 16 17) offers a telescopic view of Lisbon's history. Highlights include an enormous model of pre-earthquake Lisbon, maps and prints from before and after the quake, and azulejo panels of city scenes. Also here are Almada Negreiros' portrait of the poet Fernando Pessoa, and the shoes and shawl of Amália Rodrigues, Portugal's foremost fado singer. The museum occupies the 18th century Palácio Pimenta (said to have been built by Dom João V for one of his mistresses) at Campo Grande 245. It's open daily except Monday, from 10 am to 1 pm and 2 to 6 pm; admission costs 330$00 (free on Sunday morning). Take the metro to Campo Grande or bus Nos 1 or 36 from Rossio.

The **Museu Nacional do Traje** (National Costume Museum; ☎ 759 03 18) and the **Museu Nacional do Teatro** (National Theatre Museum; ☎ 757 25 47) both occupy 18th century palaces in the grounds of the lush Parque de Monteiro Mór (take bus No 7 from Praça da Figueira or bus No 3 from Campo Grande metro station). The Costume Museum features changing exhibits of court and common dress from the Middle Ages to the present, and the Theatre Museum has theatrical costumes, props, posters and lots of photos of actors. Both charge 400$00 for admission and are open Tuesday from 2 to 6 pm and Wednesday to Sunday from 10 am to 6 pm.

Among the legacies of Expo '98 on the former Expo site on the riverfront to the north-east of the city, the most impressive is

The Aqueduct of Free Waters

Once one of Lisbon's major attractions, the extraordinary Aqueduto das Águas Livres (Aqueduct of Free Waters) is curiously overlooked by visitors nowadays. Its 109 grey stone arches lope south across the hills into Lisbon from Caneças, over 18km away.

The aqueduct was built to bring the city its first clean drinking water, by order of Dom João V, who laid the inaugural stone at Mãe d'Água (Mother of Water), the city's main reservoir at Praça das Amoreiras. Its cost was borne by the populace through a tax on meat, olive oil and wine. Most of the work was done between 1728 and 1748, under the gaze of engineer Manuel da Maia and architect Custódio Vieira. Its construction was interrupted by the 1755 earthquake (though little was damaged) and it was not completed until 1835.

The Museu da Água (see the Santa Apolónia section earlier in this chapter) and the municipal water company jointly run walking tours (usually in Portuguese only) of the aqueduct, every Thursday and Saturday in summer only. These start at Mãe d'Água (get there on bus No 9 from Rossio) and include a visit to another reservoir, the Reservatório de Patriarcal in Praça do Príncipe Real. For meeting times, check with the museum.

The aqueduct is at its most impressive at Campolide, where the tallest arch is about 65m high. Take any train from Rossio station to the first stop, or bus No 2 from Rossio or bus No 15 from Cais do Sodré.

---

the **Oceanarium**. This is Europe's largest, with 25,000 fish, birds and mammals in a two storey aquarium which recreates the entire global scene. It's open daily from 10 am to 6 pm and admission costs 1500$00 (800$00 for children aged from 6 to 17). Take the metro to Oriente station.

BELÉM

The district of Belém, 6km west of Rossio, was one of the main launch pads for Portugal's Age of Discoveries. Most famously, this was the place from which the great explorer Vasco da Gama set sail on 8 July 1497 for the two year voyage on which he discovered a sea route to India, setting in motion a fundamental shift in the world's balance of power.

Upon Vasco da Gama's safe return, Dom Manuel I ordered the construction of a monastery on the site of the riverside chapel (founded by Henry the Navigator) in which da Gama and his officers had kept an all-night vigil before departing on their historic voyage. The Mosteiro dos Jerónimos, like its predecessor, was dedicated to the Virgin

Mary, St Mary of Bethlehem (Belém) – hence the district's name.

The monastery, and an offshore watchtower also commissioned by Manuel I, are essential viewing for every visitor to Lisbon – don't miss them. Jointly designated a UNESCO World Heritage Site in 1984, they are among the finest remaining examples of the exuberant Portuguese brand of Renaissance-Gothic architecture called Manueline (see the special section 'Portugal's Architecture' in the Facts about Portugal chapter). They are also among the few structures in Lisbon to have survived the 1755 earthquake undamaged.

This peaceful suburb, which also boasts several other historical monuments and a clutch of worthwhile museums, makes a good full-day outing from central Lisbon – but don't go on a Monday, when nearly everything in Belém is closed.

The most interesting way to get to Belém is on the No 15 tram, which takes 20 minutes from Praça do Comércio; otherwise take bus No 43 from Praça da Figueira. Trains go from Cais do Sodré station to

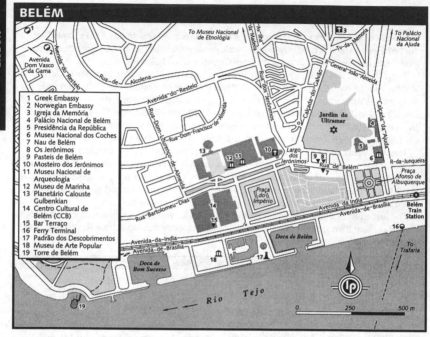

BELÉM

1 Greek Embassy
2 Norwegian Embassy
3 Igreja da Memória
4 Palácio Nacional de Belém
5 Presidência da República
6 Museu Nacional dos Coches
7 Nau de Belém
8 Os Jerónimos
9 Pasteis de Belém
10 Mosteiro dos Jerónimos
11 Museu Nacional de Arqueologia
12 Museu de Marinha
13 Planetário Calouste Gulbenkian
14 Centro Cultural de Belém (CCB)
15 Bar Terraço
16 Ferry Terminal
17 Padrão dos Descobrimentos
18 Museu de Arte Popular
19 Torre de Belém

Belém three to five times an hour weekdays, slightly less often weekends and holidays (120$00; seven minutes). From Belém station the monastery is a few hundred metres west along the riverfront.

Mosteiro dos Jerónimos

Manuel I ordered this monastery to be built in memory of Vasco da Gama's discovery of a sea route to India and, while he was at it, arranged that its church be made a pantheon for himself and his royal descendants (many of whom are now entombed in its chancel and side chapels).

Huge sums were funnelled into the project, including the so-called 'pepper money', a 5% tax levied on all income from the spice trade with Portugal's expanding African and Far Eastern colonies.

Work began in about 1502, following a Gothic design by architect Diogo de Boitaça, considered one of the originators of the Manueline style. After his death in 1517, building resumed with a Renaissance flavour under Spaniard João de Castilho and, later, with classical overtones under Diogo de Torralva and Jérome de Rouen (Jerónimo de Ruão). The monastery was only completed towards the end of the century. The huge neo-Manueline western wing and the domed bell tower, which date from the 19th century, seem out of keeping with the rest.

The monastery was populated by monks of the Order of St Jerome, whose spiritual job was to give comfort and guidance to sailors – and, of course, to pray for the king's soul. When the order was dissolved in 1833, the monastery was used as a school and orphanage until about 1940.

The façade of the **church** is dominated by João de Castilho's fantastic south portal, dense with religious and secular carvings. You enter through the west portal, designed by the French sculptor Nicholas Chanterène and now obscured by a modern connecting passage. In contrast to the extravagant exterior, the interior is sparsely adorned, spacious and lofty beneath an unsupported Baroque transept vault 25m high. Vasco da Gama is interred in the lower chancel, in a place of honour opposite the revered 16th century poet Luís de Camões.

The central courtyard of the monastery's **cloisters** is an unnervingly peaceful place, even when it's crowded; perhaps it's the fundamental harmony of its proportions that makes many visitors just sit down on the steps or lean against the columns as soon as they walk into it. In the old refectory off the western side of the cloisters, an azulejo panel depicts the Biblical story of Joseph. The sarcophagus in the echoing chapter house on the north-eastern corner belongs to the 19th century Portuguese historian Alexandre Herculano.

The monastery and church are open daily except Monday and holidays, from 10 am to 5.30 pm (5 pm in winter). Admission to the cloisters costs 400$00. There is no charge to see the church, although entry is discouraged when there are weddings (Saturday around 11 am and 3 pm and Sunday around 1 and 3 pm) or when Mass is being held (weekdays at 8 and 9.30 am and 7 pm, and Sunday at 8, 9 and 10.30 am, noon, and 7 pm).

Torre de Belém

The Tower of Belém sits just offshore, roughly 1km from the monastery. This hexagonal chesspiece – perhaps Portugal's most photographed monument – has come to symbolise Lisbon and the Age of Discoveries. Manuel I intended it as a fortress to guard the entrance to Lisbon's harbour. Before the shoreline slowly shifted south, the tower sat right out in mid-stream (and the monastery sat on the riverbank).

Designed by the brilliant Arruda brothers, Diogo and Francisco, the tower is an arresting mixture of early Gothic, Byzan-

tine and Manueline styles. Admission price and opening times are the same as for the monastery, though there's little inside that you can't see from the outside.

Padrão dos Descobrimentos

After admiring the tower, walk upriver to a modern memorial to Portuguese sea power. The huge limestone structure of the Discoveries Monument, inaugurated in 1960 on the 500th anniversary of the death of Prince Henry the Navigator, is shaped like a stylised caravel and crowded with important Portuguese figures. At the prow is Henry the Navigator; behind him are explorers Vasco da Gama, Diogo Cão and Fernão de Magalhães, poet Luís de Camões, painter Nuno Gonçalves and 27 others. Opposite the entrance is a wind rose (a device for determining the direction of the wind). Inside are exhibition rooms, and a lift and stairs to the top, which offers a bird's-eye view of the monastery and the river. It's open daily except Monday, from 9.30 am to 6.30 pm; admission costs 320$00.

Centro Cultural de Belém

The massive, squat Belém Cultural Centre, on the western side of Praça do Império, competes visually with the monastery as a moose would with a unicorn. But it's one of Lisbon's main cultural venues, with a full programme throughout the year. The interior plaza gets lots of unofficial use as a roller-blade arena and there's a pleasant rooftop terrace garden, with café and panoramic views.

Other Attractions in Belém

There are several museums worth seeing in and around Belém. Best known is the **Museu Nacional dos Coches** (National Coach Museum; ☎ 361 08 50) in the former royal riding school on Praça Afonso de Albuquerque. The focus is narrow – royal, aristocratic and church coaches of the 17th to 19th century – but the collection is one of the best in the world. There are enough gilded, painted, truly over-the-top vehicles to numb the senses and, like the Museu de

Arte Sacra in the Bairro Alto, they illustrate the ostentation and staggering wealth of the old Portuguese élite. It's open daily except Monday, from 10 am to 5.30 pm and admission costs 450$00 (free on Sunday morning).

Far more fun is the **Museu de Arte Popular** (Folk Art Museum; ☎ 301 12 82) on Avenida de Brasília opposite the Centro Cultural de Belém. This fascinating collection of clothing, ceramics, furniture, tools, toys and more from around the country, organised by region, is as good an overview as you can get of Portugal's charming and diverse folk arts. Among items you're unlikely to spot anywhere else are bagpipes from Mirando do Douro, toby jugs from Aveiro and huge spiked dog collars for the beasts of Castelo Branco. The museum is open daily except Monday, from 10 am to 12.30 pm and 2 to 5 pm; admission costs 300$00.

First opened in 1893, the **Museu Nacional de Arqueologia** (National Museum of Archaeology; ☎ 362 00 00), in the west wing of the Mosteiro dos Jerónimos, has exhibits of ceramics, sculpture, tiles, glass and coins from prehistory through Moorish times and a large collection of antique gold jewellery from the Bronze Age through Roman times. It's open Tuesday from 2 to 6 pm and Wednesday to Sunday from 10 am to 6 pm; admission costs 400$00 (free on Sunday morning).

Next door is the **Museu de Marinha** (Naval Museum; ☎ 362 00 10), with model ships from the Age of Discoveries onward, an 18th century brigantine, a late-19th century royal cabin from the yacht *Amélia*, the seaplane *Santa Cruz* that made the first crossing of the south Atlantic in 1922, and cases full of astrolabes and navy uniforms. This place often swarms with school groups, some of whom fortunately get sucked into the overpriced **Museu das Crianças** (Children's Museum) on the 1st floor, which has simple interactive exhibits (in Portuguese only). Admission to the Museu de Marinha is free for children under 10 years, 200$00 for those from 10 to 19 years,

and 400$00 for adults. It's open daily except Monday, from 10 am to 6 pm (5 pm in winter).

At the back of the Praça do Império, beside the Museu de Marinha, is the **Planetário Calouste Gulbenkian** (☎ 362 00 02). The planetarium has 40-minute shows for 400$00 (200$00 for children and 200$00 extra for headphone translations in English or French) at 11 am, 3 and 4.15 pm on Wednesday and Thursday, and at 4 and 5 pm on Saturday and Sunday. There's a special children's session on Sunday.

The often overlooked **Museu Nacional de Etnológia** (National Ethnological Museum; ☎ 301 52 64) mounts excellent temporary exhibitions from a huge collection. Past exhibitions have focussed on Portugal's former African and Asian colonies, and traditional textiles and weaving techniques from around the world. The museum is on Avenida Ilha da Madeira in the Restelo district, a relatively easy walk up from Belém. Alternatively, take bus No 32 from Praça da Figueira. It's open Tuesday from 2 to 6 pm and Wednesday to Sunday from 10 am to 6 pm; admission costs 350$00.

AJUDA

Ajuda (see Maps Belém & Greater Lisbon) is a former royal quarter on a hilltop above Belém. A 500m walk (or take bus No 27) up Calçada do Galvão from Largo dos Jerónimos is a little marble basilica, the **Igreja da Memória**, built by order of Dom José I on the site of an unsuccessful attempt on his life and now the resting place of his chief minister, the Marquês de Pombal.

If you bear right at the church and then left up Calçada da Ajuda (or take bus No 14 from Praça Afonso de Albuquerque in Belém or tram No 18 from Praça do Comércio) you'll come to the oversize Palácio da Ajuda. Begun in the late 18th century, left in limbo when the royal family fled to Brazil, used as a royal residence from 1861 to 1905 but never quite finished, it's now the **Museu do Palácio Nacional da Ajuda** (☎ 363 70 95).

The museum's vast collection of kitsch royal belongings is dominated by the furnishings of Dona Maria II and her husband Dom Ferdinand, whose lack of taste will be familiar to visitors to Sintra's Pena Palace, their summer retreat. The palace museum is open daily except Wednesday, from 10 am to 5 pm; admission costs 400$00. Also in the grounds is the Galeria de Pintura do Rei Dom Luís (Dom Luís Art Gallery), open daily except Monday from 10 am to 6 pm, with changing exhibitions.

The present official National Palace (Palácio Nacional de Belém) and the Presidential Palace (Presidência da República), just beyond the Museu Nacional dos Coches on Calçada da Ajuda, are not open to the public.

ACTIVITIES

Among Lisbon's public swimming pools, the most accessible are the indoor pools at Areeiro (☎ 848 67 94), Avenida de Roma 28 (Map Greater Lisbon), and Olivais (☎ 851 46 30), Avenida Dr Francisco Luís Gomes (Map Greater Lisbon; take bus No 21 from Campo Pequeno).

You'll need to book ahead to reserve one of the popular tennis courts at sports centres such as the Centro Desportivo Universidade de Lisboa (☎ 796 00 17) at the university (Map Greater Lisbon; metro Cidade Universitária), or Centro de Ténis de Monsanto (☎ 364 87 41) in the Parque Florestal de Monsanto (Map Estrela & Doca; bus No 24 from Alcântara).

Golfers are spoilt for choice: there are six major golf courses in the Estoril area (see the boxed text 'Golf on the Estoril Coast' in the Around Lisbon chapter), plus the Lisbon Sport Clube (☎ 431 00 77) at Casal da Carregueira, Belas (just north of Queluz). Daily green fees are around 7000$00.

ORGANISED TOURS
Bus & Tram Tours

Carris (☎ 363 20 21), the municipal transport company, runs the 1½ hour Eléctrico das Colinas tour of the hills by tram, up and around the hills on both sides of the Baixa. The tour departs up to four or five times a day and costs 2800$00 (1500$00 for children from four to 10 years). Carris also runs a Tagus Tour of the city and Belém by open-top bus for 2000$00 (1000$00 children), six or seven times a day, arranged so you can get off, explore and pick up the next bus an hour later. Both tours are in English. They depart from Praça do Comércio and there is no need to book ahead.

Cityrama (☎ 319 10 91), Portugal Tours (☎ 352 29 02) and Gray Line (☎ 352 25 94) run more or less identical sightseeing bus tours of Lisbon and the surrounding region, for identical prices. Typical Lisbon itineraries include a three hour city tour for 5250$00; Lisbon by night (12,500$00; four hours), with a restaurant meal, and Lisbon plus the Estoril coast or Lisbon plus the Costa Azul (12,500$00; full day). All buses depart from a terminal on Avenida Sidónio Pais, a block south of São Sebastião metro station in Saldanha, and pick up passengers at selected hotels. The easiest way to book a seat is through a travel agency or upmarket hotel, but if there's a space you can usually hop aboard the daytime trips without a booking.

Walking Tours

Walking Around Lisbon (☎ 340 45 39) organises two themed walks: Medieval Suburbia covers the Chiado, Bairro Alto and Carmo areas on Tuesday, Thursday and Saturday, starting at 9 am from Praça dos Restauradores. The Old Lisbon walk, visiting the Alfama and Castelo areas, sets out at 9 am on Monday, Wednesday and Friday from Casa dos Bicos. Both walks last three hours and cost 2500$00 per person. Call ahead to check meeting times and places.

River Cruises

For a relaxed look at the city from a unique point of view, Gray Line (☎ 882 03 47) runs two-hour, multilingual cruises on the Tejo (Cruzeiros no Tejo). They depart daily (at least from April to October; less often in winter) at 3 pm from the eastern end of the

Terreiro do Paço ferry terminal just beyond Praça do Comércio. The boats go down as far as Belém, cross the river and return, with no stops. Tickets cost 3000$00 if you buy them at the terminal, but more if you book through a hotel (in which case you get picked up from – but not returned to – the hotel). In summer, you can also buy tickets from a kiosk at the bottom of Rua do Carmo, in the Chiado. For student card holders, children under six years and adults over 65, the price is 1500$00.

SPECIAL EVENTS
Festas dos Santos Populares
In June the city lets its hair down with the Festas dos Santos Populares (Festivals of the Popular Saints), Christianised versions of traditional summer solstice celebrations. The highlight is the Festa de Santo António from 12 to 13 June (see boxed text 'St Anthony' earlier in this chapter). The Alfama (and to some extent Mouraria and Bairro Alto) parties through the night of the

St Anthony's Brides

In 1997 Lisbon's mayor, João Soares, revived a charming Lisbon tradition, the Noivas de Santo António (Brides of St Anthony), offering couples the chance to marry around St Anthony's day (13 June) in the Igreja de Santo António. With expenses paid by the municipal authorities and commercial sponsors, the mass wedding has been a big hit, attracting 17 couples (ranging in age from 17 to 64) in the first year and 16 in 1998.

In the past, the free marriage was offered only to less-well-off couples (and the brides had to be virgins!). The idea behind the revival is to lure youngsters into settling in Lisbon rather than heading for the suburbs: two requirements for the freebie are that the bride or groom must be living in Lisbon and must stay there once they are wed.

12th, with little *tronos* (thrones) for the saint in every square, plus parades, music, dancing, fireworks and, of course, lots of wine and grilled sardines. On the 13th, a municipal holiday, revellers rest and the devout go to church. The city then goes on buzzing for the rest of June, with concerts, exhibitions and street theatre performances sponsored by the city council.

Along with many communities across Portugal, Lisbon also celebrates the Festa de São João (St John) on the 23 to 24 June, and the Festa de São Pedro (St Peter) on the 28 to 29 June. Across the Rio Tejo at Montijo, the Festa de São Pedro is a fisher-folk celebration that dates from the Middle Ages, with a blessing of the boats, as well as bullfights and a running of the bulls in the streets.

Music Festivals
The Fundação Calouste Gulbenkian organises several annual international music festivals in Lisbon. These include Jornadas de Música Contemporânea (Journeys in Contemporary Music) at venues around the city in May, Jazz em Agosto (Jazz in August) in the foundation's gardens in early August, and Jornadas de Música Antiga (Journeys in Ancient Music) at various historical sites in October.

The Lisboa Mexe-me (Lisbon Moves Me) festival, which takes place between mid-July and mid-August, is a recent initiative by the city authorities to liven up some of the older neighbourhoods: free open-air dance, music and theatre performances are held in the streets of the Alfama, Bairro Alto, Madragoa (Alcântara) and Mouraria districts.

The Noite de Fado competition, held annually (usually in June), attracts both big names in fado, and up-and-coming artistes. Details about Lisboa Mexe-me and the Noite de Fado are available through the turismo.

Athletic Events
Lisbon hosts an international marathon, the Maratona de Lisboa (known in English as

the Discoveries Marathon), every year in late November, and a half-marathon in early March. If this sounds like a nice way to see the city, contact the organisers, Xistarca (☎ 363 36 05, fax 362 07 34), Travessa Paulo Martins 9, 1300 Lisbon, or the Federação Portuguesa de Atletismo (☎ 414 60 20), Largo da Lagoa 15-B, 2795 Linda-a-Velha.

PLACES TO STAY

In high season, advance bookings are imperative for accommodation near the city centre. Staff at the turismo at Praça dos Restauradores will make inquiries about accommodation for you, but not reservations. Prices here are for high season doubles (although some prices quoted may be unusually inflated due to Expo '98). See the Accommodation section in the Facts for the Visitor chapter for details about single room prices and discounts. Note that many top-end hotels offer weekend discounts (even at peak times).

Most budget accommodation is in the Baixa and Rossio areas, while many mid-range and top-end hotels are in the Saldanha, Marquês de Pombal and Avenida da Liberdade districts. Some of the city's most exclusive accommodation is in the upmarket Lapa district.

PLACES TO STAY – BUDGET
Camping

Six kilometres west of Rossio in the Parque Florestal de Monsanto is the big, well-equipped *Campismo de Câmara Municipal de Lisboa* (☎ 760 96 27, fax 760 74 74). It's open year round and a site costs 800/800/500$00 per person/tent/car. Take bus No 43 from Praça da Figueira.

Next nearest is a pricey site run by *Clube de Campismo de Lisboa* (☎ 962 39 60), 20km north-west of Lisbon at Almornos; prices are 850/900/850$00 per person/tent/car. There are half a dozen more on the other side of the Tejo along the Costa de Caparica, and others to the west at Sintra, Praia Grande and Praia do Guincho (see the Around Lisbon chapter).

Hostels

Lisbon's big *pousada da juventude* (☎ 353 26 96, fax 353 75 41, Rua Andrade Corvo 46, Map Saldanha) is just off Avenida Fontes Pereira de Melo (metro Picoas, bus No 46 from Santa Apolónia or the Rossio, bus Nos 44 or 45 from Cais do Sodré, or bus Nos 44, 45 or the Aero-Bus from the airport). A dorm bed costs 2900$00. Even if you don't stay there, the hostel's bulletin board is good for messages, tips and food ideas.

There are other pousadas da juventude across the Tejo at *Almada* (☎ 294 34 91, fax 294 34 97, Quinta do Bucelinho, Pragal) and on the beach at *Catalazete* (☎/fax 443 06 38, Estrada Marginal) in Oeiras, 12km west of Lisbon, accessible by frequent trains from Cais do Sodré station. The Lisbon and Catalazete hostels are open 24 hours. Reservations are essential – preferably at least a month ahead in summer. There is also a hostel in Sintra, 45 minutes from Lisbon by train from Rossio station (see the Around Lisbon chapter).

Movijovem (☎ 313 88 20, fax 352 86 21), Avenida Duque de Ávila 137 (Map Saldanha), is the central booking office for all of Portugal's Hostelling International hostels. It's open weekdays only, from 9.30 am to 6 pm.

Pensões & Residenciais
Rossio & Praça dos Restauradores All the places listed here are on Map Baixa & B Alto.

Friendly *Pensão Henriquez* (☎ 342 68 86, Calçada do Carmo 31), behind Rossio station, has bargain doubles with shared shower for 4000$00. Similarly priced is the adequate *Pensão Pérola de Baixa* (☎ 346 28 75, Rua da Glória 10), near the Elevador da Glória. Others on this road with doubles ranging in price from 4000$00 to 6500$00 include *Pensão Iris* (☎ 342 31 57, No 2-A) and the more appealing *Pensão Monumental* (☎ 346 98 07, No 21). Funicular and street-facing rooms at these places are noisy. Near the top of the Elevador the more salubrious *Pensão Globo* (☎ 346 22 79,

Rua do Teixeira 37) offers doubles for 6000$00 (4500$00 without shower).

Others falling in the upper price bracket (5000$00 to 6000$00) are the good *Pensão Duque* (☎ 346 34 44, *Calçada do Duque 53)*, the slightly noisier *Pensão Estrela de Ouro* (☎ 346 51 10, *Largo Trindade Coelho 6)* and *Residencial Nova Avenida* (☎ 342 36 89, *Rua de Santo António da Glória 87)*, near Praça da Alegria.

Baixa Many cheap places in the Baixa are on upper floors of old residential flats – warm and welcoming once you stagger up the grotty stairwells. Two good choices are *Pensão Moderna* (☎ 346 08 18, *Rua dos Correeiros 205)*, which has doubles without bathroom from around 4000$00, and *Pensão Prata* (☎ 346 89 08, *Rua da Prata 71)*, with rooms for 4000$00 to 6000$00. Plain, clean rooms at *Pensão Arco da Bandeira* (☎ 342 34 78, *Rua dos Sapateiros 226)* cost from 5000$00 to 7000$00.

Alfama *Residencial Rocha* (☎ 887 06 18, *Rua dos Bacalhoeiros 12)* has doubles without bathroom for around 4500$00.

Greater Lisbon Three blocks to the east of Arroios metro station, *Pensão Louro* (☎ 813 34 22, *Rua Morais Soares 76)* is a student hostel during the school year, but in July and August some spartan rooms with showers are available, including doubles for about 3000$00.

PLACES TO STAY – MID-RANGE
Rossio, Praça dos Restauradores & Baixa

All the places listed here are on Map Baixa & B Alto. Doubles at *Pensão Estação Central* (☎ 342 33 08, *Calçada do Carmo 17)*, behind Rossio station, are overpriced at 7500$00 (5500$00 without shower). Better value are *Pensão Residencial Florescente* (☎ 346 35 17, fax 342 77 33, *Rua das Portas de Santo Antão 99)*, with doubles for around 9000$00 (7000$00 without shower), and popular, slightly more expensive *Pensão Imperial* (☎ 342 01 66, *Praça dos Restauradores 78)*, opposite the turismo. *Pensão Aljubarrota* (☎/fax 346 01 12, *Rua da Assunção 53)*, on the 4th floor, provides spacious doubles with balconies plus great breakfasts for 8500$00 (7000$00 without shower). Old-fashioned *Pensão Residencial Alcobia* (☎ 886 51 71, fax 886 51 74, *Poço do Borratém 15)* offers spacious, quiet doubles for 9000$00 (8000$00 without bathroom). Breakfast is included in the price. Smart, security-conscious *Pensão Residencial Gerês* (☎ 881 04 97, fax 888 20 06, *Calçada do Garcia 6)* has doubles for around 9000$00 (8000$00 without bathroom) and triples from 10,000$00.

Bairro Alto & Chiado

All the places listed here are on Map Baixa & B Alto. Best value in this neighbourhood and price bracket is *Pensão Londres* (☎ 346 22 03, fax 346 56 82, *Rua Dom Pedro V 53)*. Spic-and-span upper rooms with fine views cost 8600$00 (6700$00 without shower), breakfast included. Street-facing rooms can be noisy. This popular place gets booked out a month ahead in summer. It's easy to reach on the Elevador da Glória.

At the southern end of the Chiado is *Residencial Nova Silva* (☎ 342 43 71, fax 342 77 70, *Rua Vitor Cordon 11)*, where plain rooms (some of them with river views) cost 8500$00 (7500$00 without shower).

Alfama

Just below the Castelo de São Jorge, a long climb up from the street, is *Pensão Ninho das Águias* (☎ 886 70 08, *Costa do Castelo 74)*. With a flower garden, stunning city views and 14 elegant rooms, it gets booked up a month ahead in summer and reservations are essential. Doubles/triples are about 7000/8000$00, 6000/7000$00 without bathroom.

Saldanha

Residencial Lisbonense (☎ 354 46 28, fax 354 48 99, *Rua Pinheiro Chagas 1)* has bright doubles on four upper storeys; rooms with bathroom, telephone, air-con and breakfast cost from 8000$00. *Pensão Resi-*

dencial Princesa (☎ *314 86 17, fax 314 86 19, Rua Gomes Freire 130)*, in Estefânia, has comfortable doubles/triples for 10,000/ 14,300$00; take bus No 100 from Praça da Figueira. *Pensão Residencial 13 da Sorte* (☎ *353 18 51, fax 395 69 46, Rua do Salitre 13)* gets booked up in summer; doubles/ triples with bathroom, TV and telephone are 9000/12,000$00.

PLACES TO STAY – TOP END
Rossio & Praça dos Restauradores
All the places listed here are on Map Baixa & B Alto. *Hotel Suiço-Atlântico* (☎ *346 17 13, fax 346 90 13, Rua da Glória 3)* offers adequate doubles with bathroom costing 12,000$00. *Albergaria Insulana* (☎ *342 76 25, fax 342 89 24, Rua da Assunção 52)* has simple, pleasant rooms with bathroom and breakfast for 15,000$00. An aparthotel called *Orion Eden Lisboa* (☎ *321 66 00, fax 321 66 66, Praça dos Restauradores 24)* has studio apartments for 15,000$00 and flats for up to four people (with kitchen, satellite TV and telephone) for 21,000$00. Three are wheelchair accessible.

Alfama
At the Miradouro da Senhora do Monte, *Albergaria Senhora do Monte* (☎ *886 60 02, fax 887 77 83, Calçada do Monte 39)* has comfortable rooms which cost around 25,000$00, breakfast included. Free car parking is available on the quiet street, and tram No 28 runs close by.

Down in the Alfama, behind the cathedral, is *Pensão São João da Praça* (☎/fax *886 25 91, Rua São João da Praça 97)*, where doubles with bathroom cost about 16,000$00 (10,000$00 without), but half as much in low season.

Lapa
Our vote for Lisbon's most exquisite hotel goes to *York House* (☎ *396 24 35, fax 397 27 98, Rua das Janelas Verdes 32)*, a former 17th century convent in the élite Lapa district. The 36 rooms, which are furnished with antiques, cost 30,000$00 and are in high demand.

Marquês de Pombal & Rato
All the places listed here are on Map Saldanha. *Casa de São Mamede* (☎ *396 31 66, fax 395 18 96, Rua Escola Politécnica 159)* is a small hotel in an elegant townhouse. Doubles/triples with bathroom, TV and telephone start at 16,000/17,000$00, breakfast included. Take bus No 58 from Cais do Sodré and get off a couple of blocks past the Universidade Internacional. The *Hotel Fénix* (☎ *386 21 21, fax 386 01 31, email h.fenix@ip.pt, Praça Marquês de Pombal 8)*, a traditional 1st class hotel with an old-fashioned feel, has rooms for 25,000$00.

In a quieter location, the *Hotel Miraparque* (☎ *352 42 86, fax 357 89 20, Avenida Sidónio Pais 12)* retains a personal touch despite all the tour groups. Plain rooms cost a reasonable 10,000$00 and free street parking is usually available.

A three star hotel with the facilities of a four star is the *Hotel Presidente* (☎ *353 95 01, fax 352 02 72, Rua Alexandre Herculano 13)*; rooms with TV, air-con, mini-bar and great breakfasts cost 18,000$00.

For a romantic splurge, the *Hotel Británia* (☎ *315 50 16, fax 315 50 21, Rua Rodrigues Sampaio 17)* has masses of charm. Dating from the 1940s, the hotel was designed by the Portuguese modernist architect Cassiano Branco. Its 30 rooms are huge and very pricey (35,200$00) but the atmosphere is pleasantly intimate.

PLACES TO EAT
Lisbon may not be a gastronomic paradise, but there are hundreds of restaurants, many offering great value for money. The best bargains are at lunchtime, with generous daily specials from around 800$00 (in café-restaurants it's always cheaper if you eat at the counter). Note that many places close on Sunday night; call ahead if in doubt.

Restaurants & Cafés
There are lots of good-value restaurants and cafés concentrated in the Baixa and Bairro Alto districts. At night, popular places in the Bairro Alto fill up quickly: try to bag a table by 7.30 pm.

Rossio & Praça dos Restauradores All the places listed here are on Map Baixa & B Alto.

Not for vegetarians is a good little *casa de pasto* called **Casa Transmontana** (☎ 342 03 00, Calçada do Duque 39), serving strong-tasting northern Portuguese specialities, such as chicken or rabbit cooked in its own blood, for under 1200$00 per plate. There are several other cheap lunchtime places in this lane of steps, most with outdoor seating.

Another good hunting ground is Rua da Glória: our favourite among several cheap, locally popular places is the unpretentious **Restaurante O Brunhal** (☎ 347 86 34), at No 27, with well-prepared *pratos do dia* (dishes of the day) for 700$00 to 900$00, and service beyond the call of duty.

Along Rua das Portas de Santo Antão, several restaurants offer good but seriously overpriced seafood at sunny outdoor tables. A genuinely superb fish restaurant here is **Gambrinus** (☎ 342 14 66) at No 23. Enjoy the ambience without breaking the bank by eating snacks at the counter.

Considerably more down-to-earth is **O Fumeiro** (☎ 347 42 03, Rua da Conceição da Glória 25), devoted to the cuisine of the mountainous Beira Alta and Serra da Estrela region; even the pictures on the walls are of sausages.

Baixa The Baixa has burgers and beer if that suits you, but also some of the best modestly priced food in town. A reliable standby is **Restaurante João do Grão** (☎ 342 47 57, Rua dos Correeiros 228), open daily. Tourists like its large, reasonably priced menu. Two other good-value places in the same street are **Restaurante Ena Pãi** (☎ 342 17 59) at No 180 and **Lagosta Vermelha** (☎ 342 48 32) at No 155. **Restaurante Múni** (☎ 342 89 82) at No 115 is a bit pricier.

Martinho da Arcada (☎ 887 92 59, Praça do Comércio 3) makes much of the fact that it has been in business since 1782. It was once a haunt of the literary set, but renovation has shifted its clientele from cognoscenti to tourists. Its café is good value for lunch but the restaurant is pricey.

In the Mouraria area west of the Castelo, fashionable **Algures na Mouraria** (☎ 887 24 70, Rua das Farinhas 1) offers Portuguese or African dishes at reasonable prices.

Bairro Alto & Chiado All the places listed here are on Map Baixa & B Alto.

Mention Bairro Alto and most tourists think fado, although most *casas de fado* are better known for their music than their menus. See the Entertainment section for several good fado houses with adequate food, most of them in the Bairro Alto.

One of our favourite restaurants here is venerable **A Primavera** (☎ 342 04 77, Travessa da Espera 34), where a family ambience is complemented by honest, good cooking at modest prices. Serving typical Portuguese fare, **A Transmontana** (☎ 347 88 58, Rua do Diário de Notícias 139) is another recommended budget place (like its namesake in Calçada do Duque).

Relaxed but a bit pricier is **Tasca do Manel** (☎ 346 38 13, Rua da Barroca 24), which serves tasty standards for about 1500$00 a dish. Similarly priced and with an Alentejan outlook and décor is the popular **O Cantinho do Bem Estar** (☎ 346 42 65, Rua do Norte 46); get here early. Another busy place in a similar price bracket is smart **Sinal Vermelho** (☎ 346 12 52, Rua das Gáveas 89); make sure you leave room for dessert.

On the southern fringe of the Bairro Alto, tiny **Tendinha da Atalaia** (☎ 346 18 44, Rua da Atalaia 4) specialises in fish grilled (*no carvão*) on the spot. Fancy a change from sardines and bacalhau? Try **Ali-a-Papa** (☎ 347 21 16, Rua da Atalaia 95), which serves Moroccan specialities like couscous and tagines from 1400$00.

Cavernous **Cervejaria da Trindade** (☎ 342 35 06, Rua Nova da Trindade 20-C) is a former convent building with arched ceilings, gorgeous 19th century tilework and a robust, busy atmosphere. They've been serving food here for over 150 years.

It's a bit pricey (beef and seafood specialities from the grill start at 1400$00) but makes a great lunch stop. It's open daily.

Pap'Açorda (☎ 346 48 11, *Rua da Atalaia 57*) features a startling décor and excellent, expensive *açorda* (a bread and shellfish mush served in a clay pot). It's big with celebrities and celebrity-watchers, so advance booking is essential. It's closed Saturday evening and Sunday.

Rua da Bica Duarte Belo (the street with the Elevador da Bica) has a generous sprinkling of restaurants: try *Restaurante Alto Minho* (☎ 346 81 33) at No 61, which does cheap and wholesome fare.

High on style and ambience is *La Brasserie de l'Entrecôte* (☎ 342 83 44, *Rua do Alecrim 117*), on the southern edge of the Chiado. This high-ceilinged, modernist venue offers a simple French menu – entrecôte, salad and chips (2500$00) – cooked to perfection, with some superb herb and nut sauces.

Cais do Sodré All the places listed here are on Map Baixa & B Alto.

A short walk from Cais do Sodré is zany, self-service *Pano Mania* (☎ 342 24 74, *Rua do Alecrim 47*), offering great salads, soups, hamburgers and daily specials for 700$00. *Restaurante Porto de Abrigo* (☎ 346 08 73, *Rua dos Remolares 18*) has good fish and seafood dishes costing from 800$00 to 1700$00.

For cheap snacks head for Espaço Ágora's *Ágora Café*, on the riverfront near Cais do Sodré car ferry pier; it's open 24 hours, like many other student-oriented services in this complex, and there are discounts for students.

Alfama & Castelo Just outside the castle, *Castelo Mourisco* (☎ 886 78 52, *Rua Santa Cruz do Castelo 3*) has modestly priced dishes for under 1500$00.

The Alfama's waterfront restaurants are touristy, but the outdoor seating is tempting. We like *Restaurante Leitão do Arco da Conceição* (☎ 886 98 60, *Rua dos Bacalhoeiros 4*). Or go under the Arco de Jesus

Chapitô

If you pop into *Chapitô* (☎ 887 82 25, *Costa do Castelo 1-7*), below Castelo São Jorge, you'll find it's more than an open-air café-bar with a view. It's actually part of a school of circus arts and show business run by the Collectividade Cultural e Recreativa de Santa Catarina (Santa Catarina Cultural & Recreation Collective), founded in the mid-1980s.

Next door, the collective has a library, a theatre, a gallery, recording studios, classrooms and a Ludoteca childcare centre. It runs evening courses in dance, music, singing, juggling, circus techniques and TV acting, and presents performance arts, films and exhibitions – all listed in its own monthly programme (in Portuguese), and usually in the newspapers, the *Agenda Cultural* and at the turismo.

The café-bar, serving salads, soups and sandwiches, is open in summer only from 7 pm to 2 am.

to the popular *Bacalhau de Molho* (☎ 886 37 67, *Beco dos Armazens do Linho 1*).

There are several tourist-geared places around Largo do Chafariz de Dentro, but *Restaurante Cais d'Alfama* (☎ 887 32 74) at No 24 pulls in locals too, with a big menu (including fresh sardines, grilled outside) and prices under 1000$00.

Lastly, high above it all, the outdoor tables at *Bar Cerca Moura* (☎ 887 48 59, *Largo das Portas do Sol 4*) are worth the extra escudos for the view over the Alfama.

Alcântara & Lapa All the places listed here are on Map Estrela & Doca.

Expensive *Alcântara Café* (☎ 363 71 76, *Rua Maria Luisa Holstein 15*) is a design eye-opener, combining neoclassical and Art Deco. It's open evenings only, from 8 pm to 3 am, serving international fare.

Stylish but more modest is *Picanha* (☎ 397 54 01, *Rua das Janelas Verdes 96*),

Chic & Open-Air

At last count the Doca de Santo Amaro (Map Estrela & Doca), in Alcântara, had a dozen restaurant-bars, with more on the way. Overlooking a marina and with the massive Ponte 25 de Abril overhead, it's a stunning place for alfresco dining and late boozing and schmoozing. Following is a selection of good places with both day and evening opening hours. Evening-only bars in the strip are listed under Entertainment later in this chapter.

Café da Ponte (☎ 395 76 69) – small and simple with an equally modest menu, but billed as 'Lisbon's craziest café' due to its charismatic bar staff; closed Tuesday

Café Zonadoca (☎ 397 20 10) – loopy décor, classy music and a stylish menu of salads, crêpes and ices

Cosmos (☎ 397 27 47) – pizzas, salads and pasta for under 1500$00

Doca de Santo Esplanada (☎ 396 35 22) – large outdoor dining area, extensive menu for under 1000$00 per dish (including great salads); open very late

Havana (☎ 397 98 93) – colourful décor and a simple menu of hamburgers, salads and tapas; live music from Tuesday to Friday

Tertúlia do Tejo (☎ 395 55 52) – one of the strip's poshest, with traditional Portuguese fare for 2500$00 to 5000$00 per dish

To get here, take a train from Cais do Sodré to Alcântara Mar station and follow the *marítima* signs, turning right to Doca de Santo Amaro. Alternatively, catch tram No 15 from Praça da Figueira, alighting just beyond Dock's Club and the Blues Café at Doca de Alcântara.

with a set menu of *picanha* (a Brazilian beef dish) with potatoes, salad, rice, beans and various sauces for 2200$00. There's also a good choice of desserts.

For a rundown of restaurant-bars in the trendy new Doca de Santo Amaro area, see the boxed text on this page.

Marquês de Pombal & Rato All the places listed here are on Map Saldanha.

East of Avenida da Liberdade, Travessa de Santa Marta is good hunting ground for unpretentious restaurants – which get crammed at lunchtimes). Go early to get a seat at **Restaurante Estrela de Santa Marta** (☎ 354 84 00) at No 14-A, where daily specials are under 900$00.

If you're nostalgic for pizzas and burgers, try the cheerful **Big Apple Restaurante** (*Rua Barata Salgueiro 28)*, at the rear of a shopping arcade.

Cervejaria Ribadouro (☎ 354 94 11, *Rua do Salitre 2)* is a traditional beerhall which has been modernised; the menu is still good, however, with prices from around 1300$00.

A popular café for snacks and cheap lunches is **Balcão do Marquês** (☎ 354 50 86, *Avenida Duque de Loulé 119)*. Eating is mainly stand-up (the *balcão* of the café's name means counter).

A well known Chinese restaurant in this area is **Li Yuan** (☎ 357 77 40, *Rua Viriato 23)*, near Picoas metro station, where dishes cost under 1800$00.

One of the Rato's artiest eateries is the bar and restaurant **Real Fábrica** (☎ 387 20 90, *Rua Escola Politécnica 275)*. This converted 19th century silk factory, now famous for the home-brewed beer it serves, looks expensive, but this is deceptive – many of the lunchtime specials cost less than 1000$00. There's a pleasant outdoor terrace, too.

Belém A fine place for an outdoor snack and coffee is *Bar Terraço* on the roof of the Centro Cultural.

Rua de Belém's many eateries get packed out with tourists. Among less expensive options are *Os Jerónimos* (☎ 363 84 23) at No 74, with tasty lunches for around 700$00, and *Nau de Belém* (☎ 363 81 33) at No 29, slightly more expensive but with a pleasant outdoor area.

Another place worth visiting is *Pasteis de Belém* (see the following Pastelarias & Confeitarias section). One to avoid is the over-priced *Café Astrolabio*, opposite the Museu da Marinha.

Vegetarian

Thankfully in a country that so loves its meat, the capital has some good, modestly priced vegetarian restaurants. Our choice for value is *Restaurante Os Tibetanos* (☎ 314 20 38, Rua do Salitre 117, Map Saldanha), part of a school of Tibetan Buddhism in an old house topped with prayer flags, on the northern side of the botanical garden (metro Avenida). On offer is a daily rice and vegetable dish for 750$00, plus soups, salads and pastries, in a peaceful setting. It's closed Sunday.

Also recommended is *Restaurante Espiral* (☎ 357 35 85, Praça da Ilha do Faial 14-A, Map Saldanha), open daily, with macrobiotic rice and vegetable dishes and light meals for around 700$00 per course, plus lots of desserts – and sometimes live music.

Centro de Alimentação e Saúde Natural (☎ 315 08 98, Rua Mouzinho da Silveira 25, Map Saldanha) has a weedy, peaceful courtyard and a small selection of vegetarian and macrobiotic dishes for under 1000$00; it's open weekdays and Saturday until 2 pm. Next door is a health-food shop.

Celeiro (Rua 1 de Dezembro 65, Map Baixa & B Alto) is a health-food shop, open weekdays to 8 pm and Saturday to 7 pm. The self-service macrobiotic restaurant downstairs (☎ 342 24 63) is open weekdays only from 9 am to 7 pm, with everything from herbal teas to Chinese crêpes. On the

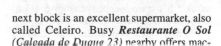

Azulejos for Lunch?

A fine setting for a light lunch is the restaurant in the *Museu Nacional do Azulejo*, in the old convent of Igreja de Nossa Senhora da Madre de Deus (see under Santa Apolónia earlier in this chapter). Choose from a small menu of salads, crêpes or meat and fish dishes which cost from 1100$00 to 1500$00, and eat in the bright, traditional kitchen (tiled with azulejos, of course) or the plant-filled garden.

next block is an excellent supermarket, also called Celeiro. Busy *Restaurante O Sol* (Calçada do Duque 23) nearby offers macrobiotic and other vegetarian fare.

Restaurante Yin-Yang (Rua dos Correeiros 14), in the Baixa, is open weekdays only from noon to 3 pm and 6.30 to 8.30 pm; macrobiotic meals start at 750$00.

The restaurant at the *Centro de Arte Moderna* in the Gulbenkian museum (see Rato, Marquês de Pombal & Saldanha earlier in this chapter) is open daily for lunch, serving great salads.

Pastelarias & Confeitarias

Lisbon has enough pastry shops and coffee shops to keep you buzzing all day, and the Portuguese love them. Many restaurants also have a separate area devoted to this excellent Portuguese pastime. Note that you'll pay quite a lot more to have your coffee or snack outside.

One of the grandest pastelarias – also serving rather expensive meals – is *Versailles* (☎ 354 6340, Avenida da República 15A, Map Saldanha), with splendidly over-the-top chandeliers and marble columns.

Another elegant setting, with strong literary associations and art all over the walls, is *Café A Brasileira* (☎ 346 95 47, Rua Garrett 120, Map Baixa & B Alto), open daily to 2 am. The bronze statue sitting outside (by Lagoa Henriques) is of the poet and writer Fernando Pessoa, a frequent habitué of the café in his day.

The Art Deco *Café Nicola (Rua 1 de Dezembro 16-26 & Rossio 24, Map Baixa & B Alto)* was once the grande dame of Lisbon's cafés, its maroon walls lined with paintings. A recent tarting-up has robbed it of its charm, though service is still slick.

Beloved of students and old dears from the neighbourhood for its pastries and big coffees is cheerful *Confeitaria Císter (Rua da Escola Politécnica 107, Map Baixa & B Alto)*.

In Cais do Sodré there's a fine bakery and pastelaria called *Caneças (Rua Bernardino Costa 34-36, Map Baixa & B Alto)* serving hot fresh bread, croissants, cakes and light snacks. It's open weekdays from 6 am to 7.30 pm and Saturday from 8 am to 2 pm.

Finally, when you go to Belém, don't miss *Pasteis de Belém (Rua de Belém 88)*, opposite the tram stop, where the traditional custard tarts called *pastéis de Belém* are made on the premises and consumed in vast quantities.

Self-Catering

The biggest and best market for fresh fruit, vegetables, cheese, olives and various Portuguese products is the *Mercado da Ribeira*, near Cais do Sodré, although there are supermarkets and groceries (*minimercados*) scattered everywhere.

For the easiest pick-up food supplies, try the well-stocked *Celeiro* health-food shop, near Rossio station. It even has freshly grilled chicken, as well as foreign brands of cereal, chocolate and other luxuries. The big shopping complexes such as Amoreiras and Colombo also have supermarkets.

ENTERTAINMENT

Bars and clubs abound in the traditional nightlife neighbourhoods of Bairro Alto, Alcântara and Avenida 24 de Julho, and in booming riverside areas like Doca de Santo Amaro. We note our choices here, but places come and go like the wind, and your best bet may be to do what everybody else does: trawl the neighbourhoods till you find what you like. Evenings start late – 11 pm at the earliest – and can go on until dawn.

For information about personal safety see under Dangers & Annoyances earlier in this chapter.

Lisbon's most famous entertainment (among visitors at any rate) is fado, the melancholy Portuguese equivalent of the blues; much of it has been expensively packaged for tourists, but you can still find more authentic places. Other traditional Portuguese entertainment, such as folk music and dancing, parades and processions, is best enjoyed during the month-long Festas dos Santos Populares in June (see Special Events earlier in this chapter).

For current listings, pick up the free monthly *Agenda Cultural* from turismos or see the listings in the *Público* newspaper. The Gulbenkian and the Centro Cultural de Belém publish their own schedules. The city also operates a 24 hour 'what's on' hotline (☎ 790 10 62) in Portuguese.

The ABEP ticket agency, on Praça dos Restauradores, is fine for bookings for bullfights, films football, and stadium concerts, but you're better off buying concert tickets at the venues.

Fado

Listening to Portugal's 'blues' in its authentic form is a wonderfully melancholy way to drink your way through the night, and the Alfama district is said to be its true home (for more about fado, see Arts in the Facts about Portugal chapter).

However, the sad truth is that with large numbers of tourists all wanting to hear fado, many of Lisbon's casas de fado offer pale imitations of the real thing – 'tour-bus meets Greek taverna', as one travel writer put it – and often at prices to make you moan along with the *fadista*. Nearly all are restaurants, most insisting that you spend a minimum (*consumo mínimo*) of between 2000$00 and 4500$00 on their food and drinks in order to stay and hear the music. You may spend twice that if you have dinner there.

Following are some better known fado houses (and a few lesser-known ones), and an indication of minimum charges. The hours listed in this section are for music, though food may be on offer earlier.

A Severa (☎ 346 40 06, *Rua das Gáveas 55, Map Baixa & B Alto*) – 9.30 pm to 3.30 am (closed Thursday); 3500$00

Adega do Machado (☎ 322 46 40, *Rua do Norte 91, Map Baixa & B Alto*) – 9.30 pm to 3 am (closed Monday); 2750$00

Adega do Ribatejo (☎ 346 83 43, *Rua Diário de Notícias 23, Map Baixa & B Alto*) – reasonable food prices, better value than most; 8.30 pm to midnight (closed Sunday); 1800$00

Adega Mesquita (☎ 321 92 80, *Rua Diário de Notícias 107, Map Baixa & B Alto*) – 8 pm to 3.30 am; 2500$00

Café Luso (☎ 342 22 81, *Travessa da Queimada 10, Map Baixa & B Alto*) – jazz at weekends; 8 pm to 3.30 am (closed Sunday); 2000$00

Lisboa à Noite (☎ 346 26 03, *Rua das Gáveas 69, Map Baixa & B Alto*) – 8 pm to 3 am daily; 3000$00

Nono (*Rua do Norte 47, Map Baixa & B Alto*) – 8 pm to 3.30 am (closed Sunday); 1500$00

O Forcado (☎ 346 85 79, *Rua da Rosa 219, Map Baixa & B Alto*) – 8 pm to 2 am (closed Wednesday); 3000$00

Os Ferreiras (☎ 885 08 51, *Rua de São Lázaro 150, Map Saldanha*) – 9 pm to 2 am Friday and Saturday; 2500$00

Parreirinha de Alfama (☎ 886 82 09, *Beco do Espírito Santo 1, Map Alfama*) – 8 pm to 3 am; 2000$00

Restaurante Numero Um (*Rua Dom Francisco Manuel de Melo, Map Greater Lisbon*) – a favourite with local enthusiasts and amateur fadistos, who turn up late to give impromptu performances

Senhor Vinho (☎ 397 26 81, *Rua do Meio à Lapa 18, Map Estrela & Doca*) – one of the better-known fado venues; 8.30 pm to 3 am (closed Sunday); 3000$00

Taverna do Embuçado (☎ 886 50 88, *Beco dos Cortumes 10, Map Alfama*) – 9 pm to 2.30 am (closed Sunday); 4500$00

Tímpanas (☎ 397 24 31, *Rua Gilberto Rola 24, Map Estrela & Doca*) – 8 pm to 2 am (closed Wednesday); 2000$00

Bars

This section is for those looking mainly for a watering hole. Many places also have music (sometimes live) and dancing (see also nightclubs and music in this secion). The Doca de Santo Amaro is the trendiest new area for late-night restaurants and bars.

Bairro Alto & Chiado Numerous bars line the narrow streets of this quarter, which is renowned for its nightlife. A few of the best are listed here:

A Capela (☎ 347 00 72, *Rua da Atalaia 45*) – in a former chapel; live jazz sometimes; 10 pm to 3 am (Friday and Saturday to 4 am)

Arroz Doce (☎ 346 26 01, *Rua da Atalaia 117*) – young, cheerful and unpretentious; 6 pm to 2 am (closed Sunday)

Café Suave (☎ 347 11 44, *Rua do Diário do Notícias 6*) – futuristic décor, very chic crowd; 9 pm to 2 am

Ma Jong (☎ 342 10 39, *Rua da Atalaia 3*) – trendy bar-restaurant; intellectual, artsy crowd; 11 pm to 4 am

Nova (☎ 346 28 34, *Rua da Rosa 261*) – jazz, funk and soul; trendy, with sushi snacks; 6 pm to 2 am

Pavilhao Chines (☎ 342 47 29, *Rua Dom Pedro V 89*) – idiosyncratic early-20th century décor and pre and post-war art; pool tables; not gay-friendly; 6 pm to 2 am (from 9 pm Sunday)

Primas (☎ 342 59 25, *Rua da Atalaia 154*) – noisy local pub with pinball machines; 10 pm to 3 am

Snob Bar (☎ 346 37 23, *Rua do Século 178*) – a favourite with journalists and the advertising crowd; serves food; 4.30 pm to 3 am

Soul Factory Bar (*Rua das Salgadeiras 28*) – music from reggae to soul, hip hop to funk and rap; 9.30 pm to 3.30 am, closed Tuesday

Cais do Sodré All the places listed here are on Map Baixa & B Alto.

Bar do Rio (☎ 346 72 79, 347 09 70, *Armazém 7*), just west of Cais do Sodré station – trendy haunt of advertising crowd; minimum charge 5000$00; 11 pm to 6 am nightly

British Bar (☎ 342 23 67, *Rua Bernardino Costa 52*) – crammed with British pub paraphernalia, serves a variety of foreign beers; noon to midnight (2 am weekends)

California (☎ 346 79 54, *Rua Bernardino Costa 39*) – bar-restaurant with dance floor; 7 pm to 4 am (closed Monday)

Hennessy's Irish Pub (☎ 343 10 64, *Rua Cais do Sodré 38*) – live music nightly, plus a great atmosphere and traditional pub grub; 11 pm to 2.30 am daily

Ó Gilíns Irish Pub (☎ 342 18 99, *Rua dos Remolares 8-10*) – draft Guinness; 11 am to 2 am daily; live traditional Irish music most Saturday nights, live jazz with brunch on Sunday

Solar do Vinho do Porto

The Instituto do Vinho do Porto (Port Wine Institute) is an autonomous, Porto-based agency with the job of maintaining the reputation of the port-wine appellation by controlling its quality and output, and promoting it generically. Among other things, it operates the *Solar do Vinho do Porto* (☎ 347 57 07, *Rua de São Pedro de Alcântara 45*) in an old palace right at the top of the Elevador da Glória, in the Bairro Alto. Here, in a refined, living-room-like setting, you can select from 300 varieties of port wine, costing from 200$00 a glass, and peruse (or buy) books and other information on port wine. It's open weekdays from 10 am to 11.45 pm and Saturday from 11 am to 10.45 pm.

There's another *solar* in Porto. See the Douro chapter for details of visits, and also for a special section on port.

Avenida 24 de Julho & Lapa There are numerous bars along this fashionable strip, and one of Lisbon's oldest clubs is nearby. All the places listed here are on Map Estrela & Doca.

Café Central (☎ 395 61 11, *Avenida 24 de Julho 112*) – rock and blues, live on Saturday; 10 pm to 4 am (closed Monday and Tuesday)
Gringo's Café (☎ 396 09 11, *Avenida 24 de Julho 116*) – Tex-Mex café-bar, margarita-land; food served to 1 am; open to 4 am (closed Sunday)
Paulinha (☎ 396 47 83, *Avenida 24 de Julho 82-A*) – all ages; 10.30 pm to 4 am (closed Sunday and Monday)
Stones (☎ 396 45 45, *Rua do Olival 1*) – haunt of Lisbon's blue-blood jet-set, one of the city's first nightclubs, still crazy after all these years, 60s and 70s rock; 10 pm to 4 am (closed Monday)

Doca de Santo Amaro & Doca de Alcântara There are dozens of new (and rather pricey) restaurant-bars along these redeveloped docks. This is a great place for an evening sundowner overlooking the marina and the river. In addition to the following establishments, see the boxed text 'Chic & Open-Air' under Places to Eat earlier in this chapter.

Blues Café (☎ 395 70 85, *Rua da Cintura do Porto de Lisboa, Armazém H*) – daily except Sunday with Cajun food and a Louisiana atmosphere; live music Thursday, disco Friday and Saturday from 2 am to 5 am
Santo Amaro Café (☎ 397 99 04, 395 35 35, *Armazém 9*) – modernist chrome and rattan décor, snooker room, tropical and salsa music; until 2 am daily

Alfama This tangle of old lanes isn't a very safe or salubrious place to go drinking late at night, but it does have a few pleasant watering holes. See also the boxed text on Chapitô earlier in this chapter.

Costa do Castelo (☎ 888 46 36, *Costa do Castelo*) – bar-restaurant with terrace, city views, occasional live music; 10 pm to 2 am (closed Monday)
O Esboço (☎ 887 78 93, *Rua do Vigário 10*) – also does cheap food; 11 pm to 2 am (closed Sunday)
Ópera (☎ 886 23 18, *Travessa das Mónicas 65*) – cheap meals and occasional art exhibits; 10 pm to 2 am (Friday and Saturday nights to 3.30 am)

Gay & Lesbian Bars There are many gay bars and clubs clustered in the hills of Rato and the northern Bairro Alto.

Bar Áqua no Bico (☎ 347 28 30, *Rua de São Marçal 170*) – 9 pm to 2 am
Bar 106 (☎ 342 73 73, *Rua de São Marçal 106, Map Baixa & B Alto*) – one of the best and busiest, with a friendly atmosphere; 9 pm to 2 am
Bric-a-Bar (or *O Brica*; ☎ 342 89 71, *Rua Cecilio de Sousa 84, Map Baixa & B Alto*) – the oldest and one of the largest gay bars in town, two floors and two bars; 9 pm to 4 am
Finalmente (☎ 347 26 52, *Rua da Palmeira 38, Map Baixa & B Alto*) – famous drag shows nightly (around 2 am), gets crowded; 10 pm to 5 am
Memorial (☎ 396 88 91, *Rua da Gustavo de Matos Sequeira 42-A, Map Baixa & B Alto*) – very popular, predominantly lesbian; 11 pm to 3.30 am (closed Monday)

Portas Largas (☎ 346 63 79, Rua da Atalaia 105, Map Baixa & B Alto) – converted old tavern, often patronised by fashion world types and new generation of fado singers; 8 pm to 4 am

7° Céu (☎ 346 64 71, Travessa da Espera 54, Map Baixa & B Alto) – small, with an easy-going atmosphere and mixed youthful crowd, gay icon music, occasionally fado; 10 pm to 2 am

Tatoo (☎ 395 27 26, Rua de São Marçal 15, Map Baixa & B Alto) – older crowd, leather and jeans; 9 pm to 2 am (closed Sunday)

Trumps (☎ 397 10 59, Rua da Imprensa Nacional 104-B, Map Baixa & B Alto) – largest, best known gay club in town, with a huge dance floor, pool tables, café and three bars; 10 pm to 6 am

Nightclubs

Lisbon's nightlife comes alive after midnight with scores of clubs and bars offering everything from classic rock to African, Brazilian to funk, acid jazz to techno. Venues vary from solid old clubs to trendy, short-lived hangouts.

Door charges can range from 1000$00 to 5000$00 (usually including a couple of drinks). Several upmarket clubs (such as Kapital and Kremlin) advertise door charges as high as 10,000$00 to scare off the riff-raff, but these are usually waived unless it's a special night, the club is crowded or the doorman doesn't like the look of you!

Bairro Alto Although this is no longer the trendiest area of the city, the Bairro Alto is still a great area for nightlife, with a good choice of clubs.

Absoluto (☎ 395 50 09, Rua de Dom Luís I 5) – 10 pm to 4 am, Friday and Saturday only

Frágil (☎ 346 95 78, Rua da Atalaia 126-128) – crumbling exterior with revamped, trendy club inside; mostly techno; 11.30 pm to 4 am (closed Sunday and Monday); plans to relocate to Doca de Santa Apolónia

Incógnito (☎ 390 87 55, Rua dos Poiais de São Bento 37) – unmarked door; very trendy young crowd; 11 pm to at least 4 am (1 to 4 am Tuesday, closed Sunday and Monday)

Os Três Pastorinhos (☎ 346 43 01, Rua da Barroca 111-113) – for trendy intellectuals; 11.30 pm to 4 am (closed Sunday)

Avenida 24 de Julho Until Doca de Santo Amaro took off, this was the liveliest nightlife area in town. Many of the clubs have now closed, but you can still find some great places to spend an evening here. All the places listed here are on Map Estrela & Doca.

Kapital (☎ 395 59 63, Avenida 24 de Julho 68) – one of Lisbon's priciest, most venerable and fashionable clubs, with a strict door policy; three floors, with roof terrace in summer; 11.30 pm to 4 am (closed Monday and Wednesday)

Kremlin (☎ 390 87 68, Escadinhas da Praia 5) – acid and techno, young and very trendy; 1 am to 7 am (8 am Friday and Saturday, closed Sunday and Monday)

Metalúrgica (☎ 397 14 88, Avenida 24 de Julho 110) – blues, rock and pop for all ages, good vibes; 10 pm to 4 am Tuesday to Saturday

Plateau (☎ 396 51 16, Escadinhas da Praia 7) – prestigious venue with great music and décor of frescoes and gold-leaf columns; 11 pm to 6 am Tuesday to Saturday

Alcântara This riverfront area is the hottest place for trendy young Lisbon nightlife. You can get here by bus or train (see the boxed text 'Chic & Open-Air' under Places to Eat earlier in this chapter); late-night revellers are better off taking a taxi from the station. All the places listed here are on Map Estrela & Doca.

Alcântara Mar (☎ 363 64 32, Rua da Cozinha Económica 11) – rock, dance and techno for twenty-somethings until 2 am, increasingly gay after that; 11.30 pm to 6 am Thursday to Saturday; café-restaurant (☎ 363 71 76) open till 1 am

Benzina (Travessa de Teixeira Júnior 6) – soul, funk, acid jazz, rock and pop; midnight to 6 am

Cais S (☎ 395 81 10, Doca de Santo Amaro, Armazém 1) – bizarre décor, giant screen with radical sports; 9 pm to 4 am

Dock's Club (☎ 395 08 56, Rua da Cintura do Porto de Lisboa 226, Armazém H) – plenty of open-air space, overlooking Doca de Alcân-tara; 10 pm to around 6 am (closed Sunday and Monday); restaurant open till 1.30 am

Gartejo (☎ 395 59 77, Rua João de Oliveira Miguens 48) – young and very trendy, some live bands; 10 pm to at least 4 am (closed Sunday)

Kings & Queens (☎ 395 58 70, Rua da Cintura do Porto de Lisboa) – crowds of heteros gaping at the drag queens, lively and loud; 10.30 pm to 5 am (closed Sunday)

Music

Lisbon has a thriving music scene, with a wide range of venues for everything from African to Irish rhythms.

African The African music scene (with roots predominantly in Cape Verde, but also Mozambique, Guinea-Bissau and Angola) bops in bars all over town.

B.Leza (☎ 396 37 35, Largo do Conde Barão 50, Map Baixa & B Alto) – up-and-coming live-music venue; 11 pm to around 4 am (closed Monday)

Discoteca A Lontra (☎ 395 69 68, Rua de São Bento 155, Map Estrela & Doca) – well known venue with music after midnight (closed Monday)

Jamaica (☎ 342 18 59, Rua Nova do Carvalho 5, Map Baixa & B Alto) – 11 pm to 4 am (closed Sunday); reggae on Tuesday

Kussinguila (☎ 363 35 90, Rua dos Luisadas 5, Map Estrela & Doca) – one of the hippest African clubs; 11 pm to 6 am

Ritz Clube (☎ 342 51 40, Rua da Glória 57, Map Baixa & B Alto) – mainly live Cape Verdean, midnight to 4 am (closed Sunday and Monday); late meals from 9 pm

Irish Homesick Dubliners, along with anyone who wants to drink Guinness and listen to good live Irish music, should head for *Ó Gilíns Irish Pub* or *Hennessy's Irish Pub* (see Cais do Sodré under Bars earlier in this section).

Jazz The Fundação Calouste Gulbenkian and Hot Clube de Portugal jointly organise an excellent annual international jazz festival at the Fundação's open-air amphitheatre in early August.

Hot Clube de Portugal (☎ 346 73 69, Praça da Alegria 39, Map Baixa & B Alto) – the centre of the jazz scene, small and often crowded; live music at least three nights a week and jam sessions on Tuesday; 10 pm to 2 am (closed Sunday and Monday)

Speakeasy (☎ 396 42 57, Cais da Rocha do Conde de Óbidos 115, Map Estrela & Doca) – 8 pm to 3 am Monday to Wednesday, 8 pm to 4 am Thursday to Saturday, jam sessions Tuesday

Tertúlia (☎ 346 27 04, Rua do Diário de Notícias 60, Map Baixa & B Alto) – some live jazz, easy going, all ages; 8.30 pm to 3 am (closed Sunday)

Latin American Some of the best Latin American music in town can be heard at these places:

Havana Bar (☎ 397 98 93, Doca de Santo Amaro, Armazém 5, Map Estrela & Doca) – Cuban bar and pricey restaurant with live Brazilian music Tuesday to Friday; midday to 4 am daily

Pé Sujo (☎ 886 56 29, Largo de São Martinho 6, Map Alfama) – live Brazilian rhythms; closed Monday

Salsa Latina (☎ 395 05 55, Gare Marítima de Alcântara, Map Estrela & Doca) – restaurant-cum-dance hall with live music nightly and a salsa dance teacher on hand Friday; weekdays from noon to 4 am, Saturday from 8 pm to 4 am (closed Sunday)

Rock & Pop Fancy some good old baby-boomer boogie? Try these.

Álcool Puro (☎ 396 74 67, Avenida Dom Carlos I 59, Map Estrela & Doca) – live rock and dancing; 11 pm to 4 am (closed Sunday)

Anos 60 (☎ 887 34 44, Largo do Terreirinho 21, Map Alfama) – live 60s music on Friday and Saturday; 9.30 pm to 3 am (closed Sunday)

Até Qu'Enfim (Rua das Janelas Verdes 2, Map Estrela & Doca) – small, serves meals too; 10 pm to 2 am daily

Rock City (☎ 342 86 40, Rua Cintura do Porto de Lisboa, Armazém 225, Map Baixa & B Alto) – live rock; restaurant, two bars (one in a tropical garden), great riverfront terrace; midnight to 4 am (closed Monday)

Theatres & Concerts

Lisbon's main concert halls are at the Fundação Calouste Gulbenkian (☎ 795 02 36), the Centro Cultural de Belém (☎ 361 24 00) and the Coliseu dos Recreios (☎ 343 16 77) at Rua das Portas de Santo Antão 92 (Map Baixa & B Alto). The opera house, the

Teatro Nacional de São Carlos (☎ 346 59 14) at Rua Serpa Pinto 9, and the neighbouring Teatro Municipal de São Luís (☎ 342 71 72) at Rua António Maria Cardoso 54, in the Chiado (Map Baixa & B Alto), have their own concert, opera and theatre seasons. If you're here with children, Teatro Infantil de Lisboa (TIL) occasionally puts on shows during school term time at Teatro Maria Matos (☎ 849 70 07), Avenida Frei Miguel Contreiras 52 (Map Greater Lisbon).

The Sony Place (Map Greater Lisbon), formerly the Expo '98 Open Air Amphitheatre, is Lisbon's largest open-air theatre, used for concerts and special events.

Cinemas

Lisbon has some 60 cinemas, many showing current blockbusters (with Portuguese subtitles). There are at least seven multiscreen theatres, of which the biggest are in shopping centres: Colombo (☎ 711 32 00) by Colégio Militar-Luz metro station and Amoreiras (☎ 387 87 52) on Avenida Engenheiro Duarte Pacheco. *Público* gives comprehensive lisitings. A ticket at these complexes costs 800$00 (550$00 on Monday).

The Instituto da Cinemateca Portuguesa (☎ 354 62 79), Rua Barata Salgueiro 39 (Map Saldanha), shows international classics twice-daily for a bargain 350$00.

SPECTATOR SPORTS
Football

Lisboêtas are as obsessed as anybody with football (soccer). Of Portugal's three good national teams, two – Benfica and Sporting – are based in Lisbon. The two have been rivals ever since Sporting beat Benfica, 2-1, on 1 December 1907.

The season runs from September to May, and most league matches are on Sunday; check the papers or ask at the turismo about upcoming contests. Tickets are cheap and are sold at the stadium on match day or you can buy them, for slightly inflated prices, at the ABEP ticket agency on Praça dos Restauradores.

Benfica (Sport Lisboa e Benfica in full) plays at Estádio da Luz in the north-western Benfica district (Map Greater Lisbon; metro Colégio Militar-Luz or take bus No 41 from Rossio). For ticket information call ☎ 726 60 53 or contact Benfica's inquiries office (☎ 726 61 29, fax 726 47 61).

Sporting (Sporting Clube de Portugal in full) plays at Estádio José de Alvalade, just north of the university (Map Greater Lisbon). The nearest metro station to the staduim is Campo Grande or take bus Nos 1 or 36 from Rossio. For information call ☎ 758 90 21 or fax 759 93 91.

Bullfighting

Bullfights are staged at the Moorish-style *praça de touros* (bullring) across Avenida da República from Campo Pequeno metro station (or take bus Nos 1, 21, 36, 44, 45 or 83 from Rossio; Map Greater Lisbon). The season runs from May to October, with fights usually on Thursday or Sunday. Tickets, on sale outside the bullring, range in price from 2500$00 to 4000$00, depending on where you sit. You can also buy tickets for a bit more from the ABEP ticket agency on Praça dos Restauradores.

See Bullfighting under Spectator Sports in the Facts for the Visitor chapter for more about bullfights, and Treatment of Animals under Society & Conduct in the Facts about Portugal chapter for a discussion of the treatment of the bulls.

SHOPPING
Azulejos & Ceramics

Lisbon has many azulejo factories and showrooms. One of the finest (and priciest) is Fábrica Sant'Ana, at Rua do Alecrim 95 (Map Baixa & B Alto). The street-level showroom is open weekdays from 9 am to 7 pm and Saturday from 10 am to 2 pm.

Another good showroom for azulejos (including made-to-order items) and other ceramic ware is Cerâmica Viúva Lamego (☎ 885 24 02) at Largo do Intendente Pina Manique 25 (Map Greater Lisbon). Pottery fanatics will also like the venerable, family-run Olaria do Desterros (☎ 885 03 29), a few blocks west in a neighbourhood of warehouses and hospitals. The factory (there's no obvious showroom) is at entry F in an alley, seemingly within the grounds of the Hospital do Desterro, at Rua Nova do Desterro 14 (Map Saldanha).

The attractive Museu Nacional do Azulejo (see Santa Apolónia under Alfama, Castelo & Graça earlier in this chapter) has a small shop, which also sells more affordable azulejo souvenirs.

The most famous name in ceramics is Vista Alegre, whose finely crafted products can be found at a number of stores including one at Largo do Chiado 20 (Map Baixa & B Alto).

Wine

Portuguese wine of any variety – red, white or rosé; *maduro* (mature) or semisparkling young vinho verde – is very good value. You needn't hunt for specialist shops: in most supermarkets you can buy something that should please the snobbiest taste buds for between 800$00 and 900$00 (US$4 to US$5).

If it's port wine you want, have a taste at the Solar do Vinho do Porto (see the boxed text under Entertainment earlier in this chapter) and then head for the supermarket or a wine speciality shop, such as Napoleão at Rua dos Fanqueiros 70 or Manuel Tavares at Rua da Betesga 1A (both on Map Baixa & B Alto). It helps to know roughly what you want but staff can offer recommendations. Failing that, the Instituto do Vinho do Porto has its own shop in the international departures concourse at the airport.

See Drinks in the Facts for the Visitor chapter for more about Portuguese wines, and also the special section on port in the Douro chapter for more about that.

Handicrafts & Textiles

A fascinating, if rather overpublicised, *artesanato* (handicrafts shop) is Santos Ofícios, Rua da Madalena 87, at the edge of the Baixa district. It stocks an eclectic range of folk art from all around Portugal and is open daily except Sunday, from 10 am to 8 pm. Another good source of select, high-quality handicrafts is Pais Em Lisboa at Rua do Teixeira 25. For bronzeware, check out Casa Achilles, at Rua de São Marçal 194, and for cork objects of all kinds, head straight for Casa das Cortiças, Rua da Escola Politécnica 4.

Hand-embroidered linen from its most famous source, Madeira, can be found at

---

Markets

For something decidedly downmarket, but good entertainment, browse the sprawling Feira da Ladra, or Thieves Market, which materialises every Tuesday morning and all day Saturday at Campo de Santa Clara, beside the Igreja de São Vincent de Fora in the Alfama district. In addition to cheap clothes and old books you'll find a motley array of junk, from nuts and bolts to old buttons and brassware, second-hand spectacles and 78-rpm records.

Another regular Lisbon market is the Feira do Relógio (Map Greater Lisbon), held Sunday on Rua Pardal Monteiro in the Bairro de Relógio district (take bus No 59 from Praça da Figueira or bus No 103 from Areeiro metro station). You can find almost anything here – fruit, vegetables, household goods, clothes, toys, shoes, and so on. The best market for food, however, is the daily Mercado da Ribeira near Cais do Sodré (see Self-Catering under Places to Eat earlier in this chapter).

A good place for cheap shoes, clothes, toys and CDs is the rough-and-ready complex of market stalls open daily except Sunday on the north-western corner of Praça de Espanha (metro Praça de Espanha).

Madeira House, Rua Augusta 131. Teresa Alecrim, Rua Nova do Almada 76, also has excellent examples.

All the above can be found on Map Baixa & B Alto.

Music

A well-established Lisbon outlet for CDs and cassettes covering the spectrum from pop-rock to classical is Valentim de Carvalho, Rossio 57. There's also a Virgin Megastore in the Teatro Eden building on Praça dos Restauradores. Smaller outlets include Loja da Música at Rua das Portas de Santo Antão 92 and Discoteca Amália, Rua de Áurea 272, which specialises in fado and cheap classical CDs.

All these shops are shown on Map Baixa & B Alto.

Shoes

These are a bargain all over Portugal and Lisbon abounds in *sapaterias* (shoe shops). Trawl Avenida de Roma, in the north of the city (metro Roma), or the Amoreiras shopping centre (see the next section) to find renowned shops such as Hera or Mocci. Rua Augusta, in the Baixa district, is also a shoe-shopper's paradise.

Shopping Centres

The colossal Centro Comercial Colombo – the Iberian peninsula's biggest mall – is on Avenida Colégio Militar, by Colégio Militar-Luz metro station. Housing 500 shops, 20 banks, 50 restaurants, 10 cinemas and a Playcenter (Portugal's largest indoor funfair, which even has a go-kart track and bowling alley), it has stolen the limelight from the Complexo das Amoreiras, which was once Portugal's biggest mall. It's open daily till midnight.

But the chrome-plated Complexo das Amoreiras, open daily until 11 pm on Avenida Engenheiro Duarte Pacheco (Map Greater Lisbon), is still popular. Most buses heading west from Marquês de Pombal metro station on Rua Joaquim António de Aguiar go past it, or take the No 11 from Praça do Comércio.

GETTING THERE & AWAY

Air

Over two dozen carriers operate scheduled international services to Lisbon, with flights from London, Paris, Frankfurt, Berlin, Dresden, Hamburg, Munich, Amsterdam, Brussels, Madrid and New York at least once-daily in summer, and less frequent connections from other cities.

From Lisbon, both PGA Portugália Airlines and TAP Air Portugal have multiple flights daily to Porto and Faro, year-round. TAP has a daily evening flight to Faro and a morning one back, scheduled to connect with international arrivals and departures in Lisbon.

For more on international and domestic air links and fares, see the Getting There & Away and Getting Around chapters.

Among useful airline booking numbers in Lisbon are the following:

AB Airlines
  ☎ 313 95 65
Air France
  ☎ 790 02 02
Alitalia
  ☎ 353 61 41
British Airways
  ☎ 346 43 53
  toll-free ☎ 0808 21 21 25
Delta Air Lines
  ☎ 353 76 10
Iberia
  ☎ 355 81 19

Arriving in Lisbon by Air

As you exit from the arrivals concourse at the airport, you'll find a helpful turismo (☎ 849 43 23, 849 36 89), open daily from 6 am to 2 am. Further on is a desk maintained by ANA, the city airport authority, with arrivals and departures information, its own handy mini-guidebook to the city called *Your Guide: Lisboa* and a useful *Taxi Information* pamphlet to help you avoid getting stung by the drivers who hang out here.

KLM-Royal Dutch Airlines
☎ 847 63 54
Lufthansa Airlines
☎ 840 44 49
PGA Portugália Airlines
☎ 847 20 92
Sabena
☎ 346 55 72
Swissair
☎ 322 60 00
TAP Air Portugal
☎ 841 69 90
toll-free ☎ 0808 21 31 41
TWA
☎ 314 71 41
Varig
☎ 353 91 53
toll-free ☎ 0500 12 34

Lisbon airport is only 20 minutes from the city centre when there's no traffic, but 45 minutes or more in rush hour; see the following Getting Around section for airport transport information.

For flight arrival and departure information call ☎ 841 37 00.

Bus

Express coaches connect Lisbon daily with almost every major town in Portugal, including Porto (around a dozen buses daily, 3½ to four hours, around 2000$00; plus four fast *alta qualidade* services), Coimbra (at least 11 daily around 1500$00), Évora (at least ten daily around 1500$00), Faro (seven daily, 4½ hours, around 2200$00; plus five faster alta qualidade services), and Viano do Castelo (two daily, around 2100$00).

Most long-distance buses, including those run by Rede Expresso (and its affiliates) and EVA (from the Algarve), operate from the Arco do Cego bus terminal (☎ 352 33 84) on Avenida João Crisóstomo (Map Saldanha). This is the best bet for almost any destination within Portugal.

It's also the place for Eurolines (here called InterCentro) international coaches; they go to Paris and London five times a week in summer (less often to other European cities). The InterCentro office is open weekdays and Saturday morning. Informa-

tion and tickets for international departures are scarce at weekends, so avoid that last-minute Sunday dash out of Portugal.

Renex (☎ 887 48 71, 888 28 29), which includes the southern bus lines Caima, Frota Azul and Resende, operates from Rua da Alfândega, a few blocks east of Praça do Comércio (Map Alfama); the ticket office is nearby at Rua dos Bacalhoeiros 12. Several regional companies with destinations in the north, including Mafrense (for Ericeira and Mafra), Barraqueiro Oeste (for Malveira and Torres Vedras) and Rodoviária do Tejo (for Peniche), operate from outside Campo Grande metro station (Map Greater Lisbon). Buses to the Setúbal Peninsula go from the bus station at Praça de Espanha (Map Greater Lisbon).

Train

Lisbon is linked by train to all major cities in Portugal. Alfa and IC fares include compulsory seat reservation charges. For more information on Caminhos de Ferro Portugueses (CP) domestic services, see the Getting Around chapter. Prices for trains to three major destinations are given here:

Destination	Class	Duration	Cost	No/day
Coimbra	Alfa	2	2300	3
	IC	2¼	1800	6
	IR	2½	1450	4
Faro	IC	3½	2000	3
	IR	4½	1850	2
Porto	Alfa	3	3150	4
	IC	3½	2550	4
	IR	4¼	2000	4

There's a daily Lisbon-Paris service (the *Rápido Sud-Expresso*) through northern Spain, and a nightly service to Madrid (the *Talgo Lusitânia*). For more on international train links and some fares to/from Lisbon, see under Train in the Getting There & Away chapter.

Lisbon has five major train stations. Santa Apolónia is the terminal for trains from northern and central Portugal, and for all international services. Cais do Sodré is the station for Cascais and Estoril, while

Rossio serves Sintra and Estremadura.
Barreiro, across the river, is the terminal for
suburbano services to Setúbal and all long-
distance services to the south of Portugal;
connecting ferries leave frequently from the
pier at Terreiro do Paço. Barreiro will
become redundant once the new North-
South Railway Line is extended (see the
boxed text above). Lisbon's newest major
station is the intermodal Oriente station; all
services to/from Santa Apolónia pass
through here.

Santa Apolónia has a helpful CP information desk (☎ 888 40 25, 888 50 92) at
door No 8, open from 8 am to 10 pm (telephones until 11 pm). The international
section at door No 47 includes an international ticket desk (and machines for buying
certain domestic IC and Alfa tickets with
credit cards); a bank, cash exchange
machine and credit card ATM; a snack bar
and restaurant (open 7 am to 11 pm); and
car rental agencies. The baggage office is at
door No 25.

Rossio station also has an information
office, open from 9 am to 8 pm. All major
stations have luggage lockers. At the Terreiro do Paço pier, travellers bound for
southern Portugal buy two tickets: a 170$00
ferry ticket to Barreiro plus their onward
train ticket.

Car & Motorcycle

The best unlimited-mileage car rental rate
we found was from Eurodollar (☎ 940 52
47, fax 940 52 49). Other local operators
with reasonable multiday rates include
Mundirent (☎ 313 93 60, fax 313 93 69),
Nova Rent (☎ 387 08 08, fax 387 31 30),
Rentauto (☎ 846 22 94, fax 846 22 95),
Rupauto (☎ 793 32 58, fax 793 17 68) and
Solcar (☎ 315 05 26, fax 356 05 05). International firms include Avis (☎ 356 11 76,
toll-free ☎ 0500 1002), Budget (☎ 353 77
17), Europcar (☎ 940 77 90, fax 942 52 39)
and Hertz (☎ 849 27 22).

You can rent a motorcycle from Gesrent
(☎ 385 27 22), Rua Nova de São Mamede
29-31.

Ferry

The Transtejo ferry has several riverfront
terminals. Two are adjacent to Praça do
Comércio: Terreiro do Paço, from where
passenger ferries cross the Rio Tejo to
Montijo and Seixal (about once an hour)
and to Barreiro (approximately every 10
minutes); and, next to it, Cais da Alfândega, from where passenger ferries go to
Cacilhas every 10 minutes. Car ferries (also
for bicycles) go to Cacilhas from a pier at
Cais do Sodré. The ferry line serving the
Barreiro train terminal is called Soflusa.

Further along, in Belém, ferries depart
for Trafaria, several kilometres west of
Cacilhas.

GETTING AROUND
To/From the Airport

Bus No 91, the Aero-Bus, is a special
service departing from outside the arrivals
hall roughly every 20 minutes from 7 am to
9 pm. It takes from 20 to 45 minutes (depending on traffic) to get from the airport to
Cais do Sodré station, with a stop near the
turismo on Praça dos Restauradores. The
price is 430/1000$00 for a one/three day
Bilhete Turístico that you can continue to
use on all city buses, trams and funiculars.
Note that the Passe Turístico (see the following Bus, Tram & Funicular section) is
for some reason not valid for this bus. For

TAP Air Portugal passengers who show their air tickets, the ride to the city is free.

Local bus Nos 8, 44, 45 and 83 also run right past the turismo, but you have to walk further at the airport to board them, and they're a nightmare in rush hour if you have baggage.

For a taxi, figure on paying about 1500$00, plus an extra 300$00 if your luggage needs to go in the boot. Taxi rip-offs are common on the airport-to-city route; ANA, the airport authority, has a good pamphlet on this at its desk in Arrivals. Avoid long taxi queues by flagging down a taxi at Departures.

Bus, Tram & Funicular

Companhia Carris de Ferro de Lisboa, or Carris, is the municipal department in charge of all transport except the metro. Its buses and trams run from about 5 or 6 am to 1 am; there are some night bus and tram services.

You can sometimes get a transport map, *Planta dos Transportes Públicas da Carris* (including a welcome map of night-time services) from the turismo or from Carris kiosks, but thanks to the chaos caused by the city's latest metro-improvement, route changes were so frequent that the map was not always reliable.

Individual tickets cost 160$00 on board or half that price if you buy a BUC (*Bilhete Único de Coroa* – a one zone ticket for the city centre) beforehand. These prepaid tickets are sold at Carris kiosks, most conveniently at Praça da Figueira, at the foot of the Elevador de Santa Justa, and at Santa Apolónia and Cais do Sodré stations.

From these kiosks (open daily from 8 am to 7.30 pm) you can also get a one day (430$00) or three day (1000$00) Bilhete Turístico, valid for all buses, trams and funiculars. Another type of pass is the Passe Turístico (1640$00/2320$00 for four/seven days), available from Carris kiosks and metro stations, and valid for buses (except the Aero-Bus), trams, funiculars *and* the metro. You must show your passport to get the (non-transferable) Passe Turístico.

However, none of these is a great bargain unless you're planning on a lot of travel far from the centre. A better deal is the Lisboa Card (see the boxed text under Information earlier in this chapter), which is good for most tourist sights as well as bus, tram, funicular and metro travel.

Buses Useful bus routes include: Nos 32, 44 and 45 (Praça dos Restauradores-Praça do Comércio-Cais do Sodré), Nos 35 and 107 (Cais do Sodré-Santa Apolónia), Nos 9, 39 and 46 (Praça dos Restauradores-Santa Apolónia), No 11 (Amoreiras-Praça do Comércio) and No 37 (Praça da Figueira-Castelo do São Jorge). Lisboêtas are surprisingly orderly in bus queues.

Trams The clattering, antediluvian trams (*eléctricos* or *tranvías*) are an endearing component of Lisbon. Don't leave the city without riding the No 28 through the narrow streets of the Alfama and back around to Largo Martim Moniz; the best place to catch it is east-bound on Rua da Conceição in the Baixa. West-bound from Rua da Conceição, it clanks through the Bairro Alto to Estrela peak.

Two other useful lines are the No 15 from Praça da Figueira and Praça do Comércio via Alcântara to Belém, and the No 18 from Praça do Comércio via Alcântara to Ajuda. The No 15 line now features huge space-age articulated trams, which also have on-board machines for buying tickets and passes. Tram stops are usually marked by a small *paragem* (stop) sign hanging from a lamppost or the overhead wires.

Funiculars The city has three *elevadors* (funiculars) which labour up and down its steepest hills, plus the extraordinary Elevador de Santa Justa, a huge wrought-iron lift that raises you from the Baixa straight up to eyelevel with the Convento do Carmo ruins.

Santa Justa is the most popular with tourists, but the most charming ride is on the Elevador da Bica through the Santa Catarina district, at the south-western corner of Bairro Alto. The other two funiculars are the Elevador da Glória, from Praça dos Restauradores up to the São Pedro de Alcântara viewpoint, and the Elevador de Lavra from Largo de Anunciada, on the eastern side of Avenida da Liberdade.

The Elevador de Santa Justa operates daily from 7 am to 11.45 pm (Sunday and holidays from 9 am to 11 pm), the Elevadors da Bica and do Lavra from 7 am to 10.45 pm, and the Elevador da Glória from 7 am to 1 am daily. They're not for anyone in a hurry!

Transport for Disabled Travellers
For disabled people, Carris operates a 24 hour dial-a-ride service (☎ 361 30 40, 758 56 76) at a cost comparable to taxis. Try to book your rides a day or two in advance. Carris may have adapted coaches with wheelchair space for hire; ☎ 363 92 26.

Metro
The rapidly expanding *metropolitano* (underground) system, which currently has 28km of track and 37 stations, is useful not only for short hops across the city, but also to reach the intermodal Oriente station at the former Expo site. By the year 2001 – when a Santa Apolónia link is expected to be completed – there will be 37km of track and 47 stations.

Individual tickets cost 80$00, a *caderneta* of 10 tickets costs 600$00. Tickets can be purchased from windows or automatic dispensers in metro stations. Single tickets must be validated in the little machine at the entrance to the platform; don't forget to do it – there *are* ticket inspectors. A one day metro pass costs 200$00 (620$00 for seven days), and both the Passe Turístico and the Lisboa Card are valid on the metro.

The system runs from 6.30 am to 1 am. Entrances are marked by a big red half-M. Travel is quite straightforward. Useful signs to know include *correspondência* (transfer between lines) and *saída* (exit to the street).

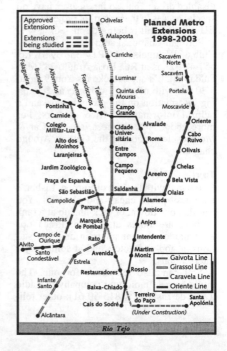

Be extra vigilant during rush hours, when pickpockets are more likely to be operating.

Car & Motorcycle

Lisbon isn't much fun for drivers, thanks to heavy traffic, metro roadworks and manic drivers. There are two ring roads, both useful for staying out of the centre. On maps, the inner one is marked CRIL (Cintura Regional Interna de Lisboa), the outer one CREL (Cintura Regional Externa de Lisboa).

If you do venture into the city centre you'll find parking scarce and car parks expensive: all-day rates in underground car parks (such as those at Restauradores or Praça Marquês de Pombal) are around 1000$00, but hotel car parks are often twice that. Hotels with (free) street parking are mentioned under Places to Stay. Always lock the car and don't leave any valuables inside.

The city has a few permit-only spaces for disabled drivers but, so far, visitors have no special access to them. A pilot project for an EU-wide permit is being discussed.

Portugal's national auto club, Automóvel Club de Portugal, or ACP (☎ 356 39 31, fax 357 47 32), is at Rua Rosa Araújo 24 (Map Saldanha). It's open weekdays from 9 am to 5.30 pm, with maps, guidebooks and camping information on the ground floor, and a helpful information office upstairs. For more about ACP services, see the Car & Motorcycle section of the Getting Around chapter.

Taxi

Compared with the rest of Europe, Lisbon's *táxis* are quick, cheap and plentiful. You can flag one down, or pick one up at a rank – there are ranks at Rossio, Praça dos Restauradores, near all train and bus stations, at top-end hotels and at some major intersections.

You can also telephone for one. The city's biggest radio-taxi company is Rádio Táxis de Lisboa (☎ 815 50 61); other reli-

able ones are Autocoope (☎ 793 27 56) and Teletáxis (☎ 815 20 76, 815 20 16). A reliable tourist-taxi outfit (for excursions, at fixed standard rates) is Unidos de Lisboa (☎ 816 00 00). For an air-con Mercedes with chauffeur who speaks English, French or Spanish, call Manuel Calado (☎ 385 09 93, mobile ☎ 0936 70 10 51).

All taxis have meters, but rip-offs do happen, in particular with some taxis that haunt the airport. Keep an eye on the meter and the map. A good brochure, with information about rates and telephone numbers for complaints, is free from the ANA office at the airport. If you think you may have been cheated, get a receipt from the driver and make a claim with the tourist subsection of the police (☎ 346 61 41, ext 279).

See under Local Transport in the Getting Around chapter for more about taxis and taxi fares.

Bicycle

Lisbon traffic is a nightmare for cyclists. You're better off stashing your bike with left-luggage at the train station or airport and seeing the city by public transport. Better hotels and pensões may have a storage room. See the Bicycle section in the Getting Around chapter for information on transporting your bike between cities.

The only dedicated bike lane in Lisbon is a 5km stretch along the Rio Tejo from 1km west of Doca de Santo Amaro (Map Estrela & Doca) to Belém and Praia d'Algés. You can rent a bike specifically to ride this route from Tejo Bike (☎ 887 19 76), near the start of the bike lane, for 750$00 an hour (or 5000$00 for 10 hours). Tandems and bikes for kids are also available. It's open daily in summer from 10 am to 8 pm (weekends only in winter).

The nearest place to rent a mountain bike (for about 1500$00 a day) is Gesrent (☎ 486 45 66, fax 483 27 34) in Cascais (see the Around Lisbon chapter).

Around Lisbon

The area around Lisbon, officially named the Área Metropolitana de Lisboa (AML), covers 3128 sq km and is one of the most densely populated regions of the country, inhabited by 1.9 million people (2.5 million including Lisbon). It stretches as far north as Azambuja, on the Rio Tejo, and as far south as Sesimbra, on the southern coast of the Setúbal Peninsula.

Although the AML's commuter suburbs of Amadora, Oeiras and Loures hold nothing much of interest, it takes only an hour or so by train or bus to reach some delightful destinations, several of which are worth considering for more than just a day trip. Top of the list is Sintra, just 45 minutes by train from Lisbon's Rossio station, a verdant cultural spot within the Parque Natural de Sintra-Cascais and a favourite of royals and romantics in times past. There are several good beaches near Sintra, including Praia Grande and Praia das Maçãs, while Praia do Guincho, a few kilometres further south, is famous for its crashing surf.

Continue south and east around this coastline (or take a bus directly south from Sintra) and you'll hit the Costa de Estoril's liveliest seaside resort, Cascais. You won't find great beaches here, but there are plenty of pubs and restaurants, and a bopping weekend and summertime nightlife scene. Nearby Estoril itself is more staid but if you're a gambler you'll love its casino, the biggest in Europe. Both Cascais and Estoril are less than 30 minutes away by train from Lisbon's Cais do Sodré station and services run frequently day and night.

For culture, in addition to Sintra's picturesque palaces and monuments, there are a couple of other palaces to visit on day trips from Lisbon. The nearby Palácio de Queluz is just 5km from the city and is easily accessible by train from Rossio station; it recalls Versailles in France with its formal gardens and rococo elegance. The massive Palácio-

HIGHLIGHTS

- Explore the enchanting wooded area around Sintra, with its palaces, museums and villas

- Go on a pub-crawl around Cascais, the liveliest seaside resort on the Costa de Estoril

- Crash through the surf at Praia do Guincho (for serious surfers only) or loll on the sands of Praia Grande

- Hike around the hills of the Parque Natural da Arrábida, then dine in one of Setúbal's superb seafood restaurants

Convento de Mafra, about an hour away by bus from Lisbon, is a mind-boggling 18th century extravaganza.

Further afield, and best considered for an overnight stay, is Setúbal, the largest and liveliest town on the Setúbal Peninsula. It's a great place for reasonably priced seafood and makes a good base for exploring the Parque Natural da Arrábida (there are plenty of organised biking and hiking trips available; see the Setúbal section for details).

Several fine beaches run west along the coast from Setúbal; Sesimbra is the liveliest and largest beach resort in the area. Other beaches can be found nearer to the city along the Costa da Caparica, an 8km stretch of beach on the peninsula's west coast. Places on the peninsula are most easily reached from Lisbon by bus from the Praça de Espanha bus station.

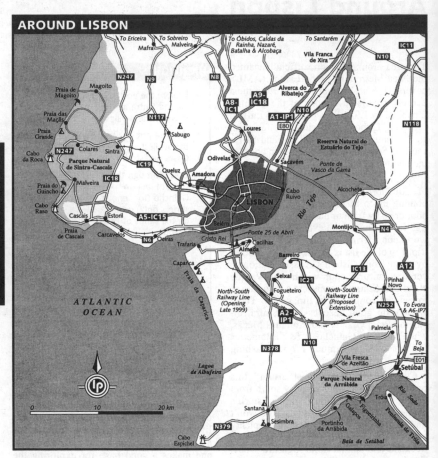

AROUND LISBON

SINTRA

☎ 01 • pop 20,600

If you're able to make only trip out of Lisbon, Sintra should receive top priority. Cool and verdant, and just 28km north-west of Lisbon, a visit Sintra makes one of the most enchanting day-trip excursions from the city; it's also a worthwhile destination in its own right for several days of exploration or relaxation.

Situated on the northern slopes of the craggy Serra de Sintra, its lush vegetation and spectacular mountaintop views towards the coast have lured admirers since the times of the early Iberians: they found the ridge so mystical they called it the Mountain of the Moon and made it a centre of cult worship. The Romans and the Moors were equally captivated – the remains of a Moorish castle overlook the town. For 500 years the kings of Portugal chose Sintra as their summer resort, and the nobility built extravagant villas and surrealist palaces on its wooded hillsides.

Not rush hour – participants in the Discoveries Marathon cross the Tejo on the Ponte 25 de Abril.

CARLOS COSTA

The Torre de Belém – built during the Age of Discoveries and symbolising the spirit of the Age.

VÍTOR VIEIRA

The magnificent 19th century Palácio Nacional da Pena, Sintra's own Disney castle.

The streets of Sintra.

Palácio Nacional da Pena.

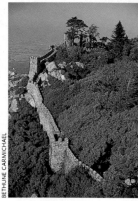

Castelo dos Mouros in Sintra.

Laid-back street in the beach resort of Cascais.

Checking for holes on the Rio Sado in Setúbal.

Poets – especially the romantic English – were enraptured by its natural beauty. Even Lord Byron (who had few nice things to say about Portugal) managed to be charmed: 'Lo! Cintra's glorious Eden intervenes, in variegated maze of mount'and glen,' he wrote in his famous travel epic, *Childe Harold*.

Despite hordes of summer tourists, especially in July when the town hosts a major music festival, Sintra still has a bewitching atmosphere and offers some fantastic walks and day trips: the Parque Natural de Sintra-Cascais encompasses both the Serra de Sintra and nearby coastal attractions (including Cabo da Roca, Europe's most westerly point). Try to avoid weekends and public holidays when the narrow, winding roads groan with tour buses.

Designated a UNESCO World Heritage Site in 1995, Sintra now faces some grandiose eco-friendly 'revival' plans by local authorities who aim to make it 'the cultural capital of Portugal'.

Orientation

Arriving at Sintra by train or bus you'll find yourself in Sintra's new town, Estefânia, where most of the cheap accommodation is located. It's 1.5km (about 15 minutes walk) north-east of the heart of Sintra's cultural attractions at Sintra-Vila (also called Vila Velha: 'old town'). Two kilometres southeast of Sintra-Vila is the São Pedro district: you'll only need to go here if you are heading for the *pousada da juventude* (youth hostel) nearby, if you want to visit the big fortnightly Feira de São Pedro market held on the second and fourth Sunday of the month, or if you'd like to sample some of São Pedro's excellent restaurants.

If you're touring by car, note that you can't drive up to the Palácio Nacional da Pena and that driving and parking in Sintra-Vila can be murder at weekends and on public holidays: it's often easier to park near the station and walk. Be sure to lock up well and keep valuables with you when you park at the Castelo dos Mouros and Monserrate Gardens.

Information

There are two turismos, one at the train station (☎ 924 16 23), and the main office (☎ 923 11 57, fax 923 51 76) at 23 Praça da República in Sintra-Vila, near the Palácio Nacional de Sintra. This extremely efficient office is open daily from 9 am to 7 pm (until 8 pm from June to September). Staff provide a free map (packed with information), as well as help with accommodation. For 250$00 you can buy a foldout booklet of *Sintra Itineraries* detailing routes around town and the surrounding area.

For other books on Sintra (mostly in Portuguese) try the bookshop in the Museu do Brinquedo. Botanists may find *Sintra: A Borough in the Wild* a worthwhile read. There are plans to allow visitors to surf the internet on the two computers in this museum.

There are several laundrettes; the most convenient is Lavandaria Teclava (☎ 923 03 37), opposite the train station at Avenida Dr Miguel Bombarda 27-D. It's open weekdays from 8 am to 7.30 pm, and till noon on Saturday.

There's a post office and bank in Sintra-Vila, near the turismo (as well as others in Estefânia). The *centro de saúde* (medical centre; ☎ 923 34 00) is at Rua Visconde de Monserrate 2, but for medical emergencies it's advisable to head for the hospital in Cascais (☎ 01-484 40 71). The police station (☎ 923 07 61) is at Rua João de Deus 6.

Palácio Nacional de Sintra

The Sintra National Palace (also known as the Paço Real or Palácio da Vila) dominates the town with its two huge conical chimneys. Of Moorish origins, the palace was greatly enlarged by João I in the early 15th century, adorned with Manueline additions by Manuel I in the following century, and repeatedly restored and redecorated right up to the present day.

Historically, it's connected with a treasury of notable occasions: João I planned his 1415 Ceuta campaign here; the three-year-old Sebastião was crowned king in the

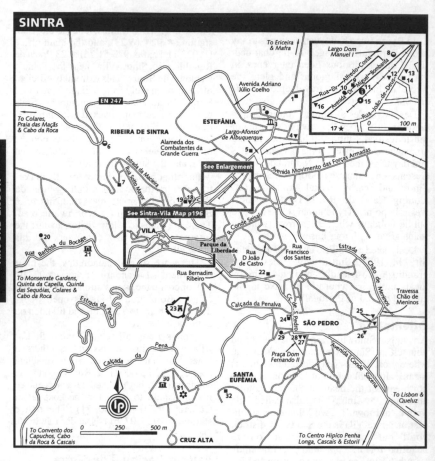

SINTRA

To Ericeira & Mafra

Largo Dom Manuel I

Rua-Dr-Alfredo-Costa

Avenida Adriano Júlio Coelho

Avenida-Dr-Miguel-Bombarda

Rua-João-de-Deus

To Colares, Praia das Maçãs & Cabo da Roca

EN 247

RIBEIRA DE SINTRA

ESTEFÂNIA

Largo Afonso de Albuquerque

Alameda dos Combatentes da Grande Guerra

Avenida Movimento das Forças Armadas

See Enlargement

Estrada da Madeira

Rua Sotto Mayor

See Sintra-Vila Map p196

VILA

Rua Barbosa du Bocage

Parque da Liberdade

R. Conde Seisal

Rua D João de Castro

Rua Francisco dos Santes

Estrada de Chão de Meninos

To Monserrate Gardens, Quinta da Capella, Quinta das Sequóias, Colares & Cabo da Roca

Estrada da Pena

Rua Bernadim Ribeiro

Calçada da Penalva

C.C. de S. Pedro

Travessa Chão de Meninos

SÃO PEDRO

Pena

Calçada   da

Praça Dom Fernando II

Avenida Conde Sucena

To Lisbon & Queluz

SANTA EUFÉMIA

To Convento dos Capuchos, Cabo da Roca & Cascais

0   250   500 m

CRUZ ALTA

To Centro Hípico Penha Longa, Cascais & Estoril

0   100 m

---

palace in 1557; and the paralytic Afonso VI, who was effectively imprisoned here by his brother Pedro II for six years, died of apoplexy in 1683 while listening to Mass in the chapel gallery.

As for the palace's aesthetic appeal, the mixed styles result in a confused architectural hotchpotch but there are some fascinating decorations inside. Highlights include: the palace's unrivalled display of 15th and 16th century azulejos (especially in the Sala dos Árabes or Arab Room),

which are some of the oldest in Portugal; the Sala das Armas (Armoury Room, also called the Sala dos Brasões or Coat of Arms Room), with the heraldic shields of 74 leading 16th century families on its wooden coffered ceiling; and the delightful Sala dos Cisnes (Swan Room), which has a polychrome ceiling adorned with 27 goldcollared swans.

Most memorable of all is the ground floor Sala das Pêgas (Magpie Room), its ceiling thick with painted magpies, each holding in its beak a scroll with the words *por bem* (in honour). The story goes that João I commissioned the cheeky decoration to represent the court gossip about his advances towards one of the ladies-in-waiting. Caught red-handed by his queen, 'por bem' was the king's allegedly innocent response.

The palace is open daily except Wednesday from 10 am to 1 pm and 2 to 5 pm; admission costs 400$00 (students 200$00). The last tickets are sold 30 minutes before closing. At weekends and public holidays the palace is crammed with tour groups.

Castelo dos Mouros

A steep 3km climb from Sintra-Vila leads to the ruins of this castle, the battlements of which snake over the craggy mountainside. First built by the Moors, the castle was captured by Christian forces under Afonso Henriques in 1147. Much restored in the 19th century, it offers some wonderful panoramas: as long as Sintra's famous sea mists aren't rolling around, you should be able to see as far as Cabo da Roca. Late afternoon is the best time for taking spectacular photographs of the nearby Pena Palace. The castle is open daily from 10 am to 6 pm (5 pm from October to May); admission is free.

Palácio Nacional da Pena

Another 20 minute walk up from the castle (or catch the bus from town – see the Getting Around section) is the most bizarre building in Sintra, the Pena National Palace. This extraordinary architectural confection, which rivals the best Disneyland castle, was cooked up by the fertile imagination of Ferdinand of Saxe Coburg-Gotha (artist-husband of Queen Maria II) and Prussian architect Ludwig von Eschwege. Commissioned in 1840 to build a 'romantic' or 'Gothick' baronial castle from the ruins of a 16th century Jeronimite monastery that stood on the site, Eschwege delivered a Bavarian-Manueline fantasy of embellishments, turrets and battlements (and added a statue of himself in armour, overlooking the palace from a nearby peak).

The interior is just as mind-boggling: the rooms have been left just as they were when the royal family fled on the eve of the revolution in 1910. There's Eiffel-designed furniture, Ferdinand-designed china, and a whole room of naughty nude paintings. More serious works of art include a 16th century carved alabaster altarpiece by Nicolas Chanterène in the original monastery chapel.

The palace is open daily except Monday from 10 am to 1 pm and 2 to 6.30 pm (5 pm in winter); admission costs 400$00 (students 160$00, people under 26 years and seniors 200$00).

Below the palace, en route from the castle if you're walking, is the enchanting **Pena Park**, open daily from 10 am to 6 pm (5 pm from October to May); admission is free. It's redolent with lakes and exotic

AROUND LISBON

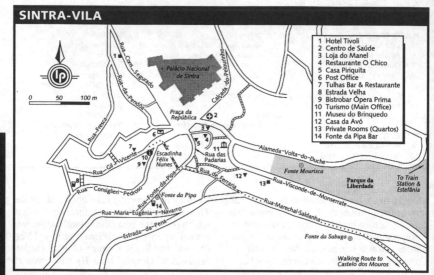

SINTRA-VILA

1 Hotel Tivoli
2 Centro de Saúde
3 Loja do Manel
4 Restaurante O Chico
5 Casa Piriquita
6 Post Office
7 Tulhas Bar & Restaurante
8 Estrada Velha
9 Bistrobar Ópera Prima
10 Turismo (Main Office)
11 Museu do Brinquedo
12 Casa da Avó
13 Private Rooms (Quartos)
14 Fonte da Pipa Bar

AROUND LISBON

plants, huge redwoods and fern trees, camellias and rhododendrons. Among the follies and cottages is a chalet built for Ferdinand's mistress, a German opera singer he titled Condessa d'Edla. An old-fashioned bus shuttles visitors from the park entrance to the palace for 200$00.

Convento dos Capuchos

If the Palácio Nacional da Pena leaves you aghast at its silly extravagance, try this atmospheric Capuchin monastery for the greatest contrast imaginable.

A tiny troglodyte hermitage, buttressed by huge boulders and darkened by surrounding trees, the monastery was built in 1560 to house 12 monks. Their child-sized cells (some little more than hollows in the rock) are lined with cork, hence the monastery's popular name, Cork Convent. Visiting the place is an Alice-in-Wonderland experience as you squeeze through low, narrow doorways to explore the warren of cells, chapels, kitchen, and cavern where one recluse, Honorius, spent an astonishing but obviously healthy 36 years (he was 95

when he died in 1596). Hermits hid away here right up until 1834 when the monastery was finally abandoned. It's now open daily from 10 am to 6 pm (5 pm from October to May); admission costs 200$00.

Monserrate Gardens

Four kilometres west of Sintra-Vila are the Monserrate Gardens. Rambling and romantic, they cover 30 hectares of wooded hillside and feature flora ranging from roses and conifers to tropical tree ferns, eucalyptus, Himalayan rhododendrons and at least 24 species of palms.

The gardens, first created in the 18th century by Gerard de Visme, a wealthy English merchant, were enlarged in the 1850s by the painter William Stockdale (with help from London's Kew Gardens), who imported many plants from Australasia and Mexico. Neglected for many years (the site was sold to the Portuguese government in 1949 and practically forgotten), the garden is still a bit of a mess but the tangled pathways and aura of wild abandon can be very appealing.

Parque Natural de Sintra-Cascais

The Sintra-Cascais Natural Park (14,583 hectares) is one of the most delightful areas in Portugal. Easily accessible from Lisbon, its terrain ranges from the verdant lushness of Sintra itself to the crashing coastline of Praia do Guincho (a champion site for modern surfers). Other coastal attractions include the lively coastal resort of Cascais and the wild and rugged Cabo da Roca, Europe's most westerly point. Sintra's mountains experience exceptional climatic conditions enjoyed by dozens of plant and tree species; a large number of exotic species were also introduced to Pena Park and Monserrate Gardens during the 18th and 19th centuries. There are no official park trails but there are plenty of walking routes in the parks and to the main points of interest. The park's headquarters (☎ 01-923 51 16, fax 923 51 41) are at Rua General Alves Roçadas 10, Sintra.

Recent EU funding can scarcely keep up with the garden's demands, though the local Amigos de Monserrate (Friends of Monserrate) group keeps up the pressure for their continued maintenance as well as for restoration of the garden's **quinta** (mansion). This bizarre Moorish-looking building – described by Rose Macauley in *They Went to Portugal* as a place of 'barbarous orientalism' – was constructed in the late 1850s by James Knowles for another wealthy Englishman, Sir Francis Cook.

The quinta's previous incarnation was as a Gothic-style villa rented by the rich and infamous British writer William Beckford in 1794 after he fled Britain in the wake of a homosexual scandal. Beckford, who loved the 'beautiful Claude-like place', added his own touch of landscaping and even imported a flock of sheep from his estate in England. Today, there are various plans for restoring it and opening it to the public: one of the most tasteful ideas is to turn it into a teahouse.

The gardens are open daily from 10 am to 6 pm (5 pm from October to May); admission costs 200$00.

Museu do Brinquedo

Sintra has several art museums of rather specialist interest, but this toy museum – in a spacious new building – is a delightful international collection of clockwork trains, lead soldiers, Dinky toys, porcelain dolls and much more, including a couple of computers on which visitors can play games. João Arbués Moreira, an engineer by profession, began this collection (now over 20,000 pieces) more than 50 years ago when he was 14. Often to be found in the museum, he is still fascinated by the toys and the history they represent, and the collection continues to grow.

The wheelchair-accessible museum – which also has a café and a small shop – is open daily except Monday from 10 am to 6 pm; admission costs 400$00 (children and students 250$00).

Museu de Arte Moderna

Sintra has put itself on the international art map with this museum, which opened in 1997 in Sintra's neoclassical former casino in Estefânia. Some of the world's best postwar art (including a particularly strong selection of pop art) has been built up by business tycoon José Berardo and his associate Francisco Capelo. Among the 350 or so pieces displayed are works by Warhol, Lichtenstein, Pollock and Kossoff. Check out the top floor café, too, with its open-air terrace and good views. The ground floor gift shop sells some classy items.

The museum is open Wednesday to Sunday from 10 am to 5.30 pm and Tuesday from 2 to 5.30 pm; admission costs 600$00 (students 300$00). On Thursday, admission is free for those under 18 and over 65 years.

Other Attractions

Between the gardens and Sintra-Vila you'll pass the brazenly luxurious **Hotel Palácio de Seteais**. Originally built in 1787 for the Dutch consul in Lisbon, its name (Palace of Seven Sighs) is said to refer to the Portuguese reaction to the 1808 Convention of Sintra, despatched from here, which gave the French reprehensibly lenient terms after their invasion. The interior has some fantastic murals (even piano lids are painted) but, unless you can fork out for a room or a meal, you probably won't get past the reception staff – they can be extremely snooty.

There's a string of lavish villas on the way back to Sintra, notably the fairytale **Quinta da Regaleira**, a collection of pseudo-Manueline buildings created by a stage designer in the early years of the 20th century for António Carvalho Monteiro, a Brazilian mining millionaire. Now belonging to the town council and finally open to the public, the quinta's showpiece is the Palâcio dos Milhões (so called because it cost so many millions to build). Also in the extensive grounds are a chapel, the Capela da Santíssima Trindade, and an initiation well, the Poço Iniciáto, which spirals down 30m to a labyrinth of underground galleries. The quinta (☎ 910 66 50) is open for guided 90-minute visits daily from 10 am to 7.30 pm (5.30 pm in winter), but admission is steep: 2000$00 (1000$00 for people under 26 years and seniors).

Activities

The Sintra region is increasingly popular for mountain-biking and hiking trips. Sintraventura, an operation run by the Sintra town council's sporting division (☎ 920 40 37, fax 920 96 46; contact Carlos Pereira) offers occasional day-long mountain biking or walking trips costing a mere 300$00 per person, but you need to contact the office in advance to reserve a place.

With a few days' advance notice Wild Side Expedições e Excursões (mobile ☎ 0931 869010, fax 443 37 44) can organise day-long hiking trips (from April to June

and September to October only) costing around 4000$00 per person. Wild Side also does mountain-biking in the Peninha region of Sintra, Cabo da Roca or Guincho (6000$00), and kayaking along the Estoril Coast (6000$00). They usually need a minimum of three people.

Another efficient operator which specialises in biking, hiking and canoeing is Cabra Montêz (mobile ☎ 0931 994 3840, fax 01-419 5315, email cabramontez@ hotmail.com); half-day trips in the area for 7000$00 including bike rental, or 4000$00 with your own bike (including a snack lunch). Prices are considerably cheaper for groups of 10 or more; it's worth calling ahead to see if you can join a group.

Two outfits arrange jeep safaris. Ozono Mais (☎/fax 924 36 73) offers a day's 'guided adventure' costing 9000$00 per person including lunch. Setúbal-based Planeta Terra (☎ 065-53 21 40) runs 'Ecotour' jeep safaris.

Horse riding is available in the grounds of Centro Hípico Penha Longa Country Club (☎ 924 90 33), costing around 3500$00 per hour. The club is about 5km south of Sintra-Vila.

Special Events

Sintra's big annual event is a classical music festival, the Festival de Música, held from around mid-June to mid-July. It features international performers playing in the palaces and other suitably posh venues. It's followed by the equally international Noites de Bailado, a classical and contemporary dance festival that goes on until the end of August. For more details about these, contact the turismo.

The more humble Feira do Artesanato (Handicrafts Fair) takes place over two weeks in early August on the shady Alameda dos Combatentes da Grande Guerra, near the train station. Stalls display various handicrafts – locally made ceramics, jewellery, Arraiolos carpets, clothes and charming model villages. Performances of traditional song and dance are also held on some evenings.

Places to Stay

The nearest camping ground is *Camping Praia Grande* (see West of Sintra), on the coast 12km from Sintra.

The *pousada da juventude* (☎ 924 12 10) is in Santa Eufémia, 4km from Sintra-Vila and 2km south-west of São Pedro, which is the closest you'll get by bus; in high season, dorm beds cost 1800$00 and doubles cost 4500$00. Advance booking is essential.

Some of the cheapest accommodation in Sintra itself can be found in the 80 or so *quartos* (private rooms); doubles cost about 5000/3500$00 with/without bathroom. The cheapest – and dampest – are probably the quartos (☎ 923 34 63) at Rua Visconde de Monserrate 60. The turismo has details of other options, including private apartments with kitchens costing about 8000$00.

Most budget guesthouses are near the train station. *Casa de Hóspedes Adelaide* (☎ 923 08 73, Rua Guilherme Gomes Fernandes 11), a 10 minute walk from the station, is the kind of place where rooms are rented by the hour, but if you don't mind that you'll find clean, simple doubles (without bathroom) costing 3500$00.

Piela's (☎ 924 16 91, Rua João de Deus 70) is justifiably popular, as much for its hospitable and informative proprietor as for its immaculate doubles (costing from 6000$00 to 7500$00). The charming *Monte da Lua* (☎/fax 924 10 29, Avenida Miguel Bombarda 51), opposite the station, offers tastefully decorated doubles with TV and bathroom costing from 8000$00 to 10,000$00. Try to get one of the quieter rooms at the back which overlook the wooded valley. Similarly priced, rooms at the popular *Quinta da Paderna* (☎ 923 5053, mobile ☎ 0931 9461261, Rua da Paderna 4) have lovely views.

In an enviably picturesque position on the high road between Sintra-Vila and São Pedro, *Residencial Sintra* (☎ 923 07 38, Travessa dos Avelares 12) is a big old mansion with 10 high-ceilinged and spacious rooms costing 15,000$00. It's perfect for families, with a rambling garden, an outdoor patio, a swimming pool and children's swings and slides. Advance booking is essential.

Among several Turihab properties in the area, the 19th century *Villa das Rosas* (☎/fax 923 42 16, Rua António Cunha 2-4) boasts some splendid décor, with azulejos in the hall and dining room. There's also a tennis court in the grounds. Doubles cost 15,000$00 including breakfast. Close to the station, the recently revamped *Pensão Nova Sintra* (☎/fax 923 02 20, Largo Afonso de Albuquerque 25) offers deluxe doubles ranging in price from 12,000$00 to 16,000$00. Its outdoor patio is a big plus.

Top-end accommodation includes the modern *Hotel Tivoli* (☎ 923 35 05, fax 923 15 72, Praça da República), right in the centre of Sintra-Vila, where deluxe doubles will set you back 24,000$00 in summer. For the same price, but with a lot more atmosphere, it's worth heading for *Quinta das Sequóias* (☎ 924 38 21, fax 923 03 42), a superb manor house just beyond the Hotel Palácio de Seteais. Nearby, in the wooded valley below Monserrate Gardens, is the 16th century former farmhouse, *Quinta da Capella* (☎ 929 01 70, fax 929 34 25), with similar prices.

Places to Eat

Estefânia Rua João de Deus, at the back of the train station, has three good choices, including *Restaurante Parreirinha* (☎ 923 12 07), a smoky locals' den at No 45 which serves great grilled fish and chicken (try the succulent grilled grouper), and the smarter *O Tunel* (☎ 923 13 86) at No 86, where dishes cost around 1200$00. There's also a good café at *Piela's* (see Places to Stay).

The unpretentious *A Tasca do Manel* (☎ 923 02 15, Largo Dr Virgílio Horta 5), next to the ornate *câmara municipal* (town hall), offers daily specials for an appetising 800$00. Nearby, the *Topico Bar & Restaurant* (☎ 923 48 25, Rua Dr Alfredo Costa 8) is pricier, especially its house wine, but it has some irresistible desserts. There's Portuguese or Afro-Brazilian live music here from 11 pm on Friday and Saturday in summer.

At the quiet end of Estefânia's market lane, Avenida Desiderio Cambournac, *Wiesbaden Restaurant (☎ 924 82 00)* offers an extensive menu of German, Portuguese and other dishes including German-style venison and *feijoada de javali* (wild boar stew). Special 'economical dishes' are on offer during the week, plus there's a kid's play area and a terrace. It's closed Sunday.

Sintra-Vila Many of the cafés and restaurants here are geared for the passing tourist trade, hence are overpriced and soulless, but *Tulhas Bar & Restaurante (☎ 923 23 78, Rua Gil Vicente 4)*, a converted grain warehouse, has maintained its character and quality. Specialities include an excellent *bacalhau com natas* (bacalhau in a cream sauce) costing 1100$00. Tulhas is closed Wednesday. Cheaper and more simple is *Casa da Avó (☎ 923 12 80, Rua Visconde de Monserrate 46)* which serves basic fare for less than 1000$00.

A classy addition is the *Bistrobar Ópera Prima (☎ 924 45 18, Rua Consiglieri Pedroso 2-A)*. This cavernous bar and restaurant serves snacks as well as main meals, and is open daily from 9 am to 2 am. There's live music here, too (see the Entertainment section).

For Sintra's famous *queijadas* (sweet cheese cakes) and *travesseiros* (apple pastries), head for the popular *Casa Piriquita* pastelaria *(Rua das Padarias 1-5)*. Picnic supplies can be bought nearby in *Loja do Manel* grocery store on Rua do Arco do Teixeira.

São Pedro In this area of town is a cluster of restaurants ideal for meat-lovers, notably *Toca do Javali (☎ 923 35 03, Rua 1 de Dezembro 12)* where you can get your teeth into a chunk of wild boar for about 2000$00. Go early to get one of the few outdoor tables in the garden. It's closed Wednesday. Down the road, at Travessa Chão de Meninos, two outlets of *Adega do Saloio (☎ 923 14 22)* have skinned goats on display, ready for cooking, as well as other standard grilled offerings. Dishes cost from 1400$00 to 2000$00 but some cheaper half-portions are also available.

Overlooking the huge cobbled Praça Dom Fernando II at the heart of São Pedro is the popular French restaurant *Solar de São Pedro (☎ 923 18 60)*. The adjacent *Restaurante Pic Nic (☎ 923 08 60)* offers cheaper, more humble fare with the added bonus of outdoor tables.

Entertainment

Fonte da Pipa (☎ 923 44 37, Rua Fonte da Pipa 11-13) is a cosy bar with snacks and inexpensive drinks; it's open nightly from around 9 pm. The central *Estrada Velha (☎ 923 43 55, Rua Consiglieri Pedroso 16)* is another popular bar, usually open until about 2 am.

Check out *Bistrobar Ópera Prima* (see Places to Eat) for its live jazz, soul and blues music on Tuesday, Wednesday and Thursday nights from around 10.30 pm to 1 am. *Restaurante O Chico (☎ 923 15 26, Rua Arco do Teixeira)* has some rather touristy fado playing nightly from July to September. There's no admission charge but meals are pricey.

Taverna dos Trovadores (☎ 923 35 48) in São Pedro is an upmarket tavern which also has fado on Friday and other types of live music on Thursday. A more casual dive popular with locals is *Mourisca Bar (☎ 923 52 53, Calçada de São Pedro 56)*, where you can play snooker, darts or chess.

Getting There & Away

Bus Services run by Stagecoach (☎ 486 76 81) or Mafrense (☎ 923 09 71) depart from outside Sintra's train station regularly for popular destinations in the region, such as Cascais (400$00 direct, 480$00 via Cabo da Roca), Estoril (400$00), Mafra (about 380$00), Ericeira (about 420$00), and the nearby beach of Praia Grande (300$00) via Colares. Reduced services operate on Sunday and public holidays.

Train Services run every 15 minutes between Sintra and Lisbon (Rossio station or Apeadeiro de Entrecampos); the last train back to Lisbon is at 1.23 am. The 45 minute journey costs 190$00.

Getting Around

Bus Stagecoach bus No 435 runs regularly from outside the train station to São Pedro via Sintra-Vila. To get to the Palácio Nacional da Pena (500$00), catch Stagecoach bus No 434 which runs from outside the train station via the turismo in Sintra-Vila daily every 30 minutes from 10.20 am to 4.55 pm except Monday when it runs every hour.

For 1200$00 you can buy a Day Rover Ticket which allows unlimited bus travel on the Stagecoach network.

Taxi You can pick up a taxi at the train station and outside the Palácio Nacional de Sintra. They aren't metered so check the fares first with the turismo. For a return trip to Palácio Nacional da Pena, the Castelo dos Mouros or Monserrate Gardens, figure on about 2000$00 (including one hour waiting time). There's a 20% supplement at weekends and on holidays.

Horse & Carriage Getting around by horse and carriage is the most romantic option. Operated by Sintratur (☎ 924 12 38), they clip-clop all over the place, even as far as Monserrate (7500$00 return). The turismo has a full list of prices, or check the table of prices on each carriage. The carriages wait by the *pelourinho* (pillory) immediately below the Palácio Nacional de Sintra.

Walking Walkers will get itchy feet in Sintra. The most popular route is from Sintra-Vila to the ruined Castelo dos Mouros above town, a relatively easy 50 minute hike. The energetic can continue to Palácio Nacional da Pena (another 20 minutes) and up to the Serra de Sintra's highest point, the 529m Cruz Alta, which offers spectacular views.

A more level route along the road to Monserrate Gardens also takes about 50 minutes, but note that this can be a nerve-wracking experience on busy weekends, with mammoth tour buses squeezing close to the roadside.

Pick up a copy of *Landscapes of Portugal: Sintra, Cascais, Estoril* by Brian & Eileen Anderson for more detailed descriptions of off-road walks (and car tours); it's available from bookshops in Lisbon or Porto. For organised walks, check out the earlier Activities section.

WEST OF SINTRA

The most alluring destinations for day trips from Sintra are the **beaches** of Praia das Maçãs and Praia Grande, about 12km to the west. Praia Grande, as its name suggests, is a big sandy beach with ripping breakers, backed by ugly apartments and a few cafés It also has an open-air swimming pool, open daily from June to September. Praia das Maçãs is more popular with Sintra's young people for its late-night revelries.

En route to the beaches, 8km west of Sintra, is the ancient village of **Colares** atop a ridge (not to be confused with traffic-clogged Várzea de Colares on the main road below). It's a laid-back spot with spectacular views, which has been famous for its wines since the 13th century, made from the only vines in Europe to survive the 19th century phylloxera plague, thanks to their deep roots and the local sandy soil. Call in advance to arrange a visit to the Adega Regional de Colares (☎ 929 12 10) and taste some of the velvety reds.

Attracting all of the tour buses, however, is **Cabo da Roca** (Rock Cape), about 18km west of Sintra. This sheer cliff, rising 150m above the roaring sea, is Europe's western-most point. A wild and rugged spot, it's surprisingly uncommercialised, perhaps because it feels too uncomfortably remote; there are only a couple of stalls, a café and a tourist office where you can buy a certificate to show you've been here.

Places to Stay & Eat

Praia Grande has one camping ground, the often crowded *Camping Praia Grande* (☎ 929 05 81), costing 390/397/247$00 per person/tent/car. Other accommodation in this area is expensive: in summer a double costs around 15,000$00 in the *Casa de Hóspedes de Piscina* (☎ *929 21 45*) in Praia Grande. Prices are similar at the *Residencial Oceano* (☎ *929 23 99*) and the *Residencial Real* (☎ *929 20 02*), both in Praia das Maçãs. For other alternatives, check out the signs advertising private *quartos* (rooms) along the road to Praia das Maçãs.

You'll have better luck with food, especially at Praia das Maçãs, where seafood restaurants such as *Buzio* (☎ *929 21 72*) and *Cai Ao Mar* (☎ *928 23 74*) are reasonably priced; both are on the main street above the beach.

Entertainment
At the last count, there were three nightclubs at Praia das Maçãs: *Concha* (☎ *929 20 67*), on the left by the GALP station; *Casino Monumental* (☎ *929 20 24*) in the centre; and *Quivuvi* (☎ *929 12 17*) further along on the right, in a modern shopping mall. They can keep you bopping till 4 am at weekends.

Getting There & Away
Bus No 441 from Sintra bus station goes frequently to Azenhas do Mar via Praia das Maçãs. In summer it also goes frequently via Praia Grande (at other times, hop off at the Ponte Ridizio junction, just before Praia das Maçãs, from where it's a short walk to Praia Grande).

The century-old tram service that used to connect Sintra with the bathing resort of Praia das Maçãs has now been revived. It runs from Ribeira de Sintra (1.5km from Sintra-Vila; take bus No 403 or 441 from Sintra station) three times daily except Monday and Tuesday (four buses at weekends); it costs 500$00 one way. Staff at the turismo can give you exact times.

You can get to Cabo da Roca from Sintra or Cascais on bus No 403 which runs between the two towns via the cape eight times daily. There are fewer buses on Sunday and public holidays.

CASCAIS
☎ 01 • pop 19,000
This former fishing village has been tuned in to tourism since 1870, when the royal court first came here for the summer, bringing a train of nobility in its wake. It's now the liveliest beach resort on the Estoril Coast, attracting a young and international crowd. If you like your home comforts (John Bull pubs and McDonald's), you'll be happy in the touristy pedestrianised centre, but there's a surprisingly unspoilt old town area which provides a pleasant afternoon's meander. The genteel resort of Estoril – just 2km along the coast to the east – boasts a pleasant beach of its own as well as Europe's biggest casino.

Orientation & Information
Everything of interest in Cascais is within easy walking distance. The train station (where buses also terminate) is a 10 minute walk north of the main pedestrianised Rua Frederico Arouca.

Near the western end of this street is the informative turismo (☎ 486 82 04, fax 467 22 80), at Rua Visconde da Luz 14. It's open daily from 9 am to 8 pm (7 pm from October to May; 10 am to 6 pm on Sunday). Pick up a copy of the free *Estoril Coast Magazine* here, which gives details of special events, restaurants and bars.

Cascais Hospital (☎ 484 40 71) is in the northern part of town.

Old Cascais
For a hint of Cascais' former life as a fishing village, head for the **fish market**, set up between Praia da Ribeira and Praia da Rainha at about 6 pm every day except Sunday, where an auctioneer sells off the day's catch in an unintelligible rapid-fire lingo.

The atmospheric back lanes and alleys to the west of the *câmara municipal* (town hall) are also well worth exploring. In a shady square south-west of the câmara municipal is the **Igreja de Nossa Senhora da Assunção**, decorated with azulejos predating the 1755 earthquake that destroyed most of the town.

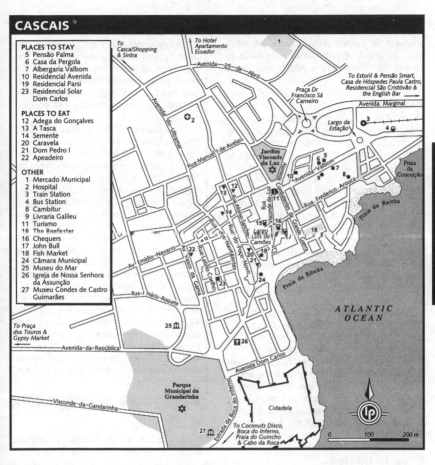

CASCAIS

PLACES TO STAY
5 Pensão Palma
6 Casa da Pergola
7 Albergaria Valbom
10 Residencial Avenida
19 Residencial Parsi
23 Residencial Solar
   Dom Carlos

PLACES TO EAT
12 Adega do Gonçalves
13 A Tasca
14 Semente
20 Caravela
21 Dom Pedro I
22 Apeadeiro

OTHER
1 Mercado Municipal
2 Hospital
3 Train Station
4 Bus Station
8 Cambitur
9 Livraria Galileu
11 Turismo
15 The Beefeater
16 Chequers
17 John Bull
18 Fish Market
24 Câmara Municipal
25 Museu do Mar
26 Igreja de Nossa Senhora
   da Assunção
27 Museu Condes de Castro
   Guimarães

Museums

The large and leafy Parque Municipal da Grandarinha is great for kids with its aviaries, duck ponds and playground; it also contains the delightful **Museu Condes de Castro Guimarães** (☎ 482 54 01). The late-19th century mansion of the Counts of Castro Guimarães is now a museum displaying the family's furnishings and *objets d'art* from the 17th and 18th centuries, including some striking Indo-Portuguese furniture and Oriental silk tapestries; its walls are liberally adorned with early azulejos. Downstairs is a small display of archaeological finds from the area. The museum is open daily except Monday from 10 am to 1 pm and 2 to 5 pm; admission (with guided tours only, every half-hour) costs 200\$00.

Walk to the north through the park and across the Avenida da República and you'll come to the excellent **Museu do Mar** (☎ 486 13 77) in Jardim da Parada. It has a small but high-quality display of model boats, fish, dolphins and whales, traditional fisherfolk's clothing and other marine artefacts. It's open daily except Monday from 10 am to 5 pm and is accessible to people in wheelchairs; admission costs 200$00.

Beaches

Most of the activity in Cascais centres around its restaurants and bars, but there are beaches if you want them: three sandy stretches (**Praia da Ribeira** is the largest and closest) tucked into little bays just a few minutes walk south of the main drag. They're nothing to write home about (nor is the water quality) but they make pleasant suntraps if you can find an empty patch.

Nearby Estoril has a pleasant beach, **Praia Tamariz**, with an ocean swimming pool (open daily in summer from 10 am to 8.30 pm) as well as showers, cafés and beachside bars.

Far more exciting waves break at **Praia do Guincho**, 9km north-west of Cascais. This long, wild beach is a surfer's and windsurfer's paradise (the site of previous World Surfing Championships) with its massive crashing rollers. Be aware that there's a strong undertow which can be dangerous for swimmers and novice surfers.

These resorts have a small but growing reputation for racist crime and assaults on tourists. Extra police were mobilised during 1998 specifically to patrol the beaches and holiday areas.

Boca do Inferno

Cascais' most famous tourist attraction, Boca do Inferno (literally Mouth of Hell), is 2km west of the centre, where the sea roars into an abyss in the coast. You can walk there in about 20 minutes and join the crowds pouring out of their tour buses, but don't expect anything dramatic unless there's a storm raging.

Estoril

Long a favoured haunt of the rich and famous (and a well known nest of spies during World War II), Estoril is very much

Golf on the Estoril Coast

As beach resorts go, Estoril is one of the dullest places west of Lisbon, but if you're a gambler or golfer (and preferably rich) you'll be in seventh heaven: Estoril not only has Europe's biggest casino, it's also got half a dozen spectacular golf courses within 25km.

The closest is just 2km to the north: Golf do Estoril has two courses overlooking the sea – one has 18 holes (par 69) and the second has 9 holes (par 34). The Quinta da Marinha course, 9km to the west, was designed by Robert Trent Jones to give both high handicappers and scratch golfers a challenge, with the course rolling over wind-blown dunes and rocky outcrops.

Ten kilometres to the north-west is the 18-hole, par 72 Penha Longa golf club, a well-equipped Trent Jones Jr creation with superb views of the Serra de Sintra and Atlantic Ocean. Nearby are Golf Estoril-Sol, designed by John Harris and Ron Fream, and the 18-hole Quinta da Beloura, designed by Rocky Roquemore, who's also responsible for the newest course in the region, the 18-hole Belas Clube de Campo, 22km north-east of Estoril in the Carregueira hills. Estoril's turismo has full details of all courses.

in the shadow of its livelier neighbour, Cascais, these days. However, if you fancy a discreet break gambling away the escudos or playing golf on one of half a dozen courses nearby, there's accommodation to suit most pockets (the deeper the better). The turismo (☎ 466 38 13, fax 467 22 80), opposite the train station, can provide details.

Activities

There are horse-riding facilities at the Centro Hípico da Quinta da Marinha (☎ 487 14 03), 2km inland from Praia do Guincho, where you can hire horses for around 4000$00 per hour.

Cascais also boasts Portugal's largest *praça de touros* (bullring), where bullfights take place regularly during the summer. Check with the turismo for dates and times.

Special Events

Summertime musical events include the Estoril Festival de Jazz and the Festival de Música da Costa do Estoril, held in both Cascais and Estoril during July.

Sometime between July and September (there's no fixed date), Cascais honours the patron saint of its fisherfolk, the Senhora dos Navegantes, with a day-long procession through the streets. In August, there's a Verão de Cascais (Cascais Summer) programme of free outdoor music and dance events, usually at 10 pm on Largo Luís de Camões or Largo da Misericórdia.

A *feira do artesanato* (handicrafts fair) takes place in Estoril, beside the casino, from 6 pm to midnight daily throughout July and August, with ceramics, rugs, sculpture and embroidery for sale. Open-air food stalls provide Portuguese snacks.

Estoril Casino's Art Gallery (on the 1st floor) is the venue for an annual International Naïve Painting Salon held in early October. It's been going strong for some 20 years and is now acknowledged as the biggest and best such exhibition in Iberia.

Racing fanatics might like to check whether the Grand Prix Formula 1 World & European Championships are back on track at the Autodromo do Estoril, 9km north of Estoril. Usually held in late September or early October, the races haven't been held for the last two years due to track repairs and lack of interest from the competing teams.

Places to Stay

Camping Orbitur do Guincho (☎ 487 04 50, fax 487 21 67) is in Areia, about 1km inland from Praia do Guincho and 9km from Cascais. Rates are 700/630/620$00 per person/tent/car. Hourly buses run to Guincho from Cascais train station.

Accommodation in town is expensive and scarce in August; you'll be hard pushed to find a place at all without advance reservations. The best budget bets are quartos (private rooms), usually costing from about 5000$00 to 6000$00 for a double. The turismo can help you to locate them. The prices listed are for early summer; add another 2000$00 for July and August.

The popular *Residencial Avenida (☎ 486 44 17, Rua da Palmeira 14)* is the best budget bet, with just four prettily decorated doubles without bathroom costing 6000$00. *Residencial Parsi (☎ 484 57 44, fax 483 71 50, Rua Afonso Sanches 8)* is a crumbling old building overlooking the waterfront; doubles without bathroom cost 6000$00.

Closer to the station is the *Pensão Palma (☎ 483 77 97, fax 483 79 22, Avenida Valbom 13)*. It's one of a pair of dainty town villas and is as pretty as a doll's house, with a fragrant flower garden at the front. Doubles range from 6500$00 (without bathroom) to 11,500$00 (with bathroom and breakfast). Next door, *Casa da Pergola (☎ 484 00 40, fax 483 47 91)* is a much more upmarket Turihab establishment with an ornate façade decorated with hand-painted tiles. Doubles with bathroom start at 15,500$00 including breakfast. More modern and less inspired accommodation can be found at *Albergaria Valbom (☎ 486 58 01, fax 486 58 05)*, across the road at No 14, where comfortable doubles cost 10,000$00.

In a quiet part of the old town, *Residencial Solar Dom Carlos (☎ 482 81 15, fax 486 51 55, Rua Latino Coelho 8)* is a 16th century former royal residence featuring a chapel where Dom Carlos used to pray. Rooms are 20th century (all with private bathroom) and cost 13,000$00.

There are several *hotel apartamentos* (apartment hotels) if you want your own cooking facilities. One of the most reasonably priced is *Hotel Apartamento Ecuador (☎ 484 05 24, fax 484 07 03, Alto da Pampilheira)*. Singles/doubles in this high-rise on the northern outskirts of town cost 10,200/13,300$00.

In Estoril, the pick of the pensões is *Pensão Smart (☎ 468 21 64, Rua José Viana 3)* in a quiet residential area about 10 minutes walk from the station. Prices for double rooms start at 10,000$00 including breakfast. There are cheaper digs nearby, at *Casa de Hóspedes Paula Castro* (☎ 468 06 99, *Rua da Escola 4*), where basic doubles without bathroom cost about 5000$00.

More upmarket guesthouses can be found along the busy Avenida Marginal, a few minutes walk east of Estoril station; turn right on leaving the station. One of them, the welcoming *Residencial São Cristóvão* (☎/fax 468 09 13) offers doubles without/ with bathroom for 8000/10,000$00 (including breakfast), and a spacious triple costs 15,000$00.

Places to Eat

There are plenty of restaurants serving unmemorable tourist-oriented stodge and overpriced seafood in the town centre, but it's worth heading away from the crowds for something better. *Dom Pedro I* (☎ 483 37 34, *Beco dos Invalides 5*), tucked into a backstreet corner of the old town, serves tasty and reasonably priced dishes starting at 900$00; go early to grab one of the few prized outdoor tables on the cobbled steps.

Further west, *Apeadeiro* (☎ 483 27 31, *Avenida Vasco da Gama 32*) is renowned locally for its grilled fish. Another popular haunt is the more upmarket *Adega do Gonçalves* (☎ 483 02 87, *Rua Afonso Sanches 54*), where hearty servings cost around 1200$00. Cheaper and more simple is *A Tasca* at No 61; try the delicious fish kebabs. Seafood splurges are best had at *Caravela* (☎ 483 02 80, *Rua Afonso Sanches 19*), where you can indulge in crab, lobster or prawns. Expect to pay at least 1300$00 per dish.

The only vegetarian restaurant in town is the modest *Semente* (☎ 483 23 92, *Rua do Poço Novo 65*), a snack bar where you can find tofu pies, quiches, millet salads and fresh fruit juices. It's closed Sunday.

On the western edge of Estoril, the *English Bar* (☎ 468 04 13, *Avenida Sabóia 9*), near Monte Estoril train station, is very popular for its seafood.

Entertainment

There's no lack of bars to keep the nights buzzing, especially on Rua Frederico Arouca and in the Largo Luís de Camões area, just down the road from the turismo, where the bars triple as cafés, restaurants and discos. For British-style establishments with imported beers and bopping music, check out *John Bull (Praça Costa Pinto 32)*, *Chequers* (☎ 483 09 26) on Largo Luís de Camões, and *The Beefeater* (☎ 484 06 96, *Rua Visconde da Luz 1*).

The most popular nightclub around is *Coconuts* (☎ 484 41 09, *Avenida Rei Humberto II de Itália 7*), about 1km south-west of Cascais, which has seven bars, two dance floors and an esplanade by the sea. It's open nightly from 11 pm to 4 am. Wednesday is Ladies' Night, featuring a male stripper.

The *casino* in Estoril, a short walk from the turismo across the Parque do Estoril, is open daily from 3 pm to 3 am. There's an admission charge of 500$00 for the gaming room (everything from roulette to baccarat, French bank and blackjack), though it's free to play the slot machines and bingo. The vast restaurant (☎ 468 45 21) attached to the casino puts on an international floor show nightly at 11 pm. Tickets cost 9000$00 with dinner, 5000$00 without.

Shopping

A good source of second-hand books in English, Spanish, Italian, French and German is Livraria Galileu, at Avenida Valbom 24-A. Serious shoppers should head for CascaiShopping, a massive shopping complex en route to Sintra. Bus No 417 passes by regularly.

The town's mercado municipal, on the northern outskirts of town, is open on Wednesday and Saturday morning, while a Gypsy market fills the area next to the bullring, 2km west of town, on the first and third Sunday of the month.

Getting There & Away

Trains from Lisbon's Cais do Sodré station frequently make the 25 minute trip to Estoril, then go on to Cascais (190$00).

Buses run regularly throughout the day from outside both Estoril and Cascais train stations to Sintra and Cabo da Roca, and also every hour from Cascais to Praia do Guincho and Mafra (bus tickets cost less when pre-purchased from the bus station kiosk).

Both places are included in most regional bus tours from Lisbon (see the Organised Tours section in the Lisbon chapter).

Getting Around

Daily throughout the summer a free electric train ferries tourists on a 45 minute round trip to Boca do Inferno, leaving every hour from 7 am to 10 pm from the Jardim Visconde da Luz, just north of the turismo.

There's also a couple of horse carriages which do half-hour trips to Boca do Inferno (about 4000$00 return); they wait beside the Jardim Visconde da Luz. There are several car rental agencies including Auto Jardim (☎ 483 10 73) and Transrent (☎ 486 45 66); all-inclusive rates start at around 6600$00 per day. You can book these through Cambitur (☎ 486 75 28) on Rua Frederico Arouca 73A, which also organises sightseeing trips.

To rent bikes or motorcycles contact Gesrent (☎ 486 45 66), Centro Comercial Cisne, Loja 15, or AA Castanheira (☎ 483 42 59), Edificio Sol de Cascais, Loja 11, Avenida 25 de Abril. Prices range from about 1500$00 per day for a mountain bike to 6500$00 for a Yamaha 125 (cheaper for longer rental periods).

QUELUZ

The only reason to stop at this dull town 5km north-west of Lisbon, en route to Sintra, is to see the pink-hued **Palácio de Queluz**, which was converted in the late 18th century from a hunting lodge to a summer residence for the royal family. It's the most elegant example of rococo architecture in Portugal, a miniature Versailles with feminine charm and formal gardens of whimsical fancy. One wing of the palace is often used to accommodate state guests and visiting dignitaries but the rest is open to the public from 10 am to 1 pm daily except Tuesday and Wednesday; admission costs 400$00.

The palace has witnessed some extraordinary royal scenes. Built for Prince Dom Pedro between 1747 and 1752, and designed by the Portuguese architect Mateus Vicente de Oliveira and French artist Jean-Baptiste Robillon, it was Dom Pedro's niece and wife, Queen Maria I, who inspired the most scintillating gossip about the place: she lived here for most of her reign, going increasingly mad. Her fierce, scheming daughter-in-law, the Spanish Carlota Joaquina, supplied even more bizarre material for the wealthy British visitor William Beckford to write about – most famously, an occasion when she insisted that Beckford run a race with her maid in the garden and then dance a bolero (which he did, he related, 'in a delirium of romantic delight').

Today the interior still shows hints of the eccentric characters of its owners through the furnishings typical of the period: English and French-style furniture, porcelain chinoiserie, Arraiolos carpets and floors inlaid with exotic woods. Highlights are the mirror-lined Throne Room, the Ambassador's Room, with a floor of chequered marble and a ceiling painting of the royal family attending a concert, a wood-panelled Music Room still used for concerts, and Pedro IV's 'circular' bedroom (actually a circular ceiling over a square room) with scenes from *Don Quixote* painted on the walls. The palace's vast kitchens have been converted into an expensive restaurant, *Cozinha Velha* (☎ 01-435 02 32).

The garden is a delightful medley of box hedges, fountains and lead statues, and features an azulejo-lined canal where the royal family went boating.

Getting There & Away

It's a 20 minute train ride (160$00) on the Sintra line from Lisbon's Rossio station to Queluz-Belas, followed by a 15 minute walk downhill (follow the signs) to the palace.

MAFRA
☎ 061 • pop 44,450 (municipal)

The otherwise unremarkable town of Mafra, 39km north-west of Lisbon, is famous for the massive Palácio Nacional de Mafra, the most awesome of the many extravagant monuments created during the reign of Dom João V in the 18th century, when money was no problem. Unless you want to explore the Tapada de Mafra park, it's best to come here on a day trip from Lisbon, Sintra or Ericeira since there's nothing else of interest in town.

Bikers and hikers might be interested in the twice-monthly trips into the countryside organised by the local council (see Activities later in this section).

Orientation & Information

You can't miss the palace: its huge grey façade dominates the town. The poorly signposted turismo (☎ 81 20 23, fax 81 51 04) is on Avenida 25 de Abril, five minutes walk north from the palace along the main street, beside the Auditorio Municipal Beatrix Costa. It's open weekdays from 9.30 am to 7 pm and weekends from 9.30 am to 1 pm and 2.30 to 7.30 pm (6 pm in winter). The turismo sells a decent map of the Mafra area (250$00) and provides useful information on nearby attractions.

The vast new Parque Desportivo Municipal Engenheiro Ministro dos Santos, on Avenida Dr Francisco Sá Carneiro, 1.5km north-west of the turismo, has an Espaço Jovem or youth centre (☎ 81 92 00, fax 81 36 64, email espacojovemcmm@mail .telepac.pt) where you can surf the Internet or send emails free of charge, for limited periods and by prior appointment. It's open weekdays from 9.30 am to 12.30 pm and 2.30 to 5.30 pm.

Palácio Nacional de Mafra

The Mafra National Palace is a combination of palace, monastery and basilica, a huge Baroque and neoclassical monument covering 10 hectares. It was begun in 1717 on the birth of a male heir to Dom João V, in order to fulfil a vow. As the king's coffers filled with newly discovered gold from Brazil, the initial design – meant for 13 monks – was expanded to house 280 monks and 140 novices, and to incorporate two royal wings. No expense was spared to build its 880 halls and rooms, 5200 doorways, 2500 windows and two bell towers boasting the world's largest collection of bells (57 in each). Indeed, when the Flemish bellfounders queried the extravagant order for a carillon of bells, Dom João is said to have doubled the order and to have sent the money in advance.

Under the supervision of the German architect Friedrich Ludwig, up to 20,000 artisans (including Italian carpenters and masons) were working on the monument at any given time. That figure rose to a mindboggling 45,000 workers in the last two years of construction, all of them kept in order by 7000 soldiers. The presence of so many outstanding artists spurred João V to establish a school of sculpture in the palace; open from 1753 to 1770, it employed many of Portugal's most important sculptors. Though the building may have been an artistic coup, the expense of its construction and the use of such a large workforce helped destroy the country's economy.

It was only briefly used as a palace: in 1799, as the French prepared to invade Portugal, Dom João VI and the royal family fled to Brazil, taking most of Mafra's furniture with them. In 1807, General Junot billeted his troops in the monastery, followed by Wellington and his men. From then on, the palace became a favourite military haven. Even today, most of it is used as a military academy.

One-hour tours (excluding the basilica) take you through innumerable galleries of polished wooden floors, down 230m-long corridors, through interminable salons and apartments, and up and dozens of flights of stairs – and you only see a fraction of the place.

It's easy to get dazed by it all but a few things stand out: the amusing 18th century pinball machines in the games room; grotesque hunting décor in the dining room, where chandeliers are made of antlers and chairs are upholstered in deerskin; and the monastery's infirmary where insane monks were locked away. Most impressive is the magnificent barrel-vaulted Baroque library, housing nearly 40,000 books dating from the 15th to 18th centuries. At 88m it's the longest room in the building. According to the original plan its ceiling was to have been gilded, but at this point the money ran out.

The central basilica, with its two bell towers, is wonderfully restrained in comparison with the rest of the palace, featuring multihued marble floors and panelling, and Carrara marble statues.

The palace-monastery is open daily except Tuesday and public holidays from 10 am to 5 pm (closed from 1 to 2 pm in winter); admission costs 400$00. The one-hour guided tours are actually little more than an escort by a (Portuguese-speaking) guard; for tours in English, French or German, book in advance at the turismo.

Tapada de Mafra

The palace's park and hunting ground, Tapada de Mafra, was originally created in 1747 and is still partly enclosed by its 20km-long perimeter wall. There are 90-minute minibus tours of the park at 10 am, 11 am, 3 pm and 4 pm on Friday, Saturday and Sunday (10 am and 3 pm on Saturday and Sunday in winter) which take visitors to see the park's deer and wild boar, plus its falcon-recuperation centre. Tours cost 950$00 for adults and 500$00 for children under 10 years. It's best to call ☎ 81 70 50 a day in advance to reserve a place.

More attractive for walkers is the well-signposted 7.5km-long *percurso pedestre* (walkers' trail) through the park; you should catch glimpses of deer and numerous birds. A leaflet (in Portuguese only) dispensed at the park entrance also illustrates the animal footprints you might come across – along with their *excremento*.

The park opens its gates to walkers (and cyclists or horse riders) only at specific times: from 9 to 10 am and 1.30 to 2 pm

daily. Whatever time you enter, you can stay until 5 pm. Admission costs 400$00 for walkers and 600$00 for cyclists. The entrance (poorly-signed) for both the minibus tours and the walking trail is about 6km north of Mafra, along the road to Gradil (look for the *Patrimonio do Estadio* sign at the gate).

Sobreiro

An unusual excursion from Mafra is to the village of Sobreiro, about 4km to the north-west (take any bus heading towards Ericeira), where sculptor José Franco has created an enchanting and extensive **craft village** dotted with small windmills and watermills, and with model figures 'working' in numerous little shops including a traditional bakery, a cobbler's and a tailor's. José Franco himself can be seen crafting clay figures at the entrance. Kids love it here; so do adults, especially when they discover the rustic *adega* (winery) serving good red wine, snacks and meals. There's also a restaurant and a shop selling ceramics and craft souvenirs. The craft village is open daily (free admission) from 9.30 am to around 7.30 pm.

Activities

Horse Riding At the Escola de Equitação de Alcainça (☎ 966 21 22), about 5km south-east of Mafra at Rua de São Miguel, Alcainça, you can hire horses for around 350$00 per hour. You can also take an intensive four day riding course on Lusitanos horses, costing around 19,500$00 per day (including meals and accommodation).

Walking & Cycling The admirable Câmara Municipal de Mafra organises a *pedestre* (hiking) or *bicyclete tudo terrano* (BTT; mountain-biking) trip one weekend each month between April and December. The 10km trips (lasting from 10 am to 1 pm) cost 500$00 per person. To register, visit the Espaço Jovem here or in Ericeira a day before (see Orientation & Information earlier in this section or under Ericeira in the Estremadura & Ribatejo chapter).

Centro de Recuperação de Lobo Ibérico

Ten kilometres north-east of Mafra is the Iberian Wolf Recovery Centre, established in 1989 to provide a home for wolves that have been trapped, snared or kept in dire conditions and are unable to function in the wild any longer. The centre's 17 hectares of secluded woodland provide a refuge for some 26 wolves, all from the north of the country where Portugal's last 300 Iberian wolves roam.

You can visit the low-profile centre at weekends or on holidays from 3 to 7 pm (2.30 to 6.30 pm in winter) if you call in advance (mobile ☎ 0931 532312). The best time is around 5 pm when the wolves emerge in the cool of the dusk, though even then sightings are never guaranteed: on our visit, we waited in the pouring rain for an hour before giving up ('wolves are afraid of umbrellas,' said our guide, one of six workers at the centre).

To support the centre's activities you can 'adopt' a wolf for about 5000$00 a year. There are also T-shirts and postcards for sale at the entrance. See Endangered Species under Flora & Fauna in the Facts about Portugal chapter for more on the Iberian wolf.

The centre isn't signposted so it's tricky getting there, even with your own transport: from Mafra, head east to Malveira then take the Torres Vedras road for 3km, and turn off to Picão just after Vale da Guarda. At the end of the village there's a steep cobbled track to the left (opposite Picão's only café). The last part of this 1km-long track is badly potholed, dangerously so after heavy rain.

By public transport, catch one of the frequent buses from Mafra to Malveira where you have to change to a Torres Vedras bus. The centre is 2km from the Picão turn-off.

Getting There & Away

There are regular buses to Mafra from Ericeira (20 minutes) and Sintra (45 minutes, about 380$00). Frequent buses from Lisbon take 75 minutes (about 550$00), leaving from the terminal by Lisbon's Campo Grande metro station.

SETÚBAL PENINSULA

The Setúbal Peninsula – the northern spur of the region the tourist board calls the Costa Azul – is an easy hop from Lisbon by ferry across the Tejo river, with regular bus connections to all the major points of interest. You can laze on the vast beaches of the Costa da Caparica, join trendy Lisbonites in the beach resort of Sesimbra's further south or eat great seafood in nearby Setúbal, where express bus connections make it a convenient stopover if you're heading south or east.

There are two major nature reserves as well: the Reserva Natural do Estuário do Sado and the Parque Natural da Arrábida, both worth exploring; several local operators offer jeep safaris, canoeing, mountain biking and hiking trips.

Cacilhas

This suburb across the Rio Tejo from Lisbon is notable mainly for its fish restaurants and the **Cristo Rei**, the immense statue of Christ with outstretched hands visible from almost everywhere in Lisbon. The 28m-high statue (a smaller version of the one in Rio de Janeiro) was built in 1959 and partly paid for by Portuguese women grateful for the country having been spared the horrors of WWII. A lift (which operates from 9 am to 7 pm in summer; 250$00) takes you right to the top from where you can gasp at the panoramic views.

Getting There & Away Ferries to Cacilhas (100$00) run every 10 minutes from Lisbon's Cais da Alfândega river terminal by Praça do Comércio. The trip takes about

10 minutes; the last boat departs from Lisbon at around 10.30 pm. A car ferry also runs every 20 minutes from Cais do Sodré (this one runs all night). To reach the statue, take Bus No 101 from the bus station opposite Cacilhas ferry terminal.

Costa da Caparica

This 8km-long stretch of beach on the west coast of the peninsula is Lisbon's favourite weekend escape, with cafés, restaurants and bars catering for every age group. During the summer a narrow-gauge railway runs along the entire length of the beach from Caparica town, giving you the option of jumping off at any one of 20 stops; northern parts of the beach attract families, southern areas gays and nudists. The turismo (☎ 01-290 00 71) on Praça da Liberdade in Caparica can fill you in on accommodation options (including several camp sites), which tend to be expensive.

Getting There & Away Buses run regularly to Costa da Caparica from Lisbon's Praça de Espanha (taking about one hour) and from Cacilhas bus terminal (stand No 17 or 25).

SETÚBAL

☎ 065 • pop 80,000

Once an important Roman settlement, Setúbal is now the largest town on the Setúbal Peninsula and Portugal's third-largest port (after Lisbon and Porto). Situated on the northern bank of the Sado estuary 50km south of Lisbon, it's refreshingly untouristy, concentrating more on its commercial port and industries (mainly cement and salt) than on visitors.

With its easy-going atmosphere, nearby beaches and excellent fish restaurants, Setúbal makes an ideal weekend escape from Lisbon. It's also a suitable base for exploring the Parque Natural da Arrábida and the Reserva Natural do Estuário do Sado, either with your own transport (this is great cycling country) or on one of the adventure trips listed under Activities in this section.

Orientation

The main train station, serving trains from Lisbon, is opposite Praça do Brasil, 700m north of the city centre. There's a local station (serving only Praia do Sado, by the Rio Sado) at the eastern end of Avenida 5 de Outubro. The main bus station is also on this avenida, five minutes walk from the municipal turismo.

Drivers should save themselves headaches (and meter charges) by heading for the free parking in Largo José Afonso.

Information

The helpful and conscientious municipal turismo (☎/fax 53 42 22) on Praça do Quebedo is open weekdays from 9 am to 7 pm and weekends from 9.30 am to 12.30 pm and 2 to 5.30 pm.

The larger regional turismo (☎ 53 91 20, fax 53 91 27) is tucked away at Travessa Frei Gaspar 10, near the town's pedestrianised shopping centre. It's open from 9 am to 7 pm daily, except Sunday when it closes at 12.30 pm. Frighteningly brisk, the office has stacks of publications about the Setúbal region and there's a touch-screen information terminal outside.

Banks and shops are plentiful in the pedestrian area near the regional turismo office. The police station (☎ 53 52 31) is on Avenida General Daniel de Sousa while the hospital (☎ 52 21 33) is near the bullring off Avenida Dom João II.

The local Instituto Português da Juventude (☎ 53 27 07, fax 53 29 63, email ipj.setubal@mail.telepac.pt), on Largo José Afonso, has several computers in its library, officially only for local students, but you may be able to surf the Internet or send emails at slack times (no charge). It's open weekdays from 9.30 am to 7 pm.

The headquarters for the Parque Natural da Arrábida and the Reserva Natural do Estuário do Sado (☎ 52 40 32, fax 3 72 56), on Praça da República, is open weekdays only.

Igreja de Jesus

There's only one major cultural site in Setúbal: the Igreja de Jesus on Praça Miguel

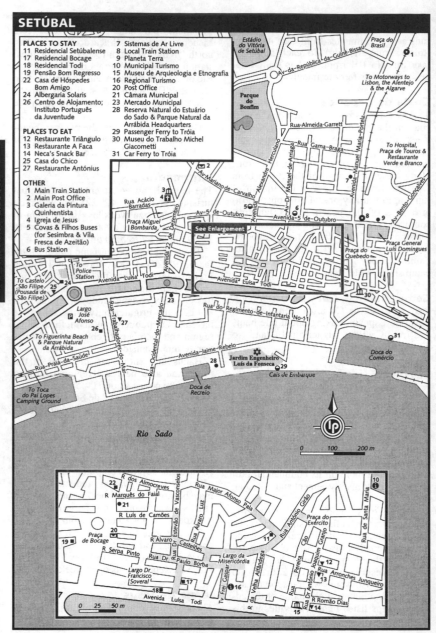

SETÚBAL

PLACES TO STAY
11 Residencial Setúbalense
17 Residencial Bocage
18 Residencial Todi
19 Pensão Bom Regresso
22 Casa de Hóspedes
     Bom Amigo
24 Albergaria Solaris
26 Centro de Alojamento;
     Instituto Português
     da Juventude

PLACES TO EAT
12 Restaurante Triângulo
13 Restaurante A Faca
14 Neca's Snack Bar
25 Casa do Chico
27 Restaurante Antónius

OTHER
1 Main Train Station
2 Main Post Office
3 Galeria da Pintura
    Quinhentista
4 Igreja de Jesus
5 Covas & Filhos Buses
    (for Sesimbra & Vila
    Fresca de Azeitão)
6 Bus Station

7 Sistemas de Ar Livre
8 Local Train Station
9 Planeta Terra
10 Municipal Turismo
15 Museu de Arqueologia e Etnografia
16 Regional Turismo
20 Post Office
21 Câmara Municipal
23 Mercado Municipal
28 Reserva Natural do Estuário
     do Sado & Parque Natural da
     Arrábida Headquarters
29 Passenger Ferry to Tróia
30 Museu do Trabalho Michel
     Giacometti
31 Car Ferry to Tróia

Bombarda, at the western end of Avenida 5 de Outubro. Constructed in 1491, it was designed by Diogo de Boitac, better known for his later work on Belém's Mosteiro dos Jerónimos. The small church is late-Gothic in style but walk inside and you'll see the earliest examples of Manueline decoration: extraordinary twisted pillars, like writhing snakes, made from delicately coloured Arrábida marble. The walls of the nave and chancel are more conservative, decorated with fine 18th century azulejos depicting the life of the Virgin. The church is open Tuesday to Saturday from 9 am to 12.30 pm and 2 to 5.30 pm.

Galeria da Pintura Quinhentista

While the Museu de Setúbal undergoes extensive renovations, its renowned Gallery of 16th Century Paintings – displaying some of the finest Renaissance art in the country – can still be found around the corner from the Igreja de Jesus, on Rua do Balneário Paula Borba. The set of 14 panels from the Lisbon school of Jorge Afonso (sometimes attributed to the anonymous 'Master of Setúbal') and four other later panels attributed to Gregório Lopes show extraordinarily rich colours and detail.

The gallery is open Tuesday to Saturday from 9 am to noon and 2 to 5 pm; admission is free.

Museu do Trabalho Michel Giacometti

A Museum of Work doesn't sound too enthralling, but the setting of this museum – a huge, cavernous former sardine-canning factory – is itself intriguing. Not only is there a realistic display of the former canning factory's activities, there's also an upper floor display of rural crafts and professions (bread-making, weaving, fishing, ploughing and so on), collected in northern and central Portugal in 1975 by local ethnographer Michel Giacometti with the help of a hundred youngsters.

The museum, at Largo Defensores da República (go east along Rua Arronches Junqueiro to the end) is open daily except

Monday and Saturday from 9.30 am to an extraordinary 11 pm; admission is free. The pleasant upstairs café is also open till late.

Museu de Arqueologia e Etnografia

The Museum of Archaeology & Ethnography, at Avenida Luísa Todi 162, houses an impressive collection of Roman remains. Setúbal was founded by the Romans after their fishing port of Cetobriga (now Tróia), on the opposite side of the river mouth, was destroyed by an earthquake in 412 AD. The museum is open from 9.30 am to 12.30 pm and 2 to 5 pm Tuesday to Saturday, and 9.30 am to 12.30 pm on Sunday. Serious archaeologists might want to inquire at the turismo about the museum's guided tours to the Roman ruins in Tróia (several of the tour operators listed under Jeep Safaris in the Activities section also visit the site).

Castelo São Filipe

Worth the half-hour stroll to the west of town is this castle built by Filipe I in 1590 to fend off an English attack on the invincible Armada. Converted into a *pousada* (upmarket inn) in the 1960s, its ramparts are still huge and impressive and its chapel boasts 18th century azulejos depicting the life of São Filipe.

Beaches

For good beaches, head west of Setúbal along the coast road until you reach Figuerinha, Galapos or Portinho da Arrábida. Buses from Setúbal run regularly in the summer to Figuerinha and sometimes further (inquire at the Covas & Filhos bus company: see Getting There & Away later in this section). More crowded are the beaches of Tróia (across the mouth of the Sado estuary), which has become hideously overdeveloped.

Activities

Walking & Cycling Sistemas de Ar Livre (SAL; ☎/fax 2 76 85, email sal@cpsi.pt, Web site www.sal.jgc.pt), Avenida Manuel Maria Portela 40, organises regular Sunday walks in the region, costing 1000$00 per person. Check their flyers at the turismos for details.

Planeta Terra (☎ 53 21 40, fax 52 79 21, email planeta.terra@mail.telepac.pt), Praça General Luís Domingues 9, also organises hiking and cycling trips in the Serra da Arrábida, costing from 4000$00 to 5000$00 per person for half a day (minimum of four people).

US-based Easy Rider Tours (see the Organised Tours section in the Getting There & Away chapter) runs a Costa Azul biking tour that includes a day's biking through the Serra da Arrábida.

Hot-Air Balloon Trips Contact Hemisférios (☎ 53 20 86, mobile ☎ 0931 944 5868) for balloon trips over the beautiful landscape of nearby Alcácer do Sal. The 25,000$00 charge includes an after-flight celebration with champagne, strawberries and cream.

Jeep Safaris Four-wheel-drive tours through the Tróia Peninsula to Alcácer do Sal, or around the Setúbal Peninsula via Palmela, are offered by Mil Andanças (☎ 53

29 96, fax 3 96 63), Rua Detraz da Guarda 40, for 3900$00 per person.

Safari Foto (☎ 063-65 17 57) organises a combination of jeep safari and horse-riding excursion in the Reserva Natural do Estuário do Tejo; it costs 7900$00 per person including lunch (500$00 extra for pick-up in Lisbon or Setúbal).

Planeta Terra (see under Walking & Cycling earlier) runs half-day trips through the Serra da Arrábida for 3500$00, or full-day trips as far as Alcácer do Sal costing 11,000$00, including lunch. It also offers an 'Arrábida by night' three hour tour costing 3500$00.

Cruises & Canoes Another unusual way to experience the area is aboard a modern galleon, the *Riquitum*, which sails along the Sado Estuary on four-hour trips (2500$00 per person) leaving every Friday at 9 am from the Cais de Embarque, just west of the Doca do Comércio (commercial dock). The trips are organised by Troiacruze (☎/fax 2 84 82). Cruises on a modern vessel are also offered by Nautur (☎ 2 49 63).

By taking a Planeta Terra half-day canoe trip through the Reserva Natural do Estu-

---

Parque Natural da Arrábida

The Arrábida Natural Park stretches along the south-eastern coast of the Setúbal Peninsula from Setúbal to Sesimbra. Covering the 35km-long Serra da Arrábida mountain ridge, with its sweeping views of the Atlantic, this is an area rich in Mediterranean thickets and plants (more than 1000 different species), butterflies, beetles and birds, especially birds of prey. Even seaweed comes in 70 different varieties.

The variety of flora makes for great local honey, especially in the gardens of the Convento da Arrábida, a 16th century former convent overlooking the sea just north of Portinho (to visit – preferably on Tuesday or Thursday – call ☎ 01-352 70 02). Cheese and wine are other famous local products; see Organised Tours in this section for details of wine-cellar tours.

Public transport through the park is sparse: buses between Setúbal and Sesimbra mostly skirt its northern boundary although there are occasional summertime buses from Figuerinha to Vila Nogueira de Azeitão (check with the turismo). Your best option is to rent a car or motorcycle and walk. For rough ideas of where to go (but don't trust its maps), read the English-language *Walking Guide to Arrábida and Sado*, published by the Região de Turismo da Costa Azul. It's available at the regional turismo and from park headquarters, both in Setúbal (see Information in this section).

Reserva Natural do Estuário do Sado

The Sado Estuary Natural Reserve encompasses a vast coastal area (23,160 hectares) around the Sado river and estuary, stretching from Setúbal at the northern end to near Alcácer do Sal at the south-east. Its mud banks and marshes, lagoons, dunes and former salt pans are a vitally important habitat for mammals, molluscs and migrating birds. The mammal species that attracts the most attention is the Bottlenose Dolphin (*Tursiops truncatus*, known in Portuguese as Roaz-Corvineiro) often found in coastal waters. There are thought to be only about 30 dolphins left in this area, fighting for survival as the mouth of the estuary becomes increasingly developed. Among the 100 or so bird species worth looking out for are flamingos (over a thousand of the birds regularly winter here), white storks (spring and summertime) and resident marsh harriers and little egrets.

Without your own transport, explorations of the park are inevitably limited. The park's headquarters in Setúbal (see Information) sells vague maps as well as T-shirts, postcards and CD-ROMs.

ário do Sado (6500$00 per person; see under Walking & Cycling) you can see the salt pans of the area and visit the old fishing village of Gâmbia.

Wine Tours Wine buffs may be interested in the free wine-cellar tours of the José Maria da Fonseca adega and museum (☎ 01-218 00 02) at Rua José Augusto Coelho 11, Vila Fresca de Azeitão, where the famous *moscatel* wine of Setúbal is made. From Setúbal, buses leave almost every half-hour to Vila Fresca de Azeitão. The adega is open weekdays from 9 am to noon and 2.30 to 4.30 pm.

Places to Stay
Camping The adequate *Toca do Pai Lopes* (☎ 52 24 75) municipal camping ground is 1.5km west of the town centre on Rua Praia da Saúde (near the shipyards); it costs 260/220/240$00 per person/tent/car. During the summer, the regular Covas & Filhas bus going to Figuerinha beach passes close to this camping ground. There's another *parque de campismo* (☎ 3 83 18) 2km further along the coast at Outão.

Hostel At the *centro de alojamento* (☎ 53 27 07, fax 53 29 63, Largo José Afonso) there are dorm beds costing 1700$00 in the high season, plus some doubles which cost 4200$00. Reception is open from 8 am to noon and 6 pm to midnight.

Pensões & Residenciais One of the cheapest options in town is the friendly *Residencial Todi (☎ 2 05 92, Avenida Luísa Todi 244)*, where dowdy but spacious doubles with/without bathroom start at 4000/3000$00; a triple is good value at 4500$00.

Two budget places overlook the pleasant Praça de Bocage. *Casa de Hóspedes Bom Amigo (☎ 52 62 90)* has adequate doubles with pokey windows and without bathroom, costing around 5000$00. *Pensão Bom Regresso (☎ 2 98 12)* offers doubles with TV, without bathroom but with some good views of the Praça, for an overpriced 5500$00.

Up several notches, with doubles costing from 7000$00 to 9000$00 including breakfast, are the comfortable *Residencial Bocage (☎ 2 15 98, fax 2 18 09, Rua São Cristovão 14)* and the smart, pretentious *Residencial Setúbalense (☎ 52 57 90, fax 52 57 89, Rua Major Afonso Pala 17)*, in another central pedestrianised lane. The four star *Albergaria Solaris (☎ 52 21 89, fax 52 20 70, Praça Marquês de Pombal 12)* offers doubles with all the frills for

14,000$00. Free car parking is available in the praça.

Most luxurious of all is the *Pousada de São Filipe* (☎ *52 38 44, fax 53 25 38*), within the walls of the town's hilltop castle; some of the rooms are in the old dungeons. Doubles will set you back a tidy 29,600$00.

Places to Eat

There are lots of cheap little eateries in the lanes just east of the regional turismo office. *Neca's Snack Bar* (☎ *3 77 13, Rua Dr António Joaquim Granjo 10*) is a welcoming little place which, despite its name, serves regular meals, including bargain daily specials costing around 700$00 and special titbits such as a delicious *queijo de ovelha* (sheep's milk cheese). On the nearby Rua Arronches Junqueiro there's a string of cheap café-restaurants, including *Restaurante A Faca* at No 71 and *Restaurante Triângulo* (☎ *3 39 27*), opposite at No 76, which pack in the locals at lunchtime.

For excellent seafood dishes, head for the western end of Avenida Luísa Todi, where there's a string of seafood restaurants. *Casa do Chico* (☎ *3 95 02*) at No 490 is small and friendly and offers weekend specialities such as *caldeirada à Setúbalense* (Setúbal-style seafood stew). It's closed Monday. Down a grubby street you'll find the popular *Restaurante Antónius* (☎ *52 37 06, Rua Trabalhadores do Mar 31*), which has an extensive fish menu; dishes cost around 1300$00. It's closed Wednesday.

For some of the best grilled fish you'll eat anywhere in Portugal, the place to try is *Restaurante Verde e Branco* (☎ *52 65 46, Rua Maria Batista 33*), beside the bullring. This restaurant, famous for miles around, is only open at lunchtimes (you'll be lucky to get a seat before 2 pm) and only serves grilled fish with potatoes and salad: simple and superb.

Getting There & Away

Until Lisbon's new North-South Railway Line links up with the line from Barreiro (see the Getting There & Away section in the Lisbon chapter), train connections are complicated since you must first cross the Rio Tejo to Barreiro. It is easier to take one of the buses that leave frequently from Praça de Espanha in Lisbon or from Cacilhas (stand No 13), a quick ferry-hop from Lisbon's Cais de Alfândega terminal. Buses leave from Setúbal for Lisbon every 15 to 30 minutes.

Buses from Setúbal to Sesimbra leave about nine times a day from outside the office of Covas & Filhos bus company on Avenida Alexandre Herculano 5-A. This is also the place to get Solexpresso tickets for buses to the Algarve, Elvas, Peniche and Portalegre.

Ferries to Tróia depart every 30 to 45 minutes daily. The fare is 150$00 per person (600$00 for a car). Note that car ferries depart from a different point from passenger ferries.

Getting Around

You can rent bikes for 3500$00 a day from Planeta Terra (see the earlier Activities section).

Car rental agencies include Avis (☎ 52 69 46), Avenida Luísa Todi 96, and Alucar (☎ 53 32 85, fax 52 54 05), Avenida Combatentes da Grande Guerra 60.

SESIMBRA
☎ 01 • pop 8100

This former fishing village sheltering under the Serra da Arrábida, at the western edge of the Parque Natural da Arrábida, 30km west of Setúbal, has become a favourite seaside resort with Lisbonites. At weekends and in high season the traffic, jet skis and bar music hardly provide a tonic of tranquillity but if you like your beaches to buzz, this little resort may fit the bill.

Orientation & Information

The bus station is on Avenida da Liberdade; from there, it's five minutes walk south to the seafront. Turn right when you reach the bottom of the avenue, pass the small 17th century Forte de Santiago (not open to the public) and you'll reach the turismo (☎ 223 57 43) at Largo da Marinho, just off the main Avenida dos Náfragos. It's open daily from 9 am to 8 pm in summer (10 am to 12.30 pm and 2 to 5.30 pm in winter) and can help you to find accommodation.

Things to See & Do

Eating and drinking seem to be the main activities in Sesimbra, though **water sports** attract a few sober souls during the day: windsurfing boards and paddle boats can be rented along the beach in summer, and swimming is good on either side of the Forte de Santiago.

The unusually energetic can hike up to the ruined Moorish **castelo** (allow at least an hour), which was taken from the Moors by Dom Afonso Henriques in the 12th century, retaken by the Moors, and finally snatched back by the Christians under Dom Sancho I in the following century. Perched 200m above the town, it's a great spot for coastal panoramas.

To see the last vestiges of Sesimbra's traditional fishing lifestyle, head for the **Porto de Abrigo**, 1km or so west of the town centre, where fishermen auction off their catch in the late afternoon.

Places to Stay

The nearest camping ground is at *Forte de Cavalo* (☎ 223 36 97), just 1km west of town, but it's often packed out in summer; it costs 220/350/120$00 per person/tent/car. The next nearest options are the municipal *parque de campismo* (☎ 268 53 85) at Maçã, 4km to the north (take any Lisbon or Setúbal bus) or the better equipped *Valbom* camping ground (☎ 268 75 45) at Cotovia, 1km further north.

Accommodation is sparse and expensive: your best bet is to seek out a private rooms (ask at the turismo); they're available in the summer and cost around 5500$00 for a double. More expensive options include the spacious doubles with bathroom costing 7000$00 which belong to *Senhora Garcia*

(☎ 223 32 27, Travessa Xavier da Silva 1). Opposite, *Residencial Chic* (☎ 223 31 10, Travessa Xavier da Silva 2-6), above Restaurante Chic, has adequate doubles without bathroom costing about 6000$00.

In the upper price bracket is the comfortable *Residencial Nautico* (☎ 223 32 33, Bairro Infante Dom Henrique 3), a 10 minute walk uphill from the waterfront, where doubles cost 9000$00 including breakfast. More attractive is the *Casa da Terrina* (☎ 268 02 64), a 19th century converted farmhouse about 3km from Sesimbra at Quintola de Santana (take the bus to Cabo Espichel). There are five doubles costing 10,000$00, and there's a swimming pool in the grounds.

Places to Eat

You're spoilt for choice if you want fish restaurants, especially along Avenida 25 de Abril, east of the Forte de Santiago. Prices aren't cheap, though, and can often escalate alarmingly if you make anything other than a run-of-the-mill choice.

Along the waterfront in the other direction, a pleasant option is *Restaurant Baia* (☎ 223 20 12, Avenida dos Náfragos 45), next to the Hotel do Mar. For cheaper fare, head for the backstreets around the bus station where *Restaurante Chic* (see Places to Stay), a bar-restaurant favoured by resident expats, serves pizzas and salads.

Entertainment

Among the many bars and cafés along the waterfront, *Sereia* (☎ 223 20 90, Avenida dos Náufragos 20) attracts a lively crowd and is open until at least 2 am.

Getting There & Away

Buses to Sesimbra depart from Lisbon's Praça de Espanha three or four times a day and at least nine times a day from Setúbal and Cacilhas.

The Algarve

Loud, boisterous and full of foreigners, the Algarve is about as far from quintessential Portugal as you can get. It's been the country's major tourist resort area since Faro airport opened in the 1960s, leading to a flood of package tours from Britain and, increasingly, Germany and France. The big attraction? Almost year-round sun, great beaches and low prices.

Those are still the Algarve's major selling points, though rampant development during the late 1970s between Lagos and Faro destroyed much of the coastline's picturesque quality and polluted inland and offshore areas. In recent years tourism has gone increasingly upmarket, with more environmentally conscious developers and a clutch of luxurious villa resorts complete with designer golf courses and marinas.

Not all of the Algarve's 270km of coastline is a built-up disaster zone. West of Lagos there are wild and almost deserted beaches. The coast east of Faro has many unspoilt towns and villages, as well as a string of sandy offshore islands which make up the Parque Natural da Ria Formosa, favoured by wildlife and beach bums alike.

And for those who've had their fill of seascapes and the packed resorts of Lagos and Albufeira, there are the forested slopes of the Serra de Monchique, with its old spa village of Caldas de Monchique, the fortified town of Silves, and the market town of Loulé tucked away in the hills. Even less

HIGHLIGHTS

- Cycle along the dramatic coastline at Sagres
- Bird watch or sunbathe on the offshore islands of the Parque Natural da Ria Formosa
- Wander through the attractive, unspoilt town of Tavira
- Explore off the beaten track with a jeep safari in Parque Natural do Sudoeste Alentejano e Costa Vicentina
- Step back in time in Silves, the former Moorish capital of the Algarve

touristy are the Algarve's fringes – the west coast from Sagres to Odeceixe, and the eastern inland road wriggling north near the Rio Guadiana, which forms the border with Spain.

HISTORY

The Algarve's sunny disposition and long, warm coastline has attracted foreigners since the time of the Phoenicians, some 3000 years ago. The Phoenicians, who made their mark by establishing trading posts along the coast, were followed by the Carthaginians, who founded several major entrepôts, including Portus Hannibalis (Portimão) in 550 BC.

But as in the rest of Portugal, the Romans were the most serious and influential early settlers. During their 400 year presence they spread the cultivation of wheat, barley and grapes; built roads and luxurious palaces (check out the remains at Milreu, near

What's an Algarve?

The name Algarve comes from the days of Moorish occupation. While most of the new arrivals to the area around Beja and Faro came from Egypt, the territory east of Faro to Seville (in present-day Spain) was settled largely by Syrians, who called it *al-Gharb al-Andalus* (western Andalusia).

Faro); and gave the Portuguese language its Latin foundations.

In the wake of the Romans came the Visigoths, and then in 711 the first wave of Moors from North Africa. The Algarve was to remain their stronghold for 500 years. Silves (called Xelb by the Moors) became their opulent capital.

The Moors of the Algarve were a mixed ethnic bunch: around Faro they were mostly Egyptians but elsewhere they included Persians, Syrians and Berbers from Morocco. Among them were notable historians, philosophers, astronomers and poets, including two outstanding female poets, Xilbia and Mariam. By the mid-9th century the powerful, prosperous Algarve had become quite independent of the larger Muslim emirate to the east, which was centred around what is now Seville and Córdoba in Spain.

As the Christian Reconquista got underway in the early 12th century, the Algarve became the ultimate goal for a succession of crusaders and kings. Though Dom Sancho I captured Silves and territories to the west in 1189, the Moors staged a comeback in the Algarve and it wasn't until the first half of the 13th century that the Portuguese finally wrested this last part of the country back for keeps.

Two centuries later came the Algarve's age of importance, when Prince Henry the Navigator chose windswept Sagres, at the furthest south-western corner of Europe, as the base (or at any rate as a point of inspiration) for a pioneering effort to extend the field of knowledge in cartography, navigation and ship design. He had his ships built, equipped and staffed in Lagos for the daring expeditions that soon followed to Africa and Asia, raising Portugal to the status of a major imperial power. See also the boxed text 'Prince Henry the Navigator' under History in the Facts about Portugal chapter.

Nothing since then has put Portugal so firmly on the world map. Today the Algarve has a far more modest place on this map as a premier sun-and-surf destination and expatriate haven.

GEOGRAPHY

The Algarve divides neatly into five regions: the leeward coast (or Sotavento), from Vila Real de Santo António to Faro; the central coast, from Faro to Portimão; the windward coast (or Barlavento), from Lagos to Sagres; the Costa Vicentina, facing west into the teeth of Atlantic gales; and the interior.

Much of the leeward coast is fronted by a chain of sandy or boggy offshore *ilhas* (islands), most of them now part of the wildlife-rich Parque Natural da Ria Formosa. The beach, golf, bar and nightclub scenes – as well as the heaviest resort development – are concentrated along the central coast. West of Lagos, the shore grows increasingly steep and rocky, culminating in the wind-scoured grandeur of the Cabo de São Vicente, Europe's southwestern corner.

The interior, along the border with the Alentejo, is surprisingly hilly and verdant, rising to two high mountain ranges. Best known to visitors is the Serra de Monchique, north of Portimão, topped off with the 902m Fóia. Less visited is the Serra do Caldeirão, running north from Faro into the Alentejo.

The Algarve's capital and largest town is Faro. Its easternmost town, Vila Real de Santo António, is a border crossing to Ayamonte in Spain. The two countries are linked by car ferry and by the nearby E01 motorway bridge across the Rio Guadiana.

INFORMATION
Tourist Offices

Every town of any size has a turismo where you can get free leaflets, maps and information. They also sell good regional maps of the Algarve (250$00) as well as expanded town maps for 50$00. Some may also still stock the old *Algarve: Guide to Walks* booklet (250$00) which details 20 rural walks of varying difficulty. Look out, too, for the monthly *Events* pamphlet and a free glossy booklet called *Algarve Tips*, which has stacks of useful information including recommended shops and restaurants. *Your*

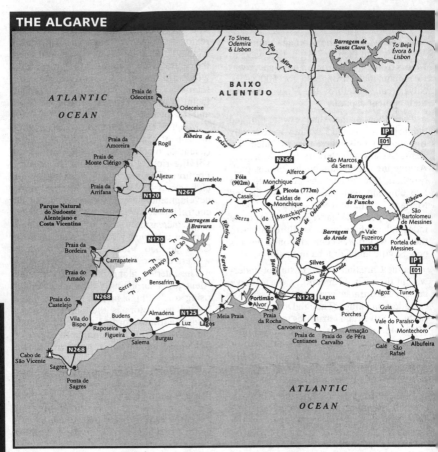

THE ALGARVE

ALGARVE

Guide Algarve, produced by the airport authority, ANA, is particularly good on bar, club and hotel listings. There's also a privately produced *Free Map* of popular resorts (often available at bars and shops too), which is great for up-to-date tips on places of entertainment.

Newspapers & Magazines

In addition to the general English-language newspapers *APN* and the *News*, several Algarve-specific magazines, in English and German, are available in most major towns. These include *Algarve Resident*, *Algarve Living* and *Entdecken Sie Algarve*.

For longer-term visitors, useful publications include the *Discover* series of pocket guides to the Algarve, and *Great Nights Out* and *Great Days Out* by resident Len Port.

Dangers & Annoyances

The Algarve has one of Portugal's higher levels of petty crime, mainly theft. Paranoia is unwarranted, but don't leave anything of

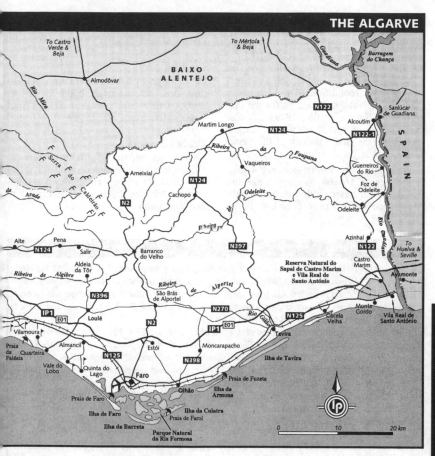

THE ALGARVE

value in your vehicle or unattended on the beach. More worryingly, a reader recently reported a nasty unprovoked attack by a gang of Portuguese males in Lagos. The police commented that such attacks are not uncommon, particularly in the summer.

Swimmers should beware of dangerous ocean currents, especially on the west coast. Beaches are marked by coloured flags: red means the beach is closed to all bathing, yellow means swimming is prohibited but wading is fine, green means anything goes.

ACTIVITIES
Walking

Os Caminheiros do Algarve/Walkers (☎ 089-36 02 70, fax 36 05 61) is an informal club that convenes every third Saturday of the month between September and May for a gentle trek, mainly around Silves and areas of the eastern Algarve. Visitors are welcome (400$00 per person). The club also arranges Discovery trips to places of interest further afield (around 5000$00 per person including lunch).

Almargem (☎/fax 089-41 29 59) is a Loulé-based Portuguese environmental group that welcomes *estrangeiros* (foreign visitors) on its frequent walks of 10km or so. This group is pioneering walks along the coast and the Rio Guadiana, and a network of pathways around Salir. The Liga para a Proteção da Natureza (League for the Protection of Nature; ☎ 082-78 93 59) also organises short walks to areas of natural interest on the first Saturday of the month (except January and August).

For times of club meetings, check listings in the weekly *Algarve Resident* magazine. For details of other guided walks, see the Monchique and Tavira sections later in this

chapter. See also the boxed text below about the newly established Via Algarviana (Trans-Algarve Way).

Cycling

Zebra Safari in Albufeira organises adventure trips with mountain bikes as well as canoes. Other small operators do trips from Lagos, Monchique and Tavira.

Water Sports

There's an organised diving centre in Sagres, and you can also do scuba diving at various other places along the coast, including Albufeira, Armação de Pêra, Luz and Vilamoura.

Via Algarviana

Compared with its neighbours, Portugal is ambling very slowly indeed in providing facilities for walkers. Helped by the EU (which, unbeknown to most, provides funds for walking trails as well as motorways to link EU countries), the European Ramblers Association has helped instigate a number of long-distance footpaths known as Euro Routes (ERs) for the use of walkers, mountain bikers and horse riders.

Some of these now stretch across vast areas of Europe: the ER4, for instance, strides from Greece to Gibraltar, and the Spanish Federaçion Espanola de Deportes de Montana y Escalada is busy extending it towards Seville. From here it will probably head via Barrancos in Portugal (48km east of Moura) to join the ER7 from Madrid which will terminate at Lisbon (and eventually, it's hoped, link up with Europe's coast-hugging ER9).

The Federação Portuguesa de Campismo e Caravanismo is finally getting Portugal involved by establishing the first tiny part of the ER7 in Portugal, from the border town of Termas de Monfortinho 20km south-westwards to Idanha-a-Nova (near Castelo Branco). But progress is slow.

Meanwhile, two walking clubs in the Algarve have got their own act together to establish the 200km Via Algarviana trail right across the Algarve. In October 1998, the Loulé-based environmental group Almargem and Os Caminheiros do Algarve/Walkers (OCDAW) christened the 10 day trail, which runs from Alcoutim to Cabo de São Vicente. The enthusiastic bunch are now hoping that they can connect the Spanish part of the ER4 with their new Via Algarviana by creating an 80km spur from Val Verde del Camino in Spain to Alcoutim, thereby being able to benefit from EU funding to waymark, publicise and maintain the new route.

For more details, contact the two clubs directly (see Walking in the Activities section of this chapter), or the Federação Portuguesa de Campismo e Caravanismo (☎ 01-812 68 90, fax 812 69 18), Avenida C Eduardo Galhardo 24-D, 1170 Lisbon.

There's a useful Web site on hiking in Europe at www.bibloset.demon.co.uk. Look out, too, for the dedicated guide to the Algarve Way by Brian & Eileen Anderson, which should hit the shelves by the new millennium.

Water-skiing is easily arranged through resorts around Albufeira, Armação de Pêra, Portimão and Vilamoura, or with outfits in Alvor, Luz, Quarteira and Sagres. There is an *escola de ski* (ski school) at Meia Praia, east of Lagos.

Sailing & Deep-Sea Fishing

Numerous outfits (including resort hotels) offer half-day or full-day sailing trips along the central coast. Points of embarkation include Sagres, Lagos, Alvor, Portimão and Armação de Pêra. Deep-sea fishing trips depart during the summer from Alvor, Portimão and Vilamoura.

Horse Riding

The Algarve has more than a dozen *centros hípicos* (riding centres) and *centros de equitação* (equestrian centres), concentrated mainly between Faro and Albufeira. Ask at the turismos for a list.

Golf

At the last count, there were 19 golf courses in the Algarve, most of them along the stretch of coast between Faro and Albufeira. The top courses are probably Quinta do Alto (Alvor), Vilamoura I, II and III (Vilamoura), Vila Sol (Vilamoura) and the deluxe Quinta do Lago (Almancil). At the Faro turismo you might be able to bag a copy of the ICEP's glossy booklet on Portugal's golf courses.

Among several resorts offering golfing packages is the David Leadbetter Golf Academy in Carvoeiro.

Tennis

Most top-end resort hotels in the Algarve have tennis courts, and there are clubs, with professional instructors, at Vilamoura, Vale do Lobo and Carvoeiro.

Jeep Safaris

Several companies run one-day jeep trips into the hills or along the west coast. Steer clear of the cowboy outfits with their massive, insensitive convoys. The best of tour operators take time to show you what is a fast-disappearing rural way of life, along with surprisingly wild scenery. Horizonte (☎ 082-69 59 20, fax 69 58 55), in Salema, which specialises in the Parque Natural do Sudoeste Alentejano e Costa Vicentina, is probably the most environmentally conscientious of the lot. A one-day jeep trip costs about 7000$00 per person. Other reliable companies are the long-established Riosul (☎ 081-51 02 01, fax 51 02 09) and Mega Tur (☎ 089-80 76 48, fax 80 74 89). Both Riosul and Mega Tur do a combined jeep safari and river cruise day trip for around 9500$00.

River & Coastal Trips

You can cruise the Rio Arade between Portimão and Silves, or the Rio Guadiana between Vila Real de Santo António and Foz de Odeleite. You can also do the Rio Guadiana trip from Portimão: several different operators have stalls by the river. A good agency for Rio Guadiana trips is Riosul, which has pick-up points in Albufeira and Tavira.

Mega Tur and Turalgarve (☎ 089-46 21 93, fax 41 29 98) run boat trips through the coastal Parque Natural da Ria Formosa to watch the fishermen catch fish and clams.

Activities for Children

Programmes at the Zoomarine aquatic park (☎ 089-56 11 04) at Guia include a good half-hour dolphin show three times a day, plus less captivating seal and parrot 'performances'; there are also two public swimming pools. The park is open daily from 10 am to 8 pm between mid-June and mid-September (5 pm in winter). Admission is 2450$00 for adults and 1500$00 for children from three to 10 years.

The Algarve has at least three huge water-slide parks along the N125 – Slide & Splash (☎ 082-34 16 85) west of Lagoa, The Big One (☎ 082-32 28 27) near Albufeira, and Atlântico Parque (☎ 0800 20 47 67) between Almancil and Loulé. Parcolândia/Planeta Aventura (☎ 089-39 58 03) is a night-time theme park near Quarteira, open daily from 7 pm to 2 am.

At Dutch Crazy Golf (☎ 082-54 134), not far from São Bartolomeu de Messines, there's an exotic animal farm, and a swimming pool and playground. It's open daily during summer from 9.30 am to 11 pm (7 pm in winter).

SPECIAL EVENTS

The Algarve's most important religious festival is at Loulé: the Romaria da Nossa Senhora da Piedade, held on the second Sunday after Easter, when the image of Our Lady of Pity (or Piety) is returned to its shrine atop the Monte da Piedade on a massive float carried up the mountain by devotees. One of Portugal's biggest Carnaval celebrations is also held at Loulé in late February/early March, with parades, mask competitions and dancing.

On the first or second weekend in September, the Algarve Folk Music & Dance Festival takes place in over a dozen towns in the region, culminating on Sunday evening with a big show at Praia da Rocha (Portimão).

Tourist-oriented bullfights are staged at Lagos, Albufeira and Vila Real de Santo António during the summer; the real ones are all further north, especially in the Ribatejo. See Spectator Sports in the Facts for the Visitor chapter for more on bullfighting.

SHOPPING

Although Algarve factories turn out fine azulejos, and the leatherworkers of Loulé consider themselves among the country's best, the Algarve is chiefly a booming outlet for souvenirs produced elsewhere.

The region's main handicrafts centre is around Loulé. Look out for locally produced woollens and Moorish-influenced ceramics. For more on the crafts of the Algarve, see the excellent guide by John & Madge Measures, *Southern Portugal: Its People, Traditions & Wildlife*, available in bookshops in Faro and elsewhere.

Lagoa is the centre of the Algarve's modest wine-growing region (see the boxed text). You may also want to try Algarviana, a local bitter almond liqueur, or the salubri-

Wines of the Algarve

The Algarve has long been an important wine-making area: the Mediterranean climate, rich soil and high-quality vines produce full-bodied wines with low acidity and a high alcohol content. The whites are traditionally very dry, the reds light and young. Although 20th century development has erased many vineyards, there are still about 40,000 acres of them in the Lagoa area, producing the Algarve's best known wines. Other wine-producing areas are Lagos, Tavira, and Portimão.

ous bottled waters of Monchique, which are on sale everywhere.

Markets

These are some of the biggest and best markets in the Algarve:

Every Saturday – Loulé, Olhão, São Brás de Alportel, Tavira
Every Wednesday – Quarteira
1st Saturday of the month – Lagos
1st Sunday – Almancil, Azinhal (Castro Marim)
1st Monday – Portimão
1st Tuesday – Albufeira
2nd Tuesday – Alvor
2nd Friday – Monchique
3rd Monday – Aljezur, Silves, Tavira
3rd Tuesday – Albufeira

For a full listing check out the what's-on pages of the English language papers or the turismo's monthly *Events* pamphlet.

GETTING THERE & AWAY
Air

Faro is one of Portugal's three international airports, and the only place in the Algarve that has scheduled flights, including direct ones several times daily from Lisbon and London. Scheduled international carriers serving Faro are TAP Air Portugal, Lufthansa Airlines, British Airways (BA) and PGA Portugália Airlines. For more information see the Faro section, the Getting

There & Away chapter (for international connections) or the Getting Around chapter (for domestic connections).

Air Pass (☎ 082-41 66 50, fax 41 66 60), Rua Júdice Biker 11, Portimão, has bargain outbound airfares.

Bus

Several companies, including Renex and EVA, operate regular and express services between the Algarve's major towns and elsewhere in Portugal. By express coach, Faro is about four hours from Lisbon; the fare is 2200$00 (2550$00 for *alta qualidade* – deluxe). Some services involve changing at Vale do Paraíso, near the IP1 motorway north of Albufeira.

EVA runs coaches twice a day, year-round, between Faro and Huelva (in Spain), with immediate connections between Faro and Albufeira and between Huelva and Seville. The journey from Faro to Seville takes five hours and costs 2050$00. In summer, Intersul runs a direct express coach service between Lagos and Seville, departing four times a week in April and May and six times a week from June to October; the six hour trip, via Portimão, Albufeira, Faro, Tavira and Vila Real de Santo António, costs about 3000$00.

Train

From Lisbon (Barreiro) there are at least five fast trains a day to Lagos and Faro; *interregional* (IR) services take five to 5½ hours, *intercidade* (IC) services four to 4½ hours. A once-weekly fast service (called the *Comboio Azul*, or Blue Train) links Faro to Porto via Beja, Évora and Coimbra.

From Spain, four trains a day go west as far as Huelva, where you must change for Ayamonte and then bus across the Rio Guadiana (or walk 1km or so to the ferry across the river) to pick up a Portuguese train at Vila Real de Santo António.

Car & Motorcycle

The most direct route from Lisbon to Faro takes about five hours. For motorists arriving via Ayamonte in Spain, the E01/IP1

motorway bridge, 4km north of Vila Real de Santo António, bypasses the old ferry crossing of the Rio Guadiana.

GETTING AROUND
Bus

The Algarve's two main coach lines are EVA and Frota Azul. Between them they cover the main destinations fairly frequently, throughout the year. EVA's Linha Litoral (Coastal Line) links Lagos, Portimão and Albufeira six times a day; it goes as far east as Faro twice a day, and to Vila Real de Santo António and Ayamonte (Spain) once a day. There are also buses to Sagres and into the interior.

If you plan to bus around the Algarve a lot, consider buying the Passe Turístico, good for either three (2600$00) or seven (3850$00) days of unlimited travel on most main routes (but not everywhere) on both lines. It's available from most ticket offices.

Train

There's a train line across the Algarve from Vila Real de Santo António in the east to Lagos in the west. For more on train services between towns in the Algarve, see the Getting There & Away sections of individual towns.

Car

By car you can blast your way west from Vila Real de Santo António as far as Albufeira on the E01/IP1 motorway, or you can nose along through every coastal town on the two-lane N125. Several roads wiggle slowly and scenically through the interior, in particular the N266 through the Serra de Monchique, the N124 across the Serra do Caldeirão and the N122 along the Spanish border.

Heavy competition has pushed average car rental rates in the Algarve below those elsewhere in Portugal. Typical peak rates are about 18,000/38,000$00 for three/seven days. Major local operators are Auto Jardim do Algarve (☎ 089-58 97 15, fax 58 77 80), City Tour (☎ 089-58 99 99, fax 58 84 29) and Luzcar (☎ 082-76 10 16, fax 76 77 25).

ALGARVE

Motorcycle & Bicycle

You can rent motorcycles, scooters and mountain bikes all over the Algarve, especially on the central coast; see individual town listings. Typical three/seven day charges are about 15,000/29,000$00 for a Yamaha 125 motorbike, 9000/18,000$00 for a scooter or 3500/7000$00 for a mountain bike.

Organised Tours

The Algarve's veteran coach-tour agency is Miltours (☎ 089-890 46 00) in Faro. It also has offices in Lisbon (☎ 01-352 41 66) and Porto (☎ 02-619 80 70). Others include Pandatours (☎ 082-41 55 41) in Portimão and Mega Tur (☎ 089-80 76 48, fax 80 74 89) in Faro. Regional trips include the leeward coast as far as Ayamonte in Spain; Silves and the Serra de Monchique; Lagos and Sagres; the Saturday market at Loulé and the Wednesday market at Quarteira. Typical prices are from 3000$00 to 4500$00 for a half-day tour or from 5600$00 to 7000$00 for a full-day tour, depending on the pick-up point. The turismos at Faro and elsewhere have brochures with details.

Faro & the Leeward Coast

FARO
☎ 089 • pop 51,600 (municipality)

Faro is the Algarve's capital and main transport hub; it's also a thriving commercial centre – but surprisingly pleasant for all that. With the region's best-equipped turismo, it's also a useful place to get your bearings. The main sights of historical interest are within the compact old town centre.

History

The Phoenicians and Carthaginians maintained a trading post here on the site of an older fishing village. The Romans in turn built this into a major port and administrative centre which they called Ossonoba.

When the Christian Visigoths built a cathedral dedicated to St Mary the town became known as Santa Maria or Santa Maria de Ossónoba.

But the town's maturation came under the Moors. Santa Maria became the cultured capital of a short-lived 11th century principality founded by Mohammed ben Said ben Hárun, from whose name 'Faro' is said to have evolved. Afonso III took the town in 1249 (it was the last major Portuguese town to be recaptured from the Moors), and walled it.

The first works produced on a printing press in Portugal came from Faro in 1487 – books in Hebrew made by a Jewish printer named Samuel Gacon.

A brief golden age – heralded by a city charter in 1544 and an episcopal seat transferred from Silves in 1577 – was brought to an abrupt end in 1596, during the period of Spanish rule. Troops under the Earl of Essex, en route to England from Cadiz in Spain, plundered the city, burned most of it to the ground and carried off hundreds of volumes of priceless theological works from the bishop's palace.

A rebuilt Faro was shattered by an earthquake in 1722 and, except for its sturdy old centre, flattened by the big one in 1755. Its present form dates largely from post-quake rebuilding.

Orientation

The town's hub is Praça Dr Francisco Gomes, with a traffic roundabout, a marina and a tidy little park called Jardim Manuel Bívar, or just Jardim. From here the town's main shopping and restaurant zone extends eastwards, centred on the pedestrianised Rua Dr Francisco Gomes and Rua de Santo António; what remains of the old town is just to the south.

The bus and train stations, on Avenida da República, are an easy walk from Praça Dr Francisco Gomes. The airport is about 6km west of the centre, off the N125 highway.

Offshore is the widest stretch of the Parque Natural da Ria Formosa. While many of the near-shore sandbars along here simply disappear at high tide, two of the bigger sea-facing islands – Ilha de Faro to the south-west and Ilha da Culatra to the south-east – have small summer settlements and good beaches. In between them, on Ilha da Barreta, is wind-blasted Cabo de Santa Maria, Portugal's southernmost point.

Information

Tourist Offices The very good municipal turismo (☎ 80 36 04) is beside the Arco da Vila, the gate to the old town, at the southern end of the Jardim Manuel Bívar. It's open daily from 9.30 am to at least 7 pm. There is also a turismo, usually open from 8 am to midnight, at the airport.

The separate, regional turismo administrative office (☎ 80 04 00, fax 80 04 89, Web site www.rtalgarve.pt) is in a flashy building at Avenida 5 de Outubro 18. There is also an information desk here, where staff dispense advice and regional brochures from 9 am to 6 pm on weekdays only, but it's of minimal use.

Money Faro's most central banks and ATMs are on and around Rua Dr Francisco Gomes and Rua de Santo António. There's also a private exchange bureau at Avenida da República 14, which offers commission-free (but low-rate) deals. It's open weekdays from 9.30 am to 5.30 pm and Saturday from 10 am to 1 pm.

Post & Communications The main post office is on Largo do Carmo, nearly 500m from the centre. It's open weekdays from 8.30 am to 6.30 pm and Saturday from 9 am to 12.30 pm. Closer to the centre, there's a smaller post office on Rua Dr João Lúcio.

The local Instituto Português da Juventude (☎ 80 15 56, fax 80 14 13, email ipj.faro@mail.telepac.pt), Rua da Polícia de Segurança Pública 1, has terminals where anyone can log onto the Internet for free. For Internet access or help with computer repairs, contact Nexus (☎ 39 39 77, fax 39 39 30, email nexus@nexus-pt.com), Portugal's first commercial Internet services provider, in nearby Almancil.

Travel Agencies The venerable travel agency Miltours (☎ 890 46 00) is based at Rua Veríssimo de Almeida 20; it primarily organises coach tours in the Algarve. At Rua Conselheiro de Bívar 36 is Space Travel (☎ 0800 20 44 43, fax 80 32 06), which arranges both local and overseas trips. Abreu Tours (☎ 80 53 35, fax 80 54 70), Avenida de República 124, organises tours of the Algarve and further afield destinations such as Lisbon.

Bookshops Two big shops with a few English-language books on the Algarve are Arty's on Rua de Santo António and Livraria Bertrand on Rua Dr Francisco Gomes. Opposite the latter is the small Livraria Rés do Chão.

Universities Faro has two universities: the Universidade do Algarve (Penha campus), beyond the hospital on Estrada da Penha, and the Universidade de Gambelas, on the road to the airport. An unnumbered municipal bus serves both, departing from Jardim Manuel Bívar every half-hour on weekdays from October to June.

Cultural Centres The closest thing the city has to a French cultural centre is the Alliance Française (☎ 2 88 81) on Rua 1 de Maio.

Laundry Lavandaria Modelo, at Rua Dr Cândido Guerrero 23, calls itself self-service but isn't, though it does have a same-day wash-and-dry service at normal prices. At least five other laundries around the town centre offer next-day service.

Medical Services The Faro district hospital (☎ 80 34 11, 80 25 55) is on Rua Leão Penedo, over 2km north-east of the centre, beside the N125 highway. Bus No 15 does the 15 to 20 minute trip every hour or two from Jardim.

Emergency The main police station (☎ 82 20 22) is east of the centre at Rua da Polícia de Segurança Pública 32.

ALGARVE

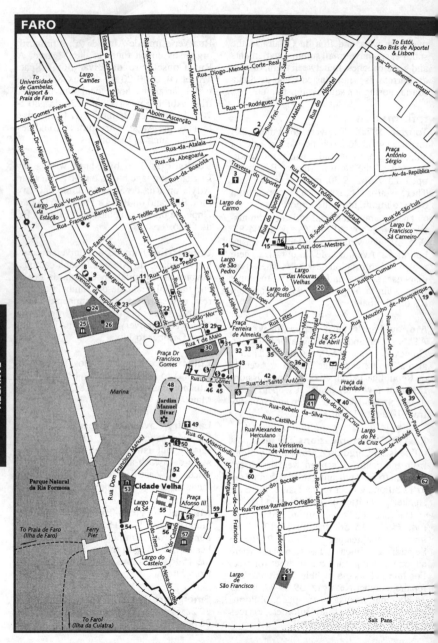

FARO

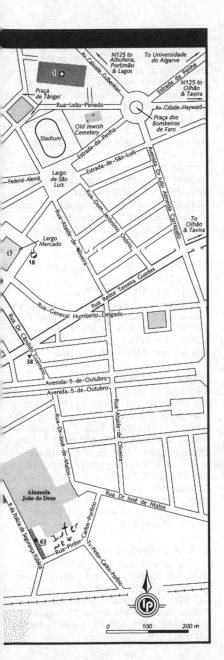

FARO

PLACES TO STAY
5 Apartmentos Vitória
9 Residencial Avenida
11 Residencial Madalena
16 Residencial Adelaide
26 Hotel Eva
30 Hotel Faro
31 Residencial Oceano
34 Pensão Residencial Central
35 Vasco da Gama
36 Hotel Santa Maria
63 Centro de Alojamento; Instituto
   Português da Juventude

PLACES TO EAT
12 A Garrafeira do Vilaça
13 Casa de Pasto
15 Restaurante A Taska
17 Mercado Municipal
32 Gal a Jardim
33 Adega Dois Irmãos
38 Minimercado
40 Restaurante Green
47 Café Aliança
48 Cafés

OTHER
1 Hospital
2 Canadian Consulate
3 Igreja de Nossa Senhora do Carmo &
  Capela dos Ossos
4 Main Post Office
6 Automóvel Club de Portugal (ACP)
7 Train Station
8 German Consulate
10 Abreu Tours
14 Igreja de São Pedro
18 Dutch Consulate
19 Lavandaria Modelo
20 Teatro Lethes
21 Emporium
22 Space Travel
23 Frota Azul, Caima &
   Renex Bus Ticket Office
24 Bus Station
25 Museu Maritimo
27 Foreign Exchange Bureau
28 Alliance Française
29 Porto Fino
37 Post Office
39 Regiònal Turismo
41 Museu Regional do Algarve
42 Arty's
43 Banks & ATMs
44 Livraria Bertrand
45 Livraria Rés do Chão
46 TAP Air Portugal

continued ...

ALGARVE

Cidade Velha

Within the medieval walls of the small Cidade Velha (Old Town) is what little of Faro survived the Earl of Essex and the two big earthquakes, most of it renovated in a jumble of styles. Nevertheless, it has a pleasantly shabby, lived-in feel, and plenty of gift and handicrafts shops to browse in.

You enter through the Renaissance-style **Arco da Vila**, built by order of Bishop Francisco Gomes, Faro's answer to the Marquês de Pombal, who saw to the city's brisk reconstruction after the 1755 earthquake. At the top of the street is Largo da Sé, lined with orange trees, with the *câmara municipal* (town hall) on the left and the ancient **Sé** (cathedral) in front of you.

The cathedral was completed in 1251, on what was probably the site of a Moorish mosque, an earlier Visigoth cathedral and, before that, a Roman temple. Badly damaged in 1755, the building's original Romanesque-Gothic exterior has been submerged in subsequent Gothic renovations and extensions, except for its tower gate and two chapels. The stubby sandstone tower was probably taller before the earthquake. The interior, a hotch-potch of architectural styles (Gothic, Renaissance and Baroque), has some fine azulejos and gilded woodwork.

To the right of the cathedral is the 18th century former **bishop's palace** (now offices), finished in multicoloured azulejos.

At the southern end of the square is a little 15th century town gate, the **Arco da Porta Nova**, facing the sea. Around to the left of the cathedral, in a small square, is a bronze **statue** of Dom Afonso III, the king who recaptured the Algarve from the Moors. Facing this square is the 16th century **Convento de Nossa Senhora da Assunção**. The convent's cloisters now house the town's Museu Arqueológica (Archaeological Museum; see Museums later).

From here you can leave the old town through the medieval **Arco de Repouso**, or Gate of Rest, named in reference to the story that Afonso III, after taking Faro from the Moors, rested and heard Mass in a nearby chapel. Around the gateway are some of the oldest sections of the town walls, Afonso III's improvements on the Moorish defences.

Igreja de Misericórdia

The main attraction of the 16th century Misericórdia church, across the road from the Arco da Vila, is its striking Manueline portico, the only part of an earlier chapel that withstood the 1755 earthquake.

Igreja de Nossa Senhora do Carmo

The twin-towered, vanilla and butterscotch Church of Our Lady of Carmel was completed in 1719 under João V and paid for with (and spectacularly gilded inside with) Brazilian gold. Many visitors overlook this in favour of a more ghoulish attraction in the cemetery behind the church – the **Capela dos Ossos**. This 19th century chapel was built from the bones and skulls of over a thousand monks as a pointed reminder of earthly impermanence.

Other Churches

If you haven't seen enough gilded woodwork yet, have a look at the dazzling 18th century Baroque interior of the Igreja de São Francisco, which also includes azulejo panels depicting the life of St Francis. Its old cloisters now serve as barracks for the Faro Infantry.

At the southern end of Largo do Carmo is the 16th century Igreja de São Pedro. Its interior is filled with 18th century azulejos and carved woodwork.

Museums

The municipal **Museu Arqueológica** (Archaeological Museum), in the Convento de Nossa Senhora da Assunção in the Cidade Velha, features Phoenician and Carthaginian relics, Roman mosaics (including a huge panel found in 1968 on a Faro building site) and, upstairs, a splendid collection of azulejos from every period since the 15th century. The museum is open weekdays only, from 9 am to 12.30 pm and 2 to 5 pm; admission costs 110$00.

In the left entrance of the district assembly building at Praça da Liberdade is the **Museu Regional do Algarve** (Algarve Regional Museum). On display are ceramics, fabrics, lots of baskets and straw mats, photos and little dioramas of 20th century home life – with not a word anywhere, in Portuguese or any other language, about what, when or who. With a 300$00 admission fee it's a poor bargain. The museum is open weekdays from 10 am to 12.30 pm and 2 to 5.30 pm.

In the harbourmaster's building at the northern end of the marina is the modest **Museu Maritimo** (Maritime Museum), full of maps, model ships, fish and nautical gear. It's open weekdays from 2 to 4 pm; admission costs 100$00.

Teatro Letes

This little Italianate theatre on Rua Letes is Faro's most charming cultural venue, it hosts drama, music and dance programmes. Built in 1874, the theatre was once the Jesuit Colégio de Santiago Maior and is now the property of the Portuguese Cruz Vermelha (Red Cross).

Beaches

The town's beach, Praia de Faro, with miles of sand, windsurfing and half a dozen cafés, is on the nearby Ilha de Faro. Take bus No 14 or 16 from Jardim (25 minutes; buses depart about every half-hour in summer) or, between April and September, a ferry from near the Arco da Porta Nova. There are also ferries out to Praia de Farol (marked on some maps as on Ilha do Farol, actually the western end of Ilha da Culatra). See Ferry under Getting Around later in this section for ferry information.

Horse Riding

Among horse-riding centres in the region are Centro Hípico Quinta do Lago (☎ 39 43 69) and Paraíso dos Cavalos (☎ 39 41 89), both in nearby Quinta do Lago.

Special Events

Faro's two big fairs are the Festa e Feira da Senhora do Carmo (Our Lady of Carmel) in mid-July, with a religious procession on the first day, and the Feira de Santa Iria in mid-October. Neither is particularly true to its roots: the former has evolved into a big agricultural fair, the latter into a modest craft fair. Faro's main fairground is the big Largo de São Francisco on the eastern side of the Cidade Velha.

Faro also hosts an international summer music festival, O Verão Músical do Algarve (Algarve Musical Summer), in July and August.

Places to Stay – Budget

Camping, pensão and hotel rates are very seasonal; we give midsummer rates here.

Camping There is a big, cheap municipal *parque de campismo* (☎ 81 78 76) at Praia de Faro. It is open year-round, costs 75/75/50$00 per person/tent/car, and there's a restaurant on-site. Take bus Nos 14 or 16 from Jardim.

Hostels The *centro de alojamento* (☎ 80 15 56, Ruà da Polícia de Segurança Pública 1) has some double rooms (4200/3400$00 with/without private bathroom) as well as dorm beds for 1700$00 during high season. It's open from 8 am to noon and 6 pm to midnight (you can leave luggage at the bus station while the hostel is closed).

Pensões & Boarding Houses In the town centre there's a run-down old rooming house called *Vasco da Gama* (☎ 82 38 41, *Rua Vasco da Gama 37*), which has doubles with shared shower and toilet for just 2500$00. Singles/doubles at the cheerful *Residencial Adelaide* (☎ 80 23 83, *fax 82 68 70, Rua Cruz dos Mestres 7*), cost 2000/3500$00 with shared shower and WC, or 3000/4000$00 with private facilities. There are also four-bed rooms for 4000$00.

Places to Stay – Mid-Range

Faro has about 16 residenciais, and staff at the municipal turismo can make recommendations and call them. The most conveniently central, with singles for about 5000$00 and doubles from 7000$00 to 8000$00 (with private shower or bath), are the *Residencial Oceano* (☎ 82 33 49, *fax 80 55 90, Rua Ivens 21*) and *Pensão Residencial Central* (☎ 80 72 91, *Praça Ferreira de Almeida 12*) which has spacious, spic-and-span rooms. *Residencial Avenida* (☎ 82 33 47, *Avenida da República 150*) has a few doubles without bathroom for 6000$00 (8000$00 with). Slightly pricier and friendlier is *Residencial Madalena* (☎/fax 80 58 06, *Rua Conselheiro de Bívar 109*).

Places to Stay – Top End

Hotels As central as you can get is the boxy *Hotel Faro* (☎ 80 32 76, *fax 80 35 46, Praça Dr Francisco Gomes 2*), overlooking the marina; singles/doubles with bathroom, satellite TV, air-con and breakfast cost 8200/11,500$00. The ageing *Hotel Santa Maria* (☎ 82 40 64, *fax 82 40 65, Rua de Portugal 17*) has earnest service and comfortable rooms from 9000/10,000$00, though street-facing rooms are noisy. The recently renovated, four star *Hotel Eva* (☎ 80 33 54, *fax 56 524, Avenida da República*), overlooking the marina, has swish rooms for 19,900/23,100$00, including breakfast.

Apartments If you want to hunker down in a flat for a while, try *Apartamentos Vitória* (☎ 80 65 83, *fax 80 58 83, Rua Serpa Pinto 60*), where a furnished studio/apartment for two, with kitchenette, linen and cleaning service, costs around 35,000/46,000$00 a week.

Places to Eat

Restaurants Those on a tight budget can check out *A Garrafeira do Vilaça* (☎ 80 21 50, *Rua de São Pedro 33*), which serves cheap Portuguese food and is popular with locals; it's closed Sunday. Nearby, at No 55, is a traditional *casa de pasto* with dishes for around 1000$00. Also recommended is the locally famous *Restaurante A Taska* (☎ 82 47 39, *Rua do Alportel 38*). It gets booked out quickly so go early or late. Two big, lively establishments, popular for seafood, are the funkily decorated *Sol e Jardim* and its next-door sister-restaurant, *Adega Dois Irmãos* (☎ 80 39 12, *Praça Ferreira de Almeida 13*).

In the higher price range, *Restaurante Green* (☎ 2 13 03, *Rua do Pé da Cruz 9*) offers tasty seafood specialities. Reservations are essential. It's closed Sunday.

You can also choose from several restaurants on Praia de Faro.

Cafés A fine place to linger over coffee and pastries or breakfast is the wood-panelled, late-19th century *Café Aliança* (*Rua Dr Francisco Gomes*). It also has sandwiches, salads, crêpes, juices and shakes, and service is snappy. Slightly downmarket, but also good for people-watching, are the plain *cafés* in the Jardim Manuel Bívar.

Self-Catering Check out Faro's big *mercado municipal* in Largo Mercado; it's especially lively in the early morning. There's also a decent little *minimercado* a couple of blocks down Rua Dr Cândido Guerrero.

Entertainment

Rua do Prior has a string of bar-clubs, liveliest at weekends, including *Emporium* (☎ 82 36 28, *No 23*) and *24 de Julho* (☎ 81 23 10, *No 38*). A more upmarket bar is *Porto Fino* (☎ 82 50 88, *Rua 1 de Maio 21*).

In the old town, nose in for a beer or a *bica* (cup of coffee) at the little ***Taverna da Sé*** *(Praça Afonso III)*. It also does food.

Getting There & Away

Air PGA Portugália Airlines has three flights daily to/from Lisbon and TAP Air Portugal two to three daily, year-round. Both cost 14,791$00 one way. Both airlines have frequent flight connections to Porto from Lisbon.

In summer TAP and BA have several flights a day from London to Faro; Lufthansa flies twice a week from Frankfurt and weekly from Düsseldorf; and TAP goes twice a week from Paris, Zürich and Geneva. Most charter flights into Portugal come to Faro.

For flight inquiries, call the airport on ☎ 80 08 00/01.

Other useful airline booking numbers in Faro are:

British Airways
    toll-free ☎ 0808 21 21 25
KLM-Royal Dutch Airlines
    ☎ 81 89 10 (no flights to Faro)
Lufthansa Airlines
    ☎ 80 07 50
PGA Portugália Airlines
    ☎ 80 08 51
TAP Air Portugal
    ☎ 80 02 10
    toll-free ☎ 0808 21 31 41

TAP also has a booking office in the town centre, on Rua Dr Francisco Gomes.

Bus At Avenida da República 106, across the street from the big EVA bus station (☎ 89 97 60), is a small ticket office (☎ 81 29 80) for the Frota Azul, Caima and Renex lines.

From Lisbon to Faro, EVA has at least seven express coaches daily (2200$00, four hours), including a night run, plus four to five quicker alta qualidade services (2550$00). Renex also runs three coaches a day from Lisbon.

There are at least seven buses a day to Tavira and Vila Real de Santo António, plus four alta qualidade services. There are two Linha Litoral services to Lagos and seven *trans rápido* (express) services via Portimão (weekdays only). For Sagres, change at Lagos.

EVA coaches for Seville (2050$00) in Spain, via Huelva (1950$00), depart at 8.10 am and 4.15 pm daily; the journey takes four hours. The daily alta qualidade express service (2500$00) takes just under four hours.

Train There are six trains a day to Faro from Lisbon including one very slow regional services, two IR services (4½ hours) and two IC services (4½ hours). The 2nd class IR/IC fare is 2020/2170$00. A once-weekly Comboio Azul service links Faro directly to Porto (seven hours), departing Faro on Friday afternoon and Porto on Sunday evening.

From Faro there are five fast trains a day to Vila Real de Santo António, eight to Albufeira and three to Lagos. Additional fast services to Lagos involve a change at Tunes junction.

For timetable information, call the train station on ☎ 80 17 26. The information kiosk at the station is open daily from 9 am to 1 pm and 2 to 7 pm.

Getting Around

To/From the Airport Buses No 14 and 16 make the 18 minute trip between the airport and Jardim every 15 minutes until about 9 pm in summer. A taxi will cost around 1100$00 during the day (1300$00 at weekends).

Car & Motorcycle Portugal's national auto club, Automóvel Club de Portugal (ACP), has a branch office (☎ 89 89 50) at Rua Francisco Barreto 26-A; it's open weekdays from 9 am to 12.45 pm and 2 to 4.30 pm. The major car rental agencies are all represented at the airport. Other reasonable local car rental agencies include Luso Rent (☎/fax 81 22 65) and Auto Jardim do Algarve (☎ 81 84 91). They can usually deliver cars to hotels/pensões if you order by telephone.

Taxi Taxi fares jump up 20% between 10 pm and 6 am and on weekends and holidays. To call a taxi, ring ☎ 82 22 89 or 82 35 37. There's also a taxi rank at the northern end of Jardim Manuel Bívar.

Bicycle Bikes (including tandems) can be rented through Megarent (☎ 80 21 36) for 2000$00 a day (750$00 junior size). Child seats are available for an extra 1000$00 a day.

Ferry From April to September, Tavares e Guerreiro (☎ 70 21 21, mobile ☎ 0931 63 48 13) operates ferries from the pier, next to Arco da Porta Nova, to Praia de Faro on the Ilha de Faro (a 20 minute ride) or Praia de Farol (45 minutes) on Ilha da Culatra. For exact times and prices check with the turismo or ask directly at the pier.

SÃO BRÁS DE ALPORTEL

☎ 089 • pop 7600 (municipality)

Few visitors think of staying overnight in this friendly little town 17km north of Faro but, if you've got the time, it makes a pleasantly untouristy base for visiting Estói, 7km to the south, and the surrounding countryside. This is part of the so-called Barrocal region, a fertile limestone belt between the mountains and the sea, which stretches all the way from Cabo de São Vicente. It is characterised by an abundance of olive, carob, fig and almond trees.

Orientation & Information

The ugly new town area is centred around Largo de São Sebastião, where buses stop and where you'll find the turismo (☎ 84 22 11) in a kiosk at the corner of Rua Luís Bívar, the road to Loulé. The turismo is open weekdays from 9.30 am to 12.30 pm and 2 to 5.30 pm, and Saturday from 9.30 am to noon.

Museu Etnográfico do Trajo Algarvio

This unexpectedly delightful museum (☎ 84 26 18) is 10 minutes walk east of the turismo, at Rua Dr José Dias Sancho 61. A rambling collection of local costumes, handicrafts, agricultural implements and household goods (with occasional special exhibitions) is displayed in an old mansion with lots of dark and musty corners. It's open Monday to Friday from 10 am to 1 pm and 2 to 5 pm, weekends and holidays from 2 to 5 pm; admission costs 100$00. Check out the miniature handmade Algarvian figures for sale at the entrance.

Old Town

Another surprise is the peaceful old town area south of the turismo. Follow Rua Gago Coutinho from Largo de São Sebastião to the 16th century Igreja Matriz, which has breezy views of orange groves from its doorstep. Nearby, below what used to be a bishop's palace (now a nursery school), is a pleasantly landscaped municipal swimming pool (open in summer daily from 10 am to 7 pm) and children's play area.

Places to Stay

The cheapest option is *Residencial São Brás* (☎/fax 84 22 13, Rua Luís Bívar 27), with doubles around 5500$00. Slightly spiffier and pricier is *Estalagem Sequeira* (☎ 84 34 44, fax 84 37 92, Rua Dr Evaristo Gago 9), next to the turismo. The *Pousada de São Brás* (☎ 84 23 05, fax 84 17 26) bags a panoramic hilltop site 2km from town on the Lisbon road. Deluxe doubles in this renovated 1950s building are 20,300$00.

Places to Eat

Luís dos Frangos (☎ 84 26 35, Estrada de Tavira 134), one of several restaurants along the Tavira road leading off the main square, is an unpretentious *churrasqueira* with great grilled chicken and turkey (*bife de peru*) from 700$00. It's closed Monday.

For something more special, head 1.5km in the opposite direction, along the Loulé road, for the *Restaurante Lena* (☎ 84 24 94). This small *casa típica*, decorated in traditional rustic style, gets packed out at lunch time; try the excellent *cabrito a casa* (roast kid). It's closed Sunday.

Golf & Gallinules

The purple gallinule (also known as the purple swamp-hen or, far more exotically, as the sultan chicken) is one of Europe's rarest and most elusive birds. It's an extraordinary violet-blue water bird the size of a large domestic fowl and has a massive red bill and red legs. In Portugal, its only confirmed nesting place is in an isolated fragment of wetland which is partly in the grounds of the exclusive Quinta do Lago villa estate, at the western end of the Parque Natural da Ria Formosa, about 12km west of Faro.

Some five years ago, the bird was facing local extinction with just two pairs recorded. But when the estate built a freshwater lake to help irrigate its new São Lourenço golf course, the gallinule's fortunes dramatically improved. The normally shy birds – now numbering about 60 – often strut around the fairways before the first golfers arrive.

You can get a good look at the sultan from an elevated public hide overlooking the lake, about 1km along the estate's São Lourenço Nature Trail. To reach the start of the trail, at a wooden bridge crossing the lagoon, head for roundabout 6 from the estate's entrance.

Clive Viney

In Mesquita Baixa, just off the Tavira road, 2.5km east of São Brás de Alportel, is the unusual *Lagar de Mesquita*. Run by an Estonian woman with support from LEADER (an organisation promoting rural tourism), it offers a weekend-only buffet of Portuguese dishes with live music (everything from big bands to classical piano, and flamenco to Afro-Brazilian). Tickets cost 2500$00 per person, including dinner; to book ring ☎ 82 49 99 weekdays, ☎ 84 18 88 weekend evenings.

Getting There & Away
During the week there are nine buses a day to São Brás de Alportel from Faro (via Estói) and three a day from Loulé. Reduced services run on weekends and holidays.

ESTÓI
A rewarding day trip from Faro is to the enchantingly derelict palace at Estói, 10km north of Faro, and on to the nearby Roman ruins at Milreu.

Palácio do Visconde de Estói
This 18th century palace (now owned by the Faro municipal council) is a short walk from Estói's village square, where the bus from Faro stops. Down a palm-shaded avenue, past abandoned stables and outhouses, are the overgrown gardens fronting the palace. The pink Rococo palace, like a smaller version of Queluz palace, near Lisbon, is under restoration (as it has been for years) and open only for pre-arranged group visits. But the intimate gardens are a delight, with busts of poets, 19th century azulejos depicting naked mythological ladies and an ornamental pool with equally voluptuous statues.

The gardens are open Tuesday to Saturday from 10 am to 12.30 pm and 2 to 5 pm (admission free).

Milreu
Some 800m down the main road from Estói's square are the ruins of Milreu, a Roman equivalent of the Estói palace. Dating from the 1st century AD, the ruins show the characteristic form of a peristyle villa, with a gallery of columns around a courtyard. In the surrounding rooms geometric motifs and friezes of fish were found, although these have now been removed for restoration. The most tantalising glimpses left of the villa's former glory are the fish mosaics in the suite of bathing chambers to the west of the villa's courtyard.

The bathing rooms include the *apodyterium*, or changing-room (note the arched niches and benches for clothes and post-bath massage), and the *frigidarium*, which had a marble basin to hold cold water for cooling off after the bath. Other luxuries were underground heating and marble sculptures (now in the museums of Faro and Lagos).

To the right of the entrance is the most interesting aspect of the site: its *nymphaerium*, or water sanctuary – a temple devoted to the cult of water. The interior was once decorated with polychrome marble slabs and its exterior with fish mosaics (some are still visible). In the 3rd century the Visigoths converted it into a church, adding a baptismal font and a small mausoleum.

The site is open Tuesday to Sunday from 10 am to 12.30 pm and 2 to 5 pm (admission free). You can pick up an information sheet (in English, French or German) at the entrance.

Getting There & Away
During the week, nine buses a day make the 20 minute run from Faro to Estói (continuing on to São Brás de Alportel). The last bus back to Faro is at 7 pm.

OLHÃO
☎ 089 • pop 37,000 (municipality)

Olhão, the Algarve's biggest fishing port, is a clamorous, sprawling town beside a vast precinct of docks, canning factories and the Sopursal salt works. But buried at the historical centre is an appealing little kernel of town, surprisingly well preserved and untouristy, which could still stand alone as the fishing village it once was. Not surprisingly, there's also plenty of good, cheap seafood. Saturday is the biggest and best day for the colourful fish market on Avenida 5 de Outubro.

Offshore are the numerous sandy islands of the Parque Natural da Ria Formosa. There are good beaches on Ilha da Culatra and Ilha da Armona, both of which can be reached by boat. Central Olhão seems to have more funeral parlours per square kilometre than any other Portuguese town – perhaps owing to the funerals-only Capela de Nossa Senhora da Soledade, right behind the parish church.

Orientation
From the small EVA bus station on Rua General Humberto Delgado, turn right (or from the train station, turn left), east, and it's one block to the inner town's main avenue, Avenida da República. Turn right and look for the clock tower of the parish church, two or three blocks along, at the edge of the central, pedestrianised shopping zone.

At the far side of this zone, Avenida 5 de Outubro runs along the waterfront. Across it are the twin-domed brick buildings of the fish market and just to the left (east) is the town park, Jardim Patrão Joaquim Lopes.

Information
Olhão's turismo (☎ 71 39 36) is on Largo Sebastião Martins Mestre, in the centre of the pedestrian zone (bear right at the prominent fork beside the parish church). It's open weekdays from 9.30 am to 5.30 pm and Saturday from 9.30 am to noon.

The post office is on Avenida da República, a block north of the parish church. The police can be reached on ☎ 70 21 44 and the local *centro de saúde* (medical centre) on ☎ 70 20 55.

Bairro dos Pescadores
Just back from the fish market and park is the so-called Fishermen's Quarter, a knot of compact, cubical houses decorated with window boxes, caged canaries and fading pastel whitewash or tile fronts. The bairro is threaded by roughly cobbled lanes too narrow for cars and is all (so far) mercifully ungentrified. From a distance it looks charmingly North African, although the Moors left in the 13th century and none of these houses is more than a few hundred years old. Nobody seems to have a good explanation for this style, found elsewhere in the Algarve only at Fuzeta (10km east).

Beaches

Good beaches nearby include Farol (said to be the best of the lot) and Hangares on Ilha da Culatra, and Armona and Fuzeta on Ilha da Armona. There are ferries to both islands from the pier just east of Jardim Patrão Joaquim Lopes; see Getting Around later in this section.

Special Events

Olhão hosts a seafood festival, with food stalls and folk music, in the Jardim Patrão Joaquim Lopes during the second week of August. The townsfolk also let down their hair for the Feira de Maio on 30 April and 1 May and the Feira de San Miguel at the end of September.

Places to Stay

Camping The well-equipped, 800 site *Camping Olhão* (☎ 700 13 00, fax 700 13 90, email sbsicamping@mail.telepac.pt) is about 2km east of Olhão and 800m off the N125. It's open year-round and costs 600/400/500$00 per person/tent/car during high season. A bus goes there from beside Jardim Patrão Joaquim Lopes every hour or two weekdays and Saturday morning, but not on Sunday or holidays.

Open between mid-January and mid-November, Orbitur's *Camping Ilha da Armona* (☎ 71 41 73, Ilha da Armona) consists of four-person bungalows only (priced around 8000$00 in July and August). Tents are not allowed and free camping is forbidden on the beaches. Bookings can be made from Lisbon on ☎ 01-811 70 00 or fax 815 80 45. See Getting Around later in this section for ferry information.

Cheapest at 250/300/500 per person/tent/car is the small, plain municipal *Parque de Campismo de Fuzeta* (☎ 79 34 59, fax 79 40 34), right on the waterfront at the end of the main street in tiny Fuzeta, about 10km east of Olhão.

Residenciais There are fewer places to stay here than you would expect, and they fill up in summer. Your best bet is to head straight for the turismo, where staff can advise you on what's available.

Cheapest in town are the basic 3000$00 rooms (without private bathroom) at *Pensão Torres* (☎ 70 26 81, Rua Dr Paulo Nogueira 13). A notch up (4000$00 without bathroom) are rooms at the central *Pensão Bicuar* (☎ 71 48 16, Rua Vasco da Gama 5); across the street is the similarly priced *Alojamentos Vasco da Gama* (☎ 70 31 46). Rua Vasco da Gama is to the left (east) of the parish church.

Nicest of all are the renovated rooms at *Pensão Boémia* (☎/fax 71 45 13, Rua da Cêrca 20). They all come with private bathroom, and the 1st floor rooms have balconies with good views. From the EVA bus station, turn left and left again into Rua 18 de Junho; Rua da Cêrca is the third street on the right. Rua Paulo Nogueira (for Pensão Bicuar) is two blocks beyond Rua Cêrca.

Places to Eat

The pedestrian zone around Rua Vasco da Gama has plenty of *cafés* to choose from. Head towards the market and you'll find dozens of seafood restaurants. The most reasonably priced eateries are the two *casas de pasto – Dionísio* and *Restaurante Barra Nova* – on Praça Patrão Joaquim Lopes, right across Avenida 5 de Outubro from the market.

East along Avenida 5 de Outubro you'll find one upscale fish restaurant after another. Recommended are the generous portions at *Papy's* (☎ 70 71 44) at No 56 and also the *Restaurante Isidro* (☎ 71 41 24) at No 68. A slightly pricier place away from the waterfront is *O Aquário*; from the Capela de Nossa Senhora da Soledade at the rear of the parish church, walk two blocks east on Rua Dr João Lúcio.

Getting There & Away

Bus Renex coaches run to/from Lisbon (2500$00, four to five hours) seven times daily on weekdays (less frequently at weekends). There's also an EVA alta qualidade service four times daily.

EVA runs coaches from Faro to Olhão (a 15 to 20 minute trip) roughly every 20 minutes on weekdays. Some of the weekday buses continue from Olhão station to the waterfront at Bairro dos Pescadores. Weekend services are less frequent.

Train Olhão is 10 to 15 minutes from Faro on the Faro-Vila Real de Santo António line, with trains coming through every two hours or so. Fuzeta is a further 15 minutes down the line.

Getting Around

Ferries run out to the ilhas from the pier at the eastern end of Jardim Patrão Joaquim Lopes. There are boats to Ilha da Armona nine times a day (starting at 7.30 am) during June and September (with more at weekends), and hourly during July and August; the last trip back from Armona in summer

leaves at 8.30 pm. In winter boats run just twice a day.

For Ilha da Culatra and Farol, boats go about six times a day from June to the end of September, and three times a day in winter; the last boat back in summer leaves Culatra at 8 pm and Farol at 8.20 pm.

TAVIRA
☎ 081 • pop 24,500 (municipality)

Sick and tired of the Algarve's tourist ghettos? Head 30km east of Faro and you'll find relief in Tavira. This picturesque little town straddling the Rio Gilão 3km from the coast is still remarkably unspoilt. Elegant 18th century houses border the river, castle ruins overlook at least 37 churches in a tangle of old streets, 16th century mansions with Manueline window flourishes line the back streets, and fishing boats bob at the quay, where a traditional market takes place daily.

Parque Natural da Ria Formosa

The Ria Formosa Natural Park is primarily a lagoon system stretching for 60km along the Algarve coastline from just west of Faro to Cacela Velha.

The park's string of dune islands and sandbars enclose a vast area of marsh (*sapal*), salt pans (*salinas*), sea channels, creeks and islands. Near the western boundary of the park there are also two freshwater lakes, at Ludo and Quinta do Lago, which constitute a vital habitat for migrating and nesting birds. At any time of the year a huge variety of wetland birds can be seen here, as well as many species of ducks, shorebirds, gulls and terns. This is also the favoured nesting place of the little tern and rare purple gallinule (see the boxed text 'Golf & Gallinules' earlier in this chapter).

And it's not only birds who fancy the place: you'll find some of the Algarve's quietest, biggest beaches on the sandbank ilhas of Faro, Culatra, Armona and Tavira (see the Faro, Olhão and Tavira sections).

The park headquarters (☎ 089-70 41 34, fax 70 41 65) at Quinta de Marim, 3km east of Olhão, has a visitor centre, open daily from 9 am to noon and 2 to 5 pm. It provides bountiful information (in English, French and German) about the park's flora and fauna, and there is a 2.4km nature trail across the dunes. Admission to the park is 300$00 for adults, 150$00 for children from 13 to 18 years, and free for younger ones.

To get to the park headquarters take any Tavira-bound bus from Olhão, get off at the Cepsa petrol station, and walk seaward for about 1km (it's 200m beyond the Camping Olhão camping ground). Alternatively, a bus goes to the camping ground every hour or two on weekdays and Saturday morning, from beside Jardim Patrão Joaquim Lopes in Olhão.

You'd hardly call the place lively, though there are bars and clubs for those who want them and bikes to rent for exploring further afield. There's also a superb, undeveloped beach (with camp site) on the nearby Ilha de Tavira. If you're looking for a quiet, relaxing base in an attractive setting, Tavira is hard to beat.

History

Tavira's origins are vague: it's likely that the area was inhabited in Neolithic times, and later by Phoenicians, Greeks and Carthaginians. The Romans left more traces – their settlement of Balsa was just down the road, near Santa Luzia (3km west). The seven-arched bridge the Romans built at Tavira (then called Tabira) was an important link in the route between Baesuris (Castro Marim) and Ossonoba (Faro).

In the 8th century, Tavira was occupied by the Moors. They built the castle (probably on the site of a Roman fortress) and two mosques. Their downfall came in 1242 when Dom Paio Peres Correia reconquered the town. Those Moors who remained were segregated into the *mouraria* (Moorish quarter) outside the town walls. Recent excavations have discovered some important Phoenician and Moorish remains, including a unique 11th century marriage vase.

Tavira's importance was established during the Age of Discoveries: as the port closest to the Moroccan coast it was the base for Portuguese expeditions to North Africa, supplying provisions (especially salt, wine and dried fish) and providing a hospital for sick soldiers. Its maritime trade also expanded, with exports of salted fish, almonds, figs and wine to northern Europe. In 1520, by then the most populated settlement in the Algarve and rich in churches and the houses of Portuguese nobles, it was raised to the rank of city.

Decline set in during the early 17th century when the North African campaign was abandoned and the Rio Gilão became so silted up that large boats couldn't enter the port. In 1645 came the devastating effects of the plague, followed by the 1755 earthquake.

After a brief spell producing carpets in the late 18th century, Tavira found a more stable income in its tuna fishing and canning industry, although this, too, declined in the 1950s when the tuna shoals moved elsewhere. Today it relies increasingly on tourism.

Salt of the South

Take plenty of sea water. Add weeks of hot sun. Let the water evaporate in specially enclosed areas. Add more water and let it evaporate. Keep the sun shining. And hey presto, you've got salt! This is the process, more or less, that has been followed in Portugal and elsewhere for thousands of years in order to make salt.

The Algarve's long coastline, vast salt marshes and long hot summers make it ideal for salt production. Near Olhão, the huge Sopursal factory uses modern mechanical methods to produce some 10,000 tonnes of salt a year (that's about half of Portugal's entire consumption). The best quality stuff is reserved for table salt; the rest is used to produce an extraordinary variety of products, from bleach to baking soda to glass.

Just outside Tavira, en route to Quatro Águas, you can see extensive salt pans – each as big as a football field – and enormous heaps of salt piled up by tractors and left to dry. Salt collection usually starts around the end of August. Here and elsewhere, salt is still collected by hand, but this is becoming less common as salt pans are transformed into more lucrative fish farms to cultivate expensive species, such as sole and bream, for export to northern Europe.

ALGARVE

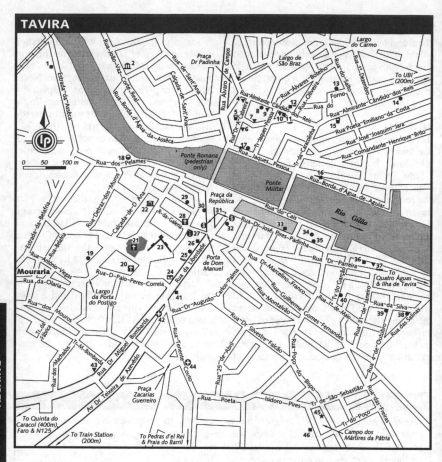

Orientation

The train station is on the southern edge of town, 1km from the centre. The bus terminal is by the river on the western edge of town, a five minute walk from the town centre (around Praça da República). Most of the town's shops and facilities are here, on the southern side of the river.

Information

Tourist Office The turismo (☎ 32 25 11) at Rua da Galeria 9 can provide all kinds of local and regional information, and help with accommodation. In summer it's open daily from 9.30 am to 7 pm; in winter, from 9.30 am to 6 pm weekdays and until 5 pm at weekends.

Money There are numerous banks with ATMs around Praça da República and along Rua da Liberdade.

Post & Communications The post office is at the top of Rua da Liberdade. At Paste-

TAVIRA

PLACES TO STAY	37	Casa de Pasto A	22	Palácio da Galeria
1 Casa do Rio		Barquinha	23	Castelo
11 Pensão Residencial Lagôas	43	Casa Pirica	24	Post Office
12 Pensão Residencial Almirante			25	Kioskau
16 Residencial Princesa do Gilão	**OTHER**		27	Turismo
26 Pensão Residencial Castelo	2	Lagar Museu	28	Igreja da Misericórdia
33 Residencial Imperial	5	Patrick's	29	Lorisrent
36 Mare's Residencial	8	Lavandaria Alagoa	30	Mota Rent
41 Pensão Residencial Mirante	13	Rent a Bike	31	Banks
46 Convento de Santo António	14	Tavira Health Club	32	Câmara Municipal
	15	Bar Toque	34	Mercado Municipal
PLACES TO EAT	17	Pastelaria Anazu	35	Casa Dias
3 Cantinho do Emigrante	18	Bus Terminal	38	Lavandaria Lavitt
4 Churrasqueira O Manel	19	Convento da Nossa	39	Tavira Moto Rent
6 Restaurante O Patio		Senhora da Graça	40	Azulejo Azul Artesenato
7 Restaurante Aquasul	20	Igreja de Santiago	42	Clinica Medica
9 Snack-Bar Petisqueira-Belmar	21	Igreja de Santa Maria	44	Centro de Saúde
10 Restaurante Bica		do Castelo	45	Police Station

laria Anazu, on the riverfront, visitors can use a computer for 650$00 an hour for sending emails or surfing the net. It's open daily from 8 am to around midnight.

Bookshops Near the post office, at Rua da Liberdade 24, is Kioskau, a well-stocked bookshop with English, French and German newspapers and local guidebooks. Recommended are the locally produced *Walking Tours of Tavira* (in English, French and German) and *Your Guide to Tavira*.

Laundry Lavandaria Alagoa (☎ 32 58 23), at Rua Almirante Cândido dos Reis 12, charges around 350$00 per kilogram (wash and dry) for next-day service. The self-service Lavandaria Lavitt, Rua das Salinas 6, charges 550$00 for 6kg (plus 550$00 for drying). It's open from 9 am to 1 pm and 3 to 7 pm daily except Wednesday.

Medical Services The centro de saúde (☎ 320 10 00, 32 40 23) is at Rua Tenente Couto. A 24 hour private clinic, Clinica Medica (☎ 32 17 50), at Avenida Dr Teixeira de Azevêdo 5, provides speedier (and pricier) treatment.

To soothe aching limbs after a long bike ride, book yourself a sauna at the Tavira Health Club (☎ 32 26 28), across the river

at Rua Almirante Cândido dos Reis 170. It's open weekdays from 10 am to 8 pm.

Emergency The main police station (☎ 32 20 22) is on Campo dos Mártires da Pátria, at the southern edge of town.

Old Town
The main entrance to the old town these days is through the town gate, **Porta de Dom Manuel** (by the turismo), built in 1520 when Dom Manuel I made Tavira a city. Facing you at the end of the lane is the **Igreja da Misericórdia**. Built in the 1540s, this church is considered the Algarve's most important Renaissance monument, thanks largely to its finely carved (though now worn and weather-beaten) arched doorway, which is topped by statues of Nossa Senhora da Misericórdia, São Pedro and São Paulo.

At the end of Rua da Galeria, to the left of the church, is the 16th century Palácio da Galeria, now very dilapidated. There are plans to restore it and turn it into an exhibition centre.

Circling round the back of the palácio on Calçada de Dona Ana brings you to the **Igreja de Santa Maria do Castelo**. This 13th century church was built on the site of a Moorish mosque (its clock tower still has some Arabic-style windows). Inside, you'll find a plaque marking the tomb of the conqueror – Dom Paio Peres Correia – as well as those of the seven Christian knights whose murder by the Moors precipitated the final attack on the town.

Beside the church is the entrance to the **castelo**. Now more of a prim little garden than a defensive bulwark, the castle's restored octagonal tower is a great place to look out over Tavira's attractive tiled rooftops, which probably owe their wave-like Oriental style to ideas brought back by 15th century explorers. The castle is open daily from 9.30 am to 5.30 pm (admission free).

Just south of the castle is the whitewashed **Igreja de Santiago**, built in the 17th century where a small mosque probably once stood. The area beside it was formerly the Praça da Vila, the old town square.

On the other side of the square is the **Convento da Nossa Senhora da Graça**. Founded in 1568 on the site of the former Jewish quarter, this convent was largely rebuilt at the end of the 18th century. Once used by the military, it has now fallen into disrepair.

Downhill from here is the **Largo da Porta do Postigo**, at the site of another old town gate and the town's Moorish quarter.

Ponte Romana
This Roman bridge near the Praça da República owes its present design to a 17th century restoration. The latest touch-up job was in 1989, after floods knocked down one of its pillars.

Lagar Museu (Casa das Artes)
This former private house by the river has been converted into an exhibition hall with a small display about traditional olive-pressing techniques. It's open during the summer only.

Mercado Municipal
Tavira's municipal market is one of the best in the Algarve. Every morning there's a wonderful assortment of fresh fish, fruits and vegetables, home-made cakes, goat's cheese and honey. On Saturday morning, it extends outside along the quayside on Rua do Cais, with everything from sacks of potatoes to quivering rabbits. The biggest market day is on the third Monday in the month.

Quatro Águas
More energetic visitors can walk 2km east along the river, past the market and the salt pans (see the boxed text 'Salt of the South' earlier in this section) to Quatro Águas, distinguished by its abandoned tuna-canning factory. As well as being the jumping-off point for Ilha de Tavira (see Around Tavira later in this chapter), this seaside hub has some excellent seafood restaurants and a couple of small cafés by the pier.

For information on buses to Quatro Águas, see under Ilha de Tavira.

Activities
Passo a Passo (☎/fax 32 68 73, mobile ☎ 0936 270 6596) organises three to four-hour walking tours inland, finishing with lunch at a local restaurant (2000$00 per person plus lunch).

Rent a Bike (☎ 32 19 73, mobile ☎ 0931 330 861), Rua do Forno 22, not only rents bikes but organises bike tours (1500$00 per person), lasting around four hours, in and around Tavira and the Parque Natural da Ria Formosa.

Riosul (☎ 51 02 01) has a pick-up point in Tavira for its Rio Guadiana cruises and jeep safaris. Turalgarve (☎ 089-46 21 93) arranges 2½ hour boat trips through the Parque Natural da Ria Formosa (from nearby Santa Luzia to Tavira); a combined boat and jeep safari costs 10,000$00 (including lunch).

Special Events
Tavira's biggest festival is its Festa de Cidade on 24 and 25 June. Myrtle and paper flowers decorate streets througout the entire town, free sardines are provided by the municipal authorities, and dancing and frolicking in the street continue until the wee hours.

Places to Stay – Budget

Camping The nearest camping ground, *Parque de Campismo de Ilha de Tavira* (☎ 32 44 55) is ideally located on Ilha de Tavira (see Around Tavira), a step away from the island's huge beach. It's open from May to October and costs 380/600$00 per person/tent (no car access).

Private Rooms & Apartments In the town, your best bet during high season may be *quartos* (private rooms), which usually cost about 4500$00 a double. Self-catering flats are also available, though usually for a minimum stay of a week. The turismo has all the contact details.

Pensões & Residenciais Among budget pensões, the long-standing favourite is *Pensão Residencial Lagôas* (☎ 32 22 52, *Rua Almirante Cândido dos Reis 24*). Clean singles/doubles are priced at 3000/4000$00 without bathroom (6000$00 for a double with bathroom). Across the street at No 51, *Pensão Residencial Almirante* (☎ 32 21 63) is a dark but cosy family house full of clutter, with just six rooms costing 2000/3500$00.

Bang in the centre are *Residencial Imperial* (☎ 32 22 34, *Rua Dr José Pires Padinha 24*), with rooms at 4000/6000$00 (including bathroom and breakfast), and the similarly priced *Pensão Residencial Castelo* (☎ 32 39 42, *Rua da Liberdade 4*). The fancy-looking *Pensão Residencial Mirante* (☎ 32 22 55, *Rua da Liberdade 83*) has doubles from 5000$00 to an overpriced 7000$00, all with bathroom.

Places to Stay – Mid-Range

Smarter places by the river include the dull but efficient *Residencial Princesa do Gilão* (☎/fax 32 51 71, *Rua Borda d'Água de Aguiar 10*), where rooms with thin walls cost 6000/7000$00, and the posher *Mare's Residencial* (☎ 32 58 15, fax 32 58 19, *Rua Dr José Pires Padinha 134*), where high-season prices soar to 12,000$00 a double. The charming riverside *Casa do Rio* (☎/fax 32 65 78, *Estrada da Assêca 39*) has similarly priced rooms (and a swimming pool).

Places to Stay – Top End

There are several attractive Turihab properties, including *Quinta do Caracol* (☎ 32 24 75, fax 32 31 75, *São Pedro*), a converted 17th century farmhouse with a spacious garden. Its seven rooms have been converted into separate quarters with typical Algarve furnishings (all but one with a kitchenette) for 15,400$00 each.

On the south-eastern edge of town, the *Convento de Santo António* (☎/fax 32 56 32, *Campo dos Mártires da Pátria*) is hidden behind high walls next to its church. This former Franciscan monastery, founded in 1606, has been owned by the same family since the 1870s. The seven furnished rooms were formerly monks' cells (now costing 19,000$00) and are set around a sunlit cloister where breakfast is served. Unfortunately, resident barking Great Danes can destroy the monastic calm.

Places to Eat – Budget

Despite a failing tuna-fishing industry, tuna is still Tavira's speciality. It's especially good at riverside restaurants such as *Casa de Pasto A Barquinha* (☎ 32 28 43, *Rua Dr José Pires Padinha 142*), where prices are reasonable and the service is friendly (the salads are great too). More basic (with a TV blaring) is the locals' hang-out, *Casa Pirica* (*Rua Dr Miguel Bombarda 22*), where dishes start as low as 700$00; it's closed Sunday.

There are several unpretentious places along Rua Almirante Cândido dos Reis, including *Restaurante Bica* (☎ 32 38 43) at No 24, where you can eat well for under 1500$00 (try the house speciality – sole with orange), and *Snack-Bar Petisqueira-Belmar* (☎ 32 49 95), at No 16, with rustic décor and half-portion prices from 700$00. The latter is closed Monday.

The nearby *Churrasqueira O Manel* (☎ 32 33 43, *Rua Dr António Cabreira 39*) is the place for *frango no churrasco* (grilled chicken) and other grilled offerings (it has

ALGARVE

a takeaway service too). Further up at Praça Dr Padinha 27, a tiny eight table den, *Cantinho do Emigrante* (☎ 32 36 96), has a surprisingly big menu despite its rough-and-ready appearance, with dishes from 800$00.

The popular café *Pastelaria Anazu* (☎ 32 22 59, Rua Jaques Pessoa 13) has a pleasant riverside location and Internet facilities. See Post & Communications earlier in this section.

Places to Eat – Mid-Range

For more salubrious surroundings and tourist-oriented service, head for *Restaurante O Patio* (☎ 32 30 08, Rua Dr António Cabreira 30), which has a popular rooftop terrace and some tasty *cataplanas* (a shellfish and ham dish typical of the Algarve) from 4000$00 for two. Another upmarket fish restaurant is the riverside *Mare's Restaurante* (see Mare's Residencial in Places to Stay – Mid-Range). *Restaurante Aquasul* (☎ 32 51 66, Rua Dr Augusto da Silva Carvalho 11) serves some great pizzas and French fare.

For the best seafood splurges – at not too extravagant prices – head 2km east of town to Quatro Águas' famous seafood restaurant *Marisqueira 4 Águas* (☎ 32 53 29), where you can indulge in specialities such as shark steak or octopus.

Entertainment

There is a clutch of lively bars on the north side of the river on Rua Poeta Emiliano da Costa and at the eastern end of Rua Almirante Cândido dos Reis. For Guinness on tap, 'flaming bomb' cocktails and high-quality music, check out *Bar Toque* (☎ 32 66 43, Rua Almirante Cândido dos Reis 118). More cocktails and satellite TV, plus bar snacks, are on offer at *Patrick's* (☎ 32 59 98, Rua Dr António Cabreira 25).

There's one huge nightclub in town – *UBI* (☎ 32 45 77, Rua Almirante Cândido dos Reis), with an open-air bar and music until 5 am. Other clubs in the vicinity include *Joy Disco* at kilometre post 121 en route to Faro on the N125.

Shopping

For classy Algarve handicrafts (azulejos, woollens and basketwork), check out Azulejo Azul Artesanato; it's tucked away at Travessa do Garção 27.

A reasonable range of camping, hiking and biking supplies are available at Casa Dias, Rua Dr José Pires Padinha 56.

Getting There & Away

There are 15 trains a day between Faro and Tavira (35 to 60 minutes) and frequent buses, including six express runs (30 minutes).

Getting Around

Tavira has a surprising number of bicycle and motorbike rental places, including Tavira Moto Rent (☎ 32 30 95, mobile ☎ 0936 63 59 28), Rua da Silva 18; Lorisrent (☎ 32 52 03, mobile ☎ 0931 27 47 66), Rua Damião Augusto de Brito 4; Rent a Bike (see the earlier Activities section); and Mota Rent (☎ 32 56 47) at Praça da República 10, where you can also rent cars. Expect to pay at least 1000$00 a day for a mountain bike or 2200$00 a day for a Suzuki automatic (less for longer periods).

For buses to Quatro Águas, see Getting There & Away under Ilha de Tavira in the next section.

Taxis line up on Praça da República.

AROUND TAVIRA
Ilha de Tavira

Part of the Parque Natural da Ria Formosa, this is one of a string of similar sandy islands stretching along the coast from Cacela Velha to just west of Faro. The huge beach at this island's eastern end, opposite Tavira, has a camp site and a string of café-restaurants, as well as water sports facilities in summer. Off season, it feels incredibly remote and empty. Don't forget the sunscreen: the low dunes offer no shade.

Further west along the ilha is **Praia do Barril**, accessible by a miniature train that trundles over the mud flats from Pedras d'el Rei, a classy chalet resort 4km west of Tavira. There are a couple of eateries where the train stops but the rest is just sand, sand, sand as far as the eye can see.

Getting There & Away Ferries make the five minute hop to the ilha (200$00 return in summer) from Quatro Águas, 2km east of Tavira. They run from mid-April to October, daily from around 8 am, leaving every 15 minutes between June and mid-September. The last boat back leaves at about 9 pm in April, May and September, 11 pm in June and July and midnight or later in August – but check with the ferryman! A bus goes hourly to Quatro Águas from the Tavira bus terminal in peak season. A taxi to Quatro Águas costs about 500$00.

In peak season there's often a direct boat to the island, departing from near Tavira's market up to six times a day. In the low season, ferries are erratic; you could try bargaining with the fishermen at the quayside for a ride to Quatro Águas, or even to Ilha de Tavira.

For Barril, take a bus from Tavira to Pedras d'el Rei Tavira (10 minutes), from where the little train runs regularly to the beach from March to September (100$00). In the low season the timetable is subject to the whim of the driver. Walking takes around 15 minutes.

Cacela Velha

Once completely overlooked by tourists, and only recently discovered by the tour-bus brigade, this hamlet 12km east of Tavira is still remarkably untouched by the 20th century. All you'll find are a clutch of cottages next to gardens, olive and orange groves, a church, an old fort, a little café and a splendid view of the sea. Magically, there's nothing to do here but follow a path down the scrubby hillside to the beach, or sit on the church walls, listen to the surf and watch pigeons wheel above the olive trees.

Getting There & Away There's no direct bus service from Tavira, but Cacela Velha is only 1km inland from the N125 (2km before Vila Nova de Cacela), which is the Faro-Vila Real de Santo António bus route. Coming from the direction of Faro, there are two turn-offs to Cacela Velha; the second is the more direct.

VILA REAL DE SANTO ANTÓNIO
☎ 081 • pop 8000

Ever since a bridge was completed over the Rio Guadiana 4km north of town in 1991, Vila Real de Santo António's importance as a frontier post and ferry-crossing point for

ALGARVE

Now You See Me, Now You Don't ...

The strictly protected Mediterranean chameleon (*Chamaeleo chamaeleon*) isn't native to Portugal. This bizarre 25cm-long reptile, with independently moving eyes, a tongue longer than its body and a skin which changes colour according to its environment (from bright yellow to jet black), only started creeping around southern Portugal about 70 years ago; it was probably introduced from North Africa where it's common. This particular species is the only type of chameleon found in Europe, and its habitat is restricted to Crete and the Iberian Peninsula. In Portugal it's got no further than the leeward Algarve, where it hides out in pine groves and coastal shrub lands.

Your best chance of coming across the slow-moving beast is either in the Quinta de Marim area of the Parque Natural da Ria Formosa or in Monte Gordo's conifer woods (6km west of Vila Real de Santo António), which have been designated a protected area in order to preserve the species. In hibernation from December to March (the only other time it comes down to ground level is in October to lay its eggs), the chameleon is most commonly seen on spring mornings, slowly clambering along branches or among shrubs.

Spain has declined. But it's still a popular shopping destination, both for tourists from the nearby Monte Gordo resort and Spaniards on day trips who come here to buy cheap linen, towels and booze.

For travellers, it's mainly interesting as the starting point for boat or biking trips along the Guadiana (see the boxed text 'Cruising and Biking Along the Guadiana').

The town itself is architecturally impressive, thanks to the Marquês de Pombal who, in a few brisk months in 1774, stamped the town with his hallmark grid pattern of streets (just like Lisbon's Baixa district) after the original town was destroyed by floods.

Orientation

The seafront Avenida da República is one of the town's two main shopping and eating thoroughfares; the other is the pedestrianised Rua Teofilio de Braga, which leads straight up from the seafront and past the spacious main square, Praça Marquês de Pombal.

The quaint little train station is on the riverfront, just beyond the ferry terminal, about 100m east of Rua Teofilio de Braga. Buses pull into the adjacent terminal on Avenida da República.

Information

The nearest turismo (☎ 54 44 95) is at the tourist resort of Monte Gordo, 6km west of town (a 10 minute bus ride). In summer it's open daily from 9.30 am to 12.30 pm and 2 to 7 pm.

Places to Stay

If you're after a beach and tourist facilities, go to nearby Monte Gordo. There's a shady municipal *parque de campismo* (☎ 54 25 88) there too, but it gets clogged with campers in summer.

In Vila Real itself, good budget accommodation is scarce. You could try the *pousada da juventude* (☎ 54 45 65, Rua Dr Sousa Martins 40), which charges 1500$00 for a dorm bed or 3200$00 for a double room (without bathroom); there's also the *Residência Matos Pereira* (☎ 54 33 25, Rua Dr Sousa Martins 57), near the Praça Marquês de Pombal, which offers tidy doubles for 5000/4500$00 with/without bathroom.

Places to Eat

Cruise Avenida da República for plenty of tempting options (mostly with outdoor seating), including the popular (though rather expensive) *Caves do Guadiana* at No 90. Cheaper fare can be found along Rua Teofilio de Braga and adjoining streets: *Churrasqueira Arenilha (Rua Cândido dos Reis)*, opposite the post office, is one of the better bets, with dishes starting from 1000$00.

Getting There & Away

Bus There are at least eight services a day to Tavira, Olhão and Faro, and regular runs to nearby Castro Marim and Monte Gordo. There's a daily Linha Litoral service to Lagos, too, but at 3½ hours it's 80 minutes slower than the fastest train service. Long-haul coach services include a twice-daily 12 hour marathon to Braga, at the other end of the country; and four alta qualidade runs to Lisbon (five hours).

If you're aiming to get further afield in Spain than Ayamonte, either pick up connections in Ayamonte itself or take the twice-daily express coach service to Huelva (2¼ hours), with connections on to Seville (another hour).

Train Vila Real de Santo António is the eastern terminal of the Algarve railway line, with services to/from Lagos at least eight times a day. The fastest IR service takes 2½ hours and the slowest regional (R) service, with changes at Faro and/or Tunes, takes an hour longer.

Ferry To hop across the border to whitewashed Ayamonte, the most enjoyable route is still by ferry. It runs every 30 minutes in summer from about 8 am to 8 pm, and the fare is 150$00 per person and 650$00 per car.

Cruising & Biking Along the Guadiana

A great way to see Portugal and Spain at the same time is on a boat up the Rio Guadiana (which serves as the border for some 50km). The route from Vila Real de Santo António to Foz de Odeleite passes some delightful villages, including Castro Marim with its formidable hilltop castle.

Several tour operators run the river trip, including Riosul (☎ 081-54 40 77 in Monte Gordo or ☎ 089-80 72 59 in Faro) and Três Dês (☎ 081-51 28 19), for around 7000$00 per person (half-price for children from four to 10 years) including barbecue lunch and time for a swim.

The quiet back road that hugs the river for 14km beyond Foz de Odeleite to Alcoutim (see the last section in this chapter) is increasingly popular with bikers. Along this scenic route are several villages worth visiting including Álamo, with its Roman dam, and Guerreiros do Rio, which has a small Museu do Rio (River Museum) open daily except Monday.

You can rent bikes in Monte Gordo (see Information in the Vila Real de Santo António section on the previous page), 26km from Foz de Odeleite.

Getting Around

You can rent bicycles from the Hotel Atlântico in Monte Gordo or through the specialist travel agency Turalgarve (☎ 51 27 89, fax 51 27 70) at the Hotel Apartamento Neptuno.

CASTRO MARIM

☎ 081 • pop 6630 (municipality)

This tiny village 5km north of Vila Real de Santo António is entirely dominated by its huge castle. The battlements provide a ringside seat for gazing out over the fens and marshes of the **Reserva Natural do Sapal** (see the boxed text on the next page), the bridge to Spain, and the pretty little village below.

There are few facilities in the village itself, but it makes a pleasant stopover en route north or as a day trip from Vila Real, and is especially rewarding if you're a birdwatcher – the nature reserve is famous for its flamingos.

Information

The efficient little turismo (☎ 53 12 32), in the centre of the village at Praça 1 de Maio 2-4, right below the castle, is open weekdays from 9.30 am to 12.30 pm and 2 to 5.30 pm, and Saturday from 9.30 am to noon.

Castelo

Castro Marim's castle was built by Dom Afonso III in the 13th century on the site of Roman and Moorish fortifications. In 1319 it became the first headquarters of the religious military order known as the Order of Christ, a revamped version of the Knights Templar (see the boxed text 'The Order of the Knights Templar' under Tomar in the Estremadura & Ribatejo chapter). Until they moved their base to Tomar in 1334, the soldiers of the Order of Christ used this castle to keep watch over the estuary of the Rio Guadiana and the frontier with Spain – where the Moors were still in power.

The ruins you see today, however, date from the 17th century, when Dom João IV ordered the addition of vast ramparts. At the same time a smaller fort, the **Castelo de São Sebastião**, was built on a nearby hilltop. Much in the area was destroyed in the 1755 earthquake, but the hilltop ruins of the main fort are still pretty awesome.

There's little to see inside the wonderfully derelict castle walls except a restored 14th century church, the **Igreja de Santiago**, where Henry the Navigator, who was Grand Master of the Order of Christ, is said to have prayed.

The castle is open daily (admission free) from 9.30 am to 5 pm.

ALGARVE

Reserva Natural do Sapal de Castro Marim e Vila Real de Santo António

Established in 1975, this nature reserve is the oldest in Portugal, covering some 2000 hectares of marshland, brackish fens and commercial salt pans bordering the Rio Guadiana just north of Vila Real. Among its most important winter visitors are greater flamingos, spoonbills, avocets and Caspian terns. In spring you can see dozens of white storks.

The park's administrative office (☎ 081-53 11 41, fax 53 12 57), currently inside Castro Marim's castle, is due to move to a new base and interpretative centre in Montinho (a five minute bus ride to the north), which is open weekdays from 9 am to 12.30 pm and 2 to 5.30 pm. There's some park accommodation (including a two room house for 4300$00) in Montinho already. It's popular with botanists and groups of birdwatchers so you need to book ahead. Another rewarding area for spotting the park's birdlife is around Cerro do Bufo, about 2km south-west of Castro Marim. Staff at the park office can provide a map and more details.

Places to Stay & Eat
There's no accommodation in the village. If you're keen to hang out to study the flora or fauna of the park, your best bet are the quiet Vila do Sol self-catering villas (☎ 081-53 15 97) in Vista Real, a few kilometres north of Castro Marim, costing about 10,000$00. The turismo has details. There are several reasonable restaurants on Rua de São Sebastião, a short walk from the turismo.

Getting There & Away
Buses from Vila Real de Santo António make the eight minute run to Castro Marim and on to Montinho, a short distance north, at least eight times a day.

The Central Coast

LOULÉ
☎ 089 • pop 9000
Loulé, one of the Algarve's largest inland towns, is a former Roman and Moorish settlement with an attractive old quarter and castle ruins. Just 16km north-west of Faro, it's become a popular destination for tour groups every Saturday, thanks to its big weekly Gypsy market and its reputation as a long-established centre for handicrafts. Its laid-back atmosphere and good range of restaurants make it worth an overnight stay.

Orientation
The bus station is on the northern edge of town, about 1km from the centre. The train station is 5km south-west of the centre (take any Quarteira-bound bus).

If you're arriving by car (especially on a Saturday), try to arrive very early in the morning or you'll have some nightmare parking problems.

Information
Inside the converted ruins of the castle in the old town area is the turismo (☎ 46 39 00), open Monday to Friday from 9.30 am to 7 pm, and Saturday from 9.30 am to 5.30 pm. There's a Ciber Espaço (Internet area) in the 1st floor café of the Casa da Cultura (☎ 41 58 60) at Praça da República 36. It's open from 3 pm to midnight Monday to Saturday. It costs 450$00 for an hour on the computers here (this includes sending emails).

Castelo
The restored castle ruins house the **Cozinha Tradicional Algarvia**, a traditional Algarve kitchen display up the steps from the turismo, and the small **Museu Municipal de Arqueológica,** next to the turismo. The museum's attractive displays feature some fine fragments of Bronze Age and Roman

ceramics, including an eye-catching 10th century bowl with swirling patterns. The museum is open Monday to Saturday from 9 am to 5.30 pm (admission free).

Activities

Quinta do Azinheira (☎ 41 59 91, mobile ☎ 0676 75 71 30) at Aldeia da Tôr, about 12km north, offers horse riding, plus special outings such as night rides with a barbecue included. Turalgarve (☎ 46 21 93), Praça da República 98, can arrange boat trips or combined boat-jeep safaris (see Activities under Tavira earlier in this chapter).

Special Events

Weekdays and out of high season, Loulé is a pretty dozy place. But come Carnaval time (late February or early March), it's livelier than almost anywhere else in the Algarve, with parades and tractor-drawn floats, dancing and singing, and lots of jolly, high-spirited behaviour.

Another major but far more sombre event in Loulé's calendar is the *romaria* (religious festival) of Nossa Senhora da Piedade. Linked to ancient maternity rites, it's probably the Algarve's most important religious festival. On Easter Sunday, a 16th century image of Our Lady of Pity (or Piety) is carried down from its hilltop chapel 2km north of town to the Igreja Matriz (parish church). Two weeks later, a much larger procession of devotees lines the steep route to the chapel to witness and accompany the return of the image to its home. The eye-catching new Igreja de Nossa Senhora da Piedade next to this old chapel was completed in 1995 and now dominates the skyline.

Places to Stay

Near the Gypsy market, the glass-fronted *Hospedaria José Viegas* (☎ 46 33 85, Rua Nossa Senhora da Piedade 61) has spacious singles/doubles with bathroom for 2000/4000$00 and triples for 8000$00. Another good budget place is *Pensão Cidem* (☎ 41 55 53, Travessa do Mercado 1), which has doubles without/with bathroom from 3000/4500$00. If the door's closed, ask at the nearby Restaurante Pescador (see Places to Eat following).

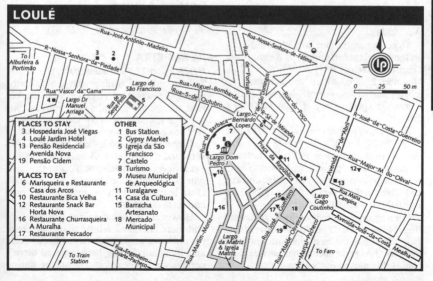

LOULÉ

0   25   50 m

PLACES TO STAY
3 Hospedaria José Viegas
4 Loulé Jardim Hotel
13 Pensão Residencial Avenida Nova
19 Pensão Cidem

PLACES TO EAT
6 Marisqueira e Restaurante Casa dos Arcos
10 Restaurante Bica Velha
12 Restaurante Snack Bar Horta Nova
16 Restaurante Churrasqueira A Muralha
17 Restaurante Pescador

OTHER
1 Bus Station
2 Gypsy Market
5 Igreja da São Francisco
7 Castelo
8 Turismo
9 Museu Municipal de Arqueológica
11 Turalgarve
14 Casa da Cultura
15 Barracha Artesanato
18 Mercado Municipal

ALGARVE

Similarly central is *Pensão Residencial Avenida Nova (Rua Maria Campina 1)*; ring ☎ 41 50 97 daytime, ☎ 41 64 06 in the evening. The big, squeaky-floored rooms here are good value, especially for trios or families. Doubles with/without shower are 4500/3500$00.

Top of the range is the *Loulé Jardim Hotel (☎ 41 30 94, fax 46 31 77, Largo Dr Manuel Arriaga)*, a late-19th century building with modernised rooms in a quiet square. A single/double room with all the frills (there's a small swimming pool too) will set you back a reasonable 9000/11,000$00.

Places to Eat
Restaurante Pescador (☎ 46 28 21), in the lane right next to the mercado municipal, is the place to head for at Saturday lunch time if you like a good family hubbub. Big helpings, lots of fish dishes and reasonable prices make this a popular choice with the locals.

For open-air dining in a walled garden, head for *Restaurante Snack Bar Horta Nova (☎ 46 24 29, Rua Major Manuel do Olival)*, which specialises in home-made pizzas (costing from as little as 650$00), charcoal-grilled meat and fish. It's closed Wednesday.

More expensive but still pleasantly unpretentious is *Marisqueira e Restaurante Casa dos Arcos (☎ 41 67 13, Rua Sá de Miranda 23-25)*, where you can feast on lobster and crabs, swordfish steak or filet mignon. Expect to pay at least 1200$00 a dish.

Restaurante Churrasqueira A Muralha (☎ 41 26 29, Rua Martim Moniz 41), in the shadow of the old town walls, is a tastefully decorated little nook with brick floors and azulejo-adorned niches. Grilled chicken and fish dishes range from 750$00 to 1400$00. It's closed Tuesday.

For a splurge, try the nearby *Restaurante Bica Velha (☎ 46 33 76, Rua Martim Moniz 17)*, which has the best reputation in town for typical Algarve specialities such as cataplanas. It's closed for Sunday lunch.

Shopping
Many of Loulé's finest arts and crafts – especially leather goods, brass and copperware, wooden and cane furniture – are made and sold in craft shops along Rua da Barbaca (behind the castle). Loulé's biggest copperware shop, Barracha Artesanato, is right by the mercado municipal, which also has a few craft stalls.

On Saturday mornings the market has far more Portuguese atmosphere and produce than the tourist-geared Gypsy market the other side of town (for this, follow the crowds along the pedestrianised Rua 5 de Outubro). Head for the Gypsy market only if you want the usual cheap clothes, t-shirts and plastic junk you'll find in all other Algarve Gypsy markets. It winds down around noon.

Getting There & Away
Both Faro and Lagos-bound trains stop at Loulé station (5km out of town) at least eight times a day. Buses are far more convenient: there are regular connections from Faro, and at least seven buses a day from Albufeira and Portimão.

Getting Around
You can rent bikes through Megarent (☎ 39 30 44) or Turalgarve (☎ 46 21 93).

ALBUFEIRA
☎ 089 • pop 22,500 (municipality)
This once-pretty fishing village now epitomises the worst of Algarve mass-market tourism, catering almost entirely for package tours, with overpriced restaurants, raucous bars and discos, and ugly towers of apartment hotels and holiday flats on all the surrounding hillsides. Albufeira's modern extension is Montechoro, 3km to the east, where 'The Strip' leading up from Praia da Oura is packed with yet more hotels, bars and restaurants.

However, the beaches are still pleasant and there is at least a little character left in the old town's steep and narrow back streets and its small fishing harbour. And there's certainly a lively resort atmosphere during

Where Eagle Owls Fly

In the foothills of the Serra do Caldeirão, 21km north-west of Loulé, is the Rocha da Pena, a 479m-high limestone outcrop that was made a classified site in 1993 because of its rich flora and fauna. Orchids, narcissi and native cistus cover the slopes, where red foxes and Egyptian mongooses are common. Among many bird species seen here are the huge eagle owl, Bonelli's eagle and buzzard.

A *centro ambiental* (environmental centre) has been established in the village of Pena, and there is a 4.7km circular trail starting from Rocha, 1km from Pena.

the summer, with buskers and artisan stalls in the street by day and plenty of late-night entertainment.

If you want to forget you're in Portugal (you'll hear more English and German than Portuguese), Albufeira may be just the ticket for a hassle-free holiday with guaranteed bacon-and-egg breakfasts, beer on tap and football on TV.

Orientation

The bus station is about 500m from the turismo and a few minutes walk from the town's focal point, Largo Engenheiro Duarte Pacheco, where most of the cafés, bars and restaurants are clustered. The main street is Rua 5 de Outubro. The train station is an inconvenient 6km north, reached by shuttle bus from the bus station (see Getting Around later in this section). If you're arriving by car, the best place to park is the free car park just above the bus station.

Information

Tourist Office The overworked turismo (☎ 58 52 79) is at the southern end of Rua 5 de Outubro, near the tunnel to the beach. In summer it's open daily from 9.30 am to 7 pm (in winter it closes for lunch on Monday, Friday and weekends).

Money In and around Largo Engenheiro Duarte Pacheco you'll find plenty of banks with Multibanco ATMs, and several no-commission private exchange bureaux.

Post & Communications The post office next to the turismo is open weekdays only. There's a phone office around the corner, on Rua Joaquim Mendonça Gouveia, open Monday to Saturday from 10.30 am to 7 pm.

Bookshops For second-hand books in languages from English to Swahili, check out Centro de Livros do Algarve (☎ 51 37 73), at Rua da Igreja Nova 6. The kiosks around Largo Engenheiro Duarte Pacheco stock a wide range of international newspapers and magazines.

Childcare There's a Ludoteca kindergarten (see Childcare under Travel with Children in the Facts for the Visitor chapter) on Travessa Pedro Samora, just off Largo Engenheiro Duarte Pacheco. It's open daily in term time from 9 am to 12.30 pm and from 2 to 7 pm.

Medical Services The 24 hour centro de saúde (☎ 58 69 33) is 2km north of town on the road to the train station. The nearest major hospital is in Faro. There's also the private Clioura Clinic (☎ 58 70 00; open 24 hours) in Montechoro.

Emergency The main police station (☎ 51 54 20, 54 14 34) is way north of town, on Estrada Vale Pedras, near the mercado municipal.

Beaches

People come to Albufeira mainly to swim, sunbathe, eat and drink (and drink and drink, if the number of bars is any indication). The town's beach, **Praia do Peneco**, through the tunnel near the turismo, is pleasant but often packed. For a bit of local flavour, head 400m east to **Praia dos Pescadores** (Fishermen's Beach, also called Praia dos Barcos). There's still a hint of

ALGARVE

Albufeira's fishing past, with fishermen mending their nets beside their high-prowed and brightly painted boats. But it's also become the place for some trendy bars and seafood restaurants (see Places to Eat later in this section).

Further afield – both east and west of the town – there are numerous beautifully rugged coves and bays, though the nearest are heavily developed and often crowded. The easiest to reach is **Praia da Oura**, 2km to the east (roughly 30 minutes on foot; follow Avenida 25 de Abril and climb the steps at the end to reach the road to the beach).

Between Praia da Oura and **Praia da Falésia**, 10km to the east, is a string of less crowded beaches, including **Balaia** and **Olhos de Água**. They're all accessible by local bus from the main bus station; there's a dozen buses every weekday to Olhos de Água, all but three of which continue to Praia da Falésia.

One of the best beaches to the west, **Praia da Galé**, about 6km away, is a centre for jet-skiing and water-skiing. There's no direct bus service to this beach or the others en route, though local buses to Portimão do run along the main road about 2km above the beaches.

Activities

Summertime activities in Albufeira include tourist-oriented bullfights held from Easter to September, early evening every Saturday in the Praia da Oura bullring, and live dance or music shows every night in Largo Engenheiro Duarte Pacheco.

For more adventurous trips out of Albufeira, ask any travel agency about mountain bike, canoe and jeep excursions organised by Zebra Safari (☎ 58 68 60, fax

ALBUFEIRA

PLACES TO STAY
2 Residencial Pensão Limas
3 Pensão Albufeirense Residencial
7 Hotel California
8 Pensão Polana
18 Pensão Restaurante Silva
21 Pensão Residencial Vila Recife
24 Residencial Vila Bela
26 Pensão Dianamar Residencial

PLACES TO EAT
9 Restaurante O Cantinho Algarvio
10 Restaurante O Painel
11 Restaurante Tipico A Ruína
12 Tasca do Viegas
25 Restaurante Lenita

OTHER
1 Bus Station & Car Park
4 Sir Harry's Bar
5 JC Bar
6 Classic Scandinavian Bar
13 Ludoteca
14 Bank
15 Turismo
16 Post Office
17 Telephone Office
19 Centro de Livros do Algarve
20 Igreja Matriz
22 Zansi Bar
23 Igreja de São Sebastião

58 87 96, email zebrasafari@mail.telepac .pt), which also organises treasure hunts and expeditions to the Alentejo. Riosul (☎ 081-51 02 01, fax 51 02 09) does a one-day Super Safari, including a cruise up the Rio Guadiana.

Travel agents can also arrange trips to the Zoomarine aquatic park at Guia, 8km north-west of Albufeira on the N125, and the other nearby water parks (for more on these see Activities in the introduction to this chapter).

Special Events

The major local festival is the Festa da Ourada on 14 August, which honours the fishermen's patron saint, Nossa Senhora da Ourada (Our Lady of the Oracle), with a beach procession.

Places to Stay

You'll need to book well ahead to be sure of getting accommodation if you're visiting in the high season.

Camping The nearest camping ground is the well-equipped and pricey *Parque de Campismo de Albufeira* (☎ 58 95 05, 58 76 29, fax 58 76 33) near Alpouvar, 2km north of town off the Estrada de Ferreiras (the road to the train station). Prices are 795/795/795$00 per person/tent/car.

Private Rooms There are dozens of private quartos, most costing from 4000$00 to 5000$00 for a double. If you're not approached by touts at the bus station or around town, it probably means there are no vacancies.

Pensões & Residenciais Recommended budget residenciais include the central *Residencial Pensão Limas* (☎ 51 40 25, Rua da Liberdade 25) and the nearby *Pensão Albufeirense Residencial* (☎ 51 20 79) at No 18, both with doubles for about 7000$00. *Pensão Restaurante Silva* (☎ 51 26 69, Travessa 5 de Outubro 21) also has cheap rooms but in high season only offers full board (11,000$00).

A 10 minute walk west along the seafront to the picturesque old fishing quarter brings you to several quieter residenciais, including the quaintly old-fashioned *Pensão Dianamar Residencial* (☎ 51 23 79, Rua Latino Coelho 36). With 14 simple rooms, it's a bargain at around 5500$00 a double. Nearby, the pretty and popular *Residencial Vila Bela* (☎ 51 55 35, fax 51 21 01, Rua Coronel Águas 32) has doubles (most with balconies) for 11,000$00, as well as a swimming pool.

In the same price bracket is the more central *Pensão Residencial Vila Recife* (☎ 58 67 47, fax 58 71 82, Rua Miguel Bombarda 12). It looks cute and tiny but has a surprising 92 rooms, often block-booked by tour groups.

Pensão Polana (☎ 58 71 68, Rua Cândido dos Reis 32) is also popular with package tour groups. Noisy doubles cost 12,000$00. The same management runs the upmarket *Hotel California* (☎ 58 68 33, fax 58 68 50, Rua Cândido dos Reis 12), where doubles soar in summer to 18,000$00.

Places to Eat

Spaghetti, fish and chips, pizzas, burgers, and bacon and eggs are everywhere. Finding decent alternatives at reasonable prices is more difficult, though there is a wide choice of cuisines, from standard Portuguese to Chinese, Indian, Italian and even Irish.

If you're prepared to walk 10 minutes from the centre, you'll come across little places like *Restaurante Lenita* (Rua Latino Coelho 14-A), which has a reasonable tourist menu for 1650$00 and other dishes for under 1200$00.

Another good hunting ground is around Praia dos Pescadores, where there are some great seafood restaurants on the waterfront and cheaper options in the backstreets. *Restaurante Tipico A Ruína* (☎ 51 20 94, Largo Cais Herculano) is the most traditional of the seafood restaurants. It isn't cheap but you get superb sea views from the rooftop terrace (or a pleasantly rustic setting inside). *Tasca do Viegas* (☎ 51 40 87) nearby is another pretty spot, with a reasonably priced menu.

In the street behind, Rua São Gonçalo de Lagos, check out *Restaurante O Painel* (☎ *51 36 61)* for its varied menu of Italian and Portuguese dishes. Around the corner, *Restaurante O Cantinho Algarvio (☎ 58 51 50, Travessa São Gonçalo de Lagos 6)*, serves Angolan specialities at weekends.

Entertainment
Bars are a dime a dozen around Largo Engenheiro Duarte Pacheco and nearby Rua Cândido dos Reis. Nearly all offer happy hours (at various times of the day) and are open until at least 2 am.

For noise volume that drowns out conversation and a long list of zany cocktails, check out *Classic Scandinavian Bar (Rua Cândido dos Reis 10)* or *JC Bar* opposite. *Zansi Bar (Rua Miguel Bombarda)* offers darts, snooker and satellite TV (including sports channels), as well as pizzas, hamburgers and English breakfasts. *Sir Harry's Bar (Largo Engenheiro Duarte Pacheco 37)* is one of the older British-style pubs, with the best of British brews on tap.

Shopping
A Gypsy market where you can buy mostly clothes and shoes is held on the first and third Tuesday of the month in the Orada district, about 1.5km south-west of the town centre.

Getting There & Away
The main bus station (☎ 51 43 01, 58 97 55) is crowded and confusing, and some services tend to slip in and out very quickly. There are regular weekday services to Lagos (including six trans rápido services) and to Faro (including seven trans rápido and two express Linha Litoral services), about eight buses a day to Portimão and Silves, and about six regular and four alta qualidade buses a day to Loulé. All weekend services are limited.

Long-distance coaches include regular services to Lisbon (some requiring a change of bus at Vale do Paraíso), including four

express alta qualidade services, four daily to Évora, and two daily services across the border to Huelva in Spain (with onward connections to Seville). The Huelva run (changing at Faro) takes about 3½ hours and costs about 1600$00.

Trains include three daily IR services to Lagos (about 430$00) and seven IR or IC services a day to Faro (about 300$00) – beware of the tedious local services. There are six trains daily to nearby Tunes, from where you can pick up connecting services to Lisbon (about 1900$00).

Getting Around
To reach the train station, take the *estação* (station) shuttle bus (185$00), which leaves twice an hour from the main bus terminal.

Among several car rental agencies is Auto Jardim do Algarve (☎ 58 97 15, fax 58 77 80) in the Edifício Brisa on Avenida da Liberdade. You can rent bikes and motorbikes from Vespa Rent (☎ 54 23 77). Prices are about 1300$00 a day for a bicycle and 9,126$00 for three days for a Honda Scoopy. Megarent (☎ 57 19 71) also rents bicycles.

CARVOEIRO
☎ 082
Flanked by cliffs, backed by hills and surrounded by an ever-expanding collection of shops, bars and restaurants, this small seaside resort 5km south of Lagoa has grown in 20 years from a little known fishing village to one of the Algarve's most popular self-catering holiday areas, with estates of foreign-owned villas sprawled across the hillsides. The town itself is a laid-back spot compared to resorts like Albufeira, though the summertime tourist invasion tends to suffocate the place.

Orientation & Information
Buses from Lagoa stop right by the beach, beside a small turismo (☎ 35 77 28) which doesn't offer much information. The post office and several banks are on Rua dos Pescadores (the one-way road in from Lagoa).

The geometric patterns in these ornate white-washed chimney pots show Moorish influence.

Beaches

The town's little beach, **Praia do Carvoeiro**, bordered by several cafés, is set in a picturesque cove. One kilometre east on the coast road is the bay of **Algar Seco**, a favourite stop on the tour-bus itinerary thanks to its dramatic rock formations.

If you're looking for a stunning swimming spot, it's worth continuing several kilometres east along the main road, Estrada do Farol, to **Praia de Centianes**, where the secluded cliff-wrapped beach is almost as dramatic as Algar Seco. Buses heading for Praia do Carvalho (nine a day from Lagoa, via Carvoeiro) pass nearby – ask for Colina Sol Aparthotel, the massive Moorish-style hotel on the clifftop.

Activities

For aquatic action, head for the Slide & Splash water-slide park, open daily from 10 am to 7 pm. It's 2km west of Lagoa (though its access road from the N125 is just 300m west of Lagoa). If you don't have a car, many travel agencies offer regular organised trips.

If you play golf, you have a choice of three nearby courses: the 18 hole Vale da Pinta (☎ 5 26 70), set in a centenarian olive grove; the neighbouring nine hole Quinta do Gramacho (☎ 5 26 70), which is part of the Carvoeiro Club west of town; and the challenging nine hole Clube de Golfe do Vale de Milho (☎ 35 85 02) near Praia de Centianes, east of town, with some of the Algarve's best value play (about 2950$00 for nine holes). The David Leadbetter Golf Academy, at the Hotel Almansor (☎ 35 80 26, fax 35 87 70, email almansor@mail.telepac.pt), Praia Vale Covo, offers golfing packages.

At Centro Hípico Casa Galaraz (☎ 35 80 55), just off the Estrada de Benagil a few kilometres north-east of town, horse riding (including a Shetland pony for the kids) is available for around 3000$00 an hour. If you don't have a car you'll have to take a taxi; there's no bus connection.

Places to Stay

You'll be lucky to find any vacancies in high season. The turismo has a list of places but no prices.

Among the most attractive quartos and studios are those belonging to a Canadian woman, *Brigitte Lemieux* (*☎/fax 35 63 18, Rampa da Nossa Senhora da Encarnação 4*) – facing the sea take the steep road up to the left from the beach. A double costs 9000$00 (50,000$00 for a week) with sea view, fridge and toaster.

Slightly cheaper are the five rooms at the pretty *Casa von Baselli* (*☎ 35 71 59, Rua da Escola*), around the corner. In the low season, prices in even the swishest hotels and villa complexes can drop 50%.

Places to Eat

There are plenty of restaurants to choose from in the main part of town and along Estrada do Farol. *Curva do Casino* (*☎ 35 75 96, Rua do Casino 36*), near the post office, is a friendly little place popular for its fish dishes.

Slightly more upmarket is *O Chefe António* (*☎ 35 89 37, Estrada do Farol*), where you can indulge yourself with dishes such as prawns flambé or paella.

Getting There & Away

Buses run to Carvoeiro at least five times a day from Portimão and almost every hour from Lagoa.

Getting Around

There's a taxi rank at the bottom of Estrada do Farol. You can rent bicycles, scooters and motorbikes from Motorent (☎ 35 65 51). For car hire call the Travel Shop (☎ 35 79 47); it's on Rua dos Pescadores, close to the turismo.

SILVES

☎ 082 • pop 33,400 (municipality)

It's hard to believe now, but this dozy town beside the Rio Arade, 15km north-east of Portimão, was once the Moorish capital of the Algarve. Its imposing red stone castle towers above the surrounding orange and almond groves, a powerful reminder of the past. More recently, Silves has started to embrace tourism with enthusiasm, its cobbled pedestrianised streets sporting an increasing number of restaurants and souvenir shops.

History

From the mid-11th to mid-13th centuries, Shelb (or Xelb) as it was then known, rivalled Lisbon in prosperity and influence: according to the 12th century Arab geographer Idrisi, there was a population of 30,000, a port and shipyards, and 'attractive buildings and well-furnished bazaars'.

Its downfall began in June 1189, when Dom Sancho I laid siege to it, supported by a horde of (mostly English) hooligan crusaders who had been persuaded (with the promise of loot) to pause in their journey to Jerusalem and give Sancho a hand. The Moors holed up inside their impregnable castle, but after three hot months of harassment they finally ran out of water and were forced to surrender. Sancho was all for mercy and honour, but the crusaders would have none of it: they stripped the Moors of their possessions as they left (including the clothes on their backs), tortured those remaining and wrecked the town.

Two years later the Moors exacted their revenge by recapturing the place. It wasn't until 1249 that the Christians gained control once and for all. But by then Silves was a shadow of its former self.

Orientation & Information

Silves train station is 2km south of town (the walk into town is mostly downhill for those arriving). Buses stop on the riverfront road at the bottom of town, crossing the Rio Arade on a modern bridge slightly upriver from a picturesque 13th century version (now for pedestrians only).

It's a steep but short climb from here to the efficient turismo (☎ 44 22 55) on Rua 25 de Abril. It's open Monday to Friday from 9.30 am to 12.30 pm and 2 to 7 pm and Saturday from 9.30 am to noon. Staff at the office can provide a town map and information on accommodation.

The post office is on Rua do Correio, a short walk west of the turismo.

Castelo

The castle is, of course, the town's highlight, commanding great views over the town and surrounding countryside. Restored in 1835, its chunky red sandstone walls enclose a rather dull interior, where unkempt gardens serve as a playground for hordes of visiting school children. Archaeological digs are in progress to discover more of the site's Roman and pre-Roman past. The Moors' occupation is recalled by a deep well and a vaulted water cistern (still in use today). The castle is open daily from 9 am to 7 pm (6 pm in winter); admission costs 250$00.

Sé

Just below the castle is the Sé (cathedral), built in 1189 on the site of an earlier mosque, rebuilt after the 1249 Reconquista and subsequently restored several times. The stark, fortress-like building has only a few of its original Gothic touches left, including the nave and aisles. Apart from several fine tombs (probably of 13th century crusaders) there's little of interest inside. It's open daily from 8.30 am to 1 pm and 2.30 to 7 pm except Tuesday when it closes at 12.30 pm, re-opening for mass at 6 pm.

Museu de Arqueologia

Just below the cathedral, in Rua das Portas de Loulé, this impressive archaeological museum offers some intriguing glimpses into Silves' illustrious history. Its centrepiece is an original Moorish water cistern and well. The museum is open daily from 10 am to 7 pm, and admission is 300$00 (free for students).

Activities

See Portimão for information on river cruises up the Rio Arade to Silves. Horse riders can contact Quinta Penedo (☎ 33 24 66) for rides through fruit farm countryside, some 13km to the north-east at Vale Fuzeiros.

Special Events

In late July or early August the slightly rowdy Festival da Cerveja (beer festival) is held within the castle walls to the sound of brass bands and folk-dance groups.

Places to Stay

In the heart of the old town, old-fashioned *Residencial Sousa* (☎ 44 25 02, Rua Samoura Barros 17) has spacious singles/doubles for 3500/5000$00. Similarly priced but noisier is *Pensão-Restaurante Ladeiro* (☎ 44 28 70) on the main road on the other side of the river. Another restaurant-cum-hotel is the eye-catching *Residencial Ponte Romana* (☎ 44 32 75) beside the old bridge, which offers frilly double rooms for around 6000$00.

If you're after rural peace and quiet, head 5km north-east (en route to São Bartolomeu de Messines) to Sitio São Estevão, where you'll find the delightful, Italian-run *Quinta do Rio* (☎/fax 44 55 28), a restored farmhouse set among orange groves, with plenty of space for kids to romp around. Doubles range from 7000$00 to 9000$00 (including breakfast).

Places to Eat

There are plenty of café-restaurants to choose from down by the river or in the pedestrianised streets leading up to the castle. Try *Ú Monchiqueiro* (☎ 44 21 42) by the river for piri-piri chicken (see the boxed text 'Piri-Piri' later in this chapter), or *A Mesquita 2* (☎ 44 27 47, Rua Policarpo Dias), in a pedestrianised street opposite the old bridge, for dishes under 1200$00. On the other side of the river, *Restaurante Ladeiro* (☎ 44 28 70) packs in the locals at lunch time with hearty Portuguese fare.

Restaurante Rui (☎ 44 26 82, Rua Comendador Vilarinho 27), in the old town, is famed for its seafood. This is the place to try *arroz de marisco* (seafood and rice stew). It's closed Tuesday. *Café Inglês* (☎ 44 23 89), just below the castle entrance is a relaxing place to indulge in home-made soups, fruit juices and cakes (there's an outdoor terrace too). It's closed Saturday.

Getting There & Away

Seven buses a day (five at weekends) shuttle between Silves and its train station, timed to meet some of the dozen or so trains a day that arrive from Lagos and Vila Real de Santo António (via Faro). On weekdays, there are also regular bus connections to Albufeira (six), Lagoa and Portimão (nine). All buses leave from the riverfront.

PORTIMÃO

☎ 082 • pop 40,000 (municipality)

This unattractive fishing port and sardine canning centre 16km east of Lagos hogs the west bank of the Rio Arade 3km inland from Praia da Rocha.

Portimão's past sounds rather more glorious than its present: inhabited by successive settlers – Phoenicians, Greeks and Carthaginians (Hannibal himself is said to have set foot here) – it was called Portos Magnus by the Romans and fought over by Moors and Christians. In 1189 crusaders under Dom Sancho I sailed up the Rio Arade from here to besiege Silves. The 1755 earthquake practically flattened the place.

Today it's the Algarve's second most important fishing port (after Olhão) and a popular destination for day-trippers from nearby holiday resorts, who come mainly for the shopping. In addition to a clutch of quality handicrafts shops, there's also a big Gypsy market.

The only other reasons to come here are to take a boat trip up the river to Silves or to enjoy a slap-up sardine lunch; overnight accommodation, tourist facilities and nightlife are far better in the nearby resort of Praia da Rocha.

Orientation

There's no bus station, but buses stop at various points along Avenida Guanaré (look for the Shell petrol station) and Avenida Afonso Henriques (look for the Agip station). The train station is a 15 minute walk north of the town centre.

Several streets in the centre are pedestrianised, including the main shopping street Rua do Comércio. Drivers should be prepared for a devilish one-way system that shunts you all over the place: try and reach the free parking in Largo do Duque.

Information

The turismo (☎ 41 91 31) is on Rua Zeca Afonso, opposite the football stadium. It's open daily from 9.30 am to 12.30 pm and 2 to 6 pm.

There are several Multibanco ATMs around the central Praça Manuel Teixeira Gomes. The police can be contacted on ☎ 41 75 10.

Things to See

The town's parish church, the **Igreja Matriz**, stands on high ground to the north of the town centre and features a 14th century

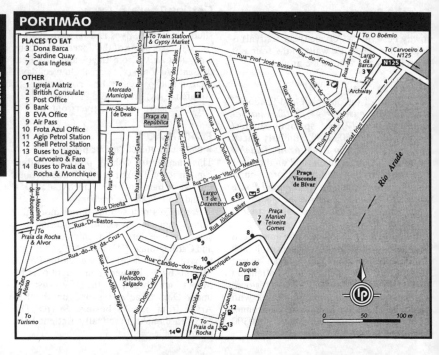

PORTIMÃO

PLACES TO EAT
3 Dona Barca
4 Sardine Quay
7 Casa Inglesa

OTHER
1 Igreja Matriz
2 British Consulate
5 Post Office
6 Bank
8 EVA Office
9 Air Pass
10 Frota Azul Office
11 Agip Petrol Station
12 Shell Petrol Station
13 Buses to Lagoa,
   Carvoeiro & Faro
14 Buses to Praia da
   Rocha & Monchique

Gothic portal – all that remains of the original structure after the 1755 earthquake. More interesting echoes of the past can be found in the narrow streets of the **old fishing quarter** around Largo da Barca, just before the old highway bridge.

Portimão's **Gypsy market** is held on the first Monday of every month, behind the train station. A **flea market** also takes place on the first and third Sunday of the month (mornings only) in front of the new mercado municipal on Avenida São João de Deus.

Activities

A number of operators along the quay offer boat trips upriver to Silves for about 3000$00 per person (4½ hours in total). Lunch and soft drinks are included in the price. Three and four-hour coastal cruises (3000/5000$00) and four-hour fishing trips (5000$00 anglers; 3500$00 spectators) are also available.

You can go horse riding at Centro Hípico Vale de Ferro (☎ 96 84 44), near Mexilhoeira Grande (turn off the N125 4.2km west of Portimão). There's a free pick-up service from Portimão as long as there are at least two of you riding for a minimum of two hours. The centre organises day trips as well as overnight excursions into the Serra de Monchique.

Places to Eat & Drink

The best hunting ground is in the old quarter, especially along the 'sardine quay', a riverside strip of stalls and humble restaurants where you can buy some of the best charcoal-grilled sardines in the Algarve for a bargain 350$00 per half-dozen.

There are several more upmarket seafood restaurants in nearby Largo da Barca (under the arches of the bridge), including *Dona Barca* (☎ 8 41 89), famous for its Algarve specialities. For cakes, snacks and simple Portuguese fare, head for the popular *Casa Inglesa* (☎ 41 62 90, *Praça Manuel Teixeira Gomes*). A recommended bar (which is also gay-friendly) is *O Boémio* (*Rua de São José 28*).

Getting There & Away

Portimão has good bus connections to other destinations in the Algarve, including half a dozen weekday services to Albufeira and Faro, eight services daily to Silves and Monchique, and hourly services to Lagos. There are at least eight express buses a day to Lisbon. Information and tickets for EVA, Intersul and Eurolines services are available at the EVA office (☎ 41 81 20) at Largo do Duque 3. There is a Frota Azul bus office nearby.

Air Pass (see Getting There & Away at the start of this chapter) advertises bargain airfares out of Portugal.

PRAIA DA ROCHA
☎ 082

This vast stretch of sand backed by towering ochre-red cliffs and scattered with bizarre rocky outcrops was one of the first beaches in the Algarve to be patronised by overseas tourists in the 1950s and 60s. Although ugly ranks of hotels and apartments, shops, bars, casinos and nightclubs have long since destroyed its charm and tranquillity, it still has a few old mansions and guesthouses (some dating from the 19th century) that give it a touch of class. And the beach itself is still one of the most impressive in the Algarve.

Orientation & Information

The esplanade, Avenida Tomás Cabreira, high above the beach and with most of the shops, hotels and restaurants, is the resort's main drag. At the eastern end is the shell of the Fortaleza da Santa Catarina, the fort built in the 16th century to stop pirates and invaders sailing up the Rio Arade to Portimão harbour.

Near the fort is the turismo (☎ 41 91 32), open daily during summer from 9.30 am to 7 pm. The post office and a taxi rank are at the centre of the esplanade, by the Hotel da Rocha.

Activities

There are numerous travel agencies offering tours and trips: Pandatours (☎ 41 55 41, fax

ALGARVE

41 23 16), on Rua Engenheiro Francisco Bívar, offers coach tours (to as far away as Évora and Lisbon) and one-day jeep safaris from about 6500$00 per person. Polo Excursions (☎ 420 18 00, fax 420 18 09), next to Hotel da Rocha, runs river cruises and trips to nearby grottoes for about 6000$00 (often with discounts for seniors).

Places to Stay

Pensão and hotel accommodation is almost impossible to find in high season without prior reservation, though it's worth asking at the turismo about private quartos. *Pensão Residencial Solar Pinguim (☎ 42 43 08, Rua António Feu)* is an old villa set back from the esplanade (behind the modern eyesore, Discoteca Katedral). Run by the same Englishwoman for 30 years, it's seen better times, but the musty atmosphere and décor are redolent of Praia da Rocha's sedate early days. Double rooms (a few with sea views) cost around 8700$00, including breakfast.

More modern but far less interesting are *Residencial Tursol (☎ 42 40 46, Rua Engheiro Francisco Bívar)* and the nearby *Residencial São José (☎ 42 40 35)*, which can also be booked through Pandatours. Doubles at both go for about 9000$00.

In the upper price bracket there are two century-old gems. The *Albergaria Vila Lido (☎ 42 41 27, fax 42 42 46, Avenida Tomás Cabreira)*, next to the turismo, is a delightful 19th century mansion with a dozen rooms and prices spiralling to as much as 16,800$00 for a double in high season. Bagging the best beach view from the middle of the esplanade is *Hotel Bela Vista (☎ 42 40 55, fax 41 53 69)*, a whimsical late-19th century creation converted to a hotel in 1936, with marvellously worked wooden ceilings and original azulejos. Only two of the 14 rooms lack a sea view. In great demand, its doubles cost 23,000$00 (dropping to 10,000$00 in winter).

Places to Eat

There are plenty of snack bars and cafés along the esplanade, as well as several on the beach. *Lena's Croissanteria*, on the esplanade opposite Hotel Bela Vista, is a pleasant spot for breakfast, vegetarian dishes, ice cream and crêpes.

For a change from standard Portuguese fare, try the North Indian and Balti cuisine at *Restaurante Ravi Indiano (☎ 41 32 68)*, at the turismo end of the esplanade, or the adjacent *La Dolce Vita Pizzaria (☎ 41 68 12)* for fresh home-made pastas. Seafood restaurants are inevitably expensive, though some, such as the elegant *Serra e Mar (☎ 26 78 10, Rua António Feu)*, opposite Hotel Bela Vista, offer a reasonable tourist menu for around 2500$00.

Entertainment

You won't have any trouble finding a decent bar with entertainment on tap. Often run by Irish or English expats, they cater for all age groups and offer everything from darts and quiz nights to satellite TV and live music.

Check out *The Celt Bar* and *Twiins* on Rua António Feu for Irish atmosphere and brews, *Kerri's Bar* (just before the turismo) for Finnish liqueurs or the popular *Shaker Bar* opposite Pensão Solar Pinguim for some boppier beats.

The classy *Casino (☎ 41 50 01)*, in the Hotel Algarve mid-way along the esplanade, has slot machines (admission free; open 4 pm to 3 am), a gambling room (500$00 admission, plus passport and respectable attire; open 7.30 pm to 3 am) and a nightly dinner show (8.30 pm dinner; 10.30 pm show) for 6500$00 (2000$00 show only).

Getting There & Away

Buses for Praia da Rocha leave Portimão every 15 minutes in summer until midnight; the fare is 190$00 (85$00 if you buy a block of five or 10 tickets). The bus terminus in Praia da Rocha is by the fort, with another stop behind the central Hotel da Rocha on Rua Engenheiro José Bívar. Change at Portimão for other destinations. The last bus back to Portimão leaves Praia da Rocha at around 11.30 pm.

Praia da Rocha is on the itinerary of several regional coach tours. You can also pick up day trips from here to other destinations in the Algarve, and even to Seville in Spain.

Getting Around

Among several motorbike/bicycle rental agencies, Citycar (☎ 41 71 41) offers some of the best deals, including 3000$00 for three days for a mountain bike and 15,000$00 for three days for a Chopper XV 250. Local car rental agencies with low rates include Auto Rent (☎ 41 71 72) and Citycar.

The Windward Coast & Costa Vicentina

LAGOS

☎ 082 • pop 22,100 (municipality)

Heaving with young people all summer, bursting with restaurants, boutiques, bars and clubs, and adjacent to some of the Algarve's best beaches and most dramatic coastline, cheerful Lagos has acquired a reputation as a good-time town (though see Dangers & Annoyances under Information at the start of this chapter).

Contrasting with this modern-day identity is its honoured history as the point of origin for most of the voyages during Portugal's extraordinary Age of Discoveries. Other than sturdy town walls and the layout of the steep and narrow streets, only a few fragments of this period survived the devastating 1755 earthquake.

History

Phoenicians and Greeks established themselves at this port (later called Lacobriga by the Romans) at the mouth of the muddy Rio Bensafrim. Afonso III recaptured it from the Moors in 1241, and it was from here that the Portuguese carried on harassing the Muslims of North Africa. In 1415 a giant fleet set sail from Lagos under the command of the 21-year-old Prince Henry (see the boxed text under History in the Facts about Portugal chapter) to seize Ceuta in Morocco – and set the stage for Portugal's groping exploration of the West African coast and the successes of its ambitious Age of Discoveries.

Lagos shipyards built and launched Prince Henry's caravels, and Henry split his time between his own trading company here and his school of navigation at Sagres. Local boy Gil Eanes left here in command of the first ship to round West Africa's Cape Bojador in 1434. Others continued to bring back information about the African coast – along with ivory, gold, and slaves. Lagos has the dubious distinction of having hosted (in 1444) the first sale of black Africans as slaves to Europeans, and it subsequently grew into a centre of the slave trade. The former customs house on a corner of Praça da República supposedly stands on the site of the first slave market.

It was also from Lagos in 1578 that Dom Sebastião, along with the cream of Portuguese nobility and an army of Portuguese, Spanish, Dutch and German buccaneers, left on his disastrous crusade to Christianise North Africa, which ended in a debacle at Alcácer-Quibir in Morocco. Sir Francis Drake inflicted heavy damage on the town a few years later, in 1587.

Lagos served as the Algarve's high-profile capital from 1576 until the 1755 earthquake, which flattened the city and brought its illustrious career to an end.

Orientation

The N125 highway comes right in along the riverfront as Avenida dos Descobrimentos. Drivers are strongly advised to leave their cars here – or head for one of the signposted free car parks – to avoid getting trapped in the inner town's web of narrow one-way lanes.

The administrative hub of Lagos is the pedestrianised Praça Gil Eanes (say 'zheel yenesh'), at the centre of which is a ridiculous statue of Dom Sebastião looking like a teenage girl astronaut.

ALGARVE

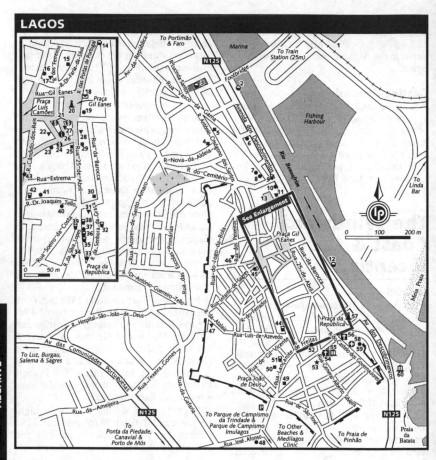

LAGOS

Both the long-distance bus station and the train station are north of the walled centre: the bus station is roughly 500m from Praça Gil Eanes and the train station is on the other side of the river, accessible by a footbridge.

Information
Tourist Offices The turismo (☎ 76 30 31) is in the centre of town on Rua Marquês de Pombal. It's open weekdays from 9.30 am to 12.30 pm and 2 to 5 pm (later in sum-

mer), and often at weekends, but with no fixed schedule. Some of the staff aren't very helpful.

For entertainment information you'll do better to check out the listings in the privately produced, frequently updated free map called *The Best of Lagos & Alvor*, available from better residenciais, shops and bars.

Lagos' big Gypsy market takes place on the first Saturday of the month, behind the train station.

LAGOS

PLACES TO STAY		OTHER			
4	Hotel de Lagos	1	Gypsy Market	36	Eddie's Bar
5	Residencial Solar	2	Boat Trips	37	Motoride
15	Residencial Lagosmar	3	Bus Station	38	Zanzibar
25	Residencial Caravela	6	Auto Jardim	39	Shaker's
29	Residencial Marazul	7	Avis	40	Loja do Livro
30	Residencial Baía;	8	Luzcar	41	Centro de Línguas
	Residencial Rubi-Mar	9	Shell Petrol Station;	42	Rosko's
49	Sra Benta Pereira		Sidecar 32	43	Caixa de Correio
	Chaves	10	Renex Ticket Office	44	Mullens
50	Pousada da Juventude	12	Ferry to Meia Praia	45	InforMédia
		13	Mercado Municipal	48	Motoride
PLACES TO EAT		14	Taxi Stand	51	Taverna Velha
11	Restaurante Bar Barros	16	Lavandaria Aida	52	Centro Cultural
17	Adega Tipica A Forja	18	Post & Telecom Office	53	Police Station
22	Restaurante Kalunga	19	Câmara Municipal	54	Igreja de Santo
27	Restaurante Piri-Piri	20	Statue of Dom Sebastião		António
28	O Cantinho Algarvio	21	Banks	55	Museu Municipal
31	Restaurante	23	Club Algarve	56	Igreja de Santa Maria
	Mediterraneo	24	Uni Câmbio	57	Statue of Henry
34	Restaurante O João	26	Turismo		the Navigator
46	Adega Ribatejana	32	Mil Copus Bar	58	Hospital
47	Restaurante A	33	Customs House	59	Manueline Window
	Muralha	35	Stones	60	Fortaleza da Ponta
					da Bandeira

ALGARVE

Money There are banks with Multibanco ATMs and currency exchange machines around Praça Gil Eanes. There's also a private exchange bureau, Uni Câmbio, opposite the turismo, open daily from 10 am to 7 pm during summer. It charges only 400$00 commission for travellers cheques and 200$00 for cash.

Post & Communications The central post and telephone office (open weekdays only) is just off Praça Gil Eanes.

At the time of research there were no cybercafés in Lagos. But at Caixa de Correio, or The Mailbox (☎ 76 89 50, fax 76 89 51, email mailbox@ip.pt), Rua Cândido dos Reis 54, you can send or receive an email for 300$00, use the computer for 500$00 (15 minutes), or send a fax for 450$00 per page (plus 40$00 per telephone unit). It also offers secretarial, translation, UPS (United Parcel Service) and post office box services. It's open weekdays from 9 am to 5.30 pm. Guests at Hotel de Lagos can send emails from the hotel office.

For computer bits and pieces, check out InforMédia (☎ 76 10 93, fax 76 19 04) at Rua Infante de Sagres 11.

Bookshop Loja do Livro bookshop, at Rua Dr Joaquim Tello 3, has a small supply of English, French and German-language paperbacks as well as some English and Portuguese-language CD Roms.

Laundry A fairly quick laundry service is available at the youth hostel (see Places to Stay later in this section). Lavandaria Aida, at Rua Conselheiro Joaquim Machado 28, does a two day service.

Medical & Emergency Services The hospital (☎ 76 30 34, 76 28 06) is on Rua do Castelo dos Governadores, just off Praça da República. One of several private clinics is Medilagos (☎ 76 01 81), which offers a 24 hour emergency service. It's south-west of town, at Amejeira de Cima, Bela Vista, Lote 2. The central police station (☎ 76 29 30) is on Rua General Alberto Silveira.

Igreja de Santo António & Museu Municipal

A block south of the Praça da República, on Rua General Alberto Silveira, is Lagos' main historical attraction, the little Igreja de Santo António. It has an astonishing interior of gilded, carved wood – a Baroque extravaganza of ripening grapes and beaming cherubs. The dome and the azulejo panels were installed during repairs made after the 1755 earthquake.

Enter from the street or from the adjacent Museu Municipal (☎ 76 23 01), an odd but appealing collection of azulejos, 16th century grave markers, pickled foetuses, coins, handicrafts and church vestments. It's open daily, except Monday and holidays, from 9.30 am to 12.30 pm and 2 to 5 pm; admission costs 340$00.

Igreja de Santa Maria

This church facing the Praça da República is of interest mainly for its 16th century entrance; most of the rest dates from the mid-19th century. Check out the spacey mural behind the altar.

Town Walls

Just south of Praça da República is a restored section of the stout town walls, built (atop earlier versions) during the reigns of Manuel I and João III in the 16th century. In fact they extend intermittently, with at least six bastions, for about 1.5km around the central town.

Tradition has it that Dom Sebastião attended an open-air Mass here and spoke to the assembled nobility from an elaborate Manueline window in the wall adjacent to the present-day hospital, before leading them to defeat at Alcácer-Quibir.

Fortaleza da Ponta da Bandeira

This little fortress at the southern end of Avenida dos Descobrimentos was built in the 17th century to protect the port. It now houses a museum on the Portuguese discoveries. The building is open daily, except Monday, from 10 am to 6 pm; admission is 340$00 (half-price for youth card holders).

Beaches

Meia Praia, the vast expanse of sand to the east of town, has sailboard rental outlets and water-skiing lessons, plus lots of laid-back restaurants and beach bars. South of town the beaches – Batata, Pinhão, Dona Ana, Camilo and others – are smaller and more secluded, lapped by calm waters and punctuated with amazing grottoes, coves and towers of coloured sandstone.

You can walk to most of them, or visit these and others on the south-facing headlands, including Canavial and Porto de Mós, by boat (see Boat Trips under Activities later in this section).

Ponta da Piedade

Aside from its beaches, Lagos' big geophysical attraction is Piety Point, a dramatic wedge of headland protruding south from Lagos. Three windswept kilometres out of town, the point is well worth a visit for its contorted, polychrome sandstone cliffs and towers, complete with lighthouse and hundreds of nesting egrets. The surrounding area is brilliant with wild orchids in spring. On a clear day you can see east to Carvoeiro and west to Sagres.

Activities

Horse Riding Tiffany's (☎ 082-6 93 95) at Vale Grifo in Almádena, about 10km west of Lagos off the N125, charges 3000$00 an hour and has various adventure trails from 6000$00. They'll come and get you if you have no wheels. Another centre with similar rates and activities (including an overnight trip to the west coast) is Quinta Paraíso (☎ 6 72 63, fax 78 83 07) at Fronteira, about 7km north of Lagos off the N120.

Boat Trips Various operators have ticket stands at the marina or along the promenade opposite the marina. Bom Dia (☎ 76 46 70, mobile ☎ 0931 81 07 61) runs near-shore trips on traditional schooners, with drinks, picnic and stops for swimming and snorkelling. Tours available include a two hour trip to the beaches and grottoes beneath Ponta da Piedade for 2500$00, a

5½ hour bay cruise for 5500$00, or a full-day sail to Sagres with a minibus tour of Cabo de São Vicente for 7900$00.

Espadarte do Sul (☎ 76 18 20) does similar jaunts to the grottoes, plus snorkelling and big-game fishing trips. Bluewater Sportsfishing (☎ 79 20 75, mobile ☎ 0931 82 00 44) specialises in half-day and full-day deep-sea fishing trips. A day of fishing costs 11,000$00 (7000$00 for spectators), plus 1500$00 for lunch. Aquabus (☎ 76 77 94), billed as 'the floating submarine', does one-hour trips throughout the day, for about 3400$00.

Local fishermen offering jaunts to the grottoes by motorboat also trawl for customers along the promenade.

Bike Trips Readers have recommended Cycle Paths, which organises full-day bike trips for around 5000$00 per person including lunch. It also does longer excursions to Morocco. Tickets and information are available from Eddie's Bar (☎ 76 83 29), Rua 25 de Abril 99.

Places to Stay

In addition to a few pensões and residenciais, Lagos abounds in resort-style hotels and *albergarias* (inns), motels and rental apartment blocks. There are more places out on Meia Praia and south on Praia da Dona Ana. Most are filled to the gunwales in summer, though you can always track down something adequate if you're only staying for a day or two. Prices are highest from July to August or September. We give midsummer rates here.

Camping The small *Parque de Campismo da Trindade* (☎ 76 38 93) is just 200m south of the Lançarote gate in the town walls. It costs 500/500/250$00 per person/ tent/car.

Pricier and more upmarket is the huge *Parque de Campismo Imulagos* (☎ 76 00 31, fax 76 00 35). Its 60 bungalows (around 9000$00 for two people) get booked out in summer, but those who have tents or caravans should have no problem finding a spot

here (there are about 1400 sites). Prices are 900/450/400$00 per person/tent/car (more in August). There's also a market, laundrette, bar and restaurant. It's on the road to Porto de Mós, about 1km from town. From June through September there is also an hourly free shuttle bus from the train station.

Hostels The *pousada da juventude* (☎ 76 19 70, Rua Lançarote de Freitas 50) is one of the best in Portugal. In addition to dorm beds for 2000$00 it's also got doubles with private bathroom (4700$00), kitchen facilities and a useful notice board. It's open 24 hours.

Private Rooms Plenty of private, unlicensed quartos are available in summer and their owners will harass you to distraction all over town; anyone wearing a daypack is a target. Figure on about 5500$00 for a double, though quality varies widely. The tidy rooms belonging to the conscientious *Sra Benta Pereira Chaves* (☎ 76 09 40, Travessa do Forno 13A) are particularly useful for those with a car: a big (free) car parking area is nearby, just outside the city walls.

Residenciais The small, glum *Residencial Baía* (☎ 76 22 92, Rua da Barocca 70) has overpriced doubles with shower for 6000$00. Upstairs at the same address is the friendlier and more comfortable *Residencial Rubi-Mar* (☎ 76 31 65, fax 76 77 49), where doubles cost 5000/7000$00 (with/ without bathroom). You need to book at least a week ahead in summer.

In the central pedestrian zone is the *Residencial Caravela* (☎ 76 33 61, Rua 25 de Abril 8) where plain doubles with shower are 6000$00. Across the way at No 13, the bigger *Residencial Marazul* (☎ 76 97 49, fax 76 99 60) has comfortable doubles costing from around 9000$00.

The friendly, professionally run *Residencial Lagosmar* (☎ 76 32 22, fax 76 73 24, Rua Dr Faria da Silva 13) has single/ double rooms with bathroom, telephone and

TV for 8000/10,000$00. Near the bus station, the modern **Residencial Solar** (*☎ 76 24 77, fax 76 17 84, Rua António Crisógono dos Santos 60*) has big, simply furnished rooms (all with bathroom and fridge) from 12,000$00.

The spiffy **Hotel de Lagos** (*☎ 76 99 67, fax 76 99 20, email hotel-lagos@mail .telepac.pt, Rua Nova da Aldeia*) charges 22,560$00 for a double in summer.

All the above prices (except for Residencial Baía) include breakfast.

Places to Eat

There's abundant good food in town, both Portuguese and international, though restaurants in the centre can be pricey. The best bargains are at lunch time when you'll find special 'light meals' for under 900$00 a dish. Also check out some of the bars under Entertainment for food options.

Restaurante Piri-Piri (*☎ 76 38 03, Rua Lima Leitão 15*) offers special prices for small dishes (from 700$00 to 900$00), and even cataplana dishes for one (1950$00). Just round the corner, **O Cantinho Algarvio** (*☎ 76 12 89, Rua Afonso d'Almeida 17*) has Algarve specialities at slightly higher prices; it's closed Sunday.

Restaurante O João (*☎ 76 10 67, Rua da Silva Lopes 15*) is a cosy nook with reasonably priced dishes (and candlelit tables at night). A modest, popular restaurant called **Adega Tipica A Forja** (*☎ 76 85 88, Rua dos Ferreiros 17*) dishes up good daily specials, in portions that will test your stomach's capacity, for around 1500$00.

Off the main tourist trail, the **Adega Ribatejana** (*☎ 76 08 06, Rua dos Peixeiros 1*) is great value for money. And for *cozinha regional* (regional cuisine), **Restaurante Bar Barros** (*☎ 76 22 76, Rua Portas de Portugal 83*), right by the mercado municipal, is a popular local choice.

Restaurante A Muralha (*☎ 76 36 59, Rua da Atalaia 15*), in the shadow of the city walls, is open from 7 pm to 4 am (except Monday), with late suppers to the sound of fado. Stylish but not extravagant dining is available at **Restaurante Mediter-**raneo (*☎ 76 84 76, Rua da Senhora da Graça 2*). And for something a little different, try the Angolan dishes at **Restaurante Kalunga** (*☎ 76 07 27, Rua Marquês de Pombal 26*).

Entertainment

Bars Lagos is chock-a-block with bars and cafés, most of them staying open to around 4 am in summer. Young people make spare cash by handing out flyers about them in summer; before you chuck these in the bin, check for the occasional good discount. Among the more popular places are **Taverna Velha** (*Rua Lançarote de Freitas 54*), a few steps along from the youth hostel, the Irish bar, **Rosko's** (*☎ 76 39 05, Rua Cândido dos Reis 79*), bars on Rua 25 de Abril including **Eddie's Bar** at No 99, **Stones** at No 101 and **Shaker's** at No 68, and **Mil Copus Bar** (*Rua da Senhora da Graça 9*).

One of the best bars serving good food plus music, too, is **Mullens** (*Rua Cândido dos Reis 86*). The bar is open in summer from noon to 2 am, with food from 7 to 11 pm. Another is **Zanzibar** (*Rua 25 de Abril 93*) which has a salad bar, vegetarian offerings, sandwiches and all-day breakfasts to the tunc of indie/alternative music.

Out at Meia Praia, the **Linda Bar** (*☎ 76 16 51*) has appealing pub grub and tunes, with a Friday night BBQ party.

Concerts & Exhibitions Lagos' main venue for classical recitals and performances, as well as art exhibitions, is the **Centro Cultural** (*☎ 76 34 03*) on Rua Lançarote de Freitas. It's open daily from 10 am to 8 pm and also has a café serving bargain pratos do dia.

Getting There & Away

Bus From the long-distance bus station (*☎ 76 29 44*) express Linha Litoral services run six times daily to Portimão and twice to Faro (about 1000$00). Only one of these continues to Vila Real de Santo António (about 1100$00). There are also faster and more frequent trans rápido services to Portimão and Faro (1¾ hours). Sagres has bus connections every hour or two.

Six EVA express coaches run to/from Lisbon each day (2200$00), plus at least four faster alta qualidade services. Renex also has a frequent express service to Lisbon (2350$00); tickets for these are available from its office at Rua das Portas de Portugal 101.

In summer, Intersul runs express coaches between Lagos and Seville (in Spain), four to six times a week for about 3000$00.

Train Lagos is at the western end of the Algarve branch line, with three IR trains a day and a host of slower ones running to Vila Real de Santo António. There are at least five trains a day to Lisbon; IR services take 5½ hours (2020$00), IC trains take around 4½ hours (2170$00). Nearly all require a change at Tunes.

Getting Around
Car Typical three/seven-day rates for a rental car are about 12,500/25,000$00. Try Auto Rent (☎ 0800 22011, fax 78 95 10), Auto Jardim (☎ 76 94 86) or Luzcar (☎ 76 10 16, next to Avis on Rua Vasco da Gama).

Alternatively, contact Club Algarve travel agency (☎ 76 31 78, fax 76 17 28) at Rua Marreiros Neto 25; staff there can arrange car or bike rental as well as tours and flights (with good discounts for seniors and students).

Motorcycle & Bicycle Motoride (☎ 76 17 20) rents out bikes, scooters and motorcycles from Rua José Afonso 23, just outside the town walls, or through agents in the centre (such as the one on Rua 25 de Abril). Typical rates for three/seven days are about 2800/5600$00 for a mountain bike, 9000/18,000$00 for a scooter, and 14,000/28,000$00 and up for a motorbike. Expect prices to rise by about 7% during August.

Sidecar 32 (☎ 76 31 77), based at the Shell petrol station at the southern end of Rua Vasco da Gama, also rents scooters and motorbikes.

Taxi There is a taxi rank at the bottom of Rua das Portas de Portugal. To call a taxi, ring ☎ 76 35 87 or 76 32 19.

Ferry Ferries run to and fro across the estuary to the Meia Praia side in summer; they leave from a landing just north of the Praça da República.

FROM LAGOS TO SAGRES
The steep and rugged shoreline west of Lagos has been the last segment of the southern coastline to fall prey to developers. Due to their fine beaches, the once-sleepy fishing hamlets are rapidly being 'resortified', but in the low season there's still a lingering sense of isolation.

Praia da Luz, just 6km from Lagos, has the most tourist facilities, villas and day-trippers. Fronting its small sandy beach is the Sea Sports Centre (☎/fax 082-78 95 38), offering scuba diving lessons, equipment for sale or rental, and fishing trips.

A more picturesque alternative, 6km further west, is tiny, cobbled **Burgau**, which sees far too many visitors in summer for its own good. Best of the lot, perhaps, is **Salema**, set on a wide bay 17km from Lagos. Despite the apartment blocks rising like mushrooms around it, Salema has an easy-going atmosphere and there are several small, secluded beaches within a few kilometres – **Praia da Salema** by the village, **Praia da Figueira** to the west and **Boca do Rio** to the east.

Salema also has a helpful travel agency called Horizonte (☎ 082-69 59 20, fax 69 58 55), in a commercial arcade about 300m uphill to the west from the boat landing. It can help with hotel and villa accommodation (often at discounted prices), moped and car rental, boat trips and bus tickets. It also runs good jeep trips within the Parque Natural do Sudoeste Alentejano e Costa Vicentina (see boxed text later in this chapter).

Places to Stay
Unless you pre-book a villa your best bet for summer accommodation is in Salema. Squads of residents there offer overpriced

ALGARVE

quartos, typically 6000$00 or more for a double with a bathroom. If money is no object, rise above it all at Salema's elegant *Estalagem Infante do Mar* (☎ 082-69 01 00, fax 69 01 09), perched high above the beach, or down below at *Hotel Residencial Salema* (☎ 082-69 53 28, fax 69 53 29). Prices for doubles at both places are around 13,000$00 and advance reservations are essential.

The nearest camp sites are the Orbitur *Valverde Camping* (☎ 082-78 92 11), at 730/630/620$00 per person/tent/car, and the cheaper, Turiscampo-run *Camping de Espiche* (☎ 082-78 82 05), both about 2km from Luz. Just 1.5km north of Salema is the comfortable *Quinta dos Carriços* (☎ 082-69 52 01, fax 69 51 22), which also has studios and apartments and even its own secluded naturist camping area. Camp site prices are 640/640/640 per person/tent/car.

Getting There & Away

Most of the Lagos-Sagres buses (around a dozen daily) call in at these villages; if not, they're only about a 2km walk from the main N125.

SAGRES
☎ 082 • pop 1500

Blasted by a steady, cutting wind and huge Atlantic waves, and with sheer cliffs facing a sea horizon on three sides, the Ponta de Sagres promontory at the western end of the Algarve seems the very edge of Europe. Its position and the austere landscape surely figured in Prince Henry the Navigator's choice of this place for a new, fortified town and a semimonastic school of navigation that specialised in cartography, astronomy and ship design, and set Portugal on course for the Age of Discoveries.

At least, that is what the current mix of history and myth says. Henry was, among other things, governor of the Algarve and had a residence in its primary port town, Lagos, from where most expeditions actually set sail. He certainly did put together a kind of nautical think-tank, though how much thinking actually went on out at

Sagres is not known. He had a house somewhere near Sagres, where he died in November 1460. In any case, he did have close links with the town and it's easy to see why.

In May 1587 the English privateer Sir Francis Drake, in the course of harassing supply lines to the Spanish Armada, captured and wrecked the fortifications around Sagres. The Ponta de Sagres was refortified after the earthquake of 1755, which had left little of verifiable antiquity standing.

Paradoxically, quirky ocean currents give Sagres some of Portugal's mildest winter weather and Atlantic winds keep the summers cool.

Orientation

From Vila do Bispo, the administrative centre of the district at the western end of the N125, a 10km gauntlet of villas along the N268 attests to the arrival of development even in this remote corner of the Algarve.

From a roundabout at the end of the N268, roads go west for 6km to the Cabo de São Vicente, south for 1km to the Ponta de Sagres and east for 250m to little Praça da República at the head of Sagres town (what there is of it). One kilometre east of the square, past age-of-tourism hotels and apartments, is the port, still a centre for boat building and lobster fishing.

Information

There's a small, knowledgeable turismo (☎ 62 48 73) 100m east of Praça da República on Rua Comandante Matoso (near a triangular monument). It's open weekdays from 9.30 am to 12.30 pm and 2 to 5.30 pm and on Saturday from 9.30 am to 12.30 pm.

In addition, there's an efficient private tourist agency on Praça da República called Turinfo (☎ 62 00 03, fax 62 00 04), where you'll find brochures, currency exchange, stamps, excursions, bicycle and car rental, and contacts for private rooms and flats. It also seems to own half the bars and eateries in town. It's open daily from 10 am to 1 pm and 2 to 7 pm.

There's a bank and ATM just beyond the turismo. The main post office is 600m north-east of the square on Rua do Mercado. The nearest medical clinic is the centro de saúde (☎ 6 61 79, ☎ 6 60 70) in Vila do Bispo.

An excellent local history booklet, called *Sagres* and published by the Vila do Bispo town council, is on sale at Turinfo.

Fortaleza de Sagres

The Sagres fortress (which dates in its present form from 1793) is more impressive from outside than inside, consisting only of a massive front wall and two bastions. Apparently there were short lateral walls inside as well once – the flat promontory's sheer cliffs were protection enough around the rest.

Just inside the gate is a stone *rosa dos ventos*, or wind rose (for measuring the direction of the wind), 43m in diameter. It was excavated in the 18th century and possibly built for Prince Henry.

It seems unlikely that much else except the foundations dates from that time, though the oldest buildings, including a cistern tower to the east, a house and the small Igreja da Nossa Senhora da Graça to the west, and the remnants of a wall running part of the way across may have been built upon what was there before. Many of the gaps between the buildings are the result of a 1950s clearance of 17th and 18th century ruins to make way for a reconstruction (later aborted) to coincide with the 500th anniversary of Henry's death.

In 1992 the state pulled down the 18th century building that housed the youth hostel and replaced it with an ugly little

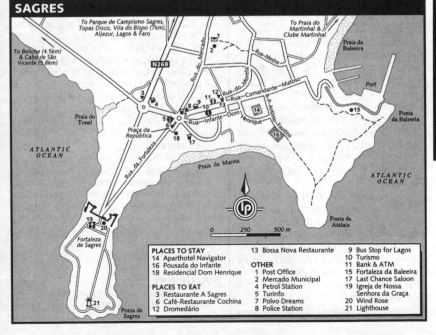

ALGARVE

PLACES TO STAY	13 Bossa Nova Restaurante	9 Bus Stop for Lagos
14 Aparthotel Navigator		10 Turismo
16 Pousada do Infante	OTHER	11 Bank & ATM
18 Residencial Dom Henrique	1 Post Office	15 Fortaleza da Baleeira
	2 Mercado Municipal	17 Last Chance Saloon
PLACES TO EAT	4 Petrol Station	19 Igreja de Nossa
3 Restaurante A Sagres	5 Turinfo	Senhora da Graça
6 Café-Restaurante Cochina	7 Polvo Dreams	20 Wind Rose
12 Dromedário	8 Police Station	21 Lighthouse

museum, next to the cistern tower. Near the southern end of the promontory is a modern lighthouse. Death-defying anglers with huge rods perch atop the cliffs all around, hoping to land bream or sea bass (though we never saw them catch anything).

Access to the fort costs 300$00.

Other Forts

Overlooking Sagres harbour are the ruins of the small **Fortaleza da Baleeira**, thought to have been built in the mid-16th century to protect the harbour.

The **Fortaleza do Beliche**, built in 1632 on the site of an older one, is 4.5km from the Sagres roundabout on the way to Cabo de São Vicente. Inside is a small chapel on the site of the ruined Igreja de Santa Catarina (and possibly an old convent), as well as a restaurant and two double rooms for rent. The rooms cost 14,300$00 and can be booked through the Pousada do Infante (see Places to Stay later in this section).

Cabo de São Vicente

No visit to Sagres would be complete without a trip to Cape St Vincent, Europe's south-westernmost point. Awesome is the only word for this barren, throne-like headland, which was the last piece of home that nervous Portuguese sailors would have seen as they headed out into the unknown sea.

The cape – a revered place even in the time of the Phoenicians and known to the Romans as Promontorium Sacrum – takes its present name from a Spanish priest martyred by the Romans (see the boxed text). The old fortifications, trashed by Sir Francis Drake in 1587, were subsequently reduced to rubble by the 1755 earthquake.

At the end of the cape are a powerful lighthouse (hundreds of ocean-going ships round this point every day) and a former convent. Some scholars place Henry the Navigator's house in a small castle to the right of the lighthouse grounds.

The best time to come here is at sunset, when you can almost hear the hissing as the sun settles into the sea. It would make a stunning clifftop walk from Sagres, though it's almost 6km each way in a stiff wind. There are cafés or restaurants in several places along the road. There is no public transport, but you can get a taxi through the turismo or Turinfo.

Beaches

There are four good beaches within a short drive or long walk from Sagres: Praia da Mareta just below the town; Praia do Martinhal to the east; Praia do Tonel on the other side of the Ponta de Sagres; and the isolated Praia de Beliche, on the way to the Cabo de São Vicente. The Praia da Baleeira, adjacent to the harbour, is pretty polluted from all the boat traffic.

Activities

Turinfo can arrange jeep trips and bike tours to beaches along the Costa Vicentina or into the Serra de Monchique, full-day minibus

---

ALGARVE

St Vincent

St Vincent (São Vicente) was a Spanish preacher killed by the Romans in 304 in Valencia. Various legends say his body was either washed up at the Cabo de São Vicente, or borne here on a boat accompanied by ravens (or perhaps carrion crows, like those still common in the area). A shrine, which Muslim chronicles refer to as the Crow Church, was built and became an object of Christian pilgrimage even in Moorish times, though it was apparently destroyed by Muslim fanatics in the 12th century.

Afonso Henriques, Portugal's first king, quick to see the saint's symbolic value, had the remains moved to Lisbon in 1173, again by ship and again supposedly accompanied by ravens. St Vincent was made Lisbon's patron saint (his remains now rest in the Igreja de São Vicente de Fora there) and there is a raven on the city's coat of arms.

tours to Monchique and Silves, boat trips along the coast east as far as Lagos and fishing trips through local operator Cabo de São Vicente Cruzeiros (☎ 62 44 42, mobile ☎ 0931 34 06 42).

Praia do Martinhal is the focus for windsurfing (the water is wetsuit-cold). At Mareta the Clube Martinhal aquatic sports centre (☎ 62 43 33) offers sea-kayaking day trips, windsurfing, snorkelling and, in

Parque Natural do Sudoeste Alentejano e Costa Vicentina

The South-West Alentejo & Costa Vicentina Natural Park is a strip of rugged, sparsely developed coastline with high cliffs and ragged coastal outcrops, isolated beaches, inlets and estuaries. It runs for about 120km from Burgau to Cabo de São Vicente and up nearly the entire western Algarve and Alentejo shore. It's rarely more than 5 or 6km wide, except where it follows the Rio Mira valley to Odemira in the Alentejo.

Established in 1995, the park was amalgamated from several protected areas in an effort to forestall development and protect an ecosystem rich and complex enough to have been designated a 'biogenetic reserve' by the Council of Europe. Here there are at least 48 plant species that are found only in Portugal, and a dozen or so found only within the park. Otters thrive in the river valleys, foxes roam in areas near the shore, and a few lynx and other wild cats lurk in the deeper valleys. The most visible wildlife is birds: some 200 species enjoy the coastal wetlands, salt marshes and cliffs, including Portugal's last remaining ospreys. Storks nest on coastal outcrops. This is also an important migratory stop in spring and autumn.

The N268/N120 road roller-coasters for long stretches along the inland edge of the pine-scented and silent park, passing through hills deeply etched by rivers on their way to the sea. The most picturesque stretches are north and south of Carrapateira and between Rogil and Odeceixe.

Information

The park headquarters (☎ 083-2 27 35, fax 2 28 30) are at Rua Serpa Pinto 32 in Odemira, in the Alentejo. There's another office in Aljezur (☎ 082-99 86 73). Colour brochures on the park are also available at Turinfo in Sagres.

Beaches

The west coast is lined with good beaches backed up against cliffs or sand dunes; some of them are huge and relatively empty, even in summer. Among good ones that are relatively accessible in a sturdy car or by public transport (see Getting There & Away under From Sagres to Aljezur later) are Castelejo (north-west of Vila do Bispo), Bordeira (by Carrapateira), Arrifana and Monte Clérigo (near Aljezur) and Odeceixe. A great many others are only accessible if you have a 4WD or a healthy appetite for walking.

Guided Tours

Access by jeeps and other vehicles has been limited since the area became a natural park, but there are a few good options. Horizonte (☎ 082-69 59 20, fax 69 58 55) in Salema is the only operator that has official permission to take jeep tours through the park. Its culturally-sensitive, low-impact 4WD trips (using no more than two jeeps at a time) visit Cabo de São Vicente, the west coast and several isolated villages to watch the locals making bread, honey and medronho firewater. A day trip with lunch costs about 7000$00.

summer, scuba diving. Also organising diving trips is the Diving Centre (☎ 62 47 36, fax 62 44 25). Surfing is possible at all beaches except Martinhal.

Places to Stay

Sagres gets crowded with tourists in summer, though it's marginally easier to find accommodation here than in the rest of the Algarve during the high season, especially if you arrive before noon. You can also try getting a room through Turinfo.

Camping The well-maintained *Parque de Campismo Sagres* (☎ 62 43 51, fax 62 44 45) is 2km from town, just off the road to Vila do Bispo. Prices are 600/500/350$00 per person/tent/car (higher in August). About 17km east from Sagres, on the beach south of Raposeira, is the basic and slightly cheaper *Ingrina Camping* (☎ 62 62 42, 63 92 42), which charges 480/480/450$00 per person/tent/car.

Other Options Every other house in Sagres seems to advertise private quartos; you may well get pounced on at the bus stop. Doubles generally go for 3500$00 to 6000$00 and flats for between 7000$00 and 15,000$00 at the height of the season. On Praça da República is the Turinfo-managed *Residencial Dom Henrique* (☎ 62 00 03, fax 62 00 04), where a double with sea view costs from 12,000$00 to 15,000$00.

At the giant *Aparthotel Navigator* (☎ 62 43 54), just off Rua Infante Dom Henrique, a double apartment in high season costs about 16,000$00. Nearby, the very elegant *Pousada do Infante* (☎ 62 42 22, fax 62 42 25) offers posh doubles for 23,000$00. The little *fortaleza* at Beliche has two double rooms for 14,300$00. You can try booking them through the pousada, but they're said to be booked up about three years ahead!

Except at the pousada, all prices drop by 50% or even more outside summer.

Places to Eat

There are several café-restaurants in and around Praça da República (of these, *Café-*

Restaurante Cochina has a large and reasonably priced restaurant menu), as well as on the main Rua Comandante Matoso. *Dromedário* bistro-bar (☎ 6 42 19, Rua Infante Dom Henrique) serves fresh juices and muesli for breakfast from 10 am, pizzas during the day and drinks till 3 am. The nearby *Bossa Nova Restaurante* (☎ 6 45 66), includes salads and vegetarian dishes on its menu; it's open from noon to midnight in summer. Cheap, filling meals can also be had at the *Restaurante A Sagres* at the roundabout as you enter the village.

Entertainment

A cheerful place for a drink with a sea view is the *Last Chance Saloon*, just down the hill from the square. Both this and *Polvo Dreams* bar-pub (which has satellite TV and video games) opposite the square are open until 4 am. For nightly live music until dawn, head for *Topas Disco*, near the Parque de Campismo.

Getting There & Away

About a dozen coaches a day run between Sagres and Lagos, with fewer services on Sunday and holidays. Buses stop at Praça da República. The stop for buses returning to Lagos is opposite the triangular kiosk (near the turismo) on Rua Comandante Matoso.

Getting Around

Turinfo can arrange for a rental car from Lagos. You can also rent mountain bikes for 1900$00 a day (1200$00 for a half-day).

FROM SAGRES TO ALJEZUR

Heading north along the Algarve's west coast you'll find some great beaches, largely free of development thanks to the Atlantic's cool, choppy, sometimes dangerous seas, and building restrictions imposed by the Parque Natural do Sudoeste Alentejano e Costa Vicentina.

The first worthwhile stop is Carrapateira, 14km north of Vila do Bispo, with two fine beaches. The dune-dominated **Praia da Bordeira** 2km to the north, is popular with casual campers and has a café-restaurant; the smaller, emptier **Praia do Amado**, is 1km south of the village down a link road.

Some 20km further north is Aljezur, a straggling riverside village in two distinct halves (one Moorish, below a ruined 10th century hilltop castle; the other, called Igreja Nova, a more modern settlement to the east). Two nearby beaches are great for surfing: **Praia de Monte Clérigo**, 7km away, has a small holiday settlement, while the grand **Praia da Arrifana** (10km) is adjacent to an unfinished tourist 'town' called Vale da Telha.

Finally, clinging to the southern side of the Ribeira de Seixe valley is tiny Odeceixe, right on the Algarve/Alentejo border. Its small, lovely, very sheltered beach, **Praia de Odeceixe**, is 3.5km down the valley: a gem out of season and an almost exclusively German hang-out in high season.

Information

You can get information on accommodation, including private rooms, from the helpful staff at the turismo (☎ 082-99 82 29) in Aljezur. It's open daily from 9.30 am to 7.30 pm (closed for lunch on Monday, Friday and weekends). In Odeceixe, Hospedaria Cláudio (see Places to Stay) serves as an information centre.

Places to Stay

Camping About 3km south of Praia de Monte Clérigo is *Camping-Caravaning Vale da Telha* (☎ 082-99 84 44), which has reasonable rates of 380/380/400$00 per person/tent/car. The slightly pricier, wheelchair-accessible *Parque de Campismo Serrão* (☎ 99 85 93, *fax 082-99 86 12*) is 4km north of Aljezur then 800m down the road to Praia de Amoreira. It charges 570/470/400$00. The beach is a further 2.5km from the camp site.

Well-equipped and wheelchair accessible, *Parque de Campismo São Miguel* (☎ 082-94 71 45, fax 94 72 45) is about 2km north of Odeceixe. Book ahead in summer. Prices are 630/650/600$00. It also has some caravans for rent.

Other Options A few quartos, some rural villas and a sprinkling of pensões are available in this area. A 15 minute walk north from Praia da Bordeira, the modern *Casa Fajarra* (☎ 082-971 23) has pricey doubles at 12,000$00.

In Aljezur, *Hospedaria São Sebastião* (☎ 082-99 80 52), just south of the bridge, offers doubles with bathroom for 7500$00, while 2km north on the Lagos road the isolated *Hospedaria O Palazim* (☎ 082-99 82 49) has doubles for 5500$00 with breakfast. Good value at 2000$00 per person are the clean rooms at *Snack-Bar Tasca Matias* (☎ 082-99 10 20), Igreja Nova.

In Odeceixe, try *Hospedaria Cláudio* (☎ 082-94 71 17, Rua do Correia 12), opposite the post office, near the N120. *Pensão Luar* (☎ 94 71 94, Rua da Várzea 28), at the rear of the village, has doubles with shower from 6000$00. There's also a *pensão* (☎ 94 75 81) at the beach.

Places to Eat

During the high season you'll find food at or near all these beaches except Praia do Amado. Aljezur has the most choice: try *Restaurante Ponte-a-Pé* (☎ 082-99 88 54, Largo da Liberdade) or *Primavera* (☎ 082-99 82 94), on the N120 south of the bridge. Near the turismo is a small morning market.

Praia da Arrifana has two seafood restaurants – the *Oceano* (☎ 082-99 73 00) and the *Brisamar* (☎ 99 84 36). It also has a supermarket. At Praia da Amoreira there's *Restaurante Paraíso do Mar* (☎ 082-99 10 88), while on the road to Praia de Odeceixe is the humble *Café O Retiro do Adelino*.

Getting There & Away

At least one daily bus runs between Vila do Bispo and Aljezur, stopping at Carrapateira. A bus goes from Aljezur to the beaches (and Vale da Telha) every morning around 9 am, returning around 6.30 pm (check with the turismo). There are three buses each weekday (plus two express services) and one on Saturday from Lagos to Aljezur, continuing to Odeceixe. Aljezur also has a twice-daily bus connection with Lisbon.

The Interior

MONCHIQUE
☎ 082 • pop 6300 (municipality)

Up in the forested Serra de Monchique, 24km north of Portimão, this busy little market town begins to feel like the real Portugal at last, the densely wooded hills surrounding it a welcome touch of wilderness after all the holiday villas further south. It makes a pleasant day trip together with Caldas de Monchique, or a longer stay if you want to take advantage of the increasing number of biking, hiking or horse-riding activities.

Orientation & Information
Buses drop you right in the town centre, the Largo dos Chorões, with its eye-catching water wheel, fountain and café. Here, too, is a well-resourced turismo (☎ 91 11 89), open weekdays from 9.30 am to 12.30 pm and 2 to 5.30 pm, and Saturday from 9.30 am to noon.

Old Town
A series of brown pedestrian signs starting near the bus station directs visitors up into the town's narrow old streets and major places of interest. The Igreja Matriz is the most notable piece of architecture, thanks to an extraordinary Manueline porch decorated with twisted columns looking like lengths of knotted rope.

Further uphill is the ruined Franciscan monastery of Nossa Senhora do Desterro, built in 1632. From below, the monastery's empty shell looks sad and spooky, but its hilltop position offers a great view of the town and surrounding hills.

Activities
Zona Verde (☎/fax 91 29 86) at nearby Casais offers everything from trekking (4000$00 per person for four-hour trips, including lunch) and mountain biking (7000$00 for five hours, summer only) to canoe tours (5500$00, summer only). Call Gordon (☎ 9 51 89) for courses in yoga and tai chi, too.

German-run Nature Walk (☎ 91 10 41) organises one-day walking trips to nearby Picota peak for 3000$00 per person (children 1500$00) and full moon walks during summer. Guided bike tours for 6000$00 (or 2000$00 on your own, with a map provided) are organised by Lúcio (☎ 0936-50 43 37) and guided horse-riding trips (2500$00 for an hour plus 1500$00 per hour extra) by Gunther (☎ 91 36 57).

To soothe aching limbs after all this activity, call on Nicole Joller (☎ 91 35 22) for a massage or Uscha Storz (☎ 91 31 08) for reflexology treatment.

Places to Stay
Os Pinheiros (☎ 91 11 22) is a small, peaceful camping ground beside the Ribeira da Perna da Negra, 8km north of Monchique. The Residencial Estrela de Monchique (☎ 91 31 11, Rua do Porto Fundo 46), near the bus station in Largo dos Chorões, has good-value singles/doubles with bathroom for 3000/5000$00, and a casual, friendly café next door. A few minutes walk in the opposite direction, up Rua dos Combatentes do Ultramar, the hilltop Residencial Miradouro (☎ 91 21 63) offers breezy views and balcony rooms for 4000/6000$00. There are more upmarket places en route to Fóia: the turismo has details.

Places to Eat
The tiny, eccentric Restaurante Central (Rua da Igreja 5) has been offering the same menu to visitors for years – hundreds of scribbled rave reviews now festoon the place. But fame seems to have gone to their heads: we found better value at A Charrete (☎ 91 21 42, Rua Dr Samora Gil 30-34). This big, comfortable place, with cabinets full of local pottery and other knick-knacks, has good service and food: you can eat well here for under 2000$00.

Entertainment
Barlefante (☎ 9 27 74, Travessa da Guerreira) is a long-established, popular bar. Another option is Bar Travessa (Travessa da Portela 37).

Monchique's Moonshine

You can find commercial brands of *medronho* (a locally made firewater) everywhere in Portugal, but according to those who have suffered enough hangovers to know, the best of all is the privately made brew from Monchique.

The Serra de Monchique is thick with medronho's raw material – the arbutus, or strawberry tree. Its berries are collected in late autumn, fermented and then left for several months before being distilled in the kind of big copper stills you see for sale as tourist souvenirs all over the Algarve.

Home-made medronho is usually clear and always drunk neat, like schnapps. It's strong, of course, but as long as you don't mix it with other drinks it doesn't give you a hangover (say the connoisseurs). Early spring (when distilling is in action) is the best time to track down some of this brew in Monchique: ask around.

Getting There & Away

Nine daily bus services (five at weekends) make the 45 minute run from Portimão to Monchique. There's also a summer-only service twice a day from Albufeira via Silves.

AROUND MONCHIQUE

Fóia

The 902m Fóia peak is the Algarve's highest point; it's 8km west of Monchique and accessible by a once-daily bus service from Monchique in summer only. Along the road, which climbs through eucalyptus and pines, is a string of restaurants specialising in piri-piri chicken (see the boxed text). The peak itself is a disappointment, bristling with ugly telecommunication towers, but its panoramic views make it a popular destination for tour buses. On clear days you can see out to the corners of the Algarve – Cabo de São Vicente (near Sagres) to the southwest and Odeceixe to the north-west.

Caldas de Monchique

☎ 082

The snug hamlet of Caldas de Monchique, at the head of a delightful valley full of eucalyptus trees 6km south of Monchique, has been a popular spa for over two millennia, and still is. The Romans loved its 32°C, slightly sulphurous waters, which are said to be good for rheumatism, backache, asthma and other ailments. Dom João II came here for years in an unsuccessful attempt to cure the dropsy that finally finished him off.

Disastrous floods in 1997 led to the closure of the spa hospital in 1998, but it was expected to reopen (for long-term patients) in 1999. Meanwhile, the hamlet is  still a quaint and peaceful place, especially after the day-trippers have gone home.

Orientation Some Portimão-Monchique buses venture off the N266 on a one-way loop road round the village centre. Others only stop on the highway, leaving you with a 500m stroll down to the centre – little more than a cluster of Victorian-style buildings around a miniature square. Here you'll find Caldas' three hotels, a restaurant, several bars, and a handicrafts shop in a grandiose former casino with ersatz battlements – nearly all of them under the same management.

The most peaceful patch is the pretty, streamside garden above the square. Down the valley are the main spa hospital buildings and below these is a huge, ugly bottling

Piri-Piri

All over the Algarve, especially in and around Monchique, you'll see restaurants advertising frango piri-piri. What is it? A spicy condiment that made its way from Africa to Portuguese kitchens decades ago, piri-piri has since become a big hot hit when cooked with that all-time Portuguese favourite, frango (roast chicken).

ALGARVE

plant where the famous Caldas waters are bottled.

Places to Stay & Eat The old *Central* hotel in the square is closed while it undergoes much-needed renovation, which may last years. A double with TV, telephone and bathroom in the adjacent *Albergaria Velha* (☎ *91 01 29, fax 91 39 20)* costs 7600$00, including a big breakfast; downstairs is the posh but not outrageously expensive *Restaurante 1692*.

Decidedly upmarket is the four star *Albergaria Lageado* (☎/fax 91 38 59), set back from the square and open during the summer only.

At the junction with Caldas' exit road, some 200m downriver, the modern *Restaurante & Residencial Granifóia* (☎ *91 05 00, fax 91 22 18)* has plain doubles with shower and breakfast for about 5500$00. There's a swimming pool here, too.

Getting There & Away At least eight buses running between Portimão and Monchique stop here daily, along with the summer-only Albufeira-Monchique service via Silves twice a day.

ALCOUTIM
☎ 081 • pop 4200 (municipality)

As the N122 twists through coarse hills towards Alcoutim, along the treeless valley of the Rio Guadiana (which forms the Algarve's entire eastern border), a fine hilltop stronghold comes into view. Rounding a final bend you discover that it's actually across the river in Alcoutim's mirror image, the Spanish village of Sanlúcar de Guadiana. It's hard to imagine that Alcoutim's lower, more humble fortress was ever a match for the Spanish one.

Like dozens of other fortified villages that face each other across the Rio Guadiana, these two castles with their whitewashed, pocket-sized towns are a reminder of centuries of mutual distrust. Forts have probably risen and decayed here ever since the Phoenicians made this village an important river port. Dom Fernando I of

Portugal and Don Henrique II of Castile signed a tentative peace treaty here in the 14th century.

Nowadays the two towns beckon to one another's visitors, and of course there's no such thing as a border post any more. There isn't really much to do here, but you can wander the pretty, cobbled lanes of both towns, poke about in their castles, photograph the many elaborate chimneys and the storks nesting on top of Alcoutim's parish church, or ride a boat across (or along) the placid river.

Information
The turismo (☎ 54 61 79) is by the central square, just a couple of minutes walk from the river, and is open Tuesday to Thursday from 9.30 am to 7 pm. Other days it opens from 9.30 am to 12.30 pm and 2 to 5.30 pm.

A Casa da Cultura has recently opened, opposite the turismo, to serve as an exhibition hall and cultural centre.

Castelo
The original Portuguese castle probably dates from pre-Moorish times; what you see now is from the 14th century. Within the ruins are a handicrafts shop, a snack bar, an incongruous green lawn and excavations in progress.

River Trips
Down by the river there are signs advertising boat trips, but you need to collar a local fisherman to make arrangements. Expect to pay at least 100$00 to hop across to the other side.

Cova dos Mouros
Although advertised in glossy brochures as *Uma Aventura em Alcoutim* (An Alcoutim Adventure), this prehistoric copper mine is actually 38km west, near Vaqueiros. The site, which dates back to around 3000BC, includes evidence of a Roman presence. It also features a reconstructed prehistoric house, local handicrafts and a souvenir shop. It's open daily from 10 am to 6 pm (5 pm in winter). Admission costs 1000$00.

Places to Stay & Eat

Accommodation is sparse, though an up-market *estalagem* (inn) was being built on the main road into Alcoutim at the time of research. For cheaper accommodation, ask staff at the turismo about private quartos.

One kilometre north of the square, across a bridge and past the fire station, is the *pousada da juventude* (☎/fax 54 60 04) – open, with military precision, from 8 am to noon and 6 pm to midnight. As well as dorm beds it also has a few double rooms (without bathroom) for 3200$00.

There are several café-restaurants around the square, and a restaurant, the *Restaurante Alcâtia*, 100m across the bridge, in the direction of the youth hostel.

Getting There & Away

Alcoutim is at the end of a branch road off the N122 highway between Vila Real de Santo António and Beja in the Alentejo. On weekdays only EVA buses leave Vila Real at 9 am and 5 pm, reaching Alcoutim about 1¾ hours later. Two buses come from Beja via Mértola on weekday afternoons.

ALGARVE

The Alentejo

Torrid summers and rolling plains characterise this vast southern province, one of the poorest and least populated parts of the country, stretching *alem Tejo* (beyond the Tejo) to cover almost a third of Portugal. Coming from Lisbon or the Algarve, you'll be struck by the emptiness and the austere, mesmerising nature of the land: mile after mile of huge agricultural estates freckled with cork and olive trees and awash with wheat. City folk may find it dull (and admittedly Baixo Alentejo, in the south, has few big attractions) but if you're looking for open spaces or for a Portugal steeped in rurual traditions, here they are.

There's culture too, though, especially in the northern part of the province, Alto Alentejo. The region's biggest attraction is the delightful Renaissance city of Évora, a UNESCO World Heritage Site with well-preserved 16th century mansions, churches and a Roman temple. Nearby are the marble towns of Estremoz, Borba and Vila Viçosa, the heavily fortified frontier town of Elvas, and scores of prehistoric stone monuments.

It's the lure of the land, however, that makes the Alentejo special. Some of the country's finest rural architecture is found here, particularly in the medieval hilltop outposts of Monsaraz and Marvão. Alentejan folk dancers and singers are among the country's best. Its cuisine is one of the most distinctive, thanks to a history of pig and sheep farming and entrenched poverty which forced farmers to conjure up entire meals out of bread. The Alentejan bread-based *açorda* soups, the *migas à Alentejana* pork stews (which look disgusting but taste OK if you're ravenous) and the inspired *carne de porco à Alentejana* (pork and clam stew) are national favourites now but are still best savoured on their home turf. Don't forget to try one of the strong local *aguardente* firewaters. Even the red table wines are punchy (the best are from Borba and Reguengos de Monsaraz).

Coastal Alentejo – which includes part of the Parque Natural do Sudoeste Alentejano e Costa Vicentina (see the boxed text in the Algarve chapter) – maintains a wild provincial allure. If you like your swimming rough and refreshing, you'll love the beaches here: try the low-key resorts west of Odemira or north of Sines.

Transport between major towns is excellent, but in the sticks you're often down to a bus or two a day – which suits the pace of the province. As long as you avoid the ferocious summer heat, cycling is a great alternative for short excursions across the plains.

HISTORY

The Alentejo's early settlers left their traces everywhere in the form of scores of dolmens, menhirs and stone circles, making the Alentejo one of the country's richest

THE ALENTEJO

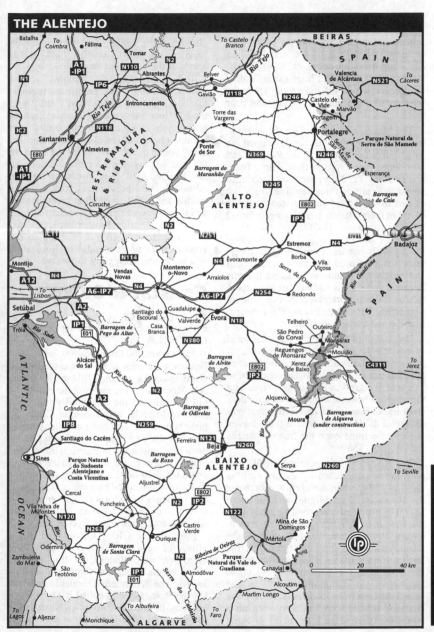

areas of prehistoric remains. It was the Romans, however, who made the greatest impact on the land, introducing crops such as vines, wheat and olives, and building dams and irrigation schemes. Most significantly, they established huge estates called *latifúndios* (which still exist today) to make the most of the region's few rivers and poor soil.

The Moors, who arrived on the scene in the early 8th century, further developed the irrigation projects set up by the Romans and introduced new crops such as citrus fruits and rice. By 1279 they were on the run to southern Spain or forced to live in special *mouraria* quarters outside town walls. Many of their citadels were later reinforced by the 'castle king', Dom Dinis, who established a chain of frontier fortresses along the Spanish border. Continuing conflicts with Spain ensured that they were rebuilt and reinforced countless times so that the Alentejo now boasts some of the most spectacular hilltop fortresses in the land at Monsaraz, Estremoz, Elvas, Beja, Serpa, Marvão and Castelo de Vide.

Despite all of the efforts of Romans and Moors, the Alentejo remained agriculturally poor and backward – increasingly so as the 15th century Age of Discoveries led to an explosive growth in maritime trade and the seaports became the focus of attention. Only Évora flourished, under the royal patronage of the House of Avis, although even this city declined once the Spanish seized the throne in 1580.

The Alentejo's low political profile was only rarely punctuated by events such as those in 1834, when the civil war between the absolutist Dom Miguel and his more liberal brother Pedro reached a climax with the defeat of Miguel's forces at Évora-monte. But with the 1974 revolution, the Alentejo stepped into the limelight: the landless rural workers who had laboured on the latifúndios for generations rose up in support of the communist rebellion and seized the land from its owners. Nearly one thousand estates were collectivised, but a lack of expertise and financial backing

meant that few of these cooperatives succeeded and, in the more conservative climate of the 1980s, they were gradually reprivatised. Most are now back in the hands of their original owners.

Today the Alentejo remains among Europe's poorest – and emptiest – regions: the consequences of Portugal's entry into the EU (increasing mechanisation meaning fewer jobs), successive droughts and greater opportunities elsewhere have led many young people to head for the cities. In the past 40 years the Alentejo's population has declined by 45% to just half a million. Although the province's cork, olives, marble and granite are still in great demand and the deep-water port and industrial zone of Sines is of national importance, this vast region contributes only a fraction to the gross national product and is still looked on as a backwater struggling to survive.

Coastal & Baixo Alentejo

MÉRTOLA
☎ 086 • pop 9000 (municipality)

Perched on a ridge between the serene Rio Guadiana and a tributary, Ribeira de Oeiras, is a Moorish castle, and wound round the hill beneath it is the delightfully flinty old heart of Mértola, a picturesque village of little houses that has hung onto its personality despite its billing as a *vila museu*, an open-air museum crammed with monuments of historic interest. An increasingly popular tourist destination (long famous for its visiting storks and rare lesser kestrels), it still manages to feel a long way from anywhere – midway between Beja and the Algarve coast, and 20km from Spain.

Mértola has a long history and, for a village of its size, is serious about it. First to arrive were Phoenician traders who sailed up the Guadiana; Carthaginians followed. The settlement's strategic position led the Romans (who called it Myrtilis) to beautify it, and the Moors (who called it Mertolah) to fortify it. Dom Sancho II captured it in 1238. The village contains several *núcleos*, or areas of historic interest, as well as a generous sprinkling of museums and plenty of archaeological digs in progress around the castle.

Local men were, until a few decades ago, heavily dependent for work on the now-exhausted copper mines at Mina de São Domingos, about 15km to the east.

In contrast with the abandoned-looking landscape to the south between Mértola and Alcoutim, the road north towards Beja is pretty, with pasture and grain, cork oaks and eucalyptus. Much of this is now part of the Parque Natural do Vale do Guadiana (see the boxed text on the next page).

Orientation

From the bus station, near a roundabout at the convergence of the Serpa and Beja roads, it's about half a kilometre south-west to the turismo and, beside it, the turn-off into the compressed old town and up to the castle. Old Mértola has few right angles or

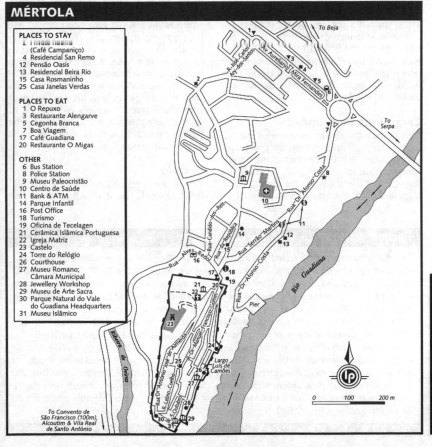

MÉRTOLA

PLACES TO STAY
1 [ ] (Café Campaniço)
4 Residencial San Remo
12 Pensão Oasis
13 Residencial Beira Rio
15 Casa Rosmaninho
25 Casa Janelas Verdas

PLACES TO EAT
1 O Repuxo
3 Restaurante Alengarve
5 Cegonha Branca
7 Boa Viagem
17 Café Guadiana
20 Restaurante O Migas

OTHER
6 Bus Station
8 Police Station
9 Museu Paleocristão
10 Centro de Saúde
11 Bank & ATM
14 Parque Infantil
16 Post Office
18 Turismo
19 Oficina de Tecelagen
21 Cerâmica Islâmica Portuguesa
22 Igreja Matriz
23 Castelo
24 Torre do Relógio
26 Courthouse
27 Museu Romano; Câmara Municipal
28 Jewellery Workshop
29 Museu de Arte Sacra
30 Parque Natural do Vale do Guadiana Headquarters
31 Museu Islâmico

To Beja

To Serpa

Rio Guadiana

Ribeira de Oeiras

Largo Luís de Camões

Pier

To Convento de São Francisco (100m), Alcoutim & Vila Real de Santo António

0   100   200 m

ALENTEJO

horizontal surfaces, and driving into it is asking for trouble: even a donkey would have trouble on its skewed, cobbled, narrow lanes. Ugly 20th century Mértola is west and north of the bus station roundabout.

Information

The helpful Posto de Informação turismo (☎ 6 25 73), in a new complex near the entrance to the old town, is open daily from 9 am to 1 pm and 2 to 5.30 pm (from 10 am at weekends). It organises a two hour guided tour covering the Igreja Matriz, the castelo, the weaving and jewellery workshops, and the Paleo-Christian and Roman museums. The tour runs at weekends at 10.30 am and 3 pm, and costs 500$00.

The local centro de saúde (medical centre; ☎ 61 10 48) is on a road leading from Rua Dr Afonso Costa, which contains the police station (☎ 6 21 27) and banks with ATMs. The post office is near the turismo on Rua Alves Redol.

Largo Luís de Camões

This is the administrative centre of the old town, a tiny, picturesque square lined with orange trees, with the *câmara municipal* (town hall) at its western end. To reach the largo, enter the town by the turismo and keep to the left at every fork in the road.

To the north of the square there's a little clock tower, **Torre do Relógio**, topped with a stork's nest overlooking the Rio Guadiana. On the river below the largo are the remains of what may have been a Moorish pier.

With its cobbled lanes and sleepy atmosphere, strolling around this part of Mértola is like entering a time warp. Cats preen on the roofs and black-clad old women sit on their doorsteps chatting and knitting.

Igreja Matriz

Walking south from the turismo, if you keep to the right at every fork, you arrive at Mértola's Igreja Matriz (parish church), which is square, flat faced and topped with little conical decorations. It's best known for the fact that it was once a mosque, among the few to have survived the Reconquista; it was reconsecrated in the 13th century. An unwhitewashed cavity in the wall on the right behind the altar is apparently the former mosque's *mihrab* (prayer niche). Note also the goats, lions and other figures carved around the peculiar Gothic portal. Admission is free.

Castelo

Above the Igreja Matriz looms Mértola's fortified castle, most of which dates from

Parque Natural do Vale do Guadiana

This relatively new park (created in 1995) comprises 600 sq km of borderland around Serpa and Mértola, an area of hills, plains and deep valleys sheltering the Rio Guadiana – one of Portugal's largest and most important rivers. Among the huge variety of flora and fauna found in the park are several rare or unusual species including the black stork (most noticeable in Mértola), Bonelli's eagle, royal owl, grey kite, horned viper and Iberian toad.

The park also has a rich cultural heritage, especially in Mértola which contains remains dating from prehistoric times as well as some Roman foundations and Islamic pottery.

For more information, visit the park's headquarters (☎ 61 10 84, fax 61 10 85), Rua Dr António José de Almeida, at the very southern edge of Mértola's old walled town. Brochures and pamphlets are available (although there's currently nothing in English). You can also inquire here about park accommodation (two double rooms plus one house sleeping 12 people) near the border town of Canavial about 20km south-east of Mértola which should be available some time in 1999.

Kestrel Haven

The kestrel commonly seen hovering alongside motorways all over Europe has a dainty Mediterranean cousin, the lesser kestrel, which nests in colonies and is much more specific in its habitat requirements. Unfortunately, it is in serious decline, due mainly to changes in agricultural practices. In Spain the population has crashed from a healthy 100,000 pairs to less than 5000 pairs in just 30 years. It's estimated that there are fewer than 200 pairs left in Portugal.

Many of the remaining birds like to congregate at the environmentally sensitive town of Mértola where strenuous efforts have been made to preserve and encourage them: nestboxes have been placed under the bridge that crosses the Ribeira de Oeiras, and in the nearby Convento de São Francisco a specially designed nesting tower has been built. All of these schemes have led to a thriving population.

The best time to see this splendid falcon is between March and September. Climb up to the castle ramparts for the best viewing spot.

Clive Viney

the 13th century, though it was built upon Moorish foundations. The castle has surviving inner and outer walls and a prominent keep, and there are ongoing archaeological digs at its feet. It's open daily except Monday from 9 am to 12.30 pm and 2 to 5.30 pm; admission is free. If the keep isn't open you may well be able to find a cheerful archaeology student or someone else on the dig who'll let you in for the climb up to a bird's-eye view over the entire town and the two river valleys.

Museums

The **Cerâmica Islâmica Portuguesa** (Exhibition of Portuguese Islamic Art) is the first museum you'll come across on the road up to the castle from the turismo. It's open from 9 am to 12.30 pm and 2 to 5.30 pm; admission costs 200$00.

In the cellar of the câmara municipal is the modest but very good **Museu Romano** (Roman Museum). Its main attraction is the foundations of the Roman house upon which the building rests, and it also contains a small collection of pots, sculpture and other artefacts. It's open weekdays only from 9 am to noon and 2 to 5.30 pm; admission costs 500$00.

At the southern end of the old town, the **Museu Islâmico** (Islamic Museum) and **Museu de Arte Sacra** (Museum of Ecclesiastical Art) are both currently closed for renovations. North of the old town, just beyond a good *parque infantil* (children's playground) is the **Museu Paleocristão** (Paleo-Christian Museum), which exhibits Roman and Moorish pottery, jewellery and strange figurines. It is only open on request; ask at the turismo.

Convento de São Francisco

This former convent across the Ribeira de Oeiras, 1km west of Mértola, has been owned since 1980 by Dutch artist Geraldine Zwannikken and her family. They have transformed it into an enchanting nature reserve and art gallery, its grounds full of herbs, horses, peacocks, tea plants, rain temples and wild flowers, its former chapel exhibiting Geraldine's extraordinary art and sculpture, and its riverside devoted to nesting storks and lesser kestrels. Occasional art workshops are held here, and limited accommodation is available (see Places to Stay). It's open daily from 10 am to 5 pm; admission costs 200$00 (students 100$00).

ALENTEJO

Special Events

Mértola's main religious festival, held annually around 24 June and lasting for two weeks, is the Festa de São João. The smaller Feira de São Mateus is held on the last weekend in September.

Places to Stay

Mértola has some excellent accommodation but it fills up in summer. Staff at the turismo can help you find a *quarto* (private room), typically costing around 5000$00 for a double, such as those belonging to Sr Domingos at *Café Campaniço* (☎ 6 22 85, *Rua José Carlos Ary dos Santos*).

Best of the guesthouses is the friendly *Residencial Beira Rio* (☎ 6 23 40, *Rua Dr Afonso Costa 18*), just below the town walls, which has a fine view of the Rio Guadiana. Rooms have recently been tastefully renovated and most have a private bathroom and TV (5000$00; two of the rooms without bathrooms cost 4000$00). Several also have large patios with a view of the river. Next door is the slightly cheaper *Pensão Oasis* (☎ 6 24 04, 6 27 01). Less atmospheric is the *Residencial San Remo* (☎ 6 21 32, *Avenida Aureliano Mira Fernandes 6*) in the new town, where three or four rooms share a bathroom; doubles cost 4000$00; there's no sign outside but an adjacent café can direct you.

There are two beautifully converted Turihab properties. *Casa Rosmaninho* (☎ 61 20 05, *Rua 25 de Abril 23*), has superb rooms (including one with a jacuzzi and another with a rooftop terrace) for a bargain 5000$00. *Casa Janelas Verdes* (☎ 6 21 45, *Rua Dr Manuel Francisco Gomes 38*), in the old town, has traditional doubles costing 8000$00, complete with a famously good breakfast.

For more unusual accommodation, *Convento de São Francisco* (☎ 6 21 19, *fax 6 25 41*) has two rooms costing 5000$00 per person.

Places to Eat

For a light meal or a *bica* (espresso coffee) in the sunshine, try the cheerful *Café Gua-* *diana* at the turn-off to the castle, near the turismo. Just inside the old town is *Restaurante O Migas*, pronounced 'oh migash', which is what you might say about the house special, *migas* – a filling but rather depressing sludge of fried bread and pork chunks – an indicator of the limited options available in this barren region. Another local dish available is fried hare, and there's a reasonably priced and sizeable fish menu.

There are several cheap and cheerful café-restaurants near the bus station roundabout, including the *Boa Viagem*, where you can eat suckling pig for 900$00 and lamprey when in season. Beyond the bus station is the excellent *Cegonha Branca* (☎ 61 10 66, *Avenida Aureliano Mira Fernandes 2-C*) which serves Alentejan specialities including *javali à Mértolense* (wild boar, Mértola style). Also on this road you'll find two other reasonable places, *Restaurante Alengarve* and *O Repuxo*.

Shopping

The tiny jewellery workshop at the southern end of the old town exhibits finely crafted (and pricey) items. Another excellent crafts centre is the Oficina de Tecelagen, an exhibition of traditional wool weaving just down some steps beside the turismo.

Getting There & Away

A Lisbon-Vila Real de Santo António express coach passes through twice daily in each direction (Lisbon is about four hours away). There is one other daily bus to Mértola from Vila Real (under two hours), and three from Beja (less than an hour).

BEJA

☎ 084 • pop 33,000 (municipality)

At its worst, Baixo Alentejo's principal town – at the heart of what the tourist authorities call the Planície Dourada (the Golden Plain) – is dull and depressing, with drunks often lounging in the main pedestrianised street and budget accommodation hard to come by. But its historic old centre has an elegant feel, with fancy wrought-iron balconies and big squares. Its various transport connections also make it a convenient stopover en route between Évora and the Algarve.

History

Built on the highest point of the surrounding plains, Beja was founded by the Romans, who called it Pax Julia after peace between the Romans and rebellious Lusitanians was restored by Julius Caesar. It soon became an important agricultural centre – as it still is today – flourishing principally on the trade in wheat and oil.

Little evidence remains of the 400 years of subsequent Moorish rule except for some distinctive 16th century azulejos in the Convento de Nossa Senhora da Conceição (now the Museu Regional). The town was recaptured from the Moors in 1162.

Beja's fame among the Portuguese rests on a scandalous series of 17th century love letters allegedly written by one of the convent's nuns, Mariana Alcoforado, to a French cavalry officer, Count Chamilly. She was said to have had a love affair with the count while he was stationed in Beja during the time of the Portuguese war with Spain. The passionate *Five Letters of a Portuguese Nun* first emerged in a French 'translation' in 1669 and later appeared in English but, as the originals were never found, the letters' authenticity has been the subject of lively controversy ever since.

Orientation

Beja's historic core is circled by a ring road and surrounded by ugly modern outskirts. The train station is at the north-eastern edge of town and the bus station is to the south-east. The main sights are all within easy walking distance of each other. Drivers are advised to try to park near the train station.

Information

The efficient turismo (☎ 32 36 93, fax 31 01 51) is at No 25 on the pedestrianised Rua Capitão João Francisco de Sousa. It's open Monday to Saturday from 10 am to 8 pm (to 6 pm in winter) and has brochures on other towns in the region as well as Beja. Locally

made leather and woollen goods are on sale here, too.

There are plenty of banks with ATMs near the turismo. The police station (☎ 32 20 22) is on Largo Dom Nuno Álvares Pereira. The hospital (☎ 31 02 00) is on Rua Dr António Covas Lima.

At the *biblioteca municipal* (municipal library; ☎ 32 99 00) on Rua Luís de Camões, there's one computer for Internet and email use (free of charge) which may have to be booked in advance. It's open weekdays from 9.30 am to 12.30 pm and 2.30 to 11 pm, and on Saturday from 2.30 to 8 pm.

Praça da República

This attractive town square with a central *pelourinho* (pillory) and an elegant Manueline arcade along its northern side is the historic heart of the old city. Dominating the square is the 16th century Igreja de Misericórdia, a hefty church with an immense porch that started life as a meat market – hence its suitably crude, hammered stonework.

Convento de Nossa Senhora da Conceição & Museu Regional

This former Franciscan convent on Largo da Conceição, founded in 1459, displays a mix of plain Gothic and fancy Manueline styles typical of the time. The interior is even more lavish, especially the Rococo chapel drowning in 17th and 18th century gilded woodwork. The cloister has some splendid 16th and 17th century azulejos, although the earliest and most interesting examples are in the chapter house, which also sports an incredible painted ceiling and carved doorway.

The museum's collection pales in comparison with the convent building itself, though it manages to exhibit a bit of something from almost every era, from Roman mosaics and stone tombs to 16th century paintings. It's open from 9.45 am to 1 pm and 2 to 5.15 pm daily except Monday and holidays; the 100$00 admission fee includes the Igreja de Santa Amaro (same opening hours).

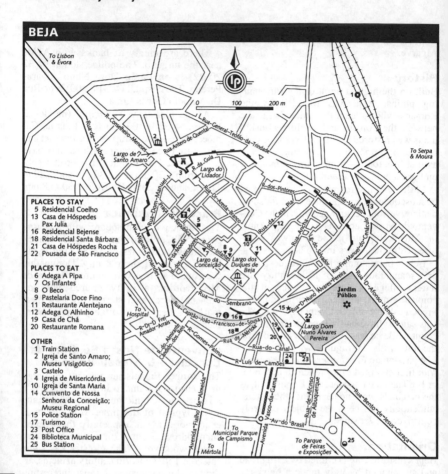

BEJA

PLACES TO STAY
5 Residencial Coelho
13 Casa de Hóspedes
    Pax Julia
16 Residencial Bejense
18 Residencial Santa Bárbara
21 Casa de Hóspedes Rocha
22 Pousada de São Francisco

PLACES TO EAT
6 Adega A Pipa
7 Os Infantes
8 O Beco
9 Pastelaria Doce Fino
11 Restaurante Alentejano
12 Adega O Alhinho
19 Casa de Chá
20 Restaurante Romana

OTHER
1 Train Station
2 Igreja de Santo Amaro;
   Museu Visigótico
3 Castelo
4 Igreja de Misericórdia
10 Igreja de Santa Maria
14 Convento de Nossa
    Senhora da Conceição;
    Museu Regional
15 Police Station
17 Turismo
23 Post Office
24 Biblioteca Municipal
25 Bus Station

Castelo

The castle was built on Roman foundations by Dom Dinis in the late 13th century. There are grand views of rolling Alentejan wheat fields from the top of the Torre de Menagem (admission 100$00). The Museu Militar (Military Museum) inside the castle consists of a few scattered cannons in the grounds. In summer the castle is open daily except Monday from 10 am to 1 pm and 2 to 6 pm (in winter it's open from 9 am to noon and 1 to 4 pm).

Igreja de Santo Amaro & Museu Visigótico

Just beyond the castle, the Igreja de Santa Amaro (or parts of it at any rate) dates from the early 6th century, when it was a Visigothic church, which makes it one of the oldest standing buildings in Portugal. Inside, some of the original columns display intriguing carvings. It now serves as a Visigothic museum and is open daily except Monday and holidays from 9.45 am to 1 pm and 2 to 5.15 pm.

Special Events

One of Beja's biggest annual events is its *ovibeja* (sheep fair) in mid-March. Held in the Parque de Feiras e Exposições on the south-eastern outskirts, it features cow and horse markets, sheep shows and an enthusiastic display of regional music, handicrafts and regional cuisine. Other major festivals are the Festas da Cidade in May and the Festa de São Lourenço e Santa Maria, a lively affair with lots of singing and dancing, which takes place in the second week of August.

Places to Stay

Beja's municipal *parque de campismo* (☎ 32 43 28) is off Avenida Vasco da Gama, not far from the bus terminal, and is part of a municipal sports area that includes a swimming pool and tennis courts. Prices are 340/250/250$00 per person/tent/car.

The cheapest digs in town are at the *Casa de Hóspedes Pax Julia* (☎ 32 25 75, *Rua Pedro Victor 8)*, near the train station. Noisy singles/doubles at the front cost 2500/4500$00 with private bathroom, 1500/3000$00 without. More central but old-fashioned is *Casa de Hóspedes Rocha* (☎ 32 42 71, *Largo Dom Nuno Álvares Pereira 12)* where singles/doubles with shared bathrooms cost 2000/4000$00.

A better option is *Residencial Coelho* (☎ 32 40 31, fax 32 89 39, *Praça da República 15)* where doubles range in price from 5000$00 to 7000$00; there are also more expensive rooms which overlook the square. Near the turismo are the similarly priced, frilly *Residencial Bejense* (☎ 32 50 01, fax 32 50 02, *Rua Capitão João Francisco de Sousa 57)* and the brisk *Residencial Santa Bárbara* (☎ 32 20 28, fax 32 12 31, *Rua de Mértola 36)*, where large carpeted doubles cost 7500$00.

Gorgeous luxury can be found in the *Pousada de São Francisco* (☎ 32 84 41, fax 32 91 43, *Largo Dom Nuno Álvares Pereira)*, where a double room – converted from a cell of the 16th century São Francisco Convent – will set you back 29,600$00 in peak season.

Places to Eat

There's no lack of places to eat in this agricultural town. Among typically cheap and modest places, try *Restaurante Romana* (☎ 32 60 34, *Rua da Biscainha 16)*. More touristy but still good is *O Beco* (☎ 32 59 00, *Beco da Rua dos Infantes)*, with dishes from around 900$00. Nearby is the classy *Os Infantes* (*Rua dos Infantes 14,* ☎ 32 27 89)*, which offers a menu of very good Alentejan specialities starting at around 1400$00. *Restaurante Alentejano* (☎ 32 38 49, *Largo dos Duques de Beja 6)*, cooks up huge and reasonably priced servings. It's closed on Saturday and is packed at lunch times.

Opposite the Red Cross headquarters is the unmarked *Adega O Alhinho* (☎ 32 46 15, *Rua da Casa Pia 20)*, a little dive stacked with huge wine jars (*adega* means wine cellar, and your table wine comes straight from the jar). You have a choice of entrance: one of the two stable doors leads into the dark, seedy bar, while the red door leads into the tiny restaurant where you'll be lucky to get a seat at lunch time. Dishes are cheap (starting at 800$00) and include a mouth-watering choice of desserts. It's closed Sunday.

Another typical Alentejan tavern, *Adega A Pipa* (☎ 32 70 43, *Rua da Moeda 8)*, serves cheap snacks, tapas and light meals costing less than 900$00, in a room as big as a barn.

For yummy regional pastries, make a beeline for *Pastelaria Doce Fino* (*Rua dos Infantes 29)* or the classier *Casa de Chá* (*Rua dos Açoutados 35)*, which serves typical *doces conventuais* just like the nuns once made them.

Getting There & Away

Bus The bus is usually quicker and more frequent than the train for nearby destinations. On weekdays there are six buses to Serpa (continuing to Moura) and Évora and four to Mértola; around half that number run at weekends. Four express coaches run to Faro via Albufeira daily and six go to Lisbon.

Train Beja is on the Lisbon to Funcheira (near Ourique) railway line. There are two direct services daily to/from Lisbon (taking two to three hours) and two more involving changes at Casa Branca and/or Éyora. You can also catch the Comboio Azul service to Porto from here (Friday only).

SERPA
☎ 084 • pop 16,600 (municipality)

Approach Serpa from Beja (30km to the north-west) on a dusky summer's evening and the striking outlines of the castle walls and aqueduct above the surrounding plains might lead you to believe you've arrived at an undiscovered medieval outpost. It's a pity the ugly grain elevator on the outskirts ruins the image.

A pity, too, that there are few decent budget places to stay and that transport connections are sparse: Serpa's untouristy, laid-back atmosphere and narrow lanes, cobbled in patterns and lined with white-washed houses, make it a tempting place for a stop en route to Spain or the Algarve.

Orientation
Those arriving by car must brave tight gateways into the old town, blind corners and streets so narrow that pedestrians often have to squeeze into doorways when cars pass.

The bus station, mercado municipal and parque de campismo are in the dull new town area, about 700m (10 to 15 minutes walk) south-west of the old town centre, Praça da República.

Information
Right in the centre at Largo Dom Jorge de Melo 2, the friendly turismo (☎ 54 47 27) has maps, brochures and a display of local handicrafts, and can help you to find accommodation. It's open daily from 9 am to 5.30 pm (at weekends it closes for lunch from 12.30 to 2 pm).

There's a bank around the corner in Praça da República, and another outside the walls on Largo 5 de Outubro. The post office is near the southern end of the aqueduct, on Rua das Lagares.

On the fourth Tuesday of each month a huge country market with clothes, toys, shoes and agricultural implements sprawls beside Rua de Santo António on the north-eastern outskirts of town.

Castelo
The courtyard of the surprisingly small castle is entered beneath a precariously balanced bit of ruined wall. In the keep is the small **Museu de Arqueologia**, housing a life-sized plaster rendition of the Last Supper and a small, poorly labelled collection of archaeological remnants revealing bits of Serpa's history, which reaches back to the arrival of the Celts over 2000 years ago.

The castle's best feature is the view from its **battlements**, with close-ups of Serpa's rooftops and cottage gardens, a detailed look at the aqueduct, and a panorama of undulating wheat fields. The castle and museum are open from 9 am to 12.30 pm and 2 to 5.30 pm daily, except holidays; admission is free.

Town Walls, Aqueduto & Palácio dos Condes de Ficalho
Walls still stand around most of the inner town, and along the west side (follow Rua dos Arcos) run the impressive remains of an 11th century aqueduct. At the southern end is a huge 17th century *noria* or wheel pump, once used for pumping water along the aqueduct to the nearby Palácio dos Condes de Ficalho (still used by the de Ficalho family as a holiday home).

Museu Etnográfico
Serpa's other major attraction is its Ethnographic Museum, which features a well-presented portrayal of aspects of traditional Alentejan life, with exhibits ranging from agricultural implements and olive presses to rural costumes; unfortunately there are no English explanations. The museum is in an elegantly converted market building on Largo do Corro and is open daily from 9 am to 12.30 pm and 2 to 5.30 pm. Admission is free.

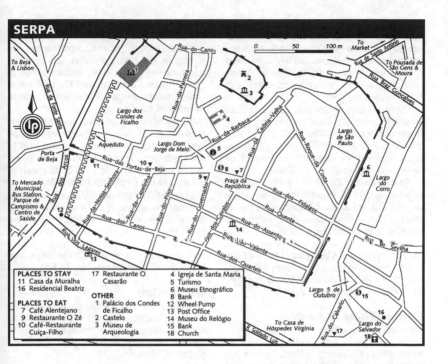

SERPA

PLACES TO STAY
11 Casa da Muralha
16 Residencial Beatriz

PLACES TO EAT
7 Café Alentejano
9 Restaurante O Zé
10 Café-Restaurante Cuiça-Filho

17 Restaurante O Casarão

OTHER
1 Palácio dos Condes de Ficalho
2 Castelo
3 Museu de Arqueologia

4 Igreja de Santa Maria
5 Turismo
6 Museu Etnográfico
8 Bank
12 Wheel Pump
13 Post Office
14 Museu do Relógio
15 Bank
18 Church

Museu do Relógio

This private museum on Rua do Assento houses a fascinating collection of watches from the 18th century. It's open Tuesday to Friday from 2 to 6 pm for guided visits only. Admission costs 400$00 (students 300$00).

Places to Stay

There is an excellent municipal *parque de campismo* (☎ 54 42 90, *Largo de São Pedro*) at the south-western edge of town near the bus station. It's open year-round and prices (150/130/150$00 per person/tent/car) include admission to the big swimming pool opposite.

Cheapest among the pensões is *Casa de Hóspedes Vírginia* (☎ 54 91 45, *Largo 25 de Abril*) where plain but clean singles/doubles without bathroom cost 2500/3500$00. The rooms above *Restaurante O Casarão* (☎ 54 92 95, *Largo do Salvador*

20) are similarly priced. Across the square is the crisply efficient *Residencial Beatriz* (☎/fax 54 44 23, fax 54 31 00), which offers comfortable singles/doubles with bathroom, TV and air-conditioning for 4800/6500$00. The price includes a generous continental breakfast.

Just within the town walls there's a Turihab property, *Casa da Muralha* (☎/fax 54 31 50, *Rua das Portas de Beja 43*), where beautifully furnished rooms cost 8500$00. Three of the five rooms open onto an enchanting garden of bougainvillea and orange trees.

For a more modern environment and superb views, head for the isolated *Pousada de São Gens* (☎ 54 47 24, fax 54 43 37) which stands on a hilltop 2km to the south of town, next to a dazzling white Moorish chapel. Doubles cost 20,300$00 in the high season.

ALENTEJO

Places to Eat

The locally popular and cheerful *Restaurante O Casarão* (see Places to Stay) has a select menu of meat and fish dishes, mostly costing less than 1000$00. Try its house speciality, *açorda* (bread-based stew) with *bacalhau* (salted cod).

There are several other attractive choices around Praça da República, including *Café-Restaurante Cuiça-Filho* (☎ 54 95 66, *Rua das Portas de Beja 18*). Its delicious Alentejan specialities include *ensopada de borrego* (lamb stew) for 1200$00.

Restaurante O Zé (☎ 54 92 46, *Praça da República 10*) is something of a tourist magnet and its bar is a favourite with young locals. The overwhelmingly friendly Zé recommends his creamy *queijo de Serpa* cheese, a local speciality. Across the square, the Art Deco *Café Alentejano* (☎ 54 41 89) is a fine place to get a buzz from bicas and locally made *queijadas de Serpa* pastries. The restaurant upstairs is pricey.

Getting There & Away

On weekdays six buses run from Beja to Serpa and continue to Moura. There's an express bus to Lisbon, via Beja, twice a day (weekdays only). The Spanish frontier at Ficalho is 55 minutes away and is accessible by one bus daily (weekdays only).

MOURA

☎ 085 • pop 16,400 (municipality)

Surrounded by a soporific landscape of undulating wheat fields and olive orchards, Moura feels a bit like a ghost town. Some 60km north-east of Beja, well off the main tourist trail, it was once patronised by the wealthy for its thermal spa (which is still in use). Now its quiet, broad streets and elegant houses seem oddly grandiose for such an out-of-the-way place.

The town's most dramatic moment in history has an element of fantasy too: legend recounts how a Moorish woman, Moura Salúquiyya, opened the gates of the town to her betrothed only to find a horde of Christians had murdered him and his escort and dressed in their victims' clothes. They sacked the town, and Moura flung herself from a tower in despair.

The Moors' 500 year occupation came to an end in 1232 with a rather less inspired takeover by Christian forces, though Moura's name lived on and the tower was incorporated into the town's coat of arms in memory of her fate.

Today Moura is gaining a questionable kind of fame as the nearest large town to the new giant dam at Alqueva, some 15km to the north (see the boxed text 'Water Wars' in this section). By the year 2002 much of the area to the north will be flooded.

Meanwhile, the town itself makes a pleasant excursion, if only to visit the immaculate Moorish quarter (one of the best preserved in Portugal) or to soak in the spa. Don't plan to stay here long – unless you're scouting for romantic film settings you could die of boredom within 24 hours.

Orientation

The bus station is by the defunct railway station at the newer, southern end of town. It's a 10 minute walk from here to the old town, where you'll find all of the main places of interest.

Information

It's a five minute walk from the bus station (turn left into the first main street, Rua das Forças Armadas, and right at the end) to the turismo (☎ 25 13 75) on Largo de Santa Clara. If you're driving from Serpa you'll pass it on your way into town. The office is open weekdays from 9 am to 1 pm and 2 to 5 pm, and at weekends from 10 am to 1 pm and 2.30 to 5.30 pm. It can provide a list of accommodation and a fairly useless town map.

Spa

The thermal spa is at the entrance to the shady Jardim Dr Santiago at the eastern end of Praça Sacadura Cabral. It's open Tuesday to Saturday from 8 am to 1 pm and 3 to 6 pm; for 100$00 you get to soak in a bath for 15 minutes. The bicarbonated calcium waters, said to be good for rheumatism, also burble from the richly marbled **Fonte das Três Bicas** (Fountain with Three Spouts) by the entrance to the jardim.

Igreja de São Baptista

Just outside the Jardim Dr Santiago you'll notice the Manueline portal of this 16th century church. It's a flamboyant bit of decoration, with carvings of knotted ropes, crowns and armillary spheres on an otherwise dull façade. There's little of interest inside the church apart from some fine 17th century Sevillian azulejos.

Mouraria

The old Moorish quarter lies at the western end of Praça Sacadura Cabral; it's a tight cluster of narrow cobbled lanes bordered by white terraced cottages with eye-catching broad chimneys. Dusk is a good time to wander here – people lean out of their stable-doors for a chat and kids play hide and seek in the streets.

Castelo

Above the old town is a ruined tower, the last remnant of a Moorish fortress. Rebuilt by Dom Dinis in the 13th century, and again by Dom Manuel I in 1510, the castle itself was largely destroyed by the Spanish in the 18th century.

Places to Stay

Closest to the bus station is rude *Pensão Italiana* (☎ 25 23 48, Rua da Vitória 8); if you manage to get a foot in the door you'll find doubles starting at 3500$00.

A better bet is the recently revamped *Residencial Alentejana* (☎ 25 00 84, fax 25 00 89, Largo José Maria dos Santos 40), just down the road. Singles/doubles cost 4000/6000$00 and all rooms in this slick new establishment come with bathroom and TV.

The posh place in town is *Hotel de Moura* (☎ 25 10 90, fax 246 10, Praça Gago Coutinho). Behind the ornate façade lies a surprisingly tacky interior, but the rooms (7000/9000$00 without breakfast, or slightly more with breakfast) come with all the frills.

Places to Eat

There are plenty of cafés and restaurants around Praça Sacadura Cabral. On Rua da República, try *Restaurante Mourense O Carlos* (☎ 25 25 98) at No 37 for regional delicacies, or *Talho Charcutaria* at No 15 for a fine selection of regional wines, cheeses and cold meats.

The *mercado municipal* is in a huge glassed building on Praça Sacadura Cabral, a 10 minute walk from the turismo.

Water Wars

The arid Alentejo is always gasping for water. One of Portugal's major agricultural regions, it employs a host of irrigation schemes and reservoirs to keep its soil from cracking up. In addition, an agreement with Spain in 1968 was meant to ensure that the waters of the Rio Guadiana (which rises in Spain and flows through the Alentejo) were fairly shared.

Unfortunately, successive droughts have strained the arrangement: Spain is accused of using more water from the Guadiana than the amount agreed, and the Alentejo is suffering. Recently, after decades of delay, the Portuguese took matters into their own hands and started work on a giant dam at Alqueva (near Moura) to guarantee both irrigation water and electricity for years to come.

The 96m-high dam will create one of the biggest reservoirs in Europe when it's finished in 2002 – so big that it could substantially reduce the average temperature of the surrounding region. One thing that's likely to heat up, on the other hand, is the dialogue with Spain, which has its own incompatible plans for making the most of the Guadiana.

Getting There & Away
Six buses a day (weekdays only) run to/ from Beja, via Serpa.

BEACHES
The Alentejo's most popular ocean resort is the small port town of **Vila Nova de Milfontes**, at the mouth of the Rio Mira, 25km north-west of Odemira. The best beaches here are along the coast, on either side of the Rio Mira estuary (but watch out for very strong river currents). In summer, whenever enough passengers have arrived to fill it, a ferry crosses the estuary to beaches on the other side.

Simpler, smaller and cheaper (but equally popular) is **Zambujeira do Mar**, lying some 20km south-west of Odemira. It has a fine Atlantic-facing beach with cool, wind-chopped waters year-round.

Information
The turismo in Vila Nova (☎ 083-965 99) is opposite the police station on Rua António Mantas; it's open daily in summer from 10 am to 7 pm (closed for lunch). There's also a smaller turismo (☎ 083-611 05) in Zambujeira.

Places to Stay – Camping
There are three camping grounds within easy reach of Vila Nova, all open year-round. Closest is *Campiférias (☎ 083-964 09, fax 965 81, Rua da Praça)*, half a kilometre north-west of the turismo, costing 460/400/280$00 per person/tent/car. The well-shaded, similarly priced *Parque de Campismo Milfontes (☎ 083-961 40, fax 961 04)* is a short distance further on. Both places have a pool, a restaurant and bungalows for rent. *Parque de Campismo Sitava (☎ 083-89 93 43, fax 89 95 71)* is 4km north of the town centre; it has good facilities, including a children's play area, but it's pricey at 520/500/300$00.

Parque de Campismo Zambujeira (☎ 083-611 72, fax 613 20) is just east of Zambujeira do Mar; it has a swimming pool and a restaurant and charges 490/520/ 400$00.

Places to Stay – Other Options
There are plenty of private rooms in both areas (ask at the turismo or look out for *quartos* signs). Recommended accommodation in Vila Nova includes *Residencial Mil-Réis (☎ 083-992 33, Largo do Rossio 2)*, the more modern *Pensão do Cais (☎ 083-962 68)* on the road to the town pier, and *Quinta das Varandas (☎ 083-961 55)*, an apartment complex about 700m west of the turismo.

In Zambujeira your options are more limited: try *Residencial Mar-e-Sol (☎ 083-611 71)*.

Places to Eat
Recommended in Vila Nova is the restaurante in *Pensão do Cais* (see Places to Stay) which serves great grilled fish, and *Restaurante Mira Mar (Largo Brito Pais)*, offering good vibes, decent music and seafood stews.

In Zambujeira, the best place to head for is *Taverna Ti Vítorio (Largo Mira Mar)*.

Getting There & Away
Vila Nova has bus connections several times each weekday with Odemira and Zambujeira do Mar. In summer there are daily coaches from Sagres and Portimão, and there are at least two coaches daily (more in summer) from Lisbon.

Zambujeira has only a few awkward bus connections a day from Odemira.

Alto Alentejo

ÉVORA
☎ 066 • pop 54,000 (municipality)

Évora, Alentejo's capital and main agricultural marketplace, is also one of Portugal's most delightful towns, with a combination of historical elegance and a lived-in feel. Its well-preserved Moorish walled centre – containing prominent remains dating back to Roman times and a trove of other architectural and artistic treasures (not to mention plenty of good cafés and restaurants) – makes it a fine spot to linger in.

Évora boasts more official monuments and buildings of public interest than any Portuguese city except Lisbon. In 1986 UNESCO declared the entire centre a World Heritage Site.

You'll need a couple of days to get the most out of it, but try not to make one of them a Monday, when most tourist attractions and many other establishments are closed.

History

Évora's history is long and rich. The Celtic settlement of Ebora was here before the Romans, who arrived in 59 BC, made it a military outpost and eventually an important centre of Roman-occupied Iberia. It was probably the headquarters of a rebel governor, Quintus Sertorius, who attempted unsuccessfully to detach most of the region from the Roman Empire.

After a depressing spell under the Visigoths, the town again flowered as a centre of trade under the Moors. In 1165 Évora's Muslim rulers were hoodwinked by a rogue Christian knight known as Giraldo Sem Pavor (Gerald the Fearless). According to one well-embellished story, Giraldo singlehandedly stormed one of the town's watchtowers by climbing up a ladder of spears driven into the walls. From there he distracted municipal sentries while his companions took the town with hardly a fight. The Moors took it back in 1192, holding on to it for another 20 years or so.

Évora's golden era came between the 14th and 16th centuries when it was favoured by the Alentejo's own House of Avis, in addition to numerous scholars and artists. It was declared an archbishopric in 1540 and got its own Jesuit university in 1559.

When the cardinal-king Dom Henrique, last of the Avis line, died in 1580 and Spain seized the throne, the royal court left Évora and the town began wasting away. The Marquês de Pombal's closure of the university in 1759 was the last straw. French forces plundered the town and massacred its defenders in July 1808.

Orientation

Évora climbs a gentle hill above the Alentejo plain. Around the walled centre runs a ring road from which you can enter on several 'spoke' roads. The town's focal point is Praça do Giraldo, 200m from the bus station on Rua da República. The train station is outside the walls, 1km south of the square.

If you're driving, save your temper by keeping out of the old town. Unless you're staying at one of the better residenciais or hotels inside the city, you'll have to pay for the very limited parking spaces. Free parking is plentiful outside the walls (for example, at one end of Rua do Raimundo).

Maps The turismo sells several glossy publications (including a set of *Historical Itineraries* for 200$00) and provides two free town maps: a poor, old affair with a few walking routes marked and a clearer new map without. To find every street, you'll need to buy the *Planta de Évora* map (700$00), easily available at Livraria Nazareth bookshop across the square from the turismo.

Information

Tourist Office The town's very helpful turismo (☎ 2 26 71, fax 2 29 55), Praça do Giraldo 73, is open during the summer from 9 am to 7 pm on weekdays and from 12.30 to 5.30 pm on weekends and holidays.

Money There are several banks with Multibanco ATMs on and around Praça do Giraldo. The town's only automatic exchange machine is outside the turismo.

Post & Communications The main post office is on Rua de Olivença, open weekdays from 8.30 am to 6.30 pm and Saturday from 9 am to 12.30 pm; the telephone office is at the back, on Rua do Menino Jesus. There's another post office (same opening times) on Largo da Porta de Moura.

At Ciber Évora (☎ 74 62 01, fax 51 96 47, email ciberevora@mail.telepac.pt), Rua Fria 7, you can log onto the Internet and

ALENTEJO

ÉVORA

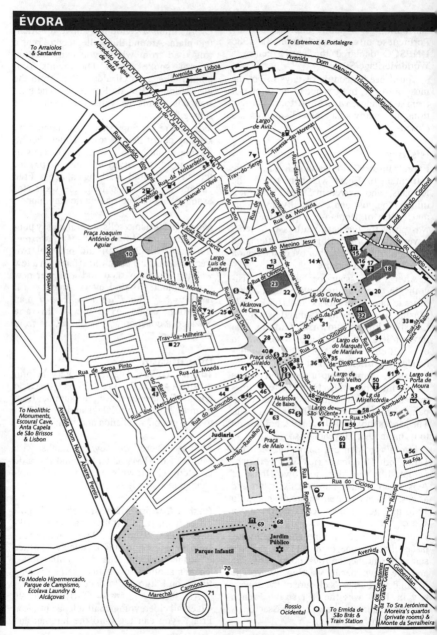

ÉVORA

PLACES TO STAY
18 Pousada dos Lóios
27 Hotel Santa Clara
30 Residencial Riviera
33 Pensão Policarpo
36 Residencial Diana
43 Pensão Portalegre
44 Pensão O Giraldo
45 Pensão Os Manueis
49 Residencial Solar Monfalim
59 Pousada da Juventude
63 Private Rooms (Quartos)

PLACES TO EAT
5 Restaurante O Portão
6 Tasca do Comendinha
7 Restaurante-Bar Molhóbico
9 Taberna Tipica Quarta-Feira
16 Jardim do Paço
26 Restaurante O Bafo
28 Café Arcada
29 Restaurante O Grémio
31 Dom João Cafetaria
35 Salão Condestável
41 Restaurante Cozinha de Santo Humberto
48 Restaurante O Túnel
61 Gelataria Zoka
64 Café Restaurante O Cruz
65 Mercado Municipal

OTHER
1 Club Dezasseis
2 Diplomata Pub
3 Evoralar
4 Pub O Trovador
8 Bar Desassossego
10 Teatro Garcia de Resende
11 Mendes & Murteira
12 Telephone Office
13 Main Post Office
14 Police Station
15 Palácio dos Duques de Cadaval
17 Igreja de São João
19 Casa dos Bonecos
20 Biblioteca Pública
21 Templo Romano (Temple of Diana)
22 Hertz
23 Câmara Municipal
24 Bank & ATM
25 TurAventur
32 Museu de Évora
34 Sé
37 Bookshop
38 Automóvel Club de Portugal (ACP)
39 Livraria Nazareth
40 Pharmacy
42 Alliance Française

continued ...

ALENTEJO

ÉVORA

46	Turismo
47	Bank & ATM
50	Igreja da Misericórdia
51	Bookshop
52	Évoratur
53	Post Office
54	Casa Cordovil
55	Hospital
56	Ciber Évora
57	Igreja do Carmo
58	Evorarent
60	Igreja da Nossa Senhora da Graça
62	Bank & ATM
66	Igreja de São Francisco; Capela dos Ossos
67	Bus Station
68	Évora Rent-a-Bike
69	Palácio de Dom Manuel; Galeria das Damas
70	Ludoteca de Évora (Kindergarten)
71	Praça de Touros

send or receive emails for 250$00 per half-hour. It's open weekdays from noon to midnight and weekends from 2 pm to midnight.

Travel Agencies TurAventur (☎/fax 74 31 34), upstairs at Rua João de Deus 21, runs adventurous hiking, biking, canoe and jeep tours of the region, but only for groups (a minimum of six).

Evoratur (☎ 74 38 60, fax 29 467, email argus@mail.telepac.pt) at Rua da Misericórdia 16, is a competent travel agency that can book flights and arrange car rental or regional tours.

Bookshops The town's biggest bookshop, Livraria Nazareth, upstairs at Praça do Giraldo 46, sells a few maps and camping guides and a limited number of books in English about Portugal. There's a smaller bookshop at the north end of Alcárcova de Baixo and a good one for guidebooks at Rua da Misericórdia 11.

University Outside the walls to the north-east are the Italian Renaissance-style courtyards of the Universidade de Évora, a descendent (reopened in the 1970s) of the original Jesuit institution founded in the 16th century.

Cultural Centre The Alliance Française (☎ 2 33 39), Rua dos Mercadores 3, is actually a language teaching centre, but it serves as a point of contact for French speakers.

Childcare In the jardim público is Ludoteca de Évora (☎ 2 17 89), a privately funded kindergarten for children aged from 5 to 14. Younger children are also welcome but must be accompanied by an adult. It's open from 10 am to noon and 2 to 6 pm (to 5 pm in winter), and at weekends from 3 to 6 pm.

Laundry Ecolava (☎ 74 45 54) at Praça Dom João III 6 (700m down the Alcáçovas road and turn right at the first roundabout) has a wash and dry service costing around 600$00 per kg. It's open weekdays from 9 am to 12.30 pm and 2.30 to 7.30 pm, and Saturday from 9 am to 1 pm.

Medical Services The Évora District Hospital (☎ 2 21 32) is east of the centre on Rua do Valasco.

Emergency The police station (☎ 2 63 41) is on Rua Francisco Soares Lusitano, near the Templo Romano.

Praça do Giraldo & Around

This square has seen some potent moments in Portuguese history, including the 1483 execution of Fernando, Duke of Bragança, the public burning of victims of the Inquisition in the 16th century, and fiery debates on agrarian reform in the 1970s. Nowadays it harbours idle tourists and hungry pigeons at all hours of the day.

The narrow lanes to the south-west once defined Évora's *judiaria* (Jewish quarter). In the other direction, Rua 5 de Outubro climbs to the Sé and the old town's smartly restored heart. On either side of Rua 5 de Outubro, handsome townhouses feature wrought-iron balconies, and alleys pass beneath Moorish-style arches. Every other place on the way up is a handicrafts shop or a restaurant.

ALENTEJO

Sé

Évora's richly endowed, fortress-like cathedral is surely one of the most imposing churches in southern Portugal. It was begun in around 1186 during the rule of Sancho I, Afonso Henriques' son, probably on the site of an earlier mosque, and was completed about 60 years later. The flags of Vasco da Gama's ships bound for India were blessed here in 1497.

You enter through a portal flanked by 14th century stone apostles, flanked in turn by massive, asymmetrical granite towers with 16th century roofs. Stout and Romanesque at first, the cathedral gets more Gothic the closer you look, starting with the front door and continuing inside. Chandeliers hang from overmined rosary chains The chancel, which was remodelled when Évora became the seat of an archdiocese, represents the only significant stylistic fiddle since the cathedral was completed.

Climb the steps in the south tower to the choir stalls and up to the **treasury**, which comprises several small galleries housing grotesquely sumptuous ecclesiastical gear including vestments, statuary, chalices and paintings.

From the cathedral you can enter the cool **cloister**, an early 14th century addition. Downstairs are the stone tombs of Évora's last four archbishops. At each corner of the cloister a dark circular staircase climbs to the top of the walls, from where there are good views across the Alentejo landscape.

The church, treasury museum and cloisters are open from 9 am to noon and 2 to 5 pm daily, except Monday. Admission to the cloisters and museum costs 350$00.

Museu de Évora

Adjacent to the cathedral, in what used to be the archbishop's palace (built in the 16th century and frequently renovated), is the small, elegant Évora Museum. Luminous fragments of old statuary and façades from around the Alentejo, including Roman, medieval, Manueline and later styles, fill the courtyard. Upstairs several rooms are filled with temporary exhibits, former episcopal

furnishings and a gallery of Flemish paintings including *Life of the Virgin*, a striking 13-panel series that was originally part of the Sé's altarpiece, created by anonymous Flemish artists, most or all of them working in Portugal around 1500. The museum also houses relics from the Neolithic sites around Évora. It's open from 10 am to 12.30 pm and 2 to 5.30 pm daily, except Monday. Admission costs 250$00 (students 125$00).

Templo Romano

Across the Largo do Conde de Vila Flor from the museum are the startling remains of a Roman temple dating from the 2nd or early 3rd century. It's Évora's visual trademark: the best preserved Roman monument in Portugal and, probably, in the Iberian Peninsula. Though it's commonly referred to as the Temple of Diana, there's no consensus about the deity to which it was dedicated.

How did these 14 Corinthian columns, capped with Estremoz marble, manage to survive in such good shape for 18 centuries? The temple was apparently walled up in the Middle Ages to form a small fortress (and even used as the town slaughterhouse for a time), its heritage only rediscovered late in the 19th century.

The Roman walls have crumbled, but the columns of Évora's Temple of Diana have stood the test of time.

Igreja de São João & Convento dos Lóios

The little Church of St John the Evangelist, facing the Templo Romano, was founded in 1485 by one Rodrigo Afonso de Melo, Count of Olivença and the first governor of Portuguese Tangier, to serve as his family's pantheon. Behind its elaborate Gothic portal is a nave lined with gorgeous azulejos produced in 1711 by one of Portugal's best known tile-makers, António de Oliveira Bernardes. Through grates in the floor you can see a cistern that predates the church, and an ossuary full of the bones of monks.

Unfortunately, the church is privately owned (by the Duques de Cadaval) and is only open for visits by arrangement, costing 500$00; contact the turismo for details.

Though it's a national monument, the former Convento dos Lóios to the right of the church, with elegant Gothic cloisters topped by a Renaissance gallery. The convent was converted in 1965 into a top-end *pousada* (upmarket inn; see under Accommodation in the Facts for the Visitor chapter). The management is clearly not thrilled to have tourists wandering around, so it's effectively out of bounds unless you can disguise yourself as a wealthy guest.

Palácio dos Duques de Cadaval

North-west of the Igreja de São João is a 17th century façade attached to a much older palace and castle, as revealed by the two powerful square towers that bracket it. The Palace of the Dukes of Cadaval was given to the governor of Évora, Martim Afonso de Melo, by Dom João I and also served from time to time as a royal residence. A section of the palace still serves as private quarters of the de Melo family; the other main occupant is the city's highway department. You can at least have a look at the inner courtyard through the open gate on weekdays. At the back the palace adjoins the town walls.

Town Walls

About a fifth of Évora's population lives within its old walls, some of them built on top of Roman fortifications from the 1st century AD (traces of which can be seen from the garden behind the Palácio dos Duques de Cadaval). Over 3km of 14th century walls enclose the northern part of the old town, while the bulwarks along the southern side (such as those running through the jardim público) date from the 17th century. Several other ranks of walls have all but disappeared.

Largo da Porta de Moura

The so-called Moor's Gate to the inner town once stood beside what is now a pleasant square, the Largo da Porta de Moura, just south of the Sé. Among several elegant mansions around the square (and contemporary with the strange-looking globular 16th century Renaissance fountain in the middle of it) is **Casa Cordovil**, built in appealing Manueline-Moorish style, at the south-eastern end. Across the road to the west, take a look at the extraordinary knotted stone doorway of the Igreja do Carmo.

Igreja de São Francisco & Capela dos Ossos

On Praça 1 de Maio is Évora's best known church, a huge Manueline-Gothic structure completed around 1510 and dedicated to St Francis, adorned with the period's exuberant nautical motifs. Legend has it that the Portuguese navigator Gil Vicente is buried here.

What draws the crowds through the dark interior is the Capela dos Ossos (Chapel of Bones), a small room behind the altar with walls and columns lined with the bones and skulls of some 5000 people. The bones were collected by 17th century Franciscan monks from the overflowing graveyards of several dozen churches and monasteries. Adding to the ghoulish atmosphere is what looks like the desiccated corpse of a child, hanging off to the right as you enter. Portugal has other ossuary chapels, but this one is the creepiest. An inscription over the entrance translates roughly as 'We bones await yours'.

The chapel is open Monday to Saturday from 8.30 to 1 pm and 2.30 to 6 pm, and Sunday from 10 to 11.30 am and 2.30 to 6 pm (unless there are services in the church); admission costs 100$00. The entrance is just to the right of the altar.

Jardim Público & Palácio de Dom Manuel

The pleasant public gardens straddle the 17th century fortifications south of the Igreja de São Francisco. Inside the walls is the so-called Galeria das Damas (Ladies' Gallery) of the 16th century Palácio de Dom Manuel, built in a pastiche of Gothic, Manueline, neo-Moorish and Renaissance styles. Tradition has it that Vasco da Gama was here given command of the ships that ultimately sailed to India.

From the town walls you can see, a few blocks to the south, the crenellated, pointy-topped, 'Arabian Gothic' profile of the Ermida de São Brás (Chapel of St Blaise), dating from about 1490, possibly an early project of Diogo de Boitac, considered the originator of the Manueline style. There's little of interest inside.

On the park's lower level outside the walls is an excellent parque infantil (playground) and the Ludoteca de Évora (see under Childcare in the Information section).

Igreja da Nossa Senhora da Graça

Down an alley off Rua da República is one of Évora's more melancholy sights, the ungainly Baroque façade of the Church of Our Lady of Grace topped by four uncomfortable-looking stone giants. It's mainly of interest to art historians, marking one of the first appearances (in the 17th century cloister of the adjoining monastery) of the Renaissance style in Portugal.

Aqueduto da Água de Prata

Marching into the town from the north-west is the Silver Waters Aqueduct, designed by Francisco de Arruda (better known for Lisbon's Tower of Belém) to bring clean water to Évora and completed in the 1530s.

Walk up Rua do Cano to the end of the aqueduct, which is almost at street level. As the street drops the aqueduct rises, with houses, shops and cafés built right into its perfect arches. The surrounding neighbourhood, plain and unbothered by tourism, has an almost village-like feel.

Organised Tours

Mendes & Murteira (☎ 2 74 68, fax 2 36 16, email m.murteira@mail.telepac.pt), which operates out of the Barafunda boutique on Rua 31 de Janeiro 15-A, offers a three hour City Tour and a four hour Megalithic Tour (both costing 2500$00 per person, usually in groups) and, with advance notice, can also arrange jeep safaris, horse riding and fishing trips.

Special Events

Évora's biggest annual bash, and one of the Alentejo's best country fairs, is the Feira de São João, held from around 22 or 23 June to 1 or 2 July. The Friday before Palm Sunday features a sizeable town fair called the Feira dos Ramos (Palm Fair).

Places to Stay

Accommodation is usually pretty tight in Évora, particularly in summer when it's wise to book ahead. Turismo staff post a list of places on the door when the office is closed, including telephone numbers and prices. We list high season prices.

Camping There is a well equipped Orbitur parque de campismo (☎ 2 51 90, fax 2 98 30) about 2km south-west of the town, open year-round (600/500/510$00 per person/tent/car). There are no local buses to the camping ground, but buses to Alcáçovas stop there. A taxi from the town centre costs about 540$00.

Youth Hostel The new pousada da juventude (☎ 74 48 48, fax 74 48 43, Rua Miguel Bombarda 40), on the site of the former Hotel Planicie, has dorm beds costing 2500$00 and doubles with private bathroom for 5500$00.

ALENTEJO

Private Rooms These are among the best budget bets. Recommended for its friendliness (and with easy parking) is the place run by *Senhora Jerónima Moreira* (☎ *2 12 14, Avenida dos Combatentes Grande Guerra 16-A)*, near the train station. Doubles here are a bargain 4000$00. More central *quartos* (☎ *74 32 59)* at Rua Romão Ramalho 27 have been recommended by readers; doubles cost 5000$00. There are others in these lanes behind the turismo: look for *quartos* signs.

Pensões & Residenciais In a quiet backstreet location but with a seedy reputation is *Pensão Portalegre* (☎ *2 23 26, Travessa do Barão 18)*, where the price of a double is about 5000$00. More salubrious is *Pensão Os Manueis* (☎ *2 28 61, Rua do Raimundo 35)*, where doubles without/with shower cost 5000/6000$00. A notch up in comfort is *Pensão O Giraldo* (☎ *2 58 33, Rua dos Mercadores 27)*, where singles/doubles cost 5500/6800$00.

To the east of Praça do Giraldo is the sombre *Residencial Diana* (☎ *74 31 13, fax 74 31 01, Rua de Diogo Cão 2)*, where doubles without/with bathroom cost 8500/10,500$00, including breakfast. Most atmospheric of all places in this price bracket is the former 16th century townhouse *Pensão Policarpo* (☎*/fax 2 24 24, Rua Freiria de Baixo 16)*. It's one of many older backstreet mansions, with quiet courtyards behind high walls. The cheapest rooms here cost 4500/7000$00 without private bathroom, or 6000/8500$00 with shower (7000/10,000$00 with bath); all prices include breakfast.

Another such place, at the upper end of the scale, is the *Residencial Solar Monfalim* (☎ *2 20 31, fax 74 23 67, Largo da Misericórdia 1)*. It has elegant rooms starting at 11,500/14,000$00, including breakfast. This place is due to be upgraded to an *albergaria* (upmarket inn), so the prices will probably rise.

Hotels Though calling itself a residencial, the professionally run *Riviera* (☎ *2 33 04,*

fax 2 04 67, Rua 5 de Outubro 49) is in effect a hotel. It's good value at 10,000$00 for doubles with bathroom and TV, including breakfast, and is bang in the centre. Offering plain, clean rooms at similar prices is the quiet *Hotel Santa Clara* (☎ *2 41 41, fax 2 65 44, Travessa da Milheira 19)*.

In a class of its own is the snooty but deluxe *Pousada dos Lóios* (☎ *2 40 51, fax 2 72 48)*, occupying the former Convento dos Lóios opposite the Templo Romano. Doubles cost 29,600$00 in high season.

Turihab On the plains around Évora are at least 10 converted *quintas* (farmhouses) registered under the Turismo de Habitação or Turismo Rural schemes. A similar place is the recommended *Monte da Serralheira* (☎ *74 12 86, fax 74 39 57)*. It's 4km south of town and has a swimming pool as well as bikes and horses to ride. Its charming self-catering apartments range from 8000$00 to 14,000$00. The turismo can help with booking this and other Turihab places.

Places to Eat

Restaurants – Budget A cheap little place tucked away near Praça do Giraldo is *Restaurante O Túnel* (☎ *2 66 49, Alcárcova de Baixo 59)* which has an extensive menu of meat courses for under 1000$00 as well as snacks and sandwiches; it's closed Sunday. Similarly priced is *Restaurante O Portão* (☎ *2 33 25, Rua do Cano 27)*, right by the aqueduct. The *Tasca do Comendinha* (☎ *2 01 00)* opposite has a pleasant outdoor area for a drink or light meal; the jukebox music isn't bad, either.

Restaurants – Mid-Range Our favourite restaurant is the locally popular *Café Restaurante O Cruz* (☎ *74 47 79, Praça 1 de Maio 20)*. It's one of several places opposite the mercado municipal; regional specialities include their unique recipe for bacalhau and tasty *carne com ameijoas* (meat with clams). Most dishes cost under 1300$00.

Restaurante O Garfo (☎ *2 92 56, Rua de Santa Catarina 13)* offers healthy servings of *ensopada de borrego alentejana* (lamb stew) and other reasonably priced traditional dishes. The jovial *Taberna Típica Quarta-Feira* (☎ 2 75 30, *Rua do Inverno 16*) is invariably packed out with locals. House specialities include *puré de espinafres* (creamed spinach) and slices of pork with sausage. Another good value place nearby is *Restaurante-Bar Molhóbico* (☎ 74 43 43, *Rua de Aviz 91*), which has a small outdoor dining area and a menu including half a dozen versions of traditional Alentejan *migas* (stews) all costing less than 1500$00.

Restaurants – Top End Pricier places with excellent service include the small *Restaurante O Grémio* (☎ 74 29 31, *Alcárcova de Cima 10*), where fish and meat courses cost around 1900$00; and *Restaurante Cozinha de Santo Humberto* (☎ 2 42 51, *Rua da Moeda 39*), offering regional specialities and a fine dessert selection in a traditional setting; advance bookings are suggested (closed Thursday).

Finally, for a splurge in historic surroundings, you can't beat the *Jardim do Paço* (☎ 74 43 00), beside the Igreja de São João, whose outdoor seating adorns the former garden of the Palácio dos Duques de Cadaval; humbler diners can retreat to the cheaper snack kiosk on the other side of the Templo Romano.

Cafés & Snacks The cavernous, busy *Café Arcada* (*Praça de Giraldo 10*), whose outdoor tables are irresistibly located in the Praça itself, serves drinks and snacks as well as reasonably priced daily specials; it's pricier if you sit outside.

Considerably less public is *Salão Condestável* (*Rua de Diogo Cão 3*), a quiet little café opposite the Residencial Diana with a menu including pizzas. A popular student hang-out that stays open late is *Dom João Cafetaria* (*Rua de Vasco da Gama 10*). If you've got a serious case of the sweet-toothed munchies, you'll enjoy the ice-cream parlour *Gelataria Zoka* (*Largo de São Vicente 14*).

Self-Catering Pick up fruit and vegetables from the *mercado municipal* on Praça 1 de Maio and eat them in the adjacent jardim público. There is a *Modelo* hipermercado just beyond the town limits on the road to the camping ground and Alcáçovas.

Entertainment

Puppet Theatre Five actors from the municipal Teatro Garcia de Resende studied for several years with the only surviving master of a traditional rural puppet style called *bonecos de Santo Aleixo* (puppets of Santo Aleixo). They offer performances of this and other styles, as well as hand-puppet shows for children, at a little theatre called *Casa dos Bonecos* (☎ 2 64 69, 2 51 99) off Largo de Machede Velho. They give shows for the general public only at weekends; tickets cost about 500$00 (300$00 for children's matinées). For current offerings, ask at the turismo.

Bars Most bars stay open until at least 2 am. Among the student hang-outs are a cluster of bars north-west of the centre: *Club Dezasseis* (☎ 2 65 59, *Rua do Escrivão da Câmara 16*); the *Diplomata Pub* (☎ 2 56 75, *Rua do Apóstolo 4*), with frequent live music; and *Pub O Trovador* (☎ 2 73 70, *Rua da Mostardeira 4*). *Restaurante-Bar Molhóbico* (see Places to Eat – Mid-Range) stays open for dinner until 1.30 am and drinks until at least 2 am. *Bar Desassossego* (☎ 2 64 75, *Travessa do Janeiro 15*) is open daily, except Sunday, from 10 pm until (so they said) 2 pm the following day.

Spectator Sports

Évora has its own *praça de touros* (bullring) outside the southern walls near the jardim público. The bullfighting season extends roughly from May to October; ask at the turismo about upcoming events.

Shopping

The lower end of Rua 5 de Outubro is a gauntlet of pricey *artesanatos* (handicrafts shops), mostly selling cork knick-knacks,

ALENTEJO

hand-painted furniture and pottery. You'll find cheaper pottery outside on the shady side of the mercado municipal. There are more upmarket shops along Rua Cândido dos Reis, including Evoralar at No 29, which sells high quality porcelain, glass and beautifully dressed porcelain dolls (typical Portuguese wedding presents).

On the second Tuesday of each month a Gypsy market sprawls across a big field called the Rossio Ocidental, just outside the walls on the road to the train station.

Getting There & Away
Bus From the claustrophobic bus station (☎ 2 21 21, 2 42 54) on Rua da República there are at least eight Évora-Lisbon express coaches (2 to 2¾ hours) each weekday (fewer at weekends) plus half-a-dozen ordinary coaches (3¾ hours). There are two direct Évora-Coimbra coaches daily (4½ hours, via Santarém), and two to Portalegre (2¼ hours).

Other daily long-distance express services include two to Faro (five hours, via Beja), one to Tomar, and two to Porto.

Train Évora station (☎ 2 21 25) is on a branch of the Lisbon-Beja railway line. There are two daily IR services to Lisbon (three hours), plus slower services, as well as trains to the Algarve (tedious and indirect) and Coimbra (changes required), and regional (R) chug-a-lug services to Beja.

Car Evorarent (☎/fax 74 60 51), Rua Miguel Bombarda 37, rents cars for around 41,000$00 a week in the high season. Hertz (☎ 2 17 67) is at Rua de Dona Isabel 11 and Europcar rents cars through the Evoratur travel agency (see Information).

There's a branch of the Automóvel Club de Portugal (see Assistance under Car & Motorcycle in the Getting Around chapter) at Alcárcova de Baixo 7 (☎ 2 75 33, fax 2 96 96).

Getting Around
Taxi Not all taxis have meters, so drivers may do their own fare calculations on the basis of fixed weekday, night and weekend rates. On a weekday expect to pay about 540$00 for a ride from Praça do Giraldo to the train station or the camping ground.

Bicycle Évora Rent-a-Bike (☎ 76 14 53) rents out mountain bikes for about 2000$00 a day (cheaper for longer periods) from a stand in the jardim público.

AROUND ÉVORA
The plains around Évora abound in prehistoric remains, including at least one cave decorated with Cro-Magnon art, and several dozen sizeable Neolithic stone monuments – menhirs (individual standing stones), dolmens (funereal temples or tombs) and cromlechs (circles of upright stones) – dating from around 4000 to 3000 BC.

Described here are among the easiest sites to find on your own; to see the most impressive – the Almendres Cromlech and Zambujeiro Dolmen – involves a round trip of about 50km.

A sheet in the *Historical Itineraries* pack (see under Maps in the Évora section) details many of the monuments. From the Évora turismo you can also pick up a briefer explanatory pamphlet, *Almendres* (100$00), or, for serious dolmen fans, the academic *Paisagens Arqueologicas A Oeste de Évora* (with summaries in English) for 2500$00. See also the boxed text 'Dolmens, Menhirs & Other Mysteries' later in this chapter.

Cromeleque dos Almendres
From Guadalupe, a dirt track winds through a beautiful landscape of olive and cork trees, ending at the Almendres Cromlech. Considering this is the most important megalithic group in the Iberian Peninsula – a veritable Portuguese Stonehenge – it's been left amazingly untouched. You're likely to be the only visitor.

The site consists of a huge oval of some 95 rounded granite monoliths spread down a rough slope. Some are engraved with symbolic markings. They were erected over different periods, probably for social gatherings, fertility rites or solar observations.

Other sacred rituals may also have taken place here in honour of a religion which (according to one of the turismo leaflets) centred on 'a female super-divinity with huge sun-like eyes'.

Anta Grande do Zambujeiro

The Great Dolmen of Zambujeiro is the largest in Europe and it's now a national monument. Under a huge sheet metal shelter in a field of wild flowers and yellow broom are seven stones, each 6m high, forming a huge chamber. The capstone was removed by archaeologists in the 1960s. Most of the site's relics (potshards, beads, flint tools and so on) are in the Museu de Évora.

Anta Capela de São Brissos

This tiny, whitewashed chapel beside the Valverde-N2 road (just beyond the turn-off to São Brissos) was assembled in the 17th century from surviving stones of an *anta* (dolmen).

Escoural Cave

About 2km east of the village of Santiago do Escoural is a cave adorned with charcoal renditions of bison, horses and other animals, thought to have been executed by Cro-Magnon artists some 15,000 years ago.

Tours, organised at the cave, require groups of around 10 people, so you might have to wait around for a while. There is no charge, but tips are appreciated. The cave is open on Tuesday from 1.30 to 5.30 pm, Wednesday to Friday from 9 am to noon and 1.30 to 5.30 pm, and at weekends from 9 am to noon and 1.30 to 5 pm.

Getting There & Away

There are no convenient buses to this area so your only option is to rent a car or bike (but note that about 5km of the route is rough and remote). Alternatively, talk to Mendes & Murteira (see under Organised Tours in the Évora section) about a guided trip.

With your own wheels, head west from Évora on the old Lisbon road (N114) for 12km, then turn south to Guadalupe. Follow the signs from here to the Cromlech dos Almendres (4km).

Return to Guadalupe and head south for 5km to Valverde, home of the Universidade de Évora's school of agriculture and the 16th century Convento de Bom Jesus. Following the signs to Anta Grande do Zambujeiro, turn into the school's farmyard and onto a badly potholed track. After 1km you'll see the Great Dolmen.

Continue west from Valverde for 12km. Before joining the N2, turn right for the cave at Santiago do Escoural.

MONSARAZ
☎ 066

One of the most famous fortified hilltop villages in Portugal, Monsaraz is visible from miles around, towering over a somnolent landscape of ploughed fields and wild meadows dotted with cork and olive trees and Neolithic monuments.

Settled long before the Moors arrived in the 8th century, Monsaraz was recaptured by the Christians under Giraldo Sem Pavor (Gerald the Fearless) in 1167 and subsequently given to the Knights Templar as a reward for their assistance. The castle was added in 1310.

You only need half an hour to meander from one end of the immaculate village to the other, but it's worth considering an overnight stay – the panorama from the castle walls is best savoured at dusk and dawn. With the town's recent application to become a UNESCO World Heritage Site, Monsaraz has even shed such 20th century trappings as TV aerials; after the daytrippers have left, a medieval aura descends on the place.

Orientation

Happily there's no room for tour coaches or cars inside the walled village, so your arrival at one of the four gates will be as it should be: on foot. From the main parking lot, the Porta da Alcoba opens directly onto the central Praça Dom Nuno Álvares Pereira. The main gate, Porta da Vila, is at the north end of town (the castle is at the other end) and leads into Rua São Tiago and the parallel Rua Direita, Monsaraz's two main streets.

Information

The staff at the turismo (☎ 55 71 36) on Praça Dom Nuno Álvares can tell you about available accommodation and bus times to Reguengos de Monsaraz. The turismo is open weekdays from 10 am to 7 pm, and weekends from 10 am to 1 pm and 2 to 5.30 pm.

Igreja Matriz

The parish church (near the turismo) was rebuilt after the 1755 earthquake and again a century later. It has just one interesting feature, a 14th century marble tomb carved with saints. An eye-catching 18th century pelourinho, topped by a Manueline globe, stands outside. The church is open daily from 9 am to 1 pm and 2 to 6 pm, as is the Igreja da Misericórdia opposite.

Museu de Arte Sacra

Housed in a fine Gothic building (perhaps once the town's courthouse) beside the Igreja Matriz, the Museum of Sacred Art houses a small collection of 14th century wooden religious figures and 18th century vestments and silverware. Its most famous exhibit is a rare example of a 14th century secular fresco (showing a good and bad judge, the latter appropriately two-faced). The museum is open from 9 am to 2 pm and 3 to 7 pm daily; admission costs 200$00.

Castelo

The castle at the south-western end of the village was one of many built by Dom Dinis as part of a defensive chain of around 50 fortresses along the Spanish border. Now converted into a small praça de touros, its ramparts offer a fine panoramic view over the Alentejan plains.

Special Events

Monsaraz is packed out during its week-long Museu Aberto (Open Museum) music festival in July, and also on the second weekend of September, when bullfights and processions take place as part of the Festa de Nossa Senhora dos Passos. Unless booked well in advance, accommodation is almost impossible to find at these times.

Places to Stay

Several villagers have cashed in on the tourist era by converting their cute little cottages into guesthouses or self-catering apartments. Two of the least expensive places – charging around 5000$00 for a double, including breakfast – are on Rua Direita: *Casa Dona Antónia* (☎ 55 71 42) is at No 15, and *Casa do Condestável* (☎ 55 71 81) is at No 4.

Casa do Paço (☎ 55 73 06, *Rua Direita 2*) has a perfect set-up for families, with two big plain rooms (5000$00 upstairs; 4000$00 downstairs, with 'special price' for students), a kitchen and plenty of space for kids to romp around.

One of several slick Turihab properties is *Casa Dom Nuno* (☎ 55 71 46, *fax 55 74 00, Rua José Fernandes Caeiro 6*), which has eight elegant doubles costing 8000$00.

Two kilometres away, en route to Mourão, the *Horta da Moura* (☎ 55 01 00, *fax 55 01 08*) is a converted Alentejan quinta where you can go horse riding, fishing, canoeing or biking; there's also a pool. Doubles cost around 16,000$00.

Places to Eat

There's a handful of restaurants geared for tourists, most offering traditional Alentejan lamb dishes such as *borrego assado* (roast lamb) costing from around 1000$00 to 1200$00. For great sunset views over the plains, check out *Café Restaurante O Alcaide* (☎ 55 71 68, *Rua São Tiago 15*). This place and the *Restaurante São Tiago* (☎ 55 71 88), on the same street at No 3, also have their own bars.

For posh ambience and prices, head for *A Casa do Forno* (☎ 55 71 90, *Travessa da Sanabrosa*). Simplest and cheapest of the lot is *Café-Restaurant Lumumba* (*Rua Direita 12*).

Self-catering options are limited to bread and cheese from a *grocery shop* at the Porta da Vila end of Rua São Tiago, and pastries from *Pastelaria A Cisterna* at the Porta da Vila end of Rua Direita.

Getting There & Away

Buses run to/from Reguengos de Monsaraz three to four times daily on weekdays only. The last one back to Reguengos (where you can pick up connections to Évora) is at 5 pm.

REGUENGOS DE MONSARAZ

☎ 066 • pop 11,000 (municipality)

This small, insignificant farming town, once famous for its sheep and wool production, is on the tourist trail today only because of its proximity and connections to Monsaraz. It's also close to the pottery centre of São Pedro do Corval and an impressive half-dozen dolmens and menhirs out of around 150 scattered across the surrounding plains (see the boxed text 'Dolmens, Menhirs & Other Mysteries' on the next page). While you're here, enjoy some of the great local wine, Terras d'el Rei.

Orientation & Information

The bus station is on the outskirts of town to the south-west, about 200m from the central Praça da Liberdade. Just off the praça, on Rua 1 de Maio, is the municipal turismo (☎ 50 33 15) which can provide general information on the region: particularly useful is the rough sketch map of nearby dolmens. The office is open weekdays from 9 am (10 am at weekends) to 12.30 pm and 2 to 5.30 pm.

Wineries

The Adega Cooperativa de Reguengos de Monsaraz (☎ 51 01 01), just outside town on the Monsaraz road, offers free group tours of its wine factory and could probably be persuaded to take individuals who sound keen enough.

More geared to visits is another major *adega*, Herdade do Esporão (☎ 51 97 50, email esporao@mail.telepac.pt), a few kilo-

metres south of town. In operation as a winery for some 700 years, with some lovely old wine cellars, it produces mostly red wines for the domestic market and now has a wine bar, restaurant and wine shop.

Places to Stay & Eat

In the heart of town, on Praça da Liberdade, there are a couple of decent places to stay. Cheapest is *Pensão Fialho* (☎ 51 92 66) at No 17, offering seven neat little doubles with bathroom for around 4000$00. *Pensão O Gato* (☎/fax 5 23 53) next door is a notch smarter; doubles cost 6000/5000$00 with/without bathroom.

Both pensões have restaurants; Gato's is the more expensive of the two. Alternatively, try *Restaurante Central* (☎ 5 22 19), also on the praça, which has a varied and imaginative menu.

Shopping

The town has a thriving handicrafts industry; *mantas*, hand-woven woollen blankets, are its speciality. You can see these and much more – ceramics, wickerware and typical hand-painted Alentejan furniture – being produced in a workshop near the Adega de Cooperativa de Reguengos. The workshop, converted from an old slaughterhouse, belongs to TEAR (Portuguese for loom), an association of young artisans founded to help preserve traditional local crafts. It's open daily from 10 am to around 7 pm (☎ 5 17 10, fax 50 11 04).

If you're particularly interested in hand-woven goods, check out the last remaining hand loom producer of *mantas Alentejanas*, Fabrica Alentejana de Lanificios (☎ 066-5 21 79); it's on the Mourão road east of town.

Serious ceramics buffs should head for São Pedro do Corval, 5km east, whose 32 workshops make it one of the largest pottery centres in Portugal. Traditional Alentejan wares made here include plates, pots and floor tiles.

For details of other handicrafts in the region, ask the turismo for its comprehensive list of local artisans.

ALENTEJO

Dolmens, Menhirs & Other Mysteries

You come across them all over the Alentejo plains, especially around Monsaraz, Elvas and Évora: faintly engraved boulders, mysterious stone circles, towering fertility objects and cave-like stone tombs. They're part of a style of construction called megalithic (literally, 'large stone' in Greek) found all along the European Atlantic coast and were built some five to six thousand years ago.

Nearly all are related to ritual worship of some kind. Dolmens (*antas* in Portuguese) are megalithic temples used as tombs, covered with a large flat stone and usually built on hilltops or near water. Menhirs (tall, upright stones) and cromlechs (stone circles) were also places of worship and their construction represents a remarkable community effort.

There are half a dozen outstanding examples between Reguengos de Monsaraz and Monsaraz including the Menhir de Bulhoa, 4km north of Monsaraz off the Telheiro-Outeiro road. This phallic stone bears intriguing traces of carved circles and lines. An even more impressive 7 tonne phallic monument stands as the centrepiece in the Cromleque do Xerez, a group of some 50 menhirs 5km south of Monsaraz, en route to Xerez de Baixo and Mourão. By the year 2000, however, the Cromleque do Xerez will have fallen victim to the flooding of this area caused by the construction of the massive Alqueva dam near Moura (see the boxed text 'Water Wars' earlier in this chapter). There are plans to relocate the stones to an open-air museum of dolmens between the villages of Monsaraz and Telheiro.

More information on these and other megaliths are available at the turismos in Évora, Reguengos de Monsaraz and Elvas.

Getting There & Away

Reguengos is connected with Évora by a bus which runs three or four times daily on weekdays (more during the school term); the journey takes 45 minutes. Three buses daily (weekdays only) go to Monsaraz; the last bus currently departs at 6.20 pm.

ESTREMOZ

☎ 068 • pop 8000

Dominated by its medieval hilltop castle, Estremoz is an elegant town of startling whiteness, thanks largely to the extensive use of marble in its construction. So plentiful is the supply of high grade marble in this region that Estremoz and its neighbouring towns of Borba and Vila Viçosa are quite blasé about it, using it even for the door-steps and window frames of its humblest cottages. But despite appearances Estremoz is basically a simple market town, famous for its earthenware pottery, large Saturday markets, preserved plums and goat cheeses.

With a plentiful supply of restaurants and pensões it makes a convenient base for visiting the other marble towns, or a suitable stopover en route to Évora or Portalegre, but it's hardly a hub of excitement – linger too long and you might calcify too.

Orientation

The lower, newer town, enclosed by 17th century ramparts, is ranged around a huge square, Rossio Marquês de Pombal (known simply as the Rossio), around which you'll find most accommodation, restaurants and shops. A 10 minute climb west of the Rossio brings you to the medieval quarter with its 13th century castle and keep (which is now a luxurious pousada).

The bus station is by the defunct train station on Avenida 9 de Abril, a 10 minute walk east of the Rossio.

Information

The excellent turismo (☎ 33 35 41, fax 2 44 89) is tucked into the southern corner of

Largo da República. It's open daily from 10 am to 12.30 pm and 3 to 6 pm. Telephone numbers were in the process of changing at the time of research; you may need to ask here for assistance with contacting pensões or hotels.

The post office is on Avenida 5 de Outubro. At the northern end of Avenida 9 de Abril is the medical centre, the *centro de saúde* (☎ 33 20 42). The police station (☎ 2 22 89) is in the câmara municipal.

The Lower Town

On the fringes of the Rossio are several imposing old churches, former convents and, to the north, some monastic buildings which have been converted into cavalry barracks. Opposite these, by Largo General Graça, is an attractive marble-edged water tank called the Lago do Gadanha (Lake of the Scythe) after its scythe-wielding statue of Neptune. Some of the prettiest marble streets in town are south of the Rossio, off Largo da República.

Câmara Municipal Peek into this 17th century building, a former convent, for a look at the imposing staircase decorated with azulejos depicting hunting scenes.

Museu Rural This delightful one room museum portraying rural Alentejan life – one of the best such museums in Portugal – suddenly closed in 1998, with no indication of whether it would reopen. Check with the turismo.

Museu de Ciências da Terra Run by the Estremoz University, the museum of earth sciences is dedicated to the area's most famous asset – its marble – with displays of old mining and cutting equipment and detailed explanations (unfortunately only in Portuguese) of other geological features. Worth the 300$00 admission fee alone is the museum's setting in the lovely cloisters of the former 16th century Convento das Maltezas. The museum is open weekdays from 9 am to 12.30 pm and 2 to 5.30 pm, and on Saturday from 9 am to 12.30 pm.

Museu Alfaia Agrícola A museum of old agricultural and household equipment doesn't sound thrilling, but this cavernous old warehouse on Rua Serpa Pinto has some fascinating stuff displayed over its three floors, from old presses and threshers to huge brass pots and pans. It's open Tuesday to Friday from 9 am to noon and 2 to 5 pm; at weekends it's open in the afternoons only. Admission costs 175$00.

The Upper Town

You can reach the upper town on foot by various tortuous routes but the easiest way is to follow the narrow Rua da Frandina from the lower town's Praça Luís de Camões to enter the inner castle walls through the Arco da Frandina.

Palace & Keep At the top of the upper town is the stark white former royal palace, now the sumptuous Pousada de Santa Rainha Isabel. The palace was built in the 13th century by Dom Dinis for his new wife, Isabel of Aragon. After her death in 1336 (Dinis had died 11 years earlier) it became an ammunition dump. An inevitable explosion in 1698 destroyed most of the palace and the surrounding castle, though in the 18th century João V restored the palace for use as an armoury.

The 27m-high keep, the **Torre das Três Coroas** (Tower of the Three Crowns), survived and is still the dominant feature. It was supposedly built by three kings: Sancho II, Afonso III and Dinis.

Visitors are welcome to look around the public areas of the pousada and climb the keep, which offers a fantastic view of the old town and surrounding plains (though a grain elevator ruins the view to the east). Sufferers from vertigo should refrain from looking down the holes intended for dumping boiling oil on invaders.

Igreja de Santa Maria & Capela de Santa Isabel The stout, square 16th century Igreja de Santa Maria near the pousada – more an art gallery displaying some mediocre, primitive Portuguese paintings

ESTREMOZ

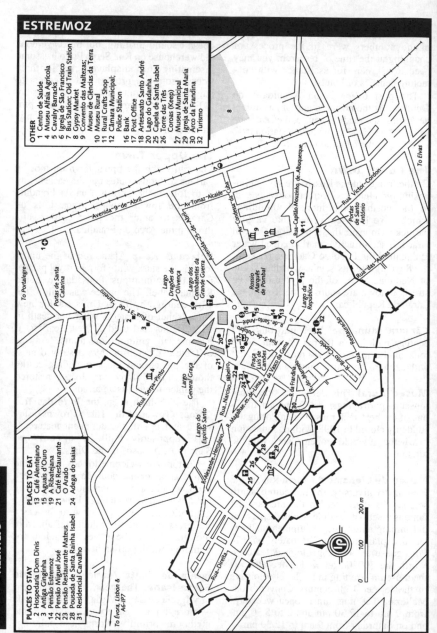

PLACES TO STAY
2 Hospedaria Dom Dinis
3 Antiga Ginginha
14 Pensão Estremoz
22 Pensão Miguel José
23 Pensão Restaurante Mateus
28 Pousada de Santa Rainha Isabel
31 Residencial Carvalho

PLACES TO EAT
13 Café Alentejano
15 Aguais d'Ouro
19 A Ribatejana
21 Café Restaurante
    O Arado
24 Adega do Isaías

OTHER
1 Centro de Saúde
4 Museu Alfaia Agrícola
5 Cavalry Barracks
6 Igreja de São Francisco
7 Bus Station; Old Train Station
8 Gypsy Market
9 Convento das Maltezas;
    Museu de Ciências da Terra
10 Museu Rural
11 Rural Crafts Shop
12 Câmara Municipal;
    Police Station
16 Bank
17 Post Office
18 Artesanato Santo André
20 Lago do Gadanha
25 Capela de Santa Isabel
26 Torre das Três
    Coroas (Keep)
27 Museu Municipal
29 Igreja de Santa Maria
30 Arco da Frandina
32 Turismo

ALENTEJO

than a church – keeps erratic hours. More interesting is the Capela de Santa Isabel behind the keep. This chapel was built in 1659 in honour of the queen, who had died, aged 65, after a journey from Santiago de Compostela in Spain. The walls are covered with panels of fine 18th century azulejo portraying scenes from the life of the saintly queen.

A legend illustrates her generosity to the poor, to the extent that (to the chagrin of her husband) she gave them her own food. According to the story, the king once demanded to see what she was carrying in her skirt; she let go of her apron and the bread she had hidden to donate to the poor was miraculously transformed into roses.

The chapel should be open to the public daily except Monday, from May to September; if it's locked, inquire at the church.

Museu Municipal Near the pousada, this museum offers an engaging view of rural Alentejan life. Housed in a 17th century almshouse, it specialises in Estremoz pottery figurines. Upstairs is a reconstruction of a typical Alentejan house interior. The museum is open daily, except Monday and holidays, from 10 am to 12.30 pm and 3 to 6.30 pm (in winter from 2 to 5 pm); admission costs 175$00.

Places to Stay
Some of the cheapest quartos can be found at *Antiga Ginginha* (☎ 2 26 43, *Rua 31 de Janeiro 4*). The two street-facing rooms here cost 1500/3000$00 for a single/double.

Another budget choice is the run-down *Residencial Carvalho* (☎ 33 93 70, *Largo da República 27*), where old-fashioned doubles without/with bathroom cost 4000/5000$00, including breakfast. Similarly priced is *Pensão Estremoz* (☎ 2 28 34, *Rossio 14*), which is part of the Café Alentejano. Despite its imposing marble staircase, the rooms (and the bed springs) have seen better days.

West of the Rossio, *Pensão Miguel José* (☎ 2 23 26, *Travessa da Levada 8*) is a warren of 13 tiny modern rooms. Neat and clean double rooms cost 4000/5000$00 without/with bathroom, including breakfast. Prices are similar at the friendlier *Pensão-Restaurante Mateus* (☎ 2 22 26, *Rua do Almeida 39*).

The upmarket choice in the lower town is *Hospedaria Dom Dinis* (☎ 33 27 17, fax 2 26 10, *Rua 31 de Janeiro 46*), offering well kitted-out doubles for 12,500$00. Surpassing everything else is the *Pousada de Santa Rainha Isabel* (☎ 33 20 75, fax 33 20 79) where you can stay in splendour, surrounded by antique furnishings and fine tapestries, for 29,600$00.

Three kilometres out of town there are also a couple of fine Turihab places with doubles for about 10,000$00; contact the turismo for more details.

Places to Eat
The upstairs restaurant at *Café Alentejano* (☎ 2 28 34 *Rossio 16*) has some good local specialities including *feijoada* (bean stew) and *javali* (wild boar) for 1200$00.

You'll need to be at the front of the queue for dinner at *Adega do Isaias* (☎ 2 23 18, *Rua do Almeida 21*). This award-winning, dark and rustic *tasca* (tavern) has outdoor grills, communal bench tables and huge terracotta wine jars from which your house wine is served. It's not cheap – grilled meat dishes start at around 950$00 – but the atmosphere is worth the extra escudos. Get here by 7.30 pm to bag a seat. It's closed Sunday.

Every other restaurant seems dull by comparison, but one that's popular with the locals is *A Ribatejana* (☎ 2 36 56, *Largo General Graça 41*). It has a long meat menu and half-portions start at 700$00. Nearby is *Café Restaurante O Arado* (☎ 33 34 71, *Rua Narciso Ribeiro 7*), which specialises in *frango no churrasco* (roast chicken).

One of the best restaurants in town is the rather pretentious, wood-panelled *Aguais d'Ouro* (☎ 33 33 26, *Rossio 27*). If you don't mind paying upwards of 1400$00 per dish, you'll eat very well. Try the house speciality, *borrego com espargos* (lamb with asparagus).

ALENTEJO

Shopping

The weekly Saturday market which sprawls along the southern fringe of the Rossio is a great display of Alentejan goodies and Estremoz specialities, especially goat and ewe's milk cheeses, and a unique style of unglazed, ochre-red pottery. On the eastern edge is a flea market and to the west a loitering crowd of Estremoz menfolk.

If you miss the Saturday market – or need horse tackle, cowbells or baskets – there's a great handicraft and rural crafts shop at Rua Victor Cordon 16, south-east of the Rossio. A smaller selection is stocked by Artesanato Santo André at Rua da Misericórdia 2.

Getting There & Away

On weekdays there are half a dozen buses between Estremoz and Évora including three express services (taking about one hour). About four buses daily run to Portalegre and Elvas, and three go to Vila Viçosa. Buses to Lisbon and Faro depart three times daily.

BORBA

☎ 068 • pop 7900 (municipality)

You'd think that a town famous for its wine, antiques and marble would be a bit pretentious, but Borba keeps a pretty low profile. It has little in the way of notable sights and has always been overlooked in favour of Vila Viçosa, 6km to the south-east.

One of the three 'marble towns' (the other two are Estremoz and Vila Viçosa), Borba is ringed by huge marble quarries and glows with marble whiteness. Even the public loos are made of marble. You can spend an agreeable few hours here, checking out the antique shops or visiting the wineries, although accommodation options are better in Estremoz.

The town comes to life once a year in early November, when it hosts a huge country fair.

Orientation & Information

Borba's main square, Praça da República, with its ornate 18th century marble fountain, the Fonte das Bicas, is the focus of town. The turismo (☎ 9 41 13, fax 9 48 06) is in the câmara municipal on Rua do Convento das Servas.

Wineries

There are three adegas in town, all producing the famous Borba full-bodied red and white *maduro* (mature) wines, which are among the best in Portugal. Two adegas offer guided tours. The turismo can help you arrange a visit.

The Adega Cooperativa de Borba (☎ 9 42 64), out on the Estremoz road, is the largest and produces over 10 million litres of wine a year. Opposite is the Sociedade de Vinhos de Borba (☎ 9 42 10), whose ornately carved portal is worth a look. The adegas are usually open weekdays only, from 9 am to noon and 2 to 5.30 pm.

Getting There & Away

There are only two or three buses a day between Borba, Estremoz and Vila Viçosa.

VILA VIÇOSA

☎ 068 • pop 9000 (municipality)

Vila Viçosa is a palatial but relaxing place and the finest of the three marble towns, with marbled streets, marble mansions, marble-adorned churches (over 20 of them) and a hilltop walled castle (alas, made only of stone). It's actually best known for its Paço Ducal, the palatial home of the Bragança dynasty, whose kings ruled Portugal until the republic was founded in 1910. You can easily cover the sights in a day trip from Estremoz.

Orientation

Regional buses stop at the huge, sloping Praça da República. At the top is the 17th century Igreja de São Bartolomeu; at the bottom is Avenida Bento de Jesus which leads to the castle. The ducal palace is five minutes walk north of the praça (follow Rua Dr Couto Jardim).

Information

The turismo (☎ 88 11 01, fax 9 26 09), Praça da República 34, is a useful stop; it dispenses maps and staff can advise on accommodation.

Paço Ducal

The austere palace of the dukes of Bragança dates from the early 16th century when the fourth duke, Dom Jaime, decided to move out of his uncomfortable hilltop castle. The Bragança family, originally from Bragança in the northern province of Trás-os-Montes, had settled in Vila Viçosa in the 15th century when they were among the wealthiest nobles in the land. After the eighth duke became king in 1640, he and his successors – especially the last of the line, Manuel I – continued to visit the palace, though it no longer hosted the banquets and festivities of Dom Jaime's time.

The interior is now pretty dull: the best furniture went to Lisbon after the eighth duke ascended the throne, and some went on to Brazil after the royal family fled there in 1807. Even so, the private apartments have a ghostly fascination – toiletries, knick-knacks and clothes of Dom Carlos and his wife, Marie-Amélia, are laid out as if the royal couple were about to return (Dom Carlos left one morning in 1908 and was assassinated in Lisbon that afternoon).

Outside, at right angles to the palace, the Convento das Chagas de Cristo, once a mausoleum for the duchesses, is now a posh pousada. The 16th century cloisters house an armoury museum, and the stables are now a coach museum.

The hour-long guided tours of the palace (usually in Portuguese) are demanding on pocket and patience. The fee of 1000$00 doesn't include the armoury museum – that's another 500$00. Opening hours are from 9 am to noon and 3 to 4.30 pm on weekdays (2.30 to 4 pm in winter) and from 9 am to noon and 3 to 5 pm at weekends (2 to 4 pm in winter). It's closed Monday.

Castelo

Dom Dinis' walled hilltop castle, south of the palace, was where the Bragança family lived before the palace was built. A few small houses (still inhabited), a 16th century pelourinho and the 15th century Igreja de Nossa Senhora da Conceição are all that remain of the town that once surrounded the castle.

Skeletons in the Bragança Cupboard

The most illustrious member of the powerful Bragança family – descended from Dom João I's illegitimate son, Afonso – was the eighth duke who in 1640 became a reluctant king, Dom João IV, sealing Portugal's liberation from Spanish rule. But there are murky corners in the dynastic history too.

The third duke, Fernando, was executed in Évora in 1483 on the orders of his brother-in-law Dom João II, who deliberately struck at the family's immense power and wealth by accusing the duke of plotting against the monarchy.

By far the nastiest episode concerns the fourth duke, Dom Jaime, who murdered his young wife Leonor de Gusmão in a fit of jealous rage on 2 November 1512. Already suspicious that his wife was having an affair, he caught a young pageboy climbing into the window of her quarters at the Paço Ducal in Vila Viçosa. Despite her pleas of innocence, the duke 'with five slashes ripped out her life'. Only later was it revealed that the pageboy was probably visiting one of the queen's ladies-in-waiting.

The most recent murderous event was the assassination of Dom Carlos and his son in Lisbon on 1 February 1908. Two years later the monarchy was overthrown and the royal Bragança line came to an end. Today's leading Bragança noble, Dom Duarte, keeps a low, politically correct profile, supervising an experimental eco-farm in the north of the country.

The castle itself has recently been transformed into a **Museu de Caça** (hunting museum) stuffed with gruesome trophies, many snared by the dukes on their 2000 hectare royal hunting ground north of Vila Viçosa and visible from the castle. The museum is open daily from 9.30 am to 1 pm and 2.30 to 6 pm (to 5 pm in winter); admission costs 400$00.

Places to Stay

The best budget option is *Hospedaria Dom Carlos* (☎/fax 9 83 18, Praça da República 25); singles/doubles (all with bathroom and TV) cost 3500/5000$00. For appropriate baronial ambience, try *Casa de Peixinhos* (☎ 9 84 72), a 17th century manor house a few kilometres out on the Borba road. Doubles furnished in tiles and antiques cost 16,000$00.

Ultimate palatial splendour is available at the new *Pousada de Dom João IV* (☎ 9 87 42, fax 9 87 47), the former royal convent next to the ducal palace. Lavishly decorated doubles cost 29,600$00 during the high season.

Places to Eat

You'll find plenty of restaurants and cafés around Praça da República and the mercado municipal. *Os Cucos* (☎ 9 88 06), hidden in the gardens near the mercado, is recommended. It boasts a long menu of fish and meat dishes; prices start at 1000$00. The *mercado municipal* itself – busiest on Wednesday – is south of the praça at the end of Rua Dr António José da Almeida.

Getting There & Away

There are two to three buses daily from Estremoz to Vila Viçosa via Borba; the trip takes 25 minutes.

ELVAS

☎ 068 • pop 15,000

This massively fortified frontier town, 15km west of Spanish Badajoz and 40km east of Estremoz, boasts the most sophisticated 17th century military architecture in Europe, with well-preserved moats, curtain walls, bastions, fortified gates and three forts. Inside the walls, though, it feels much like any other Alentejan market town, hosting Spanish day-trippers during the week (who come here for cheap linen, china and candied plums) and coming to a complete standstill on Sunday afternoons.

Walkers will have a field day following the old aqueduct or town walls, or losing themselves in the warren of narrow streets.

History

Elvas only really charged into the history books in 1230, when it was recaptured from the Moors after 500 years of relatively peaceful occupation. The following centuries saw interminable attacks from Spain, interrupted by occasional peace treaties. The only successful attack was in 1580, allowing Felipe II of Spain (the future Felipe I of Portugal) to set up court here for a few months. The garrison's honour was redeemed during the Wars of Succession when, in 1644, it held out against a nine day Spanish siege. In 1659, its numbers reduced by an epidemic to a mere one thousand men, the garrison withstood an attack by a 15,000-strong Spanish army.

The massive fortifications had their last period of glory in 1811, when the Duke of Wellington used the town as a base for attacking Badajoz during the Peninsular War.

Orientation

The town centre is surprisingly compact considering the extent of the walls. The bus station and turismo are side by side in the central Praça da República, and all of the major sights of interest are a short walk away. Those arriving by train will find themselves at Fontaínhas, 4km north of town. Drivers should park on the outskirts (or just inside Portas de Olivença) and avoid the narrow one-way streets in the centre.

Information

Tourist Office The turismo (☎ 62 22 36, fax 62 90 60) on Praça da República is open from 9 am to 6 pm daily and provides a

ELVAS

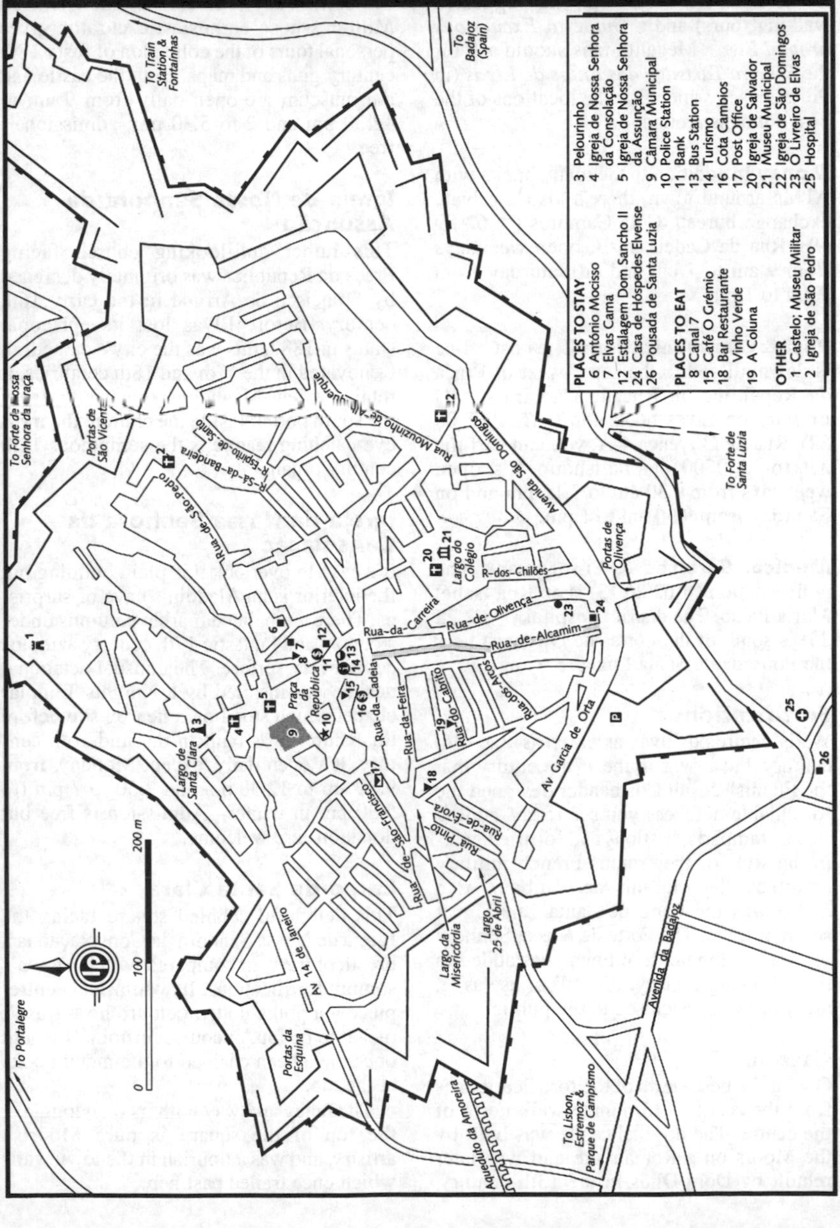

PLACES TO STAY
6 António Mocisso
7 Elvas Cama
12 Estalagem Dom Sancho II
24 Casa de Hóspedes Elvense
26 Pousada de Santa Luzia
PLACES TO EAT
8 Canal 7
15 Café O Grémio
18 Bar Restaurante Vinho Verde
19 A Coluna
OTHER
1 Castelo; Museu Militar
2 Igreja de São Pedro
3 Pelourinho
4 Igreja de Nossa Senhora da Consolação
5 Igreja de Nossa Senhora da Assunção
9 Câmara Municipal
10 Police Station
11 Bank
13 Bus Station
14 Turismo
16 Cota Cambios
17 Post Office
20 Igreja de Salvador
21 Museu Municipal
22 Igreja de São Domingos
23 O Livreiro de Elvas
25 Hospital
To Train Station & Fontaínhas
To Badajoz (Spain)
To Forte de Nossa Senhora da Graça
Portas de São Vicente
To Forte de Santa Luzia
Portas de Olivença
To Portalegre
Portas da Esquina
To Lisbon, Estremoz & Parque de Campismo
Aqueduto da Amoreira
Avenida da Badajoz
Av Garcia de Orta
Avenida São Domingos
Rua Mouzinho de Albuquerque
R-Espírito-Santo
R-Sá-da-Bandeira
Rua-de-São-Pedro
Largo de Santa Clara
Praça da República
Largo do Colégio
R-dos-Chilões
Rua-de-Olivença
Rua-de-Alcamim
Rua-da-Carreira
Rua-da-Cadeia
Rua-da-Feira
Rua-do-Cabrito
Rua-dos-Arcos
Rua-de-Évora
Rua-Pinto
Rua-de-São-Francisco
Largo da Misericórdia
Largo 25 de Abril
Av 14 de Janeiro
0 100 200 m

stack of useful material including a *Guide to the Historic Centre* (giving suggested walking tours) and a *Guide to Excursions around Elvas*. Megalith fans should ask for the *Roteiro Turístico das Antas de Elvas* (in Portuguese), which lists the locations of the best dolmens around.

Money In addition to the many banks with ATMs around town, there's also a private exchange bureau, Cota Cambios (☎ 62 89 19), Rua da Cadeia 34-B, open weekdays from 9 am to 7 pm and on Saturday from 9 am to 1 pm.

Post & Communications The post office is downhill and to the south-west of Praça da República on Rua da Cadeira. At O Livreiro de Elvas bookshop (☎/fax 62 08 82), Rua de Olivença 4-A, you can surf the net for 340$00 per half-hour. It's open weekdays from 9.30 am to 7.15 pm and on Saturday from 9.30 am to 1 pm.

Medical Services & Emergency The police station (☎ 62 26 13) is on Rua Isabel Maria Picão. The district hospital (☎ 62 22 25) is south of the Portas de Olivença near the Pousada de Santa Luzia.

Fortifications

Walls encircled Elvas as early as the 13th century, but it was in the 17th century that the Flemish Jesuit Cosmander designed the formidable defences you see today, adding moats, ramparts, bastions and fortified gates in the style of the famous French military architect, the Marquis de Vauban. Also added was the Forte de Santa Luzia, just south of town. The Forte de Nossa Senhora da Graça, 3km north of town, was added in the following century; it's still in use as an army base and is closed to the public.

Castelo

One of the best views of the fortifications is from the castle, a 15 minute walk north of the centre. The original castle was built by the Moors on a Roman site and was later rebuilt by Dom Dinis in the 13th century,

then again by Dom João II in the late 15th century. Today it houses a small **Museu Militar** whose enthusiastic curator gives personal tours of the collection of fusty 18th century guns and maps. Both the castle and the museum are open daily from 9 am to 12.30 pm and 2 to 5.30 pm; admission is free.

Igreja de Nossa Senhora da Assunção

This rather dull-looking church facing Praça da República was originally designed by Francisco de Arruda in the early 16th century. Before Elvas lost its episcopal status in 1882, this was the city's cathedral. Renovated in the 17th and 18th centuries, it retains a few Manueline touches, notably the south portal. Inside the church, the most eye-catching feature is the sumptuous 18th century organ.

Igreja de Nossa Senhora da Consolação

It's easy to overlook this plain building but the interior is an Aladdin's cave of surprises. There are painted marble columns under a cupola and fantastic 17th century azulejos cover every surface. The unusual octagonal design was inspired by a Knights Templar chapel which stood on a nearby site before this church was built in the mid-16th century. It's open daily, except Monday, from 9.30 am to 12.30 pm and 2.30 to 7 pm (to 5.30 pm in winter). Admission is free but donations are welcome.

Largo de Santa Clara

This delightful cobbled square facing the Igreja de Nossa Senhora da Consolação is a breath of fresh air compared with the town's sombre fortifications. Its whimsical centrepiece – a polka-dotted pelourinho – wasn't meant to be fun, of course: criminals would once have been chained to the metal hooks at the top.

The fancy archway with its own loggia at the top of the square is pure Moorish artistry, and was a flourish in the town walls which once trailed past here.

Museu Municipal

This excellent museum (also called the Museu Thomaz Pires), beside the biblioteca municipal in Largo do Colégio, is packed with treasures including Neolithic remnants and Roman mosaics, folk crafts and azulejos, old weapons and religious paintings, and even musical instruments from the former African colonies. Admission is a bargain 50$00 for a personalised tour. It's open daily from 9.30 am to noon and 2 to 5.30 pm.

Aqueduto da Amoreira

This massive aqueduct with huge cylindrical buttresses and several tiers of arches runs from 7km west of town to bring water to the marble fountain in Largo da Misericórdia. It took about 100 years to complete and was finally finished in 1622.

The aqueduct is best seen from the Lisbon road, west of the centre.

Special Events

Every Monday there's a big lively market around the aqueduct, just off the Lisbon road west of town.

Elvas lets its hair down for a week in late September to celebrate the Festas do Senhor da Piedade e de São Mateus, encompassing everything from agricultural markets and bullfights to folk dancing and huge religious processions (especially on the last day). You'll need to book accommodation well in advance if you want to join in.

Places to Stay

On the south-western outskirts (off the N4 Estremoz road) is the basic *Senhor Jesus da Piedade camping ground* (☎ 62 37 72), open from May to mid-September only; it costs 400$00 each for a person/tent/car.

Cheapest of the guesthouses is the cheerful *Casa de Hóspedes Elvense* (☎ 62 31 52, *Avenida Garcia de Orta 3-A*), a large old house just inside the city walls where doubles without/with bathroom cost around 3500/4500$00.

More central quartos costing 5000$00 for a double can be found along a grubby lane,

Rua João de Olivença, just east of the turismo: *Elvas Cama* (☎ 62 29 87, 62 01 22) at no 11 has new, if rather claustrophobic, rooms (all with bathroom and TV), while the well-signed *António Mocisso* (☎ 62 21 26, *Rua Aires Varela 5*) just around the corner has older and slightly more spacious rooms. Avoid the shabby and overpriced quartos at Rua João de Olivença 5 (though the owner's daughter may try to grab you at the bus station).

Mainstream accommodation can be found at *Estalagem Dom Sancho II* (☎ 62 26 84, fax 62 47 17, *Praça da República*) where homely doubles cost 7500$00. The *Pousada de Santa Luzia* (☎ 62 21 94, fax 62 21 27, *Avenida de Badajoz*) was the first of Portugal's pousadas (opening in 1942), though age hasn't mellowed its stark modern appearance. High season doubles cost 20,300$00.

Places to Eat

The obvious choice for people-watching is *Café O Grémio* (☎ 62 27 11) on the praça. It has a small indoor dining area, and main dishes start at around 950$00. Across the praça, *Canal 7* (☎ 62 35 93, *Rua dos Sapateiros 16*) is an old favourite, serving a particularly good *frango assado* (roast chicken).

Some of the town's best restaurants are in the vicinity of the post office: a cheap option is *Bar Restaurante Vinho Verde* (☎ 62 91 69, *Rua do Tabolado 4*) which offers daily specials for 600$00 and main meals from 1000$00. The nearby *A Coluna* (☎ 62 37 28, *Rua do Cabrito 11*) is a bite above the rest with azulejos on the walls and lots of bacalhau on the menu. Dishes cost upwards of 1200$00, though the *ementa turística* (tourist menu) is good value at 1500$00.

Getting There & Away

Bus Coaches run to Portalegre, Évora and Estremoz at least twice a day, with daily express services to Faro and two departures a day to Lisbon. There are three buses daily to Badajoz.

ALENTEJO

Train Forget the train for a Lisbon connection: there are only two services daily to/from Lisbon's Santa Apolónia station (with changes at Abrantes and/or Entroncamento), and there's only one connecting bus between the town and the train station. Taxis charge around 1000$00. The Lisbon-Elvas services continue across the border for the 16 minute hop to Badajoz in Spain.

PORTALEGRE
☎ 045 • pop 15,500

Portalegre, Alto Alentejo's capital and its commercial centre, is an extraordinarily run-down and old-fashioned place. You wouldn't really want to stay here – most of the accommodation is miserable – but while you're hanging around for a connecting bus (to Marvão, perhaps) it's worth walking around the small walled centre, which has a 16th century cathedral, a generous sprinkling of handsome 17th and 18th century mansions (thanks to a period of wealth from textile manufacturing) and some striking old and new azulejos adorning the streets.

Orientation

Portalegre has an hourglass shape, with the new town to the north-east and the old town clambering across a hilltop to the south-west. The waist is a traffic roundabout known to all as the Rossio, close to the bus station (☎ 33 07 23). From here it's a 10 minute walk to the old town via the pedestrianised Rua 5 de Outubro.

Information

The turismo (☎ 30 01 20, fax 33 02 35) operates from the Galerie Municipal on the Rossio. It's officially open daily from 10 am to 12.30 pm and 2 to 5.30 pm (from 9 am on weekends) but opening hours are irregular. There are numerous banks around here, too. The main post office is on Avenida da Liberdade, 250m north of the Rossio.

As in other places across Portugal, many Portalegre telephone numbers were about to change at the time of research. The turismo should be able to help with new numbers where necessary.

Sé

In 1545 Portalegre became the seat of a new diocese and soon got its own cathedral. The sombre, twin-towered 18th century façade, with a stork's nest and a broken clock, presides over the whitewashed Praça do Município. The sacristy contains an array of fine azulejos.

Museu Municipal & Mansions

Beside the cathedral, in an 18th century mansion and former seminary, is the modest town museum, featuring the obligatory period furnishings, religious art – including a huge number of figures of Santo António – and some handsome Arraiolos carpets. The museum is open daily, except Tuesday, from 9.30 am to 12.30 pm and 2 to 6 pm; admission costs 230$00.

To the south-east, Rua 19 de Junho sports numerous faded 17th century Baroque townhouses and mansions.

Fábrica de Tapeçarias

Tapestries made Portalegre famous and wealthy in the 16th century (followed by silk in the 17th), but the bubble burst after the 1703 Treaty of Methuen led to an invasion of English textiles. The town's last remaining tapestry factory is in a former Jesuit college on Rua Gomes Fernandes, just off the Rossio. Pop into the office on the 1st floor and ask about a tour of the studios and weaving room (run on weekdays from 9.30 to 11 am and 2.30 to 4.30 pm). In the showroom you can see the results: huge reproductions of classical paintings and patterns comprising 250,000 knots per square metre, in a spectrum of some 8000 colours. All tapestries are commissioned and not for sale.

Places to Stay

There's a good Orbitur *parque de campismo* (☎ 2 23 24) at Quinta da Saúde, 3km north-east of town on the N246-2 road to Reguengos, open from April to October, costing 490/410/440$00 per person/tent/car. There's also a *centro de alojamento* (☎/fax 33 09 71, Estrada do Bonfim) north of the

Rossio, with dorm beds (1700$00) and a few doubles (3400$00 without bathroom). Its doors are open from 8 to 10 am and 7 pm to midnight.

The *Residencial O Facha* (☎ 2 31 61, *Largo António José Lourinho 3*) on the Rossio has fraying doubles above its Art Deco café-restaurant costing 5500$00. Cheaper, pokey doubles (3500/5000$00 without/with shower) and pricier ones with private bathroom (6000$00) are available at *Pensão Nova* (☎ 33 12 12, fax 33 03 93, *Rua 31 de Janeiro 28-30*). Better value is the old town's friendly *Pensão Mansão Alto Alentejo* (☎ 33 06 17, *Rua 19 de Junho 61*), above Café Alenco, which offers plain, clean doubles without/with shower for 4500/5500$00.

Hotel Dom João III (☎ 33 01 92, fax 33 04 44, *Avenida da Liberdade*) has large singles/doubles with bathroom, TV and telephone for 7350/10,500$00, including breakfast.

Places to Eat

Food here is plain, sturdy and cheap. Near the Rossio are three neighbours on Rua Dom Nuno Álvares Pereira: the basic *Casa de Pasto O Casimiro* at No 7, *Restaurante Stop* at No 13 (offering meat courses under 1600$00) and the friendly *Restaurante O Cortiço* at No 17.

Inside the old town is the cheap and cheerful *Restaurante-Cervejaria O Abrigo* (*Rua de Elvas 74*); it's closed Tuesday. You can enjoy a good-value lunch at *Restaurante Casa Capote* (*Rua 19 de Junho 60*).

Getting There & Away

Bus Portalegre is most easily reached by bus, and is a useful hub for connecting buses to Castelo de Vide and Marvão. Four

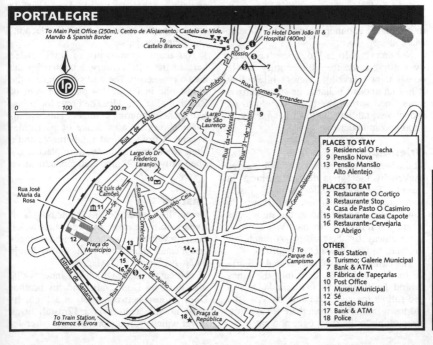

PORTALEGRE

PLACES TO STAY
5 Residencial O Facha
9 Pensão Nova
13 Pensão Mansão Alto Alentejo

PLACES TO EAT
2 Restaurante O Cortiço
3 Restaurante Stop
4 Casa de Pasto O Casimiro
15 Restaurante Casa Capote
16 Restaurante-Cervejaria O Abrigo

OTHER
1 Bus Station
6 Turismo; Galerie Municipal
7 Bank & ATM
8 Fábrica de Tapeçarias
10 Post Office
11 Museu Municipal
12 Sé
14 Castelo Ruins
17 Bank & ATM
18 Police

ALENTEJO

express coaches daily link it directly with Lisbon (4¼ hours), and there are two daily buses linking it with Évora (2¼ hours) and Beja. You can also pick up the daily Braga-Porto-Faro service here.

Train Trains from Lisbon run three times a day, taking around four hours. The Lisbon to Badajoz (Spain) service passes through Portalegre twice a day. Portalegre station is 12km south of town but shuttle buses meet all arrivals and departures.

CASTELO DE VIDE
☎ 045 • pop 4000 (municipality)

One of the Alentejo's most appealing fortified hilltop villages, Castelo de Vide sits high above the surrounding olive plains at the northern tip of the Parque Natural da Serra de São Mamede, 15km north of Portalegre and just west of the Spanish border.

Despite some modern development outside the walls, this ancient spa town has largely maintained its traditional appearance and lifestyle, leaving the day-trippers to its smaller and more stunning neighbour, Marvão.

Not that Castelo de Vide doesn't have its own attractions: its 14th century castle boasts some marvellous views while below it lies an ancient judiaria, its steep narrow lanes lined with flowerbeds. To add to its seductive qualities, the town has plenty of good accommodation.

Orientation
At the heart of town are two parallel squares backed by the Igreja de Santa Maria da Devesa. The upper 'pillory square', just a wide area in Rua Bartolomeu Álvares da Santa with a pelourinho in the middle, is where you'll find the turismo. Walk through the archway by the turismo to reach the southern square, Praça Dom Pedro V.

The castle, medieval quarter and judiaria lie to the north-west: dive into the lanes behind the Igreja de Santa Maria da Devesa and follow the signs to Fonte da Vila (the old town fountain). From there it's a short, steep climb to the synagogue and castle.

Buses stop beside the turismo; the train station is 4km north-west of town.

Information
The turismo (☎ 90 13 61, fax 90 18 27), on pillory square at Rua Bartolomeu Álvares da Santa 81, is open daily in summer from 9 am to 7 pm (to 5.30 pm in winter). Among the maps and brochures available is *Pela Serra de São Mamede* (1500$00) which describes (in Portuguese only) suggested walking routes in the area. The turismo's transport information can be shaky: it's best to check the bus timetables at the bakery opposite (see Getting There & Away).

There's a big market in Praça Dom Pedro V every Friday, with clothes, shoes, pottery, tools and toys for sale.

Judiaria
The cluster of narrow lanes just below and south-east of the castle is Castelo de Vide's most atmospheric quarter. It's a medieval enclave of cobbled paths and dazzling white cottages with Gothic doorways and window frames, potted plants and flowers decorating their doorsteps.

A sizeable community of Jews settled here in the 13th century, attracted by the area's prosperity. The tiny synagogue – the oldest one in Portugal – on the corner of Rua da Judiaria and Rua da Fonte looks just like its neighbouring cottages. The bare interior shows little evidence of its former use, apart from a wooden tabernacle and a shelf where the scriptures were placed. It's open daily from 9 am to 5.30 pm; admission is free.

Castelo
Originally, Castelo de Vide's inhabitants all lived within the castle's sturdy outer walls; even now there are some inhabited cottages and a small church, the 17th century Igreja da Nossa Senhora da Alegria.

The castle itself, within the inner walls, was built by Dom Dinis and his brother Dom Afonso between 1280 and 1365. Its most notable feature is a 12m-tall brick tower which probably predates the outer defences and which may have been used as an armoury or lookout post. There are great views from the roof of the finely-bricked and vaulted hall. The castle is open daily in summer from 9 am to 7 pm (from 9 am to 12.30 pm and 2 to 5.30 pm in winter); admission is free.

Fonte da Vila & Termas

In a pretty square just below and east of the judiaria is the well-worn 16th century marble Fonte da Vila which, along with several other fountains in the village, provides residents with the delicious mineral water for which Castelo de Vide is known. The *termas* (spa) beside the Fonte da Vila is open in summer for medical treatments; the water is said to be good for diabetes and kidney and blood pressure problems.

Special Events

Castelo de Vide's big bash is the Festa de São Lourenço on 15 August, when folk-dance groups from all over Portugal display

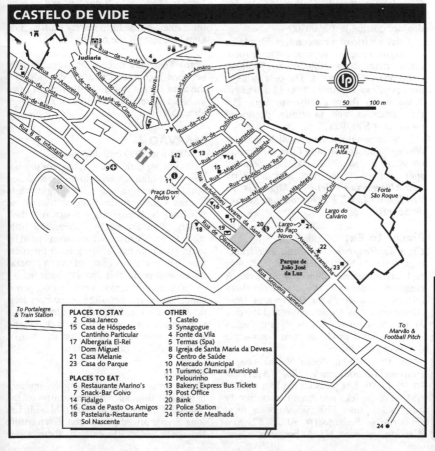

CASTELO DE VIDE

PLACES TO STAY	OTHER
2 Casa Janeco	1 Castelo
15 Casa de Hóspedes Cantinho Particular	3 Synagogue
	4 Fonte da Vila
17 Albergaria El-Rei Dom Miguel	5 Termas (Spa)
	8 Igreja de Santa Maria da Devesa
21 Casa Melanie	9 Centro de Saúde
23 Casa do Parque	10 Mercado Municipal
	11 Turismo; Câmara Municipal
PLACES TO EAT	12 Pelourinho
6 Restaurante Marino's	13 Bakery; Express Bus Tickets
7 Snack-Bar Goivo	19 Post Office
14 Fidalgo	20 Bank
16 Casa de Pasto Os Amigos	22 Police Station
18 Pastelaria-Restaurante Sol Nascente	24 Fonte de Mealhada

their skills on the football pitch on the town's south-eastern outskirts. The Easter festival is another major event, lasting four days, when hundreds of lambs are blessed (and then slaughtered), followed by processions, folk dances, band music and much revelry.

Places to Stay

The budget favourite is *Casa de Hóspedes Cantinho Particular* (☎ *90 11 51, Rua Miguel Bombarda 9*), a homely place where doubles start at around 4500$00, including breakfast. At the foot of the castle walls is *Casa Janeco* (☎ *90 12 11, Rua da Costa 56-A*), a private house with two humble doubles costing just 3500$00.

There's a trio of more comfortable places on Largo do Paça Novo, where double room prices range from 5000$00 to 7000$00 (with private bathroom). The best value is the new *Casa Melanie* (☎ *90 16 32*) at No 3, owned by fluent English-speakers. The five spacious and tastefully decorated rooms cost 5000$00.

Fancier establishments, with doubles costing 9000$00, include *Casa do Parque* (☎ *90 12 50, fax 90 12 28*), in a peaceful spot overlooking the park, and the spiffy new *Albergaria El-Rei Dom Miguel* (☎ *91 91 91, fax 9 15 92, Rua Bartolomeu Álvares da Santa*).

Places to Eat

Casa de Hóspedes Cantinho Particular (see Places to Stay) offers hearty helpings and an appealing family ambience. A couple of down-to-earth spots are the slow-moving *Casa de Pasto Os Amigos* (*Rua Bartolomeu Álvares da Santa*) and the tiny *Snack-Bar Goivo* across the square; there's no menu but it produces great home-style dishes at good prices.

On Praça Dom Pedro V, the cheery *Pastelaria-Restaurante Sol Nascente* (☎ *90 17 89*) has pleasant outdoor seating and serves snacks and main meals, mostly costing less than 1200$00. Another local favourite is *Fidalgo* (☎ *90 18 82, Rua Almeida Sarzedas 32*). At both places you

can try local specialities such as *molhinhos com tomatada* (tripe with tomato sauce), supposedly a dish once favoured by the town's Jewish community, and the earthy Alentejan delight *sarapatel*, a pork liver and blood sausage.

Posher dining ('typical dishes for special gourmets') can be found at *Restaurante Marino's* (☎ *90 14 08, Volta do Penedo 10*).

Getting There & Away

Bus Buses make the half-hour run to/from Portalegre twice daily (weekdays only). There are two express services to/from Lisbon Monday to Saturday, and one on Sunday; buy tickets for these (and check timetables) at the little bakery on Rua 5 de Outubro, just off the pillory square.

Train There are three train services daily between Lisbon and Castelo de Vide, but the train station is 4km north-west of town and there are no bus links; taxis charge about 550$00.

MARVÃO

☎ 045 • pop 3900 (municipality)

At its atmospheric best – at dusk or dawn – this 900m-high eyrie is stunning: enclosed within serpentine walls are bright white houses with vermilion-edged Manueline windows or Renaissance doorways, their lintels often graced by enchanting little stone faces. Narrow cobbled streets wind up to an awesome castle rising from the rock, from where you can gaze out over a panorama of wild peaks and Spanish horizons.

As with Portugal's other hilltop gems, summertime visitors often outnumber residents. Sadly, too, building regulations here seem slack and concern for architectural heritage minimal; greed for the tourist dollar could yet ruin Marvão.

History

Not surprisingly, considering its impregnable position and its proximity to the Spanish frontier (10km away), Marvão has long been a prized possession. Even before the walls and castle existed, there was a

Ascend to the pink Rococo Palácio do Visconde de Estói, near Faro, via this grand staircase.

Alvor, one of the Algarve's glorious beaches.

Into the bunker again at Vale do Lobo.

Looking west into Spain from the Castelo in the mountaintop village of Marvão.

This 17th century aqueduct still carries water to a fountain in Elvas.

Parque Natural da Serra de São Mamede

After the endless rolling plains of Baixo Alentejo, the Serra da São Mamede comes as a welcome change: four peaks (Fria, Marvão, Castelo de Vide and São Mamede) top off this mountain range running along the Spanish border near Portalegre. The park includes all of them, stretching from Castelo de Vide in the north to just beyond Esperança in the south.

This 40km-long massif helps provide the surrounding region with essential rainfall and humidity, and serves as a rich haven for plants and wildlife. Its combination of Atlantic forest and Mediterranean bush – craggy olive groves and the brilliant springtime blossom of yellow broom – make it an ideal habitat for the rare trumpet narcissus and stonecrop as well as dozens of bird species: more than half of the species that breed in Portugal nest here. Keep an eye out while visiting the rocky enclaves of Castelo de Vide and Marvão, especially for vultures, eagles, kites and black storks.

With your own transport you can delve right into the heart of the park on winding rural roads to traditional villages such as Alegrete and Esperança. Bus transport operates from Portalegre to Castelo de Vide and Marvão.

The park's head office (☎ 045-2 36 31, fax 2 75 01) is in Portalegre at Rua General Conde Jorge de Avilez 22.

Roman settlement in the area, and Christian Visigoths were here when the Moors arrived in 715. It was probably the Moorish Lord of Coimbra, Emir Maraun, who gave the place its present name; the Moors certainly had a hand in fortifying the village.

In 1160, Christians took control. In 1226 the town received a municipal charter, the walls were extended to encompass the whole summit and the castle was rebuilt by Dom Dinis.

Marvão's importance in the defence against the Spanish Castilians was highlighted during the 17th century War of Restoration, when further defences were added to the castle. Two centuries later it was briefly at the centre of the tug of war between the liberals and the royalists: in 1833 the liberals used a secret entrance to seize the town, the only time Marvão has ever been captured.

Orientation

Arriving by car or bus you'll find yourself approaching Portas de Ródão, one of the four village gates, opening onto Rua de Cima which has several shops and restaurants. Drivers can enter this gate and park in Largo de Olivença, just below Rua de Cima. The castle is a 10 minute walk uphill along Rua do Espiríto Santo.

Information

The turismo (☎ 9 31 04, fax 9 35 26) is on Rua Dr Matos Magalhães, just south of the street leading to the castle. In summer it's open daily from 9 am to 7 pm; at other times it's open from 9 am to 5.30 pm.

A bank and the post office face one another across Rua do Espiríto Santo.

Castelo

The formidable castle built into the rock at the western end of the village dates from the end of the 13th century, but most of what you see today was built in the 17th century. There's little left inside but if you walk along the walls you'll be rewarded with some astounding views over the sheer drop below you. Admission is free.

Museu Municipal

Just east of the castle, the Igreja de Santa Maria houses this engaging little museum with exhibits ranging from Roman remains and skeletons to gruesome old medical

ALENTEJO

implements. It's open daily from 9 am to 12.30 pm and 2 to 5.30 pm; admission costs 200$00.

Places to Stay
The turismo has details of private accommodation; singles/doubles start at 3500/5000$00 and small apartments with kitchens cost around 7000$00.

Within the town walls, other options are pricey: *Pensão Residencial Dom Dinis* (☎/*fax 9 32 36, Rua Dr Matos Magalhães*), opposite the turismo, has doubles costing upwards of 9000$00. It also operates the new eyesore *Albergaria Dom Manuel* which hogs one end of the Largo do Terreiro; although it hadn't opened at the time of research, rates will probably be high. Doubles in the elegant *Pousada de Santa Maria* (☎ 99 32 01, fax 99 34 40, Rua 24 de Janeiro) will set you back 19,200$00 in the high season.

Places to Eat
There are several bar-restaurants along and below Rua de Cima including the good *Casa do Povo Restaurante (Travessa do Chabouco)*. The nearby *Bar-Restaurante Varanda do Alentejo* (☎ 9 32 72, Praça do Pelourinho 1) serves some earthy Alentejan specialities costing less than 1200$00. For a snack or drink looking out over the hills, visit *Bar do Centro de Convivio*, just above Largo do Terreiro.

Getting There & Away
Bus Two buses run on weekdays between Portalegre and Marvão. There's currently only one late-afternoon service from Castelo de Vide (taxis charge 1500$00 one way), although two buses go there from Marvão, at 7.30 am and 1.10 pm; the latter requires a change of buses at Portagem, 7km south-west of Marvão.

Express buses to Lisbon run daily (twice on Sunday) but you must tell the turismo staff the day before if you want to catch it or the bus won't detour here to pick you up.

Train The nearest train station, Marvão-Beirã (often just Marvão on timetables), is 9km north of Marvão; it's worth a visit just to see its beautiful azulejo panels. Two trains daily run to/from Lisbon (change at Abrantes).

In addition, the daily Lisbon-Madrid *Talgo Lusitânia* stops here en route to Valencia de Alcántara just before 1 am.

Estremadura & Ribatejo

These two skinny provinces surrounding and stretching north of Lisbon are full of contrasts. They boast the country's most stunning architectural masterpieces: the monasteries of Mafra, Alcobaça and Batalha, and Tomar's Convento de Cristo. There are also the beautiful *parque natural* areas of Sintra-Cascais, Arrábida (see the Around Lisbon chapter) and Serras de Aire e Candeeiros, which are wonderful for wildlife and walking. The Estremaduran coast, a great destination for surfers and seafood-lovers, offers lively resorts interspersed with a generous sprinkling of undeveloped, empty beaches.

On the other hand, the provinces also possess a large number of dull or heavily industrialised towns. The Ribatejo (meaning Tejo riverbank) is worse in this respect than its neighbour: around Abrantes and Torres Novas there's a nasty concentration of textile, paper and chemical factories where there were once thriving river ports.

There is still plenty of countryside, though; the rich alluvial plains are important areas for growing wheat, olives and vegetables and, most famously, for breeding bulls and horses. Santarém, host of the Feira Nacional da Agricultura (National Agricultural Fair), which celebrates the agricultural lifestyle of the province with gusto, is one of the few attractive towns in the Ribatejo. Also worth visiting is Tomar, former headquarters of the Knights Templar.

Apart from Santarém and Tomar, your time is generally better spent in Estremadura, so called because it was the farthest land from the Douro (*extrema Durii*) when the Christians wrested it from the Moors. Here you can feast on culture and coastal attractions, explore the caves of the Mira de Aire region or visit the cute hilltop village of Óbidos. Most places are accessible by both train and bus, and there are quick and easy connections from Lisbon – this despite the efforts of the Tejo bus company (serving

 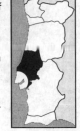
most of the region) which wins our burst tyre award for neglecting to post or publish timetables: you'll have to queue for information at ticket windows.

The Setúbal Peninsula, Sintra, Mafra and the Estoril coast are all covered in the Around Lisbon chapter.

ERICEIRA
☎ 061 • pop 4500

Ten kilometres west of Mafra, this pretty little fishing village of bright white houses edged in blue is a firm summertime favourite with the young Lisbon and European crowd thanks to an abundance of reasonably priced accommodation, seafood restaurants and lively bars and nightclubs. Another attraction is its surf, especially at nearby Praia da Ribeira de Ilhas.

The town's only claim to historical fame is a fleeting one: on 5 October 1910, as the

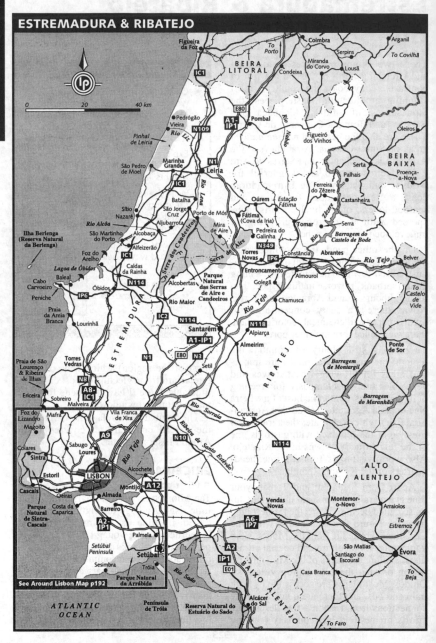

republic was being proclaimed in Lisbon, Portugal's last king, Dom Manuel II, fled here from his palace at Mafra and sailed into exile in England.

Orientation

The town sits high above the sea, its oldest buildings clustered around the central Praça da República, with a newer district to the south. There are three sandy beaches within 15 minutes walk of the praça: Praia do Sul (also called Praia da Baleia) to the south and Praia do Norte and Praia de São Sebastião to the north. A few kilometres further north is another good beach, the unspoilt Praia de São Lourenço, while Praia Foz do Lizandro is the same distance away to the south.

Buses stop at the new terminal, off the N247 highway to the east of the town centre.

Information

The gung-ho turismo runs two offices. The main one (☎ 86 31 22, fax 86 59 09) is in the beautifully ornate Casa da Cultura Jaime Lobo e Silva (named after a locally famous historian) on Rua Mendes Leal. It's open daily from 9 am to 8 pm (10 pm on Friday and Saturday).

From June to September, another turismo (☎ 86 36 68) opens at Rua Dr Eduardo Burnay 33-A for equally astonishing long hours: 9 am to 10 pm daily (midnight on Friday and Saturday).

On the 1st floor of the Casa da Cultura there's the friendly Espaço Jovem (youth centre; ☎/fax 86 05 55, email cmmej2@ip.pt) where you can surf the Internet or send emails free of charge, by prior appointment only. It's open weekdays from 10 am to 1 pm and 2.30 to 6.30 pm, and Saturday from 10 am to 1 pm. You can also register here for mountain biking and trekking tours (see under Activities later in this section).

The centro de saúde (medical centre; ☎ 86 41 00) is at the top of Rua Prudéncio Franco da Trindade. The police station (☎ 86 35 33) is on Rua 5 de Outubro.

Activities

Surfing Ericeira's big attraction is surfing. Praia da Ribeira de Ilhas, a World Championship site, is just a few kilometres north of town, though the waves at the nearer Praia de São Sebastião are challenging enough for most amateurs.

If you've arrived boardless, head for Ultimar (☎ 86 23 71), Rua 5 de Outubro 37A, where you can hire boards for 2000$00 a day. It's open Monday to Saturday from 9.30 am to 1 pm and 3 to 7.30 pm, and on Sunday from 10 am to 1 pm. It also sells fishing equipment and wetsuits.

Mountain Biking & Trekking You can register at the Espaço Jovem for mountain biking and walking trips in the area. These are organised by the câmara municipal (town hall) in Mafra and cost 500$00 per person.

Horse Riding For horse riding at Picadeiro, Quinta da Lapa, Lapa da Serra (about 5km east of Ericeira), inquire at the Adega Típica bar (☎ 86 21 49) on Rua Alves Crespo.

Places to Stay

Camping The nearest camping ground is the *Parque de Campismo Municipal de Mil Regos* (☎ 86 27 06), north-east of Praia de São Sebastião but close to the noisy main road. It costs 300/250/100$00 per person/tent/car, and there's a municipal swimming pool next door. *Clube Estrela* (☎ 81 55 25) is a camping ground at Sobreiro, 5km east of Ericeira. It's open to foreign visitors with a Camping Card International for 550/410/350$00.

Private Rooms & Apartments Although Ericeira gets packed out in summer (especially at weekends), there are plenty of *quartos* (private rooms) costing around 6500$00 for a double in summer. If the touts don't find you first, ask at the turismo. As with the pensões, the longer you stay, the more you can bargain the price down. The apartment (with sea views) belonging

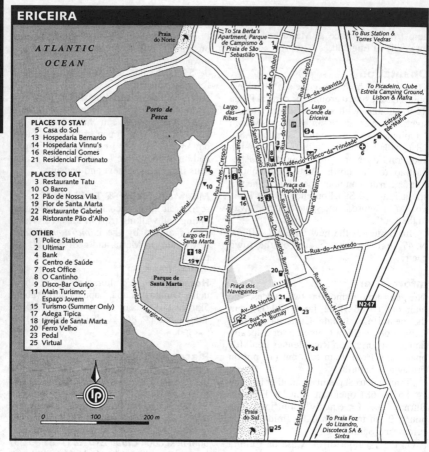

ERICEIRA

PLACES TO STAY
5 Casa do Sol
13 Hospedaria Bernardo
14 Hospedaria Vinnu's
16 Residencial Gomes
21 Residencial Fortunato

PLACES TO EAT
3 Restaurante Tatu
10 O Barco
12 Pão de Nossa Vila
19 Flor de Santa Marta
22 Restaurante Gabriel
24 Ristorante Pão d'Alho

OTHER
1 Police Station
2 Ultimar
4 Bank
6 Centro de Saúde
7 Post Office
8 O Cantinho
9 Disco-Bar Ouriço
11 Main Turismo;
   Espaço Jovem
15 Turismo (Summer Only)
17 Adega Tipica
18 Igreja de Santa Marta
20 Ferro Velho
23 Pedal
25 Virtual

to *Senhora Berta Fontão Alberto* (☎ 86 22 13, Rua de Baixo 51) has been recommended. Many shops advertise places, too.

Pensões & Residenciais Right in the centre is the fraying, old-fashioned *Residencial Gomes* (☎ 86 36 19, Rua Mendes Leal 11) where doubles with/without bathroom cost 6500/5500$00. There are other budget options along Rua Prudéncio Franco da Trindade: *Hospedaria Bernardo* (☎/fax 86 23 78) at No 17 offers spacious doubles

costing from 5000$00 to 7000$00 (plus some triples) and a cosy one bedroom apartment in the attic for 8000$00. At No 25, *Hospedaria Vinnu's* (☎ 86 38 30, fax 86 62 98) has bright, modern rooms (including a few triples with refrigerator) costing from 8000$00 to 10,000$00. Nicest of all on this street, at No 1, is the Turihab *Casa do Sol* (☎ 86 26 65, fax 86 44 02), where doubles cost 9000$00.

In the new part of town is the popular *Residencial Fortunato* (☎/fax 86 28 29,

Rua Dr Eduardo Burnay 7), where doubles are good value, costing 6500$00 (8000$00 in August) including breakfast.

Places to Eat

For seafood that isn't too outrageously expensive, try *Restaurante Gabriel* (☎ 86 33 49, *Avenida da Horta*). It's especially good for grilled fish (halibut, scabbard or mackerel) at around 1200$00 a dish. It's closed Wednesday. The nearby *Flor de Santa Marta* (☎ 86 23 68, *Largo de Santa Marta 4-A*) is another good bet – fancy squid cooked in beer? Most fish dishes cost less than 1500$00.

If you're after something classier, the sea view *O Barco* (☎ 86 27 59, *Avenida Marginal 10*) overlooking the Porto de Pesca fits the bill, albeit an expensive one, with its range of seafood specialities. It's closed Thursday.

Cheaper, more simple fare – chips and salad with almost everything – is served at the small and friendly *Restaurante Tatu* (☎ 86 47 05, *Rua Fonte do Cabo 58*).

Sick of fish? Head for the Italian *Ristorante Pão d'Alho* (☎ 86 37 62, *Zona Comercial, Estrada de Sintra 2*) where you can eat pizzas and pastas for less than 1000$00.

For pastry snacks with outdoor watch-the-world-go-by seating, the pastelarias on Praça de República are perfect. The town's best bread shop, *Pão de Nossa Vila*, is here too.

Entertainment

At last count, there were 25 bars and night-clubs in and around Ericeira. The biggest is *Discoteca SA – Sociedade Anonima* (☎ 86 23 25), housed in a cavernous former *adega* (winery) just off the N247, 3km south of town above Praia Foz do Lizandro. On the beach itself are several bars including *Limipicos* (☎ 86 41 21) and the *Koala Bar*.

If you don't fancy the late-night walk home, there are plenty of more central options including the locally popular *Disco-Bar Ouriço* (☎ 86 21 38, *Avenida Marginal 10*), the lively *Ferro Velho* (☎ 86 35 63,

Rua Dr Eduardo Burnay 7-C), and *Virtual* (☎ 86 30 71) on Praia do Sul. The tiny *O Cantinho* café-bar (☎ 86 23 47, *Rua 5 de Outubro 4*) has been recommended by a reader as 'a great place to relax, chat and try your hand at local card games'.

Getting There & Away

From around 7 am to 8 pm there are buses to Lisbon via Mafra every 30 to 45 minutes, and departures to/from Sintra every hour.

Getting Around

There are regular buses throughout the day to the Parque de Campismo and Praia da Ribeira de Ilhas from Praça dos Navegantes. About four buses a day run to Praia Foz do Lizandro.

You can hire mountain bikes from Pedal (☎ 86 58 41) in the Zona Comercial at Rua Dr Eduardo Burnay 18. It also sells bicycles and biking accessories.

PENICHE

☎ 062 • pop 15,300

There are only a couple of reasons for coming to this drab fishing port with its ugly outskirts: one is to use its ferry connections to the island Reserva Natural da Berlenga, 10km offshore, and the other is to splurge on some fantastic seafood. For surf and sand, the nearby Baleal beach is a further attraction.

Once an island, which became joined to the mainland in the late 16th century when silt created a narrow isthmus, the cramped walled town now feels rather claustrophobic – or perhaps it's just the lingering atmosphere of Salazar's notorious prison, once housed in the huge and impressive 16th century seaside fort.

Orientation

Two bridges connect Peniche to the isthmus. From the bus station on the isthmus, cross the nearest bridge, Ponte Velha, to reach the turismo on Rua Alexandre Herculano, a 10 minute walk. The main road (N114) into town also leads onto this road, branching off to run for 3km round the

Peniche peninsula to Cabo Carvoeiro and its lighthouse.

From the turismo it's a short walk south to the old town centre and fort which is close to the harbour and Avenida do Mar, where most of the seafood restaurants can be found. Passenger boats for Ilha Berlenga leave from the harbour (where there's also ample free car parking in Largo da Ribeira). The closest beaches are on the north coast of the peninsula, about 30 minutes walk away.

Information

The turismo (☎ 78 95 71) is tucked into a shady public garden alongside Rua Alexandre Herculano. It's open daily, from 9 am to 8 pm in summer, and from 10 am to 1 pm and 2 to 5 pm in winter.

Shops and banks with ATMs can be found along Rua Alexandre Herculano and Rua José Estevão. The police station (☎ 78 95 55) is on Rua Heróis Ultramar; the hospital (☎ 78 17 00) is in the northern part of town, off Rua General Humberto Delgado.

Fortaleza

Dominating the southern end of the peninsula, this imposing 16th century fortress was in use as late as the 1970s, when it was converted into a temporary home for refugees from the newly independent African colonies. Twenty years before, it played a grimmer role, as one of Salazar's notorious jails for political prisoners.

Today it houses an archaeological museum and ceramics workshop, though you can still make out some cells and solitary confinement areas. It's open daily except Monday from 10 am to 7 pm (5 pm in winter); admission costs 100$00 for the museum, though there's no charge for wandering round the desolate interior of the fort.

Lace-Making Schools

Like another of Portugal's Atlantic fishing ports – Vila do Conde in the north – Peniche is famous for its bobbin lace. There are a couple of informal 'schools' where you can

see lace being made: the Escola de Rendas De Bilros is in the turismo complex and Rendibilrosa is nearby (ask staff at the turismo to call ahead to arrange a visit). Both operate on weekdays only.

Cabo Carvoeiro

The western cape of the peninsula, marked by a lighthouse, is a rugged, breezy spot with fantastic ocean views. It's 3km from the town.

Special Events

To see Peniche at its jolliest, come here in early August for the Festa de Nossa Senhora de Boa Viagem, when a statue of the Virgin is brought ashore and paraded in the streets, accompanied by singing and dancing.

Places to Stay

Camping The municipal *parque de campismo* (☎ 78 95 29, fax 78 01 11) is 2km east of town, just after the turning to Baleal; it's open year-round and costs 350/300/300$00 per person/tent/car. The windier and pricier *Peniche Praia* camping ground (☎ 78 34 60, fax 78 94 47) is on the northern shore of the peninsula. Prices are 420/420/360$00.

Private Rooms The turismo has its own list of approved quartos (costing about 5000$00 for a double) as well as apartments, though these are often booked out during August.

Pensões & Residenciais *Residencial Katekero* (☎ 78 71 07, Avenida do Mar 70) is one of the cheaper options, offering doubles (some with sea views) for around 5000$00. Best of the town centre pensões, both offering doubles for around 6000$00 including breakfast, are the spacious *Mili Residencial* (☎ 78 39 18, Rua José Estevão 45) and the immaculate new *Residencial Rima Vier* (☎ 78 94 59, Rua Castilho 6) opposite. *Residencial Vasco da Gama* (☎ 78 19 02, Rua José Estevão 23) down the road has posher doubles costing around 7500$00 including breakfast.

For out-of-town comforts and horse riding (plus mini-golf, swimming and tennis), the *Centro Hípico A Coutada (☎/fax 75 97 33)* is around 5km east of town near Atouguia da Baleia. Doubles cost around 9000$00, though discounts are offered for long stays.

Places to Eat

Avenida do Mar is the best area for seafood restaurants; prices and standards are pretty similar at all of them but the twin restaurants *Katekero I & II (☎ 78 14 80 & ☎ 78 71 07)* at No 90 have a bright and lively atmosphere. *Restaurante Beira Mar* at No 106 is also popular and serves a filling *caldeirada* (fish stew) for 1500$00.

Getting There & Away

There are at least a dozen express coaches daily to/from Lisbon (1¾ hours) via Torres Vedras, nine to Caldas da Rainha via Óbidos and three to Coimbra via Leiria.

BALEAL
☎ 062

About 4km to the north-east of Peniche is this tiny island-village, connected to the mainland by a causeway. It has a fantastic sweep of sandy beach and some good surfing conditions.

Places to Stay

There's a reasonable *parque de campismo (☎ 76 93 33)* just west of the village. In the village itself are some well-signed *quartos (☎ 76 90 50, Rua Direita 42)* with bathrooms and great sea views – two also have kitchens; prices range from 5000$00 to 7000$00. At the end of the same lane is the imposing *Casa das Marés (☎ 76 92 55, 76 93 71, 76 92 00)*, actually three residenciais in one, owned by three sisters. Doubles here cost 13,000$00 in high season, including breakfast.

RESERVA NATURAL DA BERLENGA

Just 10km off shore from Peniche, this tiny 78 hectare island is a treeless place with weird rock formations and caverns. In the 16th century a monastery existed here, but now the most famous inhabitants are thousands of nesting seabirds which take priority over human visitors: the only developments that have been allowed are houses for a small fishing community, a lighthouse, a shop and a café. Paths are clearly marked with stones to stop day-trippers trespassing into the birds' domain.

Linked to the island by a narrow causeway is the squat 17th century Forte de São João Baptista, now one of the country's most windswept and spartan hostels.

Places to Stay

There's a small, rocky area for *camping* near the harbour but you have to book in advance at the Peniche turismo (☎ 062-78 95 71). The charge for a two person tent is around 1000$00.

You also have to make advance reservations for the *Forte de São João Baptista hostel (☎ 062-78 25 50)*. Facilities are pretty basic: you need to bring your own sleeping bag and cooking equipment.

More luxurious by far are the rooms available at *Pavilhão Mar e Sol (☎ 062-75 03 31)*. Expect to pay around 10,000$00 for a double with bathroom.

Getting There & Away

Regular ferries make the 45 minute run to the island from Peniche harbour between 1 May and 20 September (depending on the weather); the return fare is 2500$00. During high season (July and August) there are usually three sailings, at 9 and 11 am and 5 pm, with return trips at 10 am and 4 and 6 pm. Tickets tend to sell out quickly during this period as only 300 visitors are allowed each day. In the low season there's only one run, at 10 am, returning at 6 pm. For up-to-date details of the timetable, contact the Peniche turismo or Residencial Avis (☎ 062-78 21 53) opposite.

Privately organised trips operated by TurPesca (☎ 062-78 99 60, mobile ☎ 0936 37 28 18, fax 062-78 30 13) run throughout the year; they cost 3000$00 per person (minimum of six passengers). In summer you'll probably have to book at least two days ahead for these cruises, which last four to five hours. The first trip of the day usually departs at around 10 am; during the summer there are at least two more sailings a day. Tickets and information are available at the TurPesca kiosk in Largo da Ribeira at the Peniche harbour.

If you're prone to seasickness, choose your day carefully: the crossing to Berlenga can often be very rough!

ÓBIDOS

☎ 062 • pop 4800

Fortified hilltop villages don't come much prettier than this immaculate little place, 6km south of Caldas da Rainha. Entirely enclosed by high medieval walls, Óbidos perches on its limestone ridge like a fairytale watchtower, overlooking ruined windmills and a 16th century aqueduct. Until the 15th century it overlooked the sea but, when the bay silted up leaving only a lagoon, the town became landlocked.

In the half-dozen cobbled lanes, houses are bright white, edged with jolly strips of blue or yellow and draped in bougainvillea or wisteria. Pots of geraniums fill window sills where cats doze in the sun.

No wonder Dom Dinis' wife, Dona Isabel, fell in love with the place when she visited in 1228. Her husband gave the village to her as a wedding gift, establishing a royal custom which continued until the 19th century. Today day-trippers flock here in their thousands. Like them, you can see Óbidos in an hour if you're pressed but by staying overnight you can catch a hint of the town's medieval aura.

Orientation

The town's fancy main gate, Porta da Vila, leads straight into the main street, Rua Direita, where you'll find the turismo, shops and cafés. If you're arriving by train, you'll have a 20 minute climb up from the station at the northern foot of the ridge: a path leads to the Porta da Cerca, at the other end of Rua Direita from Porta da Vila.

Buses stop on the main road just outside Porta da Vila, near a small local market.

Information

The efficient turismo (☎ 95 92 31, fax 95 50 14), headquarters for the Região de Turismo do Oeste, is on Rua Direita. It's open weekdays from 9.30 am to 6 pm (probably later in high season) and weekends from 10 am to 6 pm; it has lists of accommodation and restaurants.

Castelo

Although the walls date from the time of the Moors (and were later restored), the castle is one of Dom Dinis' fine 13th century creations: a traditional, no-nonsense affair of towers, battlements and big gates. Converted into a palace in the 16th century, it's now enjoying another life as a deluxe *pousada* (upmarket inn; see Places to Stay later).

Igreja de Santa Maria

The town's main church, at the northern end of Rua Direita, was built on the site of a Visigothic temple which was later converted into a mosque. Restored several times since, it dates mostly from the Renaissance and had its greatest moment of fame in 1444 when 10-year-old Afonso V married his eight-year-old cousin Isabel here.

The church's interior is more striking than the exterior: its ceiling is painted and its walls are covered with blue 17th century azulejos. Also take a look at the fine 16th century Renaissance tomb on the left, probably carved by the French sculptor Nicolas Chanterène, and the paintings by Josefa de Óbidos to the right of the altar.

Museu Municipal

The only real reason for trudging through this dull museum of religious paintings is to see the one outstanding portrait by Josefa de Óbidos; it tends to go on visits elsewhere so check its current location with the turismo before visiting. The museum, next to the Igreja de Santa Maria, is open daily from 10 am to 12.30 pm and 2 to 6 pm; admission costs 250\$00.

Josefa de Óbidos

You'd hardly call her works masterpieces but the paintings by this 16th century Spanish-born artist are certainly among the most accomplished Iberian paintings of their time, enchanting for their personal, sympathetic interpretations of religious subjects, and for their sense of innocence.

Born in Seville in 1630 to a Portuguese painter (Baltazar Gomes Figueira) who later returned to Portugal, Josefa de Ayalla studied at the Augustine Convento de Santa Ana when she was young and, although she later left the convent without taking the vows and settled in Óbidos (hence her nickname), she remained famously chaste and religious until her death in 1684.

One of the few female Portuguese painters to win lasting recognition, she excelled in richly coloured still lifes and detailed religious works, delightfully ignoring established iconography.

Special Events

If you arrive on Tourist Day – which usually falls around 20 August – you're in for a treat: free sardines and wine are dished out to visitors by the town hall staff. A more sophisticated annual event is the festival of ancient music held each year in October. It can be difficult finding accommodation during the festival.

Places to Stay

Some of the best deals are the unofficial private rooms around town. The turismo has no specific listings for them but you'll see *quartos* signs in shop windows, including Rua Direita Nos 40 and 41, at the little shop just inside Porta da Vila, and next to the O Conquistador restaurant on Rua Josefa Óbidos. Doubles usually cost around 4000$00.

Alternatively, the cheapest guesthouse is *Residencial Martim de Freitas* (☎ 95 91 85), on the Caldas da Rainha road just outside the town walls. It obviously doesn't have the atmosphere of places inside the walls but it does have a pretty little garden and reasonable doubles starting at 8000/6000$00 with/without bathroom.

More expensive, but with considerably more charm, are several Turihab properties, including *Casa do Poço* (☎ 95 93 58, *Travessa da Rua Nova*), with four secluded doubles ranged around an inner courtyard. They cost about 8500$00 (up to 11,500$00 in high season). The similarly priced *Casa do Relógio* (☎ 95 92 82, *Rua da Graça*) is an 18th century mansion just outside the town walls.

If money's no problem, the unrivalled choice is the *Pousada do Castelo* (☎ 95 91 05, fax 95 91 48), where palatial doubles cost 29,600$00 in summer.

Places to Eat

As with accommodation, restaurants in Óbidos tend to be pricey, although there's plenty of choice. One of the cheapest options is the scruffy *Bar Esplanada das Muralhas* outside the Porta da Vila (below the Albergaria Josefa de Óbidos), which serves snacks and simple meals. Attractive choices within the walls, most offering dishes costing around 1300$00 and pleasant outdoor seating, include *Café-Restaurante 1 de Dezembro* (☎ 95 92 98), next to the Igreja de São Pedro, and the more simple *Adega do Ramada* (☎ 95 94 62) in the adjacent lane, serving snacks and grills.

The mainstream *Restaurante Alcaide* (☎ 95 92 20, *Rua Direita*) boasts a nice balcony dining area though its menu isn't very exciting. More imaginative fare is on offer at *O Conquistador* (☎ 95 95 28, *Rua Josefa de Óbidos*), where you can eat exotic dishes such as stewed river eel and grilled wild boar.

If you've got your own transport, you'll also find two excellent restaurants, *O Caldeirão* and the slightly cheaper *Vila Infante* 2km east of town, next to the eye-catching hexagonal Santuário do Senhor Jesus da Pedra down the Caldas da Rainha road.

Getting There & Away

Buses regularly make the 20 minute hop to/from Caldas da Rainha; about eight buses a day run to/from Peniche.

There are five trains a day between Lisbon and Óbidos (all except the first train requiring a change at Cacém), taking between two and 2½ hours.

CALDAS DA RAINHA

☎ 062 • pop 20,000

This quaint, old-fashioned town near Óbidos, famous for its spa and pottery, owes its existence – and its name – to the *rainha* (queen) Dona Leonor, wife of Dom João II. As she passed by one day in the 1480s she noticed people bathing in the steaming sulphuric waters and decided to build a spa hospital, now Hospital Termal Rainha Dona Leonor. Following its completion in 1484, a park and a church, Igreja de Nossa Senhora do Pópulo, were also established.

The *caldas* (hot springs) – said to be excellent for respiratory problems and rheumatism – attracted a stream of nobility and royalty to the town, its popularity reaching a peak in the 19th century. Today, although the hospital is still going strong, the town itself feels a bit dowdy; however, with its plentiful accommodation and restaurants, a great daily market and good transport connections, it makes a relaxing stopover.

Orientation

Ringed by sprawling new town development and highways, the central old town is compact in comparison. At its heart is the skinny market square, Praça da República. Most of the hotels and restaurants, and the bus station and turismo, are a short walk away. The train station is about 250m west of the turismo.

Information

The poorly-signed turismo (☎ 83 10 03, fax 84 23 20), in the corner of Praça 25 de Abril, is open weekdays from 9 am to 7 pm, and weekends and holidays from 10 am to 1 pm and 3 to 7 pm.

There are banks with ATMs around Praça 25 de Abril and on Praça da República, which also contains the police station (☎ 83 20 23). The general hospital (☎ 83 03 00) is nearby, off Rua Diário de Notícias.

In addition to the daily market in Praça da República, there's a Gypsy market every Monday in the Santa Rita neighbourhood on the north-eastern outskirts of town.

Museu da Cerâmica

The best of the town's trio of art museums, the Ceramics Museum, is in the former Palácio de Visconde de Sacavém, a delightful holiday mansion which the 19th century Viscount – a patron of the arts and something of an artist himself – filled with beautiful azulejos from other palaces. The rooms are now largely devoted to Caldas da Rainha pottery and particularly to the works of Rafael Bordalo Pinheiro, the 19th century potter who put the town on the ceramic map with his lovable clay figures. More memorable, though, are the fabulous jars and bowls (by both Pinheiro and Manuel Mafra), encrusted with animals, lobsters and swirling snakes. The top floor is devoted to contemporary works including some incredibly detailed Manueline-style carvings by José da Silva Pedro.

The museum is open from 10 am to noon and 2 to 5 pm daily, except Monday; the admission fee of 250$00 (free on Sunday mornings) includes a guided tour.

Parque Dom Carlos I

This shady central park is a pleasant place to hang out. As well as a lake and tennis courts, it also hosts the marginally interesting **Museu de Pintura José Malhoa**. The museum, which displays 19th century paintings by Malhoa and other artists, is open from 10 am to 12.30 pm and 2 to 5.30 pm daily except Monday; admission costs 250$00.

Market

The town's traditional daily market in Praça da República, mostly geared to locals, is one of the best in the region. It also caters for the tourist trade with a few stalls of basketware and famous local pottery (notably items shaped like cabbage leaves and tasteless phallic mugs).

Try to arrive at around 9 am for the best bustle; Saturday is busiest.

Special Events

Caldas da Rainha celebrates its role as a centre of pottery production by hosting the annual Feira Nacional da Cerâmica, usually in September.

Places to Stay

Caldas da Rainha has a good range of reasonably priced accommodation, though the cheapies all tend to be fraying at the edges. *Residencial Dom Carlos* (☎ *83 25 51, fax 83 16 69, Rua de Camões 39-A*) offers doubles starting at 5500$00 including breakfast; discounts are often available to seniors and students. The old *Pensão Residencial Portugal* (☎ *83 42 80, fax 84 13 33, Rua Almirante Cândido dos Reis 30*) charges similar prices.

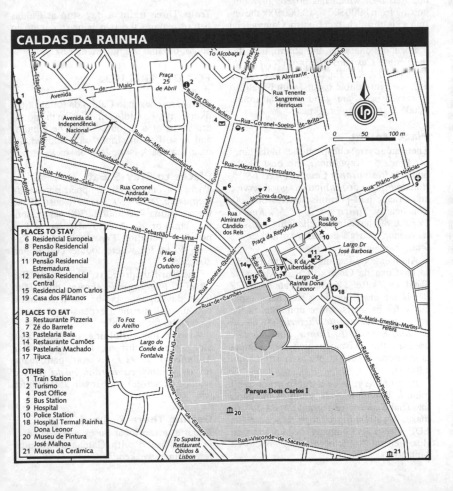

CALDAS DA RAINHA

PLACES TO STAY
6 Residencial Europeia
8 Pensão Residencial Portugal
11 Pensão Residencial Estremadura
12 Pensão Residencial Central
15 Residencial Dom Carlos
19 Casa dos Plátanos

PLACES TO EAT
3 Restaurante Pizzeria
7 Zé do Barrete
13 Pastelaria Baia
14 Restaurante Camões
16 Pastelaria Machado
17 Tijuca

OTHER
1 Train Station
2 Turismo
4 Post Office
5 Bus Station
9 Hospital
10 Police Station
18 Hospital Termal Rainha Dona Leonor
20 Museu de Pintura José Malhoa
21 Museu da Cerâmica

There are two sister-establishments on Largo Dr José Barbosa. *Pensão Residencial Estremadura (☎ 83 23 13, fax 83 36 76)* is the cheaper, with singles/doubles costing 3500/7500$00. The price includes breakfast, which you take next door at *Pensão Residencial Central (☎ 83 19 14, fax 84 32 82)*, where rooms with TV and private bathroom cost 5500/9500$00.

The most modern residencial in the town centre is *Residencial Europeia (☎ 83 47 81, fax 83 15 09, Rua Almirante Cândido dos Reis 64)*, which has dozens of rooms costing from 8000$00 to 12,000$00; the entrance is through the Centro Commercial shopping centre.

For more character and charm, head for the Turihab *Casa dos Plátanos (☎ 84 18 10, fax 84 34 17, Rua Rafael Bordalo Pinheiro 24)*. Its eight double rooms, with beautifully carved beds, are good value at around 9000$00 including breakfast.

Places to Eat

There are several cheap eateries in the lanes off Praça da República. The best of the bunch is *Restaurante Camões (☎ 83 68 56, Rua do Parque 56)*, which has good service and prices; half-portions start at 800$00. The nearby *Tijuca (☎ 2 42 55, Rua de Camões 89)* has some challenging items on its menu, such as stewed goat and cow's feet.

Another good feeding area is the Travessa da Cova da Onça, off Rua Almirante Cândido dos Reis; *Zé do Barrete (☎ 83 27 87)* is the most popular place here, especially for its grills. More upmarket is the attractive *Restaurante Pizzeria (☎ 84 56 00, Rua Engenheiro Duarte Pacheco 17)*, opposite the turismo, which serves great home-made pizzas at prices starting from 1300$00.

If you have your own transport, or don't mind a 20 minute walk south of the park, the Thai *Supatra* restaurant *(☎ 84 29 20)* makes a refreshing change. It's near the EDP (electricity company) headquarters on Rua General Amílcar Mota and is closed Monday.

Caldas is tough for dieters: its sweet *cavacas* tarts are too good to miss and pastelarias seem to be everywhere. Try the popular *Pastelaria Machado (Rua de Camões 14)*, or *Pastelaria Baia*, next to the Tijuca restaurant.

Getting There & Away

Bus There are six express buses a day to Lisbon (fewer at weekends), taking 1½ hours; three stop at Óbidos. Four buses a day run to Coimbra and five go to Porto.

Train Three trains a day stop at Caldas before making the two hour run south to Lisbon. Seven trains daily run north to the end of the line at Figueira da Foz.

FOZ DO ARELHO
☎ 062

The nearest beach to Caldas da Rainha (just 8km away), Foz do Arelho lies on the northern shore of a lagoon, Lagoa de Óbidos, and is still surprisingly undeveloped. Its main drawback is the lack of shade.

Places to Stay & Eat

There's a fairly well-equipped *parque de campismo (☎ 97 91 01)* just east of the town, costing 420/360/360$00 per person/tent/car. Foz do Arelho also has a few pensões, including *Pensão Pendedo Furado (97 96 10)*, where doubles cost around 8000$00.

The Turihab property, *Quinta da Foz (☎ 97 93 69, Largo do Arraial)*, just 500m from the lagoon, is the most romantic option – and the most expensive at around 15,000$00 for a double.

Among the sprinkling of restaurants along the beachfront, *Restaurante-Bar Atlântico (☎ 97 92 13)* is worth patronising for its yummy *caldeirada mista* (mixed seafood casserole) – a bargain 2500$00 for two.

Getting There & Away

About a dozen local buses a day connect Foz do Arelho with Caldas da Rainha; fewer run at weekends.

SÃO MARTINHO DO PORTO

☎ 062

An almost perfectly enclosed bay, ringed by a sandy beach, has made this small seaside resort, 17km north-west of Caldas da Rainha, one of the most popular hang-outs south of Nazaré: the water here is calm and warm (a plus for families with kids). The resort itself has a Mediterranean appearance and atmosphere, and seems fairly low key, although summer crowds quickly pack the place out.

Orientation & Information

The oceanside Avenida 25 de Abril (also called Avenida Marginal) is the main drag. The turismo (☎ 98 91 10) is at the northern end, it's open in summer from 9 am to 7 pm on weekdays and from 10 am to 1 pm and 3 to 7 pm at weekends and daily during the winter. The train station is about 700m to the south-east. Buses usually stop on Avenida Marechal Carmona, which leads to the main N242.

Places to Stay

Open year-round, the spacious and well-equipped **Colina do Sol** camping ground (☎ 98 97 64, fax 98 97 63) is 2km north of town; it has a swimming pool and costs 570/495/475 per person/tent/car.

The São Martinho **pousada da juventude** (☎/fax 99 95 06) is actually about 4km inland at Alfeizerão, just off the main N8 highway.

There are plenty of quartos available, ranging in price from 4000$00 to 6000$00 for a double. If the touts don't find you first, ask at the turismo which keeps a complete list of rooms and apartments.

Among pensões, the most popular choice is the **Pensão Americana** (☎ 98 91 70, fax 98 93 49, Rua Dom José Saldanha 2). It's a friendly, well-run place just back from the beach, where doubles cost around 7000$00 including breakfast. More mainstream is the similarly priced **Pensão Carvalho** (☎ 98 96 05, Rua Miguel Bombarda 6), a block from the beach. Note that prices in São Martinho soar in August.

Places to Eat

Among the seafront restaurants on Avenida 25 de Abril, the most tempting choice is **Restaurante Casa das Gambas** (☎ 98 96 33), about 300m down the road from the turismo, which has a huge selection of fish dishes, most costing around 1700$00 or more. Its **Ostra Bar & Marisqueria** downstairs serves cheaper fare.

For more humble food, retreat inland to the restaurant at the **Pensão Americana**.

Getting There & Away

From Caldas da Rainha, the 15 minute train ride (almost a dozen times a day) is a better choice than the bus service, which only runs about five times daily, taking 25 minutes. To get to Nazaré, however, choose the bus: on weekdays it makes the 20 minute run at least five times daily. Six buses also run to Alcobaça each day and five expresses depart daily for Lisbon.

Getting Around

There are four buses daily to/from the pousada da juventude at Alfeizerão. You can hire mountain bikes from the Pensão Americana for 500$00 per hour or 1500$00 per day.

NAZARÉ

☎ 062 • pop 15,000

Brash and bold, Nazaré has successfully shed its image as a cute little fishing village to become one of the most hard-selling seaside resorts on the Atlantic coast.

As soon as you arrive at the bus station you'll be pounced on by a band of aggressive local fisherwomen, many of them dressed in their traditional seven-petticoated skirts and coloured scarves, touting for guests for their private rooms. Where once the old fishermen pushed their boats out to sea along the sweeping stretch of beach, they now sell trinkets and souvenirs to tourists, backed up by another band of no-nonsense women selling sweaters, dried fruits and pistachios.

Undeniably, Nazaré looks impressive, especially when seen from the town's original site on the Promontório do Sítio (accessible by funicular); however in summer the beach is packed with sunbathers and their tents – the sea is often too rough for swimming – and the streets are clogged with cars and tour buses. Come here for the sand and seafood if that's what you fancy, but don't expect charm, tradition or tranquillity.

Orientation

Until the 18th century, the sea covered the beach and the present-day town of Nazaré, and the locals lived inland at the hilltop Pederneira and the nearer Promontório do Sítio. Today, both play second fiddle to Nazaré and its seafront Avenida da República, which is the main focus of activity. Stretching inland from here is the former fisherfolk's quarter of narrow lanes, now hosting restaurants and cafés.

The train station is 6km inland but the bus station is fairly central, on Avenida Vieira Guimarães, about 150m uphill from Avenida da República.

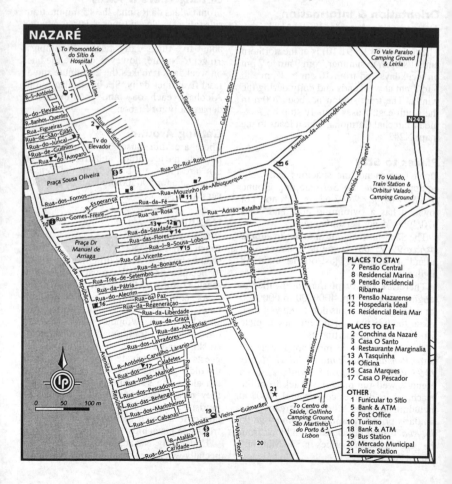

NAZARÉ

PLACES TO STAY
7 Pensão Central
8 Residencial Marina
9 Pensão Residencial Ribamar
11 Pensão Nazarense
12 Hospedaria Ideal
16 Residencial Beira Mar

PLACES TO EAT
2 Conchina da Nazaré
3 Casa O Santo
4 Restaurante Marginalia
13 A Tasquinha
14 Oficina
15 Casa Marques
17 Casa O Pescador

OTHER
1 Funicular to Sítio
5 Bank & ATM
6 Post Office
10 Turismo
18 Bank & ATM
19 Bus Station
20 Mercado Municipal
21 Police Station

Information

The turismo (☎ 56 11 94) on Avenida da República has comprehensive information on rooms, transport and events. It's open daily from 10 am to 8 pm (10 pm in July and August), closing for lunch only in winter.

There are surprisingly few banks and ATMs: the most convenient ones are opposite the bus station and on Praça Sousa Oliveira (this has a cash exchange machine, too).

The main post office, at Avenida da Independência 2, is a 10 minute walk inland from the turismo. The police station (☎ 55 12 68) is on Rua Sub-Vila. There are two options for medical emergencies: a centro de saúde (☎ 55 16 47) in Nazaré on the eastern outskirts of town or the main hospital (☎ 56 11 40) in Sítio.

Promontório do Sítio

The Sítio clifftop area 110m above the beach is popular for its tremendous views and, among Portuguese devotees, for its religious connections. According to legend it was here that the lost statue of the Virgin known as Nossa Senhora da Nazaré, brought back from Nazareth in the 4th century, was finally found in the 18th century.

Even more famously, an apparition of the Virgin is said to have been seen here one foggy day in 1182 when a local nobleman, Dom Fuas Roupinho, was out hunting a deer. When the animal disappeared off the edge of the Sítio precipice, with the nobleman's horse in hot pursuit, Dom Fuas cried out to the Virgin for help and his horse miraculously managed to stop just in time.

The small **Hermida da Memória** chapel was built by Dom Fuas on the edge of the belvedere to commemorate the event. It was later visited by a number of VIP pilgrims including Vasco de Gama. The nearby Baroque 17th century **Igreja de Nossa Senhora da Nazaré** replaced an earlier church and is decorated with attractive Dutch azulejos.

An *elevador* (funicular) climbs up the hill to Sítio throughout the day from 7 am to 1 am during summer (to midnight in winter); the fare is 90$00. The station is five minutes walk north of the turismo on Rua do Elevador.

Special Events

The Nossa Senhora da Nazaré *romaria* (pilgrimage) is Nazaré's big religious festival, taking place every year from 8 to 10 September in the square facing the church of the same name in Sítio. It features events ranging from sombre processions to folk dances and bullfights.

From July to mid-September, bullfights take place in the Sítio *praça de touros* (bullring) almost every weekend; check with the turismo for times and ticket availability.

Places to Stay

Nazaré becomes a zoo in August, with room prices rocketing; either book well ahead or stay clear during that month. Prices list here are for the high season before the August peak.

Camping The cheap municipal *Golfinho* camping ground (☎ 55 36 80) is just north of the N242. Orbitur's *Valado* (☎ 56 11 11) is 3km away, off the Valado road; prices are 590/480/500 per person/tent/car. The best-equipped is *Vale Paraíso* (☎ 56 15 46, fax 56 19 00), 2km north of town off the Leiria road. It has a swimming pool, badminton and football courts, a children's playground and bikes for hire, plus bungalows for rent; the cost is 595/490/490$00.

Private Rooms There are literally hundreds of rooms for rent in Nazaré. The turismo keeps a complete list (though they won't make bookings or recommendations) so if the touts don't find you first, check the turismo list. Expect to pay around 4500$00 for a double – possibly twice that during August.

Pensões & Residenciais There's a choice of good budget options where you can get a double (often with private bathroom) for between 3000$00 and 5000$00, including

Hospedaria Ideal (☎ 55 13 79, *Rua Adrião Batalha*) and *Residencial Marina* (☎ 55 15 41, *Rua Mouzinho de Albuquerque 6*). Further up the same road, at No 48, is the popular *Pensão Nazarense* (☎ 55 11 88), which includes breakfast in its prices. The more comfortable *Pensão Central* (☎ 55 15 10, *Rua Mousinho de Albuquerque 85*) provides doubles for 9500$00, also including breakfast.

Seafront hotels are inevitably expensive, and the ones in the centre of Avenida da República can often be noisy. *Residencial Beira Mar* (☎ 56 13 58, *Avenida da República 40*) is one of the most reasonably priced, with doubles for around 8000$00; you can expect to pay at least 10,000$00 for bright, breezy doubles in *Pensão Residencial Ribamar* (☎ 55 11 58, *fax 56 22 24, Rua Gomes Freire 9*).

Places to Eat

As you'd expect, there are dozens of seafood restaurants in Nazaré, though the ones along the seafront tend to be touristy and overpriced. Snoop around the back lanes for less pretentious places which serve other dishes as well as seafood – for example, the simple *Conchina da Nazaré* (☎ 56 15 97, *Rua de Leiria 17-D*), where budgies squawk in the corner and the price of dishes rarely rises higher than 1000$00. Around the corner, start the evening with beer and *ameijoas* (clams) at *Casa O Santo* (*Travessa do Elevador 11*), a rustic nook with tables on the street outside.

Even more down to earth is *Oficina* (☎ 55 21 61, *Rua das Flores 33*), a locals' bar and café where you can eat an *arroz de marisco* (seafood paella) for a bargain 1500$00. Nearby, *Casa Marques* (☎ 55 16 80, *Rua Gil Vicente 37*) is run by a friendly troika of typically Nazaréan women who dish up hearty meals for under 1200$00.

Slightly more upmarket are the small and rustic *Restaurante Marginalia* (☎ 56 22 03, *Rua do Amparo 13*) and the justifiably popular *A Tasquinha* (☎ 55 19 45, *Rua Adrião Batalha 54*). *Casa O Pescador* (☎ 55 33 26, *Rua António Carvalho*

Laranjo 18-A) has become more touristy in recent years but still delivers a great caldeirada for around 1000$00.

Getting There & Away

The nearest train station is 6km inland at Valado dos Frades and although there are frequent buses between Nazaré and the station, you'll generally be best off taking direct buses to other destinations. There are regular buses to/from Lisbon (1150$00), Caldas da Rainha and Alcobaça, half a dozen trips daily to Coimbra and Leiria, and two or three buses daily to Aveiro, Fátima and Batalha. The turismo holds timetables.

ALCOBAÇA

☎ 062 • pop 5400

One of Portugal's greatest architectural masterpieces (and one of Europe's most significant medieval Cistercian monuments) dominates this low-key town 26km northeast of Caldas da Rainha. The 12th century Cistercian monastery, Mosteiro de Santa Maria de Alcobaça – a UNESCO World Heritage Site – is worth going miles out of your way to see. Although the town offers little else to detain you, it's pleasant enough for a one night stopover.

Orientation

From the bus station in the new town, turn right along Avenida dos Combatentes to cross the Rio Alcôa and reach the monastery, a 10 minute walk. The turismo, restaurants and hotels are all near the monastery.

Information

The turismo (☎ 58 23 77) on Praça 25 de Abril, opposite the monastery, is open from 9 am to 7 pm on summer weekdays and from 10 am to 1 pm and 3 to 6 pm at weekends (and throughout the winter). The post office is almost next door and there are several banks with ATMs on the praça.

The hospital (☎ 59 04 00) is on the eastern edge of the new town, off Rua Afonso de Albuquerque. The police station (☎ 58 33 88) is on Rua de Olivença.

Mosteiro de Santa Maria de Alcobaça

This monastery was founded in 1153 by Dom Afonso Henriques to honour a vow he'd made to St Bernard after the capture of Santarém from the Moors in 1147. The king entrusted the construction of the monastery to the monks of the Cistercian order, also giving them a huge area around Alcobaça to develop and cultivate.

Building started in 1178 and by the time the monks actually moved in, some 40 years later, the abbey estate had already reaped the rewards of its land holdings to become one of the richest and most powerful in the country. In those early days the monastery is said to have housed no less than 999 monks who held Mass nonstop, in shifts.

Switching from farming to teaching in the 13th century, the monks later used the estate's abundant rents to carry out further enlargements and changes to the monastery: altars were remodelled to suit the fashions of the day, one of the largest libraries in the country was built, and the kitchen (which was already huge) underwent further alterations. Towards the 17th century, the monks turned their talents to pottery and the sculpting of figures in stone, wood and clay.

Although revived agricultural efforts in the 18th century made the Alcobaça area one of the most fertile and productive in the land, it was the monks' growing decadence which became famous, thanks to the bitchy writings of 18th century travellers such as William Beckford who, despite his own decadence, was shocked at the 'perpetual gormandising ... the fat waddling monks and sleek friars with wanton eyes, twanging away on the Jew's harp'. It all came to an abrupt end in 1834 with the dissolution of the religious orders.

The monastery is open daily from 9 am to 7 pm (5pm in winter). You can enter the church for free but there's an admission fee of 400$00 to see the rest.

Church Modelled on the French Cistercian abbey of Clairvaux, the Alcobaça abbey church is far more impressive inside than out. Much of the original façade was altered (including the addition of wings on either side) in the 17th and 18th centuries, leaving only the main doorway and rose window unchanged.

When you step inside, however, the combination of Gothic simplicity and Cistercian austerity hits you immediately: the nave is a breathtaking 106m long but only 23m wide, with huge pillars and truncated columns. All later decorations and alterations have been removed, leaving only beams of light filtering through from the aisle and rose windows.

Tombs of Dom Pedro & Dona Inês Occupying the south and north transepts are these intricately carved 14th century tombs, the church's greatest possessions. Perhaps it's the contrast with the surrounding simplicity that makes the tombs so stunning, or perhaps it's because of the tragic, romantic tale they commemorate (see the boxed text 'Love & Revenge' on the next page).

Although the tombs themselves were badly mutilated by rampaging French troops in search of treasure in 1811, they still show extraordinary detail and are embellished with a host of figures and scenes from the life of Christ. The Wheel of Fortune at the foot of Dom Pedro's tomb and the gruesomely realistic Last Judgement scene at the foot of Inês' tomb are especially striking.

Kitchen & Refectory The grand kitchen, described by Beckford as 'the most distinguished temple of gluttony in all Europe', owes its immense size to alterations carried out in the 18th century (which were presumably necessary to keep up with the greedy monks' lifestyle). A water channel was also built through the middle of the room so that a tributary of the Rio Alcôa could provide a constant source of fresh fish to the monastery.

Even now, it's not hard to imagine the scene when Beckford was led here by the abbey's grand priors ('hand in hand, all three together') and saw 'pastry in vast abundance which a numerous tribe of lay brothers and their attendants were rolling out and puffing up into a hundred different shapes, singing all the while as blithely as larks in a corn field'.

The adjacent refectory, huge and vaulted, is where the monks ate in silence while the Bible was read to them from the pulpit. Opposite the entrance is a 14th century *lavabo* (bathroom) embellished with a dainty hexagonal fountain.

Claustro do Silencio & Sala dos Reis

The beautiful Cloisters of Silence date from two eras. The intricate lower storey, with its arches and traceried stone circles, was built by Dom Dinis in the 14th century. The upper storey, typically Manueline in style, was added in the 16th century.

Off the north-eastern corner of the cloisters is the 18th century Sala dos Reis (Kings' Room), so called because statues of practically all the kings of Portugal line the walls. Below them are azulejo friezes depicting stories relevant to the abbey's construction, including the siege of Santarém and the life of St Bernard. A huge soup cauldron, captured from the Spanish at the battle of Aljubarrota in 1385, is also on display here; once used to feed an army, it was no doubt a useful addition to the monks' own kitchen.

Nacional Museu do Vinho

A down-to-earth alternative to the monastery, this museum provides an absorbing portrait of the region's famous wine-making history, exhibiting items ranging from huge vats and old winepresses to samples of wine to buy. Housed in an attractive, spacious old adega, it's about 1km east of town, on the Leiria road, and is open weekdays from 8.30 am to 12.30 pm and 2 to 5.30 pm. Admission is free.

Places to Stay

Camping The municipal *parque de campismo* (☎ 58 22 65) is on Avenida Professor Vieira Natividade on the northern outskirts of town. Prices are 350/180/200$00 per person/tent/car. Slightly pricier (at 400/300/300$00) but more pleasant is the shady *Parque de Campismo Rural da Silveira* (☎ 50 95 73), 3km south of town, near Évora de Alcobaça (accessible by bus).

Pensões & Residenciais The cheapest option is the rambling, run-down *Pensão Restaurante Corações Unidos (Rua Frei António Brandão 39)*, where doubles start at 5000$00 including breakfast; the quieter rooms at the back – some overlooking a claustrophobic courtyard – are a bit pricier. Around the corner on Rua Dr Francisco Zagalo is the smarter *Hotel de Santa Maria* (☎ 59 73 95, fax 59 67 15) which has

---

Love & Revenge

Portugal's most famous love story revolves around Dom Pedro, son of Dom Afonso IV, who fell in love with his wife's Galician lady-in-waiting, Dona Inês de Castro. Even after his wife's death he was forbidden by his father to marry Inês because of her Spanish family's potential influence. Various suspicious nobles continued to pressure the king until he finally sanctioned her murder in 1355, unaware that the two lovers had already married in secret.

Two years later, when Pedro succeeded to the throne, he exacted his revenge by ripping out and eating the hearts of Inês' murderers. He then exhumed and crowned her body, and (so the story goes) compelled the court to pay homage to his dead queen by kissing her decomposing hand.

On Pedro's orders, the lovers now lie foot to foot in the Mosteiro de Alcobaça so that on the Day of Judgement they will see each other as soon as they rise.

doubles costing 7000$00 including breakfast, though a new extension currently being built will probably mean higher prices.

If visiting the monastery has given you delusions of grandeur, palatial accommodation is available at the *Challet Fonte Nova* (☎ *59 83 00, fax 59 68 39, Estrada Fonte Nova)*, a 19th century mansion which has six doubles costing around 20,000$00 each.

Places to Eat

The *Pensão Restaurante Corações Unidos* (see Places to Stay) has a good restaurant with standard hearty dishes. The basement bar in the *António Padeira Cervejaria-Restaurante (☎ 58 22 95, Travessa da Cadeia 27)*, just off the Praça 25 de Abril, is more casual, as is *Cervejaria O Cantinho (☎ 58 34 71, Rua Engenheiro Bernardo Villa Nova)*, off the main Rua 15 de Outubro. More salubrious is the well-hidden *Celeíro dos Frades (☎ 58 22 81)* in Arco de Cister, under the arches near the north side of the monastery; there's a popular bar here too. The restaurant is closed Thursday.

Getting There & Away

There are frequent buses to Nazaré and Batalha, five a day to Porto de Mós (with connections at São Jorge Cruz for Leiria), and two buses daily to Caldas da Rainha. Six express buses run daily to Lisbon. The nearest train station is 5km north-west of town at Valado dos Frades, connected to Alcobaça by regular buses.

BATALHA

The Gothic-Manueline Mosteiro de Santa Maria da Vitória – usually known as Mosteiro da Batalha (Battle Abbey) – is another architectural giant, rivalling those other national masterpieces, the Mosteiro dos Jerónimos at Belém (Lisbon), and the Mosteiro de Santa Maria de Alcobaça. Like them, Batalha boasts UNESCO World Heritage status (though that didn't stop the highway authorities building the N1 motorway shockingly close). You'd be hard pressed to choose which is the finest monument of the three, but for ornate decoration and mind-boggling flamboyance, our vote goes to Batalha.

Unlike Alcobaça, there's no decent town around the abbey so you'd be better off coming here en route to (or on a day trip from) Leiria, 11km to the north, or Alcobaça, 20km to the south-west.

Mosteiro de Santa Maria da Vitória

Like Alcobaça's monastery, this abbey was founded as the result of a battle vow, though the stakes at the 1385 Battle of Aljubarrota (fought 4km south of Batalha) were considerably higher than Alcobaça's Santarém battle. On one side was the 30,000-strong force under Juan I of Castile, who was claiming the Portuguese throne; on the other was the 6500-weak Portuguese army of rival claimant Dom João of Avis, commanded by Dom Nuno Álvares Pereira and supported by a few hundred English soldiers. Defeat for João meant Portugal would slip into Spanish hands. He called on the Virgin Mary for help and vowed to build a superb abbey in return for victory. The battle was duly won and work on the Dominican abbey started three years later.

Most of the monument – the church, Claustro Real, Sala do Capítulo and Capela do Fundador – was completed by 1434 in Flamboyant Gothic style, but the dominant theme is one of Manueline flamboyance, thanks to additions made in the 15th and 16th centuries. Work at Batalha only stopped in the mid-16th century when Dom João III turned his attention to expanding the Convento de Cristo in Tomar.

The abbey is open from 9 am to 6.30 pm daily (5.30 pm in winter). There's an admission fee of 400$00 for the cloisters and Capelas Imperfeitas. A turismo (☎ 044-76 71 80) in the nearby modern shopping complex is open from 10 am to 1 pm and 3 to 7 pm daily (closing at 6 pm at weekends and an hour earlier in winter).

Exterior Set in an empty concrete plaza below the motorway, the abbey at first seems like an bizarrely out of place apparition. Confronted with the architectural detail of the building you quickly forget the surroundings: the ochre limestone monument is all pinnacles and parapets, flying buttresses and balustrades, carved windows in Gothic and flamboyant styles, and octagonal chapels and massive columns after the English perpendicular style. There's no bell tower (the Dominicans didn't like them); catching the eye instead is the main western doorway, where layers of arches are packed with carvings of the Apostles, various angels, saints and prophets, and topped by Christ and the Evangelists.

Interior The vast vaulted Gothic interior is deceptively plain, long and high like Alcobaça's church, and is warmed by light from modern stained glass windows, but step to the right as you enter and the scene changes dramatically.

The **Capela do Fundador** (Founder's Chapel) is a beautiful star-vaulted square room, lit by an octagonal lantern. In the centre is the joint tomb of João I and his English wife, Philippa of Lancaster, whose marriage in 1387 established the special alliance that exists between Portugal and England to this day. The tombs of their four youngest sons line the south wall of the chapel: furthest to the left is that of Dom Fernando who died as a hostage in Ceuta (Morocco); second from the right is that of Henry the Navigator.

Claustro Real The Royal Cloisters were first built in a restrained Gothic style by Afonso Domingues, the master of works at Batalha during the late 1380s, but it's the later Manueline embellishments by the great Diogo de Boitac, which really takes the breath away. Every arch is a tangle of detailed stone carvings of typically Manueline symbols such as armillary spheres and crosses of the Order of Christ, entwined with marine motifs such as ropes, pearls and shells, and exotic flowers. The overall effect is probably the finest marriage of Gothic and Manueline art in Portugal.

Claustro de Dom Afonso V The sober Dom Afonso V Cloister seems dull in comparison to the Royal Cloister. It's a plain Gothic affair and its main appeal lies in its austerity.

Sala do Capítulo To the east of the Claustro Real is the early 15th century chapter house. Its huge unsupported 19 sq metre vault was considered so outrageously dangerous to build that only prisoners on death row were employed in its construction. More traditional is the beautiful 16th century stained glass east window which is all purples, pinks and greens. The Sala do Capítulo contains the tomb of the unknown soldiers – one killed in Flanders in WWI, the other in Africa – now watched over by a constant guard of honour.

Capelas Imperfeitas The roofless Unfinished Chapels at the eastern end of the abbey are perhaps the most astonishing and tantalising part of Batalha. Only accessible from outside the abbey, the octagonal mausoleum with its seven chapels was commissioned by Dom Duarte (João I's eldest son) in 1437 but, as with the Claustro Real, the later Manueline additions by the architect Mateus Fernandes overshadow everything else, including the Renaissance upper balcony.

Although Fernandes' original plan for an upper octagon supported by buttresses was never completed, the staggering ornamentation gives a hint of what might have followed: not only are the unfinished pillars covered with carvings, so too is the 15m-high doorway, a mass of stone-carved thistles, ivy, flowers, snails and all manner of 'scollops and twistifications', as William Beckford noted. Dom Duarte can enjoy this extraordinary panorama for eternity: his tomb (and that of his wife) lies opposite the door.

Getting There & Away
There are regular buses from Batalha to Alcobaça and Leiria, and three a day run to Fátima.

LEIRIA

☎ 044 • pop 13,000

Despite its impressive medieval hilltop castle and location beside the Rio Lis, Leiria is a disappointingly dull town with little to get excited about except an attractive old cobbled quarter. The town was a good deal more important in medieval times: Dom Afonso III convened a *cortes* (parliament) here in 1254, Dom Dinis established his main residence in the hilltop castle in the 14th century, and in 1411 the sizeable Jewish community built Portugal's first paper mill in the town.

Today its main attraction to travellers is as a convenient base for visiting Alcobaça, Batalha and Fátima or the nearby beach of São Pedro de Muel, all easily accessible by bus.

Orientation

The life of the town focuses on the Praça Rodrigues Lobo and its elegant shops, and on the livelier Largo Cândido dos Reis to

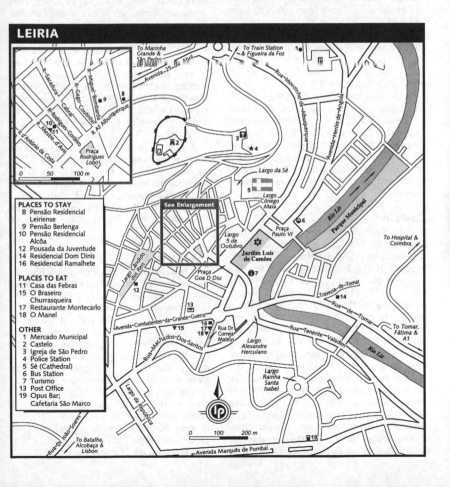

LEIRIA

PLACES TO STAY
8 Pensão Residencial Leiriense
9 Pensão Berlenga
10 Pensão Residencial Alcôa
12 Pousada da Juventude
14 Residencial Dom Dinis
16 Residencial Ramalhete

PLACES TO EAT
11 Casa das Febras
15 O Braseiro Churrasqueira
17 Restaurante Montecarlo
18 O Manel

OTHER
1 Mercado Municipal
2 Castelo
3 Igreja de São Pedro
4 Police Station
5 Sé (Cathedral)
6 Bus Station
7 Turismo
13 Post Office
19 Opus Bar; Cafetaria São Marco

the south-west, near numerous little lanes of restaurants, shops and guesthouses. The castle perches above it all on a wooded hilltop to the north.

Leiria train station is 4km north-west of the centre; there's no shuttle bus into town but taxis are usually available.

Information

The efficient turismo headquarters (☎ 82 37 73, fax 83 35 33) for the surrounding Rota do Sol region are on the edge of the Jardim Luís de Camões, open weekdays from 9 am to 7 pm, and weekends from 10 am to 1 pm and 3 to 7 pm (6 pm in winter).

The district hospital (☎ 810 70 10) is about 1.5km east of town in the Olhalvas-Pousos district (follow signs to the A1 motorway). The police station (☎ 81 37 99) is at Largo Artilharia 4.

In the basement Opus Bar (☎ 81 57 67, email opusbar@mail.exoterica.pt), below Cafetaria São Marco at Avenida Marquês de Pombal 23, you can use the one computer to surf the Internet or send emails, but it's costly at 50$00 an *impulso* (unit). This zany bar is open from 4 pm to 2 am Monday to Saturday and from 9 pm to 2 am on Sunday.

Castelo

This long-inhabited hilltop site got its first castle in the time of the Moors. After this was captured by Afonso Henriques in 1135, it stood at the frontline of the Christian kingdom until Santarém and Lisbon finally fell in 1147. The town continued to live within the castle walls until Dom Dinis decided to establish a royal residence here in the 14th century, at which time the town began to spread down towards the river.

Dom Dinis' Gothic royal palace, with its panoramic gallery, is still here, though it's been restored several times, most recently at the turn of this century by Swiss architect Ernesto Korrodi. Parts of the palace are now frequently used for exhibitions and there are plans to open a museum here, too.

Also within the walls is the ruined Igreja de Nossa Senhora da Penha, originally built in the 12th century and rebuilt by João I in the early 15th century.

The castle is open daily from 9 am to 6.30 pm (5.30 pm in winter); admission costs 135$00.

Places to Stay

There's an excellent *pousada da juventude* (☎/fax 83 18 68, Largo Cândido dos Reis 7-D), right in the heart of town.

Among the guesthouses, the best for value, service and hospitality is *Residencial Dom Dinis* (☎ 81 53 42, fax 82 35 52, Travessa de Tomar 2), where a comfortable modern double costs 6000$00, including an excellent breakfast.

Two other cheapos downtown are the friendly *Pensão Berlenga* (☎ 82 38 46, Rua Miguel Bombarda 3), which has doubles starting at 4500$00, and the nearby *Pensão Residencial Alcôa* (☎ 83 26 90, Rua Rodrigues Cordeiro 20), which offers very ordinary doubles for 5000$00 including breakfast.

A couple of more comfortable options are *Pensão Residencial Leiriense* (☎ 82 30 54, fax 82 30 73, Rua Afonso de Albuquerque 6), where doubles cost 8000$00 including breakfast, and the slightly cheaper but rather drab and run down *Residencial Ramalhete* (☎ 81 28 02, Rua Dr Correia Mateus 30).

Places to Eat

The pedestrianised Rua Dr Correia Mateus has several good restaurants to choose from, including the family-friendly, no-nonsense *Restaurante Montecarlo* (☎ 82 54 06) at No 32, which pulls in the locals with its cheap dishes, and the more upmarket *O Manel* (☎ 83 21 32) at No 50, which boasts a huge fish menu and other main dishes starting at 1200$00. *Casa das Febras* (☎ 83 23 21, Rua Mestre d'Avis 33) serves hearty dishes at cheap prices, including the house speciality, *febras de porco na brasa* (braised pork slices), costing 850$00. Another good hunting ground is Largo Cândido dos Reis, which also has a bunch of lively bars.

On Sunday evening, when many of Leiria's restaurants close, you can find some great takeaway *frangos assados* (grilled chicken) and rice dishes, as well as beer, wine and soft drinks, at *O Braseiro Churrasqueira (☎ 82 58 66, Avenida Combatentes da Grande Guerra 41)*.

Getting There & Away
Bus There are at least ten express buses on weekdays to Coimbra, Fátima and Lisboa, around four local services to Tomar, and three to Mira de Aire, via Porto de Mós.

Train Leiria is on the Lisbon to Figueira da Foz line, with one direct IC service to Lisbon's Santa Apolónia station daily and several more services to Cacém where you can pick up Lisbon connections. Nine trains daily run to Figueira da Foz.

PINHAL DE LEIRIA
☎ 044

The Leiria Pine Forest, stretching for over 11,000 hectares along the coast west of Leiria, was first planted in the reign of Dom Afonso III, some 700 years ago. However, it was his successor, Dom Dinis, who expanded and shaped the forest (subsequently called the Pinhal do Rei or Royal Pine Forest) so that it would serve not only as a barrier against the encroaching sands but also as a supply of timber for the maritime industry – especially welcome during the Age of Discoveries.

Today the pine-scented forests, stretching from Pedrógão in the north to São Pedro de Muel in the south, comprise one of the most delightful areas in the province. They are popular for their picnic and camp sites and several excellent beaches.

Orientation & Information
The nicest and nearest beach to Leiria, 20km west, is São Pedro de Muel. Two other popular beach resorts 16km north of here – Praia de Vieira and Pedrógão – have both become rather overdeveloped. The town of Marinha Grande, halfway between Leiria and São Pedro de Muel, has a useful

turismo (☎ 56 66 44), open year-round. The smaller turismos in São Pedro de Muel (☎ 59 91 52), Praia de Vieira (☎ 69 52 30) and Pedrógão (☎ 69 54 11) are only open during July and August.

Places to Stay & Eat
Camping There are two decent camping grounds at São Pedro de Muel: one belonging to *Inatel (☎ 59 92 89, Avenida do Farol)*; and the other, nearby, run by *Orbitur (☎ 59 91 68)* and costing 600/500/510$00 per person/tent/car. Praia de Vieira has a roadside municipal *parque de campismo (☎ 69 53 34)*, open June to mid-September only. Prices are 185/220/150$00. The municipal *parque de campismo (☎ 69 54 03)* in the forest at nearby Pedrógão is nicer and only costs 200/200/200$00.

Pensões & Residenciais São Pedro de Muel is your best bet for accommodation and restaurants, though the other beach resorts also have several pensões and restaurants. The turismos at Marinha Grande and São Pedro de Muel can help you locate these places or quartos (private rooms) in the high season when accommodation can get tight.

Getting There & Away
From Leiria there are frequent buses to Marinha Grande, from where you can pick up connecting services direct to the beaches. The resorts further north have fewer connections.

FÁTIMA
☎ 049 • pop 7300

Before 13 May 1917, no-one paid any attention to this unremarkable little place 22km south-east of Leiria, but on that day something happened to transform Fátima into one of the most important places of pilgrimage in the Catholic world (see the boxed text 'Apparitions & Miracles' on the next page). It now rivals Lourdes in popularity and is visited by over four million pilgrims a year. The town itself is more of a shrine to religious commercialisation than to the Virgin: it's packed with boarding houses for the pilgrims, and shops selling every kind of tasteless souvenir imaginable. Undeniably, there's an extraordinary atmosphere at the sanctuary itself, though you'd probably want to avoid coming anywhere near the place at key times, from 12 to 13 October and 12 to 13 May, when up to 100,000 pilgrims arrive to commemorate the first apparitions.

Orientation & Information

The focus of the pilgrimages, where the apparitions occurred, is Cova da Iria, just 1km or so east of the A1 motorway. Where sheep once grazed there's now a vast 1km-long esplanade dominated by a huge white basi-

---

Apparitions & Miracles

On 13 May 1917, three shepherd children from Fátima – Lúcia, Francisco and Jacinta – claimed they saw an apparition of the Virgin. Only 10-year-old Lúcia could hear what the holy lady said, including her request that they return on the 13th of every subsequent month for the next six months. The word spread and by 13 October some 70,000 devotees had gathered. What happened then has been described as the Miracle of the Sun: intense lights shooting from the sun, followed by the miraculous cure of disabilities and illnesses suffered by some of the spectators.

What the Virgin apparently told Lúcia must have seemed equally potent in those WWI days; her messages described the hell that resulted from 'sins of the flesh' and implored the faithful to 'pray a great deal and make many sacrifices' to secure peace. The most controversial of the Virgin's messages claimed that if her request were heeded, 'Russia [would] be converted and there [would] be peace'. One final message remains secret, known only to the pope.

---

lica and surrounded by streets filled with shops, restaurants and hostels.

Several major avenidas ring the area including Avenida Dom José Alves Correia da Silva to the south, where the bus station is located: turn right from the bus station and then left along Rua João Paulo II to reach the sanctuary, 500m away. The turismo (☎ 53 11 39), also on the Avenida close to this turning, is open weekdays from 9 am to 7 pm, and weekends from 10 am to 1 pm and 3 to 7 pm (6 pm in winter).

Sanctuary

The 1953 **basilica** may be gross to look at but the devout attention it receives from many of the pilgrims tends to choke any criticism. Some suppliants even shuffle across the vast esplanade on padded knees; others count the rosary or murmur prayers. En route, they usually stop at the **Capela das Apariços** (Chapel of the Apparitions), the site where the Virgin appeared, which is packed with devotees offering flowers and lighting candles.

Inside the basilica attention is focused on the tombs of Francisco (died 1919) and Jacinta (died 1920), both victims of a flu epidemic. Lúcia, who entered a convent in Coimbra in 1928, is still alive.

Seven masses are held daily in the Basilica, and there are five a day in the Capela das Apariços (in English at 3.30 pm during the summer and in Dutch or Italian at other times: a notice board nearby gives details).

Places to Stay & Eat

There are lots of reasonably priced pensões and boarding houses, many geared for groups of hundreds. Among the cheaper places are *Pensão Santa Isabel* (☎ 53 12 95, Rua de São José), where doubles cost 5000$00 including breakfast, and *Residencial Solar da Marta* (☎ 53 11 52, Rua Francisco Marto 74), which costs 6500$00.

Restaurants abound, most offering the usual fare at reasonable prices, as you'd expect in a place swarming with hungry Portuguese; try those on Rua Francisco Marto.

Getting There & Away

Buses make the 25 minute run from Leiria at least eight times daily. There are four or five buses daily from Batalha, Coimbra and Lisbon. Fátima is often referred to as Cova da Iria on bus timetables.

As for trains, Fátima is on the Lisbon-Porto line; a dozen trains stop here daily (change at Entroncamento coming from Lisbon and at Coimbra coming from Porto). The train station is actually 25km away, connected with town by irregular buses.

PORTO DE MÓS

☎ 044

At the northern tip of the Parque Natural das Serras de Aire e Candeeiros, 9km south of Batalha, Porto de Mós is an insignificant but pleasant little town beside the Rio Lena, dominated by a 13th century hilltop castle.

At the heart of a region once inhabited by dinosaurs (you can see dinosaur bones in the town's museum and dinosaur footprints on the edge of the park – see the boxed text 'Dinosaur Footprints'), Porto de Mós was a major Roman settlement. The Romans used the Rio Lena for ferrying millstones hewn from a nearby quarry and, later, iron from the mine some 10km south at Alqueidão da Serra (where you can still see a Roman road).

Today, the town serves as a jumping off point for visiting the caves in the area or exploring the scenically stunning park.

Orientation & Information

The town spreads out from a cluster of streets just below the castle to a newer area further south around the bus station on Avenida Dr Francisco Sá Carneiro. Walk west from the bus station towards the Rio Lena and you'll hit Alameda Dom Afonso Henriques, the main road from Batalha.

The turismo (☎ 49 13 23) is at the top of this road in the *jardim público* (public gardens). In addition to information on the town and the park, the conscientious tourist office also has invaluable bus timetables for the region. The office is open daily from

---

Dinosaur Footprints

For years, a huge quarry 10km south of Fátima yielded nothing more interesting than chunks of limestone. When the quarry closed in 1994, however, the local archaeologist João Carvalho discovered huge footprints embedded in the sloping rock face – the oldest and longest sauropod tracks in the world, some 175 million years old, plodding along for 147m.

The sauropods (they were those nice herbivorous dinosaurs with small heads and long necks and tails) would once have been stepping through carbonated mud here which was later transformed into limestone. As you walk across the slope you can clearly see the large elliptical prints made by the feet (*pes*) and the smaller, half-moon prints made by the hands (*manus*).

The *Pegadas de Dinossáurio* (Dinosaur Tracks) site, is at Pedreira do Galinha, 9km east of the N360 running south of Fátima; follow the brown signs marked *Pegadas da Serra de Aire*. It's open daily except Mondays from 10 am to 1 pm and 2 to 6 pm; admission costs 250$00.

---

10 am to 1 pm and 3 to 7 pm (6 pm at weekends and during the winter).

Castelo

The distinctive green-towered castle, originally a Moorish possession, was conquered in 1148 by Dom Afonso Henriques and rebuilt in 1450. At the time of research it was closed for renovations. Check with the turismo whether it's reopened.

Museu Municipal

This little museum, just off Largo Machado dos Santos, is a treasure trove of the region's prehistoric remains, with displays ranging from fossils of turtles and dinosaur bones to polished Neolithic stones and Palaeolithic flint stones. There are also some

Moorish and Roman objects and a small exhibition of local crafts.

It's open daily except Monday from 10 am to 12.30 pm and 2 to 5.30 pm.

Places to Stay & Eat

There's only one pensão in town, the friendly *Residencial O Filipe* (☎ 40 14 55, Largo do Rossio 41). Its doubles (with bathroom) currently cost 5000$00, though expansion plans may soon lead to price increases. A pleasant alternative is the *Quinta de Rio Alcaide* (☎ 40 21 24), 1km south-east of town. This converted farmhouse has one room and five small self-catering apartments, including one in a former windmill, which cost about 8500$00 per day (7000$00 without breakfast). There's a swimming pool here, too.

There are some reasonable restaurants along Avenida Dr Francisco Sá Carneiro and Alameda Dom Afonso Henriques, and around the market on Avenida de Santo António.

Getting There & Away

There are about three buses daily to Porto de Mós from Leiria via Batalha, plus three others which require you to change at São Jorge Cruz, a junction on the N1 about 5km north-west of Porto de Mós. You'll also have to change buses at this junction when coming from Alcobaça or Rio Maior.

PARQUE NATURAL DAS SERRAS DE AIRE E CANDEEIROS

This park, stretching south from Porto de Mós, occupies the most extensive and diversified limestone range in Portugal. The landscape ranges from high plateaus and peaks to huge rocky hollows and depressions. Home to several working windmills, the park is also famous for its network of caves. One of the most spectacular parts of the park is the high plateau of Serra de Santo António (in the area containing the caves) where the sweeping farmland is divided by dry stone walls.

Throughout the park are over a dozen *parques de merendas* (picnic areas), along with three short *percurso pedestre* (walking trails), described in Portuguese-language pamphlets available at the park offices.

Information

The park's head office (☎ 043-9 19 68, fax 9 26 05) is at Jardim Municipal, Rio Maior. There's also a Centro de Interpretação (☎/fax 044-40 35 55, 49 19 04) in Porto de Mós, where you can pick up information (in Portuguese only) or watch a 25 minute video about the park's attractions. The centre is open daily except Sunday morning and Monday from 9.30 am to 12.30 pm and 2 to 6 pm.

Places to Stay

The park operates several *centros de acolhimento* (lodging centres) in the southern part of the park, geared to groups of four to eight people. The smallest, near Alcobertas, costs 11,000$00 per night in high season. Officially this accommodation has to be booked at least a week in advance at the head office. There's also a summer-only *parque de campismo* (☎ 044-45 05 55) at Arrimal, about 17km south of Porto de Mós.

MIRA DE AIRE

Portugal's largest cave system, at Mira de Aire, lies 14km south-east of Porto de Mós and is the most easily accessible of the caves in the area. It was discovered in 1947 but was only made open to the public in 1971. The 45 minute guided tour leads you down through a series of colourfully lit caverns dripping with stalactites and stalagmites. The last cavern, 110m down, contains a huge lake with a dramatic fountain display.

The Mira de Aire caves are open daily from 9.30 am to 6 pm in winter and from 9 am to 7 pm in summer (8 pm in July and August). Admission costs 600$00 (350$00 for children below 12). Near the exit is the **parque aquático**, a summer-only waterslide park. The all-day (10 am to 8 pm) admission fee is 800$00 (children 600$00), or 600$00 (350$00) after 3 pm.

Grutas de Alvados & Grutas de Santo António

These caves are about 15km south-east of Porto de Mós, and about 3km and 7km, respectively, south of the N243, which runs from Porto de Mós to Mira de Aire. They're smaller, less touristy versions of the caves at Mira de Aire.

They're both open daily from 9.30 am to 8 pm between June and September (6 pm between October and March, 7 pm during April and May, and 9 pm during July and August). Admission costs 600$00 for each cave. Ticket sales stop 30 minutes before closing time.

Getting There & Away

There are three buses on weekdays from Porto de Mós to Mira de Aire (two at weekends), and two returning. If you take the first bus out (around 9.30 am) you can easily make it a day trip. Coming from Leiria or Nazaré you're in for a long day's outing: check the bus schedule at the relevant turismo.

There are no direct buses to the Alvados and Santo António caves – the closest you'll get is a point on the N243 by taking the Mira de Aire-Porto de Mós bus. A taxi from Porto de Mós should cost about 2000$00 return, including an hour's wait at the caves.

SANTARÉM

☎ 043 • pop 20,000

One of the most agreeable towns in the otherwise dull Ribatejo is Santarém, the provincial capital: 'a book made of stone,' wrote Portugal's famous 19th century novelist Almeida Garrett, 'in which the most interesting and most poetical part of our chronicles is written'.

As well as the churches and mansions to which Garrett referred, today's Santarém is famous for its bullfights and its various fairs and festivals, notably the huge agricultural fair held every June. Outside festival season its breezy panoramas and abundance of cafés and restaurants still make it a great one day stopover.

History

The town's position in a fertile area high above the Rio Tejo made Santarém a prized possession even before the times of the Romans and Moors. It was captured by Dom Afonso Henriques in 1147 in one of the watershed successes of the Reconquista – the king built the Mosteiro de Alcobaça on the strength of the victory.

Santarém subsequently became a favourite royal residence (partly because of its good hunting opportunities) and its palace served as the meeting place of the cortes during the 13th, 14th and 15th centuries. Four hundred years later, in 1833, it was again favoured by royalty when Dom Miguel used Santarém as his base during his brief (and unsuccessful) war against his brother Pedro.

Orientation

Overlooking the Rio Tejo, Santarém commands some grand views of the Ribatejan plains. At the heart of the old town are the pedestrianised Rua Serpa Pinto and Rua Capelo e Ivens, where the turismo and most of the restaurants, shops and cheap accommodation can be found. Signposts to the Portas do Sol lookout lead visitors on a pleasant walk past most of the churches of interest.

The train station is below the town, 2km to the north-east, and there's no shuttle bus to the centre. The bus station is much closer, just west of the town centre on Avenida do Brasil.

Information

Staff at the efficient turismo (☎ 39 15 12, fax 33 36 43), Rua Capelo e Ivens 63, can provide information about the region as well as about Santarém. It's open from 9 am to 7 pm Tuesday to Friday, from 9 am to 12.30 pm and 2 to 6 pm on Monday, and from 10 am to 12.30 pm and 2.30 to 5.30 pm at weekends.

The hospital (☎ 30 02 00) is on the northern edge of town; the police station (☎ 2 20 22) is on the western side of Largo Cândido dos Reis.

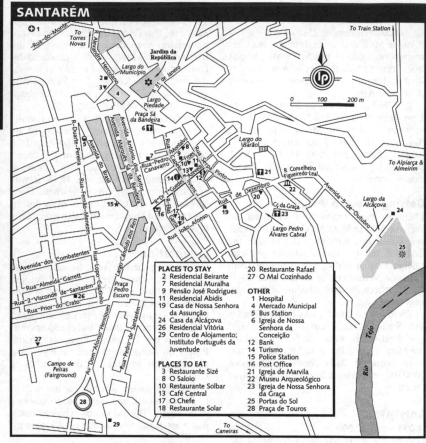

SANTARÉM

PLACES TO STAY
2 Residencial Beirante
7 Residencial Muralha
9 Pensão José Rodrigues
11 Residencial Abidis
19 Casa de Nossa Senhora
   da Assunção
24 Casa da Alcáçova
26 Residencial Vitória
29 Centro de Alojamento;
   Instituto Português da
   Juventude

PLACES TO EAT
3 Restaurante Sizé
8 O Saloio
10 Restaurante Solbar
13 Café Central
17 O Chefe
18 Restaurante Solar

20 Restaurante Rafael
27 O Mal Cozinhado

OTHER
1 Hospital
4 Mercado Municipal
5 Bus Station
6 Igreja de Nossa
   Senhora da
   Conceição
12 Bank
14 Turismo
15 Police Station
16 Post Office
21 Igreja de Marvila
22 Museu Arqueológico
23 Igreja de Nossa Senhora
   da Graça
25 Portas do Sol
28 Praça de Touros

At the Instituto Português da Juventude
(☎ 33 32 92, fax 2 78 55, email ipj
.santarem@mail.telepac.pt), on Avenida
Grupo Forcados Amadores de Santarém,
you may be able to use computers in slack
times to surf the Internet or send emails. It's
open weekdays from 10 am to 6 pm.

Igreja de Nossa Senhora da Conceição

This Baroque 17th century Jesuit seminary
church, built on the site of the former royal
palace, dominates the town's most impressive square, Praça Sá da Bandeira. Inside
the church, which now serves as the town's
cathedral, are the usual Baroque frills, including a painted ceiling and gilded carved
altars.

Igreja de Marvila

Dating from the 12th century but with
16th century overlays, the most outstanding
features of this endearing little church,
redolent with the smell of wood polish, are

its Manueline doorway and glowing 17th century azulejos. It's at the end of Rua Serpa Pinto and is open daily from 9.30 am to 12.30 pm and 2 to 6 pm (5.30 pm on Sunday); it's closed Monday and Tuesday mornings.

Igreja de Nossa Senhora da Graça

Just south of the Igreja de Marvila, on Largo Pedro Álvares Cabral, is Santarém's most impressive church. It was built in the early 15th century and features a magnificent rose window. It houses the tombs of Pedro Álvares Cabral (the 'discoverer' of Brazil) and Dom Pedro de Menezes (the first governor of Ceuta, who died in 1437). Probably because the de Menezes family founded the church, Dom Pedro's tomb is considerably more ornate than that of the explorer.

The church, which sometimes hosts temporary exhibitions, is open from 9.30 am to 12.30 pm and 2 to 5.30 pm daily except Monday.

Museu Arqueológico

This neat little archaeological museum is housed in the 12th century Igreja de São João de Alporão on Rua Conselheiro Figueiredo Leal. Among the stone carvings, azulejos, old chains and keys and other dusty relics, the showpiece is undoubtedly the elaborately carved tomb of Dom Duarte de Menezes, who died in 1464 in a battle against the Moors in North Africa. The flamboyance of the tomb is in ironic contrast to the only bit of him that was apparently saved for burial – a single tooth.

The museum (admission 200$00) is open from 9.30 am to 12.30 pm and 2 to 6 pm daily, except Monday.

Portas do Sol

The Gates of the Sun, on the site of the Moorish citadel at the south-eastern edge of town, is the town's best panoramic viewpoint and picnic site. There is a garden with aviaries and a pond, and a fantastic view over the Rio Tejo and the plains beyond.

Special Events

Santarém's Feira Nacional da Agricultura (National Agriculture Fair) is famous nationwide for its horse races, bullfights and night-time bull-running in the streets. It lasts for 10 days from the first week in June and takes place 2km west of the town centre.

Gourmets should take note of the Festival Nacional de Gastronomia, a 10 day affair at the end of October which encourages you to eat as much traditional Portuguese fare as you can. Various handicraft displays are also held at the same time.

Accommodation can be tight during both of these events: you'd be wise to book ahead.

Places to Stay – Budget

The nearest *parque de campismo* (☎ 5 50 40) is at Alpiarça, 10km to the east. It's open to visitors with CCI cards for 400/400/400$00 per person/tent/car.

There's a *centro de alojamento* (☎ 33 39 59, fax 2 78 55, Avenida Grupo Forcados Amadores de Santarém) with dorm beds (1700$00 in high season) and a few doubles available.

Among budget pensões, the most popular is the little *Pensão José Rodrigues* (☎ 2 30 88, Travessa do Froes 14), where doubles cost from 4000$00 to 5000$00.

The old-fashioned *Residencial Abidis* (☎ 2 20 17, Rua Guilherme de Azevedo 4) offers fading doubles costing 4500$00 (including a better than average breakfast). Slightly slicker, with renovated doubles starting at 5000$00 (not including breakfast), is *Residencial Muralha* (☎ 2 23 99, Rua Pedro Canavarro).

Places to Stay – Mid-Range & Top End

Away from the centre are the *Residencial Beirante* (☎ 2 25 47, Rua Alexandre Herculano 3), which is better than it looks from the outside, with doubles starting from 7000$00, and the similarly priced *Residencial Vitória* (☎ 30 91 30, fax 2 82 02, Rua 2 Visconde de Santarém 21).

Among several attractive Turihab properties, the most central is the delightful **Casa de Nossa Senhora da Assunção** (☎ 2 50 48, Rua 1 de Dezembro 55), right in the heart of the historic area. It has just two doubles costing around 11,000$00 each, plus a slightly more expensive suite.

Top of the range is **Casa da Alcáçova** (☎ 388 01 00, fax 388 01 05, email casa@mail.telepac.pt), a 17th century manor house at Largo da Alcáçova which boasts a swimming pool, superb views and eight luxury doubles ranging in price from 16,800$00 to 26,800$00.

Places to Eat

Even on a budget you'll do well in Santarém: the place is chock-a-block with cheap restaurants. The best of the rather scruffy options around the mercado municipal is **Restaurante Sizé** (☎ 2 30 30, Rua do Mercado 24-B), a jolly, busy lunchtime place.

Two places near the turismo offering bargain half-portions for around 800$00 are **Restaurante Solbar** (☎ 2 22 71, Travessa do Froes 25) and the popular **O Saloio** (☎ 2 76 56, Travessa do Montalvo 11). The well advertised **O Chefe** (Largo Emilio Infante da Câmara) is a plain, family-run place with even cheaper (and greasier) fare. A better bet on this same Largo, at No 9, is **Restaurante Solar** (☎ 2 22 39), which is popular for business lunches, as is the posher chrome and Art Deco **Café Central** (☎ 2 23 03, Rua Guilherme de Azevedo 32).

A smaller place which catches the passing tourist trade is the attractive **Restaurante Rafael** (☎ 2 65 17, Rua 1 de Dezembro 3), where dishes cost upwards of 1500$00. Similarly priced is the popular **O Mal Cozinhado** (☎ 2 35 84, Campo de Feiras). It's to the south of town, near the praça de touros.

There's a curious culinary speciality in Santarém: fataça na telha – mullet fish grilled on a tile – which occasionally appears on menus. Apparently only a few people know how to cook it properly, notably Lúcia, a villager from Caneiras, 5km

south of town. Her **O Telheiro da Lúcia** (☎ 2 85 81) is a simple riverside place where, as well as the famous fish, you can sample her home-baked bread . You need to book a day ahead: the turismo in Santarém can make the arrangements.

Getting There & Away

Bus There are hourly buses to Lisbon (80 minutes) including seven nonstop services. Around four buses a day run to Caldas da Rainha and Tomar, and three go to Setúbal.

Train There are three Alfa IC services between Lisbon's Santa Apolónia station and Santarém (45 minutes) as well as frequent slower local services. Taxis charge around 500$00 for the trip between the town and the station.

TOMAR
☎ 049 • pop 15,000

This attractive and historically outstanding town is an oasis of interest in the Ribatejo; it's home to the Convento de Cristo, former headquarters of the Knights Templar, which is one of the most significant architectural and religious monuments in the land.

The town itself, straddling the Rio Nabão, is a fine place in which to wander, with its delightful old quarter of cobbled lanes and the extensive Mata Nacional dos Sete Montes (Sete Montes National Forest) at the foot of the monastery walls. If you have your own transport, the town also makes a perfect base for exploring the surrounding area, including the nearby Castelo de Bode reservoir which is set in some very pretty countryside.

Orientation

It's easy to get your bearings: the Rio Nabão neatly divides the town, with new developments largely concentrated on the east bank and the old town to the west. The monastery looks down on it all from its wooded hilltop above the town to the west.

The bus and train station are close together at the southern end of town, a 10 minute walk from the turismo.

Salt is still produced in various areas of Portugal. Here, the salt in a salt pan is piled up to dry.

A Holy Week procession in Óbidos.

Medieval walls enclose the town of Óbidos.

Windmills dot the Portuguese countryside.

Seaweed-gathering *moliceiro*.

Traditional fishing methods are still used on Portugal's west coast.

The view across the picturesque village of Alvoco das Várzeas into the Serra da Estrela.

Folk dance outside the cheese-making town of Celorico da Beira.

The Palace Hotel do Buçaco.

Information

The conscientious staff at Tomar's turismo (☎/fax 32 24 27), at the western end of Avenida Dr Cândido Madureira, can supply a comprehensive town map and an accommodation list, along with prices. The office is open weekdays from 9.30 am to 8 pm, and weekends from 10 am to 8 pm (6 pm in winter). For information about other places in the region, head for the regional turismo (☎ 32 90 00, fax 32 43 22) at Rua Serpa Pinto 1.

In addition to a couple of medical centres, Tomar also has a district hospital (☎ 32 11 00) halfway along Avenida Dr Cândido Madureira. The police station (☎ 31 34 44) is on Rua Dr Sousa.

Convento de Cristo

Set on wooded slopes above the town and enclosed its within 12th century walls, the former headquarters of the Knights Templar reflects perfectly the power and mystique that this religious military order wielded

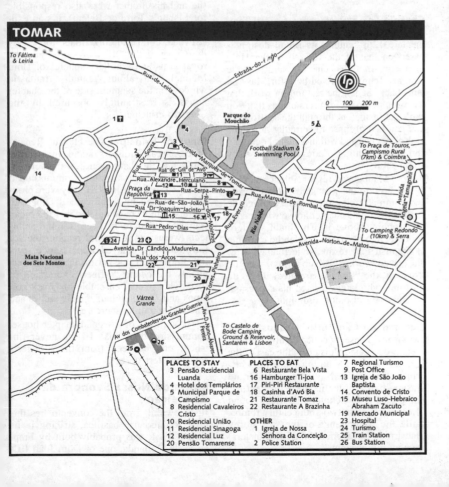

TOMAR

PLACES TO STAY
3 Pensão Residencial Luanda
4 Hotel dos Templários
5 Municipal Parque de Campismo
8 Residencial Cavaleiros Cristo
10 Residencial União
11 Residencial Sinagoga
12 Residencial Luz
20 Pensão Tomarense

PLACES TO EAT
6 Restaurante Bela Vista
16 Hamburger Ti-joa
17 Piri-Piri Restaurante
18 Casinha d'Avó Bia
21 Restaurante Tomaz
22 Restaurante A Brazinha

OTHER
1 Igreja de Nossa Senhora da Conceição
2 Police Station

7 Regional Turismo
9 Post Office
13 Igreja de São João Baptista
14 Convento de Cristo
15 Museu Luso-Hebraico Abraham Zacuto
19 Mercado Municipal
23 Hospital
24 Turismo
25 Train Station
26 Bus Station

between the 12th and 16th centuries. The monastery was founded in 1160 by Gualdim Pais, the Grand Master of the Templars. Its various chapels, cloisters and chapter houses, added over the centuries by successive kings and Grand Masters, reveal the changing architectural styles in spectacular fashion.

From 1 July to 30 September the convent is open daily from 9.15 am to 12.15 pm and 2 to 5.45 pm (5.15 pm in May and June, 5 pm from October to April). Admission costs 400$00.

Charola This extraordinary 16-sided Templar church dominates the convent. Built in the late 12th century, its round design is based on that of the Church of the Holy Sepulchre in Jerusalem. It's said that the Knights Templar arrived here for Mass on horseback. Sadly, the restoration work that has been going on for years means that you can't get inside but through the scaffolding you can just glimpse the circular aisle, the high altar enclosed within a central octagon, and some paintings dating from the early 16th century.

Dom Manuel was responsible for tacking the nave on to the west side of the Charola and commissioning the architect Diogo de Arruda to build a chapter house with a *coro alto* (choir) above it. The main western doorway into the nave – a splendid example of Spanish Plateresque style (named after the ornate work of silversmiths) – is the work of the Spanish architect João de Castilho, who later repeated his success at Belém's Mosteiro dos Jerónimos.

Claustro do Cemitério & Claustro da Lavagem These two beautifully serene, azulejo-decorated cloisters to the east of the Charola were built during the time when Prince Henry the Navigator was Grand Master of the order in the 15th century. The Claustro do Cemitério (Burial-Ground Cloisters) contain two 16th century tombs, while the water tanks of the two storey Claustro da Lavagem (Ablutions Cloisters) are now full of plants.

Chapter House The most famous feature of the entire convento – reproduced on countless postcards – is the window on the west side of the chapter house, best seen from the roof of the adjacent Claustro de Santa Bárbara (follow signs to the *janela*). Although now covered in lichen and in dire need of restoration, it's still obviously a stupendous expression of Manueline art, the confidence of the seafaring Age of Discoveries made tangible in stone.

Designed around 1510 by the master of Manueline flamboyance, Diogo de Arruda (he and his brother were also responsible for Lisbon's Torre de Belém), it's an exuberant celebration of tangled ropes, seaweed, coral and cork floats, topped by the Cross of the Order of Christ and the royal arms and armillary spheres of Dom Manuel. An almost equally fantastic window on the southern side of the chapter house is frustratingly obscured by the Claustro Principal.

Claustro Principal The elegant Renaissance Great Cloisters stand in striking contrast to the flamboyance of the convento's Manueline architecture. Commissioned during the reign of João III, they were probably designed by the Spaniard Diogo de Torralva but were completed in 1587 by an Italian, Filippo Terzi. These foreign architects were among several responsible for introducing a delayed Renaissance style into Portugal. The Claustro Principal is arguably the country's finest expression of that style: a sober ensemble of Greek columns and Tuscan pillars, gentle arches and sinuous, spiralling staircases.

The outlines of a second chapter house, commissioned by João III but never finished, can be seen from the cloister's south-western corner.

Igreja de Nossa Senhora da Conceição

Just downhill from the convento lies this little Renaissance basilica, striking in its simplicity. It was probably built by Francisco de Hollanda, one of Dom João III's

The Order of the Knights Templar

This religious military order was founded in about 1119 by a clutch of French knights who decided to devote themselves to the protection of pilgrims visiting the Holy Land from bands of marauding Muslims. King Baldwin of Jerusalem housed them in a part of his palace that was once a Jewish temple – hence the name of the order.

It soon became a strictly organised semireligious affair headed by a Grand Master. Each Templar took vows of poverty and chastity and, to emphasise their religious vows, the knights wore white coats emblazoned with a red cross. By 1139 they were placed directly under the pope's authority and soon became the leading defenders of the Christian crusader states in the Holy Land. In Portugal, their main role was in helping to expel the Moors from the country.

Rewarded with land, castles and titles, the order quickly grew very rich, owning properties all over Europe, the Mediterranean and the Holy Land. This network, and their military strength, gave them another influential role: that of bankers to kings and pilgrims alike.

By the mid-13th century, however, the primary *raison d'être* of the order was in question – the Christians had recaptured all of Portugal – and by 1300 the Moors had taken the last remaining crusader stronghold in the Holy Land. There was talk of merging the order with their age-old rivals, the Hospitallers (another military religious order), but the axe finally fell as a result of rumours and scandals involving the order's practices, probably stirred up by their enemies.

In 1307, King Philip IV of France – either eager for the order's wealth or afraid of its power – initiated an era of persecution (supported by the French pope Clement V), arresting all of the knights, accusing many of heresy and seizing their property. In 1314, the order's last Grand Master was burned at the stake.

In Portugal, however, things didn't go nearly so badly for the order. Dom Dinis did follow the trend by dissolving the order in 1314 but a few years later he cannily re-established it as the Order of Christ, under the control of the throne. It was largely thanks to the wealth of the order that Prince Henry the Navigator (Grand Master from 1417 to 1460) was able to fund the launch of the Age of Discoveries. Dom João III took the order into a more humble phase, shifting it towards monastic duties. From the 17th century its power diminished and in 1834, together with all of the other religious orders, it finally broke up.

favourite architects, in the middle of the 16th century.

It's only open from 11 am to 12.15 pm daily; at other times, ask for the key at the entrance to the convento.

Igreja de São João Baptista
The old town's most striking church faces Praça da República, itself an eye-catching ensemble of 17th century buildings. The church, mostly dating from the late 15th century, has an octagonal spire and richly ornamented Manueline doorways on its northern and western sides. The six panels hanging inside were painted specially for the church by Gregório Lopes, one of the finest of Portugal's 16th century artists.

Museu Luso-Hebraico Abraham Zacuto
At Rua Dr Joaquim Jacinto 73, a charming cobbled lane in the old town, you'll find the best preserved medieval synagogue in Portugal. Built between 1430 and 1460, it was used as a Jewish house of worship and meeting place for only a few years, until

Dom Manuel's edict of 1496 forced the Jews of Portugal to convert to Christianity or leave the country. The synagogue subsequently served as a prison, chapel, hay loft and warehouse until it was classified as a national monument in 1921.

Largely thanks to the efforts of Luís Vasco (who comes from one of two Jewish families left in Tomar), the small, plain building now serves as a Luso-Hebraic museum, displaying various tombstones engraved with 13th and 14th century Hebraic inscriptions, as well as gifts from Jewish visitors from around the world. In the house next door, women's ritual baths, discovered during 1985 excavations, are now on display under glass.

The synagogue (admission free) is open daily, except Wednesday, from 9.30 am to 12.30 pm and 2 to 6 pm (5 pm in winter).

Activities

Adventure Sports With advance planning, you could take advantage of an ambitious range of adventure sports and other activities organised by Templar, a subdivision of the Associação para o Desenvolvimento Integrado do Ribatejo Norte (ADIRN; Association for the Integrated Development of Northern Ribatejo). Its programme includes activities ranging from walking, biking and canoeing day trips to parachuting, caving, and hot-air balloon trips. They're meant for groups of at least ten people (and all have to be booked in advance) but individuals may also be able to join in. Contact Templar (☎ 32 34 93, fax 32 17 20) at Alameda 1 de Marco, Centro Commercial Templários.

Horse Riding If you'd like to go riding, contact Paulo or Sofia Mota at the Turihab Quinta da Anunciada Velha (☎ 34 55 87), 3km south-west of town.

Water Sports Although most water sports are prohibited on the nearby Castelo de Bode reservoir, 14km east of Tomar, there

---

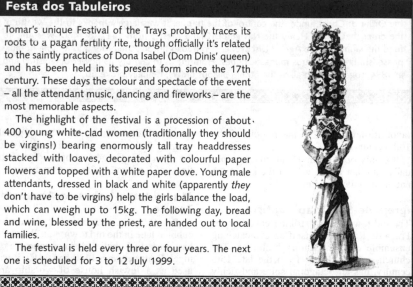

Festa dos Tabuleiros

Tomar's unique Festival of the Trays probably traces its roots to a pagan fertility rite, though officially it's related to the saintly practices of Dona Isabel (Dom Dinis' queen) and has been held in its present form since the 17th century. These days the colour and spectacle of the event – all the attendant music, dancing and fireworks – are the most memorable aspects.

The highlight of the festival is a procession of about 400 young white-clad women (traditionally they should be virgins!) bearing enormously tall tray headdresses stacked with loaves, decorated with colourful paper flowers and topped with a white paper dove. Young male attendants, dressed in black and white (apparently *they* don't have to be virgins) help the girls balance the load, which can weigh up to 15kg. The following day, bread and wine, blessed by the priest, are handed out to local families.

The festival is held every three or four years. The next one is scheduled for 3 to 12 July 1999.

are a couple of operators who arrange canoe and boat trips on the Rio Zêzere which feeds into the reservoir. Try Centro Nautico Lago Azul (☎ 049-36 15 85, fax 36 16 60), based in Castenheira (17km to the north-east), or the biggest operator in the area, Centro Naútico do Zêzere (☎ 074-99 97 45, fax 99 97 60), which offers jet skis, yachts, water-skis, canoes and kayaks at its centre in Palhais, 45km north-east of Tomar.

Special Events

Tomar's most famous event is the Festa dos Tabuleiros (see the boxed text on the opposite page). Another important religious festival is the Nossa Senhora da Piedade candle procession, held on the first Sunday in September in alternate years (the next is due in 2000). During this festival, floats decorated with paper flowers are paraded through the streets.

Places to Stay

Camping Tomar's municipal *parque de campismo* (☎ 32 26 07) is next to the football stadium and municipal swimming pool. Prices are 410/240/300$00 per person/tent/car.

There are other good camping grounds east of town. *Pelinos 77* (☎ 30 18 14), charging 480/400/250$00, is 7km to the north-east at Pelinos; bus connections are poor. *Camping Redondo* (☎/fax 37 64 21), at Poco Redondo, near Serra, 10km to the east, has a swimming pool, bar and restaurant; prices are 450/375/275$00 and bus connections are reasonably good. *Castelo de Bode* (☎ 99 22 62, 84 92 62), at 350/280/350$00, is 14km to the south-east; a few buses a day run from Tomar.

Pensões & Residenciais Close to the bus station, the old *Pensão Tomarense* (☎ 31 29 48, Avenida Torres Pinheiro 13) still offers bargain doubles for 3750$00, but they're pretty seedy. Better options in the heart of the old town include the friendly, old-fashioned *Residencial Luz* (☎ 31 23 17, Rua Serpa Pinto 144), which has singles/doubles costing 3000/5500$00, and *Resi-*

dencial União (☎ 32 31 61, fax 32 12 99), down the road at No 94, where doubles cost 6500$00, including breakfast.

In the next price bracket is the modern *Pensão Residencial Luanda* (☎ 32 32 00, fax 32 21 45, Avenida Marquês de Tomar 15) where doubles cost 7500$00, including breakfast. Nearby is the posher *Residencial Cavaleiros Cristo* (☎ 32 12 03, fax 32 11 92, Rua Alexandre Herculano 7), which offers nicely decorated doubles, all with bathroom, TV and minibar, for 10,000$00. The slightly cheaper *Residencial Sinagoga* (☎ 32 30 83, fax 32 21 96, Rua de Gil de Avô 31) is in a quiet residential area.

Top of the range in town is the new *Hotel dos Templários* (☎ 32 17 30, fax 32 21 91, Largo Cândido dos Reis 1), which has a swimming pool, a health club and doubles with all the frills for 17,400$00. There are also several lovely Turihab properties in the area; the nearest is *Quinta da Anunciada Velha* (☎ 34 52 18, fax 34 54 69), 3km south-west of town, where doubles cost 11,000$00 and an apartment 15,000$00.

Places to Eat

Winning the prize for looks and location is *Restaurante Bela Vista* (☎ 31 28 70, Rua Fonte do Choupo 6); it's often full. Overlooking the weir, it has outdoor tables under the shade of wisteria flowers. The menu comprises reasonably priced dishes starting at around 1000$00. The restaurant is closed Monday.

The brightly decorated *Restaurante Tomaz* (☎ 31 25 52, Rua dos Arcos 31) has dour service but large helpings at cheap prices. Further up the road at No 55, *Restaurante A Brazinha* (☎ 31 30 20) is a slightly more expensive option – dishes cost upwards of 1400$00, though it does have some half-portions starting at 950$00. It's closed Saturday. Cosier and cheaper is the cutely decorated *Casinha d'Avó Bia* (☎ 32 38 28, Rua Dr Joaquim Jacinto 16). The nearby *Piri-Piri Restaurante* (☎ 31 34 94, Rua dos Moinhos 54) looks posh but offers reasonably priced fare in a relaxing setting, with country music instead of TV. Across

ESTREMADURA & RIBATEJO

the road at No 49, *Hamburger Ti-joa* serves burgers and English breakfasts.

Getting There & Away

There are seven express buses daily to Lisbon and around three each to Batalha, Nazaré and Leiria. Weekday train services run hourly to/from Lisbon's Santa Apolónia station (about eight a day at weekends), taking two hours.

Getting Around

There are several car rental agencies in town, including the local Lusonabão (☎ 32 29 12), Nabantur (☎ 31 16 88) and Hertz (☎ 31 60 12).

The Beiras

At the heart of Portugal lies the Beira region, and at the heart of the Beira is the country's highest mountain range and most prominent geophysical landmark, the beautiful Serra da Estrela. This and the region's lesser ranges help to define the three Beira provinces – *litoral* (coastal), *alta* (upper) and *baixa* (lower) – that mirror Portugal's own multiple personalities.

Air masses from the Atlantic Ocean tumble against these granite ranges, spilling their moisture and giving birth to several major river systems which have laid down a rich subsoil in and west of the mountains. Unlike most of Portugal's better known rivers, which have their headwaters in Spain, the Rio Mondego rises in the Serra da Estrela and is the longest exclusively Portuguese river.

Beira Litoral's splendid coastline has so far escaped serious development; the only major resort is at cheerful Figueira da Foz. Aveiro and Ovar preside over a vast and complex estuary at the mouth of the Rio Vouga, and there's an important wildlife refuge at São Jacinto. From the coast a fertile, sometimes boggy plain stretches 30km inland to the Gralheira, Caramulo and Buçaco hills and, to the south, up to 90km into the foothills of the Serra da Estrela.

Elegant Coimbra – the provincial headquarters and the biggest town in the Beiras – is, with Lisbon and Porto, one of Portugal's historic capitals and a major centre of culture and learning. Around it lie the spa town of Luso, the holy forest of Buçaco and, at Conimbriga, Portugal's finest Roman ruins.

Beira Alta, hemmed in by mountains, was the heartland of the Lusitani who, under the legendary Viriathus or Viriato – Portugal's original national hero – put up stubborn resistance to the Romans. Its dour people see few visitors other than those who stumble upon Viseu or the provincial capital, Guarda. Most visitors head, via Seia or

HIGHLIGHTS

- Roam the lanes of the ancient, fado-loving university town of Coimbra
- Wander among the country's best-preserved Roman ruins at Conimbriga
- Hike all day in the hallowed forest of Buçaco and soak away the aches in the spa town of Luso
- Walk through the high peaks and traditional settlements of the Parque Natural da Serra da Estrela

Gouveia, straight into the Serra da Estrela. Robbed of rain, the eastern parts of the province are sparsely populated and thinly cultivated.

Beira Baixa, though hilly in the north, is much like the Alentejo, with modest, good-natured people, ferocious summer weather and hypnotically flat landscapes of cork oaks, olive groves and giant agricultural estates. Like most of the Beira Alta it's of minimal interest except to lovers of vast, quiet, open spaces – even the capital, Castelo Branco, has little to offer to visitors. A conspicuous exception is the proud, handsome hilltop town of Monsanto.

Beira Litoral

COIMBRA
☎ 039 • pop 140,000
Perched above the Rio Mondego midway between Lisbon and Porto, Coimbra is renowned as the 'Oxford of Portugal'. Its ancient university, founded in 1290, is still

BEIRAS

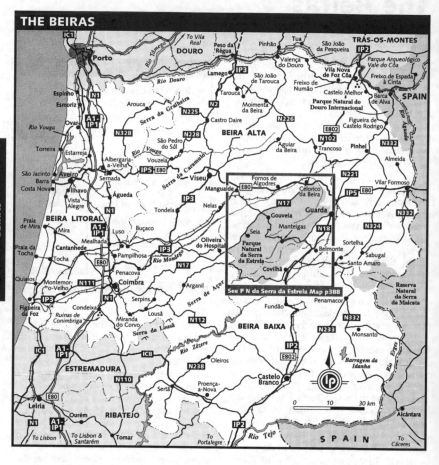

THE BEIRAS

the focus of life, though the city has many other cultural attractions, some dating back to the time some 850 years ago when Coimbra was Portugal's capital.

Although development and appalling traffic congestion have eroded the city's charm, it's still a great place to hang out for a few days: transport is good, food and accommodation are plentiful and reasonably priced, and some attractive day-trip destinations are nearby, including the country's finest Roman ruins at Conimbriga. If you're

here in May, you can throw yourself into the spirit of Coimbra's biggest bash, Queima das Fitas (see under Special Events later in this section).

All in all, this is a thoroughly enjoyable destination – romantic and cultured, lively and fun. Beware Mondays, when most museums are closed.

History

The Romans founded a major settlement at nearby Conimbriga, and the Moors settled in Coimbra itself until the Christians booted them out in the 12th century. Afonso Henriques made the city his new capital in 1145 but, just over a century later, Afonso III decided to move to Lisbon. Coimbra University, the country's first university (and among the first in Europe), was actually founded in Lisbon by Dom Dinis in 1290, but it settled here for good in 1537, attracting a steady stream of teachers, artists and intellectuals from all over Europe.

The 16th century was a particularly cultured time for Coimbra thanks to Nicolas Chanterène, Jean de Rouen (João de Ruão) and several other French sculptors who helped to create a school of sculpture which was to influence styles all over Portugal.

Today Coimbra's university has fewer students than Lisbon's but it's still the most prestigious academic establishment in the country. Coimbra itself, though respected as a traditional centre of art and culture, prospers these days thanks to its textile, tannery and tourism industries.

Orientation

Crowning Coimbra's hilltop is the university, with the old town in a tangle of lanes around and below it. Most places of interest are in this area and within easy (if steep) walking distance of one another. The new town – called Baixa (lower) by local people – sprawls at the bottom of the hill and along the Rio Mondego. Hubs of activity include Largo da Portagem and the adjacent, pedestrianised Rua Ferreira Borges (the main shopping street), and the student haunt, Praça da República. The few sights of interest across the river are accessible on foot via the Ponte de Santa Clara.

From the main bus station on Avenida Fernão de Magalhães it's a 15 minute walk south-east to the old town centre. There are three train stations: central Coimbra A (also called *estação nova* or new station); the main Coimbra B (also called *estação velha* or old station), 2km to the north-west; and Coimbra Parque, 500m south of the centre. Coimbra stations A and B are linked by a rail shuttle.

If you come by car, be ready for bad drivers and scarce parking. One place to leave your car while you hike around the town is across the river on Avenida de Conimbriga, where there's a parking area.

Information

Tourist Offices You'll get the best help from either of two amenable, efficient municipal turismos: one (☎ 83 25 91) is on Largo Dom Dinis by the university, open weekdays from 9 am to 6 pm, and weekends from 9 am to 12.30 pm and 2 to 5.30 pm; the other (☎ 83 32 02) is on Praça da República, open from 10 am to 6.30 pm on weekdays only.

A less helpful regional turismo (☎ 83 30 19 fax 82 55 76) on Largo da Portagem – the one all the signs point to – is open weekdays from 9 am to 7 pm, and weekends from 9 am to 1 pm and 2.30 to 5.30 pm.

A good town map is available from all three offices.

Money There are banks with ATMs along Avenida Fernão de Magalhães, Avenida Emídio Navarro and Rua Ferreira Borges. Outside banking hours, the Hotel Astória (see Places to Stay) also changes currency.

Post The main post office (☎ 82 81 81) is at Avenida Fernão de Magalhães 223, 500m north of Largo da Portagem. Other handy branches are on Praça da República and Rua Olímpio Nicolau Rui Fernandes near the mercado municipal.

Email & Internet Access One of the most competent 'cyberspaces' we found in Portugal is part of a graphics and publications centre called Ego Mundo (☎ 84 10 25, fax 83 70 16, Web site www.egomundo.pt) at Rua Antero de Quental 73. It's open from 10 am to midnight on weekdays (from 2 pm on Saturday and from 7 pm on Sunday). Online time costs 125$00 for 15 minutes.

Travel Agencies For student cards and youth travel discounts, go to Tagus Travel (☎ 83 49 99, fax 83 49 16), based at the

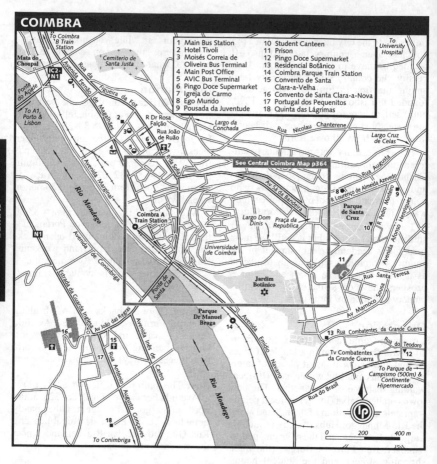

COIMBRA

1 Main Bus Station	10 Student Canteen
2 Hotel Tivoli	11 Prison
3 Moisés Correia de	12 Pingo Doce Supermarket
Oliveira Bus Terminal	13 Residencial Botânico
4 Main Post Office	14 Coimbra Parque Train Station
5 AVIC Bus Terminal	15 Convento de Santa
6 Pingo Doce Supermarket	Clara-a-Velha
7 Igreja do Carmo	16 Convento de Santa Clara-a-Nova
8 Ego Mundo	17 Portugal dos Pequenitos
9 Pousada da Juventude	18 Quinta das Lágrimas

Associação Academica de Coimbra (AAC) on Rua Padre António Vieira, open weekdays only from 9.30 am to 6 pm.

Wasteels (☎ 83 73 65) sells Inter-Rail passes from a kiosk at Coimbra A station. Other reliable agencies include Abreu (☎ 82 70 11), Rua da Sota 2, and Intervisa (☎ 82 38 73), Avenida Fernão de Magalhães 11.

Bookshops There's a cluster of good bookshops along Rua Ferreira Borges, including a branch of Livraria Bertrand.

Universities The historic Velha Universidade (Old University) is the heart of the university campus and the most interesting part. Dull modern additions contain few student rendezvous areas; the AAC (Associação Academica de Coimbra) on Rua Padre António Vieira serves that role better, with a canteen and student-oriented shops.

Language Courses The university runs a one month Portuguese language course every July; contact the Secretariádo dos

Cursos de Português (☎ 85 99 91, fax 83 46 13), Faculdade de Letras, 3049 Coimbra. Private Portuguese language courses are run by the Cambridge School (☎ 83 49 69, fax 83 39 16), Praça da República 15.

Cultural Centre You can catch up with British newspapers at the library of the British Council (☎ 82 35 49), with entrances on Rua de Tomar 4 and Rua Alexandre Herculano 34, on Monday, Thursday and Friday from 9.30 am to 12.30 pm and 2 to 8 pm, and on Wednesday from 2 to 8 pm. It's closed at weekends and on Tuesday.

Medical Services & Emergency The University of Coimbra Hospital (☎ 40 04 00) is on Praça Professor Mota Pinto. The police station (☎ 82 20 22) is on Rua Olímpio Nicolau Rui Fernandes opposite the *câmara municipal* (town hall).

Upper Town

The steep climb to the Velha Universidade from Largo da Portagem takes you into the heart and soul of Coimbra. Turn right off Rua Ferreira Borges and under the **Arco de Almedina**, once part of the old city wall. To the left, at the end of Rua Sub Ripas, is the **Torre de Anto Memória da Escrita** (☎ 83 65 92), a converted tower displaying the works of famous Coimbra writers and poets. It's open Tuesday to Friday from 10 am to 12.30 pm and 2 to 7 pm, and on Saturday from 2.30 to 7 pm. On Rua Sub Ripas you pass a magnificent Manueline doorway, part of the former **Palácio de Sub Ripas**.

Backtrack and walk to Largo Sé Velha and finally, climb Rua Borges Carneiro to the Museu Nacional Machado de Castro and the dull 'new' campus, much of which was founded by the aggressively efficient Marquês de Pombal in the 18th century. Dominating Largo da Sé Nova in front of the museum is the **Sé Nova** (New Cathedral), a severe building started by the Jesuits in 1598 but only completed a century later.

The Velha Universidade is a short walk south along Rua São João. For a glimpse of student life, stroll along any of the alleys around the Sé Velha or below the Sé Nova. Flags and graffiti identify the cramped houses known as *repúblicas*, each accommodating a group of students (traditionally 12 or 13) usually from the same region or faculty.

Velha Universidade

The Old University, packed with cultural treasures dating from the 16th to 18th centuries, lies within a compact square, the Patio das Escolas (sadly, now used as a car park). The square's most eye-catching feature is the much-photographed 18th century clock tower, nicknamed *a cabra* (the goat) by students. Here a statue of João III turns his back on a fine view of the city and the river. It was João III who re-established the university in Coimbra in 1537 and invited renowned international scholars to teach here.

As you enter the courtyard take the stairway to the right (follow the *reitoria* sign) to the **Sala dos Capelos** (Graduates' Hall), a former examination room, which is now used for degree ceremonies. Pass the dull portraits of Portugal's kings to reach the catwalk around the outside, with brilliant views of the city. Below the clock tower is the entrance to the **Capela de São Miguel**, a small, ornate chapel with a huge, gilded Baroque organ.

Everything pales before the **Biblioteca Joanina** (João V Library) behind an imposing Baroque portal next door; visits are staggered so you may have to wait to get in. A gift from João V in the early 18th century, the library's three rooms are totally unsuited for study, thanks to their extravagant and distracting riches: tables of rosewood, ebony and jacaranda, Chinoiserie designs etched in gilt, and ceilings covered with frescoes. Its 300,000 books (most of them ancient leather-bound tomes) are dedicated to law, philosophy and theology. At the far end, firmly catching the eye, is a portrait of the patron himself.

It costs 250$00 to visit each of these places, but students and teachers (including

CENTRAL COIMBRA

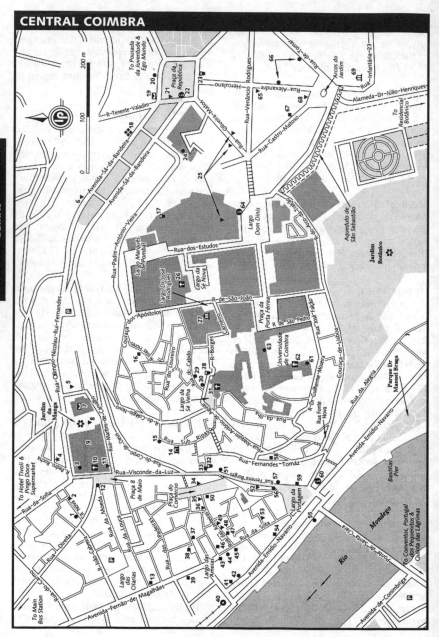

CENTRAL COIMBRA

PLACES TO STAY
12 Pensão Santa Cruz
13 Residência Lusa Atenas
16 Casa Pombal Guesthouse
37 Residência Moderna
38 Residencial Domus
39 Hotel Oslo
41 Pensão Residencial
    Internacional
43 Pensão Restaurante Vitória
45 Pensão Lorvanense
46 Pensão Flôr de Coimbra
47 Residência Coimbra
50 Pensão Residencial Rivoli
54 Hotel Astória
58 Hospedaria Simões
59 Pensão Residencial Larbelo
67 Pensão Residencial Antunes

PLACES TO EAT
2 Restaurante Democrática
5 Mercado Municipal
   Dom Pedro V
6 Restaurante Sá da Bandeira
8 Restaurante Jardim
   da Manga
11 Café Santa Cruz

21 Cartola Esplanada Bar
25 Student Canteens
34 Café Praça Velha
35 Restaurante Zé Neto
36 Adega Funchal
48 Restaurante Giro
49 Restaurante Viela
52 Pastelaria Arcadia
53 Restaurante Zé Manel
65 Bar-Restaurante ACM
68 Restaurante-Bar AAC/OAF

OTHER
1   Bar Diligência
3   Câmara Municipal
4   Police Station
7   Post Office
9   Mosteiro de Santa Cruz
10 Igreja de Santa Cruz
14 Palácio de Sub Ripas
15 Torre de Anto Memória
    da Escrita
17 Dom Dinis Bar
18 Golden Shopping Centre
19 Post Office
20 Cambridge School
22 Municipal Turismo

23 Tropical Bar
24 Associação Academica de
    Coimbra; Tagus Travel
26 Sé Nova
27 Museu Nacional Machado
    de Castro
28 Aqui Há Rato
29 Boémia Bar
30 Restaurante O Trovador
31 Sé Velha
32 Café-Galeria Almedina
33 Arco de Almedina
40 Coimbra A Train Station
42 Automóvel Club de Portugal
44 Centro Velocipédico
    de Sangalhos
51 'Chiado' & Gallery
55 Bus Kiosk
56 Valentim de Carvalho
57 Livraria Bertrand
60 Regional Turismo
61 Biblioteca Joanina
62 Capela de São Miguel
63 Sala dos Capelos
64 Municipal Turismo
66 British Council
69 Casa Museu Bissaya Barreto

BEIRAS

those from outside Portugal, provided they have appropriate identification) can visit free of charge; tickets are sold outside the Sala dos Capelos. Opening hours are from 9.30 am to noon and 2 to 5 pm daily.

Sé Velha

Coimbra's chunky Old Cathedral looks more like a fortress, and deliberately so, since it was built in the late 12th century when the Moors were still a threat. Little has been done to it since then; even the Renaissance doorway added to the north wall in the 16th century has eroded so badly you hardly notice it. What you see is pure, austere Romanesque, one of the finest Portuguese cathedrals of its time. The interior is equally simple; the most elaborate piece of decoration is an early 16th century carved and gilded altarpiece.

The Sé Velha is open daily in summer from 9.30 am to 12.30 pm and 2 to 5.30 pm, except for Friday morning cleaning; hours

are irregular in winter. There's a charge of 100$00 to visit the Gothic cloisters.

Museu Nacional Machado de Castro

Housed in this attractive former bishop's palace, with a 16th century loggia overlooking the Sé Velha and the old town, is one of the most important collections of 14th to 16th century sculpture in the country. Coimbra itself was a magnet for sculptors during this period, thanks in part to a plentiful supply of soft, easily carved Ança limestone.

The museum contains several magnificent limestone pieces, including the Gothic *Virgin & Child* by Master Pero. There is also an anonymous medieval knight on his horse, and the lovely Renaissance *A Virgem Anunciada* by Nicolas Chanterène.

The collection of paintings and ceramics is also very impressive, especially the 16th and 17th century Flemish and Portuguese paintings, including two panels by Quentin Metzys. Much preferred by school groups is the *cryptoporticus* in the basement, a series of galleries which probably served as the foundation for a Roman forum.

The museum has been undergoing major restoration and several sections are closed. The rest is open daily except Monday from 9.30 am to 12.30 pm and 2 to 5 pm; admission costs 250$00.

Mosteiro de Santa Cruz

After the trendy shops and pastelarias of the adjacent Rua Ferreira Borges and Rua Visconde da Luz, the 16th century Santa Cruz Monastery (originally founded in the 12th century) plunges you back into the Manueline and Renaissance eras.

Step through the Renaissance porch and flamboyant 18th century arch to find some of the Coimbra School's most impressive work, including an ornate pulpit and the elaborate tombs – probably carved by Nicolas Chanterène – of Portugal's first kings, Afonso Henriques and Sancho I. The most striking of the Manueline works on display here are the restrained cloisters, designed in 1524. A frieze in the choir stalls above shows Portuguese ships at their fighting best.

At the back of the church is the **Jardim da Manga** (once part of the monastery's cloisters), which contains a bizarre domed and buttressed fountain, now looking rather neglected.

The church is open daily from 9 am to noon and 2 to 5.45 pm, although groups are not welcome during daily morning mass. There's a 200$00 fee to see the cloisters.

Outside, Praça 8 de Maio is a fine place for people-watching on a sunny day; by 6 or 7 pm it's filled with unwinding students and office workers, kids, pigeons, beggars and the odd sleeping drunk.

Jardim Botânico

A pleasant place to catch your breath on the sightseeing trail is the Botanical Garden beside Alameda Dr Júlio Henriques, a 10 minute walk from the university. Estab-

lished by the Marquês de Pombal in the shadow of the 16th century Aqueduto (aqueduct) de São Sebastião, it's a combination of formal flower beds, meandering paths and elegant fountains.

Casa Museu Bissaya Barreto

Bissaya Barreto was a local surgeon, scholar and energetic collector whose handsome late-19th century mansion has been turned into a museum full of Portuguese sculpture and painting, Chinese porcelain, old azulejos, period furniture and more. The museum (☎ 37 33 39), at Rua da Infantária 23 near the Aqueduto de São Sebastião, is open daily except Monday from 3 to 5 pm (6 pm at weekends).

Across the River
Convento de Santa Clara-a-Velha

Crossing the Ponte de Santa Clara (an ideal vantage point for photographing Coimbra), you'll soon notice the convent on the left, currently being cleared of the river mud that has drowned it since the 17th century. The convent has famous connections: it was founded in 1330 by Dona Isabel (Dom Dinis' wife), whose tomb was later placed here beside that of Dona Inês de Castro, the murdered mistress of Dom Pedro (see the boxed text 'Love & Revenge' in the Estremadura & Ribatejo chapter).

Quinta das Lágrimas According to legend, Inês was killed in the gardens of this privately owned *quinta* (country estate), south of town and 200m off Rua António Augusto Gonçalves. The quinta has now been opened as a posh hotel (see Places to Stay) but even non-guests can visit the gardens and Fonte dos Amores (Lovers' Fountain) where the dastardly deed is said to have been done.

Convento de Santa Clara-a-Nova Inês' tomb now lies in the Mosteiro de Santa Maria de Alcobaça (see the Estremadura & Ribatejo chapter for details), while Isabel's is up the hill from the Santa Clara-a-Velha in the Convento de Santa Clara-a-Nova, an unattractive 17th century complex, most of which now serves as army barracks. The church that contains Isabel's solid silver tomb is devoted almost entirely to the saintly queen's memory: a series of panels shows how her tomb was moved here, wooden panels in the aisles tell her life story, and some of her clothes hang in the sacristy. Her statue here is also the focus of the Festa de Rainha Santa (see under Special Events).

The convent church is open from 9 am to noon and 2 to 5 pm (closed Saturday afternoon, Sunday morning and also all day Monday).

Portugal dos Pequenitos At this overrated theme park, coachloads of kids debouch to clamber over models of Portugal's most famous monuments. Several displays based on the former colonies seem permanently closed and many models need a lick of paint.

It's open daily from 10 am to 8 pm between July and September, to 7 pm between March and June, and to 5 pm during the rest of the year. Admission is free for those aged 6 and under, 400$00 for kids up to age 14, and 800$00 for everyone else, plus 100/200$00 for each of several small museums inside.

Prison
One of Coimbra's largest landmarks is not mentioned by the turismo at all: a huge fortified complex shaped like a cross, south-east of Praça da República. When João III moved the university here in the 16th century he also founded a number of preparatory colleges, including the Colege de São Tomar. After 1834, when religious orders were abolished, this was made into a prison, and has remained one since then.

Activities
Walking If you fancy walking in the beautiful Serra de Lousã and Serra de Açor, together arcing south-east and east almost to the Serra da Estrela, contact Dutch resident Maryke Kramer (☎ 42 30 67, ☎/fax 99 52 54), who organises guided day trips, normally for groups of four or more. The price of 2500$00 per person includes a picnic of local and home-made foods.

Canoeing In summer, O Pioneiro do Mondego rents out kayaks (3000$00 per day) for paddling down the Rio Mondego from Penacova; a free minibus takes you to the starting point at 10 am. The 25km trip takes about three hours. Inquire at their information kiosk (☎/fax 47 83 85) in Parque Dr Manuel Braga; it's open from 1 to 3 pm and 8 to 10 pm.

Boat Trips Basófias (☎ 40 41 35, mobile ☎ 0676 35 81 31) runs 75-minute boat trips on the Rio Mondego throughout the year, daily except Monday. They leave from beside Parque Dr Manuel Braga.

Horse Riding If you want to trot around Mata do Choupal (Choupal Park) on the north-western edge of town, contact the Centro de Hípico de Coimbra (Coimbra Riding Centre; ☎ 83 76 95).

Special Events
Queima das Fitas During the Burning of the Ribbons festival in May, Coimbra's students celebrate the end of the academic year with boisterous revelry. A non-stop calendar of events includes a packed midnight fado concert in front of the Sé Velha (Coimbra has its own version of fado) and a procession, with everyone in their black gowns and coloured top hats, that brings the town to a standstill. If you arrive soon after it's over, you'll find all of Coimbra in a state of utter exhaustion.

Festa de Rainha Santa Held around 4 July in even-numbered years, this major religious festival commemorates the queen-saint Isabel with a procession that takes her statue from Santa Clara-a-Nova to Igreja do Carmo and back. Events during the festival (which coincides with the Festa da Cidade or Town Festival) include folk music and dancing, and fireworks by the river.

Places to Stay – Budget

Camping At the *parque de campismo de Câmara Municipal de Coimbra* (☎ 70 14 97), by the municipal stadium east of the centre (take bus No 5 from Coimbra B station or Praça da República), you can listen to all-night traffic noise and church bells tolling every 15 minutes; it costs 231/153/294$00 per person/tent/car. A new municipal site is under construction near the river.

Hostel Coimbra's pleasant *pousada da juventude* (☎ 82 29 55, *Rua Dr António Henriques Seco 12-14)* is to the north-east of Praça da República; dorm beds/singles cost 1700/4200$00. Take bus No 7 or 29 from Coimbra A station (but No 29 takes the long way back).

Pensões & Residenciais Doubles with bathroom at the central *Hospedaria Simões* (☎ 83 46 38, *Rua Fernandes Tomáz 69)* are good value, costing 4000$00. Rooms at *Pensão Restaurante Vitória* (☎ 82 40 49, *Rua da Sota 9 & 19)* and *Pensão Lorvanense* (☎ 82 34 81, *Rua da Sota 27)*, near Coimbra A station, are similarly priced.

Pensão Residencial Internacional (☎ 82 55 03, *Avenida Emídio Navarro 4)*, around the block, doesn't offer such good value at 5500$00.

Some rooms at *Residência Lusa Atenas* (☎ 82 64 12, fax 82 01 33, *Avenida Fernão de Magalhães 68)* have handsome stucco ceilings, but all are prone to traffic noise; a double here costs 5000$00 (breakfast included in the price).

Despite a dreary exterior, *Residencial Domus* (☎ 82 85 84, fax 83 88 18, *Rua Adelino Veiga 62)* is comfortable and quiet; doubles start at 6000$00. Of a similar standard is nearby *Residência Moderna* (☎/fax 82 54 13, *Rua Adelino Veiga 49)*.

Pensão Residencial Rivoli (☎ 82 55 50, *Praça do Comércio 27)* is quiet at the back, and good value: doubles cost about 5500$00. Sunny 3rd floor rooms for the same price at *Pensão Santa Cruz* (☎ 82 61 97, *Praça 8 de Maio)* would be good value

too, except for the church bells of the Mosteiro de Santa Cruz ringing through the night.

Places to Stay – Mid-Range

Dutch-run *Casa Pombal Guesthouse* (☎ 83 51 75, fax 82 15 48, *Rua das Flores 18)* has rooms ranging from sunless, bathless cubicles (4200/6400$00) to eyries with tubs and views over the city (6900/7700$00), plus lots of local information and a buffet breakfast to please any traveller's tummy included in the price. Book ahead if you can.

The university area offers little else. *Pensão Residencial Antunes* (☎ 82 30 48, fax 83 83 73, *Rua Castro Matoso 8)* has creaky doubles; the price of 8500$00 with shower, 5500$00 without includes a minuscule breakfast and street parking at the front.

A central choice is *Pensão Residencial Larbelo* (☎ 82 90 92, fax 82 90 94, *Largo da Portagem 33)*, surprisingly cheap for its location; doubles with bathroom cost 6500$00.

Recommended near Coimbra A station is the family run *Pensão Flôr de Coimbra* (☎ 82 38 65, fax 82 15 45, *Rua do Poço 5)*, where old but well-tended singles/doubles cost 5000/7000$00 (4000/5500$00 without shower). *Residência Coimbra* (☎ 83 79 96, fax 83 81 24, *Rua das Azeiteiras 55)* offers small, quiet doubles with shower/bathtub for 7000/7500$00; it's in a street full of modest cafés and restaurants.

Honest, kid-friendly *Residencial Botânico* (☎ 71 48 24, fax 40 51 24, *Bairro São Jose 11)* at the bottom of Alameda Dr Júlio Henriques has big doubles for 7500$00 including breakfast, but there's no restaurant.

Places to Stay – Top End

Hotel Oslo (☎ 82 90 71, fax 82 06 14, *Avenida Fernão de Magalhães 25)* is good value in this range, with air-con doubles costing 10,000$00 and private parking. The Art Deco *Hotel Astória* (☎ 82 20 55, fax 82 20 57, *Avenida Emídio Navarro 21)* has more character but less warmth; double-glazed doubles cost 15,300$00. Out near the main bus station, *Hotel Tivoli* (☎ *82 69 34, fax 82 68 27, Rua João Machado)* has a pool and underground parking; doubles start at 19,500$00.

The nearest Turihab property is *Quinta das Lágrimas* (☎ *44 16 15, fax 44 16 95)*, some of whose 20,000$00 doubles look out on the garden where Dona Inês de Castro is said to have met her tragic end.

Casa dos Quintais (☎ *43 83 05)*, which overlooks Coimbra from the hamlet of Carvalhais de Cima, 6km to the south, has three overpriced but negotiable doubles (at least 7000$00), and a detached apartment with kitchen and unruly plumbing for 9000$00.

Places to Eat
Restaurants – West of the University
Take your pick of amenable budget *restaurantes*, where courses typically cost less than 1500$00, along Rua das Azeiteiras: *Giro (No 39)*, a clean *churrasqueira* with quick service; tiny *Viela* (☎ *83 26 25, No 33)*, which does a brisk local trade; *Adega Funchal* (☎ *82 41 37, No 18)*, which can be justifiably proud of its *chanfana carne de cabra* (goat stewed in red wine); and homey *Zé Neto* (☎ *82 67 86, No 8)*. Another spot with similar prices and generous portions is *Pensão Restaurante Vitória* (see Places to Stay).

The low-key *Restaurante Democrática* (☎ *82 37 84, Rua Nova)*, a family-friendly venue, provides Portuguese standards for under 1500$00 per dish; it also has a few half-portions for under 1000$00. It's closed Sunday.

Restaurante Zé Manel (☎ *82 37 90, Beco do Forno 12)* is wallpapered with knick-knacks and scribbled poems, but eccentric doesn't mean cheap; dishes run to 1800$00 or more (try their *feijoada à leitão*: beans and suckling pig). Come early or be prepared to wait.

If you're on a budget, try the cheap food at the self-service *Restaurante Jardim da Manga*, at the back of the gardens of the same name behind the Mosteiro de Santa Cruz.

Restaurants – Near Praça da República
This is not the place for high cuisine but for student low cuisine, starting with four university *canteens* where a student card will get you a meal for about 400$00. All are poorly marked, if at all. *Restaurante-Bar AAC/OAF* (☎ *82 42 51, Rua Castro Matoso)* is a student dive serving passable daily specials costing less than 1000$00.

A notch up is *Bar-Restaurante ACM* (☎ *82 36 33, Rua Alexandre Herculano 21A)*, with plain fare, quick service and prices under 800$00 per dish; the kitchen serves from noon to 2.30 pm and 7 to 9.30 pm daily except Saturday. Dishes at *Restaurante Sá da Bandeira* (☎ *83 54 50, Avenida Sá da Bandeira 89)* weigh in at 1500$00 and over.

Vegetarian The dining room at *Pensão Flôr de Coimbra* (see Places to Stay) offers a daily vegetarian dish (under 1000$00) or meal (under 1500$00) in summer.

Cafés Coimbra has some seductive cafés, including *Pastelaria Arcadia (Rua Ferreira Borges 144)*, where chic shoppers rest their feet, and *Café Praça Velha* on Praça do Comércio. One of our favourite sidewalk cafés in Portugal is *Café Santa Cruz*, a vaulted annexe of the Mosteiro de Santa Cruz: sit on creased leather chairs inside or at tables outside. The *Cartola Esplanada Bar* on Praça da República is good for student-watching and sunshine, and serves somewhat overpriced light meals.

Self-Catering The *Mercado Municipal Dom Pedro V* is east of the Mosteiro de Santa Cruz. Supermarkets include a *Pingo Doce* on Rua João de Ruão in the Baixa and another just west of the parque de campismo. The *Continente hipermercado* is on the southern outskirts; take bus No 24T (not 24) or 28 from Largo da Portagem.

Entertainment
Coimbra's version of fado is more serious and intellectual than the Lisbon variety. It's more traditional, too: a fracas erupted in

BEIRAS

Coimbra in 1996 when a woman named Manuela Bravo decided to record a CD of Coimbra-style fado, which is meant to be sung by men (see the boxed text 'Fado Uproar' in the Facts about Portugal chapter).

You'll hear fado from the students during Queima das Fitas (see under Special Events earlier), or in several *casas de fado* on just about any late Friday or Saturday evening: try *Bar Diligência* (☎ 82 76 67, *Rua Nova 30*), *Boémia Bar* (☎ 83 45 47, *Rua do Cabido 6*) or *Restaurante O Trovador* (☎ 82 54 75, *Largo da Sé Velha 15-17*). Casas de fado are often restaurants too, generally overpriced at best and usually with a minimum charge equivalent to a small meal or several pricey drinks.

For less traditional sounds and a dance floor, go to *Aqui Há Rato* (☎ 82 48 04, *Largo da Sé Velha 20*). Students like the *Tropical Bar* (*Praça da República*) and the cavernous *Dom Dinis Bar* off Praça Marquês de Pombal.

Café-Galeria Almedina (☎ 83 61 92), which nestles in the old town walls at Arco de Almedina, offers fado and other live sounds; it's open daily until 4 am.

Shopping

Upstairs at Rua Ferreira Borges 83, in a building faced in wrought iron and known to all as 'Chiado', is a bright municipally-run gallery with changing exhibitions of first-rate basketry, textiles, pottery (for which Coimbra is famous) and more. Some Wednesdays, artisans are on hand to demonstrate the making of whatever happens to be on display and sale that week. The gallery is open Tuesday to Friday from 10 am to 7 pm and at weekends from 3 to 6.30 pm.

Good tape/CD shops include Valentim de Carvalho at Rua Ferreira Borges 150 and D'artemusica in the Golden Shopping Centre at Avenida Sá da Bandeira 115.

On the fourth Saturday of each month, a flea market takes over Praça do Comércio, where you can find antiques and assorted knick-knacks.

Getting There & Away

Bus Rodoviária Beira Litoral (RBL; ☎ 82 70 81), running from the main bus station on Avenida Fernão de Magalhães, caters for most destinations. At least a dozen coaches a day go to Lisbon, with frequent express buses to Braga, Porto, Évora and Faro. In winter there are frequent services to Seia, Guarda and other points around the Parque Natural da Serra da Estrela.

AVIC (☎ 82 37 69), Rua João de Ruão 18, runs buses to Condeixa and Conimbriga (see the Conimbriga Getting There & Away section), and to the beaches at Tocha and Mira, north-west of Coimbra. Moisés Correia de Oliveira (☎ 82 82 63), Rua Dr Rosa Falção 10, runs services to Figueira da Foz.

Train A few fast trains, such as the daily Lisbon-Irún-Paris *Rápido Sud-Expresso*, stop only at Coimbra B, but most call at both Coimbra B and Coimbra A (the latter is just called 'Coimbra' on timetables). Frequent daily trains link Coimbra with Lisbon (via Santarém) and Porto (via Aveiro), including three Alfas and six IC services. Trains also run to Figueira da Foz, Luso and the Buçaco Foret.

Getting Around

Bus Although walking is the way to see Coimbra's old town, you'll need a bus for anything in the outskirts. The only direct service to the university is No 1 from Coimbra A train station, via the Baixa. Nos 11 and 24 go to Praça da República from Coimbra A. Other routes are noted in the text.

You can buy tickets on board but, if you plan to use buses a lot, you'll find it handy to pick up a booklet of 10 tickets from one of the kiosks around town; the most convenient one is across the road from Largo da Portagem, and also has timetables. It's closed Sunday and holidays.

Bicycle You can rent street bikes from Centro Velocipédico de Sangalhos (☎ 82 46 46), Rua da Sota 23. Mountain bikes can be hired from O Pioneiro do Mondego (see under Activities earlier).

Car Car rental agencies include: Salitur (☎ 82 05 94), Rua da Sota 42; Viarent (☎ 82 36 64), Hotel Oslo (see under Places to Stay); and VASC (☎ 83 59 20), Rua Padre Estêvão Cabral. International franchises include Avis (☎ 83 47 86) in Coimbra A Station and Hertz (☎ 83 74 91), Rua João de Ruão 16.

The local branch of the Automóvel Club de Portugal (ACP; ☎ 82 68 13) is at Avenida Emídio Navarro 6, by Coimbra A station.

CONIMBRIGA

The Roman ruins of Conimbriga, 16km south-west of Coimbra, are the finest you'll see in Portugal and among the best preserved in the Iberian Peninsula. The Conimbriga site actually dates back to Celtic times (*briga* is a Celtic term for a defended area) but when the Romans settled here in the 1st century AD they developed it into a major city on the route from Lisbon (Olisipo) to Braga (Bracara Augusta).

In the 3rd century, threatened by invading tribes, the townsfolk built a huge defensive wall right through the town centre, abandoning the residencial area. This wasn't enough to stop the Suevi seizing the town in 468. The inhabitants fled to nearby Aeminius (Coimbra), thereby saving Conimbriga from destruction.

Admission to the site (including entry to the museum) costs 350$00.

Museu

It's worth visiting the small museum first to get a grip on Conimbriga's history and layout. Unfortunately there are no English labels but the displays are magnificent, presenting every aspect of Roman life, from rings and hairbands to needles and hoes. Murals, mosaics and carved fragments from temples, statues and tombstones are some of the site's artistic treasures.

The museum is open daily except Monday from 10 am to 1 pm and 2 to 6 pm.

There's a pleasant café-restaurant at the back.

Ruins

The defensive wall slices through the site like a scar. Outside it, to the right, is the so-called Casa dos Repuxos (House of the Fountains); this was partly destroyed during the wall's construction but the layout of ponds and rooms is still obvious, and there are some striking mosaic floors showing the four seasons and various hunting scenes. The site's most important villa, on the other side of the wall, is said to have belonged to one Cantaber, whose wife and children were seized by the Suevi in an attack in 465. It's a palace of a place, with its own private baths, a series of pools (one encircled by columns) and a sophisticated underground heating system. Even the more humble houses nearby have mosaic floors.

Excavations are continuing in the outer areas of the city. Among eye-catching features are the remains of a 3km-long aqueduct which led up to a hilltop bathing complex, and a forum, once surrounded by covered porticoes – the museum has a model. The site, which becomes something of a playground for raucous school groups in term-time, is open daily (including Monday) from 9 am to 1 pm and 2 to 8 pm (6 pm in winter).

Getting There & Away

Buses run frequently from Coimbra to Condeixa, about 2km from the site, or you can take a direct bus at 9.05 am or 9.35 am (9.35 am only at weekends) from the AVIC terminal in Conimbriga; the bus returns at 1 pm or 6 pm (6 pm only at weekends).

LUSO & THE BUÇACO FOREST
☎ 031

For decades Portuguese tourists have been coming to the small, rather quaint old spa town of Luso, 24km north-east of Coimbra, to soak in its hypotonic waters (a balm for everything from gout to asthma). It makes an easy day trip from Coimbra, usually tagged onto a visit to the Mata Nacional do

Bussaco (Bussaco, or Buçaco, National Forest) 3km up the road, and makes a perfect base if you're tempted to linger longer in the forest. Try to avoid weekends and holidays, when you'll be swamped by hundreds of Portuguese visitors.

Orientation & Information

The spa itself nestles at the centre of town. From the train station in the northern outskirts it's a 20 minute walk downhill via Rua Dr António Granjo to the town centre. Buses stop on Avenida Emídio Navarro, just south of the centre. By road, it's about 3km south from the town centre to the *palácio* or Palace Hotel in the middle of the forest.

The efficient staff at the turismo (π/fax 93 91 33) on Avenida Emídio Navarro can provide accommodation information and good maps of the town and forest. Specialists may want to ask for the 'pedestrian circuit' leaflets (in English) detailing the forest's flora and points of historical interest. In summer (June through October) the turismo is open weekdays from 9.30 am to 1 pm and 2 to 8 pm (6.30 pm in winter), and weekends from 10 am to 1 pm and 3 to 5 pm (closed Saturday afternoon and Sunday in winter).

Termas de Luso

Unlike at many of Portugal's spas, certain therapies here are open to casual visitors, but only from May to October. These include a jacuzzi-like bath costing about 1300$00, a half-hour massage (2400$00), and a sauna and shower for (1400$00) – just the ticket after a long walk in the forest. The spa is open from 8 am to noon and 4 to 7 pm.

You can fill up your water bottle for free at the adjacent Fonte de São João.

Casino

The former casino, next to the Fonte de São João, is now a venue for exhibitions, folk dancing and fado. It's open in the summer season only, daily except Monday from 11 am to 1 pm and 3 to 10 pm.

Mata Nacional do Bussaco (Buçaco)

The 105 hectare Buçaco Forest, on the slopes of the Serra do Buçaco, is no ordinary collection of trees. For centuries it's been a religious haven, a place of sanctity and peace. Even today, overrun by picnickers at weekends and tourists in the summer, it still has a mystical appeal. There are an astounding 700 different species of trees, including huge Mexican cedars, giant ferns and ginkgo trees.

History The area was probably used as a refuge for Christians in the 2nd century, although the earliest known hermitage was established in the 6th century by Benedictine monks. In 1628 this was sold to the Barefoot Silent Carmelites who embarked on an extensive programme of forestation, introducing exotic species, marking out cobbled paths and enclosing the forest within walls. It became so famous that in 1643 Pope Urban VIII decreed that anyone who damaged the trees would be excommunicated.

Twenty years earlier, his predecessor had ensured that the monks tending the trees were protected from distracting influences: he even forbade women to enter the forest. In 1810, during the Peninsular War, the peace was briefly disrupted when Napoleon's forces under Masséna unsuccessfully clashed against the Duke of Wellington's Anglo-Portuguese army which was hidden behind the ridge above the forest. In 1834, when religious orders throughout Portugal were abolished, the forest became state property and even more tree species were introduced.

Walks The forest is threaded with trails, dotted with crumbling chapels and graced with ponds and fountains. Some of the most popular trails lead to areas of great beauty, such as the Vale dos Fetos (Valley of Ferns), but you can get enjoyably lost on more overgrown trails which eventually join up to the main ones. Among several fine viewpoints is 545m Cruz Alta; along the path to it (known as Via Sacra) are several chapels with figures depicting the stages of the Cross.

Mosteiro dos Carmelites A tiny 17th century church, almost overshadowed by the adjacent Palace Hotel do Buçaco, is all that remains of the Carmelite monastery. There's not much to see: a few cork-lined cells (in one of which Wellington spent the night before the 1810 battle) and a frieze of azulejos depicting the battle. It's open daily except Friday from 10 am to noon and 2 to 6 pm. Admission costs 100$00.

Palace Hotel do Buçaco This wedding cake of a building – all turrets and spires, arches and neo-Manueline ornamentation – was built in 1907 on the site of the monastery to serve as a royal summer residence. Three years later the monarchy was abolished, so the royals hardly got a look-in. Now a very posh hotel (see Places to Stay), staff are surprisingly tolerant of the hordes of tourists who wander in to gawp.

Museu Militar History buffs interested in the 1810 Battle of Buçaco will find maps, weapons and other paraphernalia in this small museum on the eastern outskirts of the forest, just beyond Portas da Rainha. It's open daily except Monday from 10 am to 5 pm; admission costs 200$00 (free for kids aged 10 and under).

Places to Stay

The cheapest guesthouse is grumpy *Buçaco Pensão* (☎ 93 92 74), 300m along Rua Dr António Granjo from the town centre, where plain doubles with shower cost about 3000$00. You'll be better off looking for signs advertising *quartos* (private rooms), or checking out the turismo's list; private rooms cost about 4000$00 for a double. The central *Café-Bar O Caracol* (☎ 93 94 05, *Rua Dr Francisco Diniz)* has some doubles available.

Reasonable guesthouses include the central *Pensão Central* (☎ 93 92 54, *Avenida Emídio Navarro)* where doubles cost

6000$00 (4000$00 without bathroom) including breakfast, and the *Astória* (☎ 93 91 82, *Avenida Emídio Navarro)* beside the turismo, with doubles costing 6500$00. For more genteel accommodation, try *Pensão Alegre* (☎ 93 02 56, *Avenida Emídio Navarro)* beyond the Pensão Central, a 19th century manor house with a swimming pool where doubles start at 7000$00 including breakfast.

For palatial indulgence, a double at the *Palace Hotel do Buçaco* (☎ 93 01 01, fax 93 05 09) will set you back at least 30,000$00.

Places to Eat

The Art Deco *salão de chá* (tea room) by the Fonte de São João captures the spa town atmosphere perfectly and is the place to come for tea and cakes.

Most pensões have reasonable restaurants; in summer the patio restaurant at *Pensão Central* is very pleasant. Heartier meals are available at *Restaurante O Cesteiro* (☎ 93 93 60) on the N234, a 500m hike north from the turismo towards the train station. Regional specialities include the ubiquitous *leitão a bairrada* (roast suckling pig). Or you could indulge in a splendid blowout for about 5000$00 at the *Palace Hotel do Buçaco*.

Getting There & Away

The only train of any use departs Coimbra A at about 10.15 am (check with the Coimbra turismo for current timetables) and takes about 40 minutes to reach Luso-Buçaco. The last useful train back departs at about 6.30 pm.

Bus connections between Coimbra and Luso are more convenient: there are five daily on weekdays and two at weekends, all continuing to the Palace Hotel in the forest.

In the summer season, car drivers are charged 500$00 admission to the forest.

Getting Around

In summer, Pensão Alegre (see Places to Stay) runs afternoon and evening horse and carriage rides in Luso and Buçaco on most

BEIRAS

days of the week (check with the turismo or the pensão). A one hour circuit in Luso costs at least 750$00 and a return jaunt from the Palace Hotel to Portas de Coimbra at least 1500$00. Discounts are available for guests of Pensão Alegre.

FIGUEIRA DA FOZ
☎ 033 • pop 18,000

Once top of the list for Spanish beach-seekers, this old-fashioned seaside resort and fishing port, 43km west of Coimbra at the mouth (*foz*) of the Rio Mondego, still has a faithful, mostly Portuguese, following. Some come for the casino, some for the surf (this was a venue for the 1996 World Surfing Championships) and some just to loll on its vast beach. There is plenty of accommodation, plus many restaurants and bars, though it's not easy to find a cheap room in high season.

Orientation

The best part of this place is the beach fronting Avenida 25 de Abril, near the mouth of the Rio Mondego. Inland from the 16th century Forte de Santa Catarina is tourist town: a knot of streets containing most of the accommodation and restaurants, and the casino. Seafront development continues all the way to Buarcos, a former fishing village 3km to the north which is now just an extension of Figueira.

The train station is 1.5km east of the beach, a 20 minute walk along the river. The bus station, on Rua Gonçalvo Velho, is slightly closer.

Parking is a struggle here, even in the evenings, thanks to the casino.

Information

The municipal turismo (☎ 40 28 27, 42 26 10) is right on Avenida 25 de Abril, over-

FIGUEIRA DA FOZ

PLACES TO STAY
5 Pensão Residencial Universal
8 Pensão Residencial Bela Figueira
9 Hotel Wellington
12 Pensão Astória
13 Pensão Central
15 Hotel Hispânia
18 Pensão Residencial Moderna
19 Residencial Sãozinha
20 Pensão Figueirense

PLACES TO EAT
7 Café Sylmar
10 Restaurante Caçarola II
14 Restaurante Caçarola I

OTHER
1 Bus Station
2 Museu Municipal do Dr Santos Rocha
3 AFGA Travel Agency
4 Post Office
6 Turismo
11 Casino
16 Mercado Municipal
17 Post Office
21 Train Station
22 Câmara Municipal
23 Boat Tours

shadowed by the conspicuously tall Edifício Atlântico building. From May to September it's open daily from 9 am to at least 10 pm. In winter it's open from 9 am to 12.30 pm and 2 to 5.30 pm on weekdays, and from 10 am to 12.30 pm and 2 to 6.30 pm at weekends. The parent office (☎ 40 28 20, fax 40 28 28), up in the Edifício, and a smaller turismo (☎ 43 30 19), on Largo Tomás Aquino in Buarcos, keep the same hours.

Numerous banks along Avenida Foz do Mondego and on Praça 8 de Maio have ATMs. The main post office is on the east side of the *jardim municipal* (town park).

Casino

The casino on Rua Bernardo Lopes is open daily from 3 pm to 3 am. There's an admission charge for the roulette section, and you're not welcome in your flip-flops or sports shoes. There's live entertainment nightly in the nightclub, and on Friday and Saturday in the festivities hall.

Museu Municipal do Dr Santos Rocha

This modern museum beside Parque das Abadias (a 10 minute walk north-east of the turismo) houses a rich archaeological collection and some less impressive paintings and sculptures. It's open daily except Monday from 9 am to 12.30 pm and 2 to 5.30 pm; admission is free.

Beaches

Once notorious for pollution, Figueira has cleaned up its act; in recent years local beaches have earned European Blue Flag approval. The main beach is immense and shadeless, packed and scorching in August; without shoes you might burn your feet unless you use the boardwalks that cross to the sea.

For more character, and more surf, head for Buarcos. Just around the Cabo Mondego from Buarcos (about 10km north of Figueira) you'll find considerably more seclusion at Praia de Quiaos. AVIC buses run to Buarcos about every half-hour on

weekdays and hourly at weekends (less frequently to Cabo de Mondego) from the train station and the mercado municipal. Moisés Correia de Oliveira buses run to Praia de Quaios seven times a day (five times daily in winter) from the bus station.

In the other direction, across the mouth of the Rio Mondego, is Praia de Cabedelo, a prime surfing venue; a little further south (4km from Figueira) is Praia de Gala. AVIC buses to both beaches run from the train station and the mercado municipal every half-hour from Monday to Saturday and every hour or two on Sunday.

Serra de Boa Viagem

For those with wheels this headland 4km north of Figueira carpeted in pines, eucalyptus and acacias, is a fine place for panoramic views, picnics and cool walks. Kids will like the great wooden playground at one of the forest picnic sites. Take the coast road to Buarcos, turn right at the lighthouse and follow the signs to Boa Viagem.

Boat Trips

From July to September, an outfit beside the harbourmaster's office on the Doca de Recreio (just off Avenida Foz do Mondego) offers 30-minute *passeios de barco* on motorboats, costing 4500$00 per boatload for up to seven passengers, plus 60 and 90-minute options.

Special Events

A Festival Internacional de Cinema has been held in Figueira da Foz for over 25 years. It takes place in the casino during the first 10 days of September.

Places to Stay

Camping & Hostel The municipal *parque de campismo* (☎ 40 28 10) is north of the centre; it's 2km from the beach but there's a swimming pool nearby. It costs 400/300/300$00 per person/tent/car.

The cheapest and best site is *Foz do Mondego* (☎ 43 14 96, *Praia de Cabedelo*) but you must have a Camping Card International (see under Visas & Documents in the Facts for the Visitor chapter) or belong to the Federação Portuguesa de Campismo e Caravanismo; it costs 350/280/350$00. A little further south, but 1km from the nearest bus stop, is an *Orbitur camping ground* (☎ *43 14 92, Praia de Gala*), costing 600/500/510$00.

A seaside *parque de campismo* (☎ *91 04 99, Praia de Quiaos*) 8km north of Figueira is only open from June to September; prices per person/tent/car are 80/300/300$00.

About 35km up the coast from Figueira da Foz is Mira (take any Aveiro-bound bus), with a *pousada da juventude* where dorm beds/doubles cost 1700/4000$00. Mira also has several camp sites and a fine beach at Praia de Mira.

Private Rooms The turismo has details of several officially approved quartos which usually cost around 4500$00 for a double. Touts may approach you at the bus or train station with their own offers.

Pensões & Residenciais Cheaper places (doubles costing around 5000$00) near the train station include: *Pensão Figueirense* (☎ *42 24 59, Rua Direita do Monte 10*), with shared facilities but with breakfast included in the price; the quieter *Residencial Sãozinha* (☎ *42 52 43, Ladeira do Monte 43*); and the spacious *Pensão Residencial Moderna* (☎ *42 27 01, Praça 8 de Maio 61*), with a touch of Indian décor.

Similarly priced but more central is the glum *Pensão Astória* (☎ *42 22 56, Rua Bernardo Lopes 45*). *Pensão Central* (☎ *42 23 08, Rua Bernardo Lopes 36*) across the road has nice big old doubles costing 7000$00. *Pensão Residencial Universal* (☎ *42 06 12, fax 42 04 97, Rua Miguel Bombarda 50*) and *Pensão Residencial Bela Figueira* (☎ *42 27 28, fax 42 99 60, Rua Miguel Bombarda 13*) offer doubles for about 6500$00 including breakfast; the latter has a good patio restaurant.

Hotels The plain but well-run *Hotel Hispânia* (☎ *42 21 64, Rua Dr Francisco António Dinis 61*) has doubles with shower

and toilet costing about 7500$00. Doubles with air-con and satellite TV at the genteel *Hotel Wellington* (☎ *42 67 67, fax 42 75 93, Rua Dr Calado 23*), opposite the casino, cost 9500$00. Both places have off-street parking.

Places to Eat

Younger visitors hang out at sunny *Café Sylmar* (☎ *42 29 71, Esplanada Silva Guimarães*) near the municipal turismo. Several pensões have good restaurants, including the *Pensão Astória* and *Pensão Residencial Bela Figueira* (whose Indian-Portuguese fare makes a pleasant change). The good-value *Restaurante Caçarola II* (☎ *42 69 30, Rua Bernardo Lopes 85*) stays open until 4 am. Adequate, but not up to the reputation of its progeny, is *Restaurante Caçarola I* on Rua Cândido dos Reis.

Seafood in Figueira is priced for tourists but is a bit cheaper in Buarcos: try *Dory Negro* (☎ *42 13 33, Largo Caras Direitas 16*), where you can eat well for under 2000$00.

The bountiful *mercado municipal* is a short walk from the turismo down Rua Dr Francisco António Dinis.

Getting There & Away

Bus Most services use the main terminal, including about five buses daily to Mira and Aveiro (various operators).

A daily AVIC express bus from Buarcos to Lisbon stops opposite the turismo at about 7 am, and a Rodoviário do Tejo bus runs to Lisbon three times a day from the bus station. A single express bus runs to Porto each weekday from the AFGA travel agency (see under Getting Around).

Train Two daily services link Figueira with Lisbon via Caldas da Rainha and Leiria. Trains to/from Coimbra are superior to buses, with frequent hour-long connections.

Getting Around

Bicycle The AFGA travel agency (☎ *40 22 22*), Avenida Miguel Bombarda 79, rents bicycles starting at 1500$00 a day. In high season the municipal parque de campismo (see Places to Stay) rents bikes as well.

AVEIRO

☎ 034 • pop about 40,000

One of the most attractive towns in Beira Litoral (once you pass its ugly outskirts), Aveiro lies on the south-eastern edge of a marshy lagoon known as the Ria. Canals lace the town under humpbacked bridges, giving it a genteel Dutch feel. The narrow lanes around the fish market are especially picturesque, with pastel-coloured houses bordering the canals.

Apart from one superb convent museum there's little to see or do in town, but it's a relaxing base for visiting several nearby beaches or the bird reserve at São Jacinto. The turismo's museum leaflet details other possibilities nearby, ranging from the museum of steam engines in Águeda to a collection of famous Vista Alegre porcelain in Ílhavo.

History

Aveiro's prosperity as a seaport at the mouth of the Rio Vouga took off in the 16th century, thanks to its salt pans, fishing fleet and the growing trade in *bacalhau* (salt cod). However, the mouth of the Vouga, which had gradually been narrowed by encroaching coastal sandbanks, was closed in the 1570s by a ferocious storm. The river's winter floods created fever-breeding marshes which helped decimate Aveiro's population from 14,000 to a low of 3500 by 1759.

In 1808 the old town walls were used to build the Barra Canal which re-established a passage through to the sea, draining the marshes to leave a network of salt lagoons. From that point onwards, Aveiro quickly gained importance as a fishing and industrial centre, its prosperity reflected in a spate of Art Nouveau houses and azulejo friezes around town.

Today, salt is still an economic mainstay; at one time the harvesting of *molico* (seaweed) from the estuary for use as fertiliser was too, but this is on the decline.

Many of the beautifully painted, high-prowed *moliceiros* boats tied up along the canals are now used for tourist jaunts through the Ria rather than for collecting seaweed.

Orientation

The azulejo-adorned train station is at the north-eastern end of the main street, Avenida Dr Lourenço Peixinho ('Avenida' to the locals). From the station it's about 1km to Praça Humberto Delgado, which straddles the Canal Central, and the nearby turismo.

Bus companies here seem to revel in confusion: there are at least eight, with terminals scattered all over town. The major ones tend to have terminals near the train station.

Parking is dire, though there are meters all along the Avenida. A fairly central place for overnight parking is the area on Largo do Rossio.

Information

The efficient regional turismo (☎ 2 07 60, fax 2 83 26), housed in an ornate Art Nouveau building at Rua João Mendonça 8, has lots of information on Aveiro and the region. From mid-June to September it's open daily from 9 am to 8 pm; during the rest of the year it's open weekdays from 9 am to 7 pm and on Saturday from 9 am to 1 pm and 2.30 to 5.30 pm.

In addition to several banks with ATMs on the Avenida, there's a Banco Borges e Irmão on Praça Humberto Delgado, and a branch of Barclays Bank across the Canal Central from the turismo.

The main post office is on Praça Marquês de Pombal, a five minute walk south of the turismo.

The local Instituto Português da Juventude (☎ 38 19 35, fax 38 23 95), Rua das Pombas 182, has a library with at least one terminal where visitors can log on to the Internet free of charge during weekday business hours.

The police station is on Praça Marquês de Pombal.

BEIRAS

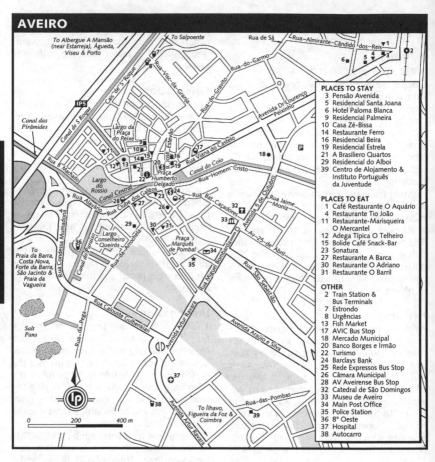

AVEIRO

To Albergue A Mansão
(near Estarreja), Águeda,
Viseu & Porto

To Salpoente

Rua de Sá

Rua–Almirante–Cândido dos–Reis

Canal das
Pirâmides

Canal de Sº Roque

Cais de Sº Roque

Rua-Vısc-da-Granja

Rua-do-Carmo

Rua-do-Gravito

Avenida Dr Lourenço
Peixinho

IP5

Largo da
Praça
do Peixe

Rua Viana do Castelo

Estevão

Canal do Coio

Rua-Homem–Cristo

Praça
Humberto
Delgado

P

Rua Bº Machado

Largo
do
Rossio

Canal Central

Rua Álvaro

Rua Clube dos Galitos

Rua Bat-Caçadores

Rua 5 de Outubro

Rua Jaime
Mônız

Av-25-de-Abril

Rua Condessa Mumadona

Largo
Conselheiro
Queirós

Rua da Arrochela

Praça
Marquês
de Pombal

Rua Miguel Bombarda

Rua São Sebastião

To
Praia da Barra,
Costa Nova,
Forte da Barra,
São Jacinto &
Praia da
Vagueira

Rua da Pega

Rua Calouste Gulbenkian

Avenida Artur Ravara

Avenida Araújo e Silva

Salt
Pans

Avenida Artur Ravara

To Ílhavo,
Figueira da Foz &
Coimbra

Rua-das-Pombas

PLACES TO STAY
3 Pensão Avenida
5 Residencial Santa Joana
6 Hotel Paloma Blanca
9 Residencial Palmeira
10 Casa Zé-Bissa
14 Restaurante Ferro
16 Residencial Beira
19 Residencial Estrela
21 A Brasiliero Quartos
29 Residencial do Alboi
39 Centro de Alojamento &
   Instituto Português
   da Juventude

PLACES TO EAT
1 Café Restaurante O Aquário
4 Restaurante Tio João
11 Restaurante-Marisqueira
   O Mercantel
12 Adega Típica O Telheiro
15 Bolide Café Snack-Bar
23 Sonatura
27 Restaurante A Barca
30 Restaurante O Adriano
31 Restaurante O Barril

OTHER
2 Train Station &
   Bus Terminals
7 Estrondo
8 Urgências
13 Fish Market
17 AVIC Bus Stop
18 Mercado Municipal
20 Banco Borges e Irmão
22 Turismo
24 Barclays Bank
25 Rede Expressos Bus Stop
26 Câmara Municipal
28 AV Aveirense Bus Stop
32 Catedral de São Domingos
33 Museu de Aveiro
34 Main Post Office
35 Police Station
36 8° Oeste
37 Hospital
38 Autocarro

0   200   400 m

Museu de Aveiro

The former Convento de Jesus, opposite the
Catedral de São Domingos, owes its best
treasures to Princesa (later beatified as
Santa) Joana, a daughter of Afonso V. In
1472, seven years after the convent was
founded, she 'retired' here and, although
she was forbidden to take full vows, she
stayed until her death in 1489.

Her 17th century tomb, a masterpiece of
marble mosaic, is set in a chancel of equally
lavish Baroque ornamentation, including

azulejos depicting the life of the princess.
Among the museum's paintings is a late-
15th century portrait of the saintly princess,
attributed to Nuno Gonçalves.

The museum is open daily except
Monday from 10 am to 5.30 pm. Admission
costs 250$00 (half price for those aged from
14 to 25 or over 65, and free for children).

Beaches

They're not the Costa de Prata's most spectacular beaches, but Praia da Barra and

nearby Costa Nova, 13km west of Aveiro, are fine for a day's outing. Although they get packed at weekends, they're surprisingly undeveloped. Costa Nova, the prettier of the two, has a beachside street lined with restaurants and traditional candy-striped cottages.

AV Aveirense buses leave the station approximately hourly for both resorts, stopping across the canal from the turismo on Rua Clube dos Galitos. The last bus back from Costa Nova is at about 8.15 pm in summer and 6.55 pm in winter. There are also about six buses a day from Costa Nova to the more remote Praia da Vagueira, about 7km away.

Wilder and less easily accessible is Praia de São Jacinto, on the northern side of the lagoon. The vast beach of sand dunes is a 1.5km walk from São Jacinto port (see the next section for details), through a residential area at the back of town.

Reserva Natural das Dunas de São Jacinto

Stretching north from São Jacinto to Torreira and Ovar, between the sea and the N327 coastal road, is a small, wooded nature reserve (☎ 33 12 82, 83 10 63) equipped with trails and bird-watching hides. It was badly scarred by a fire in 1995 and still looks rather ragged. Guided 2½ hour walking tours set off from the entrance daily except Sunday, Thursday and holidays at 9.30 am and 2 pm, and cost around 200$00. Phoning ahead to book is a good idea.

To get there, take a Forte da Barra bus from Rua Clube dos Galitos, opposite the turismo, to the end of the line, from where a small passenger ferry (no cars) crosses the lagoon to the port of São Jacinto. From there the reserve entrance is a 1.3km walk along the Torreira road.

The Aveiro turismo can tell you when to go for the best ferry connections. The last ferry back from São Jacinto is at about 6.20 pm, and the last bus back to Aveiro from Forte da Barra leaves around 7 pm on most days.

Special Events

The Festa da Ria is Aveiro's big celebration of its canals and moliceiros boats, lasting several weeks from mid-July to the end of August. The highlight is a moliceiros race, accompanied by folk dancing in the streets. Another moliceiros race features in the Festas do São Paio in Murtosa (on the northern side of the lagoon) in the first week of September.

Places to Stay

Camping At least six camping grounds are within reach of Aveiro. Nearest and cheapest are a municipal *parque de campismo* (☎ 36 94 25, Praia da Barra) at Barra (180/170/330$00 per person/tent/car), and *Parque Campismo da Gafanha da Nazaré* (☎ 36 65 65), north-west of Ílhavo (180/ 170/300$00). South of Barra are the pricier *Camping Costa Nova* (☎ 36 98 22) in Costa Nova, costing 400/400/400$00, and *Parque Campismo da Vagueira* (☎ 79 76 18, Praia da Vagueira), charging 600/550/450$00. See the earlier Beaches section for details of public transport.

At São Jacinto there's a municipal *parque de campismo* (☎ 33 12 20), 2.5km from the pier along the Torreira road, which costs 360/162/120$00 per person/tent/car, and an *Orbitur camping ground* (☎ 4 82 84) 2.5km further on, charging 590/480/ 500$00. There's no bus service along this road. See the Reserva Natural das Dunas de São Jacinto section for details of transport to São Jacinto.

Hostel Aveiro's *centro de alojamento* (☎ 2 05 36, fax 38 23 95, Rua das Pombas 182) is about 1.5km south of the centre; dorm beds cost 1700$00 in high season.

Pensões & Residenciais Summer accommodation is even tighter than parking here; if you want a choice, consider booking ahead a week or so in peak season.

The least you'll pay for a double with shared toilet and shower in summer is about 4000$00. Look for quartos signs at homes, restaurants and bars around the fish market,

BEIRAS

for example at **Restaurante Ferro** (☎ *2 22 14, Rua Tenente Resende 30)* and the seedy **Casa Zé-Bissa** (☎ *2 22 77, Rua dos Marnotos 26)*. Some may also have rooms with toilet and shower for about 5000$00, such as the family run **A Brasiliero Quartos** *(Rua Tenente Resende)*. Similarly priced, and near the train station, are the good-value **Pensão Avenida** (☎ *2 33 66, Avenida Dr Lourenço Peixinho 259)* and the plain **Residencial Santa Joana** (☎ *2 86 04, Avenida Dr Lourenço Peixinho 227)*.

The snug **Residencial Palmeira** (☎ *2 25 21, Rua da Palmeira 7)* is also good value at 6000$00. Two smart guesthouses near the turismo, **Residencial Estrela** (☎ *2 38 18, Rua José Estevão 4)* and the marginally quieter **Residencial Beira** (☎ *2 42 97, Rua José Estevão 18)*, offer doubles with shower and breakfast starting at about 7000$00. Across the canal, the frilly **Residencial do Alboi** (☎/fax *251 21, Rua da Arrochela 6)* has quiet doubles with shower/bathtub costing 8000/9000$00 including breakfast.

Top of the line is unquestionably **Hotel Paloma Blanca** (☎ *38 19 92, fax 38 18 44, Rua Luís Gomes de Carvalho 23)*, an elegant mansion where double rooms cost 14,200$00.

A rural alternative with a difference is the French-run **Albergue A Mansão** (☎ *86 50 00)*, 18km north of Aveiro and 5km from Estarreja station in the hamlet of Bunheiro. Spacious doubles costing 9500$00 come with breakfast *and* a huge dinner served *à la famille* – so count on long, conversational (French) evenings. There's a garden in which you can pitch a tent (5000$00 including breakfast and dinner). You can be met at Estarreja station if you call ahead.

Places to Eat

Two good cheapies near the train station with dishes starting from 1200$00 are **Restaurante Tio João** (☎ *72 17 85, Avenida Dr Lourenço Peixinho 235)*, offering everything from hamburgers to horse mackerel, and **Café Restaurante O Aquário** (☎ *2 50 14, Rua Almirante Cândido dos Reis 139)*. Cheap for its location – around the corner

from the turismo – **Bolide Café Snack-Bar** *(Praça Humberto Delgado 11)* is open until 10 pm and has a short menu of standards costing less than 1500$00. All three places offer some cheaper half-portions too.

Two good-value backstreet places are **Restaurante O Barril** (☎ *2 84 55, Rua 31 de Janeiro 37)* and the slightly pricier **O Adriano** (☎ *2 08 98, Rua Capitão Sousa Pizarro 4)*, the latter serving good *cabrito assado a regional* (roast kid).

Our vote for the best grilled fish in town goes to **Restaurante A Barca** (☎ *2 60 24, Rua José Rabumba 5)*, where dishes cost from 1200$00 to 2000$00. At the tourist-friendly **Restaurante-Marisqueira O Mercantel** (☎ *2 80 57, Rua António Lé 16)*, most items are in the same range. For cheaper fare in more bohemian surroundings try **Adega Típica O Telheiro** (☎ *2 94 73, Largo Praça do Peixe 22)*, beside the fish market.

Vegetarians will like the small but wholesome menu at the cafeteria-style **Sonatura** (☎ *2 44 74, Rua Clube dos Galitos 6)*. Even non-vegetarians will enjoy seeing so many vegetables on one plate in Portugal, and at earthy prices too. It's open Sunday to Friday from 8 am to 7.30 pm, and on Saturday from 9 am to 4 pm.

Self-caterers can find several **Minipreço** supermarkets on the Avenida.

Entertainment

There are three good bars along the Canal São Roque beyond the fish market: **Estrondo** at No 74 (no sign), **Urgências** (☎ *2 80 82)* just across the side-street from it, and **Salpoente** at No 83 (no sign).

Smaller places dot the streets around the fish market. **Autocarro** (☎ *2 53 09)* is a bar made out of an old bus; it's south of town, towards the youth hostel. **8° Oeste** (☎ *38 31 69, Cais do Paraíso)* is both a club and a restaurant.

Getting There & Away

Bus Long-distance timetables and stops tend to mutate, so it's worth checking with the turismo.

Services you're most likely to use include Rede Expressos (☎ 2 17 55) to Figueira da Foz (two a day), Nazaré and Caldas da Rainha; AVIC (☎ 2 37 47) to Mira (two a day); and AV Aveirense (☎ 2 35 13) to Praia de Mira (five a day in summer). All of these companies have stops in the town centre; see the map for locations. Services thin out at weekends and on holidays.

Train On the main Lisbon-Porto line, Aveiro has good connections north and south, including seven Alfa services (under an hour to Porto, two hours 40 minutes to Lisbon via Coimbra).

Getting Around
Between mid-June and mid September the turismo runs daily motorboat trips on the Ria. They leave from Aveiro's Canal Central, opposite the turismo, at 10 am for the seaside resort of Torreira (13km to the north), where you'll have a few hours on the beach before returning to Aveiro by 5 pm. Tickets, costing 2340$00 per person (1170$00 for kids aged eight to 12, younger children free), are available at the turismo.

Private trips to São Jacinto (two hours) on traditional moliceiros are also usually available in the summer; look for the kiosk by the Canal Central or ask at the turismo.

Beira Alta

Some of the towns along the Rio Douro in the far north of the Beira Alta are covered in the Douro Alto section of the Douro chapter.

VISEU
☎ 032 • pop 21,000
Underrated Viseu, capital of Beira Alta province, is a lively commercial hub, a town with the swagger of a city. At its heart is a compact – one could almost say cosy – old centre gathered around a hulking granite cathedral, symbolic of Viseu's status as a bishopric ever since Visigothic times. Its very old, crowded and partly pedestrianised market zone, punctuated with stoic 17th and

18th century townhouses, is a pleasure to squeeze through.

Viseu was the 16th century home of an important school of Renaissance art that gathered around the painter Vasco Fernandes (known as O Grão Vasco), and the town's biggest draw today is a rich museum holding his best work and that of some of his students.

You could do Viseu justice in less than a day (accommodation is tight and a bit pricey) but an overnight stop will let you while away an evening in one of several good restaurants and, if you like, the wee hours in a *casa de fado*.

History
The Romans built a fortified camp just across the Rio Pavia from Viseu, and several well-preserved stretches of their roads

---

Wines of the Dão Region

The red wines of the Dão region (an area demarcated in 1907, roughly within the watershed of the Rio Mondego in the south-western corner of Beira Alta) have enjoyed a solid reputation since the 16th century and are today considered among Portugal's best. Vines have been cultivated here since the time of the Phoenicians and Carthaginians over 2000 years ago, and possibly even before that (palaeobotanists have found vine pollens over 5000 years old in the Lagoa Comprida lagoon near Seia), though serious wine production only began with the Romans.

Although white Dão wines are available, the full-bodied reds are by far the best (and strongest in alcohol content). There are several *adegas* where you can try these velvety 'Burgundies of Portugal' including the Adega Cooperativa de Vila Nova de Tázem (☎ 038-461 82) and the Adega Cooperativa de São Paio (☎ 038-421 01), both near Gouveia. It's best to phone ahead to confirm visiting times.

survive nearby (see Roman Remains later in this section). The town, conquered and reconquered in the struggles between Christians and Moors, was finally taken by Dom Fernando I in 1057.

Viseu's sturdy walls were completed by Afonso V in about 1472. The town soon spread beyond them, having grown large and wealthy from agriculture and trade. An annual 'free fair' declared by João III in 1510 has since grown into one of the region's biggest agricultural and handicrafts expositions. Much of the town's wealth these days comes from the excellent wines of the Dão region (south-western Beira Alta), near Viseu.

Orientation

Viseu sits on the south bank of the Rio Pavia, a tributary of the Mondego. In the very middle of town is the handsome Praça da República, known to all as the Rossio. From here the shopping district stretches east along Rua Formosa and Rua da Paz,

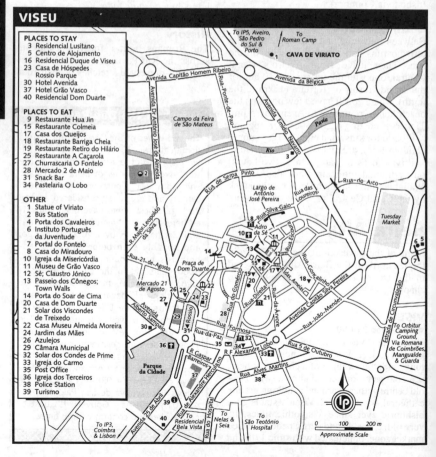

VISEU

PLACES TO STAY
3 Residencial Lusitano
5 Centro de Alojamento
16 Residencial Duque de Viseu
23 Casa de Hóspedes Rossio Parque
30 Hotel Avenida
37 Hotel Grão Vasco
40 Residencial Dom Duarte

PLACES TO EAT
9 Restaurante Hua Jin
15 Restaurante Colmeia
17 Casa dos Queijos
18 Restaurante Barriga Cheia
19 Restaurante Retiro do Hilário
25 Restaurante A Caçarola
27 Churrascaria O Fontelo
28 Mercado 2 de Maio
31 Snack Bar
34 Pastelaria O Lobo

OTHER
1 Statue of Viriato
2 Bus Station
4 Porta dos Cavaleiros
6 Instituto Português da Juventude
7 Portal do Fontelo
8 Casa do Miradouro
10 Igreja da Misericórdia
11 Museu de Grão Vasco
12 Sé; Claustro Jónico
13 Passeio dos Cônegos; Town Walls
14 Porta do Soar de Cima
20 Casa de Dom Duarte
21 Solar dos Viscondes de Treixedo
22 Casa Museu Almeida Moreira
24 Jardim das Mães
26 Azulejos
29 Câmara Municipal
32 Solar dos Condes de Prime
33 Igreja do Carmo
35 Post Office
36 Igreja dos Terceiros
38 Police Station
39 Turismo

and north into the historic centre along Rua do Comércio and Rua Direita. At the town's highest point and historical heart is the Sé (cathedral), bounded to the north, east and south by a warren of narrow lanes.

The bus station is north-west of the Rossio up Avenida Dr António José de Almeida. Drivers should avoid the old town, with its harrowing one-way lanes.

Information

The regional turismo (☎ 42 09 50) on Avenida Calouste Gulbenkian is open daily from 9.30 am to 12.30 pm and 2.30 to 5.30 pm (from 10 am at weekends).

There are numerous banks with currency exchanges and ATMs, especially along Rua Formosa. The post office is at the eastern end of Rua da Paz. The local Instituto Português da Juventude (☎ 420 34 10) at Portal do Fontelo has computer terminals where visitors can log onto the Internet free of charge during weekday business hours.

The district São Teotónio Hospital (☎ 42 05 00) is south of the centre on Avenida Dom Duarte, beside the Estrada de Circunvalação. The police station (☎ 42 20 41) is on Rua Alves Martins.

Rossio & Around

Stately Praça da República (Rossio) is so shady it almost feels like indoors. Begin your wandering here, after fortifying yourself with coffee and sweets from the snack bar in the middle.

At the southern end of the square, the late-18th century Igreja dos Terceiros has azulejo panels portraying the life of St Francis. Beyond this stretches the Parque da Cidade, also called Parque Aquilino Ribeiro. This is potentially a good place for kids to play, but its shrubs barely conceal couples at play at any hour of the day or night. In any case, it looks like a dodgy place at night.

On the western side of the Rossio is the rather grand 19th century câmara municipal. Fine modern azulejos at the northern end of the Rossio depict fairs and other scenes from regional life.

Beyond the azulejo-clad wall is the odd, sloping Jardim das Mães (Mothers' Garden), arranged around a bronze mother and child. The most elegant route into the old town is this way, past the Casa Museu Almeida Moreira, where the first director of the Museu de Grão Vasco decided to make his house, furniture and knick-knacks into a museum too; it's of limited interest.

Old Town

Walk north of the Casa Museu Almeida Moreira and through the Porta do Soar de Cima, set into a section of Afonso V's town walls, into the old town. Bear right into Adro da Sé (or Largo da Sé), the cathedral's huge forecourt, where the grandeur of the Sé is drowned in a bleak sea of parked cars.

Sé Resplendent on a rock towering above the whole town is the granite Sé, with a gloomy 17th century Renaissance façade that conceals a splendid 16th century interior, including a carved and painted Manueline ceiling. The building itself dates from the 13th century. The north chapel is graced with 18th century azulejos.

Stairs in the north transept climb to the choir, from where you can enter the upper gallery of the stately Claustro Jónico (Ionian Cloister), whose chapter house boasts 17th century azulejos outside, 18th century azulejos inside, and a collection of ecclesiastical treasures, some quite lovely. The original, lower level is one of Portugal's earliest Italian Renaissance structures. As you return to the church you pass through a Romanesque-Gothic portal, rediscovered in this century. The church is open most of the time (except lunchtime, naturally) and admission is free.

Museu de Grão Vasco Adjoining the Sé is a great square granite box, the Paço de Três Escalões (Palace of Three Steps), probably contemporary with the Sé. It was originally the bishop's palace, then a seminary, then the bishop's palace again. In 1916 it proudly reopened as a museum for the works of Viseu's own Vasco Fernandes,

BEIRAS

one of Portugal's seminal Renaissance painters (see the boxed text below).

These, together with other works of the Viseu School, are displayed on the 2nd floor. The most appealing are Grão Vasco's own *St Peter*, portrayed as a Renaissance man with an unearthly stare, and 14 panels (which once hung above the altar of the Sé next door) by Grão Vasco and his students. One panel, featuring an *Adoration of the Magi*, depicts the third wise man as an Indian from Brazil (which at that time was newly discovered).

Other displays in the museum include 13th to 18th century sculpture, 16th to 19th century furniture, 19th and 20th century Portuguese paintings, and Oriental and Portuguese ceramics. Unfortunately the only information given by the museum about the displays is in Portuguese.

The museum (☎ 42 20 49) is open daily except Monday and holidays from 9.30 am to 12.30 pm and 2 to 5 pm; admission costs 250$00 (free on Sunday until 12.30 pm) and guided tours are available.

Igreja da Misericórdia Facing the Sé across the Adro da Sé is this church dating from 1775. It's rococo, symmetrical and blindingly white outside, and neoclassical, severe and dull inside.

North of the Sé To the north of the Sé and the museum is Largo de António José Pereira (named after a 19th century Viseu artist). Behind it, along Rua Silva Gaio, is the longest remaining stretch of the old town walls. At the bottom, across Rua Emídio Navarro, is another old town gate, the **Porta dos Cavaleiros**.

South of the Sé Snug beneath the Passeio dos Cônegos (Curates' Walk) on a segment of the old wall is **Praça de Dom Duarte**, named after the Portuguese monarch, brother of Prince Henry the Navigator, who was born in Viseu. To the south on Rua Dom Duarte is a house with a beautiful Manueline window, the **Casa de Dom Duarte**, which is traditionally regarded as the king's birthplace. On and around Praça de Dom Duarte, several old **mansions** show off their wrought-iron balconies and genteel contours.

Rua Augusto Hilário (formerly Rua Nova), runs south-east through Viseu's **judiaria** (Jewish quarter), which dates from the 14th to the 16th centuries, and crosses Rua Direita, certainly Viseu's most appealing street and once the most direct route to the hilltop. It's now a lively melee of cluttered shops, souvenir stands, cafés, restaurants and old townhouses.

Old Mansions

The most handsome of Viseu's many old townhouses is the 18th century **Solar dos Condes de Prime** (the counts of Prime being its last owners), also called Casa de Cimo de Vila, on Rua dos Andrades, an extension of Rua Direita. Inside are azulejos, a little chapel and a ballroom. It's currently in use as a music conservatory; you may be able to view the interior.

Among other venerable stately homes are the 18th century **Solar dos Viscondes de**

Grão Vasco & the Viseu School

Viseu and Lisbon were the main centres of a uniquely Portuguese style of Renaissance art in the 16th century. The brightest lights in the so-called Viseu School of painting were Vasco Fernandes – known as O Grão Vasco, 'the Great Vasco' (1480-1543) – and Gaspar Vaz. Grão Vasco's work, heavily influenced by the Flemish masters, includes a range of direct, luminous, extra-realistic compositions painted for the Sé and other churches. Most of them are now at home in the Museu de Grão Vasco.

Treixedo on Rua Direita (now a bank office), and the 16th century **Casa do Miradouro** just off Largo de António José Pereira.

Roman Remains

On a shady embankment north of the centre are the remains of a Roman **military camp**. These date from around 139 BC when Viriathus (Viriato), the cunning chief of the Lusitani tribe (see the History section in the Facts about Portugal chapter), was double-crossed and murdered. Legend says that at some point he took refuge in a cave here, though there seems to be no factual basis for this. At any rate, there's a statue of him here, and the place is called **Cava de Viriato**.

A long hike or a car ride (about 5km) south-east of the town centre is **Via Romana de Coimbrões**, a well-preserved stretch of Roman road. Take the Mangualde road to Fraguzela village; then turn right and follow signs to Parque Industrial de Coimbrões; there is also access from São João de Lourosa, on the Nelas road. Another segment, about 5km north-east of the town centre, is **Via Romana de Ranhados**, in the village of Ranhados. Ask at the turismo for detailed directions. There are no bus services to or near these sites.

Market

Every Tuesday from 8 am to 2 pm a big Gypsy market sprawls across an open area a few blocks north-east of the centre. It's best visited in the morning.

Special Events

Viseu's biggest annual event is the Feira de São Mateus (St Matthew's Fair), a wine-growing, agricultural and handicrafts fair that carries on for a month from mid-August to mid-September. It features folk music and dancing, traditional food, amusements and fireworks. This direct descendant of the town's old 'free fair' still takes place on the Campo da Feira de São Mateus which was set aside for the event by João III in 1510.

Places to Stay

Camping There's a shady, wheelchair-accessible *Orbitur camping ground* (☎ 42 61 46) about 1km east of the Rossio on the Mangualde road. It's open from April to September and charges 490/410/440$00 per person/tent/car.

Hostel Viseu's *centro de alojamento* (☎ 42 06 20, fax 43 10 70) is beside the IPJ at Portal do Fontelo; dorm beds cost 1700$00 in high season. There is also a *pousada da juventude* (☎ 032-72 30 48) about 22km to the north-west in the spa centre of São Pedro do Sul; dorm beds/doubles cost 1700/4200$00.

Pensões & Residenciais The doubles at *Residencial Lusitano* (☎ 42 30 42, Avenida Emídio Navarro 167) are spacious and carpeted, but suffer from street noise; they cost 5000$00 (cheaper without bathroom) including breakfast.

Despite dodgy plumbing and chilly rooms, our mid-range choice is the staid *Casa de Hóspedes Rossio Parque* (☎ 42 20 85, Rua Soar de Cima 55) above the Rossio, where singles/doubles cost 6500/7000$00; there's a small restaurant.

Two sober guesthouses with big rooms are well south of the centre: *Residencial Dom Duarte* (☎ 42 19 80, fax 42 48 25, Rua Alexandre Herculano 214), and the child-friendly *Boa Vista* (☎ 42 20 26, fax 42 84 72, Rua Alexandre Herculano 510); doubles cost 6500$00 and 7500$00, respectively. The Bela Vista has off-street parking. Try for a quiet room at the rear of either place.

Best bet in the upper bracket is the small *Residencial Duque de Viseu* (☎/fax 42 12 86, Rua das Ameias 22), right below the Sé; air-con doubles with TV and big bathtubs cost 8500$00, and rear rooms are sunny and quiet.

Hotels Within sight of the Rossio is the well-run *Hotel Avenida* (☎ 42 34 32, fax 2 56 43, Avenida Alberto Sampaio 1), where a double with bath costs 9000$00. Top of the scale is *Hotel Grão Vasco* (☎ 42 35 11, *fax 2 70 47, Rua Gaspar Barreiros)*, offering doubles costing 13,500$00.

Places to Eat

Viseu is awash in good food. For a hit of coffee, an overpriced gooey pastry and a bit of atmosphere, go to *Pastelaria O Lobo (Rua Francisco Alexandre Lobo 37)*.

Our favourite place is *Casa dos Queijos* (☎ 42 26 43, *Travessa das Escadinhas da Sé 7-9)*, off Rua Direita, serving good *trutas grelhados* (grilled trout), decent *cozidos* (stews) and lots of greens. Bright, tiled, clean and simple *Restaurante A Caçarola* (☎ 42 10 07, *Travessa Major Teles 3)*, off the Rossio, offers lots of daily specials for under 1500$00, plus half-portions and mini-portions. *Churrascaria O Fontelo* (☎ 42 42 21, *Rua Conselheiro Afonso de Melo 45)* is good for grilled chicken, meat and fish.

For a little fado with dinner, try *Restaurante Retiro do Hilário (☎/fax 42 64 99, Rua Augusto Hilário 55)*, open daily except Monday until 2 am. There's a minimum charge of 1000$00 in the evening. Other old-town places worth a try are *Restaurante Colmeia* (☎ 42 37 18, *Rua das Ameias 12-14)* and *Restaurante Barriga Cheia (☎ 43 11 39, Rua Gonçalinho 42)*.

For a change, the peaceful Chinese *Restaurante Hua Jin (☎ 42 12 62, Rua Major Leopoldo da Silva 36)* has an immense menu of dishes under 1200$00.

Self-caterers will find fruit, vegetables and other goodies in *Mercado 2 de Maio*, the old town market on Rua do Comércio.

Shopping

Handicrafts here are noticeably cheaper than in more touristy towns. Among local specialities are black pottery, basketware and lace. Look for small handicrafts shops on or near Rua Direita, or venture into the huge, dumbbell-shaped Mercado 21 de Agosto off Rua 21 de Agosto.

Getting There & Away

The bus station hosts a number of private operators, chiefly Rede Expressos affiliate

Rodoviário de Beira Litoral (RBL; ☎ 42 28 22), Beira Alta affiliate Marquês Turismo (☎ 42 78 06) and Joalto (☎ 42 60 93). The best connections, with two or more buses each day, are: to Coimbra (about 850$00) and Lisbon (about 1400$00) with Marquês or RBL; Aveiro (about 850$00) and Porto with Marquês or Joalto; Braga with Joalto or RBL; and Guarda and Covilhã with Joalto.

Viseu is no longer on a passenger railway line, though CP runs buses to Viseu from the Coimbra-Porto line at Sernada and from the Coimbra-Guarda line at Mangualde.

SERRA DA ESTRELA

The Serra da Estrela, a glacially scoured plateau forming a conspicuous natural boundary between south and north, is the highest mountain range in mainland Portugal, topping out at 1993m Torre. At higher elevations it is decidedly alpine, with rounded peaks, boulder-strewn meadows, icy lakes and deep valleys. Lower down, the land furrows into stock trails, terraced fields lined with dry-stone walls, and plantations of pine.

The range gives birth to, and is then circumscribed by, two rivers: the Mondego (the longest river rising within Portugal) to the north and the Zêzere (a tributary of the Tejo) to the south.

Cuisine of the Beiras

Coimbra likes its roast suckling pig and Aveiro its fried eels, but the cuisine of the region is perhaps most strongly defined by the hearty, warming food of the mountains: roast lamb, roast kid and grilled trout; smoked ham, sausages and bacon; roast chestnuts and several varieties of *feijoacas* (little beans); rye bread and stout yellow corn bread; and the strong, semi-soft cheese of the Serra da Estrela. Finish your meal with an *aguardente* made from honey or juniper berries.

Serra da Estrela Cheese

Creamy, semisoft *queijo da serra* is made, usually in 1 to 2kg rounds, during the cold, humid months from November to April. Curing takes a fairly brief 40 days or so. A healthy by-product is curd cheese, made from the liquid drained during cheese manufacture.

Most serra farming families make their own cheese, though gradually the process is becoming industrialised, with certified cheese factories (offering tours and sales) springing up around the region. Towns with cheese factories include Celorico da Beira, Linhares, Carrapichana, Vale de Azares, Cadafaz, Algodres, Arcozelo, Folgosinho and São Romão.

Cheese fairs take place all over the region from November to mid-April. Best known are those at Fornos de Algodres (every other Monday), Celorico da Beira (every other Friday) and Carrapichana (every Monday), as well as those on Carnaval Saturday in Seia, Carnaval Sunday in Gouveia, and Carnaval Tuesday in Manteigas. You've got to rise early: the fairs are typically in full swing by sunrise and all over by 9 am.

A kilo of queijo da serra costs from about 2000$00 to 3000$00, depending on quality.

Mountain people – some still living in traditional one room stone *casais* (huts) thatched with rye straw, but now mostly concentrated in valley hamlets – raise sheep (for wool, meat and milk), grow vegetables, potatoes and rye, and increasingly depend on touristic variants of their traditional activities, for instance the selling of woollen goods and tasty, pungent *queijo da serra* (mountain cheese), and the renting out of rooms. Town-dwellers are concentrated at the north-eastern end, around Guarda.

The Parque Natural da Serra da Estrela (PNSE; Serra da Estrela Natural Park) was founded in 1976 to preserve not merely habitats and landscapes but also the rural character of the plateau and its people's cultural identity. Straddling the Beira Alta and Beira Baixa provinces, it's about 1000 sq km in size, with more than half of it above 700m altitude. Crisp, hyperclean air and immense vistas make this a fine place for walking, and there's greater scope for it here than anywhere else in the country, thanks to a system of well-marked trails and maps to go with them. Remoteness, harsh winters and the umbrella of natural park status have preserved fairly well the range's natural beauty and its human character.

This is not to say the Serra is untouched. Enough snow falls in winter to ski on and there are modest facilities on Torre. Every weekend (and all week in July and August), Portuguese families come up by car and bus in their thousands to play in the snow or picnic, rip branches from the trees for bonfires, leave their rubbish and create huge high-altitude traffic jams around Torre. Torre itself is defaced with a radar station and a shopping complex. Sabugueiro and a few other formerly quiet villages now bristle with pensões and souvenir shops. For the rest of the week, though, and off the road at almost any time, the mountains do indeed seem empty.

The weather constantly goes to extremes: even scorching summer days give way to freezing nights, and chilling rainstorms can arise with little warning. Mist is a big hazard because it obscures walking routes and landmarks (not to mention views) and because it can stealthily chill you, even to the point of hypothermia. You may set out on a warm, cloudless morning and in the middle of the day find yourself fogged in and shivering, so always pack for the cold and the wet too.

Wild flowers bloom in late April, and the best walking is from May to October. Winter is harsh, with snow at the higher elevations from November/December to April/May.

PARQUE NATURAL DA SERRA DA ESTRELA

Information

There are park information offices at Seia, Gouveia and Manteigas (the head office). All are equally helpful, but don't count on English being spoken. Regional turismos at Guarda and Covilhã, and local ones at Seia, Gouveia and Manteigas, have some park information too.

If you're serious about exploring the park, pick up the 1:50,000 scale, three colour topographic map called *Carta Turística: Parque Natural da Serra da Estrela*, marked with villages, roads, paths, camp sites and shelters. It costs 1050$00 and is available from any park office and most turismos, as well as the Instituto Português de Cartográfia e Cadastro in Lisbon (see Maps under Orientation in the Lisbon chapter) and Livraria Porto Editora bookshop in Porto (see Information under Porto in the Douro chapter).

The essential companion to this map is a booklet, *Discovering the Region of the Serra da Estrela*, describing the park's official walking routes, along with background information, flora and fauna basics, facilities, trail profiles and walking times; it's available at the same places as the map and costs 845$00.

Those with a more detailed interest in the park's flora and fauna can also pick up the booklet *Estrela: A Natural Approach* for 630$00.

Walking

Serra da Estrela is the only *parque natural* with a system of well-marked and mapped walking trails. Surprisingly few people use them, even in summer, and walkers often get the wonderful impression that they have the park to themselves. The park's traditional villages and agricultural way of life make a trek additionally rewarding.

Within a zone of special protection, which takes in almost everything above about 1200m altitude, camping and fires are strictly prohibited except at designated camp sites, all of them on the main trails. Cutting trees and picking plants are also prohibited in this zone.

Routes There are three main official routes that you can easily join and leave at numerous points. T1 runs the length of the park (about 90km) from Vide to Guarda, taking in every kind of terrain, including the barren summit of Torre. T2 and T3, both around 80km long, run along the western and eastern slopes of the Serra, respectively. Each of the main routes has branches and alternative trails.

It's feasible to assemble anything from a day hike to a week-long circuit of the park. The trails run through towns and villages in the park, so reaching them is relatively easy and there are sometimes accommodation options other than camping.

Manteigas is probably the best base for walkers as many of the most attractive hikes start there, including walks up the beautiful Vale do Zêzere towards Nave de Santo António (7½ to eight hours round trip); to the Poço do Inferno waterfall (3½ to four hours); to Penhas Douradas (3½ to four

hours); and to Folgosinho (about 10 hours) or on to Linhares (an additional seven hours there and back). A good alternative base is Penhas da Saúde.

Guided Walks Passeios a Pé no PNSE (Walks in the PNSE) is a programme of customised, multiday, group walks guided by park staff. There's no charge for the guide service, only for food, accommodation and other expenses. Walks should be arranged in advance through one of the park offices.

Serious hikers might also want to contact the Clube Nacional de Montanhismo (see Information in the Covilhã section later in this chapter) which organises weekend walking, riding, skiing and other trips. The club also has an office in Porto (☎ 02-200 83 23, 332 12 95).

A Porto-based adventure travel agency with experience in the Serra da Estrela is Montes d'Aventura; see Information under Porto in the Douro chapter for details.

Other Activities

The ski season typically runs from January to March, with the best conditions in February. Torre has gentle slopes, and facilities include three lifts, equipment rental, skiing lessons and a health club (with a sauna, Turkish bath and jacuzzi). Clube Nacional de Montanhismo organises ski trips.

If you'd like to go horse riding, contact Pedro Manuel Fazendeiro (☎ 075-92 18 94) in Terlamonte, about 10km north-east of Covilhã.

The Hotel Serra da Estrela (☎ 075-31 38 09, fax 32 37 89) at Penhas da Saúde organises expensive hot-air balloon trips in the region, requiring groups of at least four people.

Places to Stay

Useful bases for exploration of the Serra include Guarda, Gouveia, Seia, Manteigas and Covilhã. The best bargain accommodation includes hostels at Penhas da Saúde and Guarda, and camping grounds, of which at least eight are near the centre of the park.

BEIRAS

The Estrela Mountain Dog

The great shaggy, handsome *cão da Serra da Estrela* is a breed perfectly suited to its mountain environment. It's strong, fierce (thanks to wolf ancestry) and able to endure the cold. Though not all long-haired, they're all pretty big; an adult can weigh up to 50kg.

Traditionally used by farmers to protect their flocks from wild animals, the breed was, until recently, in danger of dying out. Now they're popular enough to have their own breeding kennel (a few kilometres south of Gouveia, off the N232) where the pedigree is preserved.

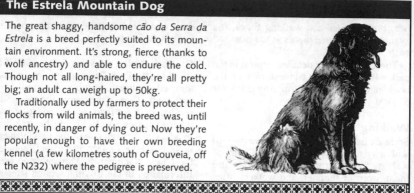

Whereas camping grounds either drop their rates or close outside the summer season, many hotels, pensões and residenciais actually raise theirs in winter to cover the extra cost of heating. Everything tends to be pricier than, for example, down in Coimbra. Contact the turismos or park offices for details of further camp sites not listed here.

Casas de Abrigo Scattered around the park are several fairly isolated *casas de abrigo* (shelter-houses) for use by park staff. Those at Covão da Ponte, Folgosinho and Videmonte are open to the public on a self-catering basis. Each has from 10 to 12 beds, a fully equipped kitchen, a fireplace and central heating, and all are accessible by car. They can only be booked in their entirety; it costs 10,000$00 at Covão da Ponte and 12,000$00 at Videmonte. A fourth, at Penhas Douradas, is open on a dormitory basis and beds cost 2000$00 (1500$00 without bedlinen). Contact any park office for details.

Turihab Turismo Habitação properties are concentrated along the Seia-Gouveia axis. They can be booked through local turismos or through ADRUSE in Gouveia (see the under Information in the Gouveia section for details).

Shopping

Souvenir shops in Serra towns sell tasty *queijo da serra*, heavy round loaves of *pão de centeio* (rye bread) and *pão de milho* (corn bread), honey, smoked hams and sausages. Non-edible items include woollen hats, slippers, rugs, coats and waistcoats (mostly made in Manteigas, Gouveia, São Romão and Folhadosa), baskets used for carrying cheese and bread (Vale de Azares and Vinhó), and miniature barrels and wooden tubs made by local wine-barrel makers (Gouveia and Seia).

Getting There & Away

There are several express coaches each day from Coimbra to Seia, Guarda and Covilhã, as well as from Aveiro, Porto and Lisbon to Guarda and Covilhã.

From Lisbon and Coimbra, IC trains run twice daily to Guarda via Celorico da Beira. Two additional IR trains each day also stop at Gouveia (2½ hours from Coimbra or five hours from Lisbon). Covilhã is on the main Lisbon-Paris line, served by two IC trains from Lisbon (4½ hours); there are numerous regional (R) services on to Guarda, plus connections from Porto.

Getting Around

Regular, though not very frequent, bus services run from Guarda along both sides of the park, though they thin out at weekends. No bus routes run across the park.

Driving can be hairy, thanks to mist and wet or icy roads at high elevations, and stiff winds. The Gouveia-Manteigas road is one of the most tortuous we found in Portugal. Don't expect empty roads at weekends, especially around Torre; on a weekend drive from Seia to Covilhã in April we found ourselves in a traffic jam that lasted for hours.

GUARDA
☎ 071 • pop 16,500

This district capital has little trouble living up to its traditional description: *fria, farta, forte e feia* (cold, rich, strong and ugly). Even in summer it seems granite-grey, dour and distant, and being at an altitude of over 1000m – making it Portugal's highest fully fledged city – it's nearly always cold. Moreover, despite an 800 year history (it was founded in 1199 to guard the frontier), there's actually little to see or do here.

So why come? With adequate accommodation, food and transport connections, Guarda is a handy base from which to explore the untouristy north-eastern corner of the Parque Natural da Serra da Estrela, as well as a rugged frontier zone dotted with medieval fortified towns. Just bring your jumper and woolly hat.

Orientation

The bus station, on Rua Dom Nuno Álvares Pereira, is about 800m south-east of Praça Luís de Camões (also called Praça Velha), heart of the old town. Most accommodation, restaurants and places of interest are near the praça. The train station is 4km north of town.

Information

The regional turismo (☎ 22 18 17), on Rua Infante Dom Henrique, is open daily from 9.30 am to noon and 2 to 6 pm (8 pm on Sunday). You can also obtain information about the Parque Natural da Serra da Estrela here.

At the time of research, the municipal turismo (☎ 22 22 51) on Praça Luís de Camões was closed for restoration of the câmara municipal which houses it.

There are several banks with ATMs around the regional turismo and on Rua Marquês de Pombal. The post office is on Largo de São João.

The local Instituto Português da Juventude, here called Casa da Juventude (☎ 21 22 10, fax 21 27 56), on Avenida Alexandre Herculano, has terminals where anyone can log onto the Internet for no charge; it's open from 8.30 am to 7 pm on weekdays only. Café Ecológico (☎ 22 70 00), Rua Comandante Salvador do Nascimento, is a non-profit gathering place with terminals you can use free of charge while chatting with local students.

Sé

This granite fortress of a cathedral on Praça Luís de Camões looks daunting even on a sunny day. It's largely in a sober Gothic style (the earliest parts date from 1390) but as it took 150 years to finish there are Manueline and Renaissance ornamentations and interior vaulting.

Inside, the most striking feature is a 16th century Renaissance altarpiece attributed to Jean de Rouen, one of a team of French artists who founded an influential school of sculpture at Coimbra. There's a small charge to climb the tower to the roof, open daily except Monday from 10 am to noon and 2 to 5.30 pm. Look out for the whimsical gargoyles up there.

Old Town

Praça Luís de Camões, the cathedral square, is the most attractive spot in Guarda, thanks to its mansions dating from the 16th to 18th centuries; see under Places to Stay for details of one you can sleep in.

Little remains of the castle, on a hilltop just above the cathedral, except the simple **Torre de Menagem** (castle keep), which was closed to visitors when we were there. Of the old walls and gates, the stalwart 17th century **Torre dos Ferreiros** (Blacksmiths' Tower) on Rua Tenente Valadim is still in good condition.

BEIRAS

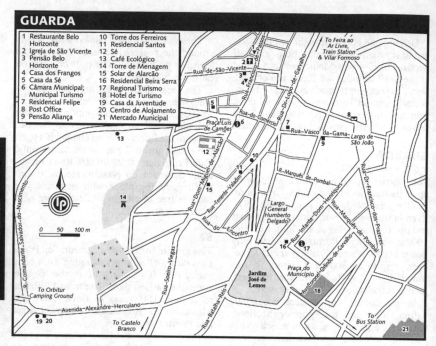

GUARDA

1 Restaurante Belo Horizonte	10 Torre dos Ferreiros
2 Igreja de São Vicente	11 Residencial Santos
3 Pensão Belo Horizonte	12 Sé
4 Casa dos Frangos	13 Café Ecológico
5 Casa da Sé	14 Torre de Menagem
6 Câmara Municipal; Municipal Turismo	15 Solar de Alarcão
7 Residencial Felipe	16 Residencial Beira Serra
8 Post Office	17 Regional Turismo
9 Pensão Aliança	18 Hotel de Turismo
	19 Casa da Juventude
	20 Centro de Alojamento
	21 Mercado Municipal

Some old-town atmosphere survives in the lanes north of the cathedral and along Rua do Comércio. At the heart of this area, around Igreja de São Vicente, was the city's former **judiaria** (Jewish quarter).

Market

A big open-air market, the Feira ao Ar Livre (local people just call it the Mercado), is held on the second and fourth Wednesdays of every month on the northern outskirts of town.

Places to Stay

Curiously, we found high season accommodation tight except at the budget end, so booking ahead might be in order.

Camping An *Orbitur camping ground* (☎ 21 14 06), open from March to October, is in the municipal park west of the cen-

tre, next to a swimming pool and sports stadium. Prices are 590/480/500$00 per person/tent/car.

Hostel Guarda's *centro de alojamento* (☎/fax 22 44 82, Avenida Alexandre Herculano) is behind a 'Pousada' sign beside the Casa da Juventude; dorm beds/doubles cost 1700/4200$00 in high season.

Private Rooms Among a small number of advertised quartos are basic doubles without bathroom costing 2500$00 at *Casa dos Frangos* (see under Places to Eat).

Pensões & Residenciais Dreary doubles at *Pensão Belo Horizonte* (☎ 21 10 36, Rua de São Vicente) cost about 3500$00.

Pensão Aliança (☎ 22 22 35, fax 22 14 51, Rua Vasco da Gama 8A) offers good-value doubles with bathroom or shower for

5000$00 including breakfast. *Residencial Filipe* (☎ 22 36 59, Rua Vasco da Gama 9) has similar rates but seems to prefer tourist groups. *Casa da Sé* (☎ 21 25 01, Rua Augusto Gil 17), within sight of the Sé, offers doubles costing 6000$00 (8000$00 for twin beds).

The pleasant, well-run *Residencial Beira Serra* (☎ 21 23 92, fax 21 13 91, Rua Infante Dom Henrique 35A), opposite the regional turismo, has doubles with bathroom which start at 7000$00, including breakfast. At the modern, charmless *Residencial Santos* (☎ 220 54 00, Rua Tenente Valadim 14), doubles with shower cost 8000$00.

Turihab The Turihab *Solar de Alarcão* (☎ 21 43 92, Rua Dom Miguel de Alarcão 25), near the cathedral, is a handsome 17th century granite mansion with its own courtyard and loggia, and three gorgeous rooms for rent, starting at 12,500$00.

Hotel If nobody else has room, the Best Western *Hotel de Turismo* (☎ 22 33 66, fax 22 33 99, Praça do Município), around the corner from the regional turismo, offers boring singles/doubles with the works for 8600/11,200$00.

Places to Eat

The food at *Casa dos Frangos* (☎ 21 27 04, Rua Francisco de Passos 47) is unexceptional but nothing (except cabrito assado) costs over 1000$00.

Restaurante Belo Horizonte (☎ 21 14 54, Largo de São Vicente 1) packs them in at lunchtime with good regional specialities, all costing under 1200$00; it's closed Saturday. *Pensão Aliança* (see Places to Stay) is another local favourite, with daily specials for 950$00 and good *cabrito assado na brasa* (braised roast kid) for 1500$00.

Getting There & Away

Bus On weekdays Rede Expressos (☎ 21 27 20) runs at least one bus to Seia, two to Coimbra, six to Viseu and nine to Guarda. Joalto (☎ 23 02 17) runs two buses to

Gouveia and Seia, two to Manteigas and four to Covilhã, plus long-distance routes. Services are less frequent at weekends.

Train Guarda is served by two lines from Lisbon. On the Beira Alta line, via Coimbra, there are five trains daily to Lisbon (five hours); change at Pampilhosa for Porto. There are three trains to Lisbon on the Beira Baixa line via Castelo Branco, but they take an hour longer and you must change at Covilhã. You might also find a seat on the daily Paris-Lisbon *Rápido Sud-Expresso*.

Four local trains trundle the 40km (one hour) between Guarda and the border at Vilar Formoso each day.

Shuttle buses run between the train station and the bus station, with a stop at Rua Marquês de Pombal, every half-hour during the day; the trip costs 100$00.

GOUVEIA

☎ 038 • pop about 7000

On the north-western edge of the Parque Natural da Serra da Estrela, 5km from the N17 between Coimbra and Celorico da Beira, this dozy town has little of interest beyond a finely manicured children's park but offers enough accommodation, food and transport to be a base for exploring this side of the park.

Orientation & Information

The town centre, where buses stop, is Praça de São Pedro. A block south, at Avenida Bombeiros Voluntários de Gouveia 8, is the Parque Natural da Serra da Estrela office (☎ 4 24 11), open weekdays only from 9 am to 12.30 pm and 2 to 5.30 pm.

A block further south, on Largo do Mercado opposite the mercado municipal, is the municipal turismo (☎ 4 21 85), open daily except Sunday and holidays from 9.30 am to noon and 2.30 to 6 pm. It's of little use except for accommodation information and a town map.

Next door to the turismo is the head office of the Associação de Desenvolvimento Rural da Serra da Estrela (ADRUSE, or Serra da Estrela Rural Development Association; ☎ 49 11 23, fax 4 02 50) which, among other things, organises Turihab accommodation and supports local handicrafts producers.

Abel Manta Museu de Arte Moderna

Gouveia's favourite son, Abel Manta (1888-1982), was an accomplished painter whose works now fill the former manor house of the Condes de Vinhós on Rua Direita, south off Praça de São Pedro. It's usually open daily except Monday from about 10.30 am to 12.30 pm and 2 to 5 pm; admission is free.

Don't confuse this with a gallery called Espaço João Abel Manta, beside the câmara municipal. This is named after the painter's son and features temporary exhibitions.

Museu Arqueologia e Etnográfico

Behind the câmara municipal is a poky museum containing a miscellany of Roman remains and medieval sculpted stones. It's only open Monday and Thursday from 9.30 am to 12.30 pm and 2 to 5.30 pm; admission is free.

Places to Stay

The simple *Curral do Negro* (☎ 49 10 08) is 3km east of Gouveia on the road to Folgosinho; rates are 500/400/350$00 per person/tent/car. *Quinta das Cegonhas* (☎/fax 74 58 86) is in the grounds of an old quinta which its Dutch owners are restoring, 6km north-east of Gouveia, between the villages of Nabais and Melo; it costs 500/400/350$00. Both sites close for 1½ to two months in winter.

Chilly, unglamorous doubles at *Pensão Estrela* (☎ 4 21 71, Rua da República 36) cost 5500/4000$00 with/without bathroom including breakfast. The modern *Hotel de Gouveia* (☎ 49 10 10, fax 4 13 70, Avenida 1 de Maio) offers soulless doubles costing 9000$00.

Pay more and get more atmosphere at several Turihab options, including *Casa da Rainha* (☎ 4 21 32, Rua Direita 74), a mansion with apartments sleeping two to six people; summer prices for two start at 9500$00. The turismo and ADRUSE have details of other Turihab places.

Places to Eat

The town's best restaurant is probably *O Júlio* (☎ 4 21 42, Travessa do Loureiro 1), where Abel Manta prints hang on the walls and regional specialities like *cabrito a serrana* (mountain kid) start at 1500$00. At the time of research it was about to move to less modest quarters opposite the park office.

The restaurant at *Pensão Estrela* (see Places to Stay) serves a few good, modestly priced local specialities and has great bird's-eye views. *Restaurante O Jardim* (☎ 4 04 27, Rua do Alto Concelho 5) serves cabrito assado for under 1200$00.

Self-caterers will find the *mercado municipal (Avenida Bombeiros Voluntários de Gouveia)* at its best on Thursday. You can buy regional cheeses, including *queijo de ovelha* (sheep's milk cheese), here or at a shop called *Cabaz Beirão* on Rua da Cadeia Velha.

Getting There & Away

On weekdays, Joalto runs two buses to Guarda and Seia (one at weekends). Rede Expressos buses pass through at least twice a day, from Guarda to Viseu and to Coimbra via Seia.

Gouveia is 'on' the northern Lisbon to Guarda line (the station is 14km north of town, near Ribamondego), with four daily trains to/from Lisbon and an evening service from Coimbra. There's no bus connection; taxis charge around 2000$00.

SEIA
☎ 038

Seia, 2km from the Coimbra to Celorico da Beira road (N17) and equipped with big shops and adequate accommodation, has become a useful stop for weekenders seeking an easy taste of the Serra da Estrela. There is no other reason to stop here.

Orientation & Information

Praça da República (where buses stop) is not a square but a street, adjacent to handsome Largo da Misericórdia and lined with shops and former mansions. Restaurants and pensões are within walking distance.

The small, poorly marked Parque Natural da Serra da Estrela office (☎ 2 55 06, fax 2 58 45), Praça da República 28, provides literature and advice on visiting the park. It's open weekdays only from 9 am to 12.30 pm and 2 to 5 pm.

Down the hill (about 500m) and behind the post office is the regional turismo, open from 9 am to noon and 2 to 6 pm (8 pm on Saturday), closed Sunday and Monday.

Places to Stay

At *Café Tumanquinhas* (☎ 2 26 17), in an industrial zone 1.5km north and downhill towards the N17, basic doubles with shower cost 5000$00. A better choice is the well-run *Hotel Camelo* (☎ 2 55 55, Rua 1 de Maio), west of the post office, where a double with satellite TV and shower costs 9200$00 including breakfast.

The grumpy *Residencial Silva* (☎ 2 23 05), 300m west of the Camelo, charges 7000$00 per double.

Places to Eat

Several restaurants on Praça da República serve regional specialities.

Snack Bar O Favo (☎ 31 16 33, Esplanada Combatentes de Grande Guerra 6), around the corner from the park office, has a downstairs restaurant where dishes start at 1000$00.

Getting There & Away

Joalto runs two buses to/from Gouveia and Guarda on weekdays (one at weekends). Auto-Transportes do Fundão has twice-daily connections to Covilhã via Unhais da Serra.

Rede Expressos passes through at least twice a day from Guarda and Gouveia, going on to Viseu and Coimbra. The Rede Expressos ticket office is at Rua da República 52.

SABUGUEIRO
☎ 038

Sabugueiro, 11km south-east of Seia on the N339 to Torre, is a typical Serra da Estrela mountain village, with chickens on the paths and sturdy mountain farmer-shepherd families living in slate-roofed houses. But it's the highest village in Portugal (1050m) and has therefore become a standard tourist magnet.

Pensões and souvenir shops have sprouted up all along the road and the village increasingly survives on tourist money. In fact, this is not a bad place to pick up queijo da serra, local smoked ham, rye bread, juniper-berry firewater, and fleecy slippers or vests made of Serra sheep's wool. Accommodation is pricey in winter but good value in summer, and the village is quiet on weekdays.

Places to Stay & Eat

Our choice is *Casa do Serrinho* (☎ 2 43 04, Largo Nossa Senhora da Fátima), just off the highway, with four rooms and a communal kitchen above a shop and café; a double costs 4000$00 (about 6000$00 in winter). *Estalagem O Abrigo da Montanha* (☎/fax 2 52 62) on the highway has comfortable doubles costing 7500$00 (going up to 10,000$00 in winter) including breakfast, and a good restaurant. Down the road, *Residencial Monte Estrela* (☎ 2 29 84) offers doubles for about 6000$00, including breakfast.

Getting There & Away

A single bus runs from Seia each week, departing from Seia on Wednesday at about midday and returning from Sabugueiro the next day at about 8 am.

MANTEIGAS
☎ 075 • pop 4050

Manteigas is probably the best base for exploring the Serra da Estrela: it's in the middle of the park and has a good park office, adequate supplies, decent food and comfortable accommodation for such a remote place.

BEIRAS

Set in a deep valley at the 700m-high confluence of the Rio Zêzere and several tributaries, it's also one of the most picturesque towns in the range. All around are dizzyingly steep, terraced hillsides clad in pine and dotted with stone casais, beehives and little meadows. The closest big attraction is the cathedral-like Vale do Zêzere, the glacial valley of the Zêzere, carpeted with small fields and ascending for 8km south-west to the foot of Torre.

There has been a settlement here since at least Moorish times, perhaps because of the hot springs around which the nearby spa of Caldas de Manteigas has grown.

Orientation

From Seia or Gouveia you approach Manteigas down a near-vertical switchback road. The town hardly seems to have a centre, though a good reference point is the turismo, which is where the bus from Guarda sets you down.

Information

The turismo (☎ 98 11 29), on Rua Dr Esteves de Carvalho near the GALP petrol station, is open from 9.30 am to noon and 2 pm to 6 pm (8 pm on Saturday), but it's closed Sunday and Monday; it's of only marginal use. Go instead to the Parque Natural da Serra da Estrela office (☎ 98 23 82, fax 98 23 84), Rua 1 de Maio 2, a two minute walk from the turismo, just beyond the petrol station. It's open weekdays from 9 am to 12.30 pm and 2 to 5.30 pm.

There are several banks with currency exchanges on the main street, Rua 1 de Maio; turn left as you approach the park office from the turismo.

Caldas de Manteigas

Two kilometres south of Manteigas is this tidy spa centre, open from May to October, with a hotel, a heated pool and two hot springs, good for rheumatic, respiratory and skin ailments. Six kilometres east of the spa, on a rough track, is Poço do Inferno (Hell's Well), a waterfall on the little Ribeira de Leandres.

Places to Stay

Camping Three camp sites run by the park authority are within reach of Manteigas: *Covão da Ponte*, on the banks of the Rio Mondego near one of the park's casas de abrigo (see the section on the Serra da Estrela earlier in this chapter); the summer-only *Covão da Ametade*, close to the road and very popular with day-trippers; and the primitive *Vale do Rossim*, north of Manteigas, which was threatened with closure at the time of writing. Contact the park office for details of these sites.

The plain municipal *Rossio de Valhelhas* (☎ 48 71 60), open from May to September, is about 18km east of Manteigas on the Belmonte road, and costs 270/235/215$00 per person/tent/car. Buses to Guarda and to Belmonte (two a day to each) pass nearby.

Private Rooms Just below and east of the turismo, *Restaurante Santa Luzia* advertises *dormidas* (rooms).

Pensões & Residenciais Adequate doubles at *Pensão Serradalto* (☎ 98 11 51, Rua 1 de Maio 15) – turn left (south) at the park office – cost 6500$00 (4500$00 and 5500$00 without bathroom). On the road above this – bear right (north) at the park office – is the more comfortable *Residencial Estrela* (☎ 98 12 88, Rua Dr Sobral 5), where doubles with/without bathroom cost 7500/6000$00, and there's a good restaurant. Breakfast is included at both places.

Turihab & Pousada At last, here's a cheap and recommendable Turihab place: *Casa de São Roque* (☎ 98 11 25, Lisbon ☎ 01-848 82 30, Rua de Santo António 51) has big, nicely furnished doubles for 5000$00, and a patio with mountain views. From the turismo, take the second left beyond Pensão Serradalto.

The *Pousada de São Lourenço* (☎ 98 24 50, fax 98 24 53) is 13km above and north of town on a ridge with stupendous views up the Vale do Zêzere, down to Manteigas and, on a clear day, east into Spain. In the high season, doubles cost 15,600$00.

Places to Eat

With a member of the Académie de Gastronomie Brillat-Savarin in the kitchen, *Residencial Estrela* (see Places to Stay) has higher aspirations, and prices, than the competition. *Pensão Serradalto* also serves good food, and for earthier prices.

Trutas de Mondego (trout from the Rio Mondego), the local speciality, is cheapest at *Café-Restaurante A Cascata (Rua 1 de Maio 10)*.

Clube de Compras is a well-stocked grocery store on Rua 1 de Maio, across from the Serradalto.

Getting There & Away

Joalto buses leave from Guarda for Manteigas on weekdays at around 11.30 am and 5 pm, returning from Manteigas at about 7 am and 1 pm; there's also a Saturday bus via Belmonte.

From Covilhã, change from Joalto's Guarda-bound bus at Vale Formoso (connections three times a day). During the school term there is one direct Covilhã-Manteigas bus each weekday.

Beira Baixa

COVILHÃ

☎ 075 • pop 22,000

This dour, polluted university town on the southern edge of the Parque Natural da Serra da Estrela is of minor interest in itself but it's the urban centre closest to the heart of the Serra da Estrela, with some modestly priced accommodation and food, and a turismo that's sometimes helpful, sometimes not.

Perhaps surprisingly, Covilhã also has at least three fairly un-touristy *casas de fado*.

Orientation

Covilhã seems pinned to the side of the Serra da Estrela foothills. The train station and a new long-distance bus station are about 2.5km downhill and south-east of the town centre, and it's a mean climb with a backpack. Every 20 to 30 minutes during the day (less frequently on Sunday), local

> ### Pêro de Covilhã
>
> Covilhã's only historical claim to fame is as the birthplace of one Pêro de Covilhã, a young Arabic-speaking Portuguese who went east in search of spice markets and perhaps to find the legendary Christian priest-king Prester John, on behalf of Dom João II. Disguised as a Muslim trader he journeyed through Egypt, India and even to the holy cities of Mecca and Medina. He was finally detained by a Coptic Christian king in what is now Ethiopia, where he married and lived out his days. His is the statue in the town's main square, beside a huge granite map showing his travels.
>
>

bus No 2 (Rodrigo) runs past both stations up to the police station, which is just up Rua António Augusto d'Aguiar from the central Praça do Município. Taxis hang out at both stations.

Information

Service at the regional turismo (☎ 32 21 70, fax 31 33 64) on Praça do Município can be rather hit or miss. The office is open weekdays only, from 9.30 am to noon and 2 to 6 pm. The Região de Turismo headquarters and a smaller information centre are by the Jardim Público.

Several banks around Praça do Município have currency exchanges and ATMs. The post office is across the square from the turismo.

The non-commercial Clube Nacional de Montanhismo (☎ 32 33 64, fax 31 35 14), upstairs at Rua Pedro Álvares Cabral 5, organises regular outings, mainly walking and mountaineering trips, and occasionally horse riding and skiing. Call by for a copy of its calendar; the office is open weekdays from 10 am to 5 pm. It also runs a spartan, summer-only camping ground at Penhas da Saúde.

The regional university, the Universidade da Beira Interior, is south of the centre on Rua Marquês d'Avila e Bolama.

BEIRAS

Things to See

There isn't much to do or look at in Covilhã, although the narrow, winding streets west of Praça do Município have a plain, quiet charm. In the midst of them you'll come across the **Igreja de Santa Maria**, the front of which is entirely covered with azulejos.

The university grounds house a **Museu de Lanifícios** (Museum of Wool-Making; ☎ 310 17 12), which looks back at a local industry that has collapsed since Portugal's entry into the EU. It's is open daily except Monday from 9.30 am to noon and 2.30 to 6 pm; admission is free.

A big Gypsy market sprawls across the plaza beside Rua Dr Júlio Maria da Costa on two Saturdays each month.

Places to Stay

Camping *Pião Camping* (☎ 31 43 12), run by Clube de Campismo e Caravanismo de Covilhã, is 4.5km north-west along the N339 towards Penhas da Saúde; it's open

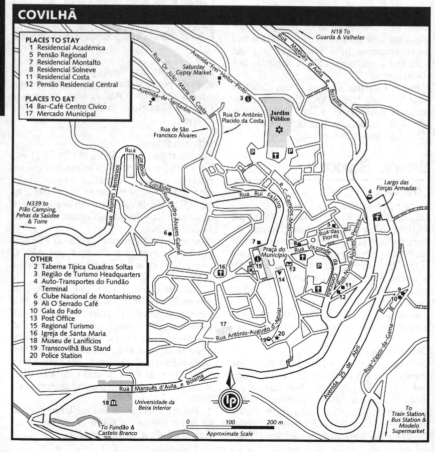

COVILHÃ

PLACES TO STAY
1 Residencial Académica
5 Pensão Regional
7 Residencial Montalto
8 Residencial Solneve
11 Residencial Costa
12 Pensão Residencial Central

PLACES TO EAT
14 Bar-Café Centro Cívico
17 Mercado Municipal

OTHER
2 Taberna Típica Quadras Soltas
3 Região de Turismo Headquarters
4 Auto-Transportes do Fundão Terminal
6 Clube Nacional de Montanhismo
9 Ali O Serrado Café
10 Gala do Fado
13 Post Office
15 Regional Turismo
16 Igreja de Santa Maria
18 Museu de Lanifícios
19 Transcovilhã Bus Stand
20 Police Station

N18 To
Guarda & Valhelas

Rua Marques d'Avila e Bolama

Avenida Frei-Heitor-Pinto

Saturday
Gypsy Market

Rua Dr Júlio Maria da Costa

Avenida-de-Santarém

Rua de São
Francisco Álvares

Rua Dr António
Placido da Costa

Jardim
Público

Rua Côa Côva

Rua Montes Hermínios

Geraldes

Rua Pedro Álvares Cabral

Rua Rui Faleiro

R.C. Campos Melo

Largo das
Forças Armadas

N339 to
Pião Camping,
Pehas da Saúdee
& Torre

Rua das
Flores

Praça do
Município

Rua Visconde

Rua Nuno-Álvares-Pereira

Universidade da
Beira Interior

Rua Marquês d'Avila e Bolama

Rua António-Augusto d'Aguiar

Avenida 25 de Abril

Rua Vasco-da-Gama

To Fundão &
Castelo Branco

To
Train Station,
Bus Station &
Modelo
Supermarket

0   100   200 m
Approximate Scale

BEIRAS

year-round. Non-members pay 350/350/270$00 per person/tent/car.

Pensões & Residenciais Rooms listed have their own showers and toilets unless noted.

If she likes you, the old dear at *Pensão Residencial Central* (☎ 32 27 27, *Rua Nuno Álvares Pereira 14*) will rent you a good-value double room for about 4500$00. *Residencial Costa* (☎ 32 20 50, *Rua Nuno Álvares Pereira 16*) next door offers mouldy rooms for similar prices. Both have good views at the back but street noise at the front. Quiet doubles at *Pensão Regional* (☎ 32 25 96, *Rua das Flores 4*) cost 5000$00, less without bathroom.

Residencial Montalto (☎ 32 16 09, *fax 31 54 24, Praça do Município 1*) has well-kept old doubles costing 6000$00 (8000$00 at weekends and in winter). The smartly run *Residencial Solneve* (☎ 32 30 01, *fax 31 54 97, Rua Visconde da Coriscada 126*) is really a hotel, with a parking garage and doubles for 7500$00 (8500$00 in winter). Prices at both places include breakfast.

At the high-rise *Residencial Académica* (☎/fax 32 75 18, *Avenida Frei Heitor Pinto*), comfortable, characterless rooms cost 6500$00 (8000$00 at weekends in winter) including breakfast. Views are grand from the upper rooms on the south-eastern side.

Places to Eat
We like *Restaurante Regional*, below the pensão of the same name (see Places to Stay), which offers a mixed menu of meaty standards starting at 900$00, plus burgers and omelettes. *Restaurante Solneve*, below the residencial of the same name, serves daily lunch specials at similar prices, plus interesting Portuguese and international dishes starting at 1500$00.

Bar-Café Centro Cívico is a cheerful student haunt in front of the Caixa Geral de Depósitos bank on Praça do Município.

Self-caterers will find fruit and vegetables available most mornings from the *mercado municipal* on Rua António Augusto d'Aguiar. There's also a big *Modelo* supermarket south of the bus station.

Entertainment
The cheerful *Taberna Típica Quadras Soltas* (☎ 31 36 83, *Avenida de Santarém 39*), well above the town centre, has fado after 10 pm on some Saturdays (minimum charge about 1200$00). Two small places in the lower reaches of town have irregular late-night fado: *Ali O Serrado Café* (☎ 32 36 11, *Rua Vasco da Gama 61*) and *Gala do Fado* (☎ 33 51 93, *Rua Vasco da Gama 59*) next door.

Getting There & Away
Bus On weekdays Rede Expressos (☎ 33 49 14) runs at least nine buses to Guarda, four to Castelo Branco, one to Seia and two or three each to Viseu, Coimbra, Braga and Lisbon. Beira Interior (☎ 33 49 14) runs four or five buses daily to Coimbra (1400$00), Porto (1400$00) and Lisbon (1500$00). Joalto (☎ 32 35 13) runs at least two buses to Guarda. Services thin out at weekends, and all run to/from the new general bus station.

Auto-Transportes do Fundão operates twice-daily connections to Seia via Unhais da Serra, from a dank terminal near Largo das Forças Armadas.

Train Two IC trains run daily to/from Lisbon (4½ hours) with connections to Porto. There is no easy train link to/from Coimbra.

PENHAS DA SAÚDE
☎ 075
Penhas da Saúde isn't a town at all, but the site of an old tuberculosis sanatorium which burned down years ago. It's now a weather-beaten collection of ski chalets and other facilities for mountain-heads, at the foot of the Barragem do Viriato dam, 10km up the N339 north-west of Covilhã.

Supplies are limited. If you're planning to go walking, do your shopping down in Covilhã.

BEIRAS

Places to Stay & Eat

Penhas has an excellent *pousada da juventude* (☎ 33 53 75, ☎ 32 75 06) with a kitchen, dining room, common room, dorm beds (1600$00) and half a dozen plain, functional doubles with shared facilities (3000$00 in summer, 3600$00 in winter); it's open year-round. Clube Nacional de Montanhismo (see under Information in the Covilhã section) runs a spartan but cheap *parque de campismo* (☎ 32 23 82), open from June to September.

At *Pensão O Pastor* (☎ 32 38 10, fax 31 40 35), doubles cost 7500$00 (more in winter) including breakfast. *Hotel Serra da Estrela* (☎ 31 38 09, fax 32 37 89) charges 19,500$00 for doubles from mid-July to August and in winter, and 14,300$00 during the rest of the year. There are several cafés along the Covilhã road.

Getting There & Away

Twice a day in August only, local buses run by Transcovilhã (☎ 33 60 17) climb to Penhas da Saúde and on to Nave Santo António, from the bus stand by the police station on Rua António Augusto d'Aguiar in Covilhã. Otherwise you must take a taxi (about 2000$00 from Covilhã), hitch (it's usually fairly easy to get a lift), cycle or walk. Except for the ever-expanding views to the east, this is a miserable climb on foot from Covilhã, much of it along the road.

SORTELHA

☎ 071 • pop 800

Sortelha is the oldest of a string of rock fortresses guarding the frontier east of Guarda and Covilhã. It's also one of the loveliest, a 12th century walled village with Arab origins, built into a boulder-strewn hillside. Although it's less immediately dramatic and less well known than Monsanto, it boasts similarly grand views over the wild landscape.

Tourism and development have arrived here, in a way that they haven't (yet) at Monsanto. With the help of EU funding, Sortelha's stout granite cottages are being restored and turned into bars, restaurants and upscale accommodation for growing numbers of Portuguese and Spanish visitors. The villagers who once clattered up the steep cobbled lanes with their donkeys – and lived rather precarious lives – can now sell their sausage, cheese and reed handicrafts at the small 'turismo' run by the Liga dos Amigos de Sortelha.

Though actually in the Beira Alta, Sortelha is included in this section because it's closer to Covilhã than to any major town in the Beira Alta.

Orientation & Information

'New' Sortelha, below the medieval hilltop fortress, borders the Santo Amaro to Sabugal road, along which are a restaurant and several Turihab properties. The fortress itself is a 10 minute walk up a newly cobbled road.

Old Village

The entrance to the fortified village is a grand stone Gothic gateway. From the square inside, a lane leads up to the heart of the village, at a *pelourinho* (pillory) in front of the remains of an old tower to the left and the parish church to the right.

Higher still is the bell tower. Climb right up to the bells to look out over the entire village (a sign begs visitors not to ring the bells), or tackle the ramparts around the village – but beware of some very precarious sections.

Special Events

The big bash of the year is a *festa* of folk dancing, merry-making and, in some years, bull-running or bullfights, on 15 August.

Places to Stay

Sortelha can boast several extraordinary Turihab properties, including some of the most atmospheric bargains in the Beiras (complete with thick stone walls and imperfect heating).

On the road below the old village is *Casa da Cerca* (☎ 38 81 13, fax 38 85 00), a 17th century mansion with air-con doubles for 10,000$00, and a four bed apartment in the adjacent **Casa do Páteo** cottage for 14,000$00, including breakfast. Within the village walls, the same owners have a cottage sleeping eight called **Casa da Vila**, though two could rent it for 10,000$00. Also within the walls is **Casa Arabe** (☎ 38 82 76), a one double-bedroomed cottage costing 6000$00. **Casa do Palheiro** (☎ 38 81 82) is similarly priced.

The most remarkable place is **Casa do Vento Que Soa** (Rua da Fontainha), a castle-like four bedroom house built into the rocks; it's a bargain at 6000$00, though ongoing renovations suggest this price can't last. The owner, Dona Maria Conceição (☎ 38 81 82) can be contacted, or the key collected, at the house on the main road opposite the turning to the fortress.

At the top of the village, **Casas do Campanário** (☎ 38 81 98) is a Turihab place where doubles cost 12,000$00; ask at the bar.

Places to Eat

Inside the gate, **Restaurante Dom Sancho I** (☎ 38 82 67) has an atmospheric bar downstairs and stratospheric food prices upstairs. **Restaurante Típico Alboroque** (☎ 38 81 29, Rua da Mesquita), behind the church, has the trappings of a medieval inn and a menu to match – lots of wild boar and kid – at somewhat lower prices. On the main road, **Restaurante O Celta** (☎ 38 82 91) can't match this ambience but does serve a hearty *ensopada de javali* (wild boar stew) costing 2200$00.

Shopping

Reed baskets and trinkets once made and sold by elderly women who hovered near the village gate can now be found, along with other handicrafts and locally produced foodstuffs, at the Liga dos Amigos de Sortelha centre (☎ 38 18 06) near the top of the old village on Rua Direita; the sign calls it a 'turismo'. It's open from 9 am to midnight, daily in summer and at weekends in winter. More durable antiques and knick-knacks can be found in several shops nearby and at Casa da Cerca.

Getting There & Away

It's nearly impossible to reach Sortelha by public transport. A daily bus service to/from Sabugal only runs during the school term. The best option is probably a train on the Lisbon to Guarda line (three daily, changing at Covilhã) to Belmonte-Manteigas station, 12km to the north-west. The local taxi (☎ 38 81 82) will bring you from the station to Sortelha for about 1800$00.

CASTELO BRANCO
☎ 072 • pop 54,000

The provincial capital of Beira Baixa is pretty and prosperous, but amazingly dull. Its excuse is that its proximity to the frontier, 20km to the south, has made it the target of so many attacks over the centuries – including a vicious one by the French in 1807 – that few historic monuments remain.

Its value for travellers is as a base for visiting the fortress village of Monsanto, though the excellent city museum is a worthwhile stop.

Orientation & Information

From the bus station, turn right and follow Rua do Saibreiro to the central Alameda da Liberdade. From the train station it's a 500m walk north on Avenida Nuno Álvares to the Alameda.

In a garden beside the Alameda is the turismo (☎ 34 10 02, fax 33 03 24), open Tuesday to Friday from 9 am to 8.30 pm, and on Monday and weekends from 9 am to 1 pm and 2 to 6 pm. Everything of interest is an easy walk from here.

The local Instituto Português da Juventude (☎ 32 69 10, fax 32 69 50) on Rua Dr Francisco José Palmeiro has a few terminals where you can log onto the Internet free of charge.

Palácio Episcopal

The Palácio (or Paço) Episcopal (Bishop's Palace), in the north of town on Rua Frei Bartolomeu da Costa, is a sober 18th century affair housing the **Tavares Proença Museu Regional** (☎ 34 42 77). In addition to an archaeological and Roman section,

BEIRAS

some fine 16th century Flemish tapestries, and 16th and 17th century paintings, there's a striking display of *colchas*, the locally famous silk-embroidered bedspreads. The museum is open daily except Monday from 9 am to 12.30 pm and 2 to 5.30 pm; admission costs 300$00.

Beside the museum is the **Jardim Episcopal** (Bishop's Garden), a Baroque whimsy of clipped box hedges, ornamental pools and little granite statues ranging from cherubic zodiac figures to the kings of Portugal. The Spanish kings Felipe I and II have been deliberately made smaller than the others! The gardens are open daily from 9 am to 7 pm; admission costs 20$00.

Castelo

There's little left of the castle, originally built by the Knights Templar in the 13th century and extended by Dom Dinis. The Miradouro de São Gens garden, which has

---

Colchas

Colchas, silk-embroidered linen bedspreads, have been a speciality of Castelo Branco for centuries. Once woven for every rich girl's bridal trousseau, their designs of exotic flora and fauna are imbued with symbolic significance (two birds symbolise lovers, trees represent families and so on).

You can see them being made in a workshop in the Museu Regional, or at the Loja da Villa (☎ 34 15 76), Rua da Misericórdia 37, where two sisters operate a small workshop for high-quality items hand-sewn with silk thread. If you're tempted to buy, you can choose from a photo album of dozens of designs (the sisters will conscientiously explain every symbol). Expect to wait up to a year for your colcha to be delivered. Prices range from 185,000$00 for a small item to a staggering 1,500,000$00 for a bedspread-sized colcha.

---

supplanted the walls, offers grand views over the town and countryside, and is a good picnic spot. The old lanes back down to the town centre are very picturesque.

Places to Stay

The spartan municipal *parque de campismo* (☎ 34 16 15) is 3km north of town, off the N18 to Covilhã. It costs 40/35/50$00 per person/tent/car.

In addition to dorm beds (1700$00 in high season), the *centro de alojamento* (☎ 32 38 38, Rua Dr Francisco José Palmeiro)* has a few plain doubles with shared facilities costing 3400$00 (2700$00 in winter).

The best budget guesthouse is *Residencial A Telhadense (☎ 33 15 45, Rua das Damas 6)*, with chattering budgies downstairs and several floors of small (often windowless) singles/doubles with shower for 2000/4000$00. In the next street, *Pensão Império (☎ 34 17 20, Rua Prazeres 20)* offers newer rooms with breakfast for 3500/5000$00. The businesslike *Residencial Arraiana (☎ 34 16 34, Avenida 1 de Maio 18)* has doubles costing 7000$00, including breakfast.

Places to Eat

There's little here to get excited about. Several cafés around Alameda da Liberdade, such as *Gelataria Pierrot*, serve snacks at outdoor tables. Nearby, the somewhat pretentious *Restaurante Kalifa (☎ 34 42 46, Rua Cadetes de Toledo 6)* serves generous portions at reasonable prices, but watch for costly extras like salads. Best of all is *Praça Velha (☎ 32 86 40, Largo Luís de Camões)*, housed in a former Knights Templar abode at the heart of the old town.

Self-caterers can find supplies, including the queijo de ovelha (sheep's cheese) for which this region is famous, in the *mercado* on Avenida 1 de Maio.

Getting There & Away

Bus On weekdays Rede Expressos runs at least four buses to Covilhã and Guarda, two of which continue to Viseu, Porto and

Braga. Two services run to Coimbra and three or four go to Lisbon. Services fade out at weekends.

Train Castelo Branco is on the Lisbon-Guarda line, with six trains daily from Lisbon, including two IC services, all continuing to Covilhã (change there for Guarda).

MONSANTO
☎ 077 • pop 2100

Once the most remote and least visited of Portugal's medieval fortress villages, Monsanto, 48km north-east of Castelo Branco, is now firmly on the tourist map, and making the most of a reputation as (allegedly) Portugal's oldest settlement. But despite a steady stream of tourists and inevitable gentrification (street lighting, souvenir shops, even a pousada), this fortified rock settlement, built on the highest peak for miles around, is still stunning. Village life here seems amazingly unaffected; elderly women still keep hens and goats and sit on their doorsteps, crocheting and chatting.

Orientation & Information
Monsanto is so small that you just need to follow the path uphill to reach the castle. Signs en route point to the *gruta* (a cavern where local men used to drink); the castle is a short climb further on.

Village
Houses near the entrance to the village are surprisingly grand, some even sporting Manueline doorways and stone crests. Since Monsanto won an award in 1939 for 'the most traditional village in Portugal', building restrictions have largely put a stop to creeping cement modernisation. Along the twisting upward path, cottages and animal sheds are built in among the boulders. Stone crosses appear at every turn.

Castelo
There was probably a fortress here even before the Romans came, but after Dom

Sancho I booted out the Moors in the 12th century it became more substantial. Dom Dinis refortified it but after centuries of attacks from across the border it finally fell into ruin.

Today it's a hauntingly beautiful site populated by lizards and wild flowers. Immense vistas from the 800m eyrie take in Spain to the east and the Barragem da Idanha lake to the south-west, but it's the sight of the village below, almost fading into the rock, that offers a glimpse of medieval Portugal at its toughest and truest.

Just below the entrance is a cement square, used for folk dances at festival time. To the right is a ruined Renaissance church and bell tower, and five stone tombs carved into the rock.

Special Events
On 3 May Monsanto celebrates the unique Festa das Cruzes, commemorating a medieval siege that failed thanks to a clever trick. The starving villagers threw their last calf over the walls as if they had them to spare, so disheartening their attackers that the siege was called off. These days, young girls throw baskets of flowers instead, after which there's dancing and singing beside the castle walls.

Places to Stay
Private rooms here are scarce and not particularly cheap; ask at souvenir shops and cafés. One gem of a place, belonging to *Sra Maria Amélia Pedroso* (☎ 34 12 63), has a double room with a sitting room, bathroom, garden and great views for 7500$00; there are downstairs rooms costing 7000$00. It's just off Largo da Barreira do Relógio, by the clock tower.

Near the village entrance is the *Pousada de Monsanto* (☎ 31 44 71, fax 31 44 81), a plain, comfortable 10 room inn where a double costs 15,600$00.

Places to Eat
Just outside the village walls is *Café Snack-Bar Jovem*, serving adequate food. Places in the village include *Adega Tipica O*

BEIRAS

Cruzeiro, with rustic wine barrels and decent fare, and the more simple *Café Monsantinho (Rua de Nossa Senhora do Castelo)*. Souvenir shops sell home-made honey cakes (some laced with aguardente!), a fine energy boost for the climb to the castle.

Getting There & Away

A single early evening bus runs here from Castelo Branco on weekdays, returning at the crack of dawn. A change at Idanha-a-Nova (35km south of Monsanto) provides a couple more options. Check bus timetable footnotes carefully.

The Douro

Douro province is dominated by Portugal's second-largest city, Porto, and by its best known river, the Douro. Rising in Spain, the Rio Douro (River of Gold) defines the eastern Spain-Portugal border from just north of Miranda do Douro in Trás-os-Montes down to Barca de Alva, then runs west for about 200km across Portugal to Porto. It's in the area reaching from the Spanish border to Peso da Régua, known as the Douro Alto, that the famous port-wine grapes are grown on steep terraced hillsides of schist that trap the region's intense summer heat.

In the early days of the port-wine trade the Douro region, especially the mountain-ringed valley itself, was rough and wild. Travellers were at the mercy of bandits, and accommodation was so primitive that British port-wine traders searching for new sources had to sleep 'on ye tables for reason of ye insects'.

Even the journey to Porto from the coastal town of Viana do Castelo in the Minho (where the earliest wine traders got their start) had its perils. 'We bestrode mules with awkward straw stuf'd saddles,' wrote a young Yorkshireman, Thomas Woodmass, in 1700. 'It was our intention to stay over ye night at Villadecon [Vila do Conde] but it was not so to be, for 6 arm'd men did stop us in ye King's name, and examined our pockets, taking all we had; our guides running away at first sight of them.'

Today the Douro valley is one of Portugal's most popular tourist destinations. The river, tamed by five dams in the 1980s, is now navigable all the way to Barca de Alva, allowing passenger cruises to slip through dramatic gorges into the heart of the port-wine country. The Douro railway, which opened in 1887 and runs from Porto to Pocinho (Beira Alta), is another fine way to travel. Although its picturesque narrow-gauge branch lines have been truncated or amputated in recent years, parts remain that

HIGHLIGHTS

- Soak up the atmosphere of Porto's Ribeira district and take bird's-eye pictures from the vertiginous Dom Luís I bridge

- Sample port wine in the crusty old lodges of Vila Nova de Gaia

- Ride a train up the Douro valley beneath its crew-cut, vineyard-terraced slopes

- Take the narrow-gauge Linha de Tâmega railway up to the handsome town of Amarante

- See Stone Age art, scratched into the rocks of the Vale do Côa tens of thousands of years ago

are worth travelling (see the Douro Alto section in this chapter).

Porto, naturally, makes an excellent base for exploring this region. The beaches immediately north and south of the city are some of the most polluted in Portugal, but Vila do Conde's fine beaches are less than an hour's train ride away. And, for the most part, 'ye insects' are no more.

PORTO
☎ 02 • pop 325,000

Portugal's second-largest city, Porto is a vibrant contrast to Lisbon: while the capital revels in its elegance, Porto is down-to-earth and hard working. This is Portugal's most important economic area, the base for most of its manufacturing and for some of its largest private enterprises. Proud *porto-enses* recite an old saying: 'Coimbra sings,

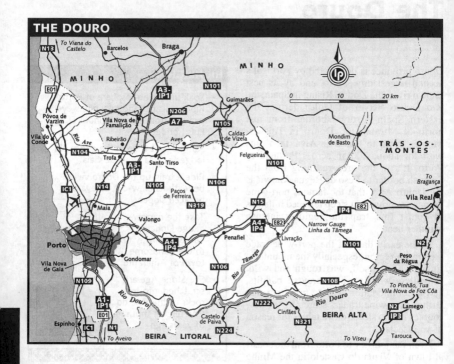

THE DOURO

Braga prays, Lisbon shows off and Porto works'. Traditionally mocked by *lisboêtas* as *tripeiros* (tripe-eaters), they refer to the southerners in turn as *alfacinhas* (lettuce-eaters).

Despite a go-getting populace, Porto (only foreigners call it Oporto: the port) is surprisingly old-fashioned. Built on steep granite hills above the Rio Douro, its heart is a 19th century tangle of grimy lanes tumbling down to the river. Straddling the river are five dramatic bridges connecting the town with Porto's 'other half', Vila Nova de Gaia, historic home of the port-wine lodges, and Porto's biggest tourist draw.

Cultural attractions are limited here, but what the city lacks in monuments and churches it makes up for in eclectic atmosphere. The riverside Ribeira district is a beguiling blend of run-down fishing quarter and tourist trap, with chic restaurants sitting alongside smoky bohemian bars. The Mercado do Bolhão (Bolhão market), a bustling, no-nonsense affair in the centre of town, is surrounded by smart shops, and everywhere there are tendon-busting steep streets with their mix of stately old mansions and back-alley dives.

You'll need at least two days to soak up the atmosphere (not to mention the port wine). This is also a natural place from which to explore not only the beautiful Douro valley but also a host of attractive towns further north in the Minho, all easily accessible by train or bus.

History

Porto is the 'Portu' in 'Portugal'. In Roman times a Lusitanian settlement called Cale, on the left (south) bank of the Douro near the river's mouth, became an important crossing on the Lisbon to Braga road. As traffic grew, another settlement, Portus (harbour), grew up on the opposite side. Portus-Cale subsequently gave its name to, and became the capital of, the county of Portucalia, which lay between the Minho and Douro rivers. This was the land given to Henri of Burgundy upon his marriage to the daughter of the King of León in 1095. From here his son Afonso Henriques launched the Reconquista, ultimately founding the independent kingdom which took Portucalia's name and became Portugal.

Porto's status grew with the building of a cathedral in 1111 and was confirmed with later royal favours: here Dom João I married his English queen, Philippa of Lancaster, in 1337, and here their most famous son, Henry the Navigator, was born in 1394. While Henry's explorers were groping round Africa for a sea route to India, British traders found a foothold in Porto with their trade in port wine.

Over the following centuries, Porto acquired a reputation for rebelliousness. In 1628 a mob of Porto women attacked the minister responsible for a tax on linen. In 1757 a 'tipplers' riot' against the Marquês de Pombal's strict new control of the port-wine trade was savagely put down. In 1808 Porto citizens arrested their French governor and set up a provisional junta. The French army which took the city back the following year was finally given the boot by the British under the future Duke of Wellington. Porto radicals soon turned against British 'control' of Portugal; they demanded a new liberal constitution, and got one in 1822.

When the absolutist Dom Miguel I usurped the throne in 1828, Porto stood by its principles and Miguel's constitutionalist brother, Dom Pedro. Miguel's forces laid siege to the city in 1832 after Pedro arrived from Brazil, but the liberal cause won through in the following year when Miguel's fleet was captured off Cabo São Vicente. Demonstrations continued to erupt in Porto in support of liberals throughout in 19th century. Portugal's first republican deputy was elected from Porto in 1878.

Orientation

Old Porto clambers up the gorge 9km from the mouth of the Douro. 'New' Porto includes the polluted seashore at Foz do Douro, at the mouth of the river, and bumps up against the commercial suburb of Matosinhos, 5km north of Foz. Vila Nova de Gaia, the port-wine centre across the river, has played such a large role in Porto's history that it's treated as part of the city, though it's actually a separate municipality.

Porto's most distinctive landmarks are its *pontes* (bridges) across the Douro. From west to east they are: the modern Ponte da Arrábida linking Porto to the A1 Lisbon highway; the two-level Ponte de Dom Luís I to Vila Nova de Gaia; two railway bridges, the Eiffel-designed Ponte de Maria Pia and the adjacent Ponte de São João to/from Campanhã station; and the newest highway bridge, Ponte do Freixo.

The city's axis is the broad Avenida dos Aliados, with a mini-park in the middle and the *câmara municipal* (city hall) looming over Praça General Humberto Delgado at its northern end. Around this square are the municipal turismo, the post office, currency exchange offices and some moderately priced accommodation. To the east and north-east is a lively shopping district. At the southern end of Avenida dos Aliados is Praça da Liberdade, a crowded bus-stop nucleus. Largo dos Lóios (commonly just 'Lóios') is a square off the south-western corner of Praça da Liberdade with more bus stops.

West from here along Rua dos Clérigos is the city's best *miradouro* (lookout), the tower of the Igreja dos Clérigos, and beyond it is the university. South of Praça da Liberdade is the Sé (cathedral), from where old lanes tumble down to the riverside Cais da Ribeira.

All of these can be reached on a steep but reasonable walk from Avenida dos Aliados. Municipal buses run to most other places of interest or use, including Vila Nova de Gaia, shopping centres around the giant hub of Praça de Mouzinho de Albuquerque (an area best known as Boavista), the youth

DOURO

PORTO

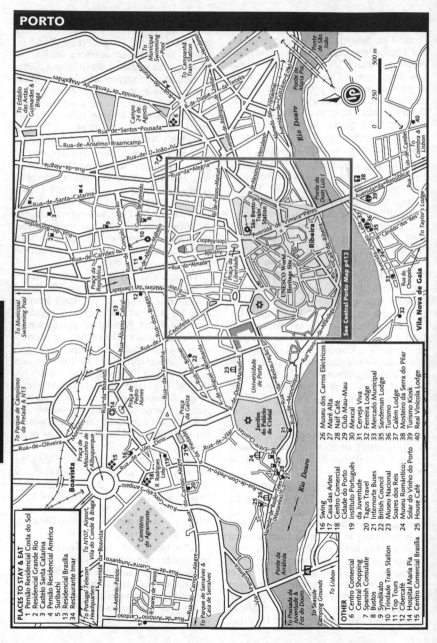

DOURO

PLACES TO STAY & EAT
1 Pensão Residencial Costa do Sol
2 Residencial Grande Rio
3 Castelo Santa Catarina
4 Pensão Residencial América
5 Suribachi
13 Residencial Brasília
34 Restaurante Imar

OTHER
6 Centro Comercial Central Shopping
7 Spanish Consulate
8 Bustos
9 Syndikato
10 Trindade Train Station
11 Top Tours
12 Cibercafé
14 Hospital Maria Pia
15 Centro Comercial Brasília

16 Swing
17 Casa das Artes
18 Centro Comercial Cidade do Porto
19 Instituto Português da Juventude
20 Tagus Travel
21 Intermote Buses
22 British Council
23 Museu Nacional Soares dos Reis
24 Museu Romântico; Solar do Vinho do Porto
25 House Café

26 Museu dos Carros Eléctricos
27 Maré Alta
28 Club Mau-Mau
29 Naif Café
30 Mexcal
31 Cerveja Viva
32 Ferreira Lodge
33 Mercado Municipal
35 Sandeman Lodge
36 Turismo
37 Calém Lodge
38 Mosteiro da Serra do Pilar
39 Turismo Kiosk
40 Real Vinícola Lodge

See Central Porto Map p412

UNESCO World Heritage Site

Rio Douro

Vila Nova de Gaia

Boavista

hostel west of town along the river, and the camping ground north-west of the centre.

Porto's Francisco Sá Carneiro airport is 20km north-west of the centre via the N13 and N107 highways. There are three train terminals: Campanhã, 2km east of the city centre; São Bento, just off Praça da Liberdade; and Trindade, a few blocks north of the câmara municipal. Bus terminals are likewise scattered all over town; see the Getting There & Away section for destinations served by each.

Maps The municipal turismo hands out a free 1:15,000 city map which is good enough for most explorations. For 100$00 it sells another that is almost identical but has additional text.

Various maps are sold at Livraria Porto Editora (see under Bookshops), other bookshops and street kiosks; the best of these maps is Dinternal's 1:16,500 *Porto: Mapa Turístico*. Porto Editora's own 1:14,000 *Planta da Cidade* has a useful street index.

If you're planning a trip along the Rio Douro, a splendid schematic map with bilingual notes, *Rio Douro: Porto-Barca de Alva*, is available for 1000$00 from many bookshops.

Information

Tourist Offices The switched-on municipal turismo (☎ 205 27 40, fax 332 33 03) is at Rua Clube dos Fenianos 25, opposite the câmara municipal. It's open weekdays from 9 am to 7 pm (5.30 pm outside the July to September summer season), and weekends from 10 am to 5 pm. It usually stocks a free monthly cultural events brochure. You can find similar listings – plus information on everything from baby-sitters and football to takeaway restaurants and late-night pharmacies –in local editions of the newspapers *Público* and *Jornal de Notícias*, on sale at newsagents.

A pocket-sized national (ICEP) turismo (☎ 205 75 14, fax 205 32 12) at Praça Dom João I 43 is better for national inquiries than Porto-specific ones. In July and August it suffers tourists on weekdays from 9 am to 7.30 pm (from 9.30 am during the rest of the year) and at weekends from 9.30 am to 7.30 pm (3.30 pm during the rest of the year). There's also an ICEP turismo at the airport (☎ 941 25 34), open from 8 am to 11 pm daily (10.30 pm from November to April).

Municipal and ICEP turismos, STCP (public transport) offices, the city's youth hostel and Parque de Campismo da Prelada sell a tourist pass, variously called the Culture Card or the Passe Porto, valid for unlimited bus and tram travel, reduced or free admission to city museums, and discounts at certain shops. There are versions valid for one day (550$00) and two days (750$00). If you prefer walking, these probably aren't very good value.

Money There are Multibanco ATMs all over Porto, most conveniently at the lower end of Avenida dos Aliados. There are also automatic currency-exchange machines at Avenida dos Aliados 21 and 138. The best rates for travellers cheques are given at private exchange bureaux such as Portocâmbios at Rua Rodrigues Sampaio 193 and Intercontinental at Rua de Ramalho Ortigão 8 (both open weekdays year-round; Portocâmbios is also open on Saturday morning). Another useful exchange is at the airport's Totta e Açores bank (open daily).

American Express (Amex) travellers cheques can be cashed commission-free at Top Tours (see under Travel Agencies), Porto's Amex representative.

Post The main post office (including poste restante) is opposite the câmara municipal on Praça General Humberto Delgado. Amex card and travellers cheque customers can have mail sent to the less central Top Tours (see Travel Agencies).

Telephone & Fax The handiest place for making long-distance or international calls is the Portugal Telecom office at Praça da Liberdade 62, open daily until midnight. There's also a telephone office (open weekdays only) in the main post office. Both

DOURO

places, plus many kiosks and newsagents, sell Credifone cards. Faxes can be sent from the post office.

Email & Internet Access Porto has at least half a dozen places where you can log onto the Internet. Several are free, including: Internet Quiosques at two Portugal Telecom offices, at Praça da Batalha, and at Telecom headquarters at Rua João de Deus 636, open weekdays from 9 am to 6 pm (no time limit); a city cultural centre called Casa das Artes (☎ 600 61 53), Rua de António Cardoso 175, open weekdays from 2.30 to 7.30 pm; and the Instituto Português da Juventude (☎ 600 41 82), Rua Rodrigues Lobo 98, with public access on Monday, Wednesday and Friday only from 3 to 5 pm, for short periods.

The helpful Cibercafé (☎ 200 82 63, fax 203 91 72, email cibercafe@cibercafe.pt), Rua dos Mártires da Liberdade 223, is open from 11 am to 2 am daily; access costs 400$00 per half-hour. Intercyber (☎ 200 59 22, email postmaster@intercyber.pt), near the municipal turismo at Praça General Humberto Delgado 291, is open from 9 am to 2 am daily (10 am on Sunday); access costs 100$00 per hour until 2 pm, 300$00 per hour after that.

Travel Agencies Youth-oriented Tagus Travel (☎ 609 41 46, fax 609 41 41), Rua do Campo Alegre 261, sells discounted plane and train tickets, plus ISIC cards. Another youth specialist is Jumbo Expresso (☎ 339 33 20, fax 339 33 29), Rua de Ceuta 47, which can also arrange discounts on car rental. Both agencies are open weekdays and on Saturday morning.

Top Tours (☎ 208 27 85, fax 332 53 67), Rua Alferes Malheiro 96, is Porto's Amex representative. If you have Amex cards or travellers cheques you can exchange currency commission-free and have mail and faxes held or forwarded here. It's open weekdays only.

Two locally based adventure travel agencies are Montes d'Aventura (☎ 830 51 57, mobile ☎ 0936 607 37 39, fax 830 51 58,

email maventura@ip.pt), offering walking and multiactivity programmes in the northern mountains (including Parque Nacional da Peneda-Gerês, the Serra da Estrela and Parque Natural do Alvão), and Trilhos (☎/fax 550 46 04, mobile ☎ 0936-71 42 77, email trilhos@trilhos.pt), a specialist in canyoning and hydrospeed (see under Activities in the Facts for the Visitor chapter for details of these sports).

Bookshops With stock of military topographic and other maps, the small Livraria Porto Editora (☎ 200 76 81), Praça Dona Filipa de Lencastre 42, may be Porto's most useful bookshop. There are other shops selling new and second-hand books in the streets just to the south of it. Livraria Bertrand (☎/fax 200 43 39), Rua 31 de Janeiro 65, offers the widest choice of foreign-language books. For educational children's books, maps and toys, go to Livraria ASA, Rua Galeria de Paris 118.

Even if you're not after books, take a look in Livraria Lello e Irmão, Rua Carmelitas 144, an Art Deco gem stacked to the rafters with new, second-hand and antique books, housed in lavish quarters more suited to a gentlemen's club.

Universities The Universidade de Porto is just west of the city centre in the neighbourhood of the Igreja do Carmo. Various faculty buildings also line nearby Rua da Restauração.

Cultural Centres The British Council (☎ 207 30 60, fax 207 30 68) is at Rua do Breiner 155. Its library, containing a good selection of English-language books and newspapers, is open Monday and Tuesday from 10 am to 1 pm and 2.30 to 8.30 pm, Wednesday from noon to 8.30 pm, Friday from 5 to 7.30 pm, and irregularly on Saturday. From about 21 June to 21 September it closes daily at 5.30 pm, and in August it shuts down entirely.

Laundry The cheapest laundry in town is the municipal Lavandaria São Nicolau

(☎ 208 46 21) in an underground complex at the junction of Rua da Reboleira and Rua Infante Dom Henrique, west of the Ribeira. Other places are Lavandaria Olimpia, on Rua de Miguel Bombarda near the University, Pinguim Lavandaria in the basement of the Centro Comercial Brasília at Boavista, and Lavandaria 5 à Sec in Centro Comercial Central Shopping, Campo 24 de Agosto. All are closed Sunday.

Medical Services There are *farmácias* everywhere; see the listings in *Público*, or call ☎ 118 for a list of places open 24 hours. Hospital Geral de Santo António (☎ 200 52 41 day, ☎ 200 73 54 night), Rua Vicente de José Carvalho, has some English-speaking staff. There's also a children's hospital, Hospital Maria Pia (☎ 609 33 27), at Rua da Boavista 82.

Emergency The police station (☎ 200 68 21) is on Rua Augusto Rosa.

Dangers & Annoyances Porto has plenty of dimly lit alleys that are best avoided after dark, in particular in the riverside areas off Rua Nova da Alfândega and Avenida de Gustavo Eiffel. Even the most central parks and squares such as Praça de Gomes Teixeira and Praça da Batalha have their share of weirdos, drunks and oddballs. Solo women travellers might feel uncomfortable taking a lunchtime picnic. São Bento train station and the Ribeira district are other areas where you might not want to be alone late at night.

Stay away from the appallingly filthy beach at Foz do Douro. You won't find a really clean beach until you reach Vila do Conde (26km to the north) or Ovar (40km to the south).

Torre dos Clérigos

One of the best places to get your bearings and photographs of the city is this 75m-high Baroque tower on Rua dos Clérigos, west of Praça da Liberdade. The Italian architect Nicolau Nasoni designed both the 240-step tower and the adjoining oval-shaped Igreja dos Clérigos in the mid-18th century. The tower is open daily from 10.30 am to noon and 2 to 5 pm; admission costs 100$00.

Sé

This fortress of a cathedral dominates central Porto from high ground above São Bento station. It was founded in the 12th

DOURO

Porto as World Heritage

In 1996 UNESCO approved the designation of the decaying medieval heart of Porto, roughly within its 14th century walls, as a World Heritage Site. The demarcated zone reaches from the Torre dos Clérigos and São Bento station to the Sé and down to the Cais da Ribeira. Also included are the Ponte de Dom Luís and the Mosteiro da Serra do Pilar in Vila Nova de Gaia.

A wider protective buffer zone, where the government has prohibited any new development, takes in the Igreja do Carmo area, Avenida dos Aliados, additional upstream and downstream riverfront areas, and the entire amphitheatre of port-wine lodges in Vila Nova de Gaia.

Many *portoenses* seem genuinely surprised and delighted that their stubborn, nose-to-the-grindstone city has been given an international pat on the back for its cultural assets. Others have seized the opportunity for a good sprucing up, and the historical zone has sprouted scaffolding and cranes.

A further jewel in this crown has been the designation of Porto as the European City of Culture for the year 2001, jointly with Rotterdam in the Netherlands. On tap for 2001 is yet more restoration in the historical centre, and a gala programme of cultural events.

CENTRAL PORTO

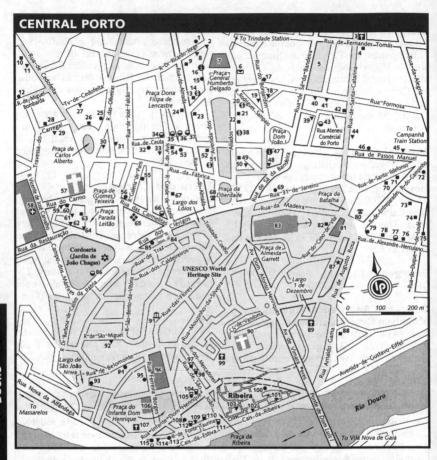

century but rebuilt a hundred years or so later and extensively altered in the 18th century. Only a Romanesque rose window and the 14th century gothic cloisters remain from its earlier incarnation; the rest is mostly Baroque, including a loggia on the northern wall (which, along with the surviving frescoes, chancel gates and sacristy door, is the work of Nicolau Nasoni) and much of the interior.

There's little that's really memorable here, though the 17th century silver altarpiece is worth a look. Best of all is the upper storey of the cloisters (reached via a Nasoni-designed stairway), decorated with 18th century azulejos and affording some fine views.

The cathedral is open daily except Sunday from 9 am to 12.30 pm and 2 to 6 pm. Admission to the cloisters costs 250$00.

Ribeira

The riverside Ribeira district is the most alluring part of Porto, a window onto the city's past, with shadowy lanes, grimy cobbled passages and boats at the quayside

CENTRAL PORTO

PLACES TO STAY
4 Pensão do Norte
9 Pensão e Restaurante Europa
10 Pensão-Residencial Estoril
13 Residencial Vera Cruz
21 Residencial Paulista
22 Pensão Chique
23 Pão de Açucar
24 Pensão Porto Rico
26 Pensão São Marino
28 Hospedaria do Carregal
42 Grande Hotel do Porto
49 Residencial Universal
52 Residencial dos Aliados
54 Hotel Infante de Sagres
63 Pensão-Residencial Douro
67 Residencial União
70 Residencial Belo Horizonte
71 Residencial Santo André
73 Pensão Aviz
74 Residencial Afonso
75 Pensão Residencial
   Henrique VIII
76 Residencial Antígua
78 Residencial Dom Filipe I
82 Pensão Mondariz
88 Pensão Astória

PLACES TO EAT
2 Café Metro da Trindade
5 Mercado do Bolhão
8 Minipreço
11 Confeitaria Rian
18 Conga Casa das Bifanas
19 Pedro dos Frangos
27 Pão de Ló Margaridense
29 Adega do Carregal
30 Restaurante Carlos Alberto
31 Solar Moinho de Vento
33 Aviz Salão de Cha
39 Restaurante Abadia
40 Confeitaria do Bolhão
41 A Pérola do Bolhão
44 Café Majestic
45 Restaurante Tripeiro
48 Café & Restaurante
   A Brasileira

50 Restaurante e Adega Flor
   dos Congregados
59 Restaurante A Tasquinha
61 Casa Zé Bota
62 Casa Leonor
64 Ervanário C Soares
92 Restaurante O Oriente
   do Porto
101 Taverna do Bebobos
102 Casa Filha da Mãe Preta
103 Restaurante da Alzira
109 Casa Cardoso
114 Restaurante Mal
   Cozinhado

OTHER
3 Capela das Almas
6 Main Post Office
7 Câmara Municipal
12 Lavandaria Olimpia
14 Intercontinental
   Currency Exchange
15 Intercyber
16 Municipal Turismo
17 Casa Januário
20 Portocâmbios
   Currency Exchange
32 Jumbo Expresso
34 IASA Office & Bus Stop
35 REDM Office & Bus Stop
36 AV Minho Office &
   Bus Stop
37 João Terreira das Neves
   Office & Bus Stop
38 Foreign Exchange Machine
43 Rodonorte Bus Terminal
47 ICEP Turismo
51 Foreign Exchange Machine
53 Livraria Porto Editora
55 Livraria ASA
56 Livraria Lello e Irmão
57 Igreja do Carmo
58 Hospital Geral de
   Santo António
60 Garrafeira do Carmo
65 Centro Comercial
   Clérigos Shopping

66 Renex Office &
   Bus Stop
68 Portugal Telecom;
   Internet Quiosque
69 Livraria Bertrand
72 TIAC Travel Agency
77 Rede Expressos
   (at Paragem Atlântico)
80 Portugal Telecom;
   Internet Quiosque
81 Teatro Nacional de
   São João
83 São Bento Train Station
84 Igreja dos Clérigos;
   Torre dos Clérigos
85 Casa Oriental
86 Airport Bus Stop (Day)
87 Police Station
89 Igreja de Santa Clara
90 Sé
91 Santa Casa da Misericórdia
95 Instituto do Vinho do Porto
96 Mercado Ferreira Borges
   Exhibition Hall
99 Igreja dos Grilos
100 Ribeira Negra Mural
106 Palácio da Bolsa
107 Igreja de São Francisco
108 Casa do Infante
113 Arte Facto
115 Lavandaria São Nicolau

ENTERTAINMENT
1 Cinema Trindade
25 Auditório Nacional
   Carlos Alberto
46 Coliseu do Porto
79 Cinema Batalha
93 O Fado Restaurante Típico
94 Teatro de Belomonte
97 Academia
98 Ribeirinha
104 Real Feytoria Bar
105 Ryan's Irish Pub
110 Anikibóbó
111 Meia-Cave
112 Está-se Bem

DOURO

(mostly for show or for tourist jaunts now, though this barely alters its appeal). Despite the bars, trendy restaurants and flocks of tourists it remains modest, easygoing and largely ungentrified.

Henry the Navigator is said to have been born in the Ribeira, in the so-called **Casa do** **Infante** on Rua da Alfândega. The building now serves as an historical archive and exhibition hall.

Palácio da Bolsa
The neoclassical Bolsa (Stock Exchange), facing Praça do Infante Dom Henrique, is a

splendidly pompous monument to Porto's past and present money merchants. It took 68 years to build (1842-1910) and is now the headquarters of the city's Commercial Association.

Just inside is the glass-domed **Great Hall**, wallpapered with international coats of arms, where the stock exchange once operated. You can see this from the entrance hall but it pales against many of the rooms deeper inside; to visit these you must join a guided tour. The undisputed highlight is a stupendous ballroom called the **Salão Árabe** (Arabian Hall), which took 18 years to complete and imitates in style the Alhambra at Granada. Its gilded stucco (18kg of gold was used) and intricate decoration include Arabic inscriptions glorifying Dona Maria II, who commissioned the building.

From April to October tours set off about every 20 minutes from 9 am to 6.40 pm on weekdays, and every half-hour (except over lunchtime) on weekends and holidays; the rest of the year, tours run every half-hour (except over lunchtime) daily. Individuals pay 700$00 and can usually join any group. For information call ☎ 339 90 00.

Igreja de São Francisco

You wouldn't guess by looking at it but this plain-faced Gothic church beside the Bolsa houses one of the country's most incredible displays of Baroque and Rococo gilt decoration. Nearly 100kg of gold leaf adorns the foliage and the dozens of carved figures covering the altars, pillars and ceiling. The extravagance was obviously too much for devotees: the church no longer holds services and is packed instead with tour groups.

There's a boring museum in the catacombs below the church. It contains a few ecclesiastical furnishings from the Franciscan monastery which once stood on the site, and a pit full of human bones dating from the 19th century (there are creepier ossuary chapels in Évora and Faro). The church and museum are open daily from 9 am to 5 pm (closed Sunday from November through March). Admission costs 500$00.

Igreja de Santa Clara

East of the Sé on Largo 1 de Dezembro, this church was part of a 15th century Franciscan convent. Gothic in shape and with a fine Renaissance portal, its interior is – like that of the Igreja de São Francisco – dense with carved and gilded woodwork.

Santa Casa da Misericórdia

Hidden away in what is now a museum at Rua das Flores 15 is the superb but anonymous Renaissance painting known as *Fons Vitae* (Fountain of Life), showing Dom Manuel I and his family around a fountain of blood from the crucified Christ. The museum is open weekdays from 9 am to 12.30 pm and 2 to 5.30 pm. Admission costs 300$00.

Azulejos

Porto is adorned with some fine, and sometimes startlingly big, azulejos. In the entrance hall of São Bento station several immense panels painted in 1930 by Jorge Colaço depict scenes ranging from daily life to historic battles (other train stations serving as azulejo art galleries are at Aveiro in Beira Litoral and Pinhão in Douro Alto).

The largest and most intricate panel, created in 1912 by Silvestre Silvestri and illustrating the legend of the founding of the Carmelite order, covers an outside wall of the **Igreja do Carmo** on Praça de Gomes Teixeira. Another church covered in blue tiles – in traditional style but dating from the start of the 20th century, by Eduardo Leite – is the **Capela das Almas** on Rua de Santa Catarina. Five 18th century panels by Vital Rifarto decorate the gothic cloisters of the Sé.

Newest of the lot is a long, multicoloured tile mural called *Ribeira Negra* by Júlio Resende, completed in 1987 and depicting life in the old Ribeira district. Appropriately, it's in the Ribeira, a few lanes back from the river.

Museu Nacional Soares dos Reis

Porto's most important museum is housed in the former Palácio das Carrancas on Rua de Dom Manuel II. This grand 18th century neoclassical mansion, once the home of a wealthy Jewish family, was later sold to Dom Pedro V. During the Peninsular War the French general Marshal Soult set up his headquarters here but was evicted so suddenly by troops under the future Duke of Wellington that he left an unfinished banquet behind, which the Duke and his officers duly polished off.

Transformed into a museum in 1940, its most notable items are works by the 19th century sculptor Soares dos Reis (see especially his famous *O Desterrado*, The Exile) and his pupil Teixeira Lopes, and the naturalistic paintings by the 19th century artists of the so-called Porto school, Henrique Pousão and Silva Porto. There's also a fine collection of Bohemian glass and Vista Alegre porcelain.

The museum (☎ 339 37 70) is open from 10 am to 12.30 pm and 1.30 to 6 pm; it's closed all day Monday and on Tuesday morning. Admission costs 350$00 (youthcard holders and seniors 175$00) and is free on Sunday mornings.

Jardim do Palácio de Cristal

This modest, leafy park, named after a longgone 19th century crystal palace, is centred on a domed sports and exhibition pavilion. In the grounds are gardens, a children's playground, a pond, and roving peacocks and small animals. The pavilion houses a reasonable self-service restaurant. The park is open daily from 8 am to 9 pm (7 pm from October to March). The main entrance is on Rua de Dom Manuel II.

Museu Romántico

On the western side of the Jardim do Palácio de Cristal at Rua Entre Quintas 220 is Quinta da Macieirinha, where the abdicated King of Sardinia, Carlos Alberto, lived in 1849.

It's now a 'Romantic Museum' (☎ 609 11 31) of marginal interest, featuring the king's belongings among dainty furnishings. It's open Tuesday to Saturday from 10 am to noon and 2 to 5.30 pm, and on Sunday from 2 to 6 pm; admission costs 150$00 (youthcard holders and seniors 75$00). The Solar do Vinho do Porto (see the boxed text under Entertainment later in this section) is in the same building.

Casa de Serralves & Parque de Serralves

The Fundação de Serralves (Serralves Foundation) is a nonprofit partnership between the Portuguese government and over 80 private organisations, founded in 1989 to stimulate public interest in contemporary art and in the environment. Its collection of modern art and architectural design, one of the country's best, is housed in Casa de Serralves, a striking 1930s Art Deco mansion off Rua de Serralves (4km west of the city centre). The landscaped garden there, the 18 hectare Parque de Serralves, is worth seeing too.

The mansion and gardens are open Tuesday to Friday from 2 to 8 pm, and weekends and holidays from 10 am to 8 pm (6 pm between November and February). Admission costs 500$00 (youth-card holders and seniors 250$00) and is free on Sunday from 10 am to 2 pm. Take bus No 35 from Lóios or bus No 78 from the bottom of Avenida dos Aliados.

The collection is displayed in the form of changing exhibitions, so check with the foundation (☎ 618 00 57) or the municipal turismo first to be sure it's not closed for its periodic two week rehanging, when only the gardens are open. A full-scale museum was under construction in the grounds at the time of research.

Museu dos Carros Eléctricos

The Tram Museum, a cavernous former switching-house with dozens of restored old trams, is beside the STCP (municipal transport agency) building on Alameda de Basílio Teles, at the (temporary) terminus of the No 18 tram line. It's open Tuesday to Friday from 2 to 8 pm, and weekends and holidays from 10 am to 8 pm; admission costs 350$00 (youth-card holders and seniors 175$00).

DOURO

Ponte de Dom Luís I

Porto's best known attraction, a hillside full of historic port-wine lodges, isn't even in Porto but lies across the river in the town of Vila Nova de Gaia (see the section following Porto). The Dom Luís I bridge, opened in 1886, is almost reason enough to go there, especially if you have the energy and the nerve to walk across the vertiginous upper deck, which offers spectacular views.

Porto for Children

Although at first sight Porto has little to offer small visitors, there are some attractions to keep them happy. Top of the list is the Jardim do Palácio de Cristal. Parque de Serralves has fountains, gardens and a small lake, and the Fundação de Serralves runs an environmental education programme for children. See the preceding sections for contact details.

Every Sunday morning a *feira dos pássaros* (bird market) materialises along the northern side of São Bento station. In early May each year, Porto hosts an international puppet festival and, though it's mainly aimed at adults, some performances are staged for children.

There are municipal swimming pools on Rua Almirante Leote do Rêgo (☎ 550 66 07), north of the centre, and on Rua Dr Sousa Avides (☎ 57 20 41), east of the centre – though each is about 2km out.

Organised Tours

River Cruises Several outfits offer 'Five Bridges' cruises lasting from 45 to 60 minutes about six times a day in summer, in imitation *barcos rabelos*, the colourful boats once used for carrying port wine down from the vineyards. Climb aboard at Praça da Ribeira on the Porto side, or from near the Ponte de Dom Luís I at Vila Nova de Gaia. Tickets cost 1500$00; children up to 12 years old go free. Some of the companies here also have trips further up the Douro; see the Peso da Régua section in this chapter for details. Turisdouro (☎/fax 375 63 89), in conjunction with the Sandeman port-wine lodge, can also organise trips.

Bus Tours Diana Tours (☎ 377 12 30, fax 379 15 08) runs a daily city tour which includes a visit to a port-wine lodge at Vila Nova de Gaia. You can linger at any of the chosen sights and hop on the next of their buses, which run at hourly intervals except at lunchtime. The tour costs 1500$00 (children from seven to 12 years 750$00). Buy tickets on the bus or at travel agencies and upper-end hotels.

Special Events

Porto's biggest bash is the Festa de São João (St John's Festival, also called the Festa da Cidade or City Festival) on 23 and 24 June, when the whole city erupts into merrymaking: dancing, drinking and hitting one another over the head with huge plastic hammers. Throughout the year there's a stream of cultural festivals; check with the municipal turismo for exact dates. Among those worth catching are:

April
   Festival Intercéltico do Porto (International Celtic Festival)
May
   Tram Parade
   Queimas das Fitas (student week)
   Festival de Marionetas (Puppet Festival)
June
   Festa de São João
   Festival Ritmos (Rhythm Festival of Ethnic Music)
   Noites Ritual Rock (Rock Festival)
July
   Festival Internacional de Folclore do Porto (International Folk Festival)
September
   Grande Noite de Fado (Fado Gala Evening)
October
   Festival de Jazz do Porto (Porto Jazz Festival)
November
   Semana do Cinema Europeu (Week of European Cinema)

Places to Stay – Budget

Camping The nearest camping ground, *Parque de Campismo da Prelada* (☎ 81 26 16), is 4km north-west of the centre on Rua Monte dos Burgos; it costs 580/480/480$00 per person/tent/car. Take bus No 6 from Praça da Liberdade or bus No 50 from

Walk the upper level of Ponte de Dom Luís I.

Vines are cultivated along the Rio Douro valley.

The colourful boats that once took port to market still sit along the quays in Vila Nova de Gaia.

Take your pick from the colourful range of market produce on offer in the Douro, from red hot chilli peppers to pumpkins and all sorts of beans.

Cordoaria (also known as Jardim de João Chagas).

There are three camping grounds across the river, linked by a seaside road (take the Ponte da Arrábida). *Campismo Salgueiros* (☎ 781 05 00, fax 781 01 36), near Praia de Salgueiros, is open from May to September and costs 220/220/120$00 per person/tent/car. *Campismo Marisol* (☎/fax 713 59 42), at the next beach south, Praia de Canide, open year-round costs 200/400/300$00). Orbitur runs *Campismo Madalena* (☎ 712 25 20, fax 712 25 34) at Praia da Madalena, Vila Nova de Gaia; it's open from June to December and costs 710/580/580$00. Bus No 57 runs to all of them from Praça de Almeida Garrett. Note that the sea at these places is far too polluted for swimming.

If everything else is full, *Parque de Medas* (☎ 476 01 61, fax 476 01 62), 25km up the Douro on the N108, is open year-round; it costs 435/1000/330$00 per person/small tent/car.

Hostel Porto's splendid *pousada da juventude* (☎ 617 72 57, fax 617 72 47, Rua Paulo da Gama 551) is approximately 4km west of the centre and is open 24 hours a day. There are doubles (two of them accessible to people in wheelchairs) costing 6000$00 and dorm-style quads, many with river views; dorm beds cost 2900$00. Reservations are essential. Take bus No 35 from Lóios; bus No 1 from the middle of Avenida dos Aliados also comes within a block or so.

Private Rooms There are numerous *dormidas* (rooming house) signs in the neighbourhood of São Bento station and down towards the river. Singles/doubles with shared facilities cost about 2000/2500$00.

Pensões & Residenciais Some of Porto's cheapest hostelries are near Praça da Batalha, a short walk east of São Bento station. Prices in this range don't include breakfast, except where noted.

Pensão Mondariz (☎ 200 56 00, Rua do Cimo de Vila 139) is the best of the bunch in this lane, with singles/doubles starting at 3000/4000$00. Near the Rede Expressos bus station on the noisy Rua de Alexandre Herculano there's a string of residenciais, including the *Dom Filipe I* (☎ 205 78 79, No 384) and the more pleasant *Antígua* (☎ 205 55 19, No 314); doubles with bathroom cost 4000$00 at both places.

On nearby Rua Duque de Loulé, a good bet is *Pensão Residencial Henrique VIII* (☎ 200 65 11, No 168), where bright double rooms with bathroom cost 5000$00; book ahead in summer. Less appealing for the same price is *Residencial Afonso* (☎ 205 94 69, No 233). Two functional, modern residenciais on Rua de Santo Ildefonso offer small doubles with bathroom: *Belo Horizonte* (☎ 208 34 52, No 100) costs 5000$00, and rooms at *Santo André* (☎ 205 58 69, No 112) start at 3500$00.

A hidden gem 10 minutes walk downhill from here is the quiet *Pensão Astória* (☎ 200 81 75, Rua Arnaldo Gama 56). The pensão's 10 elegant rooms, some with great river views, are a bargain at 3000/5000$00, with bathroom and breakfast (book well in advance).

The rambling old *Pensão do Norte* (☎ 200 35 03, Rua de Fernandes Tomás 579), in the shopping district north of Praça da Batalha, offers singles/doubles with bathroom starting at 2500/4000$00.

West of Avenida dos Aliados, singles/doubles with bathroom at friendly *Pensão e Restaurante Europa* (☎ 200 69 71, Rua do Almada 396) cost 2500/3500$00; those at *Pensão Porto Rico* (☎ 205 87 85, Rua do Almada 237) cost 4000/5000$00. *Residencial União* (☎ 200 30 78, Rua Conde de Vizela 62) offers no-frills doubles at prices starting from 4500/2000$00 with/without bathroom.

Further west, near the University, *Hospedaria do Carregal* (☎ 205 55 23, Travessa do Carregal 137) is in a backstreet that's quiet at night. It offers comfortable homey doubles with shared bathroom for 5000$00.

Places to Stay – Mid-Range

Breakfast is included in the price all the places in this section, except where otherwise noted.

Central Good value in this area is brisk, friendly *Pensão Aviz* (☎ 332 07 22, fax 332 07 47, Avenida de Rodrigues de Freitas 451), where singles/doubles with bathroom cost 5000/7500$00.

Residencial Vera Cruz (☎ 332 33 96, fax 332 34 21, Rua de Ramalho Ortigão 14) has smart singles/doubles with bathroom for 5500/7500$00. *Pão de Açucar* (☎ 200 24 25, fax 205 02 39, Rua do Almada 262) is a fine Art Deco residence with rooms starting at 6500/8500$00, including some opening onto the top-floor terrace; reservations are essential.

Residencial dos Aliados (☎ 200 48 53, fax 200 27 10, Rua Elísio de Melo 27) has old-fashioned charm but noisy rooms; doubles with bathroom cost 7500$00.

A row of handsome places on the east side of the Avenida includes *Residencial Paulista* (☎ 205 46 92, fax 600 72 76, No 214), where singles/doubles cost 5000/6000$00. The friendly *Pensão Chique* (☎ 200 90 11, fax 332 29 63, No 206) has small rooms for 5000/6500$00.

Poshest of the lot is *Residencial Universal* (☎ 200 67 58, fax 200 55 10, No 38), with a startling modern interior and doubles costing 7800$00.

North of Avenida dos Aliados

Residencial Grande Rio (☎/fax 59 40 32, Rua do Bonjardim 977) has quiet, comfortable singles/doubles costing 5500/7500$00. At the northern end of Rua de Santa Catarina is a string of guesthouses, including *Pensão Residencial Costa do Sol* (☎ 59 33 44, fax 550 19 51, No 1432), where rooms cost 6500/7500$00, and the businesslike *Pensão Residencial América* (☎ 339 29 30, fax 208 38 62, No 1018) costing 7500/9500$00. Both have free parking.

The extraordinary *Castelo Santa Catarina* (☎ 59 55 99, fax 550 66 13, Rua Santa Catarina 1347) is a late-19th century pseudo-Gothic castle in a palm-shaded garden. Rooms start at 6000/9000$00; those in the castle are small and gloomy, but there are others in a modern annexe. Bus No 20 from Praça da Liberdade and bus No 59 from Cordoaria run to this area.

The child-friendly *Residencial Brasília* (☎ 200 60 95, fax 200 65 10, Rua Álvares Cabral 221) is the best of several rambling guesthouses on this traffic-clogged street. Big doubles start at 7500$00, with breakfast; garage parking costs 800$00 per day.

University Area The prim *Pensão São Marino* (☎ 332 54 99, Praça de Carlos Alberto 59) has comfortable doubles with bathroom, very good value at 6000$00. *Pensão-Residencial Estoril* (☎ 200 27 51, fax 208 24 68, Rua de Cedofeita 193) is similarly priced but skips the breakfast. So does *Pensão-Residencial Douro* (☎ 208 12 01, Praça Parada Leitão 41), above a student café of the same name, where doubles cost 7000$00.

Places to Stay – Top End

At the *Grande Hotel do Porto* (☎ 200 81 76, fax 205 10 61, Rua de Santa Catarina 197), deluxe doubles cost 15,000$00. Top of the range is *Hotel Infante de Sagres* (☎ 200 81 01, fax 205 49 37, Praça Dona Filipa de Lencastre 62), stuffed with antiques and an air of opulence; doubles cost at least 28,000$00.

Places to Eat

Many restaurants are closed on Sunday, and seem to change their minds about it frequently, so call first.

Around Avenida dos Aliados Just east of the Avenida, the rustic *Restaurante e Adega Flor dos Congregados* (☎ 200 28 22, Travessa dos Congregados 11) offers regional specialities, such as *tripas a moda do Porto* (tripe Porto-style), for around 1500$00; some half-portions are available. Many such places also punctuate the atmospheric lanes winding down from São Bento station to the river.

A Load of Tripe

For most of us it's something to be avoided, but Porto folk can think of nothing finer than a rich stew of tripe (cow's stomach). This affection dates back to 1415 (so the story goes), when Henry the Navigator was preparing to sail for Ceuta in Morocco. The loyal citizens of Porto donated their best meat, keeping the offal for themselves and earning the nickname *tripeiros* (tripe-eaters).

Pedro dos Frangos (☎ 200 85 22, Rua do Bonjardim 219) serves good *frango no espeto* (spit-roasted chicken) to hungry crowds. Across the road, **Conga Casa das Bifanas** (☎ 200 01 13, Rua do Bonjardim 320) makes little 250$00 beef sandwiches called *bifanas*; two of them with potatoes on the side makes a good bargain lunch. Just around the corner from the municipal turismo is the glum **Café Metro da Trindade** (Rua Dr Ricardo Jorge), with lunchtime dishes from 480$00 in a clean upstairs restaurant.

At the cavernous, azulejo-lined **Restaurante Abadia** (☎ 200 87 57, Rua do Ateneu Comércial do Porto 22), business types get their tripe right for 2000$00 per dish and up. **Restaurante Tripeiro** (☎ 200 58 86, Rua de Passos Manuel 195) is similarly priced.

University Area Despite the too-folksy décor, **Restaurante A Tasquinha** (☎ 332 21 45, Rua do Carmo 23) is recommended for the attention it gives to regional specialities, with most dishes costing from 1000$00 to 2000$00. The dessert menu is almost as long as the wine list. It's closed Sunday. More modest places on the same block are **Casa Zé Bota** (☎ 205 46 97, Travessa do Carmo 20), serving good fish dishes, and **Casa Leonor** (☎ 200 68 40, Campo dos Mártires da Pátria 58-60).

The newish, quiet **Adega do Carregal** (☎ 208 12 00, Travessa do Carregal) offers garlicky appetisers and good northern dishes costing from 1400$00 to 2000$00, washed down with wines from the cask. Around the corner on Rua de Cedofeita is **Confeitaria Rian**, a plain sweet shop with good service and the best *lulas grelhadas* (grilled squid) in town.

Two other pleasant options are **Restaurante Carlos Alberto** (☎ 200 17 47, Praça de Carlos Alberto), where lunchtime dishes cost less than 900$00, and the somewhat pricier **Solar Moinho de Vento** (☎ 205 11 58, Largo do Moinho de Vento), where tripe is a speciality.

Ribeira An unpretentious place with prices of around 1500$00 per dish is **Restaurante da Alzira** (☎ 200 50 04, Viela do Buraco 3); follow the signs into this back alley. **Casa Cardoso** (☎ 205 86 44, Rua de Fonte Taurina 58), in an old high-ceilinged house, offers a menu of half-portions starting at 750$00 and main dishes costing from around 1200$00.

Riverfront restaurants in the Ribeira tend to be overpriced and touristy; the most congenial of them is **Casa Filha da Mãe Preta** (☎ 205 55 15, Cais da Ribeira 39), with Douro views upstairs, main dishes that mostly cost under 2000$00 and some half-portions under 1500$00. It's closed Sunday. Don't confuse this place with the bleak taverna of the same name, one street back.

The elevated prices at **Taverna do Bebobos** (☎ 205 35 65, Cais da Ribeira 24) are softened by a comfortable old-inn atmosphere. It's closed Monday. **Restaurante Mal Cozinhado** (☎ 208 13 19, Rua do Outerinho 11) is a *casa de fado*, open until 3 am, where dinner with fado will set you back about 4000$00 per head.

Bars around Praça da Ribeira serve modest salads, toasties and other snacks.

Vegetarian Not surprisingly in a city that's famous for tripe, vegetarians are poorly catered for. For relief from too much meat and urban stress, take yourself to contemplative **Suribachi** (☎ 510 67 00, Rua do Bonfim 136), a squeaky clean macrobiotic

DOURO

restaurant open daily except Sunday from 10 am until the food runs out, usually 2 or 3 pm. Fill up for less than 1200$00. There's a health food shop at the front too. Another vegetarian option is *Restaurante O Oriente do Porto (☎ 202 63 98, Rua de São Miguel 19)*, open weekdays from 12.30 to 3 pm in a centre for alternative therapies, a few blocks south of Clérigos and Cordoaria.

Two well-stocked health food shops are *Augusto Coutinho* in the Mercado do Bolhão and *Ervanário C Soares* at Praça Parada Leitão 21-33.

Confeitarias & Cafés Airy *Confeitaria do Bolhão (☎ 200 92 91, Rua Formosa 339)*, opposite the Mercado do Bolhão, has smart service, modestly priced lunchtime specials and a big selection of local sweets, including *pão de ló* (a sponge cake) and *bolo rei* (a rich fruit cake). For the best pão de ló, go to *Pão de Ló Margaridense (Travessa de Cedofeita 20B)*, where cooking methods have hardly changed in centuries.

An unpretentious tea salon is *Aviz Salão de Chá (Rua de Avis 17)*, around the corner from Livraria Porto Editora. Art Deco *Café & Restaurante A Brasileira (☎ 200 71 46, Rua do Bonjardim 116)* has a pavement café and a stuffier indoor restaurant.

Porto's best known tea shop is *Café Majestic (☎ 200 38 87, Rua de Santa Catarina 112)*, where gold-braided waiters will serve you a set breakfast for 1500$00 or afternoon tea for 1100$00. The interior is all prancing cherubs and gilded woodwork; splurge on a coffee (200$00) and have a look around.

Food Markets For cheese, olives, fresh bread, strawberries and more, go to the bustling municipal *Mercado do Bolhão*, off Rua de Sá da Bandeira. It's open weekdays from 7 am to 5 pm (1 pm on Saturday), and is at its best in the morning. The Art Deco shop across the street is *A Pérola do Bolhão (Rua Formosa 279)*, the place for nuts, dried fruit and other quality groceries.

A big *Modelo* supermercado is on the lower level of Centro Comercial Central Shopping (take bus No 78 from Avenida dos Aliados to Campo 24 de Agosto). Smaller *Minipreço* markets are scattered around town; one is just around the corner from the municipal turismo.

Entertainment

Porto is a lively place day and night, with a big calendar of cultural festivals (see the Special Events section). Staff at the municipal turismo can provide a free monthly cultural events brochure, and you'll find similar listings in local editions of the *Jornal de Notícias* and *Público* newspapers, on sale at newsagents.

Fado Porto hasn't got a fado tradition of its own, but among places where you can enjoy the Lisbon or Coimbra versions of 'Portugal blues' into the wee hours are *O Fado Restaurante Típico (☎ 202 69 37, Largo de São João Novo 16)* and *Restaurante Mal Cozinhado* (see under Places to Eat earlier). Both levy minimum charges but a few drinks or a light meal should cover that. They're both closed Sunday. Porto also hosts a fado festival in September; contact the municipal turismo for details and tickets.

Bars – Ribeira Area You'll find Porto's good older bars in the Ribeira, especially along Rua de Fonte Taurina and Rua de São João. Admission charges range from 400$00 to 500$00, except as noted. Take bus Nos 57 or 91 from Praça de Almeida Garrett. Our choices include:

Academia (☎ 200 57 37, Rua de São João 80) – popular student bar; 10 pm to 2 am
Anikibóbó (☎ 332 46 19, Rua de Fonte Taurina 36) – vanguard music, Thursday exhibitions and theatre performances; artistic crowd; 10 pm to 4 am (closed Sunday)
Está-se Bem (☎ 200 42 49, Rua Fonte Taurina 70/2) – low-key bar-café with cheap drinks and no admission charge; 9 pm to 4 am (closed Sunday)
Meia-Cave (☎ 208 67 02, Praça da Ribeira 6) – posh old place with a dance floor and occasional live rock music; 10 pm to 4 am; admission 1000$00

Real Feytoria (☎ 200 07 18, Rua Infante Dom Henrique 20) – rock, pop or Brazilian music downstairs, house upstairs, plus occasional live theatre; young clientele; 9 pm to 2 am daily

Ribeirinha (☎ 332 25 72, Rua de São João 70) – the Ribeira's oldest bar, with live music from Thursday to Saturday; 11 pm to 2 am daily

Ryan's Irish Pub (☎ 200 53 52, Rua Infante Dom Henrique 18) – café-bar serving up Guinness, Irish whisky and Irish tunes; 9 pm to 2 am (4 am at weekends)

Bars – Massarelos The riverside strip near the Jardim do Palácio de Cristal, known as Massarelos, is Porto's newest nightlife zone, with big, well-equipped venues that are siphoning customers away from the Ribeira. Door charges are about 500$00 except for special events. Bus No 1 from Praça de Almeida Garrett reaches all of them; the last bus back to the centre passes by at about 1.30 am. The best of the bars are:

Cerveja Viva (☎ 600 49 88, Rua da Restauração 130) – with a dance floor that jumps to radio hits and Brazilian music; 11 pm to 4 am (closed Monday); admission 1000$00 (men), 500$00 (women; free on Thursday)

Maré Alta (☎ 609 10 10, Alameda Basílio Teles) – on a boat with a dance floor and all kinds of music, including live Brazilian on Sunday; 2 pm to 6 am (closed Monday)

Naif Café (Alameda Basílio Teles 11) – occasional live rock, blues or jazz; 10 pm to 4 am Wednesday to Saturday

---

Solar do Vinho do Porto

The most salubrious place to drink port wine is **Solar do Vinho do Porto** (☎ 609 77 93, Rua Entre Quintas 220), beside the Jardim do Palácio de Cristal. Even novice port drinkers can relax in this posh bar with a riverview terrace: waiters will help you choose from hundreds of varieties (prices start at around 150$00 a glass). It's open weekdays from 10 am to 11.45 pm and Saturday from 11 am to 10.45 pm.

Bars – Elsewhere There's a good beach-front bar at Praia dos Ingleses: **Quando-Quando** (☎ 610 30 94, Avenida Brasil 56) is open daily except Sunday from 10 pm to 5 am. Take bus No 1 from Praça de Almeida Garrett.

Nightclubs – Massarelos Nightclubs are open from 11 pm or midnight to at least 4 am and usually charge 1000$00 at the door. Take bus No 1 from Praça de Almeida Garrett.

Club Mau-Mau (☎ 607 66 60, Rua do Outeiro 4) – everything but punk and metal, live music on Thursday; 11 pm to 6 am Thursday to Saturday; restaurant open 8 pm to 6 am Tuesday to Saturday

House Café (☎ 609 78 89, Rua do Capitão Eduardo Romeri 1) the place to be seen in Porto; house music downstairs, more commercial stuff upstairs; 11 pm to 4 am

Mexcal (☎ 600 91 88, Rua da Restauração 39) – Latin décor and Latin music; 10 pm to 4 am Wednesday to Saturday; admission 1000$00 Friday and Saturday, 700$00 weekdays (men only; women free)

Nightclubs – Elsewhere Most other clubs are well west of the centre.

River Café (☎ 617 11 24, Calçada João do Carmo 31) – on Rua do Ouro; old boogie-down tunes and occasional live jazz, blues and country; 10 pm to 6 am Wednesday to Saturday; admission 1500/1000$00 weekends, 1000$00 weekdays (women free); bus No 1 from Praça de Almeida Garrett

Swing (☎ 609 00 19, Praceta Engenheiro Amáro da Costa 766) – off Rua de Júlio Dinis; one of Porto's oldest clubs, playing everything but rock; 12.30 to 6 am; bus Nos 3, 52 or 78 from Praça da Liberdade

Twins (☎ 618 57 40, Rua da Passeio Alegre 994) – a club, bar and grill with a young clientele; 10 pm to 4 am Wednesday and Thursday, midnight to 6 am Friday and Saturday; bus No 1 from Praça de Almeida Garrett

Vício do Álcool (☎ 610 72 32, Avenida Fontes Pereira de Melo 449) – in the north-west commercial area; a large venue playing general dance music; midnight to 6 am Thursday to Saturday; admission 2000$00, drinks free for women Thursday; bus No 3 from Praça da Liberdade

DOURO

Gay & Lesbian Nightclubs Two clubs to check out are *Bustos* (☎ 205 48 76, *Rua Guedes de Azevedo 203, 1st floor)*, open weekends only from 10 pm to 4 am, and *Syndikato* (☎ 208 43 83, *Rua do Bonjardim 836)*; both are north of the town centre.

Brazilian Music Porto's favourite venue for live Brazilian music is a disco called *Água na Boca* (☎ 610 79 66, *Rua Prof Augusto Nobre 451)*, about 4km west of the centre; take bus No 78 from Praça da Liberdade. It's open Friday and Saturday from 11 pm to 4 am; admission costs 1000$00.

Bars which occasionally have Brazilian sounds include *Real Feytoria*, *Cerveja Viva* and *Maré Alta* (details of all three are in the Bars section).

Theatres & Concert Halls The main venues for classical music concerts, drama and occasional exhibitions are the *Auditório Nacional Carlos Alberto* (☎ 200 45 40, *Rua das Oliveiras 43)* and the *Casa das Artes* (☎ 600 61 53, *Rua de António Cardoso 175)*. Larger scale dance, rock and other performances are usually held at the *Coliseu do Porto* (☎ 205 70 87, *Rua de Passos Manuel)*.

Teatro de Belomonte (☎ 208 33 41, *Rua de Belomonte 57)*, also called Teatro de Marionetas do Porto, puts on puppet shows.

Cinemas Porto has a generous supply of cinemas, often featuring subtitled English-language films. There are multiscreen theatres are those at *Centro Comercial Central Shopping* (☎ 510 27 85, *Campo 24 de Agosto 145A)* and *Centro Comercial Cidade do Porto* (☎ 600 91 64, *Rua Gonçalo Sampaio, Boavista)*. Other central theatres include *Cinema Batalha* (☎ 202 24 07, *Praça da Batalha)* and *Cinema Trindade* (☎ 200 44 12, *Rua Dr Ricardo Jorge)*.

Spectator Sports
Porto's football (soccer) team, FC Porto, is a major rival to Lisbon's Benfica and a frequent league champion. You can watch them at Porto's Estádio das Antas (☎ 557 04

00); take bus No 6 from Praça da Liberdade. Check with the municipal turismo or the local edition of *Público* or *Jornal de Notícias* for upcoming matches.

Shopping
Porto is a great place to shop, even if you don't buy anything: establishments range from funky to chic and there are entire streets specialising in particular items: try Rua Galeria de Paris for fine art or Rua da Fábrica for bookshops.

Modern malls *(centros comerciales)* are multiplying. Big ones are Brasília at Boavista, Cidade do Porto on Rua Gonçalo Sampaio, the underground Clérigos Shopping off Rua das Carmelitas, and Central Shopping at Campo 24 de Agosto.

Port & Wine Port is an obvious purchase, and you needn't go to Vila Nova de Gaia to find it; there's plenty for sale in Porto. Garrafeira do Carmo, Rua do Carmo 17, specialises in vintage port and high-quality wines, at reasonable prices. Other good sources are Casa Januário, Rua do Bonjardim 352, and the photogenic Casa Oriental, festooned with dried *bacalhau* (salted cod), at Rua dos Clérigos 111.

Handicrafts Arte Facto, sales outlet for the Centro Regional de Artes Tradicionais (CRAT, or Regional Centre for Traditional Arts & Crafts; ☎ 332 02 01), offers appealing handmade textiles, puppets, toys, glass and pottery, and stages changing exhibitions. It's in the Ribeira district at Rua da Reboleira 37, and is open Tuesday to Friday from 10 am to noon and 1 to 6 pm, and at weekends from 1 to 7 pm (closed Monday and holidays).

The Mercado do Bolhão also sells basketry and ceramics, and in Praça da Batalha there are jewellery and craft stalls.

Shoes Porto has some great shoe bargains. You'll find *sapatarias* (shoe shops) everywhere, especially along Rua Mouzinho da Silveira, Rua 31 de Janeiro and Rua de Cedofeita.

Speciality Items For cork items, brushes, fishing tackle and more, check out the delightful shops along Rua Mouzinho da Silveira, which runs south-west from São Bento station.

Markets See the Places to Eat section for information on Porto's food markets.

Among the city's flea markets (best visited on Saturday morning) the most rewarding one is at Alameda das Fontaínhas, south-east of Praça Batalha. A touristy market along the Cais da Ribeira is good for T-shirts, woollen jumpers, tacky souvenirs and some traditional toys. A scrawny one full of junk and cheap clothes and shoes is on Calçada de Vandoma along the north side of the Sé.

Getting There & Away

Air International and domestic flights use Francisco Sá Carneiro airport (☎ 941 32 60 for flight information), 20km north-west of the city centre.

Direct domestic links include multiple daily PGA Portugália Airlines and TAP Air Portugal flights to/from Lisbon and a weekly direct Portugália flight to Faro (but none back to Porto). Direct international connections include one or more on most days to/from London, Paris, Frankfurt, Amsterdam, Brussels and Madrid. See the Getting There & Away and Getting Around chapters for more details.

Useful booking numbers include TAP (☎ 0808 21 31 41) and British Airways (☎ 0808 21 21 25) – with calls charged at local rates from anywhere in Portugal – and Portugália (☎ 600 82 80).

Bus – International The main international carrier in northern Portugal is Internorte, a Eurolines affiliate with connections throughout Europe (see the Getting There & Away chapter). Its long-distance coaches depart from the booking office (☎ 609 32 20, fax 609 95 70) at Praça da Galiza 96; bus Nos 3, 52 or 78 run between nearby Rua de Júlio Dinis and Avenida dos Aliados. The booking office is open weekdays from 7 am to 6.30 pm (noon on Saturday), though most travel agencies in town can book their coaches.

The Spanish line Ledesma uses the Rodonorte terminal (see Bus – Domestic) for thrice-weekly departures to Zamora, Valladolid and Salamanca (via Bragança) in Spain. IASA (☎ 208 43 38, fax 205 01 91), Praça Dona Filipa de Lencastre 141, runs five coaches a week to/from Paris via Braga.

Another Spanish line, ALSA, operates a weekly Porto-London connection. Tickets can be booked through the TIAC travel agency (☎ 208 85 78, fax 208 86 05) at Rua do Campinho 30.

Bus – Domestic There are at least five places to catch long-distance coaches to points within Portugal.

With the most direct routes and about a dozen departures daily, Renex (☎ 208 28 98, fax 205 04 01), Rua das Carmelitas 32, is the best option for Lisbon (2000$00). Several Renex buses go on to the Algarve, and there are also frequent connections to Braga. Coaches depart from near the ticket office, which is open 24 hours.

Rede Expressos (☎ 200 69 54, fax 208 76 12) buses depart many times a day for just about anywhere from the Paragem Atlântico terminal at Rua Alexandre Herculano 370. Under the name Rodoviária da Beira Litoral (RBL), Rede Expressos runs buses to Aveiro, Coimbra and other points in the Beiras.

For express connections the Minho, try one of three lines operating from Praça Dona Filipa de Lencastre. Rodoviária d'Entre Douro e Minho (REDM; ☎ 200 31 52) buses run mainly to Braga (about 650$00). AV Minho (☎ 200 61 21) operates buses mainly to Viana do Castelo (about 800$00), and João Terreira das Neves (☎ 200 08 81) serves Guimarães (about 650$00). Weekend services are limited.

Rodonorte (☎/fax 200 56 37), Rua Ateneu Comércial do Porto 19, has multiple daily departures for Amarante, Vila Real (about 900$00) and Bragança (1400$00).

DOURO

Its office is open seven days a week. Santos (☎ 510 49 15) buses run to Vila Real, Bragança and Miranda from the terminal in Centro Comercial Central Shopping; take bus No 78 from Avenida dos Aliados to Campo 24 de Agosto.

Train Porto is a rail hub for northern Portugal, with three train stations. Most international connections, and all IC links throughout Portugal – including the once-weekly Comboio Azul service via Beja to the Algarve – start at Campanhã, the largest station, 2km east of the centre.

Regional (R) and IR services start from either Campanhã or the central São Bento station, near the bottom of Praça da Liberdade. All lines from São Bento also pass through Campanhã. Bus Nos 34 and 35 run frequently between these two stations.

Trindade station, a few blocks north of the câmara municipal, has trains to Póvoa de Varzim and Guimarães only.

At São Bento you can book tickets for any journey departing from any station. São Bento and Campanhã have competent information offices, open daily from 8.30 am to at least 7.30 pm. For telephone information (all trains and all stations) call ☎ 56 41 41 between 8 am and 11 pm daily.

Car One of the best unlimited-mileage daily rates is at City Tour, whose only pick-up point (☎ 941 74 64, fax 941 74 65) is at the airport. Other agencies with low rates are Nova Rent (☎ 610 76 99), AA Castanheira (☎ 606 52 56) and Kenning (☎ 830 08 13). International agencies include Avis (☎ 205 59 47), Hertz (☎ 941 55 41), Europcar (☎ 205 77 37) and Budget (☎ 994 04 43).

Getting Around

To/From the Airport Bus No 56 runs roughly half-hourly between the airport and Cordoaria, via Boavista (310$00; about 50 minutes), from 6 or 7 am to 9 pm. From 9 pm to about 12.30 am the city terminus shifts to the bottom of Praça da Liberdade (with a stop at Praça de Gomes Teixeira by the Igreja do Carmo).

A taxi from Praça da Liberdade to the airport costs about 2500$00, plus possible baggage charges of 300$00. During peak traffic time, allow an hour or more.

Bus Porto's municipal transport agency, Sociedade de Transportes Colectivos do Porto (STCP; information ☎ 606 82 26, 0808 20 01 66 at local rates), operates an extensive bus system from hubs at Cordoaria, Praça Dom João I, and the area around the bottom of Avenida dos Aliados, including Lóios, Praça da Liberdade and Praça de Almeida Garrett.

There is a very out-of-date transport map, but it's hardly worth having. Current route information is available from municipal turismo staff and from STCP kiosks opposite São Bento and Campanhã stations, on Avenida dos Aliados, at Praça da Batalha and at Boavista (all open weekdays from 8 am to 7.30 pm, and Saturday from 8 am to at least 1 pm). Some handy bus routes at the time of research were:

No 1 from Praça de Almeida Garrett: Ribeira district, Massarelos (nightlife area), Tram Museum, (temporary) start of the No 18 tram line, pousada da juventude

Nos 3 or 52 from Praça da Liberdade, No 78 from Avenida dos Aliados: Instituto Português da Juventude and Boavista

Other useful bus routes are noted in the text. Tickets are cheapest if bought in advance from STCP kiosks. Fares depend on the number of zones you will cross: up to three (a short hop) costs 80$00; four to six (to outlying areas) costs 120$00; more than six zones (for example, out to the airport) costs 310$00, this last fare valid for a return journey. Tickets are available singly or in *cadernetas* of 10. A ticket bought on the bus (one way, to anywhere in the STCP system) costs160$00.

Also available are a 370$00 *bilhete diário* (day pass) and a *passe turístico* (tourist pass) valid for either four days (1850$00) or seven days (2400$00). Passes turísticos are about 10% cheaper for those aged under 26. All passes are valid for unlimited trips within the city on buses and the tram. The municipal turismo sells its own tourist pass as well (see the earlier Information section for details).

Tram Porto's trams used to be one of its delights, but only one is left. The No 18 trundles daily from beside the Museu dos Carros Eléctricos out to Foz do Douro and back to Boavista (a 45 minute trip) every half-hour from about 10 am to 7 pm. The fare is 85$00, or you can use a bus pass; the conductor sells day passes. Unfortunately neither end is close to the centre (buses run to each terminus; see the preceding Bus section), though there are plans to extend the line from the museu east towards the Ribeira district and/or back to its old terminus by the Igreja do Carmo.

Dial-a-Ride Cruz Vermelha de Portugal (CVP; Portuguese Red Cross), the Centro Regional de Segurança Social (CRSS; regional social security agency) and STCP jointly operate a dial-a-ride minibus service for disabled people. It's available daily from 7 am to 9 pm. Call CVP (☎ 606 68 72) or CRSS (☎ 600 63 53).

Taxi Taxis are good value but not easy to flag down except at taxi stands. Figure on about 500$00 across the centre, for example from Boavista to Praça da Liberdade. An additional charge is made if you cross the Ponte de Dom Luís I to Vila Nova de Gaia or leave the city limits. You can also call a radio taxi (☎ 507 39 00).

Bicycle Porto is best discovered on foot, although Nova Rent (☎ 610 76 97), Rua do Paraíso da Foz 48, sometimes has mountain bikes and child seats for hire. Take bus No 37 from Lóios.

VILA NOVA DE GAIA

Vila Nova de Gaia mainly serves as an entrepôt for port wine. Since the mid-18th century, bottlers and exporters of this highly prized, highly regulated tipple have been obliged to have their 'lodges', for storage and maturing of the wine prior to shipment, in this enclave across the Rio Douro from Porto. The lodges, now numbering around 60, are crammed cheek by jowl from the waterfront to the top of the steep slope, the oldest and biggest of them sporting huge signs. Most are open to visitors, and many offer tours and tastings.

This is the only reason to go over to Vila Nova de Gaia. Despite its crumbling Georgian façades, the part of Vila Nova down around the lodges is unattractive and full of speeding cars, loitering men and venal kids. Port-wine types and vintages are discussed in the special section on port in this chapter.

Orientation & Information

Some buses cross the lower deck of Ponte de Dom Luís I to the riverfront Avenida Diogo Leite, stopping outside the turismo, beside the Sandeman lodge. This polite office (☎/fax 375 19 02) is open weekdays from 9.30 am to 5 pm between May and October (from 10 am to 7 pm during the rest of the year), and on Saturday from 2 to 6 pm. Staff dispense a map showing which lodges are open for tours, and a list of their hours. The map is of dubious accuracy but you need only say the name of a lodge and local people will point you to it.

Buses running across the bridge's top deck go into Vila Nova's small town centre, awkwardly far above and beyond the lodges. However, a little turismo kiosk (☎ 371 25 87) is open in July and August in Jardim do Morro, right at the end of the bridge. From there you can work your way down through narrow lanes to the riverfront.

Wine Tasting & Tours

About two dozen port-wine lodges are open for tours and tastings on weekdays and Saturdays. In high season (roughly from June to mid-September) the larger ones run visitors through like clockwork and you rarely have to wait more than 10 or 15 minutes to join a tour. Outside the summer months, most will accommodate you more or less on the spot.

continued on page 430

DOURO

PORT

Vinho do Porto (port) is Portugal's most famous export, a wine made exclusively from grapes grown in the Douro valley, fortified by the addition of grape brandy, and matured in casks or large oak vats. It was traditionally produced at Vila Nova de Gaia, across the Rio Douro from Porto, from which it took its name.

History

The first British traders to set up in Porto in the 13th century had no interest in wine. Though their compatriots in Viana do Castelo did dabble with a local brew known as 'red portugal', it was olive oil, fruit and cork they were after, swapping them for woollen cloth and wheat from England and dried cod from Newfoundland.

But in 1667, Louis XIV's protectionist minister Colbert forbade the import of English cloth into France. Charles II retaliated with a ban on the import of French wines into England – a heavy blow for English gents, who were very fond of their claret. English merchants in Viana and Porto saw a chance for big bucks and shipped as much red portugal to England as they could lay their hands on.

Demand grew for finer stuff and in 1678 – so the story goes – two sons of a Liverpool wine merchant decided to investigate the wines of the upper Douro valley. They found what they wanted in a Lamego monastery (Portugal's monks had long been expert wine-makers) and shipped gallons of this new Douro red to England, via Porto. It was probably a rich, sweet wine known as 'priest's port', although the story also goes that they may have added a bit of brandy to the wine so it would travel better (thereby 'inventing' port as we know it today). In fact the addition of brandy to arrest fermentation, retain sweetness and raise the alcohol level was not standard practice until 1850, and happened only gradually in order to meet the demand from English consumers.

By the early 1700s the Viana wine merchants were on the Douro trail. Among the first to establish a base in Porto and regularly make the hazardous journey up to the Douro wine country were the founders of today's Taylor Fladgate & Yeatman, Croft's and Warre's.

The English had already clinched enormous commercial privileges in Portugal, thanks to a 1654 treaty between Cromwell and Dom João IV, and the new 'factory' of English and Scots traders grew into the most powerful group of wine merchants in Porto. Despite some competition from American, Dutch and German firms, the English had a stranglehold on the trade. The 1703 Methuen Treaty between England

and Portugal secured even greater profits by reducing the duty on Portuguese wines imported to Britain to a third less than that imposed on French wines.

By the 18th century, port was considered quite indispensable among proper Englishmen ('claret is the liquor for boys; port for men,' proclaimed Dr Johnson). But as supply lagged behind demand, growers resorted to various malpractices (such as mixing port with sweet Spanish wine or heavy doses of brandy) and by 1755 there was a crisis: the English factory refused to buy the wine unless the adulteration stopped.

In 1756 news of the fracas reached the ears of the powerful Marquês de Pombal, who seized the opportunity to loosen the English grip. He founded a state monopoly (Companhia Geral da Agricultura dos Vinhos do Alto Douro, soon to become known as the Companhia Velha or 'Old Company') which had monopoly control over port-wine standards and prices and which specified that only port from a specific region in the Alto Douro (the world's first demarcated wine region) could be exported. This probably included the designation of Vila Nova de Gaia as the place where it was to be stored, aged and bottled prior to shipment overseas.

Naturally the English were outraged. But the improved port wines regained favour in England and by the late 18th century English merchants had settled down again to a business that remained steadily profitable right up until WWII, thanks largely to port's growing popularity in Britain as a working person's drink (mixed with lemonade and drunk in bars by the mug).

When port came back onto the market after the war, it found stiff competition from sherry and cheap 'British wines' (mixtures of imported wine and grape juice). Many Porto firms sold up or amalgamated. Others, notably Sandeman, whose symbol – a black-hatted Spanish don – was a startling innovation, decided the future lay in advertising under the firm's own name.

Today's port market is very different from that of the 1700s. Ironically, the French – indirectly responsible for the English infatuation with port – are now the biggest consumers, drinking three times as much port as the English. The English get through the most vintage port, followed closely by Americans.

Vintage port may gain an even more upmarket foothold following a 1996 Portuguese ruling that bans bulk shipments of port, which will prevent the bottling of cheap blends in other countries.

Right: The best-quality ports are aged in oak barrels for 20 years or more.

Getting Port to Market

Port wine is stored, fortified, lovingly checked and fine-tuned in huge vats or 25,000L oak casks in the port lodges' cool, dark *armazéns* (warehouses). It is then matured in the cask or in black glass bottles, depending on the quality of the harvest.

For centuries, young port wine was brought to Vila Nova de Gaia from the wine estates by river (in February and March, following the autumn harvest). It came in barrels stacked on the decks of *barcos rabelos* – handsome, flat-bottomed boats with billowing square sails. But progress, initially in the form of a railway line down the valley, caught up with them. The last commercial journey by a barco rabelo was in 1956, and tanker trucks now speed the wine down modern highways. Every summer the most river-worthy of the old boats, navigated by company officials, compete in a race. Aside from that they just serve as floating advertisements for the lodges (see Vila Nova de Gaia in this chapter), and add colour to the quays.

Though the bottling and shipping firms still like to project a family-owned image, many have gobbled one another up or are in the hands of multinational companies. Since 1986 it has been legal to store and age port in the Douro valley as well. A small entrepôt has grown up at Peso da Régua, and some *quinta* (estate) owners now market their own 'estate-bottled' products.

To learn more about port wine and the port-wine region, visit the Instituto do Vinho do Porto – a rather snooty private organisation dedicated to maintaining the quality of port wine and the reputation of the port appellation. Several good booklets and brochures are available from the front desk at its headquarters (☎ 02-207 16 00, fax 208 04

Left: You may catch a glimpse of one of these traditional flat-bottomed boats on the Rio Douro.

65), opposite the Mercado Ferreira Borges exhibition hall on Rua Ferreira Borges, in Porto.

The Instituto do Vinho do Porto also has an office in Peso da Régua (☎ 054-32 11 75, fax 32 11 80), at Rua dos Camilos 90.

Types of Port

Cheapest and sweetest are the ruby and red ports, made from a blend of lesser wines, bottled early and drunk young (after about three years). Also blended are semisweet or sweet tawny ports, named after the mahogany colour they gain after years aged in wooden oak casks, and very popular as an apéritif (especially with the French, who drink several million cases of the stuff every year). Look for the label ('10 Years Old', '20 Years Old' and so on) for an indication of the best quality tawnies: the older the better. Vintage character port is a cheap version of a vintage (but with similar characteristics), blended and aged for about four years.

The single-harvest ports range from the *colheita* port, a tawny made from high-quality wines and aged for at least seven years before bottling, to late-bottled vintage (LBV) ports, which are produced from an excellent harvest and aged for four to six years before bottling. The most sublime (and most expensive) port of all – vintage port – is produced in a year of outstanding quality, bottled within two years and aged for up to two decades, sometimes more. This is your ultimate after-dinner drink, always served from a decanter (not because it's classy but because there's always sediment in the bottle).

Little known outside Portugal but well worth trying are white ports, ranging from dry to rich and sweet. The dry variety is served chilled with a twist of lemon.

Port Prices

The main difference in price and quality is between blended ports, taken from a number of different harvests, and vintage port from a single high-quality harvest. All genuine ports carry the seal of the Port Wine Institute.

You don't need to shell out for a whole bottle just to try some port (though a cheap white or ruby only costs about 800$00 a bottle): any café, bar or restaurant can serve you a glass of port for about 150$00. For better quality vintage brews, be prepared to pay at least 2500$00 a bottle, while really good port costs from 800$00 a glass and 4000$00 a bottle.

continued from page 425

Of the old English-run lodges, the venerable Taylor's (Taylor Fladgate & Yeatman), a 10 minute walk up Rua do Choupelo, offers abundant information and a taste of top-of-the-range LBV (Late Bottled Vintage) wine. Among older Portuguese-run lodges, Ferreira (on the riverfront 600m west of the turismo) runs a good tour. Recommended small, independent lodges include Calém, on the river near the bridge, and Rozès, a stiff 600m climb up Rua Cândido dos Reis past the railway, then right at Rua da Cabaça. Sandeman, Osborne and Real Vinícola (see the boxed text on this page) also run tours on Sunday.

If you can't be bothered to cross the river, the Solar do Vinho do Porto, run by the Instituto do Vinho do Porto, is a posh 'pub' where you can taste port from all of the lodges; see the boxed text under Entertainment in the Porto section.

Mosteiro da Serra do Pilar

Vila Nova de Gaia's one architectural monument is this severe 16th century monastery on a crowning hill beside the Ponte de Dom Luís I. The future Duke of Wellington made his headquarters here – probably because of the view of Porto – before crossing the river

and chasing the French out of Porto in 1809. Much of the monastery, including a striking circular cloister, now belongs to the army and is off limits, though you can get into the church – also round – when Mass is sung on Sunday morning. Take bus Nos 82 or 84 via the upper deck of the bridge.

Places to Eat

There's a cluster of grotty eateries on Avenida Diogo Leite in the block west of the mercado municipal, itself about 300m west of the turismo. One good-value exception is *Restaurante Imar* (☎ *379 27 05*), before the market at No 56. It's popular and clean, serving delicious regional specialities at modest prices.

Several of the lodges, including Taylor's, serve lunch in their own posh and pricey restaurants.

Getting There & Away

Bus Nos 57 and 91 from Praça de Almeida Garrett in the centre of Porto (by São Bento station) run via the lower deck of the bridge right to the riverfront turismo (and back); other routes are convenient only for going back. Bus Nos 82 and 84 from Boavista, Praça da República and Praça da Liberdade cross the upper deck to the centre of Vila Nova de Gaia.

VILA DO CONDE

☎ 052 • pop 20,000

Once a quiet ship-building port, and famous for its lace, Vila do Conde is now a popular seaside resort and handicrafts centre. Its beaches, about 2km south of the town centre, are some of the best north of Porto (26km away) and connections from there are easy enough to make a day trip feasible.

The town itself, at the mouth of the Rio Ave, remains charmingly unaffected by the fuss at the beach, offering a far less touristy atmosphere than the overdeveloped resort of Póvoa de Varzim, 4km to the north.

Orientation & Information

The town is completely dominated by the Mosteiro de Santa Clara and its adjacent

---

'The Old Company'

The monopoly company formed by the Marquês de Pombal to clamp down on the port-wine trade was called Companhia Geral da Agricultura dos Vinhos do Alto Douro, nicknamed Companhia Velha, the 'Old Company'. Its direct modern descendant is Real Vinícola (properly, Real Companhia Vitivinícola do Norte de Portugal), the old quarters of which are the grubby pink buildings with 'est 1756' on the outside, west along the riverfront from Ponte de Dom Luís I, just before the Ferreira lodge. Their tours, however, are of their new quarters up on Rua Luís de Camões.

aqueduct. The train station is a five to 10 minute walk across the river from the town centre. The bus station is in the town centre on Rua 5 de Outubro. There's a small turismo, which also sells handicrafts, opposite the bus station, but the main turismo (☎ 64 27 00, fax 64 18 76) is around the corner in an ivy-clad cottage at Rua 25 de Abril 103. From June to September it's open daily from 9 am to 12.30 pm and 2 to 5.30 pm; at other times it's open weekdays only.

There's an excellent market every Friday opposite the main turismo.

Mosteiro de Santa Clara

This fortress-like convent was founded in 1318 by Dom Afonso Sanches but was considerably altered and enlarged in the 18th century. At one time over 100 nuns lived here but after the 1834 decree abolishing religious orders only a few were allowed to stay; the last died in 1893. The convent served as a prison from 1902 to 1944; since then it has been a reformatory for teenage boys. The imposing aqueduct which brought water to the convent from Póvoa de Varzim reputedly once had 999 arches.

The fortified church outside the main complex is the only part to have retained its severe Gothic style. Nuns' tombstones line the path to the church door. Inside are the carved tombs of Dom Afonso Sanches, Dona Teresa Martins (his wife) and their children. A painting in the sacristy depicts the 'election' of an unpopular nun as Mother Superior on the strength of votes from the dead. The remains of a fine 18th century cloister are also worth seeing; its fountain is fed by the aqueduct.

The church is open daily from 9 am to noon and 2 to 5.30 pm; tours are led by one of the boys from the reformatory.

Igreja Matriz

This impressive Manueline parish church dates from the early 16th century. Its ornately carved doorway shows a distinctly Spanish Plateresque style (reflecting the work of Spanish *plateros,* or silversmiths) thanks to its Basque artist, João de Castil-ho. The bell tower dates from the 17th century. Outside the church there's a striking *pelourinho* (pillory), remodelled in the 18th century, with the arm of justice sticking out the top, brandishing a sword.

School of Lace-Making

Long famous for its lace, Vila do Conde is one of the few places in the country with an active school of the art, founded in 1918. Children as young as four or five years old come to learn from local experts such as Maria Beatrix Estrela, who started learning from her mother when she was three. Among a display of finished products is one sample which used 1400 bobbins of thread and took over two years to make. To arrange a visit to the school, on Rua de São Bento, inquire at the turismo.

Beaches

The two best beaches, Praia da Forno and Praia de Nossa Senhora da Guia, a couple of kilometres south of town, have lots of sand and calm seas suitable for families with young kids. Plenty of cafés and kiosks offer refreshments and meals.

Special Events

Appropriately for a town renowned for its handicrafts, a major regional *feira de arte-sanato* (handicrafts fair) is held here in the last week of July and the first week in August.

The biggest religious festival is the Festa de São João on 23 June when a candlelight procession winds through the streets to the beach.

Places to Stay

Camping The closest *parque de campismo* (☎ 63 32 37) is about 3km south of town, near the village of Árvore. It's open year-round and is close to the beach; it costs 750/800$00 per person/tent.

Private Rooms The turismo has a list of rooms, which get snapped up quickly in summer. Most owners prefer long-stay guests.

Pensões & Residenciais

The popular *Le Villageois* (☎ *63 11 19, Praça da República 94*) has clean, quiet doubles with bathroom for about 6000$00. A few doors west is *Residencial O Manco d'Areia* (☎*/fax 63 17 48, Praça da República 84*), where sparsely furnished but quiet singles/doubles cost 3000/4000$00 without bathroom and 4000/6000$00 with; the owner speaks English. *Pensão Patarata* (☎ *63 18 94, Cais das Lavandeiras 18*) is a cute riverside house where doubles with bathroom cost around 6000$00, and there's a restaurant.

The best upmarket choice is the central *Estalagem do Brasão* (☎ *64 20 16, Avenida Dr João Canavarro*), where elegant doubles cost 12,800$00 including breakfast.

Places to Eat

One of Portugal's better bargains is a *churrasqueira* (grill) called *Paul'Ana* (☎ *63 26 98, Avenida Dr João Canavarro 134*), two blocks west of the turismo and across the street, a 10 minute walk from Praça da República. *Feijoada* (pork and broad bean stew), *vitela estufada* (veal stew), grilled sardines and other dishes all cost 1200$00 (half-portions cost 700$00) and beer and wine are on tap. Service is swift but there are only a dozen counter seats, so get there by 7.30 pm or expect to wait.

The restaurants at *Le Villageois* and *Pensão Patarata* are popular with locals. Other options can be found along the riverside and on Rua 5 de Outubro.

Shopping

The Centro de Artesanato (Handicrafts Centre) on Rua 5 de Outubro is the best place to pick up pottery, wooden toys, basketry, embroidered linen and, of course, lace. Local lace-makers sometimes work here too.

The Friday market sells everything from woollen socks and lace collars to freshly made brown bread.

Getting There & Away

AV Minho's Porto to Viana do Castelo express coaches stop here up to 14 times a day (less frequently at weekends). Vila do Conde is also on the Porto to Vila Nova de Famalição railway line; trains leave at least hourly from Porto's Trindade station on the 50 minute run.

AMARANTE

☎ 055 • pop 15,000

This gracious town, which straddles the Rio Tâmega on a handsome, historical stone bridge, is a place to visit just for the setting. The river is dotted with geese and rowing boats, and the banks are lined with willows. Sturdy, balconied houses rise in tiers up the steep banks. Anchoring it all at one end of the bridge are a church and monastery dedicated to the town's patron saint, Gonçalo. Amarante is famous for its eggy pastries – not just the phallic cakes that appear during the cheerful festivals of São Gonçalo.

The most fitting and delightful way to get here is on the narrow-gauge Linha da Tâmega railway (see Getting There & Away later in this section).

History

The town may date back to the 4th century BC, but archaeological records are sparse. Gonçalo, a 13th century hermit, is credited with achievments ranging from the founding of the town to the construction of its first bridge. His hermitage grew into the trademark church by the old bridge.

Amarante's strategic position on the Tâmega and the roads to Porto, Braga and Trás-os-Montes was nearly its undoing in 1809, when the French lost their brief grip on Portugal. Marshall Soult's troops retreated to the north-east after abandoning Porto, plundering as they went. On 18 April a detachment under Générale Loison arrived at Amarante in search of a river crossing, but plucky citizens and troops led by General Francisco da Silveira (the future Conde do Amarante) held them off, allowing residents to escape to the far bank and bringing the French to a standstill. The French retaliated by trashing the upper town and burning much of it to the ground, but it was two weeks before they managed

AMARANTE

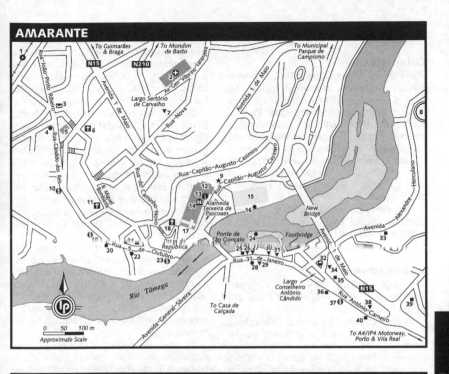

AMARANTE

PLACES TO STAY
20   Albergaria Dona Margaritta
25   Residencial Estoril
28   Casa Zé de Calçada
33   Casa da Cerca d'Além
35   Residencial A Raposeira
36   Residencial Príncipe
39   Hotel Residencial Amaranto
40   Hotel Navarras

PLACES TO EAT
7   Restaurante A Taberna
26   Restaurante Lusitania
27   Restaurante Zé de Calçada
29   Kilowat
30   Tinoca

31   Café-Restaurante Beira-
     Tâmega
34   Restaurante A Quelha
38   Adega Regional de Amarante

OTHER
1   Train Station
2   Hospital
3   Post Office
4   Pharmacy
5   Solar dos Magalhães
6   Igreja da Misericórdia
8   Praça de Touros
9   Police Station
10   Bank & ATM
11   Igreja de São Pedro

12   Câmara Municipal
13   Turismo
14   Museu Amadeo de Souza
     Cardoso
15   Mercado Municipal
16   Boat Rental
17   Igreja de São Gonçalo;
     Mosteiro de São Gonçalo
18   Igreja de São Domingos
19   Bank & ATM
21   Telephone Office
22   Pharmacy
23   Bank & ATM
24   Boat Rental
32   Rodonorte Bus Station
37   Bank & ATM

DOURO

to trick their way across. Loison withdrew from the area about a week later and the French were soon in full retreat across the Minho and Trás-os-Montes.

Amarante has also suffered frequent natural invasions by the Tâmega. Little *cheia* (high-water level) plaques in Rua 31 de Janeiro and Largo Conselheiro António

Cândido tell the harrowing story. The last big flood was in 1962.

Orientation

The Tâmega, which flows to the south-west through the middle of town, is spanned by the old Ponte de São Gonçalo and a huge modern highway bridge upstream. Planted on Praça da República at the western end of the Ponte de São Gonçalo are the Igreja and Mosteiro de São Gonçalo. In the former cloisters behind the monastery are the câmara municipal and the turismo, facing east onto the market square, Alameda Teixeira de Pascoaes.

Buses stop in Largo Conselheiro António Cândido, 300m east of the bridge. The small train station is an 800m walk northwest of the Ponte de São Gonçalo.

Information

The helpful turismo (☎ 43 22 59) is open daily from 9.30 am to noon and 2 to 7 pm (6 pm in winter).

There are several banks with ATMs along Rua 5 de Outubro and at least one on the other side of the river on Rua António Carneiro. The telephone office is a short walk up Rua 5 de Outubro from Praça da República.

There's a tiny post office near the train station on Rua João Pinto Ribeiro.

The hospital (☎ 43 76 31) is on Largo Sertório de Carvalho. The police station (☎ 43 20 15) is at the top of Alameda Teixeira de Pascoaes, near the turismo.

The biggest days at the mercado municipal, just east down the hill from the turismo, are Wednesday and Saturday.

Ponte de São Gonçalo

The granite São Gonçalo Bridge is Amarante's visual centrepiece, and a historical symbol (the defence against the French is marked by a plaque at the south-east end). It also offers one of the best views of town. The original bridge, allegedly built at Gonçalo's urging in the 13th century, collapsed in a flood in 1763; this one was completed in 1790.

Igreja de São Gonçalo & Mosteiro de São Gonçalo

The Monastery of São Gonçalo and its prominent, rather dour church, which is topped with a brick-red cupola, were founded in 1540 by João III, though the buildings weren't finished until 1620.

Beside the church's multitiered, Italian Renaissance side portal (featuring a carved figure of Gonçalo in a niche) is an arcaded gallery with 17th century statues of Dom João and the other kings who ruled while the monastery was under construction: Sebastião, Henrique and Felipe I. The bell tower was added in the 18th century.

Inside are a finely carved and gilded Baroque altar and pulpits, an organ casing held up by three giants, and Gonçalo's tomb in a tiny chapel to the left of the altar. Gonçalo is also the patron saint of marriages and tradition has it that the not-so-young-anymore in search of a mate will have their wish granted within a year if they touch the statue on the tomb. Its limestone toes, fingers and face have been all but kissed and rubbed away.

Through the north portal is the peaceful Renaissance cloister – two cloisters actually, one still attached to the church and the other now occupied by the town hall.

The church is open daily from 8 am to 6 pm.

Other Churches

Up the switchback path and steps beside São Gonçalo is the round, 18th century Igreja de São Domingos, with a little museum of church furnishings that never seems to be open. Up on Rua Miguel Bombarda, the Baroque-fronted Igreja de São Pedro has a nave decorated with 17th century blue and yellow azulejos.

Museu Amadeo de Souza Cardoso

In one of the monastery's cloisters facing the market square is a delightful, eclectic collection of contemporary art, a surprise in such a small town; it's also a bargain at only 200\$00 (students, youth-card holders and

Souza Cardoso

Amarante's Amadeo de Souza Cardoso (1887-1918) is probably the best known Portuguese artist of the 20th century. A friend of Modigliani and a student of Cézanne during his eight years in Paris, he bucked the trend among his contemporaries, abandoning naturalism for cubism and his own home-grown variety of impressionism. He died of tuberculosis at the age of 31.

seniors 100$00; free for kids aged 15 or under). It's named for and dominated by Amarante's favourite son Souza Cardoso, with his sketches, cartoons, portraits and abstracts. But there's more: don't overlook the very still portraits and landscapes of António Carneiro, and Jaime Azinheira's touching *Escultura*. Upstairs are Roman pottery, millstones and tools.

The museum is open daily except Monday from 10 am to 12.30 pm and 2 to 5.30 pm (last admission at noon and 5 pm). At the rear of the ground floor is a small, well-thumbed Gulbenkian Library.

Solar dos Magalhães
A stark, uncaptioned memento of the 'French fortnight' is this burned-out skeleton of an old manor house above Rua Cândido dos Reis, near the train station.

Casa de Calçada
Behind high walls at the south-eastern end of Ponte de São Gonçalo is Casa de Calçada, the manor house and estate of a prominent local family (who apparently own most of Rua 31 de Janeiro, once part of the estate). There were plans (and some site work) to build a five star hotel here, but that has been suspended and the grounds are currently closed to the public.

Activities
You can potter about on the peaceful Rio Tâmega in paddle boats or rowing boats, which are available for hire along the riverbank between the old and new bridges, accessible from below the market or via a narrow walkway from the southern bank. Follow the *barcos e gaivotas* signs. There are several beaches upstream, but the river is pretty polluted.

Special Events
Amarante lets its hair down during the Festas de Junho, held on the weekend of the first Saturday in June. There's an all-night drum competition (the winners are the ones who last the longest), a livestock fair, a children's parade, a handicrafts market, bullfights and fireworks, all rounded off with a procession from the Igreja de São Gonçalo. This is also a *romaria* (pilgrimage festival) in honour of São Gonçalo. The town gets into the spirit of things during the previous week too, with concerts, exhibitions and elaborate street lighting. Not surprisingly, accommodation is hard to find at this time.

During the Festas de Junho (and on São Gonçalo's day, 13 January), unmarried men and women swap little phallic pastry cakes called *falus de Gonçalo* or *bolos de Gonçalo*, a delightfully frank tradition that's probably descended from a pre-Christian fertility rite. Gonçalo is the patron saint of marriages, and this is the time to pray for a partner.

Places to Stay
Except during the Festas de Junho, there's plenty of accommodation, most of it overpriced. Try to avoid rooms overlooking the street, which tend to be noisy.

Camping A big new municipal *parque de campismo* (☎ 43 21 33) has recently opened about 1.5km upstream from the town, replacing the pokey but cheaper and more convenient camping ground near the market. Typical rates are 450/200/200$00 per person/tent/car.

Residenciais Two threadbare residenciais face one another across Largo Conselheiro

DOURO

António Cândido near the bus station. Both the *A Raposeira* (☎ *43 22 21, No 41)* and the *Príncipe* (☎ *43 29 56, No 78)* have doubles costing about 4500$00 with shower or 6000$00 with bathroom and toilet, plus their own restaurants and snack bars.

More comfortable, romantic and pricey is *Residencial Estoril* (☎ *43 12 91, Rua 31 de Janeiro)*, where a street-facing double with bathroom costs 6000$00 and one with a balcony over the river costs 7000$00, all including breakfast.

Hotels The best hotel bargain is the small, polite *Albergaria Dona Margaritta* (☎ *43 21 10, fax 43 79 77, Rua Cândido dos Reis 53)*, west of the Ponte de São Gonçalo. Air-conditioned doubles with bathroom and TV cost 7000$00 on the street side (8000$00 on the river side), including breakfast.

Uphill from the bus station is *Hotel Navarras* (☎ *43 10 36, fax 43 29 91, Rua António Carneiro)*, with a swimming pool and spotless, boring singles/doubles for 8500/10,500$00 including breakfast.

Singles/doubles at the *Hotel Residencial Amaranto* (☎ *44 92 06, fax 42 59 49)*, on the corner of Avenida 25 de Abril and Avenida 1 de Maio, cost 7600/9300$00.

Turihab *Casa Zé de Calçada* (☎ *42 20 23, Rua 31 de Janeiro)*, a former townhouse oddly categorised as 'Turismo Rural', has a few elegant doubles costing upwards of 8500$00, but street noise destroys the atmosphere. Check-in is at the restaurant of the same name across the street.

Better value and more peaceful are several converted manor houses around Amarante, including *Casa da Cerca d'Além* (☎ *43 14 49, Avenida Alexandre Herculano)*, where doubles with bathroom, bedroom and sitting room cost about 10,000$00 including breakfast. Inquire at the turismo for details.

Places to Eat

Amarante has at least three cheap, plain, very good restaurants serving regional specialities that would make the town worth a stop even if it weren't pretty. Our favourite place is a mini-adega called *A Quelha*, behind the bus station, where generous half-portions cost less than 800$00 and *petiscos* (snacks), including local *queijo* (cheese) and *presunto* (ham), start at 350$00. Wash it down with a mug of red wine and add your card or poem to hundreds stuck on the wall.

Plainer but equally packed out at lunch is *Adega Regional de Amarante* (☎ *42 45 81, Rua António Carneiro)*, opposite Hotel Navarras. A 10 minute climb above the river through the old town, but worth the effort, is *Restaurante A Taberna* (☎ *43 16 70, Rua Nova)*, open daily from 10 am to midnight, with friendly vibes and first-rate regional cooking.

Rua 31 de Janeiro is lined with eateries, notable and otherwise. *Café-Restaurante Beira-Tâmega* at No 197 is at least cheap: 500$00 buys the *prato do dia* (daily special), soup and a glass of wine. *Tinoca*, at No 137, is a teahouse with local-style pastries and a river view. Most idiosyncratic is a grumpy *tasca* (tavern) called *Kilowat* at No 104, serving sandwiches of local ham, and wine by the mug; it's open daily until about 9 pm. Most dishes at *Restaurante Lusitania* (☎ *42 67 20, No 65)* cost less than 1600$00, except the house specialities of *cabrito assado no Forno* (roast kid) and Porto-style tripe.

There's more style than substance at *Restaurante Zé de Calçada* (☎ *42 20 23)*, at the western end of Rua 31 de Janeiro, where lunchtime courses cost between 2700$00 and 3200$00.

Most residenciais have restaurants of pretty average quality. Those at *A Raposeira*, *Príncipe* and *Estoril* serve half-portions of Portuguese standards for under 1300$00.

Entertainment

There are numerous pubs and bar-clubs on Avenida General Silveira, the downstream extension of Rua 31 de Janeiro. The *praça de touros* (bullring) is east of town on Avenida Alexandre Herculano.

Getting There & Away

Bus Rodonorte coaches on the Porto to Vila Real route stop at the station (☎ 42 21 94) on Largo Conselheiro António Cândido a dozen times a day (less at weekends). Rodonorte buses also run daily to Bragança, Coimbra and Lisbon. Rede Expressos services come through en route to Porto, Vila Real and Bragança once or twice a day; ask at the snack bar of Residencial Príncipe for details. Santos links Amarante with Porto and Vila Real twice daily except Saturday; Santos buses also depart from Largo Conselheiro António Cândido.

Train The journey on the pokey narrow-gauge Linha da Tâmega, which runs from the Douro valley mainline at Livração up to Amarante, takes 25 minutes and costs 150$00 in 2nd class. There are seven to nine trains a day, most with good mainline connections. The journey between Porto and Amarante (about 600$00, five or six trains a day) takes two hours.

Car & Motorcycle Drivers planning to travel between Amarante and Braga should beware the dismal N101; see Getting There and Away under Braga in the Minho chapter for details and alternative routes.

LAMEGO

☎ 054 • pop 10,000

Called the 'cultural capital of the Douro' in turismo literature, Lamego, 12km south of the Rio Douro, is a rich, handsome town surrounded by hills terraced with vineyards and orchards. Though officially in the Beira Alta, it belongs in spirit and tradition to the Douro: the snakey road linking it with Peso da Régua was built by the Marquês de Pombal in the 18th century, specifically so that Lamego's famously fragrant wine could be shipped to Porto. Nowadays that road and bridge lie in the shadow of a giant new IP3 highway bridge and bypass.

Today Lamego's Raposeira sparkling wine (the best of Portugal's few such wines) gives it unique status among connoisseurs. And the stunning Baroque stairway of the Igreja de Nossa Senhora dos Remédios puts it on the cultural map. Well worth a digression from the Rio Douro trail, Lamego also makes a pleasant base for exploring the surrounding countryside and its half-ruined monasteries and medieval chapels.

History

Lamego was considered an important centre even in the time of the Suevi, who made it a bishopric, a status re-established in 1071. In 1143, the country's first *cortes,* or parliament, was held here, confirming Afonso Henriques as king of Portugal.

The town's wealth grew from its position on east-west trading routes and from its wines, which were already famous in the 16th century. Some of its most elegant mansions date from this time, while others date from the 18th century when Lamego's wine production took off commercially.

Orientation

From the bus station, behind the Museu de Lamego, it's a stone's throw to the heart of town, which is dominated by the Sé. The town's main axis, comprising the tree-shaded Avenida Visconde Guedes Teixeira and Avenida Dr Alfredo de Sousa, runs south-west from the Sé.

At the other end of the Avenidas, a few minutes walk from the Sé, an immense Baroque stairway ascends to the Igreja de Nossa Senhora dos Remédios, on top of one of the two hills overlooking the town.

To the north, atop the other hill, stand the ruins of a 12th century castle.

Information

The conscientious regional turismo (☎ 6 20 05, fax 6 40 14) on Avenida Visconde Guedes Teixeira has plenty of information on Lamego and the region. It's open daily except Sunday from 10 am to 12.30 pm and 2 to 7 pm (6 pm Saturday and in winter).

Igreja de Nossa Senhora dos Remédios

This 18th century church is a major pilgrimage site, especially during the Festas de

DOURO

LAMEGO

PLACES TO STAY
1 Albergaria do Cerrado
3 Ana Paula Dormidas
10 Residencial Solar da Sé
11 Residencial Império
13 Pensão Silva
16 Pensão Residencial Solar
   do Espírito Santo
19 Hotel Parque

PLACES TO EAT
6 Casa de Pasto Vitor Pinto
7 Casa de Pasto Albino
   Alves Teixeira
12 Casa Filipe
14 Restaurante Tás da Sé

OTHER
2 Castelo
4 Bus Station
5 Museu de Lamego
8 Turismo
9 Sé
15 Post Office
17 Capela do Desterro
18 Igreja de Nossa
   Senhora dos Remédios

Nossa Senhora dos Remédios (see under
Special Events), when devotees arrive in
their thousands. The church itself is of little
interest, and is completely overshadowed
by a fantastic stairway (similar to the one at
Bom Jesus near Braga), decorated with
azulejos, urns, fountains and statues, which
zigzags up the hill.

Sé

There's little left of the cathedral's 12th
century origins except the base of its square

belfry. The rest, including a brilliantly
carved Renaissance triple portal and a
lovely cloister, dates mostly from the 16th
and 18th centuries.

Museu de Lamego

Housed in the grand, 18th century former
episcopal palace is one of Portugal's best
regional museums. The collection features
some remarkable pieces: a series of five
works by the renowned 16th century Portuguese painter Vasco Fernandes (Grão

Vasco), richly worked Brussels tapestries from the same period, and heavily gilded 17th century chapels rescued in their entirety from the long-gone Convento das Chagas.

The museum is open daily except Monday and national holidays from 10 am to 12.30 pm and 2 to 5 pm. Admission costs 250$00 (free on Sunday morning).

Castelo

Climb Rua da Olaria behind the turismo and follow Rua de Almacave to the narrow Rua do Castelinho on the right, which leads to the castle. What little remains of the 12th century castle – some walls and a tower – now belongs to the Boy Scouts, who made it their local headquarters after a heroic 1970s effort to clear the site of rubbish. Lucky visitors might get a quick tour from one of the Scouts. Nip up to the roof for spectacular views.

The castle is open from June to September, daily except Monday from 10 am to noon and 3 to 6 pm; during the rest of the year it's open on Sunday only, for the same hours. Admission is free, though a small donation is always welcome.

Special Events

The Igreja de Nossa Senhora dos Remédios is the focus of Lamego's biggest festival of the year, the Festa de Nossa Senhora dos Remédios, which manages to last several weeks from the end of August to the middle of September. The highlight is a procession on 7 and 8 September when ox-drawn carts carrying religious scenes parade through the streets, and devotees climb the stairway on bended knee. Less religious aspects of the festival include rock concerts, folk dancing and car racing. The turismo has details.

Places to Stay

Camping The renovated *Parque de Campismo Dr João de Almeida* (☎ 6 20 90, mobile ☎ 0936 98 15 07), 4km south of town at Turissera, costs 200/200/200$00 per person/tent/car. Your next option is a *parque de campismo* (☎ 68 92 46) 20km

south of Lamego in Mezio, run by an organisation called the Instituto dos Assuntos Culturais (IAC; Institute of Cultural Affairs); take any Viseu-bound bus.

Private Rooms The turismo has details of some attractive dormidas. The multilingual *Ana Paula* (☎ 6 30 22, Avenida 5 de Outubro 143) offers doubles costing around 6000$00, plus apartments.

Pensões & Residenciais *Residencial Império* (☎ 6 27 42, Travessa dos Loureiros 6)* offers boring doubles for just 4000$00. *Pensão Silva* (☎ 6 29 29, Rua Tás da Sé 26) has snug doubles with bathroom for 6000$00 – charming but for the tolling of the Sé's bells every quarter-hour! Another place within earshot is *Residencial Solar da Sé* (☎ 6 20 60, Largo da Sé), where functional doubles with bathroom, and some with cathedral views, cost 7800$00 including breakfast. At *Pensão Residencial Solar do Espírito Santo* (☎ 65 53 91, fax 65 52 33, Rua Alexandre Herculano), comfortable, air-con rooms with shower cost 5000/8500$00 including breakfast.

Hotels *Hotel Parque* (☎ 60 91 40, fax 6 52 03) has an unrivalled location in a wooded park by the Igreja de Nossa Senhora dos Remédios; singles cost 6500$00, doubles 10,000$00, including a buffet breakfast. For all the trimmings, *Albergaria do Cerrado* (☎ 6 31 64, fax 6 54 64, Rua do Regim de Infantaria 9), out on the Peso da Régua road, costs a mere 10,500/14,000$00.

Turihab The turismo has details of several properties in the region. Among the closest is the modern *Quinta da Timpeira* (☎ 6 28 11, fax 6 51 76), 3km west of town, with a swimming pool and tennis courts. Figure on 11,000$00 for a double.

Places to Eat

If it's a sugar and caffeine hit you're after, Lamego is awash with cafés. For cheap local specialities (under 1000$00 per dish) you're also spoilt for choice. Behind the

DOURO

cathedral on Rua Tás da Sé are *Restaurante Tás da Sé* (☎ 6 24 68) – if you can resist the pastelaria next door – and *Casa Filipe* (☎ 6 24 28). *Casa de Pasto Albino Alves Teixeira (upstairs at Rua da Olaria 1)* is packed at lunchtime, while *Casa de Pasto Vitor Pinto (Rua da Olaria 61)* is slightly cheaper (almost nothing over 750$00) and adequate. Several grocery shops on this street sell Lamego's famous hams and wines – perfect picnic food.

Getting There & Away

The most appealing way to travel to Porto or other points in the Douro valley is by bus to Peso da Régua, where you can pick up trains along the valley.

Three companies have offices in the bus station. Empresa Automobilista de Viação e Turismo (EAVT; ☎ 6 21 16) operates regular services to Peso da Régua, and runs twice daily to Celorico da Beira on the edge of the Serra da Estrela. Empresa Soares (☎ 6 37 27) runs three buses a day to Porto. Empresa Guedes (☎ 6 26 04) has express coaches to/from Lisbon via Viseu and Coimbra twice daily, plus local services to Peso da Régua and Viseu. Rodonorte and Rodoviária Beira Litoral (RBL) express coaches also stop twice daily en route between Lisbon and Peso da Régua.

AROUND LAMEGO
Capela de São Pedro

This lovely chapel is hidden away in the hamlet of Balsemão, beside the Rio Balsemão 3km east of Lamego. Originally built by the Suevi in the 7th century, it features ornate 14th century additions, many commissioned by the Bishop of Porto, Dom Afonso Pires. The bishop's tomb, supported by angels, dominates the otherwise simple interior.

The chapel is open from 10 am to 12.30 pm and 2 to 6 pm, but is closed all day Monday and on Tuesday morning. It's a pleasant walk from Lamego: from the 17th century Capela do Desterro at the end of Rua da Santa Cruz, head south-east over the river and follow the road to the left.

Mosteiro de São João de Tarouca

In the quiet, wooded Barosa valley below the Serra de Leomil, 14km south-east of Lamego, are the remains of Portugal's first Cistercian monastery. It was founded in 1124 and fell into ruin after religious orders were abolished in 1834.

Only the church, considerably altered in the 17th century, stands intact among the eerie ruins of the monks' quarters. Inside are treasures including the imposing 14th century tomb of the Conde de Barcelos (Dom Dinis' illegitimate son), carved with scenes from a boar hunt, a larger-than-life 14th century granite Virgin and Child, gilded choir stalls, and some 18th century azulejos. The church's most famous possession, a painting by Grão Vasco, was taken away in 1978 for restoration.

Ponte de Ucanha

Just north of Tarouca, off the N226, is the unremarkable village of Ucanha. But follow the lane down as far as the Rio Barosa and this huge 12th century fortified bridge. The chunky tower was added by the Abbot of Salzedas in the 15th century, probably as a tollgate. Stonemasons' initials are clearly visible on almost every block.

Under the bridge are medieval washing enclosures made of stone – one for suds, one for rinsing. They're long since defunct, though village women still use the arch of the bridge to dry their laundry.

Mosteiro de Salzedas

Three kilometres further up the Rio Barosa valley are the ruins of another Cistercian monastery. This was one of the grandest in the land when it was built in 1168 with funds from Teresa Afonso, governess to Dom Afonso Henriques' five children.

The church, extensively remodelled in the 18th century, dominates the humble village around it. Black with mould and decay, it seems past hope of restoration, though students have been conscientiously working here each summer to bring it back to life.

Getting There & Away

From Lamego, EAVT runs buses to São João de Tarouca a dozen times each day and to Ucanha three times a day.

PESO DA RÉGUA

☎ 054 • pop about 6000

This crowded, businesslike town – Lamego's alter ego – at the confluence of the Douro and Corgo rivers is on the western edge of the demarcated port-wine region. As the largest town in that region with river access to Porto, it quickly grew into a major port-wine entrepôt. Its traditional status as capital of the trade has now been lost to Pinhão, 25km upstream.

There's little to see or do here, other than learning about (and tasting) port wine at a local lodge, but Régua, as it's usually called, is a good place from which to visit the wine country, cruise the Rio Douro or ride the Corgo railway line to Vila Real.

Orientation & Information

From the train station, or the bus stops across the road from it, head west and, at the Residencial Império, bear right into Rua dos Camilos, with most of Régua's accommodation and restaurants, then on into Rua da Terreirinha, with shops and the mercado municipal. The older part of Régua is a steep climb above these streets.

The municipal turismo (☎ 22 38 46, fax 32 22 71) is at Rua da Terreirinha 505, just before the mercado and about 1km from the station. It's open daily from 9.30 am to 12.30 pm and 2 to 6 pm (or later) from July to mid-September, and until 5.30 pm on weekdays only during the rest of the year. The area is madly congested on the morning of market day (Wednesday).

Instituto do Vinho do Porto

If you have a real interest in the details of port-wine production, you could call in on the Régua branch of the Instituto do Vinho do Porto (☎ 32 01 30, fax 32 01 49), Rua dos Camilos 90, and pick up an armful of glossy maps and brochures. As with the parent office in Porto, however, it's not really geared up for (nor very interested in) casual visitors. It's open weekdays only from 9 am to 12.30 pm and 2 to 5.30 pm. Nearby are the headquarters of Casa do Douro, the watchdog organisation that supervises all port-wine viticulture.

Quinta de São Domingos

This port-wine lodge (☎ 32 01 00) belonging to Ramos Pinto, one of the biggest port companies, is the nearest to Régua and the easiest to visit, and it offers free tours and tasting. It's just off the Vila Real road, 500m east of the train station. It's normally open daily from 9 am to 6 pm, year-round.

River Cruises

Companhia Turística do Douro (☎ 054-6 28 11, fax 6 44 58) in Lamego and Barcadouro (☎/fax 078-61 62 84) in Carrazeda de Ansiães run cruises from Régua or Cais da Barragem de Bagaúste (just upstream from Régua) to Pinhão and back.

At least three Porto companies operate copycat cruises that start, finish or pass through Régua, including:

Régua-Pinhão-Régua, half-day Saturday, 5000$00
Régua to Porto, all day Sunday, from 12,500$00
Porto-Régua-Porto, all day Sunday (train one way, boat the other), from 13,800$00
Porto-Lamego-Régua-Porto, weekend, from 32,500$00

In order of decreasing prices, operators are Douro Azul (☎ 02-339 39 50, fax 208 34 07), Via d'Ouro (☎/fax 02-938 81 39) and EnDouro (☎ 02-395 64 17, fax 395 64 18). Most cruises run between March or April and October or November. Telephone reservations are suggested.

Places to Stay

A step away from the train station is *Residencial Império* (☎ 32 01 20, fax 32 14 57, Rua José Vasques Osório 8), where singles/doubles with bathroom cost 4500/6500$00 including a big breakfast.

There are several budget options between the station and the turismo. *Pensão Douro*

DOURO

(☎ *332 12 31, Rua dos Camilos 105)* is crumbling, leaky and heavily perfumed, but cheapest at 3000$00 for a double without bathroom. Spartan doubles with shared facilities above **Restaurante Borrajo** (☎ *2 33 96, Rua Camilos 4)* cost 5000$00. **Restaurante O Maleiro** (see under Places to Eat) has basic rooms too.

If you don't mind walking, or have your own transport, try **Residencial Don Quixote** (☎ *32 11 51, Avenida Sacadura Cabral 1)*, 1km west of the turismo, where a single/double with bathroom costs 3500/6000$00. Across the road is **Residencial Columbano** (☎ *32 37 04, fax 2 49 45)*, where air-con rooms with bathroom cost 4500/6500$00. Breakfast is included in the price at both places, and some rooms have river views.

Turihab The turismo has details of some properties in the area. For a complete list of Turihab places in the Douro valley, contact Quintas do Douro (☎/fax 32 27 88).

Places to Eat

Restaurante O Maleiro (☎ *2 36 84, Rua dos Camilos)*, opposite the post office, is a friendly place with dishes from 800$00 and a big wine list. There are other budget places in the adjacent blocks. For more cheer and an upmarket menu, try **Restaurante Cacho d'Oiro** (☎ *32 14 55, Rua Branca Martinho)*, about 150m west of the turismo, where you can splurge on *cabrito no churrasco* (grilled kid) for 1400$00.

Getting There & Away

There are 15 trains daily from Porto (2½ hours; 880$00 in 2nd class) and at least five onward to Tua. Five trains leave daily for Vila Real on the Corgo line. Buses run hourly from the stops opposite the train station to Lamego and Vila Real.

THE DOURO ALTO

The Rio Douro east of Peso da Régua, defining the border between Trás-os-Montes and Beira Alta, is not actually part of the Douro province. It is included here because it's an integral part of the region and because the easiest and most natural way to get here is up the valley from Porto.

The area is dominated by terraced vineyards wrapped around every precipitous, crew-cut hillside, and dotted with the port-wine lodges' bright white *quintas* (villas). Villages are small and cultural sights are few and far between. Come here for the dramatic landscape, the port wine, or just for the train ride, which offers fantastic views once it enters the valley, some 60km east of Porto.

Small **Pinhão**, 25km east of Peso da Régua, is now considered the centre of quality port-wine production. It's surrounded by vineyards and dominated by the large signs of several port-wine lodges; even the train station has azulejos depicting the wine harvest. If you have your own wheels, a 12km hop north-east up the N322-3 to Favaios will reward you with the discovery of a little-known muscatel wine, one of only two produced in Portugal (the other comes from Setúbal).

The only reason to stop at **Tua** is to board the narrow-gauge Linha da Tua railway north to Mirandela. Alas, Mirandela itself is breathtakingly dull, though it has plenty of bus connections onward to Bragança and elsewhere in Trás-os-Montes.

See the Beiras or Trás-os-Montes regional maps in this book for locations of towns at the eastern end of the Douro valley.

Edições Livro Branco's *Rio Douro: Porto – Barca de Alva*, a handsome and useful schematic colour map of the Portugal section of the Douro valley, is available for about 1000$00 from bigger bookshops, at least in Porto.

River Cruises

See the Peso da Régua and Porto sections for information on Douro cruises, including contact details for the various operators. These companies also run boat-up, train-down trips from Porto to Pinhão and back, costing upwards of 17,000$00. Most cruises run between March or April and October or November.

Places to Stay

In addition to a few pensões in Pinhão, there are dozens of Turihab properties in the area, many marketed by a Peso da Régua company called Quintas do Douro (☎/fax 054-32 27 88). At *Pousada Barão de Forrester* (☎ *059-95 92 15, fax 95 93 04)* at Alijó, 15km north-east of Pinhão, renovated doubles cost 20,300$00.

Getting There & Away

Train The finest way to see the upper Douro valley is by train, on a route that alternatively hugs the river and clings to the valley wall. At least seven trains from Porto a day pass through Peso da Régua and on to Tua (three hours from Porto) and four go on to Pinhão (four hours from Porto) 1140$00 in 2nd class.

Two narrow-gauge lines climb out of the valley from the main line, offering slow, enchanting diversions. From Livração the Linha da Tâmega runs to Amarante (see Getting There & Away in the Amarante section for details). From Tua the Linha da Tua ascends for two hours to Mirandela (it once went all the way to Bragança); the Porto-Mirandela trip (four to five trains a day) costs 1230$00 in 2nd class.

Car, Motorcycle & Bicycle Wheeled travellers have a choice of smooth, river-hugging roads from Porto along both banks to Peso da Régua (N108 and N222), and along the south bank (N222) to Pinhão, though at weekends they're crowded with Porto escapees, driving maddeningly slowly or suicidally fast. Beyond Pinhão, the roads climb in and out of the valley. One of the most dramatic valley crossings is on a local road between Linhares and São João de Pesqueira, plunging to the Barragem de Valeira dam so fast your ears will pop.

VILA NOVA DE FOZ CÔA
☎ 079 • pop about 5000

This once-remote town, 9km south of Pocinho, was put on the map in the 1990s with

---

Death in the Douro Rapids

Squeezed into the Douro gorge 9km above Tua, the dramatic Barragem (dam) de Valeira marks the site of the dreaded Cachão da Valeira rapids. Here, in May 1862, Baron Joseph James Forrester, one of the most remarkable men in the history of the port-wine trade, died when his boat capsized.

Forrester came to Porto in 1831 to work in his uncle's firm, Offley Forrester & Co. He became thoroughly involved in the port-wine business and, among many accomplishments, produced the first good maps of the Douro region (in recognition of which he was made Barão de Forrester by the king).

In 1844, 33-year-old Forrester turned his attention to the widespread practice of adulterating port wine with brandy, sugar, elderberry juice and other 'pollutants' – in Forrester's opinion, a practice that had got out of hand. His *A Word or Two on Port Wine*, accusing the trade of encouraging the practice and of corruption among the official tasters of the Companhia Velha, caused a storm of protest.

There certainly seemed to be grounds for his accusations, but his purist approach would have meant the end of port as we know it: without the addition of brandy to stop fermentation, 'port' would simply be a thin, inferior wine. The furore eventually died down, adulteration decreased and the Companhia Velha was itself reformed in 1848. When Forrester met his death (his money belt full of gold sovereigns probably carried him right to the bottom), nearly all of Porto mourned the loss.

DOURO

the discovery of thousands of Palaeolithic rock engravings in the nearby Vale do Côa, the establishment around them of a Parque Arqueológico and the recent designation of the valley as a UNESCO World Heritage Site.

The surrounding area has other archaeological attractions too, and the town itself has a few Manueline highlights. It feels like Spain, in the way that Miranda do Douro does: clean, whitewashed, brisk, orderly and a bit boring. The night is filled with the sound of motorcycles. The hillsides are covered with almond groves and the climate is startlingly Mediterranean if you've just come from the mountains.

Orientation

Vila Nova de Foz Côa extends in a long line from west to east. Buses arriving in town deposit their passengers on Avenida Gaga Coutinho: those from Bragança stop near the twin residenciais Marina and Avenida, and those from Viseu via Pocinho (the nearest train station) stop 300m to the east, opposite the park office.

The town extends another 400m eastward through the pedestrianised Rua Juiz Moutinho de Andrade, homey Largo do Tabulado, Rua Dr Júlio de Moura and Praça do Município.

Information

The centre of things is the striking Parque Arqueológico office (☎ 76 43 17, fax 76 52 57, email pavc@mail.telepac.pt), Avenida Gaga Coutinho 19, open daily except Monday from 9 am to 12.30 pm and 2 to 5.30 pm. Staff are mostly there to shuttle visitors out to the rock engravings, but they do have some telephone numbers (though no prices) for local accommodation.

The earnest municipal turismo (☎ 76 52 43) is so far out of town that it's hardly worth visiting unless you have your own transport; from the park office, you go 1.4km west to a roundabout with a giant Vila Nova de Foz Côa sign, then south for 600m. The turismo is open daily from 9 am to noon and 2 to 5 pm.

Parque Arqueológico Vale do Côa

See the boxed text 'Rock Art in the Vale do Côa' for information about the Archaeological Park.

Although the park area is an active research zone, three sites may be visited, from three different visitor centres – Canada do Inferno from the park office in Vila Nova de Foz Côa, Ribeira de Piscos from the centre (☎ 079-76 42 98) at Muxagata on the western side of the valley, and Penascosa from the centre (☎ 079-7 33 44) at Castelo Melhor on the eastern side. A park museum is under construction at Canada do Inferno.

There is also a private site (owned by the port lodge Ramos Pinto) at Quinta da Ervamoira, with vineyards, wine tasting and a museum featuring Roman and medieval artefacts. This can be included in tours from the Muxagata visitor centre.

Visitors are taken, eight at a time in the park's own 4WDs, for a half-hour guided tour (500$00 per person). Booking is essential – about a month in advance in summer but as little as a few days in winter. There's little hope of seeing these sites without a booking, although other kinds of trips, such as by bicycle or boat, are being discussed. For information or bookings, contact the park office (☎ 76 43 17, fax 76 52 57, email pavc@mail.telepac.pt), Avenida Gago Coutinho 19, Vila Nova de Foz Côa.

The park is closed on Monday, and on Christmas day, 1 January and 1 May.

Sharing the building with the park office is Procôa, a government agency set up to fund private development such as roads, accommodation (including a youth hostel) and shops, in preparation for the expected tourist influx.

Construction is already on the rise in the area. Entrepreneurs have even entered into the spirit of things with a newly named local white wine, Vinho Paleolítico!

Other Old Sites

A Circuito Arqueológico (archaeological circuit) at Freixo de Numão, 12km west of Vila Nova de Foz Côa, includes several ex-

Rock Art in the Vale do Côa

In the rugged valley of the Rio Côa (a tributary of the Douro), 15km from the Spanish frontier, is an extraordinary Stone Age art gallery, with thousands of rock engravings dating back tens of thousands of years. A decade ago nobody knew they were there.

Initial discoveries were made in 1989 in the course of environmental studies for Electricidade de Portugal (EDP) which had proposed to build a huge hydroelectric dam that would have flooded the valley. Surveys revealed an array of ancient sites including four rock shelters with prehistoric paintings. Nevertheless, the dam proposal was approved.

It wasn't until 1992, after construction was underway, that the real discoveries began. Clusters of petroglyphs (rock engravings), mostly dating from the Upper Palaeolithic period (approximately 10,000 to 40,000 years ago), were found by 'rescue archaeologists' at the site now called Canada do Inferno. Once these finds were publicised, local people cooperated in the search for other sites, and the inventory quickly grew.

Battle commenced between EDP and archaeologists who insisted the engravings were of worldwide importance and should be preserved. Only after an international campaign was launched and the socialist government came to power in 1995 was the half-built dam formally abandoned, and the site given official protection as a National Monument. The Parque Arqueológico Vale do Côa (Côa Valley Archaeological Park) was launched in August 1996. In 1998 those stubborn archaeologists got their ultimate reward when the valley was designated a UNESCO World Heritage Site.

Today the park encompasses the largest known array of open-air Palaeolithic art in the world. Several thousand engravings found so far spread for some 17km along the valley of the Rio Côa and its tributaries. Horses, aurochs (ancestors of domesticated cattle) and long-horned ibex (a once-common wild goat which appears in petroglyphs from many parts of the world) figure prominently; some petroglyphs also depict human figures. Since 1995, surveys have been underway to locate Palaeolithic habitation sites as well.

The discovery has challenged existing theories about humankind's earliest art. Smaller open-air sites have been found in France, Spain and elsewhere in Portugal, but nothing on this scale nor covering such a time span. It was probably the valley's resistant schist bedrock and Mediterranean microclimate that saved this site from Ice Age destruction.

cavation sites (Copper and Bronze Age settlements at Castelo Velho, Roman villas at Zimbro II and Rumansil, and Neolithic, Roman and medieval remains at Prazo) and a small archaeological museum (☎ 079-78 91 17) at Casa Grande.

Old Town

Since you've come all this way, walk down to Praça do Município and have a look at the granite pelourinho topped by an armillary sphere, and the Manueline Igreja Matriz with its elaborately carved portal and painted ceiling.

River Cruises

Sociedade Hoteleira (☎ 76 50 00, fax 76 53 04) in Vila Nova de Foz Côa organises six-hour Douro cruises from Pocinho, up to Barca de Alva or down to Vesúvio and back, for groups. Porto-based Douro Azul (☎ 02-339 39 50, fax 208 34 07) runs a weekend jaunt all the way from Porto to Barca de Alva (boat up, train back), costing 45,000$00.

Places to Stay

Two charmless residenciais stand side by side near the Bragança bus stop. Singles/

DOURO

doubles with shower cost 2900/5800$00 at the *Avenida* (☎ *76 21 75, Avenida Gaga Coutinho 10).* This price includes a dreary breakfast in the bar at the front. At the more tranquil *Marina* (☎ *76 21 12, Avenida Gaga Coutinho 4)* rooms cost 4000/7000$00.

A few homes and cafés in the area around Largo do Tabulado advertise *quartos* (private rooms).

About 800m north of town on the road to Pocinho is *Residencial O Retiro* (☎ *76 21 59),* where a double with shower costs 5000$00. A *pousada da juventude* is under construction 600m further on.

Places to Eat
The friendly *Snack Bar–Restaurante A Marisqueira* (☎ *76 21 87, Rua Juiz Moutinho de Andrade)* has a small (verbal) menu of daily specials costing less than 1000$00. They made our day by scrambling some eggs in the morning.

Getting There & Away
Bus Rede Expressos buses stop two or three times a day en route between Bragança (Trás-os-Montes) and Viseu (Beira Alta).

Train Four trains a day run from Porto to the end of the Douro valley line at Pocinho (station ☎ 7 21 69), 9km north of Vila Nova de Foz Côa. A bus meets at least some of them, operating from the stop opposite the Parque Arqueológico office. A taxi to/from Pocinho costs around 2000$00.

PARQUE NATURAL DO DOURO INTERNACIONAL
In 1996 the Portuguese and Spanish governments announced plans to create a new international park, straddling the deep canyon of the Rio Douro along their common border. Though perhaps inspired by the discoveries at Vale do Côa, the park is meant to protect biological as well as archaeological resources there.

The Parque Natural do Douro Internacional is probably the best place in Portugal to observe raptors (birds of prey). Breeding species include the griffon, Egyptian vulture, kite and several species of eagle, some of them threatened.

Among other breeding species of birds in the area are the eagle owl, black stork, alpine swift, great spotted cuckoo and red-necked nightjar.

The development of the park is still in its early stages. The section in Portugal occupies about 85,000 hectares, making it the country's second-largest park after the Parque Natural da Serra da Estrela.

There is no park office, although the largest nearby town on the Portuguese side, Figueira de Castelo Rodrigo (Beira Alta), is a candidate. A temporary contact address for information is Parque Natural do Douro Internacional (☎ 0936-47 01 88), c/o Apartado 34, 6440 Figueira de Castelo Rodrigo.

FREIXO DE ESPADA À CINTA
☎ 079
Just 3km from the Rio Douro where it marks the Spanish border, and a world away from anywhere, is Freixo de Espada à Cinta. Surrounded by wild hills where black kites soar, it was in the 12th century a sanctuary for fugitives and freed prisoners who were allowed to settle here to beef up this strategic area. A century later, Dom Dinis bestowed upon the town its bizarre name ('Ash Tree of the Girth-Sword') when he stopped for a rest and hung his trusty sword in a tree – or so the story goes.

Its only modern claim to fame is blossoming almond trees, which draw Spanish tourists by the hundreds in spring. Otherwise it sees so few visitors that it doesn't even have a turismo. It's a wee bit too far to come from anywhere, but if you do, there are a few delights: an elaborate parish church, a heptagonal 13th century tower, an attractive old town of Manueline houses and a modest silk industry (the finished products are for sale in the town).

Freixo (as it's called) is in Trás-os-Montes, and is about as hard to reach from Bragança as from Porto, but it seems to have more in common with the Douro Alto than with anywhere else.

Orientation

The old town is centred around the Igreja Matriz and the Torre de Galo, with narrow streets winding their way to modern outskirts and the N221. From the bus stop near the main road, take a bead on the landmark Torre de Galo and you'll find everything of interest nearby.

Igreja Matriz

Local people brashly compare the interior of their 16th century parish church to the Mosteiro de Jerónimos in Belém, and there is a passing resemblance, with three naves of elaborate vaulting. The highlight is an altarpiece with 16 panels attributed to the renowned Vasco Fernandes or Grão Vasco (see the boxed text 'Grão Vasco & the Viseu School' in the Viseu section of the Beiras chapter).

Torre de Galo

Above the Igreja Matriz is a keep known as the Cockerel's Tower. Built by Dom Dinis, it is all that remains of the town's medieval defences.

Casa da Bicha da Seda

The House of Silk Worms at Largo do Outeiro 6 is just that: a house where thousands of silkworms munch on mulberry leaves grown in the garden at the back. The silk thread is hand-woven into cotton or linen-backed items, some of which are sold here, or you can check out the weaving room in the arched building by the church where more items are for sale.

To find Largo do Outeiro, follow Rua Sacadura Cabral from beside the Igreja Matriz.

Places to Stay & Eat

There's little on offer in the old town, though you might find someone at home at *Pensão Paris* (☎ 65 21 56, *Largo do Outeiro*), where doubles without bathroom start at about 2500$00.

Restaurante Hospedaria Cinta de Ouro (☎ 65 25 50), south of town on the N221 about 500m from the bus stop, has a few clean doubles with bathroom and TV for 4500$00. This is an adequate place for a bite too, but we prefer the *Churrasqueira Luanda* (☎ 65 21 93), around the corner, where you can have a light lunch for about 1000$00.

Getting There & Away

Four or five buses a day link Freixo with Pocinho, at the head of the Douro valley railway line, a 1½ hour trip. Two or three buses a day also pass through Pocinho en route between Bragança and Coimbra/Lisbon. One or two buses link Freixo directly with Bragança daily, costing about 1100$00.

The Minho

Portugal's north-western corner is traditional, conservative and very beautiful. Tucked under the hem of Spanish Galicia, inland mountains provide the region with plentiful rain. Rich soil encourages intensive farming, mostly on smallholdings of maize and vegetables divided by low stone walls. Despite injections of EU money, this remains a largely poor agricultural area where many farmers still rely on lyre-horned oxen to pull their carts and plough their fields. Generations of sons have left to seek fortunes in France, Germany and elsewhere, returning to flaunt their wealth with fancy new houses.

The Minho clings to its rural traditions: here you'll see some of Portugal's most vibrant country markets (most famously in Barcelos). On the calendar are dozens of festivals and *romarias* (pilgrimages) commemorating local saints. Religion plays an important part in life, and Easter in Braga, Portugal's 'ecclesiastical capital', is an extraordinary combination of fervour and merrymaking.

Minhotos have reason to be proud of their history too: this is where the kingdom of Portugal came into being. Guimarães is the birthplace of Portugal's first king, Afonso Henriques, and the place from which he launched the main thrust of the Reconquista against the Moors in 1139. In almost the same place over a millennium earlier, the Celtiberians maintained their last stronghold, the Citânia de Briteiros, against the Romans. Today this is one of the country's most fascinating archaeological sites.

Barcelos, Guimarães and Citânia de Briteiros lie within easy reach of each other in the southern Minho. Lashed by the cold Atlantic, the Minho's coastal region (sometimes called the Costa Verde, or Green Coast) has fewer attractions, though the jovial resort of Viana do Castelo and the coast north of it have good beaches and plenty of solitude.

HIGHLIGHTS

- Navigate rugged hilltop roads and explore borderland villages in the Parque Nacional da Peneda-Gerês
- Absorb the atmosphere in Braga, Portugal's spiritual capital, and climb heavenwards at nearby Bom Jesus do Monte
- Cast about in Barcelos' huge and famous weekly market
- Unwind in the cheerful seaside resort of Viana do Castelo
- Turn back the pages of time at the Celtic hill settlement of Citânia de Briteiros

The Minho's real pull is inland, along the Rio Minho (which forms the northern frontier with Spain) and the dreamy Rio Lima (so alluring the Romans reckoned it was the mythical Lethe, the river of oblivion). These areas have Portugal's highest concentration of Turismo de Habitação accommodation, offering the chance to stay in anything from manor houses to converted farmhouses.

Further inland still is the Parque Nacional da Peneda-Gerês, the only real 'national' park and the nearest thing to true wilderness in Portugal, with a cornucopia of outdoor sports and several competent outfits ready to show you around.

Don't plan on rushing through the Minho: the pace is nearly always slow and there are numerous distractions – not least of which is the local vinho verde, a young, sparkling wine that is among Portugal's most addictive.

MINHO

VITOR VIEIRA

Only the brave mount the staircase of Bom Jesus do Monte in the traditional way – on their knees.

VITOR VIEIRA

The Albufeira de Vilarinho das Furnas was formed by the damming of the Rio Homem.

Seen this somewhere before? The Solar de Mateus is depicted on the labels of Mateus rosé wine.

In remote areas of Portugal such as Trás-os-Montes, farmers still cultivate the land by hand.

THE MINHO

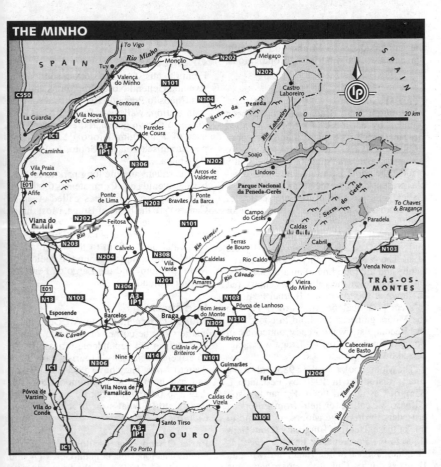

Southern Minho

BRAGA

☎ 053 • pop 65,000

The Minho's capital is one of the oldest settlements in Portugal and has genuine Celtic
roots. More importantly to the Portuguese,
Braga is their religious capital, with a
Christian pedigree dating from the 6th
century. From the 11th to the 18th centuries
this was the seat of archbishops who considered themselves Primate of All Spain, or

at any rate Primate of Portugal (these days
they minister as far south as Coimbra).

Brochures go on about 'the Portuguese
Rome', though the comparison is silly.
Braga overflows with churches – at least 35
of them, bells a-tolling all day long – but
only its ancient cathedral merits much attention, having survived wholesale Baroque
renovations that smothered most of the
others in the 18th century. The city's best
known attraction, Bom Jesus do Monte,
isn't actually in the city at all (see Around

Braga). Nevertheless, the centre of Braga is relaxing and attractive, and the students of the Universidade do Minho add youthful leavening to an otherwise proud, pious, somewhat dour city.

History

It's thought that Braga may have been founded by a tribe of Celtiberians called Bracari (hence its ancient name, Bracara). In about 250 BC the Romans moved in, renamed it Bracara Augusta and eventually made it the administrative centre of Gallaecia (present-day Douro, Minho and Spanish Galicia). Its position at the intersection of five Roman roads turned it into a major trading centre.

Braga fell to the Suevi around 410 AD, and was sacked by the Visigoths 60 years later. The Visigoths' conversion to Christianity and the founding of an archbishopric in the middle of the following century put the town at the top of the Iberian Peninsula's ecclesiastical pecking order. Though the Moors gained a foothold in about 715, the Reconquista was already underway in northern Spain and in 740 Braga was again seized by Christian forces.

The Moors took it back in 985, only to be finally dislodged in 1040 by Fernando I, King of Castile and León. Fernando's son Alfonso VI called for help from European crusaders to drive the Moors south, and to one of these, Henri of Burgundy (Dom Henrique to the Portuguese), he later gave his daughter Teresa in marriage, throwing in Braga as dowry. Out of this marriage came Afonso Henriques, first king of Portugal.

The archbishopric was restored in 1070, though prelates bickered with their Spanish counterparts for the next five centuries over who was Primate of All Spain, until the pope ruled in Braga's favour. The sturdy elegance of the city's churches and palaces reflects its subsequent power and prosperity, only curtailed when a separate Lisbon archdiocese was created in the 18th century.

It was from conservative Braga that the 1926 coup was launched which eventually put António de Oliveira Salazar in power and introduced Portugal to half a century of dictatorship.

Orientation

From the bus station it's 600m south along Avenida General Norton de Matos and Rua dos Chãos to Praça da República. From the train station, walk east for just over 1km, via the old town gate and the shopping district of Rua Dom Diogo de Sousa and pedestrianised Rua do Souto, to Praça da República.

This square and the long park to the east beside Avenida dos Combatentes (both park and street are sometimes called Avenida Central) are the heart of Braga. Most things of use or interest are within walking distance of the centre – except for the big municipal park 1.5km to the south, which includes the camping ground, Estádio 1 de Maio (stadium) and the Largo da Feira exhibition grounds.

Information

Tourist Office In fading Art Deco headquarters on the corner of Praça da República, staff at the dependable turismo (☎ 26 25 50) endure the city's tourists daily from 9 am to 7 pm. They have a decent city map and can help with accommodation. You may also be able to pick up a copy of the free monthly what's-on brochure, *Braga Cultural*.

Park Office The headquarters of the Parque Nacional da Peneda-Gerês (☎ 600 34 80, fax 61 31 69) is in the former Quinta das Parretas on Avenida António Macedo, west of the centre. The public information office, in the modern building at the back, is open weekdays only from 9.30 am to noon and 2.30 to 5 pm. It has a good park map and a booklet (in English) on the park's human and natural features; most other information is in Portuguese.

Money The city has numerous banks with currency exchange desks and ATMs; there are several around Largo de São Francisco, at the northern end of Praça da República.

Post & Communications The post and telephone office is a block south of Praça da República on Avenida da Liberdade.

Email & Internet Access Casa da Juventude (☎ 61 66 98, fax 61 66 29), the local branch of the Instituto Português da Juventude, has at least one terminal available to the public for free Internet access. It's open weekdays from 9 am to 7.30 pm; enter at the left end of the building at Rua de Santa Margarida 6. Ciberbraga (☎ 21 83 93), at Praça do Município 72, charges 600$00 per hour of online time. It's open weekdays only, from 8 am until late at night.

Travel Agencies Tagus Travel (☎ 21 51 44, fax 21 51 94), Praça do Município 7, makes budget-minded hotel and transport bookings, sells ISIC cards and organises trips in Portugal and Spain through local specialist agencies. It's open weekdays only, from 9 am to 1 pm and 2.30 to 6 pm.

Bookshops The best bookshop is Livraria Bertrand, Rua Dom Diogo de Sousa 129-133. Another good one is Livraria Diário do Minho on Rua de Santa Margarida.

Universities The Universidade do Minho, founded here in 1973, has administrative headquarters in part of the old Archbishop's Palace on Largo do Paço. There are various faculties along Rua do Castelo and Rua Abade Loureira.

Laundry Lavandaria Confiança, Rua Dom Diogo de Sousa 46, and Lavandaria 5 à Sec, Largo de Santa Cruz 35, can do wash-&-dry or dry cleaning.

Medical Services The Hospital de São Marcos (☎ 601 30 00), a block west of Avenida da Liberdade, is accessed via Rua do Raio or Rua 25 de Abril.

Emergency The police station (☎ 61 32 50) is around the left side of the Governor Civil building on Rua dos Falcões, two blocks south of the cathedral.

Praça da República

This broad square with computer-controlled fountains is a good place to start or finish your day. In an arcaded building on the western side are two of Portugal's best venues for watching the world go by, Café Astória and Café Vianna, with a tiny chapel in between and several well-stocked newsstands in front. The Astória is less posh, less touristy, and favoured by students in the evenings. The square crenellated tower visible behind the building is the **Torre de Menagem** (castle keep), the only surviving part of a fortified palace built in 1738.

Sé

Braga's cathedral – the oldest in Portugal, begun after the restoration of the archdiocese in 1070 and completed in the following century – is a rambling complex of chapels and little rooms in a jumble of architectural styles. You could spend half a day probing its corners and sorting the Romanesque bits from the Gothic attachments and the Baroque icing.

The original Romanesque survives in the overall shape, in the Porta do Sol entrance on the south side and also in the marvellous west or main entrance, carved with scenes from the medieval legend of Reynard the Fox (and now sheltered inside a Gothic porch).

The cathedral's most appealing and visible feature is its filigree Manueline towers and roof. Also outside, in a niche on the western side, there's a lovely statue of Nossa Senhora do Leite (the Virgin Suckling the Christ Child), thought to be by the 16th century expat French sculptor Nicolas Chanterène.

You enter, not straight into the church through the west door but via a courtyard on the northern side, through several Gothic chapels and, via a cloister, more chapels and the two storey *tesouro*, or treasury. The most interesting of the chapels is the Capela dos Reis (Kings' Chapel), with the tombs of Dom Henrique (Henri of Burgundy) and Dona Teresa, parents of the first king of the Portuguese, Afonso Henriques.

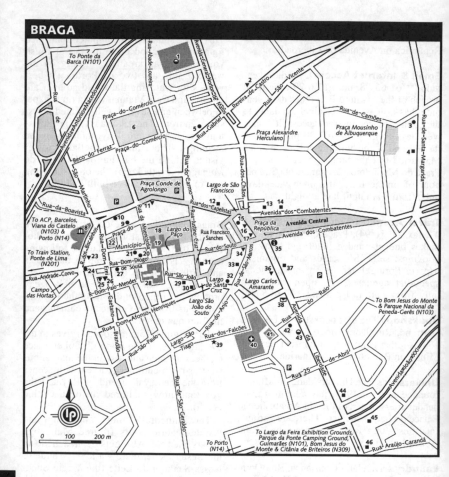

BRAGA

Not surprisingly for a cathedral of such stature, the treasury is a rich collection of ecclesiastical booty, including a 10th century Arabic-Hispanic style ivory casket and a plain iron cross used in 1500 to celebrate the first Mass in newly discovered Brazil.

In the church itself, note the fine Manueline carved altarpiece, a little chapel to the left with azulejos depicting scenes from the life of Braga's first bishop, and the extraordinary twin Baroque organs.

A ticket from the official at the entrance, admitting you to the treasury, Coro Alto (choir), Capela dos Reis and several other chapels with archbishops' tombs in them, costs 300$00. The complex is open daily from 8.30 am to 1 pm and 2 to 6.30 pm. This is the only church in town of any real interest, and everybody else will be heading for it too, so get there early.

Antigo Paço Episcopal & Around

Across Rio do Souto from the cathedral is the sprawling former Archbishop's Palace.

MINHO

BRAGA

PLACES TO STAY
4   Pousada da Juventude
12 Residencial dos Terceiros
13 Hotel Francfort
14 Hotel Residencial Centro
    Comercial Avenida
29 Casa Santa Zita
30 Hotel-Residencial
    Dona Sofia
31 Residencial Inácio Filho
33 Residencial São Marcos
37 Grande Residência Avenida
44 Hotel de Turismo
45 Hotel Carandá
46 Hotel João XXI

PLACES TO EAT
2   Retiro da Primavera
6   Mercado Municipal

11 Lareira do Conde
16 Café Vianna
17 Café Astória
23 Casa Grulha
25 Casa de Pasto Pregão
26 Taberna Rexío da Praça
34 Café Brasileira
36 Café Jolima

OTHER
1   Bus Station
3   Livraria Diário do Minho
5   AVIC Travel Agency
7   Parque Nacional da Peneda-
    Gerês Headquarters
8   Museu dos Biscaínhos
9   Ciberbraga
10 Bicycle Shop
15 Torre de Menagem

18 Jardim de Santa Bárbara
19 Antigo Paço Episcopal
20 Livraria Bertrand
21 Tagus Travel;
    Oficina d'Aventura
22 Câmara Municipal
24 Arco da Porta Nova
27 Lavandaria Confiança
28 Sé
32 Lavandaria 5 à Sec
35 Turismo
38 Post Office
39 Police Station
40 Hospital de São Marcos
41 Casa do Raio
42 Fonte do Idolo
43 Buses to Municipal Park,
    Camping Ground &
    Bom Jesus

Begun in the 14th century and enlarged in the 17th and 18th centuries, it's now occupied by the municipal library, the Braga district archives and the university rectory and administration. The gilt-ceilinged library, one of the country's wealthiest, is full of ancient documents from a score of monastic libraries.

Outside the spiky-topped north wing is the **Jardim de Santa Bárbara** which dates, like this wing of the palace, from the 17th century. Beside it, several pedestrianised blocks of Rua Justino Cruz and Rua Francisco Sanches are filled on sunny days with buskers, balloon sellers and café tables.

At the western end of neighbouring Praça do Município is Braga's *câmara municipal* (town hall), which has one of Portugal's best Baroque façades, designed by architect André Soares da Silva. (You can see a more extrovert piece of work by Soares at **Casa do Raio**, up Rua do Raio by the hospital. The Rococo front of this building is covered in azulejos.)

Arco da Porta Nova

This 18th century arch on the west side of the old centre was for some time the city's main gate. It bears the coat of arms of Archbishop Dom José de Bragança, who commissioned it. East from here to Praça da República, Rua Dom Diogo de Sousa and Rua do Souto form a narrow shopping district, heavy on religious paraphernalia.

Museu dos Biscaínhos

In a 17th century aristocrat's palace on Rua dos Biscaínhos is the municipal museum (☎ 26 76 45). Surrounded by 18th century gardens full of statuary and a fountain, this museum has an attractive collection of Roman relics, and pottery, furniture and furnishings from the 17th to 19th centuries. It is open daily except Monday, from 10 am to 12.15 pm and 2 to 5.30 pm; admission costs 250$00.

The most interesting exhibit is the building itself, a solid, handsome mansion with painted or wood-panelled ceilings and 18th century azulejos featuring hunting scenes. The ground floor is an extension of the street and was paved with ribbed stones so that carriages could drive in and continue to the stables.

Fonte do Idolo

This startling little 1st century AD Roman sanctuary, carved into solid rock, is down some stairs near the corner of Avenida da Liberdade and Rua do Raio.

MINHO

Special Events

Braga may no longer be the official religious capital, but it's still the capital of religious festivals. Easter Week here is a serious and splendid affair. The čity blazes with lights and roadside altars representing the Stations of the Cross, and the churches deck themselves out with banners. Most amazing is the torch-lit Senhor Ecce Homo procession of barefoot, black-hooded penitents on Maundy Thursday evening.

The Festas de São João on 23 to 24 June (continuing into the wee hours of the 25th) is a pre-Christian solstice bash dressed up to look like holy days, but it's still full of pagan energy. It features medieval folk plays, processions, dancing, bonfires and illuminations, a funfair in the city park, and mysterious little pots of basil everywhere.

Places to Stay

Accommodation tends to be pricey here, except for the camping ground and hostels. Bom Jesus do Monte (see Around Braga) has several additional mid-range to top-end hotels.

Camping The year-round, municipal *Parque da Ponte* (☎ 27 33 55) is almost 2km south of the centre in the big municipal park. From Avenida da Liberdade, city buses labelled 'Arcos' pass the park every half-hour (or take anything that stops at Pinheiro da Gregório); ask for *campismo*. It costs 340/260/280$00 per person/tent/car.

Hostels Braga's *pousada da juventude* (☎/fax 61 61 63, Rua de Santa Margarida 6) is a 10 minute walk from the turismo. The entrance is at the right-hand end of the building and the doors are open from 8 am to 1 pm and 6 pm to midnight. A dorm bed costs 1500$00, a double with bathroom 3700$00.

Casa Santa Zita (☎ 61 83 31) is a hostel for pilgrims (and others at non-pilgrimage times) behind the cathedral at Rua São João 20. Spartan doubles are 6500$00 (4500$00 without shower). It's unmarked but for a small tile plaque that says 'Sta Zita'.

Pensões, Residenciais & Hotels Categories are muddled, with some places calling themselves 'hotel/residencial', so we've put them all in one category.

Perhaps the best bargain in town is the charming *Hotel Francfort* (☎ 26 26 48, Avenida dos Combatentes 7), where big rooms with creaky old furniture are looked after by ladies of similar vintage. A double costs 5000$00 (3500$00 without shower). They don't take reservations, so you have to arrive early in the day, at least in summer.

Stuffy, but clean and homey, is *Residencial Inácio Filho* (☎ 26 38 49, Rua Francisco Sanches 42), where a double is 5000$00 with shower (4400$00 without). Charmless doubles at *Residencial dos Terceiros* (☎ 27 04 66, fax 27 57 67, Rua dos Capelistas 85) are overpriced at 6000$00.

Another bargain is polite, helpful *Grande Residência Avenida* (☎ 60 90 20, fax 60 90 28, Avenida da Liberdade 738), where doubles with full bathroom cost 7000$00 (6000$00 with shower but no toilet, 5500$00 without), breakfast included.

Hotel Residencial Centro Comercial Avenida (☎ 27 57 22, fax 61 63 63, Avenida dos Combatentes 27-37) has sterile doubles with air-con costing from 7500$00 (with breakfast) and pricier doubles with kitchenettes. It has its own lift at the back end of the Centro Comercial Avenida shopping mall. *Residencial São Marcos* (☎ 27 71 87, fax 27 71 77, Rua de São Marcos 80) offers carpeted rooms for 7500$00, breakfast included. *Hotel-Residencial Dona Sofia* (☎ 26 31 60, fax 61 12 45, Largo São João do Souto 131) is distinguished by the fact that its clean, boring rooms (9000$00 for a double) come with an English breakfast.

There's a further clutch of more expensive hotels 800m south of the centre at the intersection of Avenida da Liberdade and Avenida João XXI: *Hotel João XXI* (☎ 61 66 30, fax 61 66 31, Avenida João XXI) at 8500$00, *Hotel Carandá* (☎ 61 45 00, fax 61 45 50, Avenida da Liberdade 96) at 10,500$00, and *Hotel de Turismo* (☎ 61 22 00, fax 61 22 11, Praceta João XXI) at 13,000$00.

Places to Eat

Restaurants Around the corner from the bus station is one of Braga's better bargains, unpretentious *Retiro da Primavera* (☎ 27 24 82, Rua Gabriel Pereira de Castro 100), with lots of meat and fish dishes for under 1200$00; a half-portion does nicely. It's closed on Saturday.

Near the Arco da Porta Nova are two plain eateries with dishes for under 1000$00: *Taberna Rexío da Praça* (☎ 61 77 01, Praça Velha 17), with just two tasty daily specials, and *Casa de Pasto Pregão* (☎ 27 72 49, Praça Velha 18), with a larger, plainer menu. Both are closed on Sunday. Rustic, congenial and very good value is family-run *Casa Grulha* (☎ 26 28 83, Rua dos Biscaínhos 95), with excellent *cabrito assado* (roast kid).

A clean, cheap, better-than-average *churrasqueira* (restaurant serving grilled foods) is *Lareira do Conde* (☎ 61 13 40, Praça Conde de Agrolongo 56). *Café Jolima (Avenida da Liberdade)* is a giant self-service restaurant, teahouse and *confeitaria* (patisserie) with a huge array of munchies and zero atmosphere.

Cafés For light meals, coffee or beer, settle down at *Café Astória* or *Café Vianna* on Praça da República (see the Praça da República section). Around the corner at the locally favoured alternative, *Café Brasileira (Rua do Souto)*, grouchy waiters serve drinks and surprisingly awful coffee until midnight; it's closed Sunday.

Self-Catering The mercado municipal in Praça do Comércio bustles from 8 am to 6 pm (Friday 7 am to 5 pm, Saturday 7 am to 1 pm, Sunday closed). South on Avenida da Liberdade are the Minipreço and Pingo Doce supermarkets.

Shopping

A big weekly market is held on Tuesday at the Largo da Feira exhibition grounds in the big park south of the centre. Take an 'Arcos' city bus from Avenida da Liberdade (every 30 minutes).

Those planning to trek in the Parque Nacional da Peneda-Gerês can stop in at Oficina d'Aventura, a shop within Tagus Travel (see the earlier Information section) that stocks name-brand rucksacks, sleeping bags, clothes, shoes and tents, as well as topographic maps. ISIC cards get a 10% discount.

There's a small bicycle shop to the west of Praça Conde de Agrolongo if you're in need of spare parts.

Getting There & Away

Bus The bus station on Avenida General Norton de Matos is a gauntlet of private operators, including AVIC/Joalto (☎ 26 26 23), REDM/Rede Expressos (☎ 61 60 97), Renex (☎ 61 93 86), AMI/Rodonorte (☎ 27 83 54), João Carlos Soares (☎ 26 46 93), Salvador (☎ 26 34 53) and Empresa Hoteleira do Gerês (☎ 26 20 33).

For Peneda-Gerês, Empresa Hoteleira do Gerês runs every few hours daily to Rio Caldo and Caldas do Gerês, and Salvador goes to Arcos de Valdevez and on to Monção. Best bets for Guimarães are Soares and Rodonorte, the latter continuing to Amarante, Vila Real and Bragança. Take REDM to Chaves, in Trás-os-Montes. Joalto runs several times a day to Viseu, Guarda and Covilhã, with services also to Barcelos, Viana do Castelo and Vila do Conde. REDM, Renex and Soares together have over 20 daily express departures to Porto, with Renex continuing to Lisbon.

Local buses run to Bom Jesus every 30 minutes from a stop in front of the Farmácia Cristal on Avenida da Liberdade.

Train Braga station (☎ 26 21 66) is at the end of a branch line from Nine, but direct services are not bad from major centres. IC trains arrive twice a day from Lisbon, Coimbra and Porto. There are also *suburbano* trains to/from Porto: eight a day direct (one to two hours) and as many more with a change at Nine.

Car & Motorcycle The Automóvel Clube de Portugal (ACP) has a branch (☎ 21 70

51, fax 61 67 00) at Avenida Conde Dom Henrique 72. The AVIC travel agency (☎ 21 64 60), on Rua Gabriel Pereira de Castro, is an agent for Hertz Rent a Car.

Completion of the A3/IP1 motorway has made Braga an easy day trip from Porto. If you're heading to/from Amarante, unless you plan to visit Guimarães consider avoiding the N101 road, one of the most tortuous, congested and poorly signposted stretches we know of in Portugal. The alternative, via the IP1 and IP4 almost to Porto, is longer and costs almost 1000$00 in tolls, but it's faster and less aggravating.

AROUND BRAGA
Bom Jesus do Monte

Bom Jesus, 5km east of the centre of Braga on the N103, is the goal of legions of pilgrims every year. This sober, twin-towered church at the site of a (long-gone) 15th century sanctuary is on a forested hill with fine views across the countryside. It was designed in neoclassical style by Carlos Amarante and completed in 1811.

It stands atop an astonishing, and considerably more famous, granite and plaster Baroque staircase, the Escadaria do Bom Jesus, presumably built to concentrate the minds of the devout as they climb to the church.

It's actually several staircases, from several decades of the 18th century. The lowest is lined with chapels representing the Stations of the Cross, and startlingly lifelike terracotta figures. The double zigzag Stairway of the Five Senses features allegorical fountains and over-the-top Old Testament figures. At the top is the Stairway of the Three Virtues, whose further chapels and fountains represent Faith, Hope and Charity.

You can ascend by the stairs, as all pilgrims do (though you needn't go on your knees, as they usually do), and enjoy views of the whole scene; cheat and ride the adjacent *elevador* (funicular); or drive up a twisting road.

The area has become something of a resort, with luxurious hotels, tennis courts,

a little lake with boats for hire, and walks through the woods. Go on a weekday if you can.

Places to Stay Accommodation is pricey, and usually pretty full, though it's hard to see why a non-pilgrim would want to stay more than a few hours anyway.

Hotel Sul-Americano (☎ 67 67 01) has doubles with great views from about 8500$00, breakfast included. More expensive alternatives are *Hotel do Parque* (☎ 67 66 07) and *Hotel do Elevador* (☎ 67 66 11). All are within a short walk of the stairway.

Two Turihab properties here are *Casa dos Lagos* (☎ 67 67 38) and *Casa dos Castelos de Bom Jesus* (☎ 67 65 66, fax 61 71 81).

Getting There & Away Buses run to Bom Jesus via the N103 every 30 minutes all day, from in front of Farmácia Cristal on Avenida da Liberdade in Braga. If you have wheels, a longer but far more scenic route leaves the city south-eastwards on the N309.

Citânia de Briteiros

Scattered around the Minho are the remains of Celtic hill settlements called *citânias*, dating back at least 2500 years. One of the best preserved and most spectacular is at Briteiros, a 12km drive south-east of Braga.

The 3¾ hectare site, inhabited from about 300 BC to 300 AD, was probably the last stronghold of the Celtiberians against the invading Romans. When archaeologist Dr Martins Sarmento excavated the rocky hill in 1875, he discovered the foundations and ruins of more than 150 stone huts (mostly round), linked by paved paths and surrounded by the remains of multiple protective walls.

Sarmento spent years clearing away the debris, reconstructed two huts, and created one of the country's most evocative archaeological sites. Some striking remains, such as carved stone lintels and ornamental portals, are now on display in the Museu Martins Sarmento in Guimarães.

A detailed site plan available from the ticket office points out the most significant features, including a fountain, a circular community house and the so-called 'funerary monument', a deep trench initially thought to be a burial chamber when it was discovered in 1930. The more mundane recent theory is that it was a bathhouse.

The site is open daily from 9 am to 6 pm (5.30 pm in winter); admission costs 300$00.

Getting There & Away Buses run to the site frequently all day from Praça Alexandre Herculano in Braga, and less often from Guimarães (seven daily but only four returning, the last at 5 pm).

BARCELOS
☎ 053 • pop 10,400

The Minho is famous for its traditional markets, geared to the agricultural community, and none is more famous than the one in this ancient town on the banks of the Rio Cávado, 22km west of Braga. Indeed the Feira de Barcelos, held every Thursday, has become so well known that tourists now arrive by the coachload and cheap rooms can be hard to find on Wednesday and Thursday nights.

There are a few other cultural attractions, a thriving pottery tradition and several major festivals, but beyond the centre of town you're soon into industrial outskirts. If you don't make it to the market, it's scarcely worth coming.

Orientation
From the train station it's roughly 1km south-west on Avenida Alcaides de Faria to the heart of town, Campo da República (also called Campo da Feira), a huge shady square where the market is held. Various bus companies have terminals north-east or south of the Campo.

The medieval town, with museums and the parish church, is on the slopes above the river, about 500m south-west of the Campo. Food and accommodation are concentrated in this district and around the Campo.

Information
The turismo (☎ 81 18 82, fax 82 21 88) shares the Torre de Menagem (the former castle keep) on Largo da Porta Nova with a handicrafts and souvenir shop. Both are open daily from 9 am to 12.30 pm and 2.30 to 6 pm (no lunch break on market day).

Feira de Barcelos
Despite increasing tourist attention, the market, which sprawls across Campo da República, is still a local, rural affair. Villagers come from miles around to sell everything from scrawny chickens to hand-embroidered linen. Listen to Gypsy women bellowing for business in the clothes section. Snack on sausages and home-made bread as you wander among the cow bells, hand-woven baskets and carved ox yokes.

Pottery is what visitors come to see, especially the distinctive, yellow-dotted *louça de Barcelos* ware and the gaudily coloured figurines in the style of Rosa Ramalho, a local potter who put Barcelos firmly on the pottery map in the 1950s. And the trademark Barcelos cockerel (see the boxed text)

The Barcelos Cockerel

The cockerel motif that you see all over Portugal – especially in pottery form – has its origins in a 16th (some say 14th) century 'miracle'. According to the story (which also crops up in Spain), a Galician pilgrim on his way to Santiago de Compostela was wrongfully accused of theft while passing through Barcelos. Though pleading his innocence, he was condemned to hang from the gallows. In his last appearance at the judge's house the pilgrim declared that the roast cockerel that the judge was about to eat would stand up and crow to affirm his innocence. The miracle occurred, the pilgrim was saved, and the cockerel gradually became the most popular folk art motif in the country, akin to a national icon.

MINHO

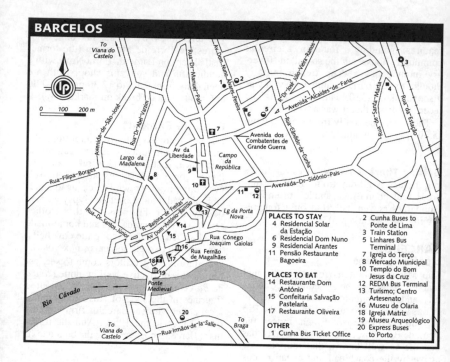

BARCELOS

To Viana do Castelo

0 100 200 m

To Viana do Castelo

Rio Cávado

Ponte Medieval

To Viana do Castelo

To Braga

Rua-Irmãos-de-la-Salle

Rua-Dr-Santos-Júnior

Rua-Filipa-Borges

Largo da Madalena

Av da Liberdade

Campo da República

Avenida dos Combatentes de Grande Guerra

Avenida-Alcaides-de-Faria

Aveniada-Dr-Sidónio-Pais

Rua Cónego Joaquim Gaiolas

Rua Fernão de Magalhães

Lg da Porta Nova

R-Barjona-de-Freitas

Av Dom-António-Barroso

Avenida-de-São-José

Rua-Dr-Abel-Varzim

Rua-Dr-Manuel-Pais

Rua-Dr-Nuno-Alves-Pereira

Av-Dom-Nuno-Alves-Pereira

Dr-José-Júlio-Vieira-Ramos

Rua-Gándão-da-Cunha

Rua-de-Santa-Marta

Rua-Dr-Estação

PLACES TO STAY			2	Cunha Buses to Ponte de Lima
4	Residencial Solar da Estação		3	Train Station
6	Residencial Dom Nuno		5	Linhares Bus Terminal
9	Residencial Arantes		7	Igreja do Terço
11	Pensão Restaurante Bagoeira		8	Mercado Municipal
			10	Templo do Bom Jesus da Cruz
PLACES TO EAT			12	REDM Bus Terminal
14	Restaurante Dom António		13	Turismo; Centro Artesenato
15	Confeitaria Salvação Pastelaria		16	Museu de Olaria
17	Restaurante Oliveira		18	Igreja Matriz
			19	Museu Arqueológico
OTHER			20	Express Buses to Porto
1	Cunha Bus Ticket Office			

is everywhere – on pots and tea towels, key rings and bottle openers, and in pottery form in every size.

The tour buses arrive by mid-morning and the market starts to wind down after midday, so it's best to get here early.

Museu Arqueológico

On a ledge overlooking the Rio Cávado and a restored 15th century bridge are the roof-less ruins of the former palace of the counts of Barcelos and Dukes of Bragança (the eighth count became the first duke). In 1755 the palace was practically obliterated by the earthquake and it now serves as an alfresco archaeological museum.

Among mysterious phallic stones, Roman columns, medieval caskets and bits of azulejos, the most famous item is a 14th century stone cross, the Crucifix O Senhor do Galo, depicting the 'Gentleman of the

Cockerel' story and said to have been commissioned by the lucky pilgrim himself. Near the entrance is a late Gothic *pelourinho* (pillory) topped by a granite lantern.

The site is open daily from 9 am to noon and 2 to 5.30 pm (admission free).

Museu de Olaria

Near the Museu Arqueológico, on Rua Cónego Joaquim Gaiolas, is a pottery museum featuring many of Portugal's regional styles, from Azores pots to figurines from Barcelos, Estremoz and Miranda do Corvo, and some striking pewter-grey ware. There's also an exhibit on techniques (though the labels are all in Portuguese). The museum is open daily except Monday, from 10 am to 12.30 pm and 2 to 6 pm (no lunch break on Thursday). The 250$00 admission charge also covers temporary exhibitions.

Igreja Matriz

It's worth peeping inside the stocky Gothic parish church, behind the Museu Arqueológico, to see its 18th century azulejos and gilded Baroque chapels.

Templo do Bom Jesus da Cruz

On the south-west corner of the Campo is this arresting circular church, also called the Igreja do Senhor da Cruz, overlooking a garden of obelisks. It was built in 1705, probably by João Antunes (who also designed Lisbon's Igreja da Santa Engrácia).

Igreja do Terço

Inside this deceptively plain church, once part of an 18th century Benedictine monastery, are some handsome azulejos on the life of St Benedict by the 18th century master, António de Oliveira Bernardes. Competing for attention are a carved and gilded pulpit and a ceiling painted with more scenes from the saint's life.

Special Events

The Festas das Cruzes (Festival of the Crosses) in early May turns Barcelos into a fairground of coloured lights, flags, flowers and street decorations.

The Festival de Folclore, a celebration of traditional folk song and dance, is held on the last Saturday of July.

Places to Stay

Booking ahead for Wednesday and Thursday nights is recommended.

Frilly doubles at *Pensão Restaurante Bagoeira* (✆ *81 12 36, fax 82 45 88, Avenida Dr Sidónio Pais 495*) start at 6000$00. Doubles at homey *Residencial Arantes* (✆ *81 13 26, Avenida da Liberdade 35*) cost 7000$00, including breakfast. Both places have cheaper rooms without bathroom, too. Rooms at *Residencial Solar da Estação* (✆ *81 17 41*), left of the train station as you exit, cost 6000$00 with breakfast.

Poshest but dullest is *Residencial Dom Nuno* (✆ *81 28 10, fax 81 63 36, Avenida Dom Nuno Álvares Pereira 76*), where modern rooms with bathroom cost 7500/8500$00, breakfast included.

Places to Eat

Pensão Restaurante Bagoeira (see Places to Stay), a market-day rendezvous for shoppers and stall-holders alike, copes with an incredible amount of jovial chaos, serving up regional items like *rojões à moda do Minho* (a casserole of marinated pork pieces) for under 1500$00 a dish.

Restaurante Oliveira (✆ *81 47 75, Largo do Município 17*) is a child-friendly, cheerful place with generous portions and prices under 1300$00 a dish. Local favourite *Restaurante Dom António* (✆ *81 22 85, Avenida Dom António Barroso 85*) has *pratos do dia* (dishes of the day) for under 1200$00. Check out the old engraved till and the famous almond sweets and cakes at *Confeitaria Salvação Pastelaria* (*Avenida Dom António Barroso 137*).

Getting There & Away

Bus REDM (✆ 81 43 10), Avenida Dr Sidónio Pais 445, has services to Braga almost hourly until 7 pm (fewer at weekends) and to Ponte de Lima several times a day. REDM is also an agent for Renex; three times a day, Renex express buses stop across the river on Rua Irmãos de la Salle, en route to Porto and Lisbon.

Linhares (✆ 81 15 71), Avenida dos Combatentes 50, runs coaches to Porto and to Viana do Castelo around four times daily. Domingos da Cunha (✆ 81 58 43), Avenida Dom Nuno Álvares Pereira (also with a major stop at the train station), has several daily services to Ponte de Lima, Ponte da Barca and Arcos de Valdevez.

Train Barcelos is on the Porto-Valença line, with 11 services daily from Porto. There are also local services from Nine (the junction to/from Braga).

GUIMARÃES

✆ 053 • pop 22,000

Known as 'the cradle of the Portuguese nation', Guimarães is chock-a-block with

MINHO

history. It was here, in 1110, that Afonso Henriques was born and from here, some 20 years later, that he launched the main thrust of the Reconquista against the Moors. Officially acknowledged as king of his new kingdom of 'Portucale' in 1143, Afonso made Coimbra the official capital, but Guimarães considers itself the first de facto capital.

Although its outskirts are now an ugly mass of industrial plants, the historic core of Guimarães is a finely preserved enclave of medieval monuments, including two convents housing excellent museums. As a university town, Guimarães also has a friendly, lively atmosphere which explodes into full scale merrymaking during the annual Festas Gualterianas.

There's enough here to warrant a day's sightseeing, though cheap accommodation is scarce so you might want to do it as a day trip from Braga. For those with escudos to spare, Guimarães' two Pousadas de Portugal are among the finest in the land.

History

Guimarães caught the royal eye as early as 840 AD, when Alfonso II of León convened a council of bishops here, but it only started to grow in the 10th century after a powerful local noblewoman, Countess Mumadona, gave it her attention. A monastery was founded and a castle built. Henri of Burgundy, Count of Portucale (the region between the Minho and Douro rivers), chose Guimarães for his court, as did his son Afonso Henriques until making Coimbra the capital of his new kingdom of Portugal in 1143.

Even in medieval times, the town was famous for its linen, as it still is today. Other industries contributing to its prosperity are cutlery, kitchenware and crafts such as gold and silversmithing, embroidery and pottery.

Orientation

Old Guimarães is in the north-east of the present-day city. Most points of interest lie within a demarcated *zona de turismo* – a tangle of medieval streets, fine monuments

and shady squares – that stretches south from the castle to an arc of public gardens variously called Alameda da Resistência do Fascismo, Alameda da Liberdade and Alameda de São Dâmaso. Around handsome Largo do Toural at the zone's southwestern corner there are restaurants, banks and hotels.

From the train station it's roughly a 10 minute walk north up Avenida Dom Afonso Henriques to the main turismo, on the right just before the gardens.

From the bus station it's a 20 minute slog east along Avenida Conde de Margaride to the centre.

Information

The main turismo (☎ 41 24 50), Alameda de São Dâmaso 86, is open weekdays from 9.30 am to 12.30 pm and 2 to 6.30 pm, and Saturday from 10 am to 1 pm. A more central, more enthusiastic turismo (☎ 51 87 90), above an art gallery on Praça de São Tiago, is open Monday to Saturday from 9.30 am to 6.30 pm, and Sunday from 10 am to 1 pm.

There are numerous banks with ATMs around Largo do Toural and on Rua Gil Vicente. The post office is at the top of Rua de Santo António.

The hospital (☎ 51 26 12) is north of the main bus station, off Avenida Conde de Margaride, and the police station (☎ 51 33 34) is on the northern edge of town, on Rua Texieira de Pascoais.

Castelo

The striking seven-towered castle on a grassy hilltop was built by Henri of Burgundy in about 1100, and is said to be the birthplace of his son Afonso Henriques. The little Igreja de São Miguel nearby is where Afonso was probably baptised. Castle and chapel are open daily, in summer from 9 am to 6.30 pm and in winter from 9.30 am to 5.30 pm. Admission is free.

Paço dos Duques

Downhill from the Igreja de São Miguel is the gross Ducal Palace, easily distinguished

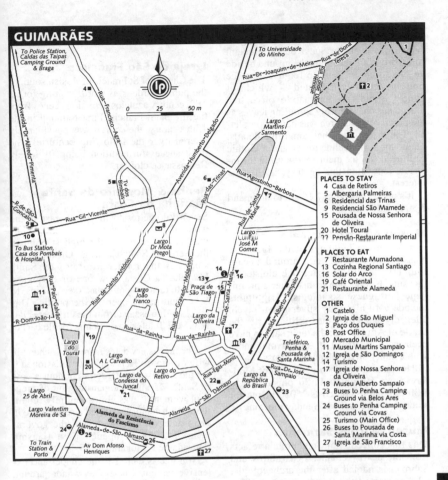

GUIMARÃES

To Police Station,
Caldas das Taipas
Camping Ground
& Braga

To Universidade
do Minho

Rua-Dr-Joaquim-de-Meira

Rua-da-Dona Teresa

Rua Conde Don Henrique

Avenida-Dr-Alfredo-Pimenta

Rua-Francisco-Agra

Tv dos Bimbais

Largo Martins Sarmento

Rua-Agostinho-Barbosa

Avenida-Humberto-Delgado

R-de São Gonçalo

Rua-Gil-Vicente

Rua-das-Trinas

Rua-de-Santa-Maria

Largo Conde José M Gomez

Rua-de-Santo-António

To Bus Station,
Casa dos Pombais
& Hospital

Largo Dr Mota Prego

Largo João Franco

Rua-do-Gravador-Molarinho

Praça de
São Tiago

Largo da Oliveira

Rua-da-Rainha

Rua-de-Santa-Maria

Rua-da-Rainha

To Teleférico,
Penha & Pousada de
Santa Marinha

Avenida-Alberto-Sampaio

Largo do Toural

Largo A L Carvalho

Largo do Retiro

Rua-Egas-Moniz

Rua-de-São-Dâmaso

Largo da República do Brasil

Rua-Dr-José-Sampaio

Largo da Condessa do Juncal

Largo 25 de Abril

Largo Valentim Moreira de Sá

Alameda da Resistência do Fascismo

Alameda-de-São-Dâmaso

To Train Station & Porto

Av Dom Afonso Henriques

PLACES TO STAY
4 Casa de Retiros
5 Albergaria Palmeiras
6 Residencial das Trinas
9 Residencial São Mamede
15 Pousada de Nossa Senhora
   de Oliveira
20 Hotel Toural
22 Pensão-Restaurante Imperial

PLACES TO EAT
7 Restaurante Mumadona
13 Cozinha Regional Santiago
16 Solar do Arco
19 Café Oriental
21 Restaurante Alameda

OTHER
1 Castelo
2 Igreja de São Miguel
3 Paço dos Duques
8 Post Office
10 Mercado Municipal
11 Museu Martins Sampaio
12 Igreja de São Domingos
14 Turismo
17 Igreja de Nossa Senhora
   da Oliveira
18 Museu Alberto Sampaio
23 Buses to Penha Camping
   Ground via Belos Ares
24 Buses to Penha Camping
   Ground via Covas
25 Turismo (Main Office)
26 Buses to Pousada de
   Santa Marinha via Costa
27 Igreja de São Francisco

0   25   50 m

by its forest of brick chimneys. Built in 1401 by Dom Afonso, the future first Duke of Bragança, it fell into ruin after the family moved to Vila Viçosa in the Alentejo. In 1933, during the Salazar era, it was tastelessly restored and has since become a museum. The only items of interest on a tedious tour are some 16th to 18th century Flemish tapestries and a couple of paintings attributed to Josefa de Óbidos (see the boxed text in the Estremadura & Ribatejo chapter for more on her work).

The palace is open during the same hours as the castle; admission costs 400$00 (free for students, and for everyone on Sunday morning).

Igreja de Nossa Senhora da Oliveira

The main attraction in the lovely medieval Largo da Oliveira is a convent-church, Our Lady of the Olive Tree, founded by Countess Mumadona and rebuilt by Dom João I four centuries later.

MINHO

In front is a Gothic canopy and cross said to mark the spot where Wamba the Visigoth (victorious over the Suevi but a reluctant ruler) drove his spear into the ground beside an olive tree, refusing to reign unless the tree immediately sprouted –' which of course it did. An alternative olive tree legend has one suddenly sprouting leaves as the porch of the church was being completed. The exterior still has some fine details, including a Manueline tower and a Gothic pediment over the main doorway, but the interior, renovated this century, is of little interest.

It's open daily from 7.15 am to noon and 3.30 to 7.30 pm.

Museu Alberto Sampaio

In the convent buildings of the Igreja de Nossa Senhora da Oliveira, around a beautiful 13th century Romanesque cloister, is this superb collection named after a prominent Portuguese sociologist. Highlights include a 14th century silver gilt triptych, allegedly taken from the Castilians after the Battle of Aljubarrota; the tunic said to have been worn by João I at Aljubarrota; and a 16th century silver Manueline cross.

The museum is open daily except Monday, from 10 am to 12.30 pm and 2 to 5.30 pm; admission costs 250$00 (free for students, and for all on Sunday morning).

Museu Martins Sarmento

This fine collection of Celtiberian artefacts from the nearby citânias of Briteiros and Sabroso is named after the archaeologist who excavated the Briteiros site in 1875. The larger pieces are dotted around the adjacent cloister of the 14th century Igreja de São Domingos.

There are some extraordinary and mysterious items here, in particular the so-called Pedra Formosa – a slab of carved stone, probably the front of a funerary monument – and the arresting 3m-high Colossus of Pedralva, an anonymous figure with one arm stretched to the sky.

The museum is open daily except Monday, from 9.30 am to noon and 2 to

5 pm; admission costs 250$00 (free for students, and for all on Sunday morning).

Igreja de São Francisco

The Church of St Francis of Assisi, south of the public gardens, is worth visiting for its 18th century azulejos depicting scenes from the life of St Francis. First founded in the 13th century, the church was considerably altered over the following centuries, the most successful addition being its lovely Renaissance cloister.

Penha & Mosteiro de Santa Marinha da Costa

Seven kilometres to the south-east is the wooded hill of Penha, overlooking Guimarães and, at 617m, the highest point in the Serra de Santa Catarina. On the lower slopes is the former Mosteiro de Santa Marinha da Costa, now one of Portugal's most luxurious pousadas (see Places to Stay) and partly open to the public. This makes a fine escape from the city, especially via the Teleférico da Penha (cable car) to the top.

The monastery dates from 1154 when the wife of Afonso Henriques commissioned it for the Augustinian Order, to honour a vow to Santa Marinha, the patron saint of pregnant women. It was almost entirely rebuilt in the 18th century, suffered a serious fire in 1834 and was finally sold to the government in 1951. It opened as a flagship Pousada de Portugal in 1985.

Non-guests can visit the chapel and extensive gardens. Guests may wander around a lovely cloister and past 18th century azulejos by the tile master Policarpo de Oliveira Bernardes, and sleep in converted monks' cells.

The cable car goes from the end of Rua de Dr José Sampaio between 10 am and 7 pm (300$00 each way). The most convenient bus to the monastery is the service to São Roque, departing every half-hour between 7 am and 11 pm from the southern side of the public gardens. Get off at Costa, a short walk away from the monastery/pousada.

Special Events

The Festas Gualterianas (Festival of Saint Walter), on the first weekend of August, is marked by a free fair (market) which has been held in Guimarães since 1452.

Places to Stay

Camping The municipal *Penha camping ground* (☎ *51 59 12*), 6km away on the Penha hill, is open from April through September and has a small swimming pool. It costs 268/213/213$00 per person/tent/car. Take an AV Mondinense bus via Covas (from opposite the main turismo) or via Belos Ares (from Largo da República do Brasil).

At Taipas, 8km north-west by the Rio Ave, is *Caldas das Taipas* (☎ *57 62 74*). It charges 420/315/315$00 per person/tent/car and is open from June through September. Take any Braga-bound bus from the bus station.

Hostel One of the starkest options in town is *Casa de Retiros* (☎ *51 15 15, Rua Francisco Agra 163*), run by Roman Catholic missionaries.

Rules include payment on arrival, entry to rooms only after 6 pm, and an 11.30 pm curfew, but at 3000/5000/7500$00 a single/double/triple (including breakfast), the hardship is bearable. Cheaper dormitory beds here are meant for youth groups but it's worth asking.

Pensões & Residenciais *Pensão-Restaurante Imperial* (☎ *41 51 63, Alameda São Dâmaso 111*), also with an entrance at Rua Egas Moniz 57, has plain doubles from 5000$00 (3000$00 without shower). Some rooms overlook the gardens.

Near the bus station, at the corner of Avenida Conde de Margaride and Rua de São Goncalo, *Residencial São Mamede* (☎ *51 30 92, fax 51 38 63*) has soulless doubles for 6500$00. Better value at 6000$00 is *Residencial das Trinas* (☎ *51 73 58, fax 51 73 62, Rua das Trinas 29*), in an atmospheric lane near the post office. Breakfast is included at both places.

Hotels On the 4th floor of Centro Comercial das Palmeiras, off Rua Gil Vicente, is *Albergaria Palmeiras* (☎ *41 03 24, fax 41 72 61*), where comfortable single/double rooms cost 9000/12,000$00, with breakfast and free parking. Take the shopping centre's side entrance on Travessa dos Bimbais, and the first lift on the left inside.

More congenial is *Hotel Toural* (☎ *51 71 84, fax 51 71 49, Largo do Toural*), at 11,000/13,000$00 (enter from Largo AL Carvalho).

Pousadas Guimarães has two splendid Pousadas de Portugal. The *Nossa Senhora de Oliveira* (☎ *51 41 57, fax 51 42 04, Rua de Santa Maria*) is a 16th century house in the heart of the old town, with doubles for 19,200$00. The jewel in the Pousada crown is the *Santa Marinha* (☎ 51 44 53, fax 51 44 59), 3km out on the slopes of Penha, where a double costs a mere 24,400$00.

Turihab The only Turihab property in town is *Casa das Pombais* (☎ *41 29 17, Avenida de Londres*), a 17th century manor house with peacocks in the garden, incongruously surrounded by shops and housing estates. The house has only three rooms, costing about 12,000$00 for a double including breakfast.

Places to Eat

There are several taverns serving cheap snacks along Rua Egas Moniz. Prices at *Cozinha Regional Santiago* (☎ *51 66 69, Praça de São Tiago 16*) are modest for the locale (for example rojões à Minhoto for under 1500$00 a dish).

Restaurante Mumadona (☎ *41 90 41, Rua de Santa Maria 48*) has dishes from about 1200$00. The upmarket *Solar do Arco* (☎ *51 30 72*), further down Rua de Santa Maria, has a select menu, mostly of seafood; it's closed Sunday.

Two good places south-west of the old town are the inexpensive *Restaurante Alameda* (☎ *41 23 72, Largo da Condessa do Juncal*) and the popular *Café Oriental* (☎ *41 40 48, Largo do Toural*), which is neither a café nor very Oriental, but serves up reasonably priced Portuguese fare until 2 am.

In the very posh dining room of the **Pousada de Nossa Senhora de Oliveira** (see Places to Stay) you can say goodbye to at least 3000$00 per person from a fixed-price menu.

For self-catering supplies, check out the mercado municipal, at the top of Rua Paio Galvão.

Getting There & Away

Bus REDM (☎ 51 62 29) runs multiple daily coaches to Viana do Castelo and to Chaves. Rodonorte has services throughout the day for Braga, Amarante and Ponte de Lima. João Ferreira das Neves (☎ 51 31 31) has eight daily express runs to Porto. João Carlos Soares (☎ 51 24 93) has as many to Braga and to Porto, and three to Lisbon.

Train Guimarães is at the end of a line via Santo Tirso from Porto's Trindade station (560$00). Trains run almost hourly and take just under two hours.

Coastal & Northern Minho

VIANA DO CASTELO
☎ 058 • pop 18,000

This is the Minho's largest and liveliest resort, an elegant town of Manueline and Renaissance houses and Rococo palaces which stretches along the northern bank of the Rio Lima estuary. It's also famous for its festivals, especially the Romaria de Nossa Senhora da Agonia, held in August.

Using Viana as a base you could comfortably explore the lower Lima valley, but the town is also an easy place just to relax and unwind, and there's a fine beach right across the river, as well as others up the coast.

History

On the wooded hill of Monte de Santa Luzia at the northern edge of town are the remains of a Celtiberian citânia, or fortified settlement, though there's little evidence of the Romans, Suevi, Visigoths and Moors who followed. The Romans called the place Diana, which over the years changed to Viana.

The town by the river was given official status by special charter in 1258 by Dom Afonso III, who wanted an urban and fishing centre at the mouth of the Rio Lima. In the 16th century Viana found fame and fortune in the exploits of its sailors, who fished for cod off Newfoundland. The resulting prosperity led to a flurry of building Manueline mansions and monasteries, and the construction of a fort at the mouth of the river.

By the mid-17th century this was northern Portugal's biggest port, its merchants trading as far afield as Russia. At the same time expatriate British cloth merchants here were beginning to export large quantities of local 'red portugal' wine to England (see the special section on port in the Douro chapter).

More money flooded into Viana in the 18th century, thanks to the Brazilian sugar and gold trade. But with Brazil's independence and Porto's increasing prominence as a wine-exporting port, Viana fell into decline. It has since revived to become a prosperous deep-sea fishing and industrial centre and an increasingly popular tourist destination.

Orientation

Viana is dominated by Monte de Santa Luzia to the north. From the train station at the foot of this hill, the river is 800m south down Avenida dos Combatentes da Grande Guerra (usually called Avenida dos Combatentes, or just Avenida). East of the Avenida is the old town, with major points of interest around Praça da República. To the west lies the old fishing quarter, with the Castelo de São Tiago da Barra at the western edge of town.

From the bus station it's a 20 minute hike west on Rua da Bandeira to the centre, though many buses from the station stop by

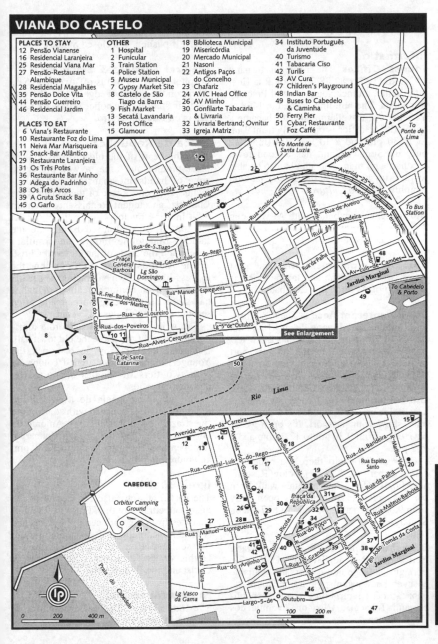

VIANA DO CASTELO

PLACES TO STAY
12 Pensão Vianense
16 Residencial Laranjeira
25 Residencial Viana Mar
27 Pensão-Restaurant Alambique
28 Residencial Magalhães
35 Pensão Dolce Vita
44 Pensão Guerreiro
46 Residencial Jardim

PLACES TO EAT
6 Viana's Restaurante
10 Restaurante Foz do Lima
11 Neiva Mar Marisqueira
17 Snack-Bar Atlântico
29 Restaurante Laranjeira
31 Os Três Potes
36 Restaurante Bar Minho
37 Adega do Padrinho
38 Os Três Arcos
39 A Gruta Snack Bar
45 O Garfo

OTHER
1 Hospital
2 Funicular
3 Train Station
4 Police Station
5 Museu Municipal
7 Gypsy Market Site
8 Castelo de São Tiago da Barra
9 Fish Market
13 Secatá Lavandaria
14 Post Office
15 Glamour
18 Biblioteca Municipal
19 Misericórdia
20 Mercado Municipal
21 Nasoni
22 Antigos Paços do Concelho
23 Chafariz
24 AVIC Head Office
26 AV Minho
30 Gonfilarte Tabacaria & Livraria
32 Livraria Bertrand; Ovnitur
33 Igreja Matriz
34 Instituto Português da Juventude
40 Turismo
41 Tabacaria Ciso
42 Turilis
43 AV Cura
47 Children's Playground
48 Indian Bar
49 Buses to Cabedelo & Caminha
50 Ferry Pier
51 Cybar; Restaurante Foz Caffé

MINHO

the riverside gardens (Jardim Marginal) south of Praça da República.

Information

Tourist Offices The regional turismo (☎ 82 26 20, fax 82 78 73) is on Rua Hospital Velho, a block south-west of Praça da República. The building opened in 1468 as a shelter for travellers and later became a hospital. The office is open daily from 9 am to 12.30 pm and 2.30 to 6 pm (morning only on Sunday), and has a good town brochure and map. You should also be able to pick up a copy of the free what's-on monthly, *Agenda Cultural*.

Money There are banks with ATMs along Avenida dos Combatentes and on Praça da República.

Post & Communications The post office, with telephone and fax facilities, is at the top of Avenida dos Combatentes.

Email & Internet Access The local Instituto Português da Juventude (☎ 810 88 00, fax 43 10 70), Rua do Poço, has a few terminals where you can log on for short periods at no charge from 5.30 to 8 pm.

The *biblioteca municipal*, or town library (☎ 82 85 80), on Rua Cândido dos Reis, also has terminals for free public Internet access, for up to 30 minutes at a time. You must show your passport. It's open weekdays only, from 9.30 am to 12.30 pm and 2 to 7 pm.

Over at Cabedelo there's a cybercafé called Cybar (☎ 33 28 51), below Restaurante Foz Caffé, a few minutes walk from the ferry pier. In summer it's open daily from 9.30 pm to at least 4 am (3 to 7 pm on Sunday).

Bookshops There's a branch of Livraria Bertrand at Rua de Sacadura Cabral 32. Foreign-language newspapers are available at several newsagents, including Gonfilarte Tabacaria & Livraria on Praça da República, and Tabacaria Ciso on Avenida dos Combatentes.

Laundry Secatá Lavandaria, Rua dos Rubins 111, can wash and dry a load within a day, if pushed. It's closed Sunday.

Medical Services & Emergency The hospital (☎ 82 90 81) is off Avenida 25 de Abril, on the northern edge of town beyond the train station. The police station (☎ 82 20 22) is on Rua de Aveiro.

Praça da República

This, the heart of the old town, is Viana's most picturesque area, a well-preserved zone of handsome mansions and monuments. The centrepiece of the square is the **Chafariz**, an elegant Renaissance fountain built in 1554 by João Lopes the Elder. At the top of its sculptured basins are the famous Manueline motifs, an armillary sphere and the cross of the Order of Christ.

The **Antigos Paços do Concelho**, the fortress-like old town hall facing the square, is another 16th century creation, though it has since been restored, its arcade often serving as a craft hawkers' venue.

The striking former **Misericórdia** almshouse is at right angles to the old town hall. Designed in 1589 by João Lopes the Younger, it features an arched colonnade with two tiers of loggias supported by monster caryatids.

The adjoining **Igreja de Misericórdia**, rebuilt in 1714, is adorned with some of the finest azulejos in Portugal, by António de Oliveira Bernardes and his son Policarpo. It's open Sunday from 11 am to 12.30 pm, and more often in August.

Igreja Matriz

The parish church (also referred to as the Sé, or cathedral), south of Praça da República, dates from the 15th century but has had several reincarnations. Its best features are the sculpted Romanesque towers and a Gothic doorway carved with figures of Christ and the Evangelists.

Museu Municipal

The 18th century Palacete Barbosa Maciel, on Rua Manuel Espregueira, houses a fine collection of azulejos, ceramics (especially blue Portuguese china) and furniture (especially Indo-Portuguese tables and ivory, teak and ebony chests) dating from the 17th and 18th centuries.

The museum (☎ 2 42 23) is open daily except Monday, from 9.30 am to noon and 2 to 5 pm; admission costs 150$00.

Castelo de São Tiago da Barra

The grandiose castle at the mouth of the river started life in the 15th century as a smallish fort, which was later integrated into a larger one which Felipe II of Spain (at that time also known as Felipe I of Portugal) commissioned in 1592 to guard the prosperous port from pirates.

Today the buildings within the walls have been converted into uninteresting office space, but it's worth taking a look at the exterior.

Monte de Santa Luzia

There are two good reasons to climb Viana's hill. The ugly basilica on top isn't one of them, but the view from the basilica is; go into the basilica at the side entrance marked 'zimbório'.

The second draw is the ruins of a Celtiberian citânia dating from around the 4th century BC, in a fenced-off area behind the basilica. The site is poorly maintained but you can make out the remains of walls and circular stone huts.

You can either climb up the hill through pine woods (the trail starts about 200m up the road from the main entrance to the hospital) or take the *elevador* (funicular) from the northern side of Avenida 25 de Abril. In summer and at weekends it runs on the hour from 9 am to noon, then at 12.30 pm, then every half-hour from 1.30 to 7 pm. At other times it runs approximately hourly from 9 am to 6 pm. The seven minute trip costs 100$00 each way.

Children's Playground

There's an excellent children's adventure playground along the riverfront near Largo 5 de Outubro.

Markets

The mercado municipal is east of the centre on Rua Martim Velho. A huge Gypsy market takes place every Friday in the wasteland beside the Castelo de São Tiago da Barra.

Beaches

Viana's beach, Praia do Cabedelo, across the river, is one of the Minho's best, with little development beyond a windsurfing school and a couple of cafés by the dock. The easiest way to get there is by passenger ferry (no cars) from the pier south of Largo 5 de Outubro. In summer only it makes the five minute crossing almost hourly until at least 7 pm, for 120$00. There are also regular buses from the Jardim Marginal.

North of Viana, all the way to Caminha, is a string of fine, undeveloped beaches, including Afife (allegedly one of Portugal's cleanest) and Moledo do Minho, and a low-key resort at Vila Praia de Âncora. Four daily train services, and regular bus services as far as Caminha (get on at the Jardim Marginal) make day trips feasible.

Boat Trips

If there are enough people to fill the boat, trips up the Rio Lima run daily in summer, from the pier south of Largo 5 de Outubro. They can last anywhere from 30 minutes (600$00) to three hours (2500$00, with lunch), with 25% off for kids from 11 to 16 years, and 50% off for ages three to 10. Call Portela & Folhos (☎ 84 22 90) for more details or check at the pier.

Special Events

The Romaria de Nossa Senhora da Agónia in August is the region's big bash of the year (see the boxed text on the next page). Viana also goes a little nuts in mid-May, during Semana Académica (or Queima das Fitas), a week of between-terms madness similar to Coimbra's.

Places to Stay

Camping *Orbitur* (☎ 32 21 67) is at Praia do Cabedelo, within walking distance of the

MINHO

Who's Sorry Now?

Viana's Romaria de Nossa Senhora da Agónia (Our Lady of Sorrows) is one of the most spectacular of the Minho's many festivals. It starts on the Friday nearest 20 August and lasts for three days, featuring everything from sombre processions to merry parades and nightly fireworks. The streets are decorated with coloured sawdust, the women come out in their jewellery and traditional dress, the men drink like there's no tomorrow and at the end of it the town collapses with a massive hangover. Of course accommodation is tight; you'll need to book well ahead.

ferry pier. It's open mid-January through November, with bungalows for rent too. Rates per person/tent/car are 600/500/510$00. The nearby Inatel site is for Inatel members only. Both get packed out in the summer.

Hostels The *Gil Eanes*, an old hospital ship from Viana's mothballed Newfoundland cod fishing fleet, is under renovation, with plans to transform it into a combined public health centre, museum (of the cod fishing era), restaurant and youth hostel. A completion date is hard to come by.

Private Rooms The turismo keeps a list of *quartos* (private rooms) around town (probably your only chance of accommodation in August, especially during the Romaria). Expect to pay at least 5000$00 a double at these times.

Pensões & Residenciais Accommodation may be tight in summer but outside the high season a little shopping around may reveal some good bargains. Prices given here are for the high season.

Droopy *Pensão Guerreiro* (☎ 82 20 99, Rua Grande 14) has basic doubles without bathroom for 5000$00. For the same price, *Pensão Vianense* (☎ 82 31 18, Avenida Conde da Carreira 79) and *Pensão Dolce Vita* (☎ 2 48 60, Rua do Poço 44) offer more character and comfort.

Doubles at friendly *Residencial Viana Mar* (☎/fax 82 89 62, Avenida dos Combatentes 215) are good value at 6500$00 (5000$00 without bathroom). *Residencial Laranjeira* (☎ 82 22 61, fax 82 19 02, Rua General Luís do Rego 45) has thin-walled doubles for 7000$00 with bath or 6000$00 with shower (4500$00 without either).

In the same range are the popular *Residencial Magalhães* (☎ 82 32 93, Rua Manuel Espregueira 62) and *Pensão-Restaurant Alambique* (☎ 82 38 94, Rua Manuel Espregueira 86). Prices at all four places include breakfast.

For a bit of pampering, try a night at *Residencial Jardim* (☎ 82 89 15, fax 82 89 17, Largo 5 de Outubro), which offers doubles with river views for 9000$00, breakfast included.

Turihab The turismo has details of several nearby cottages and manor houses (most of them hard to reach without your own wheels). Expect to pay at least 9000$00 for a double.

Places to Eat

Most mid-range pensões have restaurants that welcome non-guests and offer reasonable food at good prices. One is *Restaurante Laranjeira* (☎ 82 22 58, Rua Manuel Espregueira 24), which has a huge menu of dishes under 1300$00, though helpings are small and extras pricey.

Another is *Dolce Vita* (☎ 2 48 60, Rua do Poço 44), whose pasta and pizza make a welcome change. *A Gruta Snack Bar* (☎ 82 02 14, Rua Grande 87) is popular with students; it has a limited menu of dishes under 1200$00.

Two family-friendly places on Rua Gago Coutinho are *Restaurante Bar Minho* (☎ 82 32 61, No 103) and *Adega do Padrinho* (☎ 2 69 54, No 162), the latter with traditional dishes like *ensopada de coelho* (rabbit stew) for under 1500$00. Unpretentious *O Garfo* (☎ 82 94 15, Largo 5 de

MINHO

Outubro 28) has similarly sturdy offerings (offal-lovers will like the blood-and-meat concoction called *sarrabulho*).

Os Três Arcos (☎ 2 40 14, Largo João Tomás da Costa 25) deserves its reputation for good-value, well-prepared fish and seafood. Freshwater fish dishes are around 1500$00, seafood more, though the adjoining *cervejaria* (beer house) serves up half-portions for around 1000$00 (700$00 at lunchtime). *Os Três Potes (☎ 82 99 28, Beco dos Fornos 7)* draws the tourists with folksy décor and Saturday night folk dancing. Both restaurants are closed on Monday.

The fishing quarter between the castelo and Largo Vasco da Gama naturally has some worthy places, including *Restaurante Foz do Lima (☎ 82 92 32, Rua dos Poveiros)*, which does a good *caldeirada de peixe* (fish stew) for about 1300$00. At *Viana's Restaurante (☎ 2 47 97, Rua Frei Bartolomeu dos Mártires 179)* you can eat your fill of the *bacalhau* for which this restaurant is famous. *Neiva Mar Marisqueira (☎ 82 06 69, Largo Infante Dom Henrique 1)*, opposite the fish market, is strong on grilled dishes, with prices starting at around 1700$00.

Looking for a real breakfast? The modest *Snack-Bar Atlântico (Rua General Luís do Rego 37)* opens at 6.30 am and does good omelettes.

Entertainment

Good bars near the centre include *Glamour (☎ 82 29 63, Rua da Bandeira 177)*, with occasional live music, *Nasoni (☎ 82 72 15, Rua Espírito Santo 10)* and *Indian Bar (☎ 82 87 94, Rua de São Bento 131)*.

Getting There & Away

Bus Several long-distance bus companies operate from the bus station (☎ 82 13 92) and also have stops near their ticket offices on Avenida dos Combatentes. Buses to closer destinations (such as Cabedelo and Caminha) stop by the Jardim Marginal. Note that long-distance services thin out drastically at weekends.

AVIC (☎ 82 97 05), the largest local operator, with several offices on the Avenida including its head office at No 206, and Turilis (☎ 82 93 48), Avenida dos Combatentes 107, each have daily express services between Melgaço and Lisbon, via Viana and Porto. AV Minho (☎ 82 88 34), Avenida dos Combatentes 181, has multiple daily express coaches to Porto and up the Rio Minho to Melgaço. AV Cura (☎ 82 93 48), Avenida dos Combatentes 81, has services to Ponte de Lima and Arcos de Valdevez throughout the day.

Train Viana is on the Porto-Valença do Minho line, with at least 10 services daily to Porto and seven to Valença (including three fast international trains between Porto and Vigo in Spain). Coming from Braga, there are frequent services to Nine where you can pick up connecting trains to Viana.

Getting Around

Taxis hang out along Avenida dos Combatentes. Cars can be rented from Ovnitur (☎ 82 03 33), Avis (☎ 82 39 94) and Hertz (☎ 82 22 50).

VALENÇA DO MINHO
☎ 051 • pop 2500

From its grassy hilltop position, the 17th century fortified citadel of Valença do Minho (usually called just Valença) overlooks the Rio Minho frontier with Spain. A dull new town has spread out below, but it's the old *fortaleza* (fortress) which is the focus of attention for Spanish day-trippers. They troop across the river from Tuy in their hundreds to buy cheap linen and towels from the souvenir shops lining the cobbled streets. Once the hordes have gone, the silence seeps up over the walls from the riverbank and the citadel regains its tranquillity and sense of isolation.

Orientation

Arriving by train or bus (they share a terminal), you'd hardly guess there was anything to see: you're in the dreary new town, half a kilometre south of the citadel, without a sign in sight. Head up to the intersection and turn right into Avenida Espanha, the new town's main street. At the first crossroads, turn left and climb the hill to the citadel's southernmost gateway, Portas da Coroada. Or go straight and then bear left (a 'Centro Histórico' sign points the way) up Avenida dos Combatentes da Grande Guerra to the citadel's main pedestrian entrance, Portas do Meio.

If you're arriving from Spain, you'll cross the Eiffel-inspired Ponte Internacional (also called Ponte Velha), built in 1886, to the north-eastern end of Avenida Espanha. Drivers can also approach by the A3/IP1 motorway, which crosses the Rio Minho on a new bridge, slightly downstream from Ponte Velha.

Information

The marginally useful turismo (☎/fax 2 33 74) is housed in a poorly signposted wooden cottage in a patch of woods off Avenida Espanha (behind the Centro Histórico sign). The office is open daily from 9.30 am to 12.30 pm and 2.30 to 6 pm (morning only on Sunday).

There's a Spanish consulate (☎ 2 21 22) about 90m north-east of the turismo on Avenida Espanha. It's open weekdays only from 9 am to 5 pm.

Fortaleza

A fortress existed on this site from at least the 13th century, guarding Portugal's northern frontier. At that time Valença was called Contrasta (the fortress across the river at Tuy provided its counterpart). The well-preserved fortress you see today dates from the 16th century, its design inspired by the French military architect Vauban, as were several others in northern Portugal (such as the forts at Chaves). In fact there are two fortresses – separated by a deep ditch and joined by a single bridge – each with six bastions, watchtowers, massive gateways and defensive bulwarks.

The old churches and Manueline mansions lining the cobbled streets inside reveal how successful the fortifications were: they emerged unscathed from several sieges, as late as the 19th century. The larger north-eastern fortress contains most historic items of note, including the 14th century Igreja de São Estevão with its Renaissance façade, a nearby Roman milestone (taken from the Roman Braga-Astorga road at its Rio Minho crossing) and, outside the Capela de Bom Jesus, a statue of Santo Teotónio, a 12th century local holy man venerated by Dom Afonso Henriques.

Both forts now bulge grotesquely with predatory restaurants and shops hawking everything from trinkets to antiques; and this must be the smallest village in Europe with traffic lights. It's a bit depressing, although with a bit of imagination (and/or money for top-end accommodation) you can see the fort for what it was, most easily at the far north-eastern end.

Places to Stay

Fortaleza Private rooms are sometimes available, and campers often set up tents below the north-western ramparts, but there are only two official places to stay inside, both at the north-eastern end, both with superb views into Spanish Galicia, and both expensive.

At the *Pousada de São Teotónio (☎ 82 40 20, fax 82 43 97)* high-season doubles cost 20,300$00. The nearby Turihab *Casa do Poço de Valença (☎ 82 52 35, fax 82 54 69, Travessa da Gaviarra 4)* is a restored 18th century house that once lodged the sick from the Misericórdia hospital and now cares for the wealthy, with contemporary Portuguese and Spanish art, a library, billiard room and five doubles for 15,000$00 (13,500$00 with double bed).

New Town Relax, there are more modest places down below. Prices are for the local high season, approximately July to mid-September; outside this period they're at least a third less. All have private bathroom and include breakfast.

Restaurante-Residencial Rio Minho (☎ 2 23 31, Largo da Estação), opposite the station, has doubles from 7000$00. On the road up to the Portas da Coroada are *Residencial São Gião* (☎ *2 32 66, Centro Comercial Alvarinho, 1st floor)*, at 7000$00; *Residencial Val Flores* (☎ *82 41 06, fax 82 41 29, Centro Val Flores)* in the adjacent shopping centre, at 7500$00; and the *Hotel Lara* (☎ *82 43 48, fax 82 43 58)*, up the hill, at 11,500$00.

Around Valença At Fontoura, about 10km south of Valença on the N210, is English-run *Casa de Yavanna* (☎/*fax 83 92 11, Lugar da Insua)*, offering not only 10-day pottery workshops (see Courses in the Facts for the Visitor chapter) but also separate B&B accommodation at 6000$00 for a double with bathroom and breakfast, on a 17th century farmstead. Call ahead for directions. Public transport is scarce.

Places to Eat

Eating in the fort with Spanish tour groups isn't as bad as it sounds if you've got the dosh and the palate, and like a jolly atmosphere. *Restaurante Monumental* (☎ *2 35 57, Portas da Coroada)* has roast kid, Minho trout and other local treats for 1200$00 per dish and up. At the more easy-going *Restaurante Bom Jesus* (☎ *2 20 88, Largo do Bom Jesus)*, prices for specialities like *ameijoa à espanhola* (Spanish-style clams) and rojões à moda do Minho start at 1400$00. *Restaurante Beluarte* (☎ *82 40 42, Rua Apolinário da Fonseca)* has a nice array of desserts.

In the north-eastern fort, *A Gruta* (☎ *2 22 70)* is a simple restaurant-bar built into the walls beside the portal near Largo da República. Most items here cost less than 1500$00 a dish, and there's a decent tourist menu for 1400$00.

Outside the fort are several mid-range restaurants, along the same strip as the residenciais.

Getting There & Away

Bus From the station, Courense (☎ *82 41 75)* has eight daily services to Viana do Castelo and 11 to Monção, with fewer at weekends. AVIC and Turilis each have two

or three daily express services between Melgaço and Lisbon, via Viana and Porto. AV Minho buses to/from Melgaço and Viana pass through five or six times each weekday, and three times each weekday en route to Porto.

Train Valença is 3½ to four hours from Porto on regional trains (at least six daily), and 2½ hours away on three fast international trains that continue as far as Vigo in Spain.

MONÇÃO
☎ 051 • pop 2600

This pleasant riverside town, 16km east of Valença do Minho, is popular with Portuguese tourists for its spa, just east of the centre. Little remains of the town's 14th and 17th century fortifications but the small, atmospheric old town is a soothing place, and there's plenty of good food and wine.

Orientation

From the defunct train station, now serving as the main bus stop, it's two blocks north, straight up Rua General Pimenta de Castro, to the first of the town's two major squares, Praça da República. Praça Deu-la-Deu and the heart of the old town lie a block further along this street.

There is another bus stop by the GALP petrol station, two blocks east down Avenida 25 de Abril from the old train station, outside the town's southern gateway, Portas do Sol.

Information

The turismo (☎ 65 27 57) is on the 1st floor of the restored Casa do Curro, which also houses the town library. There are entrances on Praça Deu-la-Deu (next to the Café Escondidinho) and on Praça da República. It's open daily from 9.30 am to 12.30 pm and 2 to 7 pm (6 pm in winter).

Deu-la-Deu

Following the Deu-la-Deu history trail will lead you through the most attractive part of town. From the chestnut-shaded Praça

Deu-la-Deu

Monção's most famous daughter is one Deu-la-Deu Martins, who tricked a force of Castilians into calling off a siege in 1368 by scrabbling together enough flour from the starving town to make some cakes. She threw these to the Castilians in a brazen show of plenty and the disheartened force withdrew.

Deu-la-Deu, where a statue of Monção's famous daughter tops a fountain, head east down an arched side street to her birthplace, next to a butcher shop. Her tomb is in the Romanesque Igreja Matriz at the end of this street.

Igreja da Misericórdia
Dominating the southern end of Praça Deu-la-Deu, this church has an attractive coffered ceiling painted with cherubs, and walls of azulejos.

Special Events
The town's biggest bash is the Festa de Corpo de Deus on 18 June, with a religious procession that includes a re-enactment of the mythical battle between St George and the Dragon.

Places to Stay
Dormidas O Abrigo (☎ 65 23 29, Rua Bispo de Lemos 2), off Praça Deu-la-Deu, has comfortable doubles with bathroom for 3500$00. The owners run a second house with the same name and prices on Rua 1 de Dezembro, also off Praça Deu-la-Deu. Sunny rooms with shower above *Croissanteria Raiano* (see Places to Eat) cost 5000$00.

Cheery *Residencial Esteves* (☎ 65 23 86, Rua General Pimenta de Castro) offers modern doubles from 5500$00 (3500$00 without bathroom). Rooms at *Pensão Residencial Mané* (☎ 65 23 55, fax 65 23 76, Rua General Pimenta de Castro 5) cost 8000$00; up the street and under the same management is *Albergaria Atlântico (Rua General Pimenta de Castro 15)*, with rooms for 10,000$00. Rates at all three include breakfast.

For top-end comfort, ask the turismo about Turihab properties: closest are two manor houses, *Casa de Rodas* (☎ 65 21 05), 1km to the south, and *Solar de Serrade* (☎ 65 40 08, fax 65 40 41), a few kilometres further. Both are on the grounds of estates producing Alvarinho wine grapes.

Places to Eat
Local specialities here include salmon, shad and trout from the Rio Minho, and lamprey eels (in season from January to March). Wash them down with local Alvarinho wine, pricey but arguably the best of the Minho's vinhos verdes.

The cheapest fare is near the former train station, with several places tabling lunchtime specials for about 800$00. In the same mould is the minuscule *Café A Regional (Largo Alfândega)*, off the western corner of Praça da República. The good *Café-Restaurante Central* (☎ 65 28 05), at the south-eastern corner of Praça Deu-la-Deu (enter at the rear), has lots of grilled meat and fish plates starting from 900$00.

Croissanteria Raiano (☎ 65 35 34, Praça Deu-la-Deu 34), a few doors from the turismo, has a few modest lunchtime specials – with vegetables, hurray – and service that's about the most cheerful in town. One of the best places for fish is nearby *Restaurante Cabral* (☎ 65 17 55, Rua do 1 Dezembro).

A salubrious place en route to the spa is *Flôr do Minho* (☎ 65 14 20, Largo São João de Deus), where most of the regional specialities cost 1000$00 to 1500$00 per plate.

Getting There & Away
From the former train station, Courense (☎ 65 38 81) has at least eight daily services via Valença to Viana do Castelo, and Salvador (☎ 65 38 81) has six to Braga and Arcos de Valdevez. Services thin out at weekends.

MINHO

From the bus stop near the GALP station you can catch AVIC, Turilis and AV Minho services to Lisbon, Viana do Castelo and Porto detailed under Getting There & Away in the earlier Valença do Minho section.

PONTE DE LIMA

☎ 058 • pop 3300

This market town reclining on the south bank of the Rio Lima, 23km east of Viana do Castelo, is a relaxing, pretty place to hole up in for a few days. When the Romans passed through here on their march through Iberia they had trouble leaving because, so the story goes, the soldiers were convinced that the Rio Lima was the River Lethe – the mythical river of oblivion – and that if they crossed it they would forget everything. It was only after their leader, Decimus Junius Brutus, plunged ahead and shouted back his legionaries' names that they braved the waters.

The Roman bridge after which Ponte de Lima is named supposedly marks the very spot, and is part of the Roman road from Braga to Astorga in Spain. It's just one of several well-preserved historical features which give the town its character. But there's no pressure for major sightseeing here: the charm of the place lies in its sandy river bank (the site of fantastic bimonthly markets and annual fairs) and shady riverside walks, its rural surroundings and laid-back atmosphere.

As the heartland of Turismo de Habitação (see Accommodation in the Facts for the Visitor chapter), Ponte de Lima also has more Turihab properties than any other town in Portugal. Alas for traditionalists, a golf course and racecourse have opened too, marking Ponte de Lima's coming-of-age in upmarket tourism.

Orientation

The bus station and mercado municipal are a few steps from the 'Alameda' (Alameda Principe Real Dom Luís Filipe, also called Avenida dos Plátanos), a riverside pedestrianised avenue of huge plane trees. Upriver is the main square, Largo de Camões, with cafés, restaurants and an 18th century fountain. Everything of interest is within a few blocks of it. Downriver, the modern Ponte de Nossa Senhora da Guia carries traffic on the Braga to Valença N201 highway.

Information

The very well-organised turismo (☎/fax 94 23 35) shares space with a small handicrafts display on Praça da República, a few minutes walk from the river on Rua Cardeal Saraiva. It's open daily from 9 am to 12.30 pm and 2.30 to 6 pm (morning only on Sunday).

The headquarters of Portugal's largest Turihab owners' association, Solares de Portugal (☎ 74 16 72, fax 74 14 44), around the corner from the turismo, has information on properties around the country. Some owners belong to a smaller association based here, Privetur (☎ 74 14 93).

Several banks have ATMs, including one on Largo de Camões. The post office is across Rua Cardeal Saraiva from the turismo. There's a laundry, Lavandaria Ibérica, in Centro Ibérico, a shopping centre by the bus station.

The hospital (☎ 74 14 00) is on Rua Conde de Bertiandos and the police station (☎ 94 11 13) is on Rua Dr Luís da Cunha Nogueira, east of the old town.

Ponte Romana

The 31-arched bridge across the Rio Lima actually dates from the 14th century, when the original Roman bridge was rebuilt and extended. It was restored again in the 15th century. According to the turismo, the segment on the north bank by the village of Arcozelo is still original Roman work, apart from the road surface. The bridge is off limits to motor traffic, but watch for riders who gallop across it at dusk, instantly plunging the scene back into medieval days.

Museu dos Terceiros

Downriver from the town centre, just off the Alameda, is the Renaissance Igreja de Santo António dos Frades (formerly part of a convent). Adjacent to it, the 18th century

MINHO

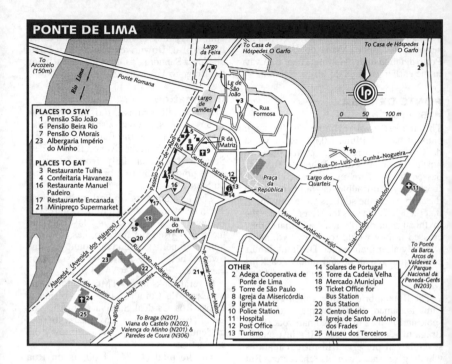

PONTE DE LIMA

To Arcozelo (150m)

Rio Lima

Ponte Romana

Largo da Feira

To Casa de Hóspedes O Garfo

Lg de São João

Largo de Camões

Rua Formosa

To Casa de Hóspedes O Garfo

0   50   100 m

PLACES TO STAY
1 Pensão São João
6 Pensão Beira Rio
7 Pensão O Morais
23 Albergaria Império do Minho

PLACES TO EAT
3 Restaurante Tulha
4 Confeitaria Havanaza
16 Restaurante Manuel Padeiro
17 Restaurante Encanada
21 Minipreço Supermarket

R da Matriz

Rua Cardeal Saraiva

Passeio 25 de Abril

Rua-Dr-Luis-da-Cunha-Nogueira

Praça da República

Largo dos Quartéis

Rua do Bonfim

Rua-Conde-de-Bertiandos

Avenida-António–Feijó

'Alameda' (Avenida dos Plátanos) r

Rua-dos-Terceiros

Rua-João-Rodrigues-de-Morais

Rua-Agostinho-José-Taveira

Rua-General-Norton-de-Matos

To Ponte da Barca, Arcos de Valdevez & Parque Nacional da Peneda-Gerês (N203)

To Braga (N201)
Viana do Castelo (N202),
Valença do Minho (N201) &
Paredes de Coura (N306)

OTHER
2 Adega Cooperativa de Ponte de Lima
5 Torre de São Paulo
8 Igreja da Misericórdia
9 Igreja Matriz
10 Police Station
11 Hospital
12 Post Office
13 Turismo
14 Solares de Portugal
15 Torre da Cadeia Velha
18 Mercado Municipal
19 Ticket Office for Bus Station
20 Bus Station
22 Centro Ibérico
24 Igreja de Santo António dos Frades
25 Museu dos Terceiros

Igreja de São Francisco dos Terceiros is now a rambling museum of ecclesiastical and folk treasures, although the highlight is the church itself, with its gilded Baroque altars and pulpits. The museum (☎ 94 25 63) offers guided tours daily except Tuesday, from 9 am to noon and 2.30 to 5 pm. Ring the bell for the curator. Admission is free.

Igreja Matriz
The parish church, off Rua Cardeal Saraiva, is one of several eye-catching medieval monuments in this part of town. It dates from the 14th century but was remodelled in the 18th century. A fine Romanesque doorway remains from earlier days.

Town Walls & Towers
Two crenellated towers – once part of the town's 14th century fortifications – face the river south of Largo de Camões. The southern one, Torre da Cadeia Velha (Old Prison Tower), is now a handicrafts and souvenir shop, where you can watch linen and cotton being embroidered. Surviving bits of the walls can be seen behind and between this and the other tower, Torre de São Paulo. You can climb onto the walls via stairs in two places (one near Restaurante Manuel Padeiro).

Markets
A huge, twice-monthly Monday market sprawls along the bank downriver of the Roman bridge, offering everything from farm tools and wine barrels to fresh fruit, cheese and bread.

Activities
Walking There are charming walks all round Ponte de Lima – through the coun-

tryside, past ancient monuments, along cobbled village lanes trellised with vines. The turismo has produced *Trilhos Alto Minho*, an illustrated folio of eight fine and easy walks of between 7 and 14km (though the maps and details are not 100% reliable). Take a picnic: cafés and restaurants are rare.

Golf Clube de Golfe de Ponte de Lima (☎ 74 34 14/5) is 2km south of town, off the Braga road at Feitosa. The 18 hole, par 71 course covers the wooded slopes above town, commanding grand views. The clubhouse includes a tee shop and restaurant.

Horse Riding At Clube Equestre (☎ 94 24 66), across the river in Arcozelo, you can hire horses by the hour. The turismo insists a better deal is the Hípodromo de Ponte de Lima (☎ 76 27 84), 12km south of town at Calvelo, where you can also watch horse races.

Wine Tasting The Adega Cooperativa de Ponte de Lima (☎ 74 14 49), north-east of the centre on Rua Conde de Bertiandos, is open weekdays for wine-tasting tours. The *adega* (literally, wine cellar) produces both red and white varieties of vinho verde, as well as two brands of *aguardente* firewater.

Special Events
One of Portugal's most ancient ongoing fairs, the Feiras Novas (New Fairs), has been a Ponte de Lima fixture for almost nine centuries, and it's a great show (see the boxed text).

Another centuries-old tradition is the Vaca das Cordas, a form of bull-running in which young men goad a hapless bull (restrained by a long rope, or *corda*) as it runs through the town and down to the river. The following day's Festa do Corpo de Deus has more religious overtones and features patterns of flowers carpeting the streets. The festival is held annually in early June.

Places to Stay
Pensões & Residenciais The riverfront *Pensão Beira Rio* (☎ 94 34 71, Passeio 25

---

de Abril 10) and the damp *Pensão O Morais* (☎ 94 24 70, Rua da Matriz 8) have doubles from about 4000$00. Turismo staff wrinkle their noses at these, but they're the cheapest in town.

Doubles at *Pensão São João* (☎ 94 12 88, Largo de São João)* cost 5000$00. Just under 1km north-east is *Casa de Hóspedes O Garfo* (☎ 74 31 47, fax 74 35 80), where comfortable doubles start at 6000$00. The modern *Albergaria Império do Minho* (☎ 74 15 10, fax 94 25 67, Avenida dos Plátanos)*, in a shopping complex on the riverfront, has rooms with air-con and satellite TV for 9000$00. Breakfast is included at all three.

Turihab There are about three dozen Turihab properties in the Ponte de Lima area, from modest farmhouses to fabulous mansions, two-thirds of them affiliated to Solares de Portugal. You can book through the turismo, Solares or Privetur, or – sometimes more cheaply – directly with the owners. For two people, figure on paying at least 9500$00 for a double room or a small self-catering cottage in high season.

Among affordable choices near Ponte de Lima are *Casa do Arrabalde* (☎ 74 24 42), a restored 18th century manor house in Arcozelo, across the Ponte Romana (or off the N306 to Paredes de Coura); *Quinta de Pomarchão* (☎ 74 17 42), also in Arcozelo, with accommodation in old farm cottages on the grounds; and **Casa de Crasto** (☎ 94 11 56), a 17th century house in São João da Ribeira, just off the Ponte da Barca road, about 1km east of Ponte de Lima.

Our choice is **Quinta da Aldeia** (☎ 94 22 68), a secluded manor house 3km from Ponte de Lima in São João da Ribeira, off the Ponte da Barca road, with a few cottage-apartments, outdoor space for kids and even a miniature playhouse. It's open from May to October.

Places to Eat

Unlike restaurants elsewhere in Portugal, some in Ponte de Lima don't seem to post prices out front.

Pensão Beira Rio and **Pensão São João** (see Places to Stay) have popular, modestly priced restaurants, run by bevies of mums and grannies. Another popular spot is **Restaurante Encanada** (☎ 94 11 89, Passeio 25 de Abril), overlooking the mercado municipal.

Restaurante Manuel Padeiro (☎ 94 16 49, Rua do Bonfim) serves the local speciality, rojões de sarrabulho (a carnivore's dream, made from minced pork and pig's blood) and local sável (shad fish) in season. Most dishes cost under 1500$00. **Restaurante Tulha** (☎ 94 28 79, Rua Formosa) is a smart spot favoured by late-night diners, with prices around 1500$00 per dish.

The best places in town for watching the world go by are the cafés on Largo de Camões, in particular the venerable **Confeitaria Havaneza**.

There's a **Minipreço** supermarket on Rua General Norton de Matos.

Getting There & Away

Each weekday, AV Minho (☎ 74 36 13) and AV Cura (☎ 94 12 44) between them have some 20 services from Viana do Castelo; REDM (☎ 94 28 70) and Domingos da Cunha (☎ 94 27 91) have several from Barcelos; REDM also has buses from Braga, along with local carrier Esteves e Andreia. AV Minho also has a once-weekly Porto express via Viana do Castelo on Sunday, returning to Ponte de Lima on Friday.

AV Cura and Salvador (☎ 6 60 01) both go to Ponte da Barca four or five times per weekday, and AV Cura has services to Arcos de Valdevez throughout the day; Domingos da Cunha also has upriver services. Weekend services are less frequent.

PONTE DA BARCA
☎ 058 • pop 2000

This pretty riverside town, named after the barca (barge) which used to ferry passengers (frequently pilgrims on their way to Santiago de Compostela in Spain) across the river, is a smaller, drowsier version of Ponte de Lima. The place comes to life, however, every other Wednesday (alternating with Arcos de Valdevez) when a huge market spreads along the riverside. The old town area has a picturesque 16th century bridge and a pleasant riverside promenade.

Ponte da Barca makes a good base for some fine local walking (see Walks later in this section).

Orientation

Just east of the bridge, the old town is packed into narrow lanes on both sides of the main road, Rua Conselheiro Rocha Peixoto. Further east, where this road becomes Rua António José Pereira, is the less appealing new town. Buses stop near the bridge.

Information

The turismo (☎/fax 45 28 99), a few minutes walk east of the bridge at Largo do Misericórdia 10 (below Rua Conselheiro Rocha Peixoto), is open weekdays from 9 am to 12.30 pm and 2.30 to 6 pm between June and September (plus Sunday morning from mid-July to mid-September). You can pick up a town map and accommodation information here.

Next door to the turismo is ADERE (Peneda-Gerês Rural Development Association; ☎ 45 22 50, ☎/fax 45 24 50, email aderepg@mail.telepac.pt), a consultancy involved in culturally sensitive development in and around the Parque Nacional da Peneda-Gerês. It's open weekdays from

9 am to 1 pm and 2 to 7 pm. For more on its work, including the booking of traditional-style accommodation in the park area, see the boxed text in the Parque Nacional da Peneda-Gerês section later in this chapter.

There are banks with ATMs along Rua António José Pereira and a post office nearby, on Rua das Fontainhas.

Ponte & Jardim dos Poetas

The lovely 10-arched bridge across the Rio Lima, dating from 1543, has been rebuilt several times since then, most recently in the 19th century. Beside it is the former arcaded marketplace and a little garden, Jardim dos Poetas, dedicated to two 16th century poets, Diogo Bernardes and his brother Agostinho da Cruz, born in Ponte da Barca.

Walks

The turismo can suggest walking routes in the area, including a strenuous 18km hike just within Parque Nacional da Peneda-Gerês, starting from Entre Ambos-os-Rios, 12km east of Ponte da Barca. In fact much of their information is from *Landscapes of Portugal: Costa Verde* (see the Books section in the Facts for the Visitor chapter), which isn't entirely up-to-date – though the old villages described en route have changed very little.

A shorter, more simple stroll is westwards 4km to Bravães, a roadside hamlet famous for its Romanesque Igreja de São Salvador, whose doorways are covered with intricate carvings of animals, birds and human figures.

Places to Stay

Camping The nearest *parque de campismo* (☎ 6 83 61) is a basic riverside site 9km upriver at Entre Ambos-os-Rios, just inside the national park. It's run by ADERE and is open year-round for 400/350/450$00 per person/tent/car.

To get there take any Lindoso-bound bus (see Soajo & Lindoso under Parque Nacional da Peneda-Gerês later in this chapter).

Pensões & Residenciais Two places offering simple doubles with shared bathroom for about 3000$00 are *Pensão Gomes* (☎ 45 22 88, Rua Conselheiro Rocha Peixoto 13), with a rooftop terrace, and the less atmospheric *Pensão Carvalho* (☎ 45 22 68, Praça Dr António Lacerda), in the new town. Also in the new town is the modern *Residencial Fontainhas* (☎ 45 24 42, Rua António José Pereira), at about 5500$00 for a double with bathroom. Breakfast is included at all three.

At *Residencial Os Poetas* (☎ 45 35 78, Jardim dos Poetas) – you can't miss the ugly roof sign – a double costs 8400$00 in August or 6400$00 the rest of the summer. Another up-scale option is *Casa Nobre* (☎ 45 21 29), a private manor house opposite the turismo (behind the arched town hall).

Turihab There are at least five Turihab properties within 5km of town, including *Quinta da Prova* (☎ 45 31 86) on the river's north bank, with several two-room apartments for 8000$00. These, and others nearer the national park, can be booked through ADERE.

Places to Eat

The lethargic restaurant attached to *Pensão Gomes* (see Places to Stay) offers regional fare, including truta à Rio Lima (river trout) for 990$00. Cheaper places in the new town include friendly *Café Snack Bar O Nicola* (☎ 45 32 86, Rua António José Pereira 32), with good-value lunchtime pratos do dia for 700$00.

Those with money to spend can settle in at the riverside *Restaurant Bar do Rio* (☎ 45 25 82) for arroz de marisco (seafood rice), snails and other luxuries for around 2000$00 a dish.

Getting There & Away

Buses all stop near the bridge: on Rua Diogo Bernardes (the Ponte de Lima road) for Ponte de Lima, opposite Pensão Gomes for Lindoso and Braga, and outside Pensão Gomes for Arcos de Valdevez.

Salvador stops about 15 times a day, en route between Braga and Arcos. AV Cura stops four or five times on the way from Viana do Castelo to Arcos via Ponte de Lima. Domingos da Cunha also has Ponte de Lima services. All of their weekend schedules are thinner.

ARCOS DE VALDEVEZ
☎ 058

Though Arcos has two comely old churches in a small, almost tourist-free old centre, and a pleasant setting on the west bank of the Rio Vez (a tributary of the Lima), it doesn't merit a special trip. But it's a gateway into the northern part of the Parque Nacional da Peneda-Gerês. You've got to buses here for Soajo or Lindoso (see Getting There & Away in the Soajo & Lindoso section later in this chapter), and there's a park information office in town.

Orientation & Information
The municipal turismo (☎/fax 6 60 01) is by the Avenida bus stop at the edge of the old town, just upriver (north-east) from the N101 bridge. It's open daily except Sunday afternoon, from 9.30 am to 12.30 and 2.30 to 6 pm (closed Sunday in winter). They'll give you an Arcos map-brochure and help you find a place to stay.

A marginally useful national park office (☎ 6 53 38, fax 52 27 07) is on Rua Padre Manuel Himalaia, two blocks uphill from the riverfront fountain, which is just downriver from the N101 bridge. It's open weekdays only, from 9 am to 12.30 pm and 2 to 5.30 pm.

The town centre is Praça Municipal, a block uphill (north-west) from the turismo. Every other Wednesday is market day, alternating with Ponte da Barca.

Churches
If you've got time on your hands, from the turismo walk half a block downriver and then turn right up to Praça Municipal. On the other side of the square is the little Romanesque Capela da Nossa Senhora da Conceição (also called Capela da Praça),

which dates from 1372. Carry on towards Largo da Lapa, which embraces the oval and oddly pretty Baroque Igreja da Nossa Senhora da Lapa (1767).

Places to Stay
Pensão Flôr do Minho (☎ 6 52 16, Rua da Valeta 106-108) has a few plain doubles without bathroom for 3000$00. It's down behind the Praça Municipal (take the lane along the left side of the Capela da Praça).

Residencial Tavares (☎ 6 62 53) opposite Nossa Senhora da Lapa has doubles with bathroom for 6000$00 to 7000$00. Two distant residenciais with similar prices are **Costa do Vez** (☎ 52 12 26), on the Monção road half a kilometre upriver from the turismo, and **Dom António** (☎ 52 10 10, Rua Dr Germano Amorim), half a kilometre downriver from the turismo, just before the big bridge to Braga.

Places to Eat
Restaurante A Cozinha da Aldeia (Rua da Valeta 75), between Capela da Nossa Senhora da Conceição and Pensão Flôr do Minho, dishes up Portuguese standards for 800$00 to 1300$00 per plate.

Getting There & Away
Salvador (☎ 52 15 04) runs to/from Braga (via Ponte da Barca) about 15 times a day, and to/from Monção about six times a day (less at weekends). AV Cura (☎ 6 52 36) has eight or nine weekday services from Viana do Castelo (via Ponte de Lima, with about half of them via Ponte da Barca too), plus further services from Ponte de Lima. Domingos da Cunha (☎ 81 58 43) has several daily services from Barcelos, and Renex (☎ 6 51 24) comes here daily from Lisbon.

Parque Nacional da Peneda-Gerês

The Peneda-Gerês National Park, the first protected area in Portugal, was established in 1971 to safeguard both the country's natural riches and the rural way of life of its people. At 70,290 hectares, it's the fourth-largest protected area in Portugal (the first three being the Serra da Estrela, Douro Internacional and Montesinho natural parks).

The crescent-shaped park takes in four major granite massifs – the Serra da Peneda, Serra do Soajo, Serra Amarela and Serra do Gerês – largely covering the north-eastern part of the Minho, but with one end in Trás-os-Montes.

It's crossed by the Rio Lima (which rises in Spain), almost dissected by the Rio Homem (which rises high in the park) and deeply etched by many more streams. Two rivers help define its boundaries: the Rio Laboreiro between the Serra da Peneda and Spain, and the Rio Cávado, which runs along the entire south-eastern end of the park. Five hydroelectric dams back up big reservoirs within the park, three of them on the Cávado.

PNPG Protected Areas

Portugal's other parks are all called *natural*. Peneda-Gerês is a *parque nacional* because it meets certain conditions of the World Conservation Union (IUCN), in particular reasonably undisturbed ecosystems of scientific/educational value which the government has taken steps to protect.

Thus there is a designated inner *área de ambiente natural* (natural environmental area) at higher elevations close to the border, parts of which are set aside for research and off limits to the general public. This is surrounded by a buffer *área de ambiente rural* (rural environment area) peppered with small villages, where controlled development is permitted. The park's roads, tracks and trails are largely in the latter area.

The most assiduously protected zone – upon which the park's 'national' status heavily depends – is an area of virgin oak, chestnut and mistletoe forest called the Mata de Albergaria, north of Caldas do Gerês. Ironically it's traversed by the N308 highway which, serving an EU-anointed international border crossing, cannot simply be closed. Satisfying both the IUCN and the EU presents park officials with a delicate job.

On a 6km stretch of the twisting road above Caldas do Gerês, from the Portela de Leonte pass to the border at Portela do Homem, motorised traffic is tolerated but not allowed to linger. At checkpoints at either end, each driver gets a time-stamped ticket and has 15 minutes to turn it in at the other end. This stretch is patrolled, and the checkpoints staffed, seven days a week from July to September, and on weekends the rest of the year. Two side roads are also no-go for vehicles: south-west down the Rio Homem valley (except for residents), and east from Portela do Homem into the high Serra do Gerês.

The rules on camping – essentially that you can only use designated sites – are most strictly enforced in heavily trafficked areas. Signs warn against *campismo clandestino* (illegal camping), and park rangers are more like police than the cheerful helpers foreign visitors might expect.

The only restrictions on walking tie in with those on camping – if you can't get as far as a designated camp site, then you're expected to come back out (although private guides apparently do break the rules with multiday treks through remote areas devoid of official sites).

There are also restrictions on boats in the park's five *albufeiras* (reservoirs): motorised boats of any kind are allowed on the Caniçada, only electric motors on the Lindoso, only non-motorised boats on the Salamonde, and no boats at all on the Vilarinho das Furnas and Paradela. Even swimming is prohibited in the Vilarinho das Furnas.

PARQUE NACIONAL DA PENEDA-GERÊS

The heights close to the Spanish frontier, especially in the Serra do Gerês where several peaks rise over 1500m, are almost free of human activity other than summertime transhumance (temporary migration of entire villages, with their livestock, to high pastures). The outer part of the crescent has some 115 villages totalling around 15,000 people. The park, sharing 80km of frontier with Spain's Orense province, embraces a corresponding Spanish reserve, the Parque Natural Serra do Xurés.

Peneda-Gerês, especially the accessible southern Serra do Gerês, offers fine hiking and other sports, some attractive rural accommodation, and a window on a vanishing rural way of life. Needless to say, the park is very popular. The main base is the little spa town of Caldas do Gerês. If your time is short and you plan to base yourself there, do it midweek if you can: Portuguese daytrippers swarm up on summer weekends (though they tend to stick to the main camping areas). There's no fee to enter the park.

Flora & Fauna

The park has a striking diversity of climate, habitat and landscape, nourished by heavy rainfall – the Serra da Peneda gets more rain than anywhere else in Portugal. In sheltered valleys there are stands of arbutus, laurel and cork oak. Forests of black oak, English oak and holly give way at higher elevations to birch, yew and Scots pine, and in alpine areas to juniper and sandwort. In a small patch of the Serra do Gerês grows the Gerês iris, found nowhere else in the world. The park's upper reaches are blanketed in purple heather in April.

In the more remote areas there are wolves, wild boars, foxes, badgers, polecats and otters, as well as roe deer and a few wild ponies. Closer to the ground are grass snakes and the occasional venomous black viper. Birds found here include red kites, buzzards, goshawks, golden eagles and several species of owls. The park's best known domestic animal is the sturdy Castro Laboreiro sheepdog.

Traditional Culture

Many of the park's oldest villages are truly in a time warp, with oxen trundled down cobbled streets by black-clad old women, and horses shod in smoky blacksmith shops. The practice of moving livestock, and even entire villages, to high pasture for up to five months still goes on in the Serra da Peneda and Serra do Gerês.

But despite the founding of the park, the building of roads, and other government and private efforts, this rustic scene is fading away as young people head for the cities. Statistics say that an astonishing 75% of local people now are over 65. The road between Cabril and Paradela, for example, reveals a deeply ironic picture – a string of sparsely populated, decaying villages, surrounded by grand scenery, fertile soil, pristine air and clean water. Tourism may, in its own way, turn out to be a friend of tradition, with entrepreneurs restoring old buildings as rustic accommodation (see Places to Stay, later in this section). But it's an uphill battle: the spruced-up village of

Sirvozelo near Paradela, for example, has just 11 permanent residents left.

Information

Park Offices There are good park information offices at the park's Braga headquarters (☎ 053-600 34 80, fax 61 31 69) and Caldas do Gerês (☎ 053-39 11 81), and less useful ones at Arcos de Valdevez (☎ 058-6 53 38) and Montalegre (☎ 076-5 22 81). Small interpretative centres at Lamas de Mouro and Mezio have basic information and occasional exhibits.

All the offices sell a map of the park (530$00) which indicates some roads and tracks (but not trails), as well as an ageing booklet (105$00) on the park's human and natural features. Most other information is in Portuguese.

Topographic Maps Military topographic sheets covering the park at 1:25,000 cost

MINHO

about 1000$00 from Oficina d'Aventura (at Tagus Travel) in Braga, and from Montes d'Aventura, based at the youth hostel in Campo do Gerês. While they include reservoirs and most highways, they're poor on current trails. For more on topographic maps of Portugal, see under Planning in the Facts for the Visitor chapter.

Several detailed orienteering maps of the Campo do Gerês region are available for 300$00 from the Cerdeira camping ground there, and occasionally from park offices. The park's own map is not reliable enough for hiking.

Megaliths
There are Stone Age dolmens (stone temple-tombs) on the high plateaus of the Serra da Peneda and Serra do Gerês: near Castro Laboreiro, Mezio, Paradela, Pitões das Júnias and Tourém. For more on Portugal's ancient stone monuments, see the boxed text 'Dolmens, Menhirs & Other Mysteries' in the Alentejo chapter.

Activities
Walking & Mountain Biking Scenery, crisp air, the rural panorama and local hospitality make walking and cycling a pleasure in Peneda-Gerês. There's a certain

Next Exit Vilarinho das Furnas

A 320km Roman military road between Bracara Augusta (Braga) and Asturica Augusta (Astorga in Spain) once ran up the valley of the Rio Homem and crossed the mountains here. A 2km stretch (a candidate for UNESCO World Heritage status) is still visible along the south side of the Albufeira (reservoir) de Vilarinho das Furnas. Milestones – each inscribed with its position and the name of the emperor during whose rule it was erected – remain at Miles XXIX, XXX and XXXI; the nearest one to Campo do Gerês is about 1km beyond the camping ground. Others have been haphazardly collected at Portelo do Homem.

amount of dead reckoning involved, though tracks of some kind (animal or vehicle) are everywhere in the área de ambiente rural, most leading within a half-day's walk to a settlement or a main road. Local people claim streams at higher elevations are safe to drink from, though anything below farmed areas is suspect.

An official long-distance footpath (*trilho pedestre de longo curso*) is being developed, with eight linked itineraries to span the park, mostly along traditional roads or tracks between villages where you can stop for the night. Park offices sell detailed 300$00 map-brochures in Portuguese for two of these itineraries (Lamas de Mouro to Soajo and Cabril to Paradela), plus two for interpretive trails at Pitões das Júnias (good for kids too) and São Miguel (Entre Ambos-os-Rios). At the time of research, these and two other trails (Campo do Gerês to Vidoeiro and Paradela to Pitões das Júnias) had been scouted and marked.

The Cerdeira camping ground at Campo do Gerês has marked some loop trails in that area and has produced their own maps for them. Day walks around Caldas do Gerês are popular but crowded; see that section for details. Further afield, Ermida and Cabril make excellent goals and both have simple accommodation and food. The high-elevation trek directly between Portela do Homem and Pitões das Júnias is said to be the finest in the park, though park maps don't show a trail there.

Two useful books setting out routes in the park are *Walking in Portugal* and *Landscapes of Portugal*; see the Books section in the Facts for the Visitor chapter.

Outfits with local expertise and small-group walking and cycling programmes are Montes d'Aventura, Trote-Gerês, PlanAlto and Água Montanha Lazer (see Getting Around in this section, which also lists places to rent mountain bikes). PlanAlto organises quarterly multiday treks right across the park.

Water Sports Except for a swimming pool at Caldas do Gerês, the only places for water sports are on the park's reservoirs. Rio Caldo, 8km south of Caldas do Gerês, is the base for the Albufeira da Caniçada. English-run Água Montanha Lazer rents single/double kayaks for 600/1000$00 for the first hour, plus four-person canoes, pedal boats, rowboats and small motor boats. It also organises water-skiing jaunts and sells sports gear.

Trote-Gerês rents out two/three-person canoes for paddling the Albufeira de Salamonde at 1000/1200$00 per hour. Both have lower half-day and day rates too. See Organised Tours later in this section for details of both companies.

Horse Riding The national park operates facilities beside its Vidoeiro camp site near Caldas do Gerês; contact the park office there. Others with horses for hire are Trote-Gerês and Montes d'Aventura (see Organised Tours). Typical rates are from 1300 to 1900$00 per hour or 7000 to 8000$00 per day; the park outfit has the cheapest rates.

Places to Stay
Unless you're camping, cheap accommodation is hard to find in the park. There's a *pousada da juventude* in Campo do Gerês.

Parques de campismo include basic park-run sites at Lamas do Mouro, Entre Ambos-os-Rios and Vidoeiro, all open from May or June to September or October; and pricier, year-round private sites at Campo do Gerês and Cabril.

A righteous alternative is *quartos*, which gives a minor but appropriate boost to the local economy; ask at turismos, park offices or ADERE (see Information in the Ponte da Barca section earlier in this chapter).

Ten plain *casas de abrigo* (shelters) around the park, formerly for park staff, can be booked through ADERE. Each has four doubles, bathrooms, hot water and either fireplace or electric heat. The entire house must be rented at 15,500$00 (less in low season, for stays of a week or more, and/or for shelters without electricity). Visits of less than a week can only be booked a week ahead. Meals cannot be cooked in the

houses, but all are in or near villages where food is available. High season for these is from the first Friday in June to the first Friday in October.

ADERE is also the place to book several *restored houses* in Soajo (see that section), as well as a dozen regional *Turihab* properties for as little as 8000$00 per double.

Caldas do Gerês has many *pensões*, but they tend to get booked out in summer. Booking ahead is a good idea. These and other options are noted under individual towns in this section.

Shopping
Local honey (*mel*) is on sale everywhere. The best – unpasteurised and unadulterated with syrup – is from small dealers (look for signs on private homes). Much of it bears a faint piney taste from certain evergreen flowers.

Getting There & Away
Bus From Braga, Empresa Hoteleira do Gerês runs at least 10 coaches a day to Rio Caldo and Caldas do Gerês, and REDM has seven to Campo do Gerês (fewer at weekends). Salvador has buses to Arcos de Valdevez from Braga and Monção, plus twice-daily onward links from Arcos to Lindoso and Soajo (see Getting There & Away in the Soajo and Lindoso section). A few buses run to Paradela from Montalegre, in Trás-os-Montes, on weekdays only.

Car & Motorcycle There are entry roads at Lamas de Mouro (from Monção and Melgaço), Mezio (from Arcos de Valdevez), Entre Ambos-os-Rios (from Ponte de Lima and Ponte da Barca), Covide, Rio Caldo and Salamonde (from Braga), and Sezelhe, Paradela and Vila Nova (from Montalegre). Four roads cross the (unstaffed) border from Spain as well.

Getting Around
No buses operate within the park. To get around inside the park without your own wheels you must bag a taxi (scarce), hitch or walk.

Drivers: back roads in the park can be axle-breakers, even when the map suggests otherwise. Note the restrictions on travel through the Mata de Albergaria (see the boxed text 'PNPG Protected Areas' earlier in this section). Even with a car there's no practical way to travel between the Peneda and Gerês sections except outside the park – most conveniently via Spain.

Bicycle Mountain bikes can be hired from Água Montanha Lazer and Cerdeira camping ground (see under Campo do Gerês) for about 2000$00 per day; from Pensão Carvalho Araújo (see under Caldas do Gerês) for 3000$00; or from Trote-Gerês in Cabril for 3700$00. See the following Organised Tours section for details of Água Montanha Lazer and Trote-Gerês, both of which are also good sources of information for cyclists. Água Montanha Lazer has trail notes for the area around Caldas do Gerês and Campo do Gerês, and a small stash of gear and spare parts.

Organised Tours Switched-on private outfits with small-group outdoor programmes (as well as their own tips on sights and accommodation) include:

Água Montanha Lazer (☎ 053-39 17 01, fax 39 15 98, email aguamontanha@mail.telepac.pt), Rio Caldo, 4845 Caldas do Gerês – walking, biking, canoeing; also water-sports equipment rental

Montes d'Aventura (☎ 02-830 51 57, mobile ☎ 0936 607 37 39, fax 02-830 51 58; email maventura@ip.pt), Alameda Dr António Macedo 19, 4200 Porto, with a representative at the youth hostel at Campo do Gerês – walking, biking, horse riding, canoeing, multiactivity

PlanAlto (☎/fax 053-35 10 05), Parque de Cerdeira, Campo do Gerês, 4840 Terras de Bouro – walks, multiactivity

Trote-Gerês (☎/fax 053-65 98 60), Outeiro Alto, Cabril, 5495 Borralha – walking, biking, horse riding; also a camping ground and equipment rental

Bus Tours For a spin past the park's major sights, Agência no Gerês (☎ 053-39 11 12), at the Hotel Universal in Caldas do Gerês,

organises two to five-hour minibus trips for 1000$00 to 1250$00 per person, from June through August. It also has an office in Braga (☎ 053-61 58 96).

SOAJO & LINDOSO
☎ 058

These two sturdy, remote villages, across the Rio Lima valley from one another, are best known for their *espigueiros*, or stone granaries (see the boxed text).

Lindoso also has its own small, restored **castelo**, founded in the early 13th century by Afonso III, beefed up in the 14th century by Dom Dinis, occupied by the Spanish from 1662 to 1664, and used as a military garrison until 1895. Now it's 'garrisoned' by the national park, with an information office and tantalising but poorly captioned exhibits on the castle, its excavations and the traditional way of life of the village.

The castle is open daily except Monday and Tuesday. Summer (April to September) hours are from 10 am to 12.30 pm and 2 to 6 pm Wednesday to Saturday, and from 10 am to noon and 2.30 to 5 pm Sunday. The rest of the year the castle's open from 9.30 am to 12.30 pm and 2 to 5.30 pm Wednesday to Saturday, and from 10 am to noon and 2 to 4.30 pm on Sunday. Admission costs 200$00.

Walk through the stony old villages, too, to see what remains of traditional life in this part of the Minho.

Places to Stay
Soajo Soajo is home to an ADERE programme called Turismo de Aldeia, under which at least 10 village houses have already been renovated and adapted for tourist accommodation. Each has a fireplace or stove (with a ration of firewood) and breakfast-only kitchen. Prices range from 7000$00 for two people to 24,000$00 for eight. Book through ADERE (see under Information in the Ponte da Barca section).

A modest Turihab property that's not part of this scheme is *Casa do Adro* (☎ 6 73 27), where a double costs 8000$00, breakfast included. This and others can be booked

Espigueiros

These huge slatted granite caskets on stilts were used in the 18th and 19th centuries for storing maize or winnowed grain and protecting it from rats – and many still are. In clusters above their villages, grizzled with moss and topped with little crosses, they look like miniature cathedrals, or giants' tombs. The brass-belled, long-horned cows grazing around them, and the washing lines tied to them, do little to dispel their eerie appearance.

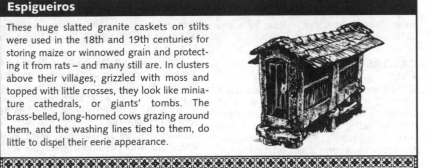

through ADERE too. Failing that, ask about quartos at the café near the bus stand.

Lindoso There is no convenient place to stay. You might drum up a private room in the village, or by asking at *Café Carril*, 700m past the Lindoso turn-off, on the N203 to Spain, or *Restaurante Lindoverde* (☎ 6 74 46), a further 100m down the N203.

Getting There & Away
At the time of writing, Salvador buses from Arcos de Valdevez ran to Soajo daily at 12.20 and 2 pm (plus 5.40 pm on weekdays), returning daily at 7.30 am and 1.15 pm. They ran to Lindoso on weekdays and Saturday at noon, and weekdays and Sunday at 5.50 pm, returning weekdays and Saturday at 7.25 am and 1.05 pm (no Sunday return).

On Wednesday (market day at Arcos de Valdevez or Ponte da Barca), two or three extra services are added to Soajo and five to Lindoso. Check with the turismo in Arcos about schedule changes.

RIO CALDO
☎ 053
Just inside the park on the Albufeira de Caniçada, Rio Caldo is little more than a base for water sports on the reservoir. It's also a fall-back if accommodation is booked up in Caldas do Gerês. English-run Água Montanha Lazer (see Organised Tours ear-

lier in this section), 100m from the roundabout on the N304 to Campo do Gerês, is a good source for park information, accommodation, and mountain bike and boat rental. About 2.5km further along the N304 is **São Bento da Porta Alberta**, a knot of trinket stands, overpriced accommodation and a church to which busloads of pilgrims come all day long. Apart from brilliant view of the reservoir, that's it: even the former convent to which the church was attached is now an inn.

Places to Stay
A few hundred metres from the roundabout, heading south-west on the N308, is *Residencial do Cávado* (☎ 39 11 57), with doubles for 4000$00 (3500$00 without bathroom); the owners also have another house near Rio Caldo with doubles for 6000$00.

The Água Montanha Lazer shop (see under Organised Tours earlier in this section) has four *houses* in the Rio Caldo area: two with two bedrooms for 9000$00, and two four-bedroom ones for 18,000$00 or 30,000$00.

Scattered along the road up to São Bento da Porta Alberta are lots of pensões offering doubles from 4000$00 to 6000$00. In the former convent at São Bento is the deluxe *Estalagem São Bento da Porta Alberta* (☎ 39 11 06, fax 39 11 17), where a double with the works costs 11,500$00.

MINHO

Getting There & Away

Empresa Hoteleira do Gerês runs every few hours daily from Braga to Rio Caldo and Caldas do Gerês.

CALDAS DO GERÊS

☎ 053

If the Gerês end of the national park has a 'centre', it's the somnolent spa town of Caldas do Gerês (or just Gerês). Wedged into the valley of the Rio Gerês, it is a centre only because of its position, bus connections and an earnest park office. The spa and many, but not all, pensões are closed from October to April.

Orientation

The town is built on an elongated loop of road with the spa centre (*balneário*) housed in the pink buildings in the middle. The original hot spring, some baths, the turismo, a bar and an ice-cream parlour are in the very staid *colunat* (colonnade) 150m away at the northern end of the loop. Buses stop about 50m below the spa, on Avenida Manuel F Costa, opposite the Universal and Termas hotels.

Information

The turismo (☎ 39 11 33), open in the colunat from 9 am to noon and 2 to 6 pm daily (less often in winter), has information about the town but little of use on the park. For that, go a block uphill to the park information office (☎ 39 11 81, fax 39 14 96); it's open daily from 8 am to 8 pm, year-round (and someone is on duty right through the night in summer).

The post office is on the roundabout at the entrance to the village. Banco Espírito Santo, with currency exchange desk and ATM, is on Avenida Manuel F Costa opposite the Hotel Universal.

Mountain bikes can be hired for about 3000$00 per day from Pensão Carvalho Araújo (see Places to Stay later).

Walks

The turismo or the park office can suggest local strolls. One pleasant (though not free) option is the spa-owned Parque das Termas, through the gate opposite the turismo. It's open from May to September and admission costs 150$00 (70$00 for children under 12 years).

About 1km up the N308 is Parque do Merendas, the start of the short, popular Miradouro walk, with good views to the south. Or you can walk, hitch or take a taxi up the N308 to the 862m pass at Portela de Leonte (about 6km).

From the Mata de Albergaria, at the point where the Rio Homem crosses the road (10km above Caldas do Gerês), a walk up the river takes you to a picturesque waterfall. At the 757m Portela do Homem border post (13km from Caldas do Gerês) is a cluster of Roman milestones.

A good choice is to head south-west from the Mata de Albergaria down the Rio Homem and the Albufeira de Vilarinho das Furnas for 8km to Campo do Gerês. This route takes you along part of the Roman road (see the boxed text 'Next Exit Vilarinho das Furnas' earlier in this section). Walking all the way from Caldas do Gerês takes a very long and rugged day, so you're better off bagging a ride up to the Mata de Albergaria. Swimming is not permitted in the Albufeira de Vilarinho das Furnas.

Swimming Pool

The swimming pool at the Parque das Termas is open to the public for 700$00 per person on weekdays, 1100$00 weekends and holidays (less for children under seven years). There's also a little lake there, with boats for hire at 600$00 for half an hour.

Spa

You can drink the local mineral water, or soak in it at several different temperatures – hottest at the colunat, cooler at the balneário – daily except Sunday from 8 am to noon and 3.20 to 6 pm. Tourists are welcome for one-off visits; buy a ticket at the main entrance to the balneário, opposite the petrol station on Avenida Manuel F Costa. A sauna or steam bath costs 1100$00, a full massage 3500$00; serious devotees can also try various arcane and uncomfortable 'intubations'.

Places to Stay

Camping One kilometre north of Caldas do Gerês, at Vidoeiro, is the good park-run *Parque Campismo Vidoeiro* (☎ 39 12 89), open year-round. It charges 400/350/450 per person/tent/car.

Private Rooms There are lots of private rooms available in summer, costing around 5000$00 per double. The owners often approach travellers at the bus stop and around town.

Pensões & Residenciais Caldas do Gerês has plenty of pensões, though during the summer you may find some block-booked for spa patients, and the others may fill up a month or more ahead. On the other hand, bargaining is definitely in order outside high season.

A line of at least 10 pensões – most with TV, heating, bath, breakfast, some sort of restaurant, and parking – climbs the west side of the valley. *Pensão da Ponte* (☎ 39 11 21, Rua da Boa Vista), by the roaring river, is the only one with any charm and, despite sloping floors and ancient plumbing, is good value with plain, well-kept doubles for 7000$00 (5000$00 without bathroom). The less appealing *Príncipe*, just up the hill, is run by the same people for the same rates.

Further up, the rather posh *Carvalho Araújo* (☎ 39 11 85, fax 39 12 25) has singles/doubles for 7000/8500$00. Doubles at the gloomy *Horizonte do Gerês* (☎ 39 12 60) and at *Flôr de Moçambique* (☎ 39 11 19) are about 7000$00.

At the top of the hill, with the best views, are *Pensão São Miguel* (☎ 39 13 60) and the less modest *Pensão Adelaide* (☎ 390 00 20, fax 390 00 29), where doubles start at 7000$00.

There are more pensões downstream from the bank, and yet more line the road up from Rio Caldo.

Hotels At the twin hotels *Universal* and *das Termas* (☎ 39 11 41, fax 39 11 02, Avenida Manuel F Costa), owned by the Empresa Hoteleira do Gerês bus company, doubles range from 9250$00 in winter to 14,500$00 in August.

Places to Eat

Most pensões provide hearty meals, which are usually available to non-guests too; *Pensão Adelaide* is popular. Guests at the *Pensão da Ponte* are summoned to dinner with a bell; choose from the usual standards for 800$00 to 1400$00 per dish.

There are several restaurants, food shops, cheap cafés and pastelarias at the lower (south) end of town. One is *Restaurante O Lurdes Capela*, with a sizeable menu and modest prices. Further down is a cheerful fast-food place called the *Green House*, with burgers and other grill items, sandwiches and ice cream, and outdoor tables.

Getting There & Away

Empresa Hoteleira do Gerês buses run every hour to 2½ hours (less often at weekends) from Braga to Caldas do Gerês.

AROUND CALDAS DO GERÊS

About 11km south-east from Parque do Merendas is **Ermida**, a sturdy village of small farms and stone houses clinging to steep hillsides. Spartan doubles with shared toilet in private houses are available for around 3000$00. Six kilometres further east is **Fafião**, which also has some rooms; ask at the Retiro do Gerês café beside the small post office.

CAMPO DO GERÊS
☎ 053

Campo do Gerês – called São João do Campo on some maps, and just Campo by nearly everybody – is barely more than a hamlet, near the Albufeira de Vilarinho das Furnas dam. The compact old centre seems entirely made of identical rugged square blocks of sandstone. The youth hostel and camping ground here make very good bases for hikes.

MINHO

Orientation & Information

The bus from Braga stops by the Museu Etnográfico, on the main road, and then continues 1.5km to the old village centre. The youth hostel is 1km up a side road from the museum. About 200m before the centre, the road to the dam branches to the right, and the camping ground is about 700m in this direction.

Vilarinho das Furnas & Museu Etnográfico

The village of Vilarinho das Furnas was once, by all accounts, an extraordinary place – a democratic community with a well-organised communal life, shared property and decisions taken by consensus. Even during the Salazar years, Vilarinho maintained its principled, independent way of life. But the village was submerged when the reservoir was created in 1972, and its people were relocated. In summer, when the reservoir level usually falls, the empty walls of the village rise like spectres from the water and the near shore.

In anticipation of the end of their old way of life, villagers donated many articles for a proposed memorial. These are now on view at a rather eloquent ethnographic museum (☎ 35 11 35), where the road to Campo forks to the youth hostel. It's (usually) open daily from 8.30 am to noon and 2.30 to 5 pm; admission costs 100$00.

This is a recommended stop before you visit the spooky remains of the village itself, about 2.5km beyond the dam, a comfortable three hour return trip walking from Campo or the camping ground.

Places to Stay

North of the centre is the good *Parque Campismo de Cerdeira* (☎ 35 70 65, ☎/fax 35 10 05). Along with camping sites (costing 600/500/550$00 per person/tent/car in August) it has two-person bungalows with kitchenette for 10,000$00 in July and August or 8500$00 the rest of the year. Book ahead for tents and bungalows in July and August. PlanAlto, a local environmental tourism organisation based here, has gone to some lengths to make a stay here interesting (see the boxed text 'Walks & Other Programmes' below).

The sprawling *pousada da juventude* (☎/fax 35 13 39) was originally a camp for dam construction workers. Along with dorms it has quads, doubles and a few bungalows with kitchenette and bathroom. A dorm bed costs 1600$00, while a double room with/without bathroom costs 4200/3400$00. Booking ahead is wise. Reception is open from 9 am to noon and 6 pm to midnight, though guests must clear out by 10 am.

Pensão Stop (☎ 35 12 91), near the turnoff for the camp site and dam, provides doubles with bathroom for 5000$00, including breakfast. A café and shop by the bus stop in the centre might be able to help find a cheap room at a pinch.

Places to Eat

The *pousada da juventude* says meals are available at fixed times by arrangement, though they have little at lunch.

The *Parque Campismo de Cerdeira* has its own good, no-frills restaurant with local

Walks & Other Programmes

An environmental tourism outfit called PlanAlto, based at the Parque Campismo de Cerdeira, has marked three loop trails around Campo do Gerês, ranging from two to five hours walking, and has printed its own walking and orienteering maps of the area. Among activities arranged throughout the year are interpretive walks (including the collection of medicinal plants), tree plantings, traditional games and orienteering competitions. It has also made an effort to arrange programmes linked to local festivals, such as Matança do Porco (a communal pork meal and other events) in January and the Desfolhada Minhota (harvest festival) in October. Ask at the camping ground.

specialities like *bersame* (a pork and vegetable stew), rojões à moda do Minho and cabrito (kid) at 1300$00 to 2300$00 per person (minimum four people), as well as omelettes, hamburgers and other snacks. Pickings are slim and pricey at the village's three small shops. The next nearest place for provisions is Rio Caldo.

Getting There & Away
REDM has seven daily coaches from Braga (fewer at weekends), stopping at the museum, the camping ground and the centre.

CABRIL
☎ 053

Though it hardly looks the part, this tiny village is the administrative centre of Portugal's biggest *freguesia* (parish), stretching from Fafião to Lapela and up to the Spanish border. It's also a fine place to stay for a few days.

Set with outlying hamlets in a wide, fertile bowl, it is peaceful and pretty, with access on foot to hardy villages like Pincães, which are struggling to maintain a traditional lifestyle but are short on young people.

An old bridge, submerged by the Salamonde reservoir half a century ago, partially rises out of the water in summer; the 'new' bridge beside it looks quite old too. Four kilometres away at Vila Nova is another handsome old bridge.

Orientation & Information
The reference point is a tiny square with a pillory and the Tasquinha do Guarda café-bar. Off to one side is a grimy but charming little church (said to have been moved five centuries ago, brick by brick, by villagers of nearby São Lourenço in search of a more propitious locale). On a rise beyond the church is a small national park work station and information office (no telephone), open on weekdays.

Places to Stay & Eat
The small, year-round *Parque de Campismo Outeiro Alto* (☎/fax 65 98 60) is run by the 'leisure-time collective' Trote-Gerês, which also has horses, bikes and canoes for hire (see Organised Tours earlier in this section). A site costs 400/450$00 per person/tent. It's 1.2km up from the village square, over the bridge and in the direction of Pincães and Ermida (follow the rearing-horse signs).

Quartos are available in the village for under 3000$00 per double; inquire about these at the *Restaurante de Ponte Nova de Cabril*, by the bridge, at *Tasquinha do Guarda*, in the square, or at *Café Aguia Real*, about 250m from the square, towards Paradela.

Getting There & Away
There are no buses to Cabril. The best option is to get off any Braga-Montalegre bus at Salamonde and ask about a taxi at the Retiro da Cabreira café.

The only crossing into the park for miles is over the Salamonde reservoir dam, way down below the N103 highway. Trote-Gerês will sometimes collect their guests at Salamonde.

PARADELA
☎ 076

There's little to do here but walk, eat and sleep to your heart's content. The town also makes a base for the park's Paradela to Pitões das Júnias trail (see under Activities earlier in this section). Paradela and the villages around it are actually in Trás-os-Montes.

Beside the parish church in Paradela, the modest *Pousadinha de Paradela* (☎ 56 61 65) has doubles costing 5500$00 (4200$00 without bathroom), breakfast included – good value except for the hourly church bell. Other meals can be specially prepared, by arrangement, for 1300$00. Book ahead through Trote-Gerês (see Places to Stay & Eat in Cabril).

Rooms at the *Restaurante Sol Rio* (☎ 56 61 67), 300m out on the Montalegre road, cost 4000 to 5000$00 (3000$00 without bathroom) and have reservoir views at the back.

Restaurante Dom Dinis (☎ 56 61 53), a few hundred metres past the Pousadinha on the Sirvozelo road, also lets rooms.

One of Portugal's finer accommodation bargains is 3.5km away, on the other side of the Paradela dam, in Sirvozelo: two compact stone *houses*, equipped with fireplace (and firewood), stove, fridge, hot shower and double bed, each costing 8000$00. Book them through Trote-Gerês.

Sirvozelo itself is a handsome village with old stone espigueiros (granaries); see the boxed text under Soajo & Lindoso for more on these.

Getting There & Away

There are buses to Paradela at about 1 and 6 pm on weekdays from Cambedo on the Braga-Montalegre road (REDM has five or six Braga-Montalegre buses a day).

There are two direct buses from Montalegre to Paradela on weekdays, departing from Montalegre at about 12.15 and 4.30 pm. There are no bus services to Paradela at weekends.

Trás-os-Montes

Portugal's north-eastern province is largely ignored, even by Portuguese travellers, who consider it too far, too uncomfortable, too backward and probably too pagan. The name means 'beyond the mountains', and indeed the Gerês, Alvão and Marão mountain ranges make it feel more walled out than walled in.

But the name implies more than geographical isolation. Here the climate tends to extremes too: the north is a *terra fria* (cold land) where winter temperatures may drop to freezing for months at a time, and the south, towards the Douro Alto, is a *terra quente* (hot land) where searing summers ripen olives, almonds, chestnuts, fruit, rye, and the port-wine grapes of the Douro and Tua valleys.

Isolation and harsh conditions have bred a culture of rock-solid self-reliance, laced with mysterious practices and beliefs. In this vast province – almost twice the size of the Minho, with less than half the population – there are still villages to which EU funds have failed to filter through and where farmers struggle to make ends meet, plough their fields with oxen and live with their hens, pigs and donkeys in the humblest of granite cottages.

For the adventurous traveller, this province's austere feel and rugged landscape are major attractions. There are few places in Europe where you'll feel such a sense of space and remoteness.

Getting to the major cities of Vila Real, Chaves, Bragança, and Miranda do Douro is no longer a problem, thanks to the IP4/E82 motorway, long-haul bus services, and even trains: the Linha da Corgo runs to Vila Real and the narrow-gauge Linha da Tua runs to Mirandela. But while these cities make useful bases and have some unique attractions, it's the smaller villages that will stick in your memory. To reach these you'll need time and patience – local bus services often disappear entirely at

HIGHLIGHTS

- Stroll across a 1900-year-old Roman bridge in Chaves

- Cool off in a tunnel of trees behind the manor house near Vila Real, pictured on the label of Mateus rosé wine

- Try the Wine of the Dead in Boticas, if you dare

- Let your imagination run wild in Bragança's lofty, ancient *cidadela*, and ponder why pigs were once important enough to be honoured with statues

- Ride a horse over the gentle, faraway hills of the Parque Natural de Montesinho, one of Portugal's unsung treasures

- Spend a few peaceful hours in Rio de Onor – half Portuguese, half Spanish, but in a world of its own

weekends and outside the school term – or your own transport.

Walkers will find the province's two *parques naturais* – Alvão, near Vila Real, and Montesinho, near Bragança – a delight. Although neither has as many facilities or trails as the Parque Nacional da Peneda-Gerês, neither sees any crowds. If serious walking is on your mind, talk to the eager and helpful staff at the park offices in Vila Real and Bragança first.

Destinations in the Rio Douro valley, where it forms the province's border with the Beira Alta, are covered in the Douro chapter.

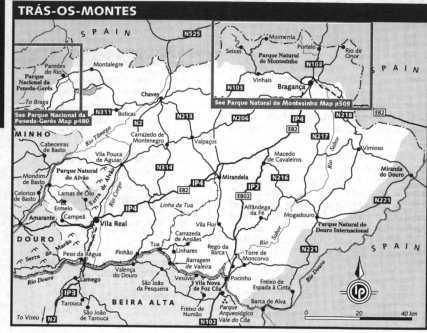

TRÁS-OS-MONTES

Western Trás-os-Montes

VILA REAL

☎ 059 • pop 15,000

High above the confluence of the Corgo and Cabril rivers lies the district capital of Vila Real, a busy university and industrial town whose population swells by 40% during the academic year. It's surrounded by the splendid mountainous scenery of the Serra do Marão to the west and Serra de Alvão to the north, with parts of the latter comprising the Parque Natural do Alvão.

The town itself has few cultural attractions, though the Palácio (or Solar) de Mateus, 4km to the east, is worth a visit. The town also makes a useful base for hikers interested in exploring the surrounding countryside. Otherwise it's best considered as a stopover en route to more intriguing parts of Trás-os-Montes.

Orientation

Most of Vila Real's accommodation, restaurants and places of interest are on or near Avenida Carvalho Araújo, a 20 minute walk north-west across the Rio Corgo from the train station.

From the Rodonorte and Santos bus stops it's a five minute walk south on Rua Dom Pedro de Castro. AV Tâmega buses stop at the southern end of the Avenida.

Information

Tourist Office The competent regional turismo (☎ 32 28 19, fax 32 17 12) is in an arresting Manueline building at Avenida Carvalho Araújo 94. It's open daily except Sunday from 9.30 am to 12.30 pm and 2 to 7 pm, April to September (5.30 pm from

October to March); there's no lunch break from June to September.

Park Office At the time of research the headquarters for the Parque Natural do Alvão (☎ 32 41 38, fax 7 38 69) was exiled to a residencial complex 1.7km north of the town centre at Praceta do Tronco, lote 17, Cruz das Almas, but new quarters were under renovation just south of the centre on Rua Camilo Castelo Branco.

The office is open weekdays only, from 9 am to 12.30 pm and 2 to 5.30 pm. Here you can find leaflets in English on the park's flora and fauna, handicrafts and rural ways of life, plus some information on walks.

Money There are banks with ATMs along Avenida Carvalho Araújo (including one next to the turismo).

Post & Communications There's a post office with fax and telephone facilities at the top of Avenida Carvalho Araújo.

Email & Internet Access The Instituto Português da Juventude (☎ 320 96 40, fax 37 47 44) on Rua Dr Manuel Cardona has terminals for Internet access available free of charge.

University The Universidade de Trás-os-Montes e Alto Douro is to the south-east of the centre, roughly 500m beyond the train station.

Medical Services The hospital (☎ 34 10 41) is 2km north-west of the town centre, across the IP4/E82 motorway.

Emergency The police station (☎ 32 20 22) is just west of Avenida Carvalho Araújo.

Sé

Once part of a 15th century Dominican monastery, the Gothic cathedral (also called the Igreja de São Domingos) is unremarkable except for its age.

Miradouro de Trás-do-Cemitério

For a fine view across the gorge of the Rios Corgo and Cabril, walk south from the town centre to a promenade just beyond a small cemetery and chapel.

Palácio de Mateus

Better known as Solar de Mateus, and famously depicted on bottles of Mateus rosé wine, this frilly Baroque creation 4km east of Vila Real was probably designed and built by the Italian Nicolau Nasoni in the mid-18th century. Its granite wings ('advancing lobster-like towards you,' wrote English poet and critic Sacheverell Sitwell) shelter a cobbled forecourt dominated by an ornate balustraded stairway and overlooked by rooftop spires and statues.

Instead of the swan on the wine label, the pond in front holds a half-submerged statue of a naked lady, created by the modern sculptor João Cutileiro. Behind the palace is the best part: an Alice in Wonderland garden of tiny box hedges and prim statues, and a dark, fragrant cypress tunnel. Inside the house you can visit just a few rooms, heavy with velvet drapes and fussy 18th century furnishings.

The palace is open daily from 9 am to 1 pm and 2 to 7 pm (6 pm in winter); admission costs an exorbitant 1000$00 to the palace and gardens. Take the 'Timpeira e Mateus' bus, which leaves five times daily from the stop near the police station, and ask for *palácio*; it's a five minute walk from the crossroads where you're dropped.

As for the rosé, it's actually made down the road by the Sogrape company (Portugal's biggest exporter of bottled wines), though the palace does produce its own range of jams and wines, sold at a shop on the premises.

Special Events

The Festa de São Pedro, held on 28 and 29 June, is one of the town's liveliest events, with a huge market in the streets east of the turismo. This is a good time to pick up samples of the region's unusual black pottery and other local handicrafts.

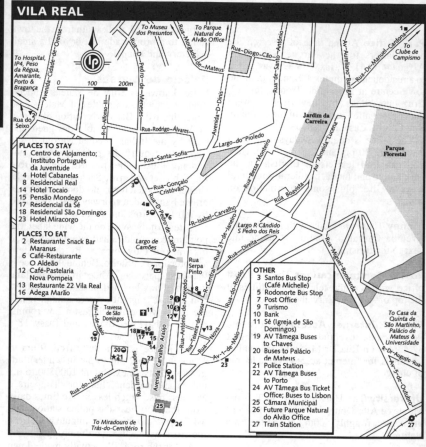

VILA REAL

PLACES TO STAY
1 Centro de Alojamento;
Instituto Português
da Juventude
4 Hotel Cabanelas
8 Residencial Real
14 Hotel Tocaio
15 Pensão Mondego
17 Residencial da Sé
18 Residencial São Domingos
23 Hotel Miracorgo

PLACES TO EAT
2 Restaurante Snack Bar
Maranus
6 Café-Restaurante
O Aldeão
12 Café-Pastelaria
Nova Pompeia
13 Restaurante 22 Vila Real
16 Adega Marão

OTHER
3 Santos Bus Stop
(Café Michelle)
5 Rodonorte Bus Stop
7 Post Office
9 Turismo
10 Bank
11 Sé (Igreja de São
Domingos)
19 AV Tâmega Buses
to Chaves
20 Buses to Palácio
de Mateus
21 Police Station
22 AV Tâmega Buses
to Porto
24 AV Tâmega Bus Ticket
Office; Buses to Lisbon
25 Câmara Municipal
26 Future Parque Natural
do Alvão Office
27 Train Station

Places to Stay

Camping The good *Clube de Campismo* (☎ 32 47 24) has a swimming pool and a prime location by the river, north-east of the town centre, but you need a carnet or Camping Card International (see the Visas & Documents section in the Facts for the Visitor chapter) to stay there. It costs 480/305/305\$00 per person/tent/car.

Hostel There's a *centro de alojamento* (☎ 7 22 01) on Rua Dr Manuel Cardona by the Instituto Português da Juventude, near the Clube de Campismo. Dorm beds cost 1700\$00 in high season.

Pensões & Residenciais A trio of down-to-earth places can be found near the Sé; fortunately the cathedral bells don't seem to ring much. *Pensão Mondego* (☎ 32 30 97, *Travessa de São Domingos 11*) and *Residencial São Domingos* (☎ 32 20 39, *Travessa de São Domingos 33*) have the same owner and rates (4000\$00 for a double with shower). The former also has cheaper rooms without bathroom, while the rooms at the latter are marginally more pleasant. Rather smarter is *Residencial da Sé* (☎ 32 45 75, Travessa de São Domingos 19), where a room with a double bed costs 5000$00 and a twin room 6000$00 or more; breakfast is included in the price.

Overlooking the pedestrianised Rua Central at No 5 is *Residencial Real* (☎ 32 58 79, fax 32 46 13), where tidy doubles cost 6500$00.

Hotels At the deceptively grand-looking *Hotel Tocaio* (☎ 32 31 06, Avenida Carvalho Araújo 45), 1960s-vintage doubles – some of which have bigger bathrooms than bedrooms – cost 6000$00 including breakfast. More comfortable places include *Hotel Cabanelas* (☎ 32 31 53, fax 7 41 81, Rua Dom Pedro de Castro), where doubles start at 8000$00, and *Hotel Miracorgo* (☎ 32 50 01, fax 32 50 06, Avenida 1 de Maio 76-78) with doubles costing 10,800$00.

Turihab There are several handsome properties near town, and some are better deals than the town's hotels. The owners can be hard to contact, but one who isn't runs *Casa da Quinta de São Martinho* (☎ 32 39 86), on the way to the Palácio de Mateus. A double costs about 9000$00, and there are apartments as well.

The turismo has information about other Turihab places.

Places to Eat

The plain *Café-Pastelaria Nova Pompeia* (☎ 7 28 76, Rua Carvalho Araújo 82) has quick *tostas mistas* (toasted ham and cheese sandwiches), pasties and burgers for under 500$00 as well as dinner specials for under 1000$00; the pastelaria is on the Rua António de Azevedo side.

Cheerful *Restaurante 22 Vila Real* (☎ 32 12 96, Rua Teixeira de Sousa 16) offers carefully prepared fish and meat dishes for under 1400$00, plus some half-portions. Another good choice with similar prices is *Café-Restaurante O Aldeão* (☎ 32 47 94, Rua Dom Pedro de Castro 70).

Museu dos Presuntos (☎ 32 60 17, Avenida Cidade de Orense 43) is not a Ham Museum but serves lots of hearty ham and bean dishes, and other meals; the 20 minute walk to the residential neighbourhood north of the town centre will get your appetite up. The cave-like *Adega Marão* (Travessa de São Domingos 17) is worth a look for its immense bottle collection.

Restaurante Snack Bar Maranus (☎ 32 15 21), lote 2 in a cluster of shops called Quinta do Seixo, 700m north-west of the centre, looks an unlikely venue but serves good grilled dishes and even fondues for under 1500$00.

Getting There & Away

Bus Among bus lines serving Vila Real are: AV Tâmega (☎ 32 29 28), Avenida Carvalho Araújo 26; Rodonorte (☎ 32 32 34), Rua Dom Pedro de Castro 19, beside the Hotel Cabanelas; and Santos (☎ 7 58 94), at Café Michelle, just past Hotel Cabanelas.

All three run several weekday expresses to Porto (about 930$00), and Rodonorte and AV Tâmega also go to Chaves and Lisbon. AV Tâmega runs nine buses a day to Peso da Régua. For Bragança, Rodonorte has five services a day and Santos three. All services are more limited at weekends; all give youth discounts, and Santos offers discounts for seniors too.

Train Vila Real is at the end of the Linha da Corgo from Peso da Régua: five services daily connect with trains to/from Porto. The only transport between the train station and the town centre, besides walking, is a taxi.

PARQUE NATURAL DO ALVÃO

This 7220 hectare natural park (Portugal's smallest) occupies the western slopes of the Serra de Alvão between Vila Real and Mondim de Basto. In a transition zone between humid coast and dry interior, the park has diverse flora and fauna, but it's the harsh landscape at the higher elevations that is most striking, especially around Lamas de Ôlo, a village of traditional slate and schist architecture at an altitude of 1000m.

An extensive granite basin here is the source of the Rio Ôlo, a tributary of the Tâmega, and a 550m drop to Ermelo gives rise to the spectacular Fisgas de Ermelo waterfalls, the park's major tourist attraction.

Exploring on your own is not simple, as maps and public transport are limited. Before setting out on foot, visit one of the park offices at Vila Real or Mondim de Basto and get some information on how to get around, what to see and where to stay in the park.

Information

The park's head office is in Vila Real; see Information in the Vila Real section for temporary and future locations. There is also a public information centre at Mondim de Basto (see that section later in this chapter for details). Both places sell leaflets on walks, flora and fauna, land use, handicrafts and local products (including linen cloth and smoked sausages).

Mondim de Basto's turismo is also a useful source of information on the park as well as on the adjacent Serra do Marão.

Ermelo & Fisgas de Ermelo

The 800-year-old slate-roofed village of Ermelo is just off the N304 between Vila Real and Mondim de Basto. You can get there on the AV Mondinense/Rodonorte bus to Vila Real, which stops on the N304.

Traditional Activities

In a restored slate-roofed granite house at Arnal, at the south-eastern corner of the Parque Natural do Alvão, is the Núcleo das Técnicas Tradicionais (Centre for Traditional Techniques). It features displays and sales of local handicrafts, and information about mountain agriculture and animal husbandry.

At Ermelo, half a dozen linen weavers have joined in a park project to open their workshops to the public. Inquire at the Vila Real park office about visiting these places.

You'll need to catch the 7 am bus if you want to walk up to the falls.

From the Ermelo turning, a picnic site and a turning to the dramatic Fisgas de Ermelo waterfall are 2km along the N304 towards Mondim. From there the waterfall is a shadeless 9km uphill walk. Take water and snacks.

The last bus back to Mondim passes Ermelo at about 7 pm (the last one back on Saturday is at about 2 pm, and none run on Sunday), but check times with the Mondim turismo.

Other Walks

A three hour hike in the vicinity of **Arnal**, plus information on traditional farming as well as geology, flora and fauna, is described in the English translation of a park leaflet, *Guia do Percurso Pedestre*. The route offers views beyond Vila Real to the Serra do Marão. Another worthy destination is **Lamas de Ôlo** village, with its old mill and thatched houses, 4km from Anta, on the park's northern boundary.

Other walks, ranging from 2.5km to 11.5km, are outlined in an older booklet called *Percurso Pedestre: Mondim de Basto/Parque Natural do Alvão*, though this is only available in Portuguese. Staff at the Vila Real park office and at the turismo at Mondim will photocopy their maps for serious hikers. There are good additional sources of information at the Turihab properties in Campeã (see under Places to Stay).

Park staff organise guided walks for groups of a dozen or more people, by arrangement with the Vila Real park office. Porto-based Montes d'Aventura (see Information under Porto in the Douro chapter) is an adventure travel agency with experience in the Serra de Alvão and Serra do Marão.

Places to Stay & Eat

The park manages a 12 bed *cottage* at Arnal, which costs 3000$00 per person (2000$00 if you bring your own sleeping bag). The minimum charge is 8000$00 and bookings must be made in advance through the Vila Real park office.

In Lamas de Ôlo, *Restaurante A Cabana* (☎ 059-34 17 45) is known for its trout dishes and has a double room for rent. Ermelo has three *cafés* where you could ask about private rooms. See additional listings in the Mondim de Basto section.

If you've got wheels, two modest Turihab properties at Campeã, 12km west of Vila Real, make fine bases for exploring the park. *Casa da Cruz* and *Casa do Mineiro* (☎ 059-7 29 95, 97 92 45, fax 7 29 95) are remodelled, fully equipped three-room cottages, owned by a local teacher with files of information on the area, including walking routes and maps. Each cottage costs around 9000$00 a night, with reductions for longer stays.

Getting There & Away
AV Mondinense and Rodonorte jointly run buses between Vila Real and Mondim de Basto, skirting the park near Ermelo: there are three services on weekdays and two on Saturday (none on Sunday). In Vila Real these depart from the Rodonorte bus stop.

There are no buses to Lamas de Ôlo: a taxi from Vila Real costs about 2000$00 one way. Taxis are also available in Lamas de Ôlo. School term sees additional services to villages inside the park. For timetables, inquire at the park offices or turismos in Vila Real or Mondim de Basto.

MONDIM DE BASTO
☎ 055 • pop 9530 (municipality)
This unattractively modernised mountain town near the intersection of Douro, Minho and Trás-os-Montes provinces, 22km northeast of Amarante, is saved by mountain surroundings, friendly people and a strong local wine for which the Terras de Basto region is famous. The town isn't worth a detour, but it's a suitable base for exploring the Parque Natural do Alvão.

Orientation & Information
The town hardly has a centre. Buses drop you near the market, from where it's a short walk west to the turismo (☎ 38 14 79), at Praça 9 de Abril, and what remains of the old town. From July to September the turismo is (usually) open daily from 9 am to 9 pm; during the rest of the year it's open weekdays only, from 9 am to 12.30 pm and 2 to 5.30 pm.

A Parque Natural do Alvão information centre (☎ 38 12 09), at Lugar do Barrio, Sítio de Retiro, is open weekdays only, from 9 am to 12.30 pm and 2 to 5.30 pm.

Activities
Walking A popular two or three hour walk from Mondim finishes at the **Capela de Senhora da Graça** on the summit of the pine-clad Monte Farinha. The path starts several kilometres east of town on the road to Bilhó; the turismo has a rough map. At the top you can reward yourself with a restaurant lunch (see Places to Eat).

To drive up, turn off the N312 3.5km out of Mondim in the direction of Cerva; from there it's a twisting 9.5km road to the summit.

Swimming Two kilometres south of town, just off the N304, is a great swimming spot at **Senhora da Ponte**, beside the Rio Cabril; follow signs to the parque de campismo and then take the track to the right. River water still powers an old flour mill by the rocky site. Follow the river upstream for shady picnic spots and walks.

Wine Tasting The nearest 'Basto' *vinho verde* wine is produced at Quinta do Fundo (see Places to Stay). Two other labels come from Quinta da Veiga (☎ 36 12 12) in Gagos and Quinta da Capela (☎ 02-49 10 76) in Veade, both a few kilometres west of town. Inquire at the turismo for opening hours for wine tasting.

Places to Stay
Camping An excellent *parque de campismo* (☎ 38 16 50) beside the Rio Cabril, 2km south of town, is open only to holders of the Camping Card International (see the Visas & Documents section in the Facts for the Visitor chapter); it costs 350/280/350$00 per person/tent/car.

Pensões & Residenciais Two adequate places just west of the turismo on Avenida Dr Augusto Brito are *Residencial Carvalho* (☎ *38 10 57*), near the petrol station, where doubles cost 5000$00, and *Residencial Arcadia* (☎ *38 14 10*), further south, which charges 6000$00 including breakfast.

Turihab *Casa das Mourôas* (☎ *38 13 94*) is a converted 19th century hayloft on Rua José Carvalho Camões near the turismo; singles/doubles start at 6000/7500$00. The much grander *Quinta do Fundo* (☎ *38 12 91, fax 38 20 17*), 2km south of town on the N304 at Vilar de Viando, has a tennis court and a swimming pool, horses and bikes for hire, and rooms costing 7500/8500$00 including breakfast; it also bottles its own wine.

Places to Eat

Restaurante Transmontana (☎ *38 12 79, Avenida da Igreja*) offers a wide selection of regional fare at reasonable prices. Atop Monte Farinha is *Restaurante Senhora da Graça* (☎ *38 14 04*), with steeper prices but splendid views. Best value of all are the cheap daily specials at the rustic, welcoming *Adega São Tiago* (☎ *38 22 69, Rua Velha*), just above the turismo; it's closed Sunday.

Getting There & Away

AV Mondinense (☎ 38 20 41) and Rodonorte jointly run buses between Vila Real and Mondim de Basto, with a change of bus and operator at Campeã, three times each weekday (two buses on Saturday, none on Sunday). Several buses daily run from Mondim de Basto to Amarante and to Porto via Guimarães.

MONTALEGRE

☎ 076 • pop 14,150 (municipality)

You're only likely to call in on this small town if you're on the way between Chaves and the Parque Nacional da Peneda-Gerês (see the Minho chapter). There's a park information office, but we had problems getting information here. Presiding over the town and the surrounding plains is a restored castle, one of Dom Dinis' necklace of frontier outposts. The Duke of Wellington rested here after chasing the French from Porto.

Orientation & Information

The *câmara municipal* (town hall) sits foursquare on a new-looking plaza at the top of a rise. The turismo is across the road to the south, by the traffic roundabout, but in several visits we have never found it open. A bank with a currency exchange and an ATM is on the square in front of the câmara municipal, and another is on the square behind it.

The park office (☎ 5 22 81) is at Rua do Regioso 17: turn left (north) to the east of Banco Crédito Predial Português, behind the câmara municipal, and go to the end of the street, then jog right a few metres to a low stone building set back from the street. You may have to hammer on the door at the back. It's open weekdays only from 9 am to 12.30 pm and 2 to 5.30 pm.

Castelo

The castle, consisting mainly of a restored 28m-high keep, three smaller turrets and some walls in a misshapen oval, is on the heights about 400m north-east of the câmara municipal; it offers good views of the countryside (and of the fairly ugly new town). Built in the 14th century by Dom Dinis, the castle was enlarged (including the addition of the biggest of the towers) by his son Afonso IV.

Horse Riding

Casa da Travessa (☎ 5 61 21) in Paredes do Rio, 15km west of Montalegre on the N308, has horses for hire by the hour or the day.

Places to Stay & Eat

There's little obvious accommodation apart from *Residencial Fidalgo* (☎ *5 24 62, Rua da Corujeira 34*), about 300m up the Braga road from the centre. Clean doubles with bathroom and TV cost 5000$00. Book ahead if possible.

A further 200m from the centre is *Restaurante Florestal (☎ 5 24 20)*, a bit pricey for the locale – fish and meat dishes cost from 1000$00 to 1500$00 – but clean and earnest.

On Rua dos Ferradores, near the park office, there's the basic *Café-Restaurante Terra-Fria* and, across the road, *Pizzeria-Restaurante O Cantinho*.

Getting There & Away

A furniture shop across the roundabout from the town hall is also the information and ticket office for regional and long-distance buses. REDM (Rodoviária d'Entre Douro e Minho) runs at least six daily buses to/from Braga (fewer at weekends), and Rodonorte's Braga-Chaves coaches stop here twice daily. Change at Chaves for Vila Real and Bragança.

CHAVES

☎ 076 • pop 12,000

This unpretentious, occasionally attractive but slightly boring spa town straddles the Rio Tâmega 10km south of the Spanish frontier. It's renowned locally not only for its waters but also for its smoked *presunto* (ham) and sausages. If you end up here on the way to eastern Trás-os-Montes or Spain, these deserve a taste. The town's old centre is also worth exploring.

The town's name (which means 'keys') reveals its importance as a frontier gateway: Romans, Suevi, Visigoths, Moors and, later, the French and Spanish have all squabbled over Chaves. The Romans, who founded it in 78 AD, called it Aquae Flaviae after the spa and their emperor, Flavio Vespasianus. Their 16-arched bridge is even now a major traffic-bearing feature of the town, as are the old medieval quarter, the 14th century castle keep and two fortresses.

Orientation & Information

The town centre is a five to 10 minute walk south-west of the AV Tâmega bus station (and defunct train station), and a few blocks north-east of the Rodonorte stop on Alameda do Tabolado.

The turismo (☎ 33 30 29, fax 2 14 19) is at Terreiro de Cavalaria, a garden at the northern end of the old town's axis, Rua de Santo António. The turismo is open weekdays from 9 am to 7 pm, and weekends from 9 am to 12.30 pm and 2 to 6.30 pm; in winter it's closed on Sunday and for lunch.

Banks with ATMs dot Rua de Santo António and Rua Direita. The district hospital (☎ 33 20 12) is north-west of the town centre on Avenida Sá Carneiro. The police station (☎ 2 31 25) is on Avenida dos Bombeiros de Voluntariós, near the turismo. Most accommodation is south of the centre.

Ponte Romana

Chaves' Roman bridge was built between 98 and 104 AD by Emperor Trajan (hence its other common name, Ponte Trajano); it probably served as a link on the important road between Braga and Astorga (in Spain). In the middle on both sides of the road are engraved Roman milestones.

Spa

The warm sodium-bicarbonated waters of Chaves spa are good for rheumatism, nutritional disorders, liver complaints and high blood pressure, but the stuff tastes pretty awful. Have a free cupful at the spa gardens. Most residenciais are full of elderly patients on long courses of treatment.

Museu da Região Flaviense

A building on Praça de Camões houses this collection of archaeological and ethnographical material from the region. Of course there are lots of Roman remains, but the most interesting items are prehistoric stone menhirs and carvings, some dating back over 2500 years. The museum is open daily except Monday from 9 am to 12.30 pm and 2 to 5.30 pm (afternoon only at weekends). A combined ticket for this and the Museu Militar costs 100$00.

Torre de Menagem & Museu Militar

Around the corner from the Museu da Região Flaviense is the Torre de Menagem

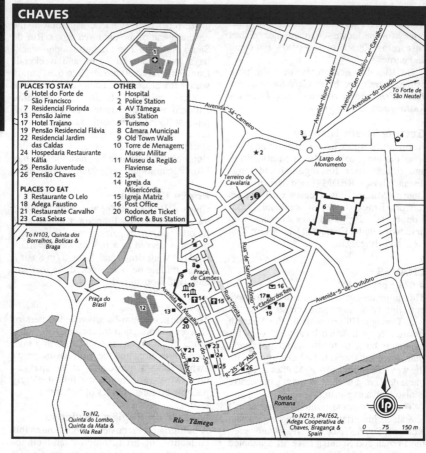

CHAVES

PLACES TO STAY
6 Hotel do Forte de São Francisco
7 Residencial Florinda
13 Pensão Jaime
17 Hotel Trajano
19 Pensão Residencial Flávia
22 Residencial Jardim das Caldas
24 Hospedaria Restaurante Kátia
25 Pensão Juventude
26 Pensão Chaves

PLACES TO EAT
3 Restaurante O Lelo
18 Adega Faustino
21 Restaurante Carvalho
23 Casa Seixas

OTHER
1 Hospital
2 Police Station
4 AV Tâmega Bus Station
5 Turismo
8 Câmara Municipal
9 Old Town Walls
10 Torre de Menagem; Museu Militar
11 Museu da Região Flaviense
12 Spa
14 Igreja da Misericórdia
15 Igreja Matriz
16 Post Office
20 Rodonorte Ticket Office & Bus Station

(keep), the only major remnant of a castle built by Dom Dinis in the 14th century and originally enclosed within defensive walls, parts of which can still be seen. After Dom João triumphed at Aljubarrota in 1385, he gave the castle to his constable, Dom Nun' Álvares Pereira. It was inherited by the House of Bragança when Nun' Álvares' daughter Beatriz married the Count of Barcelos, the future Duke of Bragança.

Today the Torre, set in manicured gardens with fine views of the countryside, houses a rather dull military museum, open the same hours as the Museu da Região Flaviense. A combined ticket valid for both museums costs 100$00.

Forte de São Neutel & Forte de São Francisco

The style of these two 17th century forts, like the one at Valença do Minho, was inspired by the work of the French military architect Vauban. Forte de São Neutel, north-east of the bus station, is open to the public during the day in summer and is the site of periodic evening *son et lumière* shows. Forte de São Francisco has been converted into a top-end hotel (see Places to Stay later in this section).

Churches

Next to the Museu da Região Flaviense, the 17th century **Igreja da Misericórdia** catches the eye with its exterior porch and columns. Inside are huge 18th century azulejos.

The Romanesque **Igreja Matriz** (parish church) was completely remodelled in the 16th century, though the doorway and belfry still retain original features. There's little of interest inside.

Activities

Horse Riding At Quinta dos Borralhos (☎ 2 83 67) in Curalha, 4km south-west of town, you can take riding lessons or hire horses.

Wine Tasting The Adega Cooperativa de Chaves (☎ 2 21 83) on Avenida Duarte, 2km south of town, is open weekdays from 9 am to 12.30 pm and 2 to 6 pm for tours and tastings of its strong local wine. For details of something a little out of the mainstream, see the boxed text.

Special Events

Feira de Santos is Chaves' major fair, lasting for a week at the end of October. The biggest days are 31 October and 1 November, when there's music and dancing, and market stalls fill the streets.

Dia de Cidade (City Day) on 8 July is another big bash, featuring brass bands, parades, fireworks and laser lights. An important religious event is the 15km pilgrimage to the Sanctuario de São Caetano on the 2nd Sunday in August.

Places to Stay

Pensões & Residenciais Built into the old town walls along Rua do Sol is a string of inexpensive restaurante-pensões. Jolly *Pensão Juventude* (☎ 2 67 13) at No 8 has eight clean, spartan doubles with shared

---

Wine of the Dead

Twenty-three kilometres south-west of Chaves, in the otherwise unremarkable town of Boticas, you can sample Portugal's most bizarrely named brew: *vinho dos mortos* (wine of the dead). This rough red wine, generously described by the local turismo as 'famous, tasty clarets', takes its name from an incident in 1809 when villagers hid their hoard of wine from the invading French by burying it underground. Discovering afterwards that the taste had noticeably improved as a result, they have continued the practice to this day, burying wine in deep underground cellars for up to a year.

You can sample this earthy wine at a number of Boticas cafés, including *Café de Armindo* (*Rua de Sangunhedo*), or inquire about it at the turismo on Rua 5 de Outubro.

---

bathroom costing 3000$00. The slicker *Hospedaria Restaurante Kátia* (☎ 2 44 46) at No 28 offers doubles with bathroom for around 5500$00 including breakfast.

The many residenciais geared to spa clientele are heavily booked in summer. A modest one is *Pensão Residencial Flávia* (☎ 2 25 13, Travessa Cândido dos Reis 12), with a gloomy restaurant and a pleasant courtyard garden; basic doubles with bathroom cost about 5500$00.

Others include the characterless *Pensão Jaime* (☎ 2 12 73), on Avenida da Muralha at the corner of Rua da Família de Camões, where singles/doubles with bathroom cost 3500/4500$00; *Residencial Jardim das Caldas* (☎ 33 11 89, Alameda do Tabolado), costing 3500/6000$00; and the rambling *Pensão Chaves* (☎ 2 11 18, Rua 25 de Abril) at 4500/5500$00. Breakfast is included in these prices, and all three places have cheaper rooms with shared facilities.

Residencial Florinda (☎ 33 33 92, fax 2 65 77, Rua dos Açougues) offers spotless, pretty rooms with double beds and large bathtubs for 7000$00, though the owners can be over-attentive.

Hotels The sturdy old *Hotel Trajano (☎ 33 24 15, fax 2 70 02, Travessa Cândido dos Reis)* has singles/doubles costing 7000/8500$00. Top of the price heap is *Hotel do Forte de São Francisco (☎ 33 37 00, fax 33 37 01)* in the tarted-up Forte de São Francisco, with singles/doubles from 15,000/18,000$00.

Turihab If you've got the wheels and the wherewithal, ask at the turismo about Turihab places. Nearest are *Quinta do Lombo (☎ 2 14 04)*, a stone house 2km to the south-east off the Valpaços road (N213) with rooms for 10,000$00 and a swimming pool; and *Quinta da Mata (☎/fax 9 62 53)* is a 17th century manor house 2km further out on the same road with doubles for 13,000$00, tennis courts and a sauna.

Places to Eat

Most residenciais and many restaurants serve generous portions of standard Portuguese fare at reasonable prices. The restaurant at *Hotel Trajano* is popular with well-heeled patrons.

At the lower end of the scale is the modest, unsignposted *Casa Seixas (☎ 2 35 70, Rua do Sol 38)*, where the atmosphere is homey, the menu short and the food very good. Hidden away by a busy roundabout is the plain *Restaurante O Lelo (☎ 2 70 33, Largo do Monumento)*, with local specialities for around 1000$00, and some half-portions – our half-portion of *feijoado* (meat, rice and black beans) would have fed two. *Adega Faustino (☎ 2 21 42, Travessa Cândido dos Reis)* is a cavernous former *adega* (winery) with a menu of light meals ranging from salads to pig's ear in vinaigrette sauce, mostly costing from 500$00 and 900$00 per dish.

One deservedly well known spot is *Restaurante Carvalho (☎ 2 17 27, Alameda do Tabolado)*, in a row of cafés and noisy bars facing the riverside park. Prices are around 1500$00 per dish but the food is good. It's closed Thursday.

Self-caterers should head for the *supermarket* upstairs from the bus station.

Getting There & Away

AV Tâmega (☎ 33 23 51) operates multiple weekday services to/from Porto, Braga (via Montalegre), Vila Real, Caldas do Gerês (Parque Nacional da Peneda-Gerês) and Bragança, often in conjunction with REDM.

Rodonorte (☎ 33 34 91), on Alameda do Tabolado, runs weekday express services to/from Lisbon (five), Porto (six) and Braga (two), all via Vila Real. The ticket office is open daily, into the evening except on Saturday, but tends to close for long meal breaks. As usual in Trás-os-Montes, weekend services are more limited.

AV Tâmega operates at least half a dozen local services daily to the frontier, where you can pick up Spanish buses to Orense.

Eastern Trás-os-Montes

BRAGANÇA
☎ 073 • pop 32,600

The name Bragança has rung down through Portuguese history since the 15th century, when Dom João I created a duchy here as a reminder to the Spanish that this remote corner was indeed part of the Portuguese kingdom. Though the dukes of Bragança came to prefer their vast holdings in the south (see the Vila Viçosa section in the Alentejo chapter), their home town's splendid isolation remained a symbol of national determination – especially after they ascended the throne in 1640 (they ruled until the fall of the monarchy in 1910).

Thanks to mountains, bad roads and poor communications, the isolation continued right into the late 20th century. An EU-designated motorway, the E82, arrived from Porto and Vila Real in the early 1990s, completing a major road link with Spain. Bragança is now – rather suddenly – a few hours from Porto as well as Madrid, and in summer its sober streets fill with Portuguese tourists and jolly Spaniards.

But despite an air of self-importance – and a walled citadel that presents, from afar, one of the most stirring views in northern Portugal – the town itself is surprisingly modest in scale, at heart a backwater where donkey carts still trundle within a few blocks of its little cathedral.

Why come all this way? Bragança still has a dollop of medieval atmosphere and one of the country's best museums, and it's the obvious base for a spin through the underrated Parque Natural de Montesinho. If you're driving or cycling, a roundabout route to Bragança through eastern Trás-os-Montes reveals some of Portugal's loveliest and least-seen landscapes.

History

The town has Celtic roots, as Brigantia or Brigantio. The Romans fortified it and called it Juliobriga. Trashed during repeated Christian and Moorish campaigns, it was solidly rebuilt in the early 12th century by Fernão Mendes, an in-law of Afonso Henriques, as the capital of a semi-independent fiefdom. It wasn't long before its brand new fortress was attacked and unsuccessfully besieged by Alfonso IX of León in 1199.

In 1442 Dom João I, determined to keep a grip on the region, assumed direct control, creating the duchy of Bragança – a thumb in the eye for Castile and León – and declaring his own bastard son Afonso the first Duke of Bragança. The House of Bragança soon became one of the wealthiest and most powerful families in the country.

Jews fled to Bragança in large numbers from the Spanish Inquisition in the 16th century, to a rather milder Portuguese version which was hardly felt in Trás-os-Montes. Unfortunately, few traces remain of the town's old Jewish community.

In 1640 the Portuguese decided that 60 years of Spanish rule was enough. They booted out Philip II's garrisons, and the eighth Duke of Bragança reluctantly took the Portuguese throne as João IV. In his

quest for alliances against the Spanish he gave his daughter Catherine in marriage to Charles II of England.

Spain and France invaded Trás-os-Montes in 1762 on the pretext of freeing Portugal from English domination. Bragança and other towns were besieged for a time before being bailed out by Portuguese and English troops. Shortly afterwards Bragança scored an ecclesiastical coup when the bishopric was transferred here from Miranda do Douro.

Orientation

Bragança sits at around 670m in undulating countryside on the edge of the Parque Natural de Montesinho. Beside it runs the Rio Fervença, a tributary of the Rio Sabor which runs right across eastern Trás-os-Montes to the Douro. The approach to the town from Braga and Chaves is through ugly outskirts, but with the citadel always floating above the scene like a mirage.

If Bragança has a centre, it is Praça da Sé, in front of the cathedral. From here one road runs to the citadel, one to Spain and one to the rest of Portugal. The axis of town is along Avenida João da Cruz (where most long-distance coaches start and stop), Rua Almirante Reis and Rua Combatentes da Grande Guerra (usually called just Rua Combatentes).

Information

Tourist Office Bragança's well-organised turismo (☎ 38 12 73, fax c/o câmara municipal 2 72 52) on Avenida Cidade de Zamora is open daily except Sunday from 9 am to 8 pm (also closed Saturday afternoon in winter).

Park Office A helpful Parque Natural de Montesinho information office (☎ 38 12 34, fax 38 11 79) is among other park offices at No 5 in Bairro Salvador Nunes Teixeira, a residential district north-east of the turismo. It's open weekdays only from 9 am to 12.30 pm and 2 to 5.30 pm. Some good Instituto da Conservação da Natureza (ICN; park service) publications are for sale,

TRÁS-OS-MONTES

BRAGANÇA

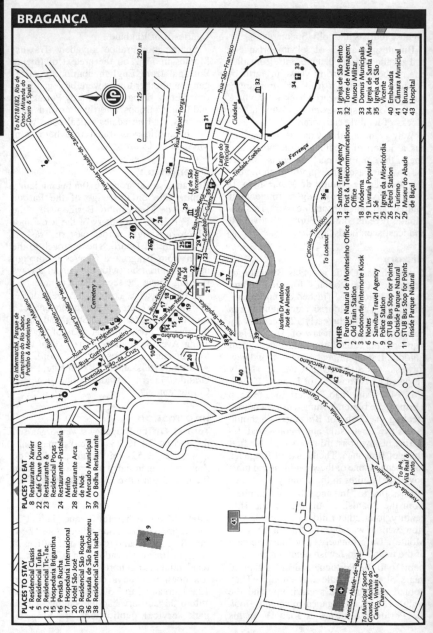

PLACES TO STAY
4 Residencial Classis
5 Residencial Tulipa
12 Residencial Tic-Tac
15 Hospedaria Brigantina
16 Pensão Rucha
17 Hospedaria Internacional
20 Hotel São José
30 Residencial São Roque
36 Pousada de São Bartolomeu
38 Residencial Santa Isabel

PLACES TO EAT
8 Restaurante Xavier
22 Café Chave Douro
23 Restaurante &
   Residencial Poças
24 Restaurante-Pastelaria
   Mérito
28 Restaurante Arca
   de Noé
37 Mercado Municipal
39 O Bolha Restaurante

OTHER
1 Parque Natural de Montesinho Office
2 Old Train Station
6 Noites
9 Police Station
10 STUB Bus Stop for Points
   Outside Parque Natural
11 STUB Bus Stop for Points
   Inside Parque Natural
13 Santos Travel Agency
14 Post & Telecommunications
   Office
18 Moderna
19 Livraria Popular
21 Sé
25 Igreja da Misericórdia
26 Petrol Station
27 Turismo
29 Museu do Abade
   de Baçal

31 Igreja de São Bento
32 Torre de Menagem;
   Museu Militar
33 Domus Municipalis
34 Igreja de Santa Maria
35 Igreja da São
   Vicente
40 Embaixada
41 Câmara Municipal
42 Bruxa
43 Hospital

Rodonorte/Internorte Kiosk
Sanvitur Travel Agency

though all are in Portuguese except a free schematic park map.

Money There are several banks with currency exchanges and ATMs along Rua Almirante Reis.

Post & Communications The post and telecommunications office is at the top of Rua Almirante Reis.

Travel Agencies Sanvitur (☎ 33 18 26, fax 2 75 36), Avenida João da Cruz 38, is also the local agent for Rede Expressos and AV Tâmega. Santos (☎/fax 2 65 52), Avenida João da Cruz 5, is also a Trás-os-Montes regional coach line.

Bookshop There is a small bookshop, Livraria Popular, at Rua Almirante Reis 16.

Medical Services & Emergency The district hospital (☎ 33 12 33) is over 1km west of the centre, on Avenida Abade de Baçal. Behind the câmara municipal and in the same complex is the police station (☎ 33 13 54).

Sé
Don't get your hopes up. This old but forgettable church, which started life in 1545 as the Igreja de São João Baptista, was declared a cathedral in 1770 when the bishopric was moved here from Miranda do Douro.

Museu do Abade de Baçal
This museum of regional archaeology, ethnography and art is one of Portugal's best museums. It houses a wide-ranging and high-minded collection based on that of its namesake, the Abbot of Baçal, Francisco Manuel Alves (1865-1947), a dedicated scholar of regional history and architecture. It's in the 16th century Paço Episcopal (former Bishop's Palace) on Rua Abílio Beça, just off Largo de São Vicente.

Downstairs, displays include ancient pottery and tools, the mysterious stone pigs called berrões (see the boxed text) and other

---

Pig Mysteries

Scattered around Trás-os-Montes and the Zamora region of Spain are hundreds of crudely carved granite pigs or boars known as berrões (singular berrão). Some date back over 2000 years, others to the 2nd or 3rd century AD. No one knows what they were for, though there are plenty of theories: they may be fertility or prosperity symbols, grave guardians, or offerings to, or representations of, Iron Age gods. Alternatively they may have marked the boundary of someone's land.

You can take a close look at these mysterious pigs in museums in Bragança, Chaves and Miranda do Douro, or in situ in Bragança castle where there's one pierced through its middle by a pillory.

---

animal totems, handsome Roman funeral stones (plus Roman milestones, tools and coins), and the papal bulls (documents) that proclaimed the diocese of Miranda in the 16th century and moved it to Bragança in the 18th.

Upstairs are the remnants of the palace's own chapels, luminous wooden church statues and other furnishings. A garden at the back is dotted with more tombstones and stone animals. There is no information in English. The museum is open daily except Monday from 10 am to 5 pm (6 pm at weekends). Admission costs 250$00 (free on Sunday morning).

Largo de São Vicente & Around
Facing this small, pretty square is the Igreja de São Vicente, Romanesque in origin but rebuilt in the 17th century. Tradition has it that the future Dom Pedro I secretly married Inês de Castro here in around 1354 (see the boxed text 'Love & Revenge' in the Estremadura & Ribatejo chapter, which is about this star-crossed, ultimately grisly affair).

Bragança's most attractive church is about a block east of Largo de São Vicente on Rua São Francisco: the Igreja de São Bento, which has a Renaissance stone portal and a trompe l'oeil ceiling over the nave, and an Arabic-style inlaid ceiling over the chancel.

Cidadela

From Largo de São Vicente, follow Rua Serpa Pinto or the cobbled Rua Trindade Coelho up to the walled and amazingly well-preserved citadel. People still live along the few narrow lanes inside, now sharing the area with *artesanatos* (handicrafts shops) and posh restaurants. There were more houses in pre-Salazar days.

Within the walls are what remains of the castle, built in 1187 by Dom Sancho I and beefed up by João I for the dukes of Bragança. The massive, square **Torre de Menagem** (built as a residence too; note the Gothic window upstairs) was garrisoned in the 19th and early 20th centuries, and now houses the marginally interesting **Museu Militar**, open daily except Thursday from 9 to 11.45 am and 2 to 4.45 pm; admission costs 200$00 (free on Sunday morning). In front is an extraordinary and primitive *pelourinho* (pillory), atop a granite boar similar to the berrões found all over the province.

The best views of the citadel are from the Pousada de São Bartolomeu across the valley (see Places to Stay later in this section), the road beyond it or, best of all, a lookout near the old Mosteiro de São Bartolomeu. Cross the river on Rua Alexandre Herculano and take the first left.

Domus Municipalis At the rear of the cidadela is an odd, severe, five-sided building known as the Domus Municipalis (Town House). This 12th or 13th century structure is one of Portugal's few examples of non-church Romanesque architecture, and its oldest town hall. Upstairs, in an arcaded room, Bragança's medieval town council met to settle land or water disputes; below is the citadel's precious cistern. It's been tidied up a bit too much, and unfortunately roofed with incongruous red tiles.

At one time one of the neighbours had the key, but at the time of research this was in doubt. Check with the turismo, or ask around: *Por favor, gostaria de visitar a domus por dentro* (please, I'd like to go inside the domus).

You may also get in the door – covered with carved vines – of the early 16th century **Igreja da Santa Maria** next door, said to have an 18th century trompe l'oeil ceiling showing the Assumption.

Market

A big thrice-monthly market, featuring animals as well as the usual clothes and homewares, takes over the municipal sports ground west of the centre on Avenida Abade de Baçal on the third, 12th and 21st of each month (or on the following Monday when any of these falls on a Saturday or Sunday).

Special Events

The Feira das Cantarinhas is the biggest market of the year: a huge street fair of traditional handicrafts held every 2 to 4 May (a *cantarinha* is a small terracotta pitcher).

Places to Stay

Camping The municipal *Parque de Campismo do Rio Sabor* (☎ 33 15 35), open from May to October, is 6km north of the town centre on the Portelo road; it costs 200/200/200$00 per person/tent/car. Municipal (STUB) bus No 7 to Meixedo runs from in front of Caixa Geral de Depósitos bank, at the southern end of Avenida João da Cruz, past the parque de campismo three to five times each weekday (once only on Saturday) in each direction. It doesn't run on Sunday. Ask at the turismo for a current timetable. The Rodonorte bus to Portelo departs from the old train station on schooldays only at 1.45 and 5.15 pm, passing the parque de campismo.

The next nearest camping ground is *Parque de Campismo de Cepo Verde* at Gondesende, 12km west of town on the Vinhais road; see the following Parque Natural de Montesinho section for details.

Private Rooms Staff at the municipal turismo can help with finding private rooms, and there are a few notices in the window of Livraria Popular at Rua Almirante Reis 16.

Pensões & Residenciais Bragança is plagued with late-night unmuffled motorcycles, so try for back rooms.

Good value at the budget end is *Residencial Poças (☎ 33 14 28, Rua Combatentes 200)*, over the restaurant of the same name, where plain doubles (some with shower) cost 4000$00. You'll find another bargain at the peaceful *Pensão Rucha (☎ 33 16 72, Rua Almirante Reis 42)*, where a small double room with shared bathroom costs 5000$00.

Two threadbare boarding houses also face one another across this street. *Hospedaria Brigantina (☎ 2 43 21, Rua Almirante Reis 48)* has doubles with shared facilities for 3000$00, and all the charm of a hospital ward. At *Hospedaria Internacional (☎ 2 26 11, Rua Almirante Reis 47)* the same price (or 4000$00 for a double with shower) buys you a modicum of atmosphere and access to a small restaurant.

Residencial São Roque (☎ 38 14 81) is on the 7th and 8th floors of a building on Rua Miguel Torga. It's some way east of the centre, but the 7000$00 doubles with bathroom, TV and fine views (and no motorcycle noise) are good value. Under the same management and with the same prices is *Residencial Santa Isabel (☎ 33 14 27, Rua da República)*.

Near the long-distance bus stops on the Avenida are three smartly run residenciais with characterless but comfortable air-con doubles with bathroom, telephone and TV: *Tic-Tac (☎ 33 13 73, Rua Emídio Navarro 85)* costs 6000$00; *Tulipa (☎ 33 16 75, Rua Dr Francisco Felgueiras 8-10)* costs 7500$00 (with big bathtubs); and *Classis (☎ 33 16 31, fax 2 34 58, Avenida João da Cruz 102)* costs 9000$00. Rates at all three include breakfast.

Hotel São José (☎ 33 15 78, fax 33 12 42, Avenida Sá Carneiro 11-15) is actually an oversized pensão. Rooms with the works (including breakfast) cost 10,000$00. Some old signs say Estalagem or Hotel Bragança.

Pousada Splash out at the *Pousada de São Bartolomeu (☎ 33 14 93, fax 2 34 53)*. It's 1.5km from the centre and has splendid views across the valley to the cidadela. Posh doubles cost 20,300$00 during the high season.

Turihab Among places staff at the turismo can tell you about is *Moinho do Caniço (☎ 2 35 77)*, a converted water mill that sleeps six and has two bathrooms, a kitchen and a fireplace. It's by the Rio Baceiro at Castrelos, 12km west of Bragança on the N103.

Places to Eat

There are several fairly ordinary cafés and pastelarias near the long-distance bus stops. Among them is *Restaurante Xavier (☎ 2 39 68, Avenida João da Cruz 12)*, with dishes for around 1300$00 and a good value 800$00 weekday special.

Residenciais *Tic-Tac* and *Tulipa* have their own restaurants serving adequate versions of Trás-os-Montes specialities. At the sharp end of Praça da Sé is the cheerful *Café Chave Douro*, where locals wash down their gossip with a coffee or a beer.

Restaurante Poças, beneath Residencial Poças (see Places to Stay earlier), has a big menu of fish and meat dishes at prices ranging from 900$00 to 1600$00; nothing is typically northern but the food is deservedly well known and the service is polite and relaxed. *Restaurante-Pastelaria Mérito (☎ 2 33 71, Rua Abílio Beça 86)* offers a few well-prepared lunch specials for about 900$00 per dish, plus sandwiches, tostas mistas and pastries, in a clean, stylish setting.

You may find the service obsequious at *O Bolha Restaurante (☎ 2 32 40, Jardim Dr António José de Almeida)* but, when they're on a roll, the northern and Portuguese specialities (costing under 1500$00 per dish) are very good. We liked their *rojões do*

TRÁS-OS-MONTES

Transmontana (a casserole of marinated pork pieces).

A *marisqueira* (seafood restaurant) and adega called **Restaurante Arca de Noé**, or Noah's Ark (☎ *38 11 59, Avenida Cidade de Zamora)*, has a big, pricey seafood menu, but some dishes cost under 1500$00.

Self-caterers can stock up at the **mercado municipal**, just south of Praça da Sé, or at the **Intermarché** supermarket, just north of the old train station.

Entertainment

There are at least four discos/clubs in town, including **Noites** *(Rua Dr Francisco Felgueiras)*, **Moderna** *(Rua Almirante Reis)* in a shopping arcade, **Embaixada** *(Avenida Sá Carneiro)* and **Bruxa** *(Rua Alexandre Herculano).*

Getting There & Away

A Rodonorte ticket kiosk (☎ 33 18 70) is on upper Avenida João da Cruz. Buy Rede Expressos tickets from Sanvitur travel agency. Santos operates a regional coach line. See under Travel Agencies earlier in this section for Sanvitur and Santos. All offer youth discounts, and Santos has discounts for seniors too. All buses depart from stops on the Avenida near the Rodonorte kiosk.

Each weekday Rodonorte has an express service to Lisbon (2700$00, seven hours) plus slower, cheaper services (2400$00); nine to Porto (1500$00); and two to Braga (1600$00). Santos runs slightly cheaper services to Porto. Weekend services with both companies are more limited. Rede Expressos operates a Lisbon-Coimbra-Bragança service seven or eight times daily, mostly via Porto, and has at least four daily runs to Braga. Almost all buses go via Vila Real.

Three times a week, Empresa Francisco Ledesma (affiliated with Rodonorte) passes through Bragança en route between Porto and Zamora (about 2200$00), Valladolid and Salamanca in Spain. Rodonorte and Santos are also agents for Internorte/Eurolines, which runs buses to further European destinations (see Eurolines under Bus in the Getting There & Away chapter).

STUB (the municipal bus company) and Rodonorte run services into the Parque Natural de Montesinho (see below).

PARQUE NATURAL DE MONTESINHO
☎ 073

Projecting into Spain, in what looks like an annex of north-eastern Trás-os-Montes, is Montesinho Natural Park, a modest and very lived-in park with dozens of small, lean villages sprinkled across 75,000 hilly hectares of grassland and deciduous forest. Its appeal is this very mixture of gentle human and natural landscapes – both of which the park seeks to protect – and minimal tourist development.

Though it was founded in 1979, regional tourist literature seems oddly low-key about it. Perhaps local people simply take it for granted. Certainly, on summer weekends, it seems that every family in north-eastern Portugal is picnicking there.

The park includes two slatey massifs: the lush, wet Serra da Corôa in the central west and the Serra de Montesinho in the central east. The finest landscapes are in these highland areas and the complex watershed between them. Elevations range from 438m on the Rio Mente at the western end of the park to 1481m near the Rio Sabor at its northernmost point.

The most convenient base from which to explore the park is Bragança. There is also some accommodation at Vinhais and at villages within the park, though transport is limited.

Flora & Fauna

In the park's immense forests of Iberian oak and chestnut, or among riverside alders, willows, poplars and hazel, you may spot roe deer, otter or wild boar; in its grasslands are partridge, kite and hunting kestrel. Above 900m the otherwise barren ground is carpeted in heather and broom. Stands of birch grow at the highest elevations of the Serra de Montesinho.

Huge state plantations of pine mar the landscape on the eastern limb of the park;

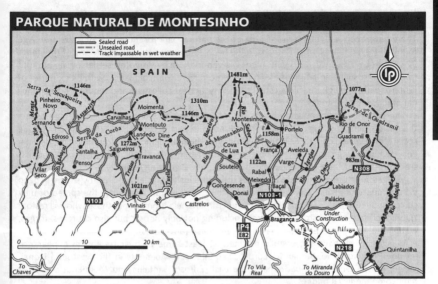

PARQUE NATURAL DE MONTESINHO

nevertheless, this and the Serra de Montesinho host the richest diversity of animals.

The park's north-eastern corner, combined with the adjoining Reserva Nacional de Sierra Culebra on the Spanish side, is the last major refuge for the endangered Iberian wolf. (For more information about the wolf, see the Flora & Fauna section in the Facts about Portugal chapter.) Other threatened species found here are the royal eagle and black stork.

There are no restricted zones in the park except for several royal eagle nesting areas, which are strictly off-limits to rock climbers. Motorised boats are not permitted in the park's waters.

Information

There is a good park information office in Bragança (see Information in the Bragança section) and another (☎ 7 14 16) at Rua Dr Álvaro Leite in Vinhais, the region's other *concelho* or county seat. Handsome publications on flora and fauna and the park's cultural and architectural heritage are all in Portuguese, but translations are in the

works, and English-speaking staff are very willing to answer questions.

Maps The free schematic park map available from the park office shows villages, roads and tracks, points of interest, camp sites and rural accommodation, but not trails. Some two dozen military topographic maps cover the park at a scale of 1:25,000; nobody seems to be selling these or the 1:50,000 civilian versions, but the park offices have these maps and staff will photocopy them at your expense.

There are also several detailed 'road books' for mountain bikers. These are on sale at both offices, and good relief maps are apparently on the way.

Rio de Onor

Little Rio de Onor, 22km up the N218 from Bragança, is one of the most interesting villages in the park, not only because of its well-preserved stone buildings but also because it has held on staunchly to the independent-minded communal lifestyle once typical of the region.

The Villages of the Parque Natural de Montesinho

There have been settlements in the area of the natural park for thousands of years: Iron Age foundations, adapted by the Romans, have been found in several places. Many of the park's 92 villages bear distinctly Germanic names, given to them by Visigothic settlers. In an attempt to create a sustainable fabric of life in this remote *terra fria* (cold land), with its extremes of climate, early Portuguese rulers established a system of collective land tenure, and communal practices persist today.

The park's overall population is only about 9000, which works out at an average of less than 100 souls per village. The park was founded in part to protect and revitalise this fragile social structure and cultural heritage, but many of the more remote villages are on the decline, deserted by young people. The main exception is Moimenta, the biggest village. It's the first stop for many of these young people and is therefore growing healthily.

Villages are more concentrated towards the park's lusher western end. Many shelter in deep valleys, peaceful gems easily overlooked by the casual visitor. To counter the spread of ugly stucco and red-tile modern construction, government help is on offer to those who will restore traditional slate-roofed stone structures, including not only houses but also churches, forges, water mills and the conspicuous, charming *pombals* (dovecotes).

Villages which have successfully retained at least some of their traditional appearance include Pinheiro Novo, Sernande, Edroso, Santalha and Moimenta in the west, and Donai, Varge, Rio de Onor and Guadramil in the east. Edroso, Santalha and Moimenta also have handsome medieval bridges.

On top of that, the Portuguese-Spanish border runs through the middle of the village (it's marked only by a stone marker with 'P' on one side and 'E' on the other), and nobody pays it a blind bit of notice. People speak a dialect that's neither quite Portuguese nor quite Spanish, and have more in common with one another than with Lisbon or Madrid.

The Rio Onor itself – just a trickle here – flows at right angles to the border. The road from Bragança ends at the village, and a footpath branches left to cross the border or right to cross the river. The prettiest part of the village is east over the bridge.

There are no pensões or restaurants in the village. With the permission of the village *presidente* (ask at the *casa de povo* or common house above the village on the east side of the river), you could pitch your tent on common land or possibly stay in the casa de povo itself.

Cervejaria Prato, across the bridge, serves snacks.

Visiting without your own transport is tricky: STUB bus No 5 departs from Praça da Sé in Bragança on weekdays only at 5.44 pm, but eight minutes after arriving at Rio de Onor, it heads back. So you either enjoy the scenery en route and look the place over in eight minutes or stay the night (there's another bus to Bragança in the morning).

On schooldays only, an additional bus leaves Bragança at 2.11 pm, which would give you about 3½ hours at the village. A taxi from Bragança and back would cost about 3000$00.

Walking

Spring and summer are the best times for walking, though visually the park is at its best in the chilly autumn. Few if any trails have been established with walkers in mind, but a network of roads and dirt tracks pushes out to villages in many remote corners. The prettiest areas with the fewest paved roads are the watersheds of the Rio

Sabor north of Soutelo and França, and the Rio Tuela between Dine and Moimenta. The park operates its own fairly comfortable *abrigos de montanha* or mountain shelters in these areas (see under Places to Stay & Eat).

Horse Riding

There's a park-run *centro hípico* or pony trekking and riding centre (☎ 91 91 41) at França, from where numerous routes go into the park. You can hire horses for 1500$00 per hour or 7000$00 per day. The centre is open from Wednesday to Saturday, and alternate Tuesdays and Sundays, from 9.30 am to noon and 3.30 to 6 pm (9.30 am to noon and 2.30 to 5 pm in winter). França is 15km along the Portelo road north of Bragança, and the centre is 800m down a track from the upper end of the village.

Places to Stay & Eat

Camping The *Parque de Campismo de Cepo Verde* (☎ 9 93 71) is 12km west of Bragança on the N103 and 600m north off the highway, just before Gondesende village. It costs 500/300/300$00 per person/tent/car and is open year-round. Rodonorte's Bragança-Vinhais bus passes the parque de campismo twice each weekday (see under Getting Around).

Villagers, if asked, will sometimes allow free camping on common land. There is also another parque de campismo north of Bragança; see under Places to Stay in the earlier Bragança section.

Abrigos de Montanha The park operates 10 *abrigos de montanha* (mountain shelters) for walkers; they're of various sizes and cost from 7500$00 for two people to 20,000$00 for nine. All are open year-round and have sheets, blankets and towels, hot water, equipped kitchens, fireplaces and firewood. Book them well in advance at either park office; you'll have to pay a 50% deposit.

Private Rooms Although not plentiful in the park, there are some private rooms, notably in Montesinho, a friendly village of 35 souls. In July and August they're all booked out, while from October to May you don't have to book at all. Montesinho is 23km from Bragança (bus almost to Portelo, plus a fine 5km walk).

Other places where you might find a room include *Café Turismo* in França, *Snack Bar O Careto* (☎ 91 92 69) in Varge and *Restaurante Fraga dos Três Reinos* (☎ 6 41 74) in Moimenta. Ask at cafés and shops, or check with park officers for current recommendations.

Hotel The *Hospedaria da Senhora da Hera* (☎ 9 94 14), near Cova de Lua, has nine doubles which cost 7000$00 (6000$00 without bathroom) and four triples with bathroom for 8000$00; there's also a restaurant, bar and swimming pool. It's about 1km off the N308 to Dine.

Getting There & Away

Main roads enter the park at around a dozen places, mainly via Bragança and Vinhais. There are also three roads to/from Spain (plus a footpath through Rio de Onor), all of them open 24 hours.

Getting Around

Moving around the park is hard without a car, bike or sturdy feet. Tracks marked on the map are mainly firebreaks, and are sometimes dicey in bad weather. The unsealed 'scenic' routes are in marginally better condition. All make suitable hiking routes, but if you plan to drive on any of them, check on current conditions with the park office.

Bus Public buses within the park are scarce (even more so at weekends) and most do not return the same day. Many services disappear outside the school term, in July, August and early September.

STUB, Bragança's municipal bus company, has routes near Bragança, departing from in front of Caixa Geral de Depósitos bank or Praça da Sé. The turismo can provide current timetables.

Rodonorte has most of the park covered, with buses from various points in Bragança:

Dine
1.45 and 5.15 pm on schooldays only, or at 11.55 am and 5.15 pm on weekdays only outside school term, from opposite the old train station

Guadramil
Monday and Friday only, at 1.45 and 5.15 pm, from opposite the petrol station on Avenida Cidade de Zamora

Portelo
1.45 and 5.15 pm on schooldays only, from opposite the old train station

Vinhais
6 and 11.55 am and 5.25 pm on weekdays only, from Rodonorte kiosk; change at Vinhais for Penso and Moimenta

Inquire at Rodonorte's kiosk on Avenida João da Cruz in Bragança for current schedules and fares.

Bicycle Given a bit of notice and a deposit of 1000$00, the park service rents mountain bikes through its centro hípico at França. See Information earlier in this section for information on bike maps.

Minibus On Tuesday and Thursday, for trips within the park only, a group of 10 or more can hire a minibus from the park office, complete with a guide-driver, for about 5000$00 per day.

MIRANDA DO DOURO
☎ 073 • pop 8200
This sleepy town, facing Spain across the Rio Douro gorge in the furthest corner of Trás-os-Montes, is one of Portugal's (and Europe's) smallest cities – for despite its small population, a 'city' is what history made it. That history is one of Miranda's few present claims to fame.

This is also the easternmost town of any size in Portugal, more accessible from Spain than from Portugal, and in a sense more Spanish than Portuguese. Local people speak *mirandês*, a dialect descended almost straight from Latin but sounding rather like that of rural Castile and León.

What is there to see here? The uninteresting ruins of a medieval castle, views of the Douro (dammed in this area into a silent lake), a cathedral without a diocese and an amateurish but charmingly eclectic ethnographic museum. Its famous Pauliteiros stick-dancers (see the boxed text below) are hard to find here anymore.

The cobbled streets of the old town, lined with identical, blindingly whitewashed 15th and 16th century houses, echo with the chatter of Spanish tour groups in summer and at weekends. Miranda's new town is for these day-trippers what the Algarve is for many English: a tidy gauntlet of handicrafts shops and pricey restaurants.

Miranda would make a pleasant day trip if it were closer to anywhere else in Portugal. It is possible to see everything worth seeing here in a couple of hours, but the vagaries of public transport make it almost essential to spend longer. Don't come on Monday, when the museum and cathedral are closed.

The Pauliteiros

Probably the most high-profile representatives of Trás-os-Montes folk customs are the 'stick dancers' of Miranda do Douro, who look rather like Britain's Morris dancers. Local men dress in white linen kilts and smocks, black waistcoats, bright flapping scarves and shawls, and black hats covered in flowers and ribbons, and do a rhythmic dance to the complex clacking of short wooden sticks (*paulitos*). It looks a bit like a sword dance, from which it may well have descended in Celtic times.

The Pauliteiros have gone big time, appearing at major festivals around the region and all over Portugal, and they are rarely seen in their home town except at local festivals. The best time to catch them in Miranda is during the Festas de Santa Bárbara (also called Festas da Cidade or City Festival) on the third weekend in August.

History

Strategic Miranda was an important bulwark during Portugal's first two centuries of independence, and the Castilians had to be chucked out at least twice: in the early days by Dom João I, and in 1710 during the Wars of the Spanish Succession. In 1545, perhaps as a snub to the increasingly powerful House of Bragança, a diocese was created here, an oversized cathedral was built, and the town was declared a *cidade*. During a siege by French and Spanish troops in 1762 the castle's powder magazine blew up, pulverising most of the castle, killing 400 people and leaving almost nothing to besiege. Twenty years later, shattered Miranda was kicked while it was down, with the transfer of its diocese to Bragança. No one ever saw fit to rebuild the castle, and nobody paid much attention to Miranda again until the Barragem de Miranda dam was built in the 1950s.

Orientation

From Largo da Moagem, a roundabout on the N218 from Bragança (where the buses stop), the new town is down to the left (north-east); it consists mainly of Rua 1 de Maio, parallel to the highway, and Rua 25 de Abril and Rua do Mercado, perpendicular to it. In this area there are handicrafts shops, pensões, restaurants, cafés (those on Rua do Mercado have views across the gorge) and, a few hundred metres down Rua do Mercado, the mercado municipal.

About 200m uphill from the roundabout are the old walls and castle ruins, and beyond them the old town and what was once the citadel. The axis is Rua da Mousinho da Albuquerque; crossing it just inside the walls and then curving parallel to it is Rua de Dom Turíbio Lopes. Between them, halfway along, is the centre of the old town, Praça de Dom João III. On a triangular *largo* at the end of Rua de Dom Turíbio Lopes is the cathedral.

Information

A small turismo (☎ 43 11 32) beside the highway is (usually) open weekdays only from 9 am to 12.30 pm and 2 to 5.30 pm. There are several banks with ATMs near Largo da Moagem, and one beside the post office, facing the cathedral at the back end of Rua da Mousinho da Albuquerque.

Museu de Terra de Miranda

The municipal ethnographic museum on Praça de Dom João III offers a charmingly miscellaneous look at the region's past, laid out with the innocence of a school project. Upstairs, past a Roman tombstone, are several halls. Highlights include a barely recognisable *berrão* (stone pig), 14th and 15th century stones with Hebrew inscriptions, rough woollen Mirandês clothing, farm tools and kitchen furnishings, and a miscellany of Portuguese and Spanish regional pottery. Best of all is a musty collection of musical instruments, masks and ceremonial costumes (including those of the Pauliteiros).

The museum (☎ 43 11 64) is open daily except Monday from 10 am to 12.15 pm and 2.30 to 5.45 pm (on winter afternoons it opens and closes half an hour earlier). Admission costs 150$00, with a 40% discount for youth-card holders and 50% off for seniors and teachers.

Old Town

The backstreets are all alike, save for a few old, unwhitewashed but dignified 15th century façades punctuating Rua da Costanilha (which runs west off Praça Dom João III), and a Gothic gate at the end of it.

The severe, twin-towered granite Sé (cathedral), dating from the founding of the bishopric in the 16th century, is unremarkable except for its size. Inside is a very grand, gilded main altarpiece. In a case in one transept stands the arresting Menino Jesus da Cartolinha, a Christ child in a top hat, whose wardrobe has more outfits than Imelda Marcos, thanks to local devotees. The cathedral is closed to tourists on Monday and when Mass is in progress.

Behind the cathedral are the roofless remains of the former bishop's palace, which burned down in the 18th century.

Barragem de Miranda

A road crawls across the 80m-high dam, about 1km east of town, and on to Zamora, 55km away. This dam is one of five on the Douro along the Spanish border, the upper three for use by Portugal.

About 20km south-west of Miranda on the N221 is the Barragem de Picote, and 35km away is the Barragem da Bemposta, the latter also a border crossing.

Places to Stay

Camping At the time of research the modest municipal *parque de campismo* (☎ 4 12 73), open from June to September, was free of charge, though this was under review. It's at the end of a residential street, west of the old town across the ravine of the Rio Fresno, 1.3km from the Rua da Costanilha gate or 1.8km from the roundabout. Houses nearby also advertise private rooms.

Pensões & Residenciais On Rua do Mercado in the new town are *Residencial Flôr do Douro* (☎ 43 11 86) at No 7, with singles/doubles for 4000/5000$00, and *Pensão Vista Bela* (☎ 43 10 54), costing 3500/4500$00. *Residencial Planalto* (☎ 43 13 62, Rua 1 de Maio 25) has 40 rooms with bathroom, TV and telephone costing 3500/4500$00. Prices at all three places include breakfast. Further on at No 49, *Restaurante Casa Pimentel* (☎ 4 14 78) also has some rooms to rent.

In the old town, just off the largo by the castle ruins, is the prettified *Pensão Santa Cruz* (☎ 43 13 74, Rua Abade de Baçal 61), where singles/doubles with bathroom start at 3000/5000$00 including breakfast.

For a deluxe treat and yawning views, take a room at the *Pousada de Santa Catarina* (☎ 43 10 05, fax 43 10 65), just east of the roundabout and perched at the edge of the gorge. Doubles cost 15,600$00 in high season.

Places to Eat

Most pensões have a restaurant of some description, open at fixed meal times.

Casual *Restaurante & Pizzeria O Moinho* (☎ 43 11 16, Rua do Mercado 47-D), less pricey than others on the street and with views across the gorge, has a big menu featuring paella, salads and pizzas, plus Portuguese standards for under 1500$00 per dish.

Restaurants in the old town include *São Pedro* (☎ 43 13 21, Rua da Mousinho da Albuquerque 20), with a vast menu of meat and fish dishes, and *Buteko* (☎ 43 12 31, Rua da Mousinho da Albuquerque 55), which also has a cheerful café and ice cream parlour on the corner of Praça de Dom João III.

Getting There & Away

In summer, Rodonorte runs three buses each weekday from Bragança to Miranda, and Santos has an afternoon departure. Santos buses also run to Miranda twice a day (except Saturday) from Porto, via Vila Real.

By car, the quickest road from Bragança to Miranda is the N218, a tortuous 85km trip. The 100km route to Miranda from the IP4/E82 motorway via Macedo de Cavaleiros and Mogadouro (N216 and N221) is one of the loveliest – and wiggliest – in Portugal. It crosses a *planalto* (high plain) dotted with olive, almond and chestnut groves, with a dramatic descent into the Rio Sabor valley.

Language

Like French, Italian, Romanian and Spanish, Portuguese is a Romance language, closely derived from Latin. It is spoken by 10 million Portuguese and 130 million Brazilians, and is the official language of five African nations (Angola, Cape Verde, Guinea-Bissau, Mozambique and São Tomé e Príncipe). In Asia it is still spoken in the former Portuguese territory of East Timor, and in enclaves around Malacca, Goa, Damão and Diu.

Visitors to Portugal are often struck by the strangeness of the spoken language, which some say sounds like Arabic. However, those who understand French or Spanish are often surprised to see how similar written Portuguese is to the other Romance languages.

The pre-Roman inhabitants of the Iberian Peninsula are responsible for the most striking traits of the Portuguese language. The vulgar Latin of the Roman soldiers and merchants, who were well established by 27 BC, gradually took over the indigenous languages and a strong neo-Latin character evolved.

After the Arab invasion in 711 AD, Arabic quickly became the prestige cultural language in the Iberian Peninsula. The influence of Arabic on the formation of the Portuguese language ended with the expulsion of the Moors in 1249.

During the Middle Ages, Portuguese underwent several changes, mostly influenced by French and Provençal (another Romance language). In the 16th and 17th centuries, Italian and Spanish were responsible for innovations in vocabulary.

As further reading, we recommend Lonely Planet's *Western Europe phrasebook* for the basics. If you want more detail, the Chambers *Portuguese Travelmate* is a useful hybrid of phrasebook and pocket dictionary: for each English word it provides not only the usual literal translation but a variety of possible English-language contexts and phrases for this word, and the corresponding Portuguese translations of these idioms. A pocket dictionary may also be useful.

Pronunciation

Pronunciation of Portuguese is difficult; as with English, vowels and consonants have more than one possible sound depending on position and stress. Moreover, there are nasal vowels and diphthongs in Portuguese with no equivalent in English.

Vowels

Single vowels should present relatively few problems:

a	short, as the 'u' sound in 'cut', or long, as the 'e' in 'her'
e	short, as in 'bet', or longer, as in French *été* and Scottish 'laird'
é	short, as in 'bet'
ê	long, as the 'a' sound in 'gate'
e	silent final 'e', like the final 'e' in English 'these'; also silent in unstressed syllables
i	long, as in 'machine', or short, as in 'ring'
o	short, as in 'off', long, as in 'note', or as the 'oo' in 'good'
ô	long, as in 'note'
u	as the 'oo' in 'good'

Nasal Vowels

Nasalisation is represented by **n** or **m** after a vowel, or by a tilde over it (eg **ã**). The nasal **i** exists only approximately in English, as the 'ing' in 'sing'; try to pronounce this and the other nasal vowels (**a**, **e**) with your nasal passages open, giving a sound similar to what you get when you hold your nose.

Diphthongs

Diphthongs (vowel combinations) are relatively straightforward:

au	as in 'now'
ai	as in 'pie'
ei	as in 'day'

eu   pronounced together
oi   similar to 'boy'

Nasal Diphthongs

Try the same technique as for nasal vowels. To say *não*, pronounce 'now' through your nose.

ão   nasal 'now' (owng)
ãe   nasal 'day' (eing)
õe   nasal 'boy' (oing)
ui   similar to the 'uing' in 'ensuing'

Consonants

Pronunciation of the following consonants is specific to Portuguese:

c   hard, as in 'cat', before **a**, **o** or **u**
c   soft as in 'cell', before **e** or **i**
ç   as in 'cell'
ch   as the 'sh' in 'ship' (variable)
g   hard, as in 'garden', before **a**, **o** or **u**
g   soft, as the 's' in 'treasure', before **e** or **i**
g   hard, as in 'get', before **e** or **i**
h   never pronounced at the beginning of a word
nh   as the 'ni' sound in 'onion'
lh   as the 'll' sound in 'million'
j   as the 's' in 'treasure'
m   not pronounced when word-final; it simply nasalises the previous vowel: *um* (oong), *bom* (bõ)
n   as per **m**
qu   as the 'k' in 'key' before **e** or **i**
qu   as the 'q' in 'quad' before **a** or **o**
r   at the beginning of a word (or **rr** in the middle of a word) a harsh, guttural sound similar to the 'r' in French *rue*, or 'ch' in Scottish 'loch'. In some areas of Portugal this **r** is not guttural, but strongly rolled.
r   in the middle or at the end of a word it's a rolled sound stronger than English 'r'
s   as in 'see' (at the beginning of a word)
ss   as in 'see' (in the middle of a word)
s   as the 'z' in 'zeal' (between vowels)
s   as the 'sh' in 'ship' (before another consonant, or at the end of a word)
x   as the 'sh' in 'ship', the 'z' in 'zeal', or the 'ks' sound in 'taxi'
z   as the 's' in 'treasure' (before another consonant, or at the end of a word)

Word Stress

Word stress is important in Portuguese, as it can change the meaning of the word. In Portuguese words with a written accent, the stress always falls on the accented syllable.

Gender

In Portuguese, things (as well as people) can be either masculine or feminine, with most masculine nouns ending in -o and most feminine ones ending in -a. This applies also to words or phrases about a person, with the ending agreeing with the person's gender – for example, *Obrigado/a* (Thank you), or *É casado/a?* (Are you married?).

The only single numbers with gender are 'one' or 'a' (*um* is masculine, *uma* feminine) and 'two' (*dois* is masculine, *duas* feminine).

Basics

Yes/No.   *Sim/Não.*
Maybe.   *Talvez.*
Please.   *Se faz favor/por favor.*
Thank you.   *Obrigado/a.*
That's fine/   *De nada.*
  You're welcome.
Excuse me.   *Desculpe/Com licença.*
Sorry/Forgive me.   *Desculpe.*

Greetings

Hello.   *Bom dia.*
Hi. (casual –   *Olá/Chao.*
  among friends)
Good morning.   *Bom dia.*
Good evening.   *Boa tarde.*
Goodbye.   *Adeus.*
Bye. (casual)   *Chao.*
See you later.   *Até logo.*

Small Talk

How are you?   *Como está?*
I'm fine, thanks.   *Bem, obrigado/a.*

What's your name?	*Como se chama?*
My name is ...	*Chamo-me ...*
Where are you from?	*De onde é?*

I'm from ...	*Sou de ...*
Australia	*Austrália*
Japan	*Japão*
the UK	*o Reino Unido*
the USA	*os Estados Unidos*

How old are you?	*Quantos anos tem?*
I'm ... years old.	*Tenho ... anos.*
Are you married?	*É casado/a?*
Not yet.	*Aindo não.*
How many children do you have?	*Quantos filhos tem?*
daughter	*filha*
son	*filho*

Language Difficulties

I understand.	*Percebo/Entendo.*
I don't understand.	*Não percebo/entendo.*
Do you speak English?	*Fala inglês?*
Could you please write it down?	*Pode escrever isso por favor?*

Getting Around

What time does the ... leave/arrive?	*A que horas parte/ chega o ...?*
boat	*barco*
bus (city)	*autocarro*
bus (intercity)	*camioneta*
metro	*metro*
train	*combóio*
tram	*eléctrico*

Where is the ...?	*Onde é a ...?*
bus stop	*paragem de autocarro*
metro station	*estação de metro*
train station	*estação ferroviária*
tram stop	*paragem de eléctrico*

I want to go to ...	*Quero ir a ...*
How long does it take?	*Quanto tempo leva isso?*
Is this the bus/train to ...?	*E este o autocarro/ combóio para ...?*

I'd like a ... ticket.	*Queria um bilhete ...*
one-way	*simples/de ida*
return	*de ida e volta*
1st class	*primeira classe*
2nd class	*segunda classe*

left-luggage office	*o depósito de bagagem*
platform	*cais*
timetable	*horário*

I'd like to hire ...	*Queria alugar ...*
a car	*um carro*
a motorcycle	*uma motocicleta*
bicycle	*bicicleta*
a tour guide	*uma guia intérprete*

Fill it up, please. (ie the tank)	*Encha a depósito, por favor.*

Directions

How do I get to ...?	*Como vou para ...?*
Is it near/far?	*É perto/longe?*

What ... is this?	*O que ... é isto/ista?*
street/road	*rua/estrada*
suburb	*subúrbia*
town	*cidade/vila*

Signs

PARQUE DE CAMPISMO	CAMPING GROUND
ENTRADA	ENTRANCE
SAÍDA	EXIT
ENTRADA GRÁTIS	FREE ADMISSION
TURISMO	TOURIST OFFICE
ABERTO	OPEN
FECHADO/ ENCERRADO	CLOSED
POLÍCIA	POLICE
PROÍBIDO	PROHIBITED
EMPURRE/PUXE	PUSH/PULL
QUARTOS LIVRES	VACANCIES
ESTAÇÃ	TRAIN STATION
PARTIDAS	DEPARTURES
CHEGADAS	ARRIVALS
LAVABOS, WC	TOILETS
h (for *homems*)	MEN
s (for *senhoras*)	WOMEN

Go straight ahead.	*Siga sempre a direito/ sempre em frente.*
Turn left ...	*Vire à esquerda ...*
Turn right ...	*Vire à direita ...*
at the traffic lights	*no semáforo/nos sinais de trânsito*
at the next corner	*na próxima esquina*
north	*norte*
south	*sul*
east	*leste/este*
west	*oeste*

Around Town

Where is a/the ...?	*Onde é ...?*
bank	*um banco*
city centre	*o centro da cidade/ da baixa*
... embassy	*a embaixada de ...*
exchange office	*um câmbio*
hospital	*o hospital*
hotel	*um hotel*
market	*o mercado*
post office	*os correios*
police station	*o posto da polícia*
public toilet	*os sanitários*
telephone office	*a central de telefones*
toilet	*os lavabos*
tourist office	*o turismo*

| What time does it open/close? | *A que horas abre/ fecha?* |
| I'd like to make a telephone call. | *Quero usar o telefone.* |

I'd like to change ...	*Queria trocar ...*
some money	*dinheiro*
travellers cheques	*uns cheques de viagem*

Accommodation

I'm looking for ...	*Procuro ...*
a camp site	*um parque de campismo*
a youth hostel	*uma pousada da juventude*
a guesthouse	*uma pensão (pl pensões)*
a hotel	*uma hotel (pl hotéis)*

Do you have any rooms available?	*Tem quartos livres?*
I'd like to book ...	*Quero fazer una reserva para ...*
a bed	*uma cama*
a cheap room	*um quarto barato*
a single room	*um quarto individual*
a double room	*um quarto de casal*
a twin-bed room	*um quarto de duplo*
a room with a bathroom	*um quarto com casa de banho*
a dormitory bed	*cama de dormitório*
for one night	*para uma noite*
for two nights	*para duas noites*
How much is it ...?	*Quanto é ...?*
per night	*por noite*
per person	*por pessoa*
Is breakfast included?	*O pequeno almoço está incluído?*
Can I see the room?	*Posso ver o quarto?*
Where is the toilet?	*Onde ficam os lavabos (as casas de banho)?*
It's very dirty/ noisy/expensive.	*É muito sujo/ ruidoso/caro.*

Shopping

How much is it?	*Quanto custa?*
Can I look at it?	*Posso ver?*
It's too expensive.	*É muito caro.*
bookshop	*livraria*
chemist/pharmacy	*farmácia*
clothing store	*boutique/confecções*
department store	*magazine*
laundrette	*lavandaria*
market	*mercado*
newsagents	*papelaria*
open/closed (shop or office)	*aberto/encerrado*

Time & Dates

What time is it?	*Que horas são?*
At what time?	*A que horas?*
When?	*Quando?*
today	*hoje*
tonight	*hoje à noite*

tomorrow	amanhã
yesterday	ontem
morning/afternoon	manhã/tarde
Monday	segunda-feira
Tuesday	terça-feira
Wednesday	quarta-feira
Thursday	quinta-feira
Friday	sexta-feira
Saturday	sábado
Sunday	domingo

Numbers

1	um/uma
2	dois/duas
3	três
4	quatro
5	cinco
6	seis
7	sete
8	oito
9	nove
10	dez
11	onze
12	doze
13	treze
14	catorze
15	quinze
16	dezasseis
17	dezassete
20	vint
21	vint e um
22	vint e dois
30	trinta
40	quarenta
50	cinquenta
60	sessenta
70	setenta
80	oitenta
90	noventa
100	cem
101	cento e um
123	cento e vinte e três
200	duzentos
300	trezentos
400	quatro centos
500	quinhentos
1000	mil
2000	dois mil

one million — um milhão (de)

Emergencies

Help!	Socorro!
Call a doctor!	Chame um médico!
Call the police!	Chame a polícia!
Go away!	Vai-te embora!
I've been robbed.	Fui roubado/a.
I've been raped.	Fui violada/ Violarem-me.
I'm lost.	Estou perdido/a.

Health

Where is ...?	Onde é ...?
a hospital	um hospital
medical clinic	um centro de saúde

I'm ...	Sou ...
diabetic	diabético/a
epileptic	epiléptico/a
asthmatic	asmático/a

I'm allergic to ...	Sou alérgico/a a ...
antibiotics	antibióticos
penicillin	penicilina

I need a doctor.	Preciso um médico.
I'm pregnant.	Estou grávida.

antiseptic	antiséptico
aspirin	aspirina
condoms	preservativo
constipation	constpaçao
contraceptive	anticoncepcional
diarrhoea	diarreia
dizzy	vertiginoso
medicine	remédio/medicamento
nausea	náusea
sanitary napkins	pensos higiénicos
tampons	tampões

FOOD

I'm looking for a ...	Ando à procura ...
food stall	quiosque de comida/ uma bancada
grocery	mercearia/ minimercado
market	mercado
restaurant	restaurante
supermarket	supermercado

Is service included in the bill?	*O serviço está incluído na conta?*
I'm a vegetarian.	*Sou vegeteriano/a.*

Where to Eat

casa/salão da chá	teahouse
casa de pasto	a casual eatery with cheap, simple meals
cervejaria	(lit: a beer house); also serves food
churrasqueira	(lit: a barbecue or grill); usually a restaurant serving grilled foods
marisqueira	seafood restaurant
pastelaria	pastry and cake shop

Menu Items

The following food and dining terms should help you decipher most menus.

almoço	lunch
balcão	counter in bar or café
conta	bill (check)
couvert	cover charge for service (bread, butter etc)
ementa	menu
ementa turística	tourist menu
jantar	evening dinner
meia dose	half-portion of a dish
pequeno almoço	breakfast
prato do dia	dish of the day

Entradas (Starters)

cocktail de gambas
  prawn cocktail
salada de atum
  tuna salad
omeleta de marisco/presunto/cogumelos
  shellfish/smoked ham/
    mushroom omelette

Sopa (Soup)

caldo verde
  potato and shredded-cabbage broth
gazpacho
  refreshing cold vegetable soup
canja de galinha
  chicken broth and rice
sopa à alentejana
  bread soup with garlic and poached egg

sopa de legumes
  vegetable soup
sopa de feijão verde
  green-bean soup

Peixe e Mariscos (Fish & Shellfish)

ameijoas	clams
atum	tuna
bacalhau	dried, salted codfish
camarões	shrimp
carapau	mackerel
chocos	cuttlefish
enguia	eel
espadarte	swordfish
gambas	prawns
lagostins	crayfish
lampreia	lamprey (like eel)
linguada	sole
lulas	squid
pargo	sea bream
peixe espada	scabbard fish
pescada	hake
polvo	octopus
robalo	sea bass
salmão	salmon
sardinhas	sardines
savel	shad
truta	trout

arroz de marisco
  rich seafood and rice stew
caldeirada
  fish stew with onions, potatoes & tomatoes
cataplana
  a combination of shellfish and ham cooked in a sealed wok-style pan and typical of the Algarve region

Carne e Aves (Meat & Poultry)

borrego	lamb
bife	steak
cabrito	kid
carne de vaca (assada)	(roast) beef
carneiro	mutton
chouriço	spicy sausage
coelho	rabbit
costeleta	chop
entrecosto	rump steak
fiambre	ham
fígado	liver
frango	young chicken

galinha	chicken
javadi	wild boar
leitão	suckling pig
lombo	fillet of pork
pato	duck
perú	turkey
presunto	smoked ham
salsicha	sausage
tripas	tripe
vaca	beef
vitela	veal

Legumes (Vegetables)

alface	lettuce
alho	garlic
arroz	rice
batatas	potatoes
cebolas	onions
cenouras	carrots
cogumelos	mushrooms
couve	cabbage
couve-flor	cauliflower
ervilhas	green peas
espargos	asparagus
espinafres	spinach
favas	broad beans
feijão	beans
lentilhas	lentils
pepino	cucumber
pimentos	peppers
salada	salad
salada mista	mixed salad

Ovos (Eggs)

cozido	hard boiled
escalfado	poached
estrelado	fried
mexido	scrambled
omeleta	omelette
quente	boiled

Frutas (Fruit)

alperces	apricots
ameixas	plums
amêndoas	almonds
ananás	pineapple
bananas	bananas
figos	figs
framboesas	raspberries
laranjas	oranges
limões	lemons
maças	apples

melões	melons
morangos	strawberries
pêras	pears
pêssegos	peaches
uvas	grapes

Condiments, Sauces & Appetisers

azeite	olive oil
azeitonas	olives
manteiga	butter
pimenta	pepper
piri-piri	chilli sauce
sal	salt

Snacks & Supplements

batatas fritas	French fries
gelado	ice cream
pão	bread
queijo	cheese
sandes	sandwiches
uma torrada	an order (two pieces) of toast

Cooking Methods

assado	roasted
cozido	boiled
ensopada de ...	stew of ...
estufado	stewed
frito	fried
grelhado	grilled
na brasa	braised
no carvão	on coals (charcoal grilled)
no espeto	on the spit
no forno	in the oven (baked)

Drinks

água mineral	mineral water
com gás	sparkling
sem gás	still
aguardente	firewater
café	coffee
chá	tea
com leite	with milk
com limão	with lemon
sumo de fruta	fruit juice
vinho da casa	house wine
branco	white
tinto	red
vinho verde	semi-sparkling young wine

Glossary

See the Food section in the Language chapter for a listing of culinary terms.

abrigo de montanha – mountain shelter
adega – cellar, especially a wine cellar; also denotes a winery, or a traditional wine bar likely to serve wine from the barrel
Age of Discoveries – the period during the 15th and 16th centuries when Portuguese sailors explored the coast of Africa and finally charted a sea route to India
aguardente – strongly alcoholic 'firewater'
albergaria – upmarket inn
albufeira – reservoir, lagoon
aldeia – village
almoço – lunch
arco – arch
armazém – riverside warehouse
armillary sphere – celestial sphere used by early astronomers and navigators to chart the stars; a common decorative motif in Manueline architecture and atop *pelourinhos*
artesanato – handicrafts shop
ATM – automated teller machine
azulejo – hand-painted tile, typically blue and white, used to decorate buildings

bagagem – left-luggage office
bairro – town district
balcão – counter in a bar or café
balneário – health resort, spa
barragem – dam
beco – cul de sac
berrão, berrões (pl) – ancient stone monument shaped like a pig, found mainly in Trás-os-Montes and the adjacent part of Spain
biblioteca – library
bicyclete tudo terrano (BTT) – mountain bike

câmara municipal – city or town hall
Carnaval – Carnival; festival which takes place over several days before Lent

cartão telefónico – plastic card used in Credifone telephones
casa de abrigo – shelter for staff in national/natural parks; sometimes open to the public
casa de banho – toilet (literally bathroom)
casa de chá – teahouse
casa de fado – fado house; a place where people gather to hear *fado* music, usually a café or restaurant
casa de hóspedes – boarding house; prices are lower than at a *pensão* or *residencial*, and showers and toilets are usually shared
casa de pasto – casual eatery serving cheap, simple meals
castelo – castle
castro – fortified hill town
CCI – Camping Card International
Celtiberians – descendants of Celts who arrived in the Iberian Peninsula around 600 BC
centro de alojamento – literally accommodation centre; a simple youth hostel
centro de comércio – shopping centre
centro de saúde – state-administered medical centre
cervejaria – literally beer house; also serves snacks
churrasqueira or **churrascaria** – restaurant serving grilled foods, especially chicken
cidade – city
citânia – Neolithic or Celtic fortified settlement
claustro – cloisters
concelho – council, municipality
conta – bill (in a restaurant)
coro alto – choir stalls overlooking the nave in a church
Correios/correio – post office
cortes – parliament
couvert – cover charge added to restaurant bill to pay for sundries

CP – Caminhos de Ferro Portugueses; Portuguese state railway company
Credifone – card-operated public telephone
cromlech – circle of prehistoric standing stones
cruz/cruzeiro – cross

direita – right; abbreviated as D, dir or Dta
dolmen – Neolithic stone tomb (*anta* in Portuguese)
Dom, Dona – honorific titles (like Sir, Madam) given to royalty, nobility and landowners; now used more generally as a very polite form of address
dormidas – sign indicating a rooming house
duplo – room with twin beds

elevador – lift (elevator), funicular
ementa – menu
ementa turística – tourist menu
entrada – entrée, starter
esplanada – terrace, seafront promenade
esquerda – left; abbreviated as E, esq or Esqa
estação – station (usually train station)
estalagem – inn; more expensive than an *albergaria*

fado – traditional, melancholy Portuguese style of singing
farmácia – pharmacy
feira – fair
festa – festival
FICC – Fédération Internationale de Camping et de Caravanning; international federation of camping and caravanning
fortaleza – fortress
FPCC – Federação Portuguesa de Campismo e Caravanismo; Portuguese federation of camping and caravanning
freguesia – parish

gelado – ice cream
GNR – Guarda Nacional Republicana, the national guard; acting police force in rural towns without PSP police
gruta – cave
Gypsy market – huge outdoor market specialising in cheap clothes and shoes, usually with many Gypsy stallholders

hipermercado – hypermarket
horários – timetables
hospedaria – see *casa de hóspedes*

IC (Intercidade) – express intercity train
ICEP – Investimentos, Comércio e Turismo de Portugal; the government umbrella organisation for tourism
IDD – International Direct Dial
igreja – church
igreja matriz – parish church
ilha – island
infantário – children's daycare centre
IR (Interregional) – fairly fast train without too many stops
IVA – Imposto sobre Valor Acrescentado; VAT (value added tax)

jantar – evening meal
jardim – garden
judiaria – quarter in a town where Jews were segregated
junta de turismo – see *turismo*

largo – small square
latifúndios – Roman system of large farming estates
lavabo – toilet
lavandaria – laundry
lista – see *ementa*
livraria – bookshop
loggia – covered area on the side of a building; porch

Manueline – elaborate Renaissance/Gothic style of art and architecture that emerged during the reign of Manuel I in the 16th century
marisqueira – seafood restaurant
meia dose – half-portion (food)
menir – menhir; individual standing stone dating from the late Neolithic Age
mercado municipal – municipal market
mesa – table
MFA – Movimento das Forças Armadas; military group which led the Revolution of the Carnations in 1974
minimercado – grocery, small supermarket
miradouro – lookout

Misericórdia – from Santa Casa da Misericórdia (Holy House of Mercy), a charitable institution founded in the 15th century to care for the poor and the sick; usually designates an old building founded by this organisation

mosteiro – monastery

mouraria – quarter where Moors were segregated during and after the Christian *Reconquista*

mudéjar – originally meant a Muslim under Christian rule; also used as an adjective to describe the art and architecture of the mujédars

museu – museum

paço – palace

parque de campismo – camping ground

parque infantil – children's playground

pastelaria – pastry and cake shop

pelourinho – stone pillory, often ornately carved; erected in the 13th to 18th centuries as symbols of justice and sometimes as places where criminals were punished

pensão, pensões (pl) – guesthouse; the Portuguese equivalent of a bed and breakfast (B&B), though breakfast is not always included

pequeno almoço – breakfast, traditionally just coffee and a bread roll

planalto – high plain

pombal – dovecote; a structure for housing pigeons

portagem – toll road

posto de turismo – see *turismo*

pousada or **Pousada de Portugal** – government-run scheme of upmarket inns, often in converted castles, convents or palaces

pousada da juventude – youth hostel; usually with kitchen, common rooms and sometimes rooms with private bathrooms

praça – square

praça de touros – bullring

praia – beach

prato do dia – dish of the day

pré-pagamento – prepayment required (as in some café-restaurants)

PSP – Polícia de Segurança Pública; local police force

quarto de casal – room with a double bed

quarto individual – single room

quarto particular – often just quarto; room in a private house

quinta – country estate or villa; in the Douro wine-growing region it often refers to a wine lodge's property

R (Regional) – slow train

Reconquista – Christian reconquest of Portugal (718-1249)

rés do chão – ground floor; abbreviated R/C

residencial, residenciais (pl) – guesthouse; slightly more expensive than a *pensão* and usually serving breakfast

ribeiro – stream

rio – river

romaria – religious pilgrimage

rua – street

salão de chá – teahouse

sanitários – public toilets

sé – cathedral; from the Latin *sedes* (seat), implying an episcopal seat

selos – stamps

sem chumbo – unleaded (petrol)

serra – mountain, mountain range

solar – manor house

supermercado – supermarket

talha dourada – gilded woodwork

tasca – simple tavern, often with rustic décor

termas – spa

torre de menagem – castle tower, keep

tourada – bullfight

Turihab – short for Turismo Habitação, a scheme for marketing private accommodation (particularly in northern Portugal) in country cottages, historic buildings and manor houses

turismo – tourist office

vila – town

vinho da casa – house wine

vinho verde – semisparkling young wine

Acknowledgments

THANKS

Many thanks to the travellers who used the last edition and wrote to us with helpful hints, useful advice and interesting anecdotes:

Sonya, Louise & Nicholas, Mohamed Al-Jabir, Rachal Allen, Suzanne K Barner, Joeri Belis, Helen Bettany, Allison Birchwood, Marie & Paul Bombeke, Peter & Sue Boyden, Liz Brant, Brooklyn Brown, Lynn Cairns, Debra Carter, Carol Christie, K Cooke, Richard Corbett, August Cosentino, Maureen A Crerar, Angela, M Crew, Jose Da Silva-Teixeira, R Degotardi, Margreet & Ronald van Deutekom, Jennifer Ditchburn, Gordon Drumm, Edna Engel, Monique van Erp, Eva Eshilsson, Steffen Fjurvik, Gabriel Gonzalez Maurazos, DA Gott, Bob Gould, Diana Hall, Vagn Asbjorn Hansen, Charles & Sarah Harmer, Adam Harris, Stephan Hasselberg, Donald Hatch, Colman Higgins, Sydney Hope, Anouk van Ingen, DA Jackson, Greg Johnson, Chun-Ha Joo, Stephanie Kaye, Karen Kepke, David & Hilary Ker, Daniel Klobucar, Manon van der Knabben, Henry Koster, Lillian Lahe, Peter Lantos, Sharon Laren, Dr Knud Lassen, Brit Lehrmann Nielsen, Myron & Carol Leiter, Almond Leung, Simon Li, Steve Little, Hans Lodewijks, Ana Luiza, Michael Madden, Carlos Madeira, Sander Martens, Lloyd McCune, Jim McKenny, Jon Moulton, Peter Nankivell, Ippolito Nievo, John van Nijnatten, Kristina Ostberg, Jacinto Pereira, Alan Pewsey, Julia Playford, Dr Herbert Plotke, Peter Ratcliffe, Sergio Rebelo, Jose Ribau, Tony Roberts, Sacha Sadan, Lorenzo Salvioni, Anthony Schneider, Ralph Scoggin, Geurs Sieraden, Eva Skyborn, Mr & Mrs Sluiter, Kara Smith, Duncan Smith, Gary Spinks, Vit Stepanek, Ichiro Sugiyama, Adam Sutcliffe, AnneMarie Thepaut, Hugo Thielemans, Nicholas Tomich, Amy Valdez de Buono, Nigel Varey, Gonzalo Velez, Clive Anthony Viney, Angelo Volandes, Sylvia Weekers, David Whittaker, Laura Wilson, Carsten Witzmann

LONELY PLANET

Phrasebooks

Lonely Planet phrasebooks are packed with essential words and phrases to help travellers communicate with the locals. With colour tabs for quick reference, an extensive vocabulary and use of script, these handy pocket-sized language guides cover day-to-day travel situations.

- handy pocket-sized books
- easy to understand Pronunciation chapter
- clear & comprehensive Grammar chapter
- romanisation alongside script to allow ease of pronunciation
- script throughout so users can point to phrases for every situation
- full of cultural information and tips for the traveller

'...vital for a real DIY spirit and attitude in language learning'
– *Backpacker*

'the phrasebooks have good cultural backgrounders and offer solid advice for challenging situations in remote locations'
– *San Francisco Examiner*

Arabic (Egyptian) • Arabic (Moroccan) • Australian *(Australian English, Aboriginal and Torres Strait languages)* • Baltic States *(Estonian, Latvian, Lithuanian)* • Bengali • Brazilian • Burmese • Cantonese • Central Asia • Central Europe *(Czech, French, German, Hungarian, Italian, Slovak)* • Eastern Europe *(Bulgarian, Czech, Hungarian, Polish, Romanian, Slovak)* • Ethiopian (Amharic) • Fijian • French • German • Greek • Hill Tribes • Hindi/Urdu • Indonesian • Italian • Japanese • Korean • Lao • Latin American Spanish • Malay • Mandarin • Mediterranean Europe *(Albanian, Croatian, Greek, Italian, Macedonian, Maltese, Serbian, Slovene)* • Mongolian • Nepali • Papua New Guinea • Pilipino (Tagalog) • Quechua • Russian • Scandinavian Europe *(Danish, Finnish, Icelandic, Norwegian, Swedish)* • South-East Asia *(Burmese, Indonesian, Khmer, Lao, Malay, Tagalog Pilipino, Thai, Vietnamese)* • Spanish (Castilian) *(also includes Catalan, Galician and Basque)* • Sri Lanka • Swahili • Thai • Tibetan • Turkish • Ukrainian • USA *(US English, Vernacular Talk, Native American languages, Hawaiian)* • Vietnamese • Western Europe *(Basque, Catalan, Dutch, French, German, Greek, Irish)*

Lonely Planet Journeys

JOURNEYS is a unique collection of travel writing – published by the company that understands travel better than anyone else. It is a series for anyone who has ever experienced – or dreamed of – the magical moment when they encountered a strange culture or saw a place for the first time. They are tales to read while you're planning a trip, while you're on the road or while you're in an armchair, in front of a fire.

These outstanding titles explore our planet through the eyes of a diverse group of international writers. JOURNEYS books catch the spirit of a place, illuminate a culture, recount a crazy adventure, or introduce a fascinating way of life. They always entertain, and always enrich the experience of travel.

MALI BLUES
Traveling to an African Beat
Lieve Joris (translated by Sam Garrett)

Drought, rebel uprisings, ethnic conflict: these are the predominant images of West Africa. But as Lieve Joris travels in Senegal, Mauritania and Mali, she meets survivors, fascinating individuals charting new ways of living between tradition and modernity. With her remarkable gift for drawing out people's stories, Joris brilliantly captures the rhythms of a world that refuses to give in.

THE GATES OF DAMASCUS
Lieve Joris (translated by Sam Garrett)

This best-selling book is a beautifully drawn portrait of day-to-day life in modern Syria. Through her intimate contact with local people, Lieve Joris draws us into the fascinating world that lies behind the gates of Damascus. Hala's husband is a political prisoner, jailed for his opposition to the Assad regime; through the author's friendship with Hala we see how Syrian politics impacts on the lives of ordinary people.

THE OLIVE GROVE
Travels in Greece
Katherine Kizilos

Katherine Kizilos travels to fabled islands, troubled border zones and her family's village deep in the mountains. She vividly evokes breathtaking landscapes, generous people and passionate politics, capturing the complexities of a country she loves.

'**beautifully captures the real tensions of Greece**' – *Sunday Times*

KINGDOM OF THE FILM STARS
Journey into Jordan
Annie Caulfield

Kingdom of the Film Stars is a travel book and a love story. With honesty and humour, Annie Caulfield writes of travelling in Jordan and falling in love with a Bedouin with film-star looks.

She offers fascinating insights into the country – from the tent life of traditional women to the hustle of downtown Amman – and unpicks tight-woven Western myths about the Arab world.

LONELY PLANET

Lonely Planet Travel Atlases

Lonely Planet has long been famous for the number and quality of its guidebook maps. Now we've gone one step further and produced a handy companion series: Lonely Planet travel atlases – maps of a country produced in book form.

Unlike other maps, which look good but lead travellers astray, our travel atlases have been researched on the road by Lonely Planet's experienced team of writers. All details are carefully checked to ensure the atlas corresponds with the equivalent Lonely Planet guidebook.

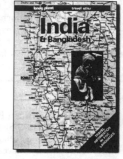

- full-colour throughout
- maps researched and checked by Lonely Planet authors
- place names correspond with Lonely Planet guidebooks
- no confusing spelling differences
- legend and travelling information in English, French, German, Japanese and Spanish
- size: 230 x 160 mm

Available now: Chile & Easter Island • Egypt • India & Bangladesh • Israel & the Palestinian Territories • Jordan, Syria & Lebanon • Kenya • Laos • Portugal • South Africa, Lesotho & Swaziland • Thailand • Turkey • Vietnam • Zimbabwe, Botswana & Namibia

---

Lonely Planet TV Series & Videos

Lonely Planet travel guides have been brought to life on television screens around the world. Like our guides, the programs are based on the joy of independent travel, and look honestly at some of the most exciting, picturesque and frustrating places in the world. Each show is presented by one of three travellers from Australia, England or the USA and combines an innovative mixture of video, Super-8 film, atmospheric soundscapes and original music.

Videos of each episode – containing additional footage not shown on television – are available from good book and video shops, but the availability of individual videos varies with regional screening schedules. ∙

Video destinations include: Alaska • American Rockies • Australia – The South-East • Baja California & the Copper Canyon • Brazil • Central Asia • Chile & Easter Island • Corsica, Sicily & Sardinia – The Mediterranean Islands • East Africa (Tanzania & Zanzibar) • Ecuador & the Galapagos Islands • Greenland & Iceland • Indonesia • Israel & the Sinai Desert • Jamaica • Japan • La Ruta Maya • Morocco • New York • North India • Pacific Islands (Fiji, Solomon Islands & Vanuatu) • South India • South West China • Turkey • Vietnam • West Africa • Zimbabwe, Botswana & Namibia

The Lonely Planet TV series is produced by: Pilot Productions
The Old Studio
18 Middle Row
London W10 5AT, UK

LONELY PLANET

Lonely Planet Online
www.lonelyplanet.com *or* AOL keyword: lp

Whether you've just begun planning your next trip, or you're chasing down specific info on currency regulations or visa requirements, check out Lonely Planet Online for up-to-the minute travel information.

As well as mini guides to more than 250 destinations, you'll find maps, photos, travel news, health and visa updates, travel advisories, and discussion of the ecological and political issues you need to be aware of as you travel. You'll also find timely upgrades to popular guidebooks which you can print out and stick in the back of your book.

There's also an online travellers' forum where you can share your experience of life on the road, meet travel companions and ask other travellers for their recommendations and advice.

And of course we have a complete and up-to-date list of all Lonely Planet travel products including travel guides, diving and snorkelling guides, phrasebooks, atlases, travel literature and videos, and a simple online ordering facility if you can't find the book you want elsewhere.

Lonely Planet Diving & Snorkelling Guides

Known for indispensible guidebooks to destinations all over the world, Lonely Planet's Pisces Books are the most popular series of diving and snorkelling titles available.

There are three series: **Diving & Snorkelling Guides**, **Shipwreck Diving** series, and **Dive Into History**. Full colour throughout, the **Diving & Snorkelling Guides** combine quality photographs with detailed descriptions of the best dive sites for each location, giving divers a glimpse of what they can expect both on land and in water. The **Dive Into History** series is perfect for the adventure diver or armchair traveller. The **Shipwreck Diving** series provides all the details for exploring the most interesting wrecks in the Atlantic and Pacific oceans. The list also includes underwater nature and technical guides.

LONELY PLANET

Guides by Region

L onely Planet is known worldwide for publishing practical, reliable and no-nonsense travel information in our guides and on our Web site. The Lonely Planet list covers just about every accessible part of the world. Currently there are nine series: travel guides, shoestring guides, walking guides, city guides, phrasebooks, audio packs, travel atlases, diving and snorkeling guides and travel literature.

AFRICA Africa – the South • Africa on a shoestring • Arabic (Egyptian) phrasebook • Arabic (Moroccan) phrasebook • Cairo • Cape Town • Central Africa • East Africa • Egypt • Egypt travel atlas • Ethiopian (Amharic) phrasebook • The Gambia & Senegal • Kenya • Kenya travel atlas • Malawi, Mozambique & Zambia • Morocco • North Africa • South Africa, Lesotho & Swaziland • South Africa, Lesotho & Swaziland travel atlas • Swahili phrasebook • Trekking in East Africa • Tunisia • West Africa • Zimbabwe, Botswana & Namibia • Zimbabwe, Botswana & Namibia travel atlas
Travel Literature: The Rainbird: A Central African Journey • Songs to an African Sunset: A Zimbabwean Story • Mali Blues: Traveling to an African Beat

AUSTRALIA & THE PACIFIC Australia • Australian phrasebook • Bushwalking in Australia • Bushwalking in Papua New Guinea • Fiji • Fijian phrasebook • Islands of Australia's Great Barrier Reef • Melbourne • Micronesia • New Caledonia • New South Wales & the ACT • New Zealand • Northern Territory • Outback Australia • Papua New Guinea • Papua New Guinea (Pidgin) phrasebook • Queensland • Rarotonga & the Cook Islands • Samoa • Solomon Islands • South Australia • Sydney • Tahiti & French Polynesia • Tasmania • Tonga • Tramping in New Zealand • Vanuatu • Victoria • Western Australia
Travel Literature: Islands in the Clouds • Sean & David's Long Drive

CENTRAL AMERICA & THE CARIBBEAN Bahamas and Turks & Caicos • Bermuda • Central America on a shoestring • Costa Rica • Cuba • Eastern Caribbean • Guatemala, Belize & Yucatán: La Ruta Maya • Jamaica • Mexico • Mexico City • Panama
Travel Literature: Green Dreams: Travels in Central America

EUROPE Amsterdam • Andalucia • Austria • Baltic States phrasebook • Berlin • Britain • Central Europe • Central Europe phrasebook • Czech & Slovak Republics • Denmark • Dublin • Eastern Europe • Eastern Europe phrasebook • Estonia, Latvia & Lithuania • Finland • France • French phrasebook • Germany • German phrasebook • Greece • Greek phrasebook • Hungary • Iceland, Greenland & the Faroe Islands • Ireland • Italian phrasebook • Italy • Lisbon • London • Mediterranean Europe • Mediterranean Europe phrasebook • Paris • Poland • Portugal • Portugal travel atlas • Prague • Romania & Moldova • Russia, Ukraine & Belarus • Russian phrasebook • Scandinavian & Baltic Europe • Scandinavian Europe phrasebook • Slovenia • Spain • Spanish phrasebook • St Petersburg • Switzerland • Trekking in Spain • Ukrainian phrasebook • Vienna • Walking in Britain • Walking in Italy • Walking in Switzerland • Western Europe • Western Europe phrasebook
Travel Literature: The Olive Grove: Travels in Greece

INDIAN SUBCONTINENT Bangladesh • Bengali phrasebook • Bhutan • Delhi • Goa • Hindi/Urdu phrasebook • India • India & Bangladesh travel atlas • Indian Himalaya • Karakoram Highway • Nepal • Nepali phrasebook • Pakistan • Rajasthan • South India • Sri Lanka • Sri Lanka phrasebook • Trekking in the Indian Himalaya • Trekking in the Karakoram & Hindukush • Trekking in the Nepal Himalaya
Travel Literature: In Rajasthan • Shopping for Buddhas

LONELY PLANET

Mail Order

Lonely Planet products are distributed worldwide.They are also available by mail order from Lonely Planet, so if you have difficulty finding a title please write to us. North and South American residents should write to 150 Linden St, Oakland, CA 94607, USA; European and African residents should write to 10a Spring Place, London NW5 3BH, UK; and residents of other countries to PO Box 617, Hawthorn, Victoria 3122, Australia.

ISLANDS OF THE INDIAN OCEAN Madagascar & Comoros • Maldives • Mauritius, Réunion & Seychelles

MIDDLE EAST & CENTRAL ASIA Arab Gulf States • Central Asia • Central Asia phrasebook • Iran • Israel & the Palestinian Territories • Israel & the Palestinian Territories travel atlas • Istanbul • Jerusalem • Jordan & Syria • Jordan, Syria & Lebanon travel atlas • Lebanon • Middle East on a shoestring • Turkey • Turkish phrasebook • Turkey travel atlas • Yemen
Travel Literature: The Gates of Damascus • Kingdom of the Film Stars: Journey into Jordan

NORTH AMERICA Alaska • Backpacking in Alaska • Baja California • California & Nevada • Canada • Florida • Hawaii • Honolulu • Los Angeles • Miami • New England USA • New Orleans • New York City • New York, New Jersey & Pennsylvania • Pacific Northwest USA • Rocky Mountain States • San Francisco • Seattle • Southwest USA • USA phrasebook • Washington, DC & the Capital Region
Travel Literature: Drive Thru America

NORTH-EAST ASIA Beijing • Cantonese phrasebook • China • Hong Kong • Hong Kong, Macau & Guangzhou • Japan • Japanese phrasebook • Japanese audio pack • Korea • Korean phrasebook • Kyoto • Mandarin phrasebook • Mongolia • Mongolian phrasebook • North-East Asia on a shoestring • Seoul • South-West China • Taiwan • Tibet • Tibetan phrasebook • Tokyo
Travel Literature: Lost Japan

SOUTH AMERICA Argentina, Uruguay & Paraguay • Bolivia • Brazil • Brazilian phrasebook • Buenos Aires • Chile & Easter Island • Chile & Easter Island travel atlas • Colombia • Ecuador & the Galapagos Islands • Latin American Spanish phrasebook • Peru • Quechua phrasebook • Rio de Janeiro • South America on a shoestring • Trekking in the Patagonian Andes • Venezuela
Travel Literature: Full Circle: A South American Journey

SOUTH-EAST ASIA Bali & Lombok • Bangkok • Burmese phrasebook • Cambodia • Hill Tribes phrasebook • Ho Chi Minh City • Indonesia • Indonesian phrasebook • Indonesian audio pack • Jakarta • Java • Laos • Lao phrasebook • Laos travel atlas • Malay phrasebook • Malaysia, Singapore & Brunei • Myanmar (Burma) • Philippines • Pilipino (Tagalog) phrasebook • Singapore • South-East Asia on a shoestring • South-East Asia phrasebook • Thailand • Thailand's Islands & Beaches • Thailand travel atlas • Thai phrasebook • Thai audio pack • Vietnam • Vietnamese phrasebook • Vietnam travel atlas

ALSO AVAILABLE: Antarctica • Brief Encounters: Stories of Love, Sex & Travel • Chasing Rickshaws • Not the Only Planet: Travel Stories from Science Fiction • Travel with Children • Traveller's Tales

LONELY PLANET

FREE Lonely Planet Newsletters

We love hearing from you and think you'd like to hear from us.

Planet Talk

Our FREE quarterly printed newsletter is full of tips from travellers and anecdotes from Lonely Planet guidebook authors. Every issue is packed with up-to-date travel news and advice, and includes:

- a postcard from Lonely Planet co-founder Tony Wheeler
- a swag of mail from travellers
- a look at life on the road through the eyes of a Lonely Planet author
- topical health advice
- prizes for the best travel yarn
- news about forthcoming Lonely Planet events
- a complete list of Lonely Planet books and other titles

To join our mailing list, residents of the UK, Europe and Africa can email us at go@lonelyplanet.co.uk; residents of North and South America can email us at info@lonelyplanet.com; the rest of the world can email us at talk2us@lonelyplanet.com.au, or contact any Lonely Planet office.

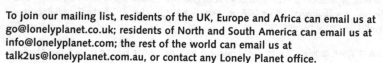

Comet

Our FREE monthly email newsletter brings you all the latest travel news, features, interviews, competitions, destination ideas, travellers' tips & tales, Q&As, raging debates and related links. Find out what's new on the Lonely Planet Web site and which books are about to hit the shelves.

Subscribe from your desktop: www.lonelyplanet.com/comet

Index

Text

Bold indicates maps.
Italics indicates boxed text.

Bold indicates maps.
Italics indicates boxed text.

Bold indicates maps.
Italics indicates boxed text.

Boxed Text

Bold indicates maps.
Italics indicates boxed text.

MAP LEGEND

BOUNDARIES

▬▬▬▬▬ .... International
▬▬▬ ▬ ▬ ▬ .... Provincial

HYDROGRAPHY

.... Coastline
.... River, Creek
.... Lake
.... Intermittent Lake
.... Salt Pans
.... Canal
◎ ⟶ .... Spring, Rapids
.... Waterfalls
▬ ▬ ▬ ▬ ▬ .... Marine Park
.... Swamp

ROUTES & TRANSPORT

▬▬▬▬▬ .... Freeway
▬▬▬▬▬ .... Highway
▬▬▬▬▬ .... Major Road
▬▬▬▬▬ .... Minor Road
═══════ .... Unsealed Road
▬▬▬▬▬ .... City Freeway
▬▬▬▬▬ .... City Highway
▬▬▬▬▬ .... City Road
▬▬▬▬▬ .... City Street, Lane

▬▬▬▬▬ .... Pedestrian Mall
⇒═══: .... Tunnel
├─┼─┼─●┼─ ..... Train Route & Station
━━━Ⓜ━━ .... Metro & Station
▬▬▬▬▬ .... Tramway
┼─┼─┼─┼─┼ ... Cable Car or Funicular
─ ─ ─ ─ ─ .... Walking Track
• • • • • • • • • • .... Walking Tour
─ ─ ─ ─ ─ .... Ferry Route

AREA FEATURES

.... Building
✿ .... Park, Gardens
+ + × × .... Cemetery

.... Market
.... Beach, Desert
.... Urban Area

MAP SYMBOLS

✈	.... Airport	🏛	..Museum or Art Gallery
⟋	....Ancient or City Wall	←	............One Way Street
∴	.......Archaeological Site	🏛	.... Palace
⊜	...................Bank	🅿	.... Parking
🏖	...................Beach	)(	.... Pass
🏰	..............Castle or Fort	★	............Police Station
▥ 🕆	....Cathedral or Church	✉	.... Post Office
⌒	....Cliff or Escarpment	❖	.......Shopping Centre
○	...Embassy or Consulate	▭	.........Swimming Pool
⚑	...............Golf Course	▦	.... Synagogue
✚	...................Hospital	☎	.................Telephone
✳	...................Lookout	❶	.... Tourist Information
👤	...............Monument	◒	.... Transport
▲ ⌢	...Mountain, Mtn Range	🐘	............................Zoo

○ **CAPITAL** .... National Capital
● **City** .... City
● **Town** .... Town
● **Village** .... Village
○ .... Point of Interest
■ .... Place to Stay
▲ .... Camping Ground
⌂ .... Caravan Park
⌂ .... Hut or Chalet
⌂ .... Shelter
▼ .... Place to Eat
🍺 .... Bar or Nightclub

Note: not all symbols displayed above appear in this book

LONELY PLANET OFFICES

Australia
PO Box 617, Hawthorn, Victoria 3122
☎ (03) 9819 1877 fax (03) 9819 6459
email: talk2us@lonelyplanet.com.au

UK
10a Spring Place, London NW5 3BH
☎ (0171) 428 4800 fax (0171) 428 4828
email: go@lonelyplanet.co.uk

USA
150 Linden St, Oakland, CA 94607
☎ (510) 893 8555 TOLL FREE: 800 275 8555
fax (510) 893 8572
email: info@lonelyplanet.com

France
1 rue du Dahomey, 75011 Paris
☎ 01 55 25 33 00 fax 01 55 25 33 01
email: bip@lonelyplanet.fr
minitel: 3615 lonelyplanet *(1,29 F TTC/min)*

World Wide Web: www.lonelyplanet.com *or* AOL keyword: lp
Lonely Planet Images: lpi@lonelyplanet.com.au